Business Ethics

Business Ethics

A Stakeholder and Issues Management Approach

Fourth Edition

Joseph W. Weiss
Bentley College

THOMSON

SOUTH-WESTERN

Australia • Canada • Mexico • Singapore • Spain
United Kingdom • United States

THOMSON

SOUTH-WESTERN ™

Business Ethics: A Stakeholder and Issues Management Approach, Fourth Edition
Joseph W. Weiss

VP/Editorial Director:
Jack W. Calhoun
VP/Editor-in-Chief: Dave Shaut
Executive Editor: John Szilagyi
Developmental Editor:
Leslie Kauffman, LEAP, Inc.
Marketing Manager: Jacque Carrillo
Production Project Manager:
Stephanie Schempp
Media Editor: Karen Schaffer

Technology Project Editor:
Kristen Meere
Manufacturing Coordinator: Doug Wilke
Production House: Graphic World Inc.
Printer: Webcom Limited,
Toronto, Canada
Art Director: Stacy Jenkins Shirley
Internal Designer: Design Matters
Cover Designer: Design Matters
Cover Images: © Getty Images

Thomson Higher Education
5191 Natorp Boulevard
Mason, OH 45040
USA

For more information about our
products, contact us at:

**Thomson Learning Academic
Resource Center
1-800-423-0563**

For permission to use material from this
text or product, submit a request online
at **http://www.thomsonrights.com.**

Student Edition: ISBN 0-324-22380-3

Library of Congress Control Number:
2005927284

Contents

Chapter 2
Stakeholder and Issues Management Approaches   47

Chapter 3
Ethical Principles, Quick Tests, and Decision-Making Guidelines   113

Chapter 4
The Corporation and External Stakeholders: Managing Moral Responsibility: From the Boardroom to the Marketplace   167

Chapter 5
The Corporation and Internal Stakeholders: Values-Based Moral Leadership, Culture, Strategy, and Self-Regulation   287

Chapter 6
Employee Stakeholders and the Corporation   361

Chapter 7
Business Ethics, Stakeholder Management, and Multinational Corporations in the Global Environment   437

Preface

Visit a major news Web site, read any major newspaper or business journal, turn on any major broadcast network like CNN, or tune into Al-Jazeera if you have satellite television, and you will find an event, a crisis, or an issue that relates a corporation's activities to global ethical implications. Questions quickly arise: Who is right? Who is wrong? Does someone stand to gain or lose? Was someone hurt? Who is liable? Should someone pay damages? Who acted responsibly? Who did not? Will justice be served? And, perhaps, how does this affect me, my work, and my life?

Business ethics is about relationships, values, justice, and identity (personal, professional, corporate, national, and global). It also concerns the intersection between business and ethics and is fundamental to the relationships between business and society at large. Why does the modern corporation exist in the first place? What is its *raison d'être*? How does it treat its stakeholders? Business ethics engage these essential questions, and it is also about the purpose, values, and transactions of and between individuals, groups, and companies and their global alliances.

With this in mind, students and professionals need straightforward frameworks to thoughtfully and objectively analyze and then sort through complex issues in order to make decisions that matter—ethically, economically, socially, legally, and spiritually. The post–9-11 world is different. Potential terrorist threats, corporate scandals, security issues, globalization, off-shoring and outsourcing, and the changing (perhaps diminishing) middle class all present business and ethical issues that can and do affect our professional and personal relationships, careers, and lives.

This fourth edition of *Business Ethics: A Stakeholder and Issues Management Approach* was revised with these concerns in mind and with at least six related goals:

- to recognize the effects of corporate scandals on business and governance practices
- to present dilemmas and ethical thinking regarding the contemporary workplace and workforce
- to cover major contemporary, international, and global topics in business ethics
- to present stakeholder and issues management frameworks and practical methods for identifying and evaluating breaking news in the business world
- to present the material in a straightforward, "reader-friendly" way

- to offer research and business press findings and stories to explain concepts and perspectives

In addition to providing concrete frameworks for analyzing and discussing a wide range of ethical issues, the fourth edition of *Business Ethics* also includes a full complement of tools for leading discussions and encouraging student participation:

- Highlighted ethical dilemmas (several new to this edition) underscore the fact that difficult business decisions are grounded in ethical dilemmas. Each dilemma asks students not only to make a choice but to defend their decisions and to consider the consequences that inattention to the ethical implications depicted might bring. Plant closings, audit disclosures, and the strategic misrepresentation of facts are among the dilemmas examined in these end-of-chapter dilemmas.

- Twenty-two cases, most new, cover breaking news topics, with special attention to corporate scandals, Sarbanes-Oxley legislation, and corporate reactions.

- New PowerPoint slides and revised chapter outlines accompany the materials for text adopters.

- Access to *Harvard Business Review* articles and cases is available to text adopters.

- Updated end-of-chapter questions and exercises are designed to motivate the reader's active participation in chapter topics.

- Boxed inserts throughout the chapters illustrate current applications of chapter content in a business context. Integrating ethical frameworks with current events provides numerous opportunities to set up problems and deliver the tools to effect solutions at the same time. Businesses face difficult problems everyday, and the media ceaselessly report on those problems. *Business Ethics* draws on this vast reservoir to make its points accessible, credible, and relevant.

This edition also expands stakeholder analysis to incorporate a values-driven management approach. For example, Chapter 5, which addresses internal stakeholders, investigates options for assessing an organization's readiness to manage from a values-driven and stakeholder-responsiveness approach.

A Proactive Approach

Although business ethics issues change daily, classic ethical principles remain constant. The challenge in writing this book was to devise an effective vehicle that integrates the two. This book presents contemporary and classic business cases and decisions that can be analyzed and interpreted using ethical principles and decision-making negotiation styles. "Hypernorms" and conflict resolution techniques are illustrated along with classic ethical principles.

As earlier editions of this book demonstrated, *Business Ethics* encourages the reader to take on the decision-maker's role. With thought-provoking cases and discussion questions that ask, "What would you do if you had to decide a course of action?" *Business Ethics* also encourages readers to articulate and share their decision-making rationales and strategies. Readers will also be able to examine changing ethical issues and business problems with a critical eye. We take a close look at the business reportage of the *Wall Street Journal, 60 Minutes, 20/20,* the *New York Times, BusinessWeek,* the *Economist,* and other online and off-line sources to learn from the challenges, practices, and mistakes of companies and organizations around the world.

Stakeholder and Issues Management Analysis

Stakeholder analysis is one of the most comprehensive orienting approaches for identifying issues, groups, strategies, and outcomes (potential or realized) revolving around complex ethical dilemmas. Stakeholder, issues management, and ethical methods can be used throughout the book. These methods are presented in an updated and more integrative Chapter 2. It offers a useful starting point for mapping the who, what, when, where, why, and how of ethical problems involving organizations and their constituencies. Issues and crisis management frameworks are explained and integrated into approaches that complement the stakeholder analysis. Several other ethical problem-solving frameworks, quick tests, and negotiation techniques are presented in Chapters 3 and 7.

Features of the Book

- *Clear and understandable presentations.* Principles, concepts, and examples are written to minimize jargon and maximize meaning. Although intended primarily for the dedicated course in business ethics, this text may also serve as a useful adjunct in other course areas, namely, introduction to business, business law, business and society, and business policy.

- *Additional contemporary cases. Business Ethics* retains and updates many of its longer cases, adding 15 new, shorter cases to the mix. The cases are grouped at the end of appropriate chapters.

- *Global scope.* Ethics, advantageously integrated into the world economy, forms the core of Chapter 7, "Business Ethics,

Stakeholder Management, and Multinational Corporations in the Global Environment."

- *Contemporary approach.* Revised sections on globalization, international ethics, stakeholder management and negotiation methods for assessing organizations, and ways business ethics has been affected since 9-11 are included in this edition. Contemporary individual and professional ethical dilemmas in business are presented throughout the text.

- *Cross-disciplinary reach.* Topics relating to philosophy, law, ethics, business and society, and management increase understanding.

- *Updated research.* Additional and updated research has been added throughout the text on the ethical implications of technology, off-shoring and outsourcing, and music file-sharing technologies and practices, along with new company profiles, including Nike, Wal-Mart, and Apple Computer.

Objectives of the Book

- to introduce basic ethical concepts, principles, and examples to enhance understanding and use of ethics in solving moral dilemmas that are occurring now at every professional level

- to introduce the stakeholder and issues management methods as strategic and practical ways for mapping corporate, group, and individual relationships so readers can understand and apply ethical reasoning in the marketplace and in workplace relationships

- to expand readers' awareness of what constitutes ethical and unethical practices in business at the individual, group, organizational, global, and multinational levels

- to instill a confidence and competence in readers' ability to think and act according to moral principles as they create, manage, and study stakeholder relationships in their own worlds at the national and international level

Structure of the Book

- Chapter 1 defines business ethics and familiarizes the reader with examples of ethics in business practices, levels of ethical analysis, and what can be expected from a course in business ethics.

- Chapter 2 introduces the stakeholder and issues management methods for studying social responsibility relationships at the individual employee, group, and organizational levels. These methods provide and encourage the incorporation of ethical principles and concepts from the entire book.

- Chapter 3 contains a discussion of the "micro-level" approach to ethical decision making. Moral principles and concepts derived from both classic and more contemporary ways of thinking and acting ethically are presented. Individual styles of moral decision making are also discussed in this section. Although this section is a micro-level approach, these principles can be used to examine and explain corporate strategies and actions as well. (Executives, managers, employees, coalitions, government officials, and other external stakeholder groups are treated as individuals.)

- Chapter 4 presents ethical issues and problems that firms face with external consumers, government, and environmental groups. The question "How moral can and should corporations be and act in commercial dealings?" is examined. Do corporations have a conscience? Classic and recent crises resulting from corporate and environmental problems are covered.

- Chapter 5 presents the corporation as internal stakeholder and discusses leadership, strategy, structure, alliances, culture, and systems as dominant themes regarding how to lead, manage, and be a responsible follower in organizations today.

- Chapter 6 addresses the individual employee stakeholder and examines new and changing moral issues and dilemmas employees and managers face and must solve in the contemporary workplace.

- Chapter 7 extends the level of analysis to global and multinational corporations (MNCs) and discusses ethical issues between MNCs, host countries, and other groups. Issues resulting from globalization are presented along with stakeholders who monitor corporate responsibility internationally. Negotiation techniques for professionals responsibly doing business abroad are presented.

Cases

Twenty-two cases are included in this edition, 15 of which are new:

- Enron: What Caused the Ethical Collapse? (new)
- Microsoft: Industry Predator or Fierce Competitor?
- The Tylenol Crisis: How Effective Public Relations Saved Johnson & Johnson

- The Plundering of Adelphia Communications: The Saga of the Rigas Family (new)
- Accounting Irregularities at WorldCom (new)
- Arthur Andersen . . . No More: What Went Wrong? (new)
- Samuel Waksal and ImClone (new)
- Aaron Feuerstein and Malden Mills: How Values Guide Actions in a Post-Crisis Situation (new)
- Ford's Pinto Fires: The Retrospective View of Ford's Field Recall Coordinator
- Napster: From Illegal Weapon to Killer Application
- Apple Computer's Online Music Venture (new)
- Dow Corning and the Silicone Breast Implant Controversy
- Colt and the Gun Control Controversy
- Wal-Mart: Problems in Paradise? (new)
- Nike's Responses to Sweatshop Charges: Protected or Unprotected Speech? (new)
- *Fortune's* Global Most Admired Companies: Do Values Make a Difference? (new)
- What's Written versus Reality: Ethical Dilemmas in a Hi-Tech Public Relations Firm
- Sotheby's Price Fixing (new)
- Sherron Watkins—Revelations of a Letter (new)
- Women on Wall Street: Fighting for Equality in a Male-Dominated Industry (new)
- Olympic Athlete Drug Testing: Creating an Anti-Doping Culture and Fair Competition (new)
- Sweatshops: Just a Problem in Developing Nations? (new)

Ancillary Package

The following ancillaries are available to instructors who adopt *Business Ethics: A Stakeholder and Issues Management Approach*:

- *Instructor's Manual with Test Bank* (0-324-32127-9). Includes lecture outlines, suggested answers to end-of-chapter discussion questions and ethical dilemmas, case notes, and test questions. Prepared by David A. Foote, Middle Tennessee State University, and Ross Mecham, Virginia Polytechnic Institute and State University. Available in print or for download at http://weiss.swlearning.com.

- *PowerPoint.* Lecture-support slides. Prepared by Christina Stamper, Western Michigan University. Available for download at http://weiss.swlearning.com.

- *ExamView Testing Software.* Contains all the questions available in the printed Test Bank. ExamView is an easy-to-use test-creation program available in Windows and Macintosh formats. Available on the Instructor's Resource CD.

- *Instructor's Resource CD* (0-324-32130-9). Includes key instructor ancillaries (instructor's manual, Test Bank, ExamView, and PowerPoint slides) on CD-ROM, giving instructor's the ultimate tool for customizing lectures and presentations.

- *Video* (VHS 0-324-31606-2; DVD 0-324-31614-3). Includes video segments selected to support the themes of the book and to deepen students' understanding of the ethical concepts presented throughout the text.

- *Web Site* (http://weiss.swlearning.com). Offers a host of ancillary materials for students and instructors, including downloadable ancillaries for the instructor.

Acknowledgments

This book has been in the making over the last several years during my teaching of MBA students and executives. My consulting work also pervades this text in numerous ways. I would like to thank all my students for their questions, challenges, and class contributions, which have stimulated the research and presentations in this text. Michael McCuddy of Valparaiso University was also very helpful in adding and revising cases to the fourth edition. I also thank my colleagues with whom I have met and worked over the years in the Academy of Management and in the Organizational Behavior Teaching Society. I also thank colleagues at Bentley College who contributed resources, ideas, and motivation for executing the writing of the text. Kathy Rusiniak, my graduate assistant, helped enormously with the first edition. Vinamra Daga and Angela Ding, Bentley College MBA students, helped make the second edition possible with their research and writing assistance. Kristin Galfetti helped with the original research and construction of the discussion questions. I also wish to thank Michael Hoffman and his staff at Bentley College's Center for Business Ethics, who shared resources and friendship in helping with research. I thank Leslie Kauffman for her invaluable editorial help, along with Keith

Roberts, Alison Trulock, and Stephanie Schempp for their management of the production process, and John Szilagyi, my principal editor, who continues to make these editions possible.

I recognize and extend thanks to those who reviewed this book and offered valuable suggestions as this edition hopefully reflects:

Albert D. Clark, Southern University

Geri L. Dreiling, Fontbonne University

Christina Eggert, South Carolina State University

Robert Giacalone, University of Richmond

Suresh Gopalan, Columbus State University

John James, University of Florida

Susan Jarvis, University of Texas–Pan American

Greg Jenkins, North Carolina State University

Mark Keppler, California State University–Fresno

Susan Key, University of Alabama at Birmingham

Nancy Landrum, Morehead State University

Tony McAdams, University of Northern Iowa

Michael McCuddy, Valparaiso University

Joan Ryan, Lane Community College

Christina Stamper, Western Michigan University

William Wines, Boise State University

Several graduate students, many of whom are not identified here, from my Management Systems in the Changing Environment course at Bentley College contributed to the research and writing of the cases. I wish to thank the following MBA students who authored drafts of the following cases used in this text: Apple Computer case—John D. MacDonald; Colt case—Dan Barton, Craig Corsetti, and Aman Datta; Hi-Tech Public Relations case—Tim Corbett and Trudy Essember; Napster case—Robert Manning, Leenuta Pola, Kristina Morin, and D. Krachev; Olympic Athlete Drug Testing case—Paula C. Greene; Sam Waksal and ImClone case—Amy Venskus; Sotheby's case—Christopher Besse and Caitlin Murray; Wal-Mart case—Keri Babajtis, Yadelyn Cordero, and Sukhenda Samaraweera; and Women on Wall Street case—Monica Meunier.

Joseph W. Weiss
Bentley College

Case Authorship

Case 1

Adapted and edited for this text by Michael K. McCuddy, The Louis S. and Mary L. Morgal Chair of Christian Business Ethics and Professor of Management, College of Business Administration, Valparaiso University.

29

Case 2

Written by Michael K. McCuddy, Valparaiso University.

34

Case 3

Written by Tamara Kaplan, Pennsylvania State University.

89

Case 4

Written by Michael K. McCuddy, Valparaiso University.

97

Case 5

Written by Michael K. McCuddy, Valparaiso University.

101

Case 11

Written by John McDonald under the direction of Professor Joseph W. Weiss and adapted and edited for this text by Michael K. McCuddy, Valparaiso University.

236

Case 12

Written by MBA students under the direction of Professor Joseph W. Weiss and adapted and edited for this text by Michael K. McCuddy, Valparaiso University.

244

Case 13

Written by MBA students from Bentley College under the direction of Professor Joseph W. Weiss and adapted and edited for this text by Michael K. McCuddy, Valparaiso University.

254

Case 14

Written by Keri Babajtis, Yadelyn Cordero, and Sukhenda Samaraweera under the direction of Professor Joseph W. Weiss and adapted and edited for this text by Michael K. McCuddy, Valparaiso University.

262

Case 15

Written by Michael K. McCuddy, Valparaiso University.

272

Case 16

Written by Michael K. McCuddy, Valparaiso University.
333

Case 17

Written by an MBA student from Bentley College under the direction of Professor Joseph W. Weiss and adapted and edited for this text by Michael K. McCuddy, Valparaiso University.
341

Case 18

Written by Christopher Besse and Caitlin Murray under the direction of Professor Joseph Weiss and adapted and edited for this text by Michael K. McCuddy, Valparaiso University.
351

Case 19

Written by Michael K. McCuddy, Valparaiso University.
418

Case 20

Written by Monica Meunier under the direction of Professor Joseph W. Weiss and adapted and edited for this text by Michael K. McCuddy, Valparaiso University.
423

Case 21

Written by Paula C. Greene under the direction of Professor Joseph Weiss and adapted and edited for this text by Michael K. McCuddy, Valparaiso University.

476

Case 22

Written by Michael K. McCuddy, Valparaiso University.

483

1

Business Ethics, the Changing Environment, and Stakeholder Management

The Recording Industry Association of America (RIAA), on behalf of its member companies, renewed its commitment to protecting the rights of copyright owners and deterring illegal file sharing, bringing a new round of copyright infringement cases today, including lawsuits against individuals at 14 additional universities.

Today's action targeted 477 illegal file sharers, including 69 individuals using university networks to illegally distribute copyrighted sound recordings on unauthorized peer-to-peer services. The university networks used for this illegal activity include schools in Connecticut, Georgia, Kansas, Michigan, Minnesota, New Jersey, Pennsylvania, Rhode Island, Texas, Virginia, and Washington. As in earlier rounds of lawsuits, the RIAA is utilizing the "John Doe" litigation process, which is used to sue defendants whose names are not known.

Citing the ongoing effort to reach out to the university community on proactive solutions to the problem of illegal file sharing on college campuses, Cary Sherman, the RIAA's President, said "it remains as important as ever that we continue to work with the university community in a way that is respectful of the law as well as university values. That is one of our top priorities, and we believe our constructive outreach has been enormously productive so far. Along with offering students legitimate music services, campus-wide educational and technological initiatives are playing a critical role. But there is also a complementary need for enforcement by copyright owners against the serious offenders—to remind people that this activity is illegal." Sherman stated, "Illegally downloading music from the Internet costs everyone—the musicians not getting compensated for their craft, the owners and employees of the thousands of record stores that have been forced to close, legitimate online music services building their businesses, and consumers who play by the rules and purchase their music legally.[1]

1.1 BUSINESS ETHICS AND THE CHANGING ENVIRONMENT

Businesses and governments operate in changing technological, legal, economic, social, and political environments with competing stakeholders and power claims. As the opening story shows, there is more than one side to every complex issue and debate involving businesses, consumers, families, other institutions, and professionals. The RIAA does not wish to alienate too many college students because they are also the music industry's best customers. At the same time, the association believes it must protect those groups it represents. Who is right and who is wrong? Who stands to lose and gain from this case? Who gets hurt by these transactions? Which group's ethical positions are the most defensible?

Stakeholders are individuals, companies, groups, and even nations that cause and respond to external issues, opportunities, and threats. Corporate scandals, globalization, deregulation, mergers, technology, and global terrorism have accelerated the rate of change and the uncertainty in which stakeholders must make business and moral decisions. Issues concerning questionable ethical and illegal business practices confront everyone, as the following examples illustrate:

- The corporate scandals at Enron, Adelphia, Halliburton, MCI WorldCom, Tyco, Arthur Andersen, Global Crossing, Dynegy, Qwest, Merrill Lynch, and other firms jarred shareholder and public confidence in Wall Street and corporate governance. One survey found 75% of the public had limited confidence in large firms. Now, effective corporate governance is a global concern.[2]

- The debate continues over excessive CEO pay and poor corporate performance. "CEOs running 100 of the USA's biggest companies pulled in a median 2002 compensation of $33.4 million." The disconnect between pay and performance is exemplified by Walt Disney's 19% shares loss in 2002—the stock was off 60% from 2000. Still, Michael Eisner took a $5 million bonus for that period. Also, CEO Tom Engibous of Texas Instruments had a salary and bonus of $1.3 million with a 2002 grant of $44 million, although the company's stock lost 80% since early 2000—40% in 2002. His stock options are worth $142 million.[3]

- Are companies becoming over-regulated since the scandals? The Sarbanes-Oxley Act of 2002 is one response to the corporate scandals. This act states that corporate officers will serve prison time and pay large fines if they are found guilty of fraudulent financial reporting and of deceiving shareholders. Implementing this legislation requires companies to create accounting oversight boards, establish ethics codes, and show financial reports in greater detail to investors. Implementing these provisions is costly for corporations. Some claim their profits and global competitiveness are negatively affected and "unenforceable."[4]

- U.S. firms are outsourcing work to India and other countries to cut costs and improve profits. Estimates of U.S. jobs outsourced range between 104,000 to 400,000 from 2000 to 2004, to a projected 3.3 million by 2015. Do U.S. employees who are laid off and displaced need protection, or is this another expected societal business transformation?[5]

These are a sample of larger, macrolevel issues that occur among stakeholders in rapidly changing business environments. Add the ongoing issues resulting from disruptive technologies and increased working hours on professional and personal stress levels, and you can see the pressures created on stakeholders. Large issues, like the open-file-sharing story, can get personal quickly depending on who is involved and who is at risk. Before discussing stakeholder management, we take a brief look at the broader environmental forces that affect industries, organizations, and individuals.

Seeing the "Big Picture" Pulitzer Prize-winning journalist Thomas Friedman, in *The Lexus and the Olive Tree*,[6] has written a vivid account of the accelerating trend toward globalization. A macro environmental perspective provides a first step using stakeholder and issues approaches to map out and analyze interactions between organizations and groups. Friedman notes,

> Like everyone else trying to adjust to this new globalization system and bring it into focus, I had to retrain myself and develop new lenses to see it. Today, more than ever, the traditional boundaries between politics, culture, technology, finance, national security, and ecology are disappearing. You often cannot explain one without referring to the others, and you cannot explain the whole without reference to them all. I wish I could say I understood all this when I began my career, but I didn't. I came to this approach entirely by accident, as successive changes in my career kept forcing me to add one more lens on top of another, just to survive. (pp. 2, 20)

Quoting Murray Gell-Mann, the Nobel laureate and former professor of theoretical physics at Caltech, Friedman continues,

> "We need a corpus of people who consider that it is important to take a serious and professional look at the whole system. It has to be a crude look, because you will never master every part or every interconnection. Unfortunately, in a great many places in our society, including academia and most bureaucracies, prestige accrues principally to those who study carefully some [narrow] aspect of a problem, a trade, a technology, or a culture, while discussion of the big picture is relegated to cocktail party conversation. That is crazy. We have to learn not only to have specialists but also people whose specialty is to spot the strong interactions and entanglements of the different dimensions, and then take a crude look at the whole." (p. 28)

Environmental Forces and Stakeholders
Organizations are embedded in and interact with multiple changing local, national, and international environments, as the previous excerpts illustrate. These environments are increasingly merging into a global system of dynamically interrelated interactions among businesses and economies. We must "think globally before acting locally" in many situations. The macrolevel environmental forces shown in Figure 1.1 affect the performance and operation of industries, organizations, and jobs. This framework can be used as a starting point to identify trends, issues, opportunities, and ethical problems that affect people and stakes in different levels. A first step toward understanding stakeholder issues is to gain an understanding of environmental forces that influence stakes. As we discuss an overview of these environmental forces here, think of the effects and pressures each of the forces has on you.

The *economic environment* continues to evolve into a more global context of trade, markets, and resource flows. Large and small U.S. companies are expanding businesses and products overseas. Stock and bond market volatility and interdependencies across international regions are unprecedented. The European market has consolidated currencies in order to facilitate competitiveness and monetary flow. The rise of China presents new trade opportunities and business practices.

Technologically, the advent of electronic communication and the Internet is changing economies, industries, companies, and jobs. U.S. jobs that are based on routine technologies and rules-based procedures are vulnerable to outsourcing. Online technologies facilitate changing corporate "best practices." Company supply chains are also becoming virtually integrated online. While speed, scope, economy of scale, and efficiency are transforming transactions through information technology, privacy and surveillance issues continue to emerge. The boundary between surveillance and convenience continues to blur.

Politically, the emergence of China as an economic power and the rise of global terrorism are also changing trading and business partners.

FIGURE 1.1	Environmental Dimensions Affecting Industries, Organizations, and Jobs

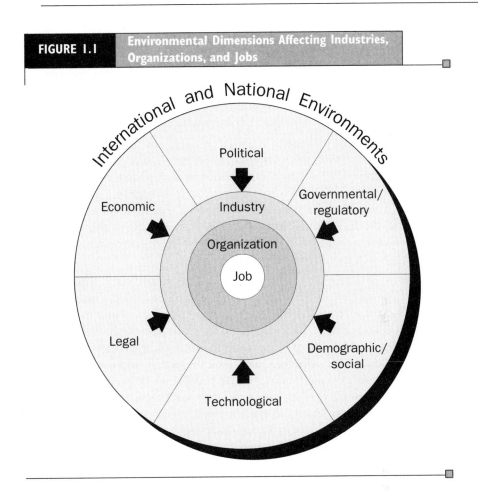

Electronic democracy is changing the way individuals and groups think and act on political issues. Instant Web surveys, which are broadcast over CNN and interactive Web sites, have created a global chatroom for political issues. Creation of online communities in the 2004 campaign proved an effective political strategy for both U.S. parties' fundraising.

Many *governmental and regulatory* laws and procedures also are changing. Since Enron and other corporate scandals, the Sarbanes-Oxley Act of 2002 and the revised 2004 Federal Sentencing Guidelines were created to audit and constrain corporate executives from blatant fraudulence on financial statements. Several federal agencies are also changing or ignoring standards for corporations. The U.S. Food and Drug Administration (FDA), for example, speeds the required market approval time for new drugs sought by patients with life-threatening diseases, but lags behind in taking some unsafe drugs off the market.

Uneven regulation of fraudulent and anticompetitive practices affects competition, shareholders, and consumers. Executives from Enron and other large U.S. firms involved in scandals have been and are being tried and sentenced. Should the banks that loaned funds to these also be have not been charged with wrongdoing? Should U.S. laws be enforced more evenly? Who regulates the regulators?

Legal questions and issues affect all of these environmental dimensions and every stakeholder. How much power should the government have to administer laws to protect citizens and ensure that business transactions are fair? Also, who protects the consumer in a free market system? These issues are exemplified in the Firestone defective tire crisis and the file-sharing controversy as summarized in the opening story; all of which question the nature and limits of consumer and corporate law in a free market economy.

Demographically, the workforce has become more diverse. Employers and employees are faced with sexual harassment and discrimination issues and the effects of downsizing and outsourcing on morale, career changes, productivity, and security. How can companies effectively integrate a workforce that is increasingly both younger and older, less educated and more educated, and technologically sophisticated and technologically unskilled? Also, should companies be pressured to pay insurance to employees' partners in same sex unions, which are not legal in some states? As these environmental factors continue to force adaption by stakeholders, a stakeholder management approach can benefit all constituencies in developing collaborative and socially responsible actions.

Stakeholder Management Approach How do companies, the media, political groups, consumers, employees, competitors, and other groups respond when they are affected by an issue, dilemma, threat, or opportunity from the environments just described? The stakeholder management approach is a way of understanding the ethical effects of environmental forces and groups on specific issues that affect real-time stakeholders and their welfare.

The stakeholder approach begins to address these questions by enabling individuals and groups to articulate collaborative, win–win strategies based on

1. Identifying and prioritizing issues, threats, or opportunities

2. Mapping who the stakeholders are

3. Identifying their stakes, interests, and power sources

4. Showing who the members of coalitions are or may become

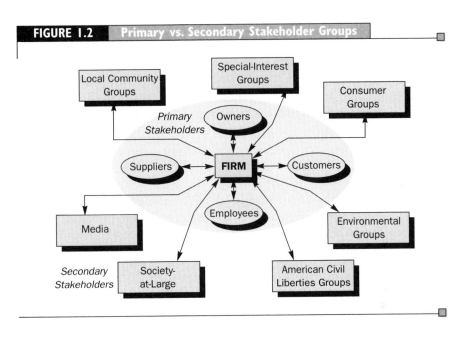

FIGURE 1.2   Primary vs. Secondary Stakeholder Groups

5. Showing what each stakeholder's ethics are (and should be)

6. Developing collaborative strategies and dialogue from a "higher ground" perspective to move plans and interactions to the desired closure for all parties

Chapter 2 lays out specific steps and strategies for analyzing stakeholders. Here, our aim is to develop awareness of the ethics and social responsibilities of different stakeholders. As Figure 1.2 illustrates, there can be a wide range of stakeholders in any situation. We turn to a general discussion of "business ethics" in the following section to introduce the subject and motivate you to investigate ethical dimensions of organizational and professional behavior.

1.2 WHAT IS BUSINESS ETHICS? WHY DOES IT MATTER?

Business ethicists ask, "What is right and wrong, good and bad, and harmful and beneficial regarding decisions and actions in organizational transactions?" Ethical "solutions" to business and organizational problems may have more than one alternative, and sometimes no right solution may seem available.

Learning to think, reason, and act ethically can enable us to first be aware of and recognize a potential ethical problem. Then, we can evaluate values, assumptions, and judgments regarding the problem before we act. Ultimately, ethical principles alone cannot answer what the noted theologian Paul Tillich called "the courage to be" in serious ethical dilemmas or crises. We can also learn from business case studies, role playing, and discussions how our actions affect others in different situations. Acting accountably and responsibly is still a choice.

Laura Nash defined business ethics as "the study of how personal moral norms apply to the activities and goals of commercial enterprise. It is not a separate moral standard, but the study of how the business context poses its own unique problems for the moral person who acts as an agent of this system." Nash stated that business ethics deals with three basic areas of managerial decision making: (1) choices about what the laws should be and whether to follow them; (2) choices about economic and social issues outside the domain of law; and (3) choices about the priority of self-interest over the company's interests.[7]

Unethical Business Practices of Employees   The third National Business Ethics Survey (NBES) that surveyed 1,500 employees in 48 contiguous American states[8] found the following types of ethical misconduct have occurred:

- "Nearly a third of respondents say their coworkers condone questionable ethics practices by showing respect for those who achieve success using them.

- The types of misconduct most frequently observed in 2003 include: abusive or intimidating behavior (21%); misreporting hours worked (20%); lying (19%); and withholding needed information (18%).

- Employees in transitioning organizations (undergoing merger, acquisition, or restructuring) observe misconduct and feel pressure at rates that are nearly double those in more stable organizations.

- Compared with other employees, younger managers (under age 30) with low tenure in their organizations (less than three years) are twice as likely to feel pressure to compromise ethics standards (21% versus 10%).

- Despite an overall increase in reporting misconduct, nearly half of all non-management employees (44%) still do not report the misconduct they observe. The top two reasons given for not reporting misconduct are: (1) a belief that no corrective action will be taken and (2) fear that the report will not be kept confidential.

- Younger employees with low tenure are among the least likely to report misconduct (43% as compared with 69% for all other employees). They are also among the most likely to feel that management and coworkers will view them negatively if they report it.

- Less than three in five employees (58%) who report misconduct are satisfied with the response of their organizations.

- In many areas, views of ethics remain "rosier at the top." For example, senior and middle managers have less fear of reporting misconduct and are more satisfied with the response of their organizations. They also feel that honesty and respect are practiced more frequently than do lower level employees."[9]

Signs of positive change since the corporate scandals and the year 2000 include:

- Employees perceived that top management does keep promises, discusses the importance of ethics, and exemplifies ethical behavior more since 2000. "For example, 82% of employees in 2003 said that top management in their organizations keeps promises and commitments, as compared with 77% in 2000. In addition, the increases between 2000 and 2003 tend to be more substantial in larger (over 500 employees) versus smaller organizations." Observed misconduct and pressures that compromise ethics standards declined since the NBES 2000 survey. "Observed misconduct dropped from 31% in 2000 to 22% in 2003, and pressure fell from 13% to 10% during this time period."

- Non-management employees had the greatest decline in observed misconduct and pressures.

- Misconduct reported by employees increased in the surveys conducted as follows: 1994 (48%), 2000 (57%), and 2003 (65%).

- Employees reported that honesty and respect values were practiced more frequently in their organizations in 2003.[10]

Unethical Business Practices by Industry   The most unethical behavior, one survey showed, happens in the following areas (listed in rank order, starting with the organization that has the most instances of unethical behavior)[11]:

1. Government
2. Sales
3. Law
4. Media
5. Finance
6. Medicine
7. Banking
8. Manufacturing

The sales profession, in particular, is under significant pressure to meet quotas. A survey by Sales & Marketing Management of 200 sales managers showed that 49% reported that their representatives lied on a sales call; 34% said that they heard representatives make unrealistic promises on sales calls; 22% said that their representatives sold products that customers did not need; 30% said that customers demanded a kickback for buying their product; and 54% said that the drive to meet sales goals does a disservice to customers.[12]

It is interesting to note the differences in the size of an organization and employees' perceptions of business ethics. Quoting from the National Business Ethics Survey, size matters:

- Smaller organizations (fewer than 500 employees) are less likely to have key elements of ethics programs in place than larger ones. For example, 41% of employees in smaller organizations say ethics training is provided, as compared with 67% in larger organizations. Similarly, 77% of employees in larger organizations say that mechanisms to report misconduct anonymously are available, versus 47% in smaller organizations.

- Employee perceptions of ethics in smaller and larger organizations converged in 2003. This finding contrasts with the 2000 survey findings, which showed employees in smaller organizations generally holding more positive views of ethics. The convergence is due primarily to more positive ethics trends in larger organizations between 2000 and 2003.[13]

These ethical issues in business suggest that any useful definition of business ethics must address a range of problems in the workplace, including relationships among professionals at all levels and among corporate executives and external groups.

Other issues discussed in this book include the ethical effects of *information technology* on the economy, workplace, and workforce (e.g., the "digital divide," rights and justice during transformations); *sexual harassment* (e.g., events at Wal-Mart, Mitsubishi, Astra USA, and Texaco); *invasion of privacy on the Internet* (e.g., workplace surveillance, individual identity theft, unauthorized use of personal information); limits of a company's *competitiveness*; employee rights and issues (e.g. employment laws, "just cause," standards to avoid wrongful dismissal, gift giving, same-sex marriage benefits); international human rights and sweatshop labor (e.g., Nike and other large retail firms); the ethics of *diversity* (e.g., the fair and equitable treatment of minorities in the international workforce, the changing perceptions and reality of a "level playing field" in businesses); and the future of *capitalism* (especially with regard to government regulation of U.S. companies doing business internationally).[14]

Why Does Ethics Matter in Business?   "Doing the right thing" matters. To companies and employers, acting legally and ethically means saving billions of dollars each year in lawsuits, settlements, and theft.

Studies have shown that corporations have paid significant financial penalties for acting unethically.[15] It is estimated that theft costs companies $600 billion annually, and that 79% of workers admit to or think about stealing from their employers. Also, CNN reported that an estimated one out of three businesses closes because of employee theft. The so-called cheating culture creates an environment that discourages whistle blowers from stepping up and telling what they know.[16]

Costs to businesses also include deterioration of relationships; damage to reputation; declining employee productivity, creativity, and loyalty; ineffective information flow throughout the organization; and absenteeism. Companies that have a reputation of unethical and uncaring behavior toward employees also have a difficult time recruiting and retaining valued professionals.

For business leaders and managers, managing ethically also means managing with integrity.[17] Integrity cascades throughout an organization. It shapes and influences the values, tone, and culture of the organization; the communications among all members; and the realism, commitment, and imagination of everyone in a company.

Working for the Best Companies   Employees care about ethics because they are attracted to ethically and socially responsible companies. *Fortune* magazine regularly publishes the 100 best companies for which to work (http://www.fortune.com). Although the list continues to change, it is instructive to observe some of the characteristics of good employers that employees repeatedly cite. The most frequently mentioned characteristics include profit sharing, bonuses, and monetary awards. However, the list also contains policies and benefits that balance work and personal life and those that encourage social responsibility. Consider these policies described by employees:

- "When it comes to flextime requests, managers are encouraged to 'do what is right and human.'"
- "An employee hotline to report violations of company values"
- "Will fire clients who don't respect its security officers"
- "Employees donated more than 28,000 hours of volunteer labor last year."

The public and consumers benefit from organizations acting in an ethically and socially responsible manner. Ethics matters in business because all stakeholders stand to gain when organizations, groups, and individuals seek to do the right thing, as well as do things the right way. Ethical companies create investor loyalty, customer satisfaction, and business performance and profits.[18] The following section presents different levels on which ethical issues can occur.

1.3 LEVELS OF BUSINESS ETHICS

Because ethical problems are not only an individual or personal matter, it is helpful to see the different levels at which issues originate, and how they often move to other levels. Because business leaders and professionals must manage a wide range of stakeholders inside and outside their organizations, understanding the issues that stakeholders face facilitates our understanding of the complex relationships between participants involved in solving ethical problems.

Ethical and moral issues in business can be examined from at least five levels. Figure 1.3 illustrates these five levels: individual, organizational, association, societal, and international.[19] Aaron Feuerstein's story as former CEO of Malden Mills exemplifies how an ethical leader in his seventies turned a disaster into an opportunity. His story also shows how his actions reflect his person, faith, allegiance to his family and community, and sense of social responsibility, which made an impact beyond the nation.

FIGURE 1.3   Business Ethics Levels

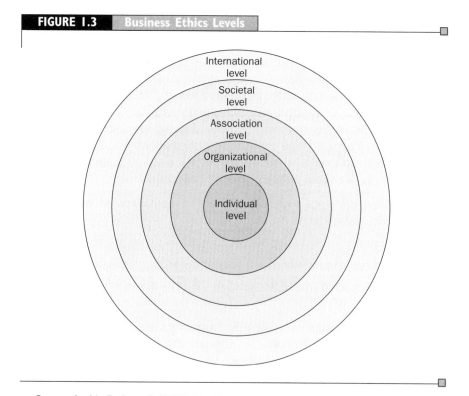

Source: Archie B. Carroll. (1978). Linking business ethics to behavior in organizations. SAM *Advanced Management Journal,* vol. 43, no. 3: 7. Reprinted with permission from Society for Advancement of Management, Texas A&M University, College of Business, 6300 Ocean Drive, FC111, Corpus Christi, Texas, 78412.

On December 11, 1995, Malden Mills in Lawrence, Massachusetts—manufacturer of Polartec and Polarfleece fabrics and the largest employer in the city—was destroyed by fire. Over 1,400 people were out of work. Feuerstein stated, "Everything I did after the fire was in keeping with the ethical standards I've tried to maintain my entire life, so it's surprising we've gotten so much attention. Whether I deserve it or not, I guess I became a symbol of what the average worker would like corporate America to be in a time when the American dream has been pretty badly injured." Feuerstein announced shortly after the fire that the employees would stay on the payroll, while the plant was rebuilt, for 60 days. He noted, "I think it was a wise business decision, but that isn't why I did it. I did it because it was the right thing to do." Mrs. Feuerstein personally signed off on all the rebuilding plans and ran a division of Malden Mills.

Feuerstein could have taken the $300 million in insurance and retired, or even offshored the entire operation. Instead, he paid out $25 million and helped rebuild the plant. Feuerstein spent the insurance funds, borrowed $100 million more, and built a new plant that is both environmentally and worker friendly. It is also unionized. Feuerstein commented, "You are not permitted to oppress the working man, because he's poor and he's needy, amongst your brethren and amongst the non-Jew in your community." Feuerstein was invited to President Clinton's State of the Union address and serves as an icon in the business ethics and leadership community, regardless of the fate of Malden Mills going forward.[20]

Asking Key Questions   It is helpful to be aware of the ethical levels of a situation and the possible interaction between these levels when confronting a question that has moral implications. The following questions can be asked when a problematic decision or action is perceived (before it becomes an ethical dilemma):

- What are my core values and beliefs?
- What are the core values and beliefs of my organization?
- Whose values, beliefs, and interests may be at risk in this decision? Why?
- Who will be harmed or helped by my decision or by the decision of my organization?
- How will my own and my organization's core values and beliefs be affected or changed by this decision?
- How will I and my organization be affected by the decision?

Figure 1.4 offers a graphic to help identify the ethics of the system (i.e., a country or region's customs, values, and laws), your organization (i.e., the written formal and informal acceptable norms and ways of doing business), and your own ethics, values, and standards.

FIGURE 1.4   A Framework for Classifying Ethical Levels

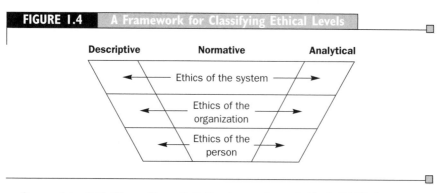

Source: John B. Matthews, Kenneth E. Goodpaster, Laura L. Nash. (1985). *Policies and Persons: A Casebook in Business Ethics,* p. 509. New York: McGraw-Hill. Reproduced with permission of the McGraw-Hill Companies.

In the following section, popular myths about business ethics are presented to challenge misconceptions regarding the nature of ethics and business. You may take the "Quick Test of Your Ethical Beliefs" before reading this section.

1.4 FIVE MYTHS ABOUT BUSINESS ETHICS

Not everyone agrees that ethics is a relevant subject for business education or dealings. Some have argued that "business ethics" is an *oxymoron,* or a contradiction in terms. Although this book does not advocate a particular ethical position or belief system, it argues that ethics is relevant to business transactions. However, certain myths persist about business ethics. The more popular myths are presented in Figure 1.5.

FIGURE 1.5   Five Business Ethics Myths

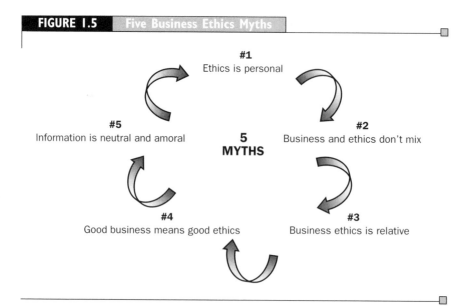

Answer each question following with your first reaction. Circle the number, from 1 to 4, that best represents your beliefs if 1 represents "completely agree" and 4 represents "completely disagree."

1. I consider money to be the most important reason for working at a job or in an organization.   1 2 3 4

2. I would hide truthful information about someone or something at work to save my job.   1 2 3 4

3. Lying is usually necessary to succeed in business.   1 2 3 4

4. Cutthroat competition is part of getting ahead in the business world.   1 2 3 4

5. I would do what is needed to promote my own career in a company, short of committing a serious crime.   1 2 3 4

6. Acting ethically at home and with friends is not the same as acting ethically on the job.   1 2 3 4

7. Rules are for people who don't really want to make it to the top of a company.   1 2 3 4

8. I believe that the "Golden Rule" is that the person who has the gold rules.   1 2 3 4

9. Ethics should be taught at home and in the family, not in professional or higher education.   1 2 3 4

10. I consider myself the type of person who does whatever it takes to get a job done, period.   1 2 3 4

Total your scores by adding up the numbers you circled. The lower you score, the more questionable your ethical principles regarding business activities. The lowest possible score is 10, the highest score is 40. Be ready to give reasons for your answers in a class discussion.

A myth is "a belief given uncritical acceptance by the members of a group, especially in support of existing or traditional practices and institutions." Myths regarding the relationship between business and ethics do not represent truth but popular and unexamined notions. Which myths have you accepted as unquestioned truth? Do you agree that the following myths are indeed myths? Do you know anyone who holds any of these myths as true?

Myth 1: "Ethics Is a Personal, Individual Affair, Not a Public or Debatable Matter"
This myth holds that individual ethics is based on personal or religious beliefs, and that one decides what is right and wrong in the privacy of one's conscience. This myth

is supported in part by Milton Friedman, a well-known economist, who views "social responsibility," as an expression of business ethics, to be unsuitable for business professionals to address seriously or professionally, because they are not equipped or trained to do so.[21]

Although it is true that individuals must make moral choices in life, including business affairs, it is also true that individuals do not operate in a vacuum. Individual ethical choices are most often influenced by discussions, conversations and debates and made in group contexts. Individuals often rely on organizations and groups for meaning, direction, and purpose. Moreover, individuals are integral parts of organizational cultures, which have standards to govern what is acceptable. Therefore, to argue that ethics related to business issues is mainly a matter of personal or individual choice is to belittle the role organizations play in shaping and influencing member's attitudes and behavior.

Studies indicate that organizations that act in socially irresponsible ways often pay penalties for unethical behavior.[22] In fact, integrating ethics into the strategic management process is advocated (e.g., "doing well by doing good"). It is argued that integrating ethics into the strategic management process is the right thing and the profitable thing to do. Corporate social performance has been found to increase financial performance. One study clearly showed that "analysis of corporate failures and disasters strongly suggests that incorporating ethics in before-profit decision making can improve strategy development and implementation and ultimately maximize corporate profits."[23] Moreover, the popularity of books, training, and articles on learning organizations and the habits of highly effective people among *Fortune* 500 and 1000 companies suggests that organizational leaders and professionals have a need for purposeful, socially responsible management training and practices.[24]

Myth 2: "Business and Ethics Do Not Mix"   This popular myth[25] holds that business practices are basically amoral—not necessarily immoral—because businesses operate in a free market. This myth also asserts that management is based on scientific, rather than religious or ethical, principles.

Although this myth may have thrived in an earlier industrializing U.S. society and even during the 1960s, the myth has eroded over the past two decades. The widespread consequences of computer hacking on individual, commercial, and government systems that affect the public's welfare, like identity theft on the Internet (stealing others' Social Security numbers and using their bank accounts and credit cards); and kickbacks, unsafe products, oil spills, toxic dumping, air and water pollution, and improper use of public funds have contributed to the erosion. The international and national infatuation with a purely scientific understanding of U.S. business practices, in particular, and of a value-free marketing system has been undermined by these events. As one saying goes, "A little experience can inform a lot of theory."

The ethicist Richard DeGeorge has noted that the belief that business is amoral is a myth because it ignores the business involvement of all of us. Business is a human activity, not simply a scientific one and, as such, can be evaluated from a moral perspective. If everyone in business acted amorally or immorally, as a pseudoscientific notion of business would suggest, businesses would collapse. Employees would openly steal from employers; employers would recklessly fire employees at will; contractors would arrogantly violate obligations; chaos would prevail. Business and society share the same U.S. values: rugged individualism in a free-enterprise system, pragmatism over abstraction, freedom, and independence. When business practices violate these American values, society and the public are threatened.

Finally, the belief that businesses operate in totally "free markets" is debatable. Although the value or desirability of the concept of a "free market" is not in question, practices of certain firms in free markets are. At issue are the unjust methods of accumulation and noncompetitive uses of wealth and power in the formation of monopolies and oligopolies (i.e., small numbers of firms dominating the rules and transactions of certain markets). The dominance of AT&T before the breakup is an example of how one powerful conglomerate could control the market. Microsoft and Wal-Mart may be other examples. The U.S. market environment can be characterized best as a "mixed economy" based on free-market mechanisms, but not limited to or explained only by them. Mixed economies rely on some governmental policies and laws for control of deficiencies and inequalities. For example, protective laws are still required, such as those governing minimum wage, antitrust situations, layoffs from plant closings, and instances of labor exploitation. In such mixed economies in which injustices thrive, ethics is a lively topic.

Myth 3: "Ethics in Business Is Relative"   This is one of the more popular myths, and it holds that no right or wrong way of believing or acting exists. Right and wrong are in the eyes of the beholder.

The claim that ethics is not based solely on absolutes has some truth to it. However, to argue that all ethics is relative contradicts everyday experience. For example, the view that because a person or society believes something to be right makes it right is problematic when examined. Many societies believed in and practiced slavery; however, in contemporary individuals' experiences, slavery is morally wrong. When individuals and firms do business in societies that promote slavery, does that mean that the individuals and firms also must condone and practice slavery? The simple logic of relativism, which is discussed in Chapter 3, gets complicated when seen in daily experience. The question that can be asked regarding this myth is, "Relative to whom or what? And why?" The logic of this ethic, which answers that question with "Relative to me, myself, and my interests" as a maxim, does not promote community. Also, if ethical relativism were carried to its logical extreme, no one could disagree with anyone about moral issues because each person's values would be true for him or her. Ultimately, this logic would state that no right or wrong exists apart from an individual's or society's principles. How could interactions be completed if ethical relativism was carried to its limit? Moreover, the U.S. government, in its vigorous pursuit of Microsoft, certainly has not practiced a relativist style of ethics.

Myth 4: "Good Business Means Good Ethics"   The reasoning here[26] is that executives and firms that maintain a good corporate image, practice fair and equitable dealings with customers and employees, and earn profits by legitimate, legal means are de facto ethical. Such firms, therefore, would not have to be concerned explicitly with ethics in the workplace. Just do a hard, fair day's work and that has its own moral goodness and rewards.

The faulty reasoning underlying this logic is that ethics does not always provide solutions to technical business problems. Moreover, as Buchholz[27] argued, no correlation exists between "goodness" and material success.

It also argues that "excellent" companies and corporate cultures have created concern for people in the workplace that exceeds the profit motive. In these cases, excellence seems to be related more to customer service, to maintenance of meaningful public and employee relationships, and to corporate integrity than profit motive.[28]

The point is that ethics is not something added to business operations; it is necessary to managing successfully. A more accurate, logical statement from business experience would suggest that "good ethics means good business." This is more in line with observations from successful companies that are ethical first and also profitable.

Finally, "What happens, then, if what should be ethically done is not the best thing for business? What happens when good ethics is not good business?"

The ethical thing to do may not always be in the best interests of the firm. We should promote business ethics, not because good ethics is good business, but because we are morally required to adopt the moral point of view in all our dealings with other people—and business is no exception. In business, as in all other human endeavors, we must be prepared to pay the costs of ethical behavior. The costs may sometimes seem high, but that is the risk we take in valuing and preserving our integrity.[29]

Myth 5: "Information and Computing Are Amoral"

This myth holds that information and computing are neither moral nor immoral but are amoral. They are in a "gray zone," a questionable area regarding ethics. Information and computing have positive dimensions, such as empowerment and enlightenment through the ubiquitous exposure to information, increased efficiency, and quick access to online global communities. It is also true that information and computing have a dark side: Information about individuals can be used as "a form of control, power, and manipulation.[30]

The point here is to beware of the dark side: the misuse of information and computing. Ethical implications are present but veiled. Truth and accuracy must be protected and guarded: "Falsehood, inaccuracy, lying, deception, disinformation, misleading information are all vices and enemies of the Information Age, for they undermine it. Fraud, misrepresentation, and falsehood are inimical to all of them.[31]

Logical problems occur in all five of these myths. In many instances, the myths hold simplistic and even unrealistic notions about ethics in business dealings. In the following sections, the discussion about the nature of business ethics continues by exploring two questions:

- Why use ethical reasoning in business?
- What is the nature of ethical reasoning?

1.5 WHY USE ETHICAL REASONING IN BUSINESS?

Ethical reasoning is required in business for at least three reasons. First, many times laws do not cover all aspects or "gray areas" of a problem.[32] How could tobacco companies have been protected by the law for decades until the settlement in 1997, when the industry agreed to pay $368.5 billion for the first 25 years and then $15 billion a year indefinitely to compensate states for the costs of health care for tobacco-related illnesses? What gray areas in federal and state laws (or the enforcement of those laws) prevailed for decades? What sources of power or help can people turn to in these situations for truthful information, protection, and compensation when laws are not enough?

Second, free-market and regulated-market mechanisms do not effectively inform owners and managers how to respond to complex issues that have far-reaching ethical consequences. Enron's CEO Jeffrey Skilling believed that his new business model of Enron as an energy trading company was the next big breakthrough in a free-market economy. The idea was innovative and creative; the executive's implementation of the idea was illegal. Perhaps Skilling should have followed Enron's ethics code; it was one of the best available.

A third argument holds that ethical reasoning is necessary because complex moral problems require "an intuitive or learned understanding and concern for fairness, justice, due process to people, groups, and communities."[33] Company policies are limited in scope in covering human, environmental, and social costs of doing business. Judges have to use intuition and a kind of learn-as-you-go in many of their cases. In the example of the Microsoft alleged monopoly case, for example, there were no clear precedents in the software industry or with a company of Microsoft's size and global scope to offer clear legal direction. Ethics, then, plays a role in business because laws are many times insufficient to guide action.

1.6 Can Business Ethics Be Taught and Trained?

Because laws and legal enforcement are not always sufficient to help guide or solve complex human problems relating to business situations, the questions arise: Can ethics help? If so, how? And can business ethics be taught? This ongoing debate has no final answer, and studies continue to address the issue. One study, for example, that surveyed 125 graduate and undergraduate students in a business ethics course at the beginning of a semester showed that students did not reorder their priorities on the importance of ten social issues at the end of the semester, but they did change the degree of importance they placed on the majority of the issues surveyed.[34] What, if any, value can be gained from teaching ethical principles and training people to use them in business?

This discussion begins with what business ethics courses cannot or should not, in my judgment, do. Ethics courses should not advocate a set of rules from a single perspective or offer only one best solution to a specific ethical problem. Given the circumstances of situations, more desirable and less desirable courses of action may exist. Decisions depend on facts, inferences, and rigorous, ethical reasoning. Neither should ethics courses or training sessions promise superior or absolute ways of thinking and behaving in situations.

Informed and conscientious ethical analysis is not the only way to reason through moral problems.

Ethics courses and training can do the following[35]:

- Provide people with rationales, ideas, and vocabulary to help them participate effectively in ethical decision making processes
- Help people "make sense" of their environments by abstracting and selecting ethical priorities
- Provide intellectual weapons to do battle with advocates of economic fundamentalism and those who violate ethical standards
- Enable employees to act as alarm systems for company practices that do not meet society's ethical standards
- Enhance conscientiousness and sensitivity to moral issues and commitment to finding moral solutions
- Enhance moral reflectiveness and strengthen moral courage
- Increase people's ability to become morally autonomous, ethical dissenters and the conscience of a group
- Improve the moral climate of firms by providing ethical concepts and tools for creating ethical codes and social audits

Other scholars argue that ethical training can add value to the moral environment of a firm and to relationships in the workplace in the following ways[36]:

- Finding a match between an employee's and employer's values
- Managing the push-back point, where an employee's values are tested by peers, employees, and supervisors
- Handling an unethical directive from a boss
- Coping with a performance system that encourages cutting ethical corners

Teaching business ethics and training people to use them does not promise to provide answers to complex moral dilemmas. However, thoughtful and resourceful business ethics educators can facilitate the development of awareness of what is ethical, help individuals and groups realize that their ethical tolerance and decision making styles decrease unethical blind spots, and enhance discussion of moral problems openly in the workplace.

Finally, a useful framework for evaluating ethics training is Lawrence Kohlberg's study[37] of the stages of moral development, as well as studies on the relevance of Kohlberg's study for managers and professionals.[38]

Stages of Moral Development   Kohlberg's three levels of moral development (which encompass six stages) offer a guide for observing a person's level of moral maturity, especially as he or she engages in different organizational transactions. Whether, and to what extent, ethical education and training contribute to moral development in later years is not known. Most individuals in Kohlberg's 20-year study (limited to males) reached the fourth and fifth stages by adulthood. Only a few attained the sixth stage. Still, this framework is used in ethics classrooms and training centers around the globe.

> Level 1: Preconventional Level (Self-Orientation)

- Stage 1: Punishment avoidance: avoiding punishment by not breaking rules. The person has little awareness of others' needs.

- Stage 2: Reward seeking: acting to receive rewards for oneself. The person has awareness of others' needs but not of right and wrong as abstract concepts.

> Level 2: Conventional Level (Others Orientation)

- Stage 3: Good person: acting "right" to be a "good person" and to be accepted by family and friends, not to fulfill any moral ideal.

- Stage 4: Law and order: acting "right" to comply with law and order and norms in societal institutions.

> Level 3: Postconventional, Autonomous, or Principles Level (Universal, Humankind Orientation)

- Stage 5: Social contract: acting "right" to reach consensus by due process and agreement. The person is aware of relativity of values and tolerates differing views.

- Stage 6: Universal ethical principles: acting "right" according to universal, abstract principles of justice and rights. The person reasons and uses conscience and moral rules to guide actions.

Kohlberg's Study and Business Ethics   One study of 219 corporate managers working in different companies found that managers typically reason at moral stages 3 or 4, which, the author noted, is "similar to most adults in the Western, urban societies or other business managers."[39] Managers in large- to medium-sized firms reasoned at lower moral stages than managers who were self-employed or who worked at small firms. Reasons offered for this difference in moral reasoning include that larger firms have more complex bureaucracies and layers of structure, more standard policies and procedures, and exert more rule-based control over employees. Employees tend to get isolated from other parts of the organization and feel less involved in the central decision making process.

On the other hand, self-employed professionals and managers in smaller firms tend to interact with people throughout the firm and with external stakeholders. Involvement with and vulnerability to other stakeholders may cause these managers to adhere to social laws more closely and to reason at stage 4.

This study also found that managers reasoned at a higher level when responding to a moral dilemma in which the main character was not a corporate employee. It could be that managers reason at a higher level when moral problems are not associated with the corporation. The author suggested that the influence of the corporation tends to restrict the manager to lower moral reasoning stages. Or it could be that the nature of the moral dilemma may affect the way managers reason (e.g., some dilemmas may be appropriately addressed with stage 3 or 4 reasoning, other dilemmas may require stage 5 logic). This study raises the question: "How can organizations use these findings in training and managing people?"

Another important study argued that moral decision making is "issue dependent" and, more specifically, that "the moral intensity of the issue itself has a significant effect on moral decision making and behavior at all stages of the process." In fact, the authors argue that "issues of high moral intensity will be recognized as moral issues more frequently than will issues of low moral intensity."[40] The study suggests that people who do not recognize moral issues will not act morally regarding those issues. This conclusion supports a serious need for business ethics education and training with specific emphasis on identifying stakeholder and issues management.

1.7 PLAN OF THE BOOK

This book focuses on applying stakeholder and issues-management approaches along with your own critical reasoning to situations that involve groups and individuals who often have competing interpretations of a problem or opportunity. Because stakeholders are people, they generally act on beliefs, values, and financially motivated strategies. For this reason, ethics and values-based thinking is an important part of a stakeholder issues-management approach. It is important to understand why stakeholders act and how they make decisions. The stakeholder management approach ideally aims at having all parties reach win–win outcomes through communication and collaborative efforts.

FIGURE 1.6   Plan of the Book

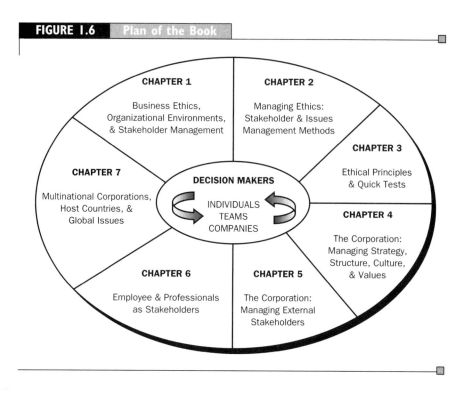

Unfortunately, this does not always happen. If we do not have a systematic approach to understanding what happens in complex stakeholder relationships, we cannot learn from past mistakes or plan for more collaborative, socially responsible future outcomes. A schematic of the book's organization is presented in Figure 1.6.

Chapter 2 provides a systematic approach for structuring and evaluating stakeholder issues, strategies, and options at the outset. Step-by-step methods for collaborating and for forming and evaluating strategies are identified. Chapter 3 provides ethical principles, "quick tests," and scenarios for evaluating motivations for certain decisions and actions. A stakeholder management approach involves knowing and managing stakeholders' ethics, including your own. Chapter 4 examines an organization's management of external stakeholders, including the environment. Chapter 5 looks at organizations as stakeholders, leadership, culture, and a collaborative approach for integrating ethics into organizations. Chapter 6 looks at the twenty-first-century workforce and discusses rights and obligations of employees and employers as stakeholders. Chapter 7 views nations as stakeholders and looks at how multinational corporations operate in host countries and different systems of capitalism.

Summary

Businesses and governments operate in numerous environments, including technological, legal, social, economic, and political dimensions. Understanding the effects of these environmental forces on industries and organizations is a first step in identifying stakeholders and the issues that different groups must manage in order to survive and compete. This book explores and illustrates how stakeholders can manage issues and trends in their changing environments in socially responsible, principled ways. Thinking and acting ethically is not a mechanical process; it is also very personal. It is important as a professional in an organization to integrate personal with professional experiences and values.

Business ethics deals with what is "right and wrong" in organizational decisions, behavior, and policies. Business ethics provides principles and guidelines that assist people in making informed choices that balance economic interests and social responsibilities. Being able to think of other stakeholders' interests can better inform the moral dimension of your own decisions. This is one aim of using a stakeholder approach.

Seeing the "big picture" of how ethical issues begin and transform requires imagination and some "maps." Because business ethics apply to several levels, this chapter presents these levels to illustrate the complexity of ethical decision making in business transactions. When you can "connect the dots" among these dimensions, more options for solving problems morally are opened.

The stakeholder approach also provides a means for mapping complicated relationships between the focal and other stakeholders, a means of identifying the strategies of each stakeholder, and a means for assessing the moral responsibility of all the constituencies.

Five myths often held about business ethics are discussed. Each myth is illustrated and refuted. You are invited to identify and question your own myths about business ethics. Ethical reasoning in business is explained with steps to guide decision making. Three reasons why ethical reasoning is necessary in business are: (1) Laws are often insufficient and do not cover all aspects or "gray areas" of a problem; (2) free-market and regulated-market mechanisms do not effectively inform owners and managers how to respond to complex crises that have far-reaching ethical consequences; and (3) complex moral problems require an understanding and concern for fairness, justice, and due process. Ethical reasoning helps individuals sort through conflicting opinions and information in order to solve moral dilemmas.

Ethical education and training can be useful for developing a broad awareness of the motivations, values, and consequences of our decisions. Business ethics does not, however, provide superior or universally correct solutions to morally complex dilemmas. Principles and guidelines are provided that can enhance—with case analysis, role playing, and group discussion—a person's insight and self-confidence in resolving moral dilemmas that often have two right (or wrong) solutions. Kohlberg's stages of moral development are presented and discussed as a means of assisting professionals and managers with ethical decision making by identifying underlying moral arguments and motivations.

QUESTIONS

1. Refer to Figure 1.1 to identify three specific environmental influences that the organization for which you work (or study) must address to survive and be competitive. Explain. How do these influences, pressures, and opportunities affect you and how ethically you get your work and goals accomplished?

2. What are the three major ethical issues you face now in your work or student life? What is "ethical" about these issues?

3. Identify some benefits of using a stakeholder approach in ethical decision making. How would using a stakeholder approach help you plan and/or solve an ethical issue in your working life? Explain.

4. Which, if any, of the five business myths in the chapter do you not accept as a myth (i.e., that you believe is true)? Explain.

5. Identify one myth you had/have about business ethics. Where did it originate? Why is it a "myth?" What led you to abandon this myth; or do you still believe in it? Explain.

6. Identify three reasons presented in this chapter for using ethical reasoning in business situations. Which of these reasons do you find the most valid? The least valid? Explain.

7. Is the law sufficient to help managers and employees solve ethical dilemmas? Explain and offer an example from your own experiences or from a contemporary event.

8. What are some important distinctive characteristics of ethical problems? What distinguishes an ethical from a legal problem?

9. What (if any) specific attitudes, values, beliefs, or behaviors of yours do you think could be changed from an ethics course? Explain.

10. Identify and describe a specific belief or behavior of yours that you would like to be changed from an ethics course.

EXERCISES

1. Invent and state your own definition of "business ethics." Do you believe that ethics is an important factor in business transactions today? If you were the chief executive officer (CEO) of a corporation, how would you communicate your perspective on the importance of ethics to your employees, customers, and other stakeholder groups?

2. Conduct your own small survey of two people regarding their opinions on the importance of unethical practices in businesses today. Do your interviewees give more importance to economic performance or socially irresponsible behavior? Or do they think other factors are more important? Summarize your results.

3. You are giving a speech at an important community business association meeting. You are asked to give a presentation called "an introduction to business ethics" for the members. Give an outline of your speech.

4. Explain how a major trend in the environment has affected your profession, job, or skills—as a professional or student. Be specific. Are any ethical consequences involved, and has this trend affected you?

5. Review Kohlberg's levels and stages of moral development. After careful consideration, briefly explain which stage, predominantly or characteristically, defines your ethical level of development. Explain. Has this stage influenced a recent decision you have made or action you have taken? Explain.

6. How can Kohlberg's framework assist professionals in organizations to see, prevent, and solve ethical problems and dilemmas?

7. You are applying to a prestigious organization for an important, highly visible position. The application requires you to describe an ethical dilemma in your history and how you handled it. Describe the dilemma and your ethical position.

Ethical Dilemma   You're in the Hot Seat

You are a staff associate at a major public accounting firm and graduated from college two years ago. You are working on an audit for a small, non-profit religious publishing firm. After performing tests on the royalty payables system, you discover that for the past five years, the royalty payable system has miscalculated the royalties it owes to authors of their publications. The firm owes almost $100,000 in past due royalties. All of the contracts with each author are negotiated differently. However, each author's royalty percentage will increase at different milestones in books sold (i.e., 2% up to 10,000 and 3% thereafter). The software package did not calculate the increases, and none of the authors ever received their increase in royalty payments. At first you can't believe that none of the authors ever realized they were owed their money. You double check your calculations and then present your findings to the senior auditor on the job. Much to your surprise, his suggestion is to pass over this finding. He suggests that you sample a few additional royalty contracts and document that you expanded your testing and found nothing wrong. The firm's audit approach is well documented in this area and is firmly based on statistical sampling. Because you had found multiple errors in the small number of royalty contracts tested, the firm's approach suggested testing 100% of the contracts. This would mean: (1) going over the budgeted time/ expense estimated to the client; (2) possibly providing a negative audit finding; and (3) confirming that the person who audited the section in the years past may not have performed procedures correctly.

Based on the prior year's work papers, the senior auditor on the job performed the testing phase in all of these years just before his promotion. For some reason, you get the impression that the senior auditor is frustrated with you. The relationship seems strained. He is very intense, constantly checking staff's progress in the hope of coming in even a half-hour under budget for a designated test/audit area. There's a lot of pressure, and you don't know what to do. This person is responsible for writing your review for your personnel file and bonus or promotion review. He is a very popular employee who is "on the fast track" to partnership.

You don't know whether to tell the truth and risk a poor performance review and jeopardize your future with this company or to tell the truth, hopefully be exonerated, and be able to live with yourself by "doing the right thing" and facing consequences with a clean conscience.

Questions

1. What would you do as the staff associate in this situation? Why? What are the risks of telling the truth for you? What are the benefits? Explain.

2. What is the "right" thing to do in this situation? What is the "smart" thing to do for your job and career? What is the difference, if there is one, between the "right" and "smart" thing to do in this situation? Explain.

3. Explain what you would say to the senior auditor, your boss, in this situation if you decided to tell the truth as you know it.

Case 1

Enron: What Caused the Ethical Collapse?

Introduction   Kenneth Lay, former chairman and chief executive officer (CEO) of Enron Corp., is quoted in Michael Novak's book *Business as a Calling: Work and the Examined Life* as saying, "I was fully exposed to not only legal behavior but moral and ethical behavior and what that means from the standpoint of leading organizations and people." In an introductory statement to the revised *Enron Code of Ethics* issued in July 2000, Lay wrote: "As officers and employees of Enron Corp., its subsidiaries, and its affiliated companies, we are responsible for conducting the business affairs of the companies in accordance with all applicable laws and in a moral and honest manner." Lay went on to indicate that the 64-page *Enron Code of Ethics* reflected policies approved by the company's board of directors and that the company, which enjoyed a reputation for being fair and honest, was highly respected. Enron's ethics code also specified that "An employee shall not conduct himself or herself in a manner which directly or indirectly would be detrimental to the best interests of the Company or in a manner which would bring to the employee financial gain separately derived as a direct consequence of his or her employment with the Company."

Enron's ethics code was based on respect, integrity, communication, and excellence. These values were described as follows:

> Respect. We treat others as we would like to be treated ourselves. We do not tolerate abusive or disrespectful treatment. Ruthlessness, callousness and arrogance don't belong here.

> Integrity. We work with customers and prospects openly, honestly and sincerely. When we say we will do something, we will do it; when we say we cannot or will not do something, then we won't do it.

> Communication. We have an obligation to communicate. Here we take the time to talk with one another . . . and to listen. We believe that information is meant to move and that information moves people.

> Excellence. We are satisfied with nothing less than the very best in everything we do. We will continue to raise the bar for everyone. The great fun here will be for all of us to discover just how good we can really be.

Given this code of conduct and Ken Lay's professed commitment to business ethics, how could Enron have collapsed so dramatically, going from reported revenues of $101 billion in 2000 and approximately $140 billion during the first three quarters of 2001 to declaring bankruptcy in December 2001? The answer to this question seems to be rooted in a combination of the failure of top leadership, a corporate culture that supported unethical behavior, and the complicity of the investment banking community.

Enron's Top Leadership   In the aftermath of Enron's bankruptcy filing, numerous Enron executives were charged with criminal acts, including fraud, money laundering, and insider trading. For example, Ben Glisan, Enron's former treasurer, was charged with two-dozen counts of money laundering, fraud, and conspiracy. Glisan pled guilty to one count of conspiracy to commit fraud and received a prison term, three years of post-prison supervision, and financial penalties of more than $1 million. During the plea negotiations, Glisan described Enron as a "house of cards."

Andrew Fastow, Jeff Skilling, and Ken Lay are among the most notable top-level executives implicated in the collapse of Enron's "house of cards." Andrew Fastow, former Enron chief financial officer (CFO), faced 98 counts of money laundering, fraud, and conspiracy in connection with the improper partnerships he ran, which included a Brazilian power plant project and a Nigerian power plant project that was aided by Merrill Lynch, an investment banking firm. Fastow pled guilty to one charge of conspiracy to commit wire fraud and one charge of conspiracy to commit wire and securities fraud. He agreed to a prison term of 10 years and the forfeiture of $29.8 million. Jeff Skilling was indicted on 35 counts of wire fraud, securities fraud, conspiracy, making false statements on financial reports, and insider trading. Ken Lay was indicted on 11 criminal counts of fraud and making misleading statements. Both Skilling and Lay pled not guilty and are awaiting trial.

The activities of Skilling, Fastow, and Lay raise questions about how closely they adhered to the values of respect, integrity, communication, and excellence articulated in the *Enron Code of Ethics*. Before the collapse, when Bethany McLean, an investigative reporter for *Fortune* magazine, was preparing an article on how Enron made its money, she called Enron's then-CEO, Jeff Skilling, to seek clarification of its "nearly incomprehensible financial statements." Skilling became agitated with McLean's inquiry, told her that the line of questioning was unethical, and hung up on McLean. Shortly thereafter Andrew Fastow and two other key executives traveled to New York City to meet with McLean, ostensibly to answer her questions "completely and accurately."

Fastow engaged in several activities that challenge the foundational values of the company's ethics code. Fastow tried to conceal how extensively Enron was involved in trading for the simple reason that trading companies have inherently volatile earnings that aren't rewarded in the stock market with high valuations—and a high market valuation was essential to keeping Enron from collapsing. Another Fastow venture was setting up and operating partnerships called related party transactions to do business with Enron. In the process of allowing Fastow to set and run these very lucrative private partnerships, Enron's board and top management gave Fastow an exemption from the company's ethics code.

Contrary to the federal prosecutor's indictment of Lay, which describes him as one of the key leaders and organizers of the criminal activity and massive fraud that lead to Enron's bankruptcy, Lay maintains his innocence and lack of knowledge of what was happening. He blames virtually all of the criminal activities on Fastow. However, Sherron Watkins, the key Enron whistleblower, maintains that she can provide examples of Lay's questionable decisions and actions. As Bethany McLean and fellow investigative reporter Peter Elkind observe: "Lay bears enormous responsibility for the substance of what went wrong at Enron. The problems ran wide and deep, as did the deception required in covering them up. The company's culture was his to shape." Ultimately, the actions of Enron's leadership did not match the company's expressed vision and values.

Enron's Corporate Culture   Enron has been described as having a culture of arrogance that led people to believe that they could handle increasingly greater risk without encountering any danger. According to Sherron Watkins, "Enron's unspoken message was, 'Make the numbers, make the numbers, make the numbers—if you steal, if you cheat, just don't get caught. If you do, beg for a second chance, and you'll get one.'" Enron's corporate culture did little to promote the values of respect and integrity. These values were undermined through the company's emphasis on decentralization, its employee performance appraisals, and its compensation program.

Each Enron division and business unit was kept separate from the others, and as a result very few people in the organization had a "big picture" perspective of the company's operations. Accompanying this emphasis on decentralization were insufficient operational and financial controls as well as "a distracted, hands-off chairman, a compliant board of directors, and an impotent staff of accountants, auditors, and lawyers."

Jeff Skilling implemented a very rigorous and threatening performance evaluation process for all Enron employees. Known as "rank and yank," the annual process utilized peer evaluations, and each of the company's divisions was arbitrarily forced to fire the lowest ranking one-fifth of its employees. Employees frequently ranked their peers lower in order to enhance their own positions in the company.

Enron's compensation plan "seemed oriented toward enriching executives rather than generating profits for shareholders" and encouraged people to break rules and inflate the value of contracts even though no actual cash was generated. Enron's bonus program encouraged the use of non-standard accounting practices and the inflated valuation of deals on the company's books. Indeed, deal inflation became widespread within the company as partnerships were created solely to hide losses and avoid the consequences of owning up to problems.

Complicity of the Investment Banking Community

According to investigative reporters McLean and Elkind, "One of the most sordid aspects of the Enron scandal is the complicity of so many highly regarded Wall Street firms" in enabling Enron's fraud as well as being partners to it. Included among these firms were J.P. Morgan, Citigroup, and Merrill Lynch. This complicity occurred through the use of *prepays*, which were basically loans that Enron booked as operating cash flow. Enron secured new prepays to pay off existing ones and to support rapidly expanding investments in new businesses.

One of the related party transactions created by Andrew Fastow, known as LJM2, used a tactic whereby it would take "an asset off Enron's hands—usually a poor performing asset, usually at the end of a quarter—and then sell it back to the company at a profit once the quarter was over and the 'earnings' had been booked." Such transactions were basically smoke and mirrors, reflecting a relationship between LJM2 and the banks wherein "Enron could practically pluck earnings out of thin air."

Epilogue   The *Enron Code of Ethics* and its foundational values of respect, integrity, communication, and excellence obviously did little to help create an ethical environment at the company. The full extent and explanation of Enron's ethical collapse is yet to be determined as legal proceedings continue. Fourteen other Enron employees—many high level—have pled guilty to various charges; 12 of these are awaiting sentencing, while the other two, one of whom is Andrew Fastow's spouse, have received prison sentences of at least one year. Juries have convicted five individuals of fraud, as well as Arthur Andersen, the accounting firm hired by Enron that shared responsibility for the company's fraudulent accounting statements. Three of the convicted individuals were Merrill Lynch employees involved in the Nigerian barge deal with Fastow. Ken Lay and Jeff Skilling, along with Richard Causey, Enron's former chief accounting officer, are awaiting trial. Lay faces 11 criminal counts, Skilling faces 35 criminal counts, and Causey faces 31 criminal counts. Five executives from Enron's broadband division are also awaiting trial. Three bank executives from Britain who had been involved in a complicated series of deals in a Fastow partnership are fighting extradition.

In addition, there are 114 unindicted co-conspirators in the federal government's case against Lay and Skilling.

Questions for Discussion

1. What led to the collapse of Enron under Lay and Skilling?

2. How did the top leadership at Enron undermine the foundational values of the *Enron Code of Ethics*?

3. Given Kenneth Lay's and Jeff Skilling's operating beliefs and the *Enron Code of Ethics*, what expectations regarding ethical decisions and actions should Enron's employees reasonably have had?

4. How did Enron's corporate culture promote unethical decisions and actions?

5. How did the investment banking community contribute to the ethical collapse of Enron?

Sources

This case was developed from material contained in the following sources:

Elkind, P., McLean, B. (July 12, 2004). Ken Lay flunks ignorance test. *Fortune*, http://www.fortune.com, accessed December 15, 2004.

Enron Code of Ethics. The Smoking Gun Web site, http://www.thesmokinggun.com, accessed December 15, 2004.

Enron: Houston Chronicle Special Report. (Dec. 11, 2004). *Houston Chronicle*, http://www.chron.com/cs/CDA/story.hts/special/enron/1624822, accessed December 15, 2003.

Enron Timeline. *Houston Chronicle*, http://www.chron.com/content/chronicle/special/01/enron/timeline.html, accessed December 15, 2003.

Fowler, T. (October 20, 2002). The pride and the fall of Enron. *Houston Chronicle*, http://www.chron.com/cs/CDA/story.hts/special/enron/1624822, accessed November 25, 2003.

Flood, M. (September 10, 2003). Ex-Enron executive going to prison: Glisan plea may speed cases. *Houston Chronicle*, http://www.chron.com/cs/CDA/story.hts/special/enron/2090943, accessed November 25, 2003.

McLean, B. (December 9, 2001). Why Enron went bust. *Fortune*, http://www.fortune.com, accessed December 15, 2004.

McLean, B., Elkind, P. (October 13, 2003). Partners in crime. *Fortune*, http://www.fortune.com, accessed December 15, 2001.

McLean, B., Elkind, P. (October 13, 2003). Partners in crime, part 2. *Fortune*, http://www.fortune.com, accessed December 15, 2001.

Mehta, S.N. (October 14, 2003). Employees are the best line of defense. *Fortune*, http://www.fortune.com, accessed December 15, 2004.

Novak, M. (1996) *Business as a Calling: Work and the Examined Life*. New York: The Free Press.

Strip clubs, daredevil trips, $1 million paychecks. (October 2, 2003). Excerpt from B. McLean and P. Elkind, *The Smartest Guys in the Room*, printed in *Fortune*, http://www.fortune.com, accessed December 15, 2004.

CASE 2

MICROSOFT: INDUSTRY PREDATOR OR FIERCE COMPETITOR?

Introduction   Microsoft, one of the most influential software companies of the twentieth century, was founded by Bill Gates, Paul Allen, and several other friends to fill a niche in the personal computer (PC) operating system and software business. The phenomenal growth of this company did not happen by luck. Events that led the United States Department of Justice (DOJ) and 20 state attorneys general to file class action lawsuits against Microsoft for illegally bundling its Internet Explorer with Windows 95 were very controversial. The company's business practices came under close scrutiny. District Judge Thomas Penfield Jackson released his finding on November 5, 1999, declaring that Microsoft held a monopoly in the PC industry. Several months later, Jackson ordered a breakup of Microsoft, but this order was overturned on appeal. Numerous subsequent events eventually led to a resolution of the antitrust allegations.

The Road to Monopoly   Microsoft enjoys a monopoly in the market for Intel-compatible PC operating systems. No products currently in the market or anticipated in the near future can be substituted for the Intel-compatible operating system without incurring substantial costs. Three facts bolster arguments by DOJ and Judge Jackson that Microsoft exerted monopoly power in the market for PC operating systems: Microsoft's market share and high barriers to entry and the lack of viable alternatives to Microsoft products.

Market Share   Microsoft maintains a dominant and increasing market share for Intel-compatible PC operating systems. In each of the 10 years preceding the lawsuits, Microsoft has had a 90% market share in operating systems for Intel-compatible PCs. In the last two years of that period, Microsoft's market share stood at 95% and is expected to increase even further. Microsoft has effectively argued that it has just been successful and competitive.

High Barriers to Entry   Microsoft managed to maintain its monopoly in PC operating systems because of persistent high barriers to entry for competing operating systems. Consumer interest is based on the ability of the operating system to run software applications. Consumers also prefer an operating system that has several software vendors' applications in different software categories. Microsoft has more than 70,000 software applications written for it.

Two examples illustrate the difficulty in overcoming Windows' dominant market share and applications. In 1994, IBM introduced the OS/2 Warp operating system. IBM spent tens of millions of dollars on attempts to get software developers to produce applications for OS/2. However, IBM was unsuccessful, and by 1996, OS/2 supported only 2,500 applications, with 10% of the market for Intel-compatible PC operating systems. IBM realized it could not generate enough software applications for OS/2 to make it a viable alternative to Windows. Instead, IBM marketed OS/2 as a specialized operating system that did not compete head to head with Windows. Apple's Mac OS operating system also does not compete effectively with Windows. Although Mac OS has more than 12,000 applications written for it, consumers still lack adequate software options compared with the number of applications written for Windows. Consumers could not rely on Mac OS as a replacement for Windows.

Lack of Viable Alternatives   The fixed costs of developing software applications are high, although the margins for selling software applications are low. Producing software to run on multiple operating systems is time consuming and expensive. Software developers produce software for an operating system that has the largest base of users. A goal is quick recovery of net costs. Windows has the largest market share for PC operating systems, which means software developers profit by producing applications for Windows.

Barriers to entry do not prevent Microsoft's competitors from attracting consumer interest, nor do the barriers prevent software vendors from making a profit. However, the high barriers to entry do prevent competing operating systems from drawing a large percentage of users away from Windows. There are several operating systems on the market today that serve niche markets but do not pose a direct threat to Windows. For example, Be Inc. sells an Intel-compatible operating system that is designed to support multimedia functions. The operating system supports 1,000 software applications and has an installed base of 750,000. Be OS's market share is minuscule compared to Windows', and it is marketed as a complement to Windows rather than a substitute.

Another PC operating system on the market today is the Linux open-ended operating system, which has an estimated 15 million users. Linux programs run on servers and not PCs. Linux was created and is updated by a global network of software developers who contribute their labor free of charge. There are only a limited number of software developers willing to convert applications to Linux, and it does not pose a significant threat to Windows' market position yet. Consumers have shown little desire to abandon Windows and its reliable development support in favor of Linux and its uncertain future.

Strategic Alliance or Hostages to Microsoft?   Several companies that transacted business with Microsoft acquiesced to Microsoft's dominance in the market because Microsoft's corporate practices threatened them. How? These companies claimed that Microsoft forced them to freeze the development of software applications that directly competed with Microsoft's software products by threatening to change technologies so non-Microsoft applications, chips, and systems would be incompatible with Microsoft's. On the other hand, Microsoft argued that its cross-marketing agreements with firms were based on industry standard contracts that were legal and competitive.

Intel   By early 1995, Intel Architecture Labs was in the advanced stage of development of its Native Signal Processing (NSP) software, which would provide Intel microprocessors with substantially superior video and graphics quality. Microsoft was alarmed because Intel's development of software for non-Microsoft operating systems had the potential of weakening the barrier to entry that protected Microsoft's monopoly.

At a meeting between Microsoft's CEO Bill Gates and Andrew Grove, then the CEO of Intel, Gates tried to talk Grove into not shipping NSPs and decreasing the number of people working on software at Intel. In a second meeting between Gates and Grove, Gates informed Grove that Microsoft would withdraw its support of the next generation of microprocessors if Intel continued to develop platform-level software that competed with Windows. Intel was in an awkward situation; if Microsoft did not support Intel chips and told its original equipment manufacturers (OEMs) likewise, or if Microsoft made the chips incompatible with Windows, Intel would have had a tough time selling its PC microprocessors. Faced with this threat, Intel stopped the development of platform-level interfaces.

Apple   QuickTime (QT) was Apple's software for creating, editing, publishing, and playing back multimedia content. Apple's versions of QT could run on Mac OS and Windows, which competed with Microsoft's multimedia software DirectX. Microsoft therefore considered QT a potential threat to its applications barrier to entry and from mid-1997 to 1998 tried to stop Apple from producing a Windows 95 version of its multimedia software.

Microsoft informed Apple that if it did not stop marketing the multimedia software with a platform for content development, Microsoft would enter the authoring business in order to ensure that those writing multimedia content for Windows 95 would concentrate on Microsoft's Application Programming Interfaces (APIs) instead of Apple's. Microsoft further informed Apple that if the company developed and marketed its authoring tools, Microsoft would render the technologies in its tools incompatible with Apple's tools. Furthermore, Microsoft would invest in whatever means and resources needed to ensure that developers would use Microsoft's tools.

Microsoft met with Apple to persuade them to stop the development of multimedia software for Windows. A few weeks after the meeting, Apple rejected Microsoft's proposal.

IBM   During the summer of 1994, IBM informed Microsoft that IBM wanted the same favorable terms that Microsoft gave Compaq for licensing Microsoft's OS products. Compaq paid the lowest rate in the market and had strong marketing and technical support from Microsoft. Microsoft asked IBM to enter into a "Frontline Partnership," which existed between Microsoft and Compaq. If IBM accepted the terms, it meant that it would have to abandon its own operating system.

At an industry conference in November 1994, Microsoft and IBM met, and IBM rejected the terms. IBM then went on to acquire Lotus Development Corporation. Lotus, according to Microsoft, was a threat because it offered users a common interface across platforms.

After IBM's acquisition of Lotus, there was trouble in paradise. On July 20, 1995, three days after IBM announced its intention of installing SmartSuite—which directly competed with MS Office—Microsoft informed IBM that it was ceasing negotiations with IBM for the licensing of its Windows 95 and refused to release the "golden master" code of Windows 95. Microsoft stated that it first wanted to settle the ongoing audit of IBM's previous royalty payments to Microsoft for different OS systems. Because IBM needed the code for its product planning and development, this type of ultimatum prevented IBM from having enough time to get its product ready for the "back-to-school" season. Finally, 15 minutes before the start of Microsoft's official launch event on August 24, 1995, Microsoft granted IBM a license to pre-install Windows 95. On the same day, IBM paid Microsoft $31 million to close the issue of the audit. The delay caused IBM to miss the back-to-school season, and they lost substantial revenue.

Sun's Implementation of Java Technologies   Sun's aim with Java technology was to permit applications written in Java language to run on a variety of platforms with minimal porting (creating a software designed for one platform available to run on another platform—the process involves changing programming details within software to enable it to run on a different platform). More applications would be written for operating systems other than Windows if developers found it easier to link their applications to different operating systems. The ultimate ambition of Sun was to have the Java technology be an end-user-oriented application written cross-platform. If this were to happen, the applications barrier to entry would be diminished. In May 1995, Netscape agreed to include the Java runtime environment with every Navigator, and this soon became the main mode by which Java was placed on the PCs of Windows users. This laid the foundation for a non-Microsoft OS to emerge as an acceptable substitute for Windows. By late spring of 1996, Microsoft was concerned about Java's potential.

Monopoly Through Pricing?   Microsoft charged different OEMs different prices for Windows. The pricing strategy was dependent on the extent to which the OEMs acted in accordance with Microsoft's terms. Of the five largest OEMs, Gateway and IBM have not always complied with Microsoft's terms and paid higher prices than Compaq, Dell, and Hewlett-Packard, who have had less problematic issues with Microsoft. The Windows license conditions curbed OEMs from promoting software that would weaken the applications barrier to entry. Lower prices were charged to OEMs who ensured that their machines were powerful enough to run Windows NT for Workstations.

When Microsoft launched Windows 98, it did not consider other vendors' prices for competing operating systems. In a competitive market, a firm pays close attention to what other firms are charging for competing products. Microsoft conducted a study in November 1997, which found that Microsoft could have charged $49 for a Windows 98 upgrade. Microsoft chose instead to charge the revenue-maximizing price of $89. Microsoft's alleged monopoly in pricing was demonstrated when Microsoft raised the price it charged OEMs for Windows 95 to the same level charged for Windows 98 just before it released Windows 98. In a competitive market, one could expect the price for an older operating system to decrease. Microsoft's primary concern was getting OEMs to ship the new operating system. It is highly unlikely that Microsoft would have imposed price increases if it were concerned that OEMs might shift business to competing operating systems.

Microsoft's Perspective   Microsoft argued that its agreements, contracts, and pricing have evolved with the fast pace of the PC and software industries. Prices in these industries fluctuate widely. Microsoft acknowledges that although it has been a leader in the PC and software areas, it is not the only dominant player. It is only one of more than 10,000 companies in the world. IBM, Hewlett-Packard, Sun

Microsystems, Apple, and AOL remain active competitors in an industry with $1 trillion in revenues (Microsoft claims its revenues are less than 1% of this).

Bundling: Competitive Strategy or Monopoly Ploy?

Microsoft used bundling (i.e., combining new or untested, and even weaker, products with market leading name brands) as a strategy by distributing its Web browser Internet Explorer (IE) free with its Windows 95 and 98 operating systems. Microsoft required PC makers to accept IE as a condition of receiving Windows. Through this practice, consumers were automatically introduced to IE exclusive of any other browser, most notably Netscape Navigator, which was the market leader at the time. Microsoft viewed Netscape Communications Corporation of Mountain View, California, as a competitor after Netscape declined to collaborate with Microsoft on a browser deal that would have left Netscape with a narrow niche market for its product. The rationale behind the bundling strategy was that Netscape's browser could be developed as a platform to be used as an alternative to the Windows operating system. Had Netscape Navigator been allowed to compete freely and succeed, application writers would no longer have had an incentive to write only for Windows.

With Microsoft's operating system running on about 85% of personal computers in the United States, distributing Internet Explorer in this way potentially constituted an unfair advantage. This practice was considered by the DOJ under President Clinton and by Judge Jackson as a use of monopolistic power to stifle competition. The DOJ requested that Microsoft include Netscape's browser in its Windows system.

Microsoft's Perspective   From Microsoft's perspective, customers were just given another option (IE) without paying for it—the same strategy (a "product design" decision, as Microsoft vice president James Allchin stated) as giving away free software as a way to win over customers—a standard industry practice. Customers did not and do not have to adopt and use IE; they can delete it from their operating system. Also, Netscape was available to customers through Microsoft's Windows operating system.

Microsoft also claimed that the DOJ's request to force Microsoft to include Netscape Navigator, a competitor's product, in its operating system was like forcing Coca-Cola to distribute Pepsi or McDonald's to sell Burger King hamburgers or Sears to provide floor space for Wal-Mart products. In direct testimony, an MIT economist argued that Netscape's browser's market share was related to the superiority of Microsoft's IE—"A rising tide lifts all ships" argument.

Browser Battle: Internet Explorer Versus Netscape Navigator

The events that led to the DOJ's charges that Microsoft engaged in bundling started as soon as Netscape released Navigator, and it received dramatic acceptance by the public. Microsoft, critics claimed, feared that the enthusiastic acceptance of Navigator could embolden Netscape to develop its browser into an alternative platform for applications development. Microsoft executives expressed deep concern (as internal memos revealed) that Netscape was pursuing a multi-platform strategy where the underlying operating system's applications development tools would be released. Netscape was moving its business in a direction that could diminish the applications barrier to entry that existed with Microsoft's Windows.

Talks with Netscape   The first response by Microsoft was to persuade Netscape to structure its business so that the company would not distribute platform-level browsing software for Windows. So long as Navigator was written for Windows 95 and relied on Microsoft's Internet-related APIs instead of exposing its own, developing for Navigator would not mean cross-platform development. The meeting with Netscape executives was intended by Microsoft to make a deal that would limit Navigator's development.

Microsoft made it clear that it would be releasing its own browser for Windows 95 based on its own platform-level Internet technologies, and if Netscape marketed browsing software for Windows 95 based on different technologies, Netscape would be considered a competitor, not a partner. If Netscape agreed to the deal, it would acquire preferential treatment and access to technical information. Although both sides left the meeting agreeing to keep the channels of communication open, Microsoft's Thomas Reardon convinced Bill Gates that Netscape would compete with almost all of Microsoft's platform-level Internet technologies. The effort to reach a strategic agreement with Netscape failed.

Netscape continued to request the applications development tools despite having declined the special relationship with Microsoft. It was not until three months later that Microsoft released the tools to Netscape. Microsoft gained an edge in releasing Windows 95 with its own browser significantly ahead of Navigator's release. Netscape was therefore excluded from the holiday sales. This monopolistic tactic, combined with the bundling of IE with Windows 95 at no cost to consumers, gave Microsoft power to reduce Navigator's market share and make consumers use their browser.

Since then, a dramatic increase occurred in new usage of IE. Despite the fact that most users considered Netscape Navigator a superior product compared to the initial release of IE, users continued to use IE at Netscape's expense. According to estimates that Microsoft executives cited to support their testimony in the trial, and those on which Microsoft relied in the course of its business planning, the shares of all browser usage changed dramatically in favor of IE after Microsoft began its campaign to protect the applications barrier to entry. Navigator's share fell from 80 to 55%, while IE's share rose from 5 to 36%. Before long, IE's usage was above 55%, and Navigator's was at 40%. An internal Microsoft presentation concluded that many customers see IE and Navigator as parity products, providing no strong reason to switch. That IE experienced such a dramatic increase in usage share was a result of Microsoft's practice of bundling IE with its Windows operating system.

One interpretation of these events and relations is as follows: Microsoft not only prevented Navigator from lowering the applications barrier to entry, but also did considerable damage to Netscape's business. An opposing argument is this: Microsoft's IE helped open up the entire market for browsers, which helped Netscape's browser increase market share. Netscape originally lost market share because IE became a preferred product over Netscape Navigator.

Evolution and Resolution of the Antitrust Case Against Microsoft

In May 1998, 20 states joined the DOJ in a suit against Microsoft claiming violation of antitrust laws. The ensuing trial, which lasted nearly a year, commenced on October 19, 1998. On November 5, 1999, U.S. District Judge Thomas Penfield Jackson released his finding of fact, which declared that Microsoft routinely used its monopoly power to crush competitors; he portrayed the software giant as nothing less than a social menace. On June 7, 2000, Judge Jackson ordered Microsoft to spilt into two companies—a Windows operating systems company and a content company for the PC and Internet. On June 28, 2001, the Circuit Court of Appeals for the District of Columbia reversed Judge Jackson's breakup order but upheld the finding that Microsoft illegally defended its Windows monopoly. Concurrent with the appeals process, settlements were reached with South Carolina and New Mexico.

On August 24, 2001, District Judge Coleen Kollar-Kotelly was picked to take over the case. On September 6, 2001, the DOJ indicated it did not seek a breakup of Microsoft but did want a quick remedy. On October 15, 2001, Judge Kollar-Kotelly appointed arbitration specialist Eric Green, a Boston University professor, to the case, giving him until November 2, 2001, to come up with a settlement solution. In November 2001, Microsoft entered into a proposed agreement with the DOJ and nine states (New York, Ohio, Illinois, Kentucky, Louisiana, Maryland, Michigan, North Carolina, and Wisconsin), known as the New York group.

This settlement agreement addressed client middleware choice and two key aspects of technical information disclosure. Under the client middleware choice remedy of the settlement agreement, "Microsoft will allow end users and OEMs to enable or remove access to certain windows components or competing software (e.g., Internet browsers, media players, instant messaging clients, e-mail clients) and designate a competing product to be invoked in place of that Microsoft software." Under the client middleware API aspect of technical information disclosure, Microsoft agreed to make available internal Windows interfaces "for third parties to use solely to interoperate with Windows." The communication protocol program aspect of technical information disclosure required Microsoft to make "available for license more than 110 proprietary protocols . . . to third parties, on a royalty basis solely to interoperate or communicate with Windows 2000 Professional, Windows XP, and successor client operating systems."

In November 2002, following a remedy trial and district court ruling by Judge Kollar-Kotelly, seven states (California, Connecticut, Florida, Iowa, Kansas, Minnesota, and Utah) and the District of Columbia, collectively known as the California group, accepted the settlement agreement previously endorsed by the New York group. In June 2003 West Virginia dropped its appeal and accepted the settlement agreement. In June 2004, the U.S. District Court of Appeals for the District of Columbia denied the challenge brought by Massachusetts and upheld the antitrust remedies that were approved in late 2002 by District Judge Kollar-Kotelly. Status conferences continue to occur periodically to monitor and ensure that Microsoft is effectively implementing the specified remedies.

More recently, Microsoft has been charged by the European Union (EU) commission on questionable monopoly practices with regard to bundling a built-in media player with its Windows XP operating system. A Washington Post article noted that,

> Microsoft Corp. said yesterday [1/24/05] it will comply with a European antitrust ruling and within weeks begin offering a version of its Windows XP operating system without a built-in media player. The decision by Microsoft, which was not a surprise, is consistent with the firm's strategy these days on antitrust matters: Get them resolved quickly so the software giant can focus on its business, rather than on legal wrangling. The company plans to continue to pursue a long-term legal appeal on the merits of its antitrust case in Europe. That legal appeal could take years. In addition to offering its Windows operating system without a pre-installed media player, it is also revealing some source code to make it easier for European software developers to make Windows-compatible products.

Questions for Discussion

1. Was and is Microsoft guilty of being a monopoly? Explain.

2. What are the major issues in this case? How have these issues evolved?

3. Do you agree or disagree with the legal and court decisions made in the case? Explain.

4. How have the environments changed in this case? Explain.

5. What are the lessons from this case?

Sources

This case was developed from material contained in the following sources:

Bank, D., Clark, D. (July 23, 1999). Microsoft broadens vision statement to go beyond the PC-centric world. *The Wall Street Journal,* A3.

Becker, G. (April 6, 1998). Let the marketplace judge Microsoft. *Business Week,* 26.

Bork, R. (May 22, 1998). The most misunderstood antitrust case. *The Wall Street Journal,* A6.

Bork, R. (Nov. 8, 1999). Manager's journal—US vs. Microsoft: Judge Jackson's finding of fact—a predatory monopoly. *The Wall Street Journal,* A50.

Carlson, C. (July 5, 2004). Antitrust decision is upheld. *eweek,* 16.

Defendant Microsoft Corporation's Answer to the Complaint Filed by the U.S. Department of Justice, *United States of America* v. *Microsoft Corporation,* United States District Court for the District of Columbia, No. 98-1232 (TPJ), July 28, 1998; and Defendant Microsoft Corporation's Answer to Plaintiff States' First Amended Complaint and Counterclaim, *State of New York* v. *Microsoft Corporation,* United States District Court for the District of Columbia, No. 98-1232 (TPJ), July 28, 1998.

D.C. Circuit Court Upholds District Court Ruling in Microsoft Case. (September 2004). *The Computer & Internet Lawyer, 21(9),* 28.

France, M., Burrows, P., and Himelstein, L., et al. (Nov. 22, 1999). Does a break up make sense? *Business Week,* 28.

Geralds, John (Oct. 15, 2001) Mediator to sort out Microsoft/DOJ battle. Newswire (VNU), VNU Business Publications, Ltd. Source: World Reporter, *Wall Street Journal.*

Government Antitrust Suits. Microsoft Web site. http://www.microsoft.com/presspass/legal/10-28settlementFS.asp, accessed Dec. 14, 2004.

Jackson, T. P. (Nov. 5, 1999). *United States of America v. Microsoft Corporation,* CA 98–232, Findings of Fact, 1–141.

Joint Status Report on Microsoft's Compliance with the Final Judgments. (April 17, 2003). Filing in the United States District Court for the District of Columbia.

Kerber, R. (April 29, 2000). U.S. asks judge to break up Microsoft. *Boston Globe,* A-1, A-12.

Krim, Jonathan, (December 23, 2004). E.U. orders Microsoft to modify Windows, one version must omit Media Player, *Washington Post,* A01.

Lohr, S., Harmon, A. (Jan. 28, 1999). Microsoft executive defends folding browser into Windows." *New York Times,* C2.

Rill, J. (Nov. 20, 1997). Why Bill Gates is wrong. *The Wall Street Journal,* A22.

Schmalensee, R. (January 13, 1999). Direct Testimony, in the United States District Court for the District of Columbia, *United States of America Plaintiffs* v. *Microsoft Corporation,* Defendant, Civil Action No. 98-1232 (TPJ), 322.

Settlement Program. Microsoft Web site, http://www.microsoft.com/legal/settlementprogram/, accessed Dec. 14, 2004.

Shiver, Jr., J. (Dec. 8, 1998). United front cracks in case against Microsoft. *Los Angeles Times*, C1.

Technology briefing software: Microsoft's new MP3 venture. (July 17, 2001). *New York Times*, 6.

Vise, David, (January 25, 2005). Microsoft acts on antitrust ruling Windows without Media Player to be available in Europe, *Washington Post*, E05.

Weil, N., Haney, C. (Dec. 6, 1999). DOJ appoints adviser as Microsoft reshuffles. *Infoworld*, *21(49)*, 3.

Wilke, J. (Nov. 9, 2001). Negotiating all night, tenacious Microsoft won many loopholes. *The Wall Street Journal*, A1, A6.

Notes

1. Recording Industry Association of America. (April 28, 2004). New wave of illegal file sharing lawsuits brought by RIAA. *Collegiate Presswire*, http://www.cpwire.com/archive/2004/4/28/1559.asp.
2. Langer, G. (July 1, 2002). Confidence in business: Was low and still is. *ABC News*, http://abcnews.go.com/sections/business/DailyNews/corporatetrust_poll020701.html.
3. Strauss, G., Hansen, B. (March 31, 2003). Bubble hasn't burst yet on CEO salaries despite the times. *USA Today*, http://www.usatoday.com/money/companies/management/2003-03-31-ceopay2_x.htm.
4. Smith, P. (November 3, 2004). Sarbanes bill is "unenforceable." http://www.accountancyage.com/News/112993.
5. O'Sullivan, K., Durfree, D. (June 1, 2004). Offshoring by the numbers. *CFO Magazine 20(7)* 49–54, http://www.cfo.com/article.cfm/3014067/c_3046613; Ricciuti, M., Yamamoto, M. (May 5, 2004). Outsourcing: Where to draw the line. *CNET News*, http://zdnet.com.com/2100-1104-5206031.html; A richer future for India. (June 10, 2004). *The McKinley Quarterly*.
6. Friedman, T. (2000). *The Lexus and the Olive Tree*, 17, 20, 24. New York: Anchor Books.
7. Nash, L. (1990). *Good Intentions Aside: A Manager's Guide to Resolving Ethical Problems*, 5. Boston: Harvard Business School Press.
8. The Ethics Resource Center. (2003). 2003 National Business Ethics Survey—Executive Summary. http://www.ethics.org/nbes2003/2003nbes_summary.html.
9. Ibid.
10. Ibid.
11. Gordon et al. (1990); Gordon (1999).
12. Marchetti, M. (Dec. 1997). Whatever it takes. *Sales & Marketing Management*, 28–38.
13. The Ethics Resource Center. (2003). 2003 National Business Ethics Survey—Executive Summary. http://www.ethics.org/nbes2003/2003nbes_summary.html.
14. Colvin, G. (March 6, 2000). The amazing future of business. *Fortune*, F6–F10.
15. Frooman, J. (1997). Socially irresponsible and illegal behavior and shareholder wealth. *Business & Society*, 36(3), 221–229.
16. The Cheating Culture. Workplace Theft. http://www.cheatingculture.com/workplacetheft.htm; Callahan, D. (2004). *The Cheating Culture: Why More Americans Are Doing Wrong to Get Ahead*. New York: Harcourt.
17. Ibid.
18. Graves, S., Waddock, S. (1993). Institutional owners and corporate social performance: Maybe not so myopic after all. Proceedings of the International Association for Business and Society, San Diego; Graves, S., Waddock, S. (1997). The corporate social performance–financial performance link. *Strategic Management Journal*, *18*, 303–319.
19. Carroll, A. (1993). *Business & Society: Ethics and Stakeholder Management*, 3rd ed., 110–112. Cincinnati: South-Western.
20. Kalwall Corporation. Malden Mills: Daylight from ashes. http://www.kalwall.com/1.htm; CBS 60 Minutes. (July 6, 2003). The mensch of Malden Mills. *CBSNews.com*, http://www.cbsnews.com/stories/2003/07/03/60minutes/main561656.shtml.

21. Friedman, M. (Sept. 13, 1970). The social responsibility of business is to increase its profits. *New York Times Magazine, 33.*
22. Frooman.
23. Key, S., Popkin, S. (1998). Integrating ethics into the strategic management process: Doing well by doing good. *Management Decision, 36(5),* 331–338. See Colvin and Frooman. Also see Allinson, R. (1993). *Global Disasters: Inquiries into Management Ethics.* New York: Prentice Hall; and Arthur, H. (1984). Making business ethics useful. *Strategic Management Journal, 5,* 319–333.
24. Senge, P. (1990). *The Fifth Discipline: The Art and Practice of the Learning Organization,* New York: Doubleday. Also see the following sources: In search of the holy performance grail. (April 1996). *Training & Development,* 26–32. Also see Covey, S. R. (1989). *The Seven Habits of Highly Effective People.* New York: Simon & Schuster.
25. DeGeorge, R. (1999). *Business Ethics,* 5th ed. Upper Saddle River, NJ: Prentice Hall.
26. Stone, C. D. (1975). *Where the Law Ends.* New York: Harper & Row.
27. Buchholz, R. (1989). *Fundamental Concepts and Problems in Business Ethics.* Englewood Cliffs, NJ: Prentice Hall. For more information, see Buchholz, R. A. (1995). *Business Environment and Public Policy,* 5th ed. Englewood Cliffs, NJ: Prentice Hall.
28. Newton, L. (1986). The internal morality of the corporation. *Journal of Business Ethics, 5,* 249–258.
29. Hoffman, M., Moore, J. (1995). *Business Ethics: Readings and Cases in Corporate Morality,* 3rd ed. New York: McGraw-Hill.
30. DeGeorge, R. (2000). Business ethics and the challenge of the information age. *Business Ethics Quarterly, 10(1),* 63–72.
31. Ibid.
32. Stone.
33. Carroll.
34. Stead, B., Miller, J. (1988). Can social awareness be decreased through business school curriculum? *Journal of Business Ethics, 7(7),* 30.
35. Jones, T. (1989). Ethics education in business: Theoretical considerations. *Organizational Behavior Teaching Review, 13(4),* 1–18.
36. Hanson, K. O. (Sept. 1987). What good are ethics courses? *Across the Board,* 10–11.
37. Kohlberg, L. (1969). State and sequence: The cognitive developmental approach to socialization. In Gosline, D. A. (1969). *Handbook of Socialization Theory and Research.* Chicago: Rand McNally.
38. Jones, T. (1991). Ethical decision making by individuals in organizations: An issue-contingent model. *Academy of Management Review, 16(2),* 366–395.
39. Weaver, G., Trevion, L., Cochran, P. (1999). Corporate ethics practices in the mid-1990s: An empirical study of the *Fortune 1000. Journal of Business Ethics, 18,* 283–294.
40. Jones, 383, 391.

2

Stakeholder and Issues Management Approaches

Microsoft employs more than 37,000 people in 80 countries. The company was featured in the news when a report found that it has been outsourcing high-wage jobs since 2001. WashTech, a Seattle-based labor union, received an anonymous package containing three-year-old documents outlining contracts between Microsoft and Infosys Technologies and Satyam Computer Sciences, two of India's largest outsourcing companies.[1] Microsoft had agreed to pay these firms to provide "software architects" for various Microsoft initiatives. Software architects are instrumental in developing ways to make original software work. Much of the work Microsoft outsources is so-called lower level, such as testing, preparation of user guides, and creating technology tools to help solve problems with software.

Microsoft's actions were seen in the media as part of an ongoing debate regarding the extent to which technology and other companies are "exporting America," i.e. sending jobs and tax revenue overseas at the expense of U.S. communities. Ronil Hira, an assistant professor of public policy at the Rochester Institute of Technology, stated that "It's important to dispel the myth that work is not immune to offshore outsourcing . . . What is not clear, is how much of that high end work will go abroad."[2] Trying to dispel further criticism, Stacey Drake, a Microsoft spokeswoman, said that it is company policy not to talk about its contracts with vendors. She also stated, "we often use companies for projects,"[3] and noted that of the $7 billion that Microsoft spends on research and development (R&D) for new products, 4% is accomplished by outside companies, and 1% by companies overseas.[4]

Bill Gates has said Microsoft will invest $400 million over the next three years to expand its activities in India; $100 million of which would go to its facility in Hyderabad.[5]

The extent and endgame of U.S. firms' outsourcing of jobs, work, and operations is debatable. Microsoft is not the only firm using international labor and operational resources. Hewlett–Packard (HP) shifted 1,200 Compaq customer service jobs from Florida to the existing HP center in India. A 2003 survey by The Information Technology Association of America reported that "22% of respondents [IT firms] have moved work offshore and 15% have opened operations overseas." A similar survey conducted by Forrester Research estimates that at the current rate, "about 3.3 million U.S. service jobs, or about $136 billion in wages, will be located in countries such as India, Russia, China, and the Philippines by 2015, with the IT industry leading the mass off-shore exodus."[6] The outsourcing debate is ongoing. The extent and effects of global outsourcing on the U.S. economy, including ethical implications, is explored in Christopher Clott's article, "Perspectives on Global Outsourcing and the Changing Nature of Work."[7] This chapter introduces frameworks and methods that enable you to systematically argue this and other complex organizational and business ethics issues and their effects on individuals, organizations, and societies.

2.1 WHY USE A STAKEHOLDER MANAGEMENT APPROACH FOR BUSINESS ETHICS?

The stakeholder management approach is a response to the growth and complexity of contemporary corporations and the need to understand how they operate with their stakeholders and stockholders. Stakeholder theory argues that corporations should treat all their constituencies fairly and that doing so can enable the companies to perform better in the marketplace.[8] "If organizations want to be effective, they will pay attention to all and only those relationships that can affect or be affected by the achievement of the organization's purposes."[9]

This chapter applies stakeholder management not only in its theoretical form, but also as a practical method to analyze how companies deal with their stakeholders. We therefore use the term "stakeholder analysis" (which is part of stakeholder management) to identify strategies, actions, and policy results of firms in their management of employees, competitors, the media, courts, and stockholders. Later in the chapter, we introduce "issues management" as another set of methods for managing stakeholders. Issues management and stakeholder management are complementary theories that use similar methods, as we show later. Starting with a major issue or opportunity that a company faces is one way to begin stakeholder analysis.

A more familiar way of understanding corporations is the "stock-holder approach," which focuses on financial and economic relationships. By contrast, a stakeholder management approach is a descriptive method that studies actors.[10] The stakeholder management approach takes into account nonmarket forces that affect organizations and individuals, such as moral, political, legal, and technological interests, as well as economic factors.

Underlying the stakeholder management approach is the ethical imperative that mandates that businesses in their fiduciary relationships to their stockholders: (1) act in the best interests of and for the benefit of their customers, employees, suppliers, and stockholders, and (2) respect and fulfill these stakeholders' rights. One study concluded that "our analysis clearly reveals that multiple objectives—including both economic and social considerations—can be and, in fact, *are* simultaneously and successfully pursued within large and complex organizations that collectively account for a major part of all economic activity within our society."[11]

There is an ongoing debate among some scholars regarding the legitimacy of the stakeholder management model.[12] Heugens and Van Riel (2002) present evidence showing that stakeholder management may result in both organizational learning and societal legitmacy.[13] Our view here is grounded in Key's (1999) stakeholder theory of the firm[14] and summarized by Mitchell, Agle, and Wood (1997)[15]:

> We argue that stakeholder theory must account for power and urgency as well as legitimacy, no matter how distasteful or unsettling the results. Managers must know about groups in their environment that hold power and intend to impose their will upon the firm. Power and urgency must be attended to if managers are to serve the legal and moral interests of legitimate stakeholders.

The ethical dimension of this approach is based on the view that profit maximization is constrained by justice, regard for individual rights should be extended to all constituencies that have a stake in a business, and organizations are not only "economic" in nature, but can act in socially responsible ways. To this end, companies "should" act in socially responsible ways, not only because it's the "right thing to do," but also to ensure their legitimacy.[16]

The Outsourcing Debate   Competing stakeholder claims are common in leading and managing organizations. The debate gets heated when executives must choose between an action that could profit the company and one that could benefit the welfare of some or all stakeholders. For example, when Microsoft, Dell, Hewlett–Packard, and so many other U.S. firms lay off large numbers of workers and outsource to other countries, are they violating a trust and responsibility to their communities, employees, and the U.S. economy? Outsourcing provides opportunities for understanding different stakeholders' interests, power, and ethics.

Studies argue the pros and cons of outsourcing. For example, a McKinsey Global Institute study stated that, "every dollar of corporate spending shifted offshore by an American firm—mostly, now, to India—generates $1.13 in new wealth for America's economy."[17] The study stated that 70% of workers whose jobs are shipped abroad find new work within six months, as opposed to 40% in places like Germany. The study claims this is evidence that America's economy is still producing jobs, while other countries struggle to replace jobs that have been sent to other low-cost countries.

On the other hand, a Forrester Research report stated that U.S. workers may lose $120 billion in wages by 2015, and that 1.7 million jobs are estimated to be lost by 2015. Harris Miller, president of the Information Technology Association of America, a trade group representing 500 technology concerns, believes "a perfect storm" is gathering over the outsourcing issue in America.[18] Arguments against significant outsourcing of jobs and work include these points:

1. Jobs are not presently being created in the private sector, which has not happened before in U.S. history.

2. The U.S. trade deficit continues to escalate, with no trade surplus in the United States for more than 20 years.

3. At least three million jobs have been lost over the last three years, with no end in sight. The job loss is not only at lower levels, but also at middle and administrative levels.

4. Local communities and states depend on individual and corporate taxes to survive. Massive outsourcing threatens the American middle class as well as local communities.[19]

In this and other cases with complex issues, we ask what methods can be used to evaluate who is right and who is wrong, and what costs must be incurred and by whom in resolving issues of justice, rightness, and fairness. "Rightness" and "wrongness" are not always easy to determine in moral dilemmas. As Abraham Lincoln said, "The true role, in determining to embrace or reject anything . . . is not whether it have any evil in it, but whether it have more evil than of good. There are few things wholly evil or wholly good."

In fact, no central or absolute source of authority exists to evaluate competing interests between a company and its stakeholders, especially in a democratic, pluralistic, and capitalist society such as the United States.

Governmental and legal systems often play roles in this process, but, more often than not, these entities enter the fray after the fact. In an open-market system, special interests, lobbyists, and communications media are significant forces that influence corporate decisions. In a pluralistic society, corporate leaders need a method that helps them understand and "keep score" on each of their stakeholders' *strategies, ethics,* and *power relationships.*

2.2 STAKEHOLDER MANAGEMENT APPROACH DEFINED

The *stakeholder management approach* is based on an instrumental theory that argues "a subset of ethical principles (trust, trustworthiness, and cooperativeness) can result in significant competitive advantage."[20] At the same time, this approach includes analytical concepts and methods for identifying, mapping, and evaluating corporate strategy with stakeholders. We refer to these methods as "stakeholder analysis." The stakeholder management approach, including frameworks for analyzing and evaluating a corporation's relationships (present and potential) with external groups, aims ideally at reaching "win-win" collaborative outcomes. Here, "win-win" means making moral decisions that benefit all constituencies within the constraints of justice, fairness, and economic interests. Unfortunately, this does not always happen. There are usually winners and losers in complex situations where there is a perceived zero-sum game (i.e., a situation in which there are limited resources, and what is gained by one person is necessarily lost by the other).

Scholars and consultants, however, have used the stakeholder management approach as a means for planning and implementing collaborative relationships to achieve win-win outcomes among stakeholders.[21] Structured dialogue facilitated by consultants is a major focus in these collaborative communications. The aim in using the stakeholder approach as communication strategy is to change perceptions and "rules of engagement" to create win-win outcomes.

A stakeholder approach does not have to result from a crisis, as so many examples from ethics literature and the news provide. It can also be used as a planning method to anticipate and facilitate business decisions, events, and policy outcomes. A stakeholder analysis is also not limited to large enterprises. Business units, teams, and groups can use this approach.

A stakeholder management approach also begins, as indicated in Chapter 1, by asking what external forces in the general environment are affecting an organization. This context can often provide clues to responses by stakeholders to opportunities, crises, and extraordinary events. Corporate scandals revealed following the Enron debacle suggest that there were several factors in the general environment that were at play in addition to certain corporate executives' greed. For example, the dot-com bubble created a financial environment where investment funds followed innovative ideas in exorbitant and exuberant ways. Investment banks loaned large amounts to Enron and other companies without due diligence. Stock analysts lied and encouraged deceptive investing from the public. Boards of directors abandoned their fiscal responsibilities, as did large accounting firms like Arthur Andersen, which is no longer in existence. The general legal and enforcement environment during the 1990s appeared indifferent to monitoring corporate activities and protecting shareholders. This all changed after Enron. Let's define two major terms before explaining how to do a stakeholder analysis.

Stakeholders   A *stakeholder* is "any individual or group who can affect or is affected by the actions, decisions, policies, practices, or goals of the organization."[22] We begin by identifying the *focal stakeholder*. This is the company or group that is the focus of our analysis.

The primary stakeholders of a firm include its owners, customers, employees, and suppliers. Also of primary importance to a firm's survival are its stockholders and board of directors. The CEO and other top-level executives can be stakeholders, but in the stakeholder analysis, they are generally considered actors and representatives of the firm. In the opening Microsoft outsourcing scenario, stockholders have a stake in the economic advantages of outsourcing. Cutting expenses and gaining market share through value-added, low-cost technological expertise from India and other countries increases profits— a primary goal of executives and stockholders. However, those employees who are laid off because of lower labor costs in other countries may be losing with the outsourcing strategy.

Secondary stakeholders include all other interested groups, such as the media, consumers, lobbyists, courts, governments, competitors, the public, and society. Microsoft outsources in part to outperform its competitors. Consumers may or may not gain an advantage from Microsoft's outsourcing, depending on the prices and quality of products. In some instances, consumers may be at a disadvantage through lower product or service quality. (Dell Computer, because of continuing complaints from corporate customers regarding language misunderstanding and low level service, announced on November 25, 2003, that it would direct calls for corporate customers only to call centers in Texas, Idaho, and Tennessee.)[23]

Stakes   A *stake* is any interest, share, or claim that a group or individual has in the outcome of a corporation's policies, procedures, or actions toward others. Stakes may be based on any type of interest. The stakes of stakeholders are not always obvious. The economic viability of competing firms can be at stake when one firm threatens entry into a market. The physical health of a community can be at stake when a corporation decides to empty toxic waste near residential sites.

Stakes also can be present, past, or future oriented. For example, stakeholders may seek compensation for a firm's past actions, as occurred when lawyers argued that certain airlines owed their clients monetary compensation after having threatened their emotional stability when pilots announced an impending disaster (engine failure) that, subsequently, did not occur. Stakeholders may seek future claims; that is, they may seek injunctions against firms that announce plans to drill oil or build nuclear plants in designated areas or to market or bundle certain products in noncompetitive ways.

2.3 HOW TO EXECUTE A STAKEHOLDER ANALYSIS

The stakeholder analysis is a pragmatic way of identifying and understanding multiple (often competing) claims of many constituencies. As part of a general stakeholder approach, the stakeholder analysis is a method to help understand the relationships between an organization and the groups with which it must interact. Each situation is different and therefore requires a map to guide strategy for an organization dealing with groups, some of whom may not be supportive of issues such as outsourcing jobs. The aim here is to familiarize you with the framework so that you can apply it in the classroom and in news events that appear in the press and in other media. Even though you may not be an executive or manager, the framework can enable you to see and understand more clearly complex corporate dealings. Former students of mine who are now professional consultants, owners, and managers have reported that their having studied the stakeholder approach helped them see the "big picture" and clients differently in their careers. Although this chapter focuses on upper-level and functional area managers as stakeholders who formulate and direct corporate strategy, Chapter 3 discusses the individual employee and the organization as stakeholders. Chapter 3 also provides ethical principles you can use to evaluate the moral criteria of strategies used by managers when responding to different stakeholders.

Taking a Third-Party Objective Observer Perspective   In the following discussion, you are asked to assume the role of a chief executive officer (CEO) of a company to execute a stakeholder analysis. However, it is recommended that you take the role of "third-party objective observer" when doing a stakeholder analysis. Why? In this role, you will need to suspend your belief and value judgments in order to understand the strategies, motives, and actions of the different stakeholders. You may not agree with the focal organization or CEO whom you are studying. Therefore, the point is to be able to see all sides of an issue and then objectively evaluate the claims, actions, and outcomes of all the parties. Being more objective helps determine who acted responsibly, who won and who lost, and at what costs.

Part of the learning process in this exercise is to see your own blind spots, values, beliefs, and passions toward certain issues and stakeholders. Doing an in-depth stakeholder analysis with a group enables others to see and comment on your reasoning. For the next section, however, take the role of a CEO so you can get an idea of what it feels like to be in charge of directing an organization-wide analysis.

Role of the CEO in Stakeholder Analysis   Assume you are the CEO, working with your top managers, in a firm that has just been involved in a major controversy of international proportions. The media, some consumer groups, and several major customers have called you. You want to get a handle on the situation without reverting to unnecessary "firefighting" management methods. A couple of your trusted staff members have advised you to adopt a planning approach quickly while responding to immediate concerns and to understand the "who, what, where, when, and why" of the situation before jumping to "how" questions. Your senior strategic planner suggests you lead and participate in a stakeholder analysis. What is the next step?

The stakeholder analysis is a series of steps aimed at the following tasks[24]:

1. Map stakeholder relationships.
2. Map stakeholder coalitions.
3. Assess the nature of each stakeholder's interest.
4. Assess the nature of each stakeholder's power.
5. Construct a matrix of stakeholder moral responsibilities.
6. Develop specific strategies and tactics.
7. Monitor shifting coalitions.

Each step is described in the following sections. Let us explore each one and then apply them in our continuing scenario example.

Step 1: Map Stakeholder Relationships   In 1984, R. Edward Freeman offered questions that help begin the analysis of identifying major stakeholders (Figure 2.1). The first five questions in the figure offer a quick jump-start on the analysis. Questions 6 through 9 may be used in later steps, when you assess the nature of each stakeholder's interest and priorities.

Let's continue our example with you as CEO. While brainstorming about questions 1 through 5 with employees you have selected who are the most knowledgeable, current, and close to the sources of the issues at hand, you may want to draw a stakeholder map and fill in the blanks. Note that your stakeholder analysis is only as valid and reliable as the sources and processes you use to obtain your information. As more controversial, incomplete, or questionable issues arise, you may wish to go outside your immediate planning group to obtain additional information and perspective. A general picture of an initial stakeholder map is shown in Figure 2.2. You would identify and complete the stakeholder map, inserting each relevant stakeholder involved in the particular issue you are studying. For example, if you were examining Microsoft's practice of outsourcing, you would place the Microsoft Corporation (or perhaps one of its divisions) in the center (or focal) stakeholder box, then continue identifying the other groups involved with that issue.

Step 2: Map Stakeholder Coalitions   After you identify and make a map of the stakeholders who are involved with your firm in the incident you are addressing, the next step is to determine and map any coalitions that have formed. Coalitions among stakeholders form

---

FIGURE 2.1   Sample Questions for Stakeholder Review

1. Who are our stakeholders currently?
2. Who are our potential stakeholders?
3. How does each stakeholder affect us?
4. How do we affect each stakeholder?
5. For each division and business, who are the stakeholders?
6. What assumptions does our current strategy make about each important stakeholder (at each level)?
7. What are the current "environmental variables" that affect us and our stakeholders (inflation, GNP, prime rate, confidence in business [from polls], corporate identity, media image, and so on)?
8. How do we measure each of these variables and their impact on us and our stakeholders?
9. How do we keep score with our stakeholders?

Source: R. Edward Freeman. 1984. *Strategic Management: A Stakeholder Approach.* Boston: Pitman, 242. Reproduced with permission of the author.

FIGURE 2.2   Stakeholder Map of a Large Organization

Source: R. Edward Freeman. 1984. *Strategic Management: A Stakeholder Approach.* Boston: Pitman, 25. Reproduced with permission of the author.

around stakes that they have—or seek to have—in common. Interest groups and lobbyists sometimes join forces against a common "enemy." Competitors also may join forces if they see an advantage in numbers. Mapping actual and potential coalitions around issues can help you, as the CEO, anticipate and design strategic responses toward these groups before or after they form.

Step 3: Assess the Nature of Each Stakeholder's Interest
Steps 3 and 4, which assess the nature of each stakeholder's power, overlap to some extent. Figure 2.4 is explained in more detail in step 6, but observe in that figure the four different types of stakeholders you face as a company—the "supportive," "nonsupportive," "mixed blessing," and "marginal." The supportive and nonsupportive are with and against you. With the "mixed blessing" and "marginal," you are less sure about their support for your strategy. Briefly identify each of these groups' interests or stakes with regard, for example, to your outsourcing practice and strategy—if you were Microsoft.

In the opening Microsoft example, a hypothetical CEO, along with his or her staff, might determine that supporters of Microsoft's outsourcing plans would be a few members of the board of directors and a lobbyist. Their interests are to make a profit and see that you do. Nonsupportive stakeholders, or those who may seek to prevent, disrupt, and/or change Microsoft's outsourcing strategies, may include employees that would be laid off, suppliers who might be let go, a local politician, and an anti-globalist group against outsourcing. Their interests are to protect their jobs, their beliefs, and their constituents' beliefs. Who else would you add to those in opposition to Microsoft? By systematically completing this audit through brainstorming, you, as a CEO in crisis, can create a broader, more objective picture of the situation, the players and their interests, and your firm's role in the situation.

Step 4: Assess the Nature of Each Stakeholder's Power
This part of the analysis asks, "What's in it for each stakeholder? Who stands to win, lose, or draw over certain stakes?" Three types of stakeholders you can use are those with (1) voting power, (2) political power, and (3) economic power.[25] Note that the power and influence is two-way: Microsoft toward its stakeholders, and each stakeholder toward Microsoft on a given issue. For example, owners and stockholders can vote on the firm's decisions regarding a particular issue or opportunity, such as outsourcing. On the other hand, federal, state, and local governments can exercise their political power by voting on privileges and responsibilities of Microsoft in their communities. New legislation may emerge with regard to outsourcing. Consumers can exercise their economic power by boycotting Microsoft's products or buying other operating systems, browsers, and software. What other sources of stakeholder power exist?

Step 5: Identify Stakeholder Ethics and Moral Responsibilities
After you map stakeholder relationships and assess the nature of each stakeholder's interest and power, the next step is to determine the responsibilities and moral obligations your company has to each stakeholder. A matrix of stakeholder responsibilities is shown in Figure 2.3. For example, Microsoft's CEO may see the firm's *economic responsibility* to the owners (as stakeholders) as "preventing as many costly lawsuits as possible." *Legally,* the CEO may want to protect the owners and the executive team from liability and damage; this would entail proactively negotiating disputes outside the courts, if possible, in a way that is equitable to all. *Ethically,* the CEO may keep the company's stockholders and owners current as to his or her ethical thinking and strategies to show responsibility toward all stakeholders. Chapter 3 explains ethical principles and guidelines that can assist in this type of decision making. *Voluntarily,* the CEO may advise shareholders to show responsibility by publicly announcing their plans for resolving the accusations about the firm's "next steps" in more open and conscientious marketing and distribution of products.

This part of the analysis should continue until you have completed matching the economic, legal, ethical, and voluntary responsibilities

| FIGURE 2.3 | Stakeholder Moral Responsibility Matrix |

	Legal	Economic	Ethical	Voluntary
Owners				
Customers				
Employees				
Community interest groups				
Public (citizens at large)				

Stakeholders

you have for each stakeholder, so that you can develop strategies toward each stakeholder you have identified.

Step 6: Develop Specific Strategies and Tactics   Using your results from the preceding steps, you can now proceed to outline the specific strategies and tactics you wish to use with each stakeholder.

First, you should consider whether to approach each stakeholder directly or indirectly. Second, you need to decide whether to do nothing, monitor, or take an offensive or defensive position. Third, you should determine whether to accommodate, negotiate, manipulate, resist, avoid, or "wait and see." Finally, you should decide what combination of strategies you want to employ.

A useful typology for both identifying and deciding on strategies to employ in a complex situation is shown in Figure 2.4.[26] This diagnostic typology of organizational stakeholders shows two dimensions: potential for threat and potential for cooperation. Note that stakeholders can move among the quadrants, changing positions as situations and stakes change.

The ideal strategic situation for the focal corporation is type 1, the *supportive* stakeholder with a low potential for threat and high potential for cooperation. Here the strategy of the focal company is to *involve* the supportive stakeholder. Think of both internal and external stakeholders who might be supportive and who should be involved in the focal organization's strategy.

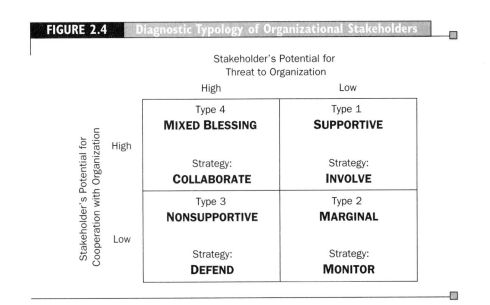

FIGURE 2.4   Diagnostic Typology of Organizational Stakeholders

Source: Academy of Management Executive: *The Thinking Manager's Source,* by G. Savage et al. Copyright 1991 by Academy of Management. Reproduced with permission of Academy of Management in the format Textbook via Copyright Clearance Center.

In contrast, there is type 3, the *nonsupportive* stakeholder who shows a high potential for threat and a low potential for cooperation. The suggested strategy in this situation calls for the focal organization to *defend* its interests and reduce dependence on that stakeholder.

A type 4 stakeholder is a *mixed blessing,* with a high potential for both threat and cooperation. This stakeholder calls for a *collaborative* strategy. In this situation, the stakeholder could become supportive or nonsupportive. Collaborative attempts to move the stakeholder to the focal company's interests is the goal.

Finally, type 2 is the *marginal* stakeholder. This stakeholder has a low potential for both threat and cooperation. Such stakeholders may not be interested in the issues of concern. The recommended strategy in this situation is to *monitor* the stakeholder, to "wait and see" and minimize expenditure of resources, until the stakeholder moves to a mixed blessing, supportive, or nonsupportive position.

Figure 2.5 presents an illustration of the typology in Figure 2.4, using the Microsoft outsourced opening case as an example. Indicate other stakeholders who might be or were influenced by Microsoft's decision to outsource. Using your objective "third-party perspective," determine the movement among stakeholder positions: Who influenced whom, by what means, and how? Using arrows on this diagram, suggest who might move from one quadrant to another. As you look at Figure 2.5, ask yourself: Do I agree with this diagram as it is completed? Who is likely

FIGURE 2.5   Diagnostic Typology of Stakeholders for Microsoft Corporation

Offshore hires *Some strategic partners* *Most shareholders* *Bush administration*	*Many employees* *Some customers*
Some shareholders *Some customers* *Some suppliers*	*Employees who lost jobs* *Unions* *Some competitors* *Lou Dobbs* *Some U.S. Congress persons*

to move from Supportive to Unsupportive? From a Mixed Blessing position to Unsupportive or Supportive? Why? How? Support your logic and defend your position.

From the point of view of the focal stakeholder, while you as CEO are developing specific strategies, keep the following points in mind:

1. Your goal is to create a win-win set of outcomes, if possible. However, this may mean economic costs to your firm if, in fact, members of your firm are responsible to certain groups for harm caused as a consequence of your actions.

2. Ask: "What is our business? Who are our customers? What are our responsibilities to the stakeholders, to the public, and to the firm?" Keep your mission and responsibilities in mind as you move forward.

3. Consider the probable consequences of your actions. For whom? At what costs? Over what period? Ask: "What does a win-win situation look like for us?"

4. Keep in mind that the *means* that you use are as important as the ends you seek; that is, how you approach and treat each stakeholder can be as important as what you do.

Specific strategies now can be articulated and assigned to corporate staff for review and implementation. Remember, social responsibility is a key variable; it is as important as the economic and political factors of a decision because social responsibility is linked to costs and benefits in other areas. At this point, you can ask to what extent your strategies are just and fair and consider the welfare of the stakeholders affected by your decision.

Executives use a range of strategies, especially in long-term crisis situations, to respond to external threats and stakeholders. Their strategies often are short-sighted and begin as a defensive. In observing and using a stakeholder analysis, question why executives respond to their stakeholders as they do. Following the questions and methods in this chapter systematically helps you understand why key stakeholders respond as they do.

Step 7: Monitor Shifting Coalitions Because time and events can change the stakes and stakeholders, and their strategies, you need to monitor the evolution of the issues and actions of the stakeholders, using Figure 2.4. Tracking external trends and events and the resultant stakeholder strategies can help a CEO and his or her team act and react accordingly. How would you feel if you were Bill Gates as he explains to his employees, his board of directors, and to a local Rotary Club his company's need to outsource jobs and business processes to cut costs, take advantage of global low-cost resources, and increase market share and profit?

Summary of Stakeholder Analysis   You have now completed the basic stakeholder analysis and should be able to proceed with strategy implementation in more realistic, thoughtful, interactive, and responsible ways. The stakeholder approach should involve other decision makers inside and outside the focal organization.

The stakeholder analysis provides a rational, systematic basis for understanding issues involved in complex relationships between an organization and its constituents. It helps decision makers structure strategic planning sessions and decide how to meet the moral obligations of all stakeholders. The extent to which the resultant strategies and outcomes are moral and are effective for a firm and its stakeholders depends on many factors, including the values of the firm's leaders, the stakeholders' power, the legitimacy of the actions, the use of available resources, and the exigencies of the changing environment. Many CEOs and top management teams could benefit from managing their constituencies using this analytical method, with everyone's rights and responsibilities in mind.

2.4 NEGOTIATION METHODS: RESOLVING STAKEHOLDER DISPUTES

Disputes are part of stakeholder relationships. Most disputes are handled in the context of mutual trusting relationships between stakeholders; others move into the legal and regulatory system.[27]

Disputes occur between different stakeholder levels: for example, between professionals within an organization, consumers and companies, business to business (B2B), governments and businesses, and among coalitions and businesses. It is estimated that *Fortune* 500 senior HR executives are involved in legal disputes 20% of their working time. Also, managers generally spend 30% of their time handling conflicts. The hidden cost of managing conflicts between and among professionals in organizations can result in absenteeism, turnover, legal costs, and loss of productivity.[28]

It is estimated that more than $1 trillion was spent in B2B eCommerce last year, with a projected $5 trillion by 2005. With that volume, there will be business disputes. A study by The American Arbitration Association found that:

1. 58% of companies have no plans in place to handle B2B eCommerce disputes.

2. Seven out of 10 executives and general counsel state that additional guidelines are required to handle online disputes.

3. Only 41% of companies have guidelines for conducting B2B eCommerce relationships.

4. Most executives surveyed said that placing supply chains online creates different and new types of disputes.[29] Stakeholder conflict and dispute resolution methods are necessary.

Stakeholder Dispute Resolution Methods Dispute resolution is an expertise also known as "alternative dispute resolution" (ADR). Dispute resolution techniques cover a variety of methods intended to help potential litigants resolve conflicts. The methods can be viewed on a continuum ranging from face-to-face negotiation to litigation, as Figure 2.6 illustrates. Advocates of alternative resolution methods argue that litigation need not be the standard for evaluating other dispute techniques.[30] Figure 2.6 illustrates the degree to which disputing parties give up control of the process and outcome to a neutral third party.

The left side of the continuum is based on consensual, informal dispute resolution methods. Negotiating, facilitation, and some mediation

---

FIGURE 2.6   The ADR Continuum

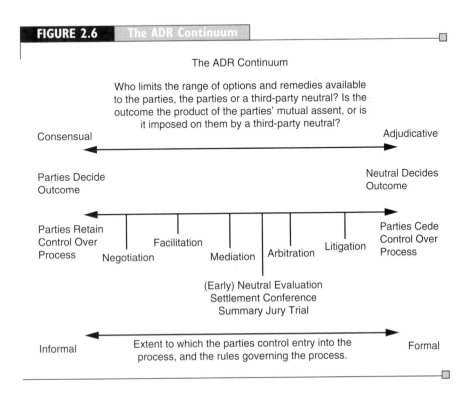

The ADR Continuum

Who limits the range of options and remedies available to the parties, the parties or a third-party neutral? Is the outcome the product of the parties' mutual assent, or is it imposed on them by a third-party neutral?

Consensual — Adjudicative

Parties Decide Outcome — Neutral Decides Outcome

Parties Retain Control Over Process — Facilitation — Negotiation — Mediation — Arbitration — Litigation — Parties Cede Control Over Process

(Early) Neutral Evaluation
Settlement Conference
Summary Jury Trial

Informal — Extent to which the parties control entry into the process, and the rules governing the process. — Formal are methods where the parties maintain control over the conflict resolution process. Moving to the right side of the spectrum (adjudicative), disputing parties give up control to third-party arbitrators and then litigators (courts, tribunals, and binding arbitration). For example, with regard to outsourcing issues discussed earlier in the chapter, most companies have the authority to make outsourcing decisions. However, with regard to outsourcing control over who and what types of contracts will be used to rebuild Iraq, Congress is debating the use of external contractors doing federal work. Halliburton received several exclusive outsourced contracts in this effort. Congress is using the fiscal 2005 defense authorization bill to enable civil service employees in the Departments of Defense, Homeland Security, the Internal Revenue Service, and the Pentagon to control the use of external contractors. Although Republican and Democratic senators debate this issue, some argue that private company bidders have appeal rights.[31]

The stakeholder management approach involves the full range of dispute resolution techniques, although ideally more *integrative* and *relational* rather than *distributive* or *power-based* methods would be attempted first. (Power-based approaches are based on authoritarian and competition-based methods where the more powerful group or individual "wins" and the opposing group "loses." This approach can cause other disputes to arise.) Integrative approaches are characterized as follows:

- Problems are seen as having more potential solutions than are immediately obvious.
- Resources are seen as expandable; the goal is to "expand the pie" before dividing it.
- Parties attempting to create more potential solutions and processes are thus said to be "value creating."
- Parties attempt to accommodate as many interests of each of the parties as possible.
- The so-called "win-win" or "all gain" approach.[32]

Distributive approaches have the following characteristics:

- Problems are seen as "zero sum."
- Resources are imagined as fixed: "divide the pie."
- "Value claiming."
- Haggling or "splitting the difference."[33]

Relational approaches (which consider power, interests, rights, and ethics) include and are based on:

- "Relationship building"
- "Narrative," "deliberative," and other "dialogical" (i.e., dialogue-based) approaches to negotiation and mediation
- Restorative justice and reconciliation (i.e., approaches that respect the dignity of every person, build understanding, and provide opportunities for victims to obtain restoration and for offenders to take responsibility for their actions)
- Other "transformative" approaches to peacebuilding[34]

The process of principled negotiation from Roger Fry and William Ury's book, *Getting to Yes*, continues to be used for almost any type of dispute. The four principles include:

1. Separate the people from the problem.
2. Focus on interests rather than positions.
3. Generate a variety of options before settling on an agreement.
4. Insist that the agreement be based on objective criteria.[35]

Adjudicative, legislative, restorative justice, reparation, and rights-based approaches are necessary when rights, property, or other legitimate claims have been violated and harm results. Leaders and professionals practicing a stakeholder management approach incorporate and gain proficiency in using a wide range of conflict and alternative dispute resolution methods.[36]

2.5 STAKEHOLDER APPROACH AND ETHICAL REASONING

Ethical reasoning in the stakeholder analysis involves asking: "What is equitable, just, fair, and good for those who affect and are affected by business decisions? Who are the weaker stakeholders in terms of power and influence? Who can, who will, and who should help weaker stakeholders make their voices heard and encourage their participation in the decision process?" Finally, the stakeholder analysis requires the principal stakeholders to define and fulfill their ethical obligations to the affected constituencies.

Chapter 3 explains major ethical principles that can be used to examine individual motivation for resolving an ethical dilemma. That chapter explains several ethical frameworks and principles, including the following: (1) rights, (2) justice, (3) utilitarianism, (4) relativism, and (5) universalism, all of which can be applied to belief systems, policies, and motives. You may want to refer to Chapters 2 and 3 when using ethical principles to describe actual individuals' and groups' observed moral policies, motives, and outcomes in cases that you are studying or creating from your experience or research.

2.6 MORAL RESPONSIBILITIES OF CROSS-FUNCTIONAL AREA PROFESSIONALS

One goal of a stakeholder analysis is to encourage and prepare organizational managers to articulate their own moral responsibility, as well as the responsibilities of their company and their profession, toward their different constituencies. Stakeholder analysis focuses the enterprise's attention and moral decision making process on external events. The stakeholder approach also applies internally, especially to individual managers in traditional functional areas. These managers can be seen as conduits through which other external stakeholders are influenced.

Because our concern is managing moral responsibility in organizational stakeholder relationships, to illustrate moral dilemmas that can arise, this section briefly outlines some of the responsibilities of selected functional area managers. With the Internet, the transparency of all organizational actors and internal stakeholders increases the risk and stakes of unethical practices. Chat rooms, message boards, and breaking news sites provide instant platforms for exposing both rumor and truth about companies. (In the tobacco controversy, it was an anti-smoking researcher and advocate who first posted inside information from a whistle-blower on the Internet. This action was a first step toward opening the tobacco companies' internal documents to public scrutiny and the resulting lawsuits.)

Figure 2.7 illustrates a manager's stakeholders. The particular functional area you are interested in can be kept in mind while you read the descriptions discussed next. Note that the same procedures, steps 1 through 7, presented in the stakeholder analysis can also be used for this level of analysis.

Functional and expert areas include marketing, R&D, manufacturing, public relations, and human resource management (HRM). The basic moral dimensions of each of these are discussed. Even though functional areas are often blurred in some emerging network organizational structures and self-designed teams, many of the responsibilities of these managerial areas remain intact. Understanding these managerial roles from a stakeholder perspective helps to clarify the pressures and moral responsibilities of these job positions. This section can be read and revisited after reading Chapter 3, which presents ethical principles and quick ethical tests for professionals.

FIGURE 2.7   A Manager's Stakeholders

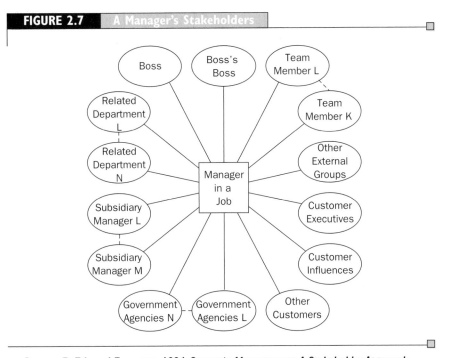

Source: R. Edward Freeman. 1984. *Strategic Management: A Stakeholder Approach.*
Boston: Pitman, 218. Reproduced with permission of the author.
Note: The letters **K, L, M** and **N** are hypothetical designations in place of real
department names. Dotted lines refer to hypothetical linkages.

Marketing and Sales Professionals and Managers as Stakeholders

Sales professionals and managers are continuously engaged—electronically and/or face-to-face—with customers, suppliers, and vendors. Sales professionals are also evaluated by quotas and quantitative expectations on a weekly, monthly, and quarterly basis. The stress and pressure to meet expectations is always present. Sales professionals must continually balance their personal ethics and their professional pressures. The dilemma often becomes: "Who do I represent? What weight do my beliefs and ethics have when measured against my department's and company's performance measures for me?" Another key question for sales professionals particularly is: "Where is the line between unethical and ethical practices for me?" Also, because customers are an integral part of business, these professionals must create and maintain customer interest and loyalty. They must be concerned with consumer safety and welfare, while increasing revenue and obtaining new accounts. Many marketing and sales professionals also are responsible for determining and managing the firm's advertising and the truthfulness (and legality) of the data and information they issue to the public about products and services. They must interact with many of the other functional areas and with advertising agencies, customers, and consumer groups. Moral dilemmas can arise for marketing managers who may be asked to promote unsafe products or to implement advertising campaigns that are untrue or not in the consumer's best interests.

Several equity traders during and after the corporate scandals were involved in lying to customers about "dogs"—stocks which they knew were underperforming. Part of their motive was to keep certain stocks popular and in a "buy" mode so their own sales performance would be valued higher, giving them better bonuses.

A major moral dilemma for marketing managers is having to choose between a profitable decision and a socially responsible one. The stakeholder analysis helps marketing managers in these morally questionable situations by identifying stakeholders and understanding the effects and consequences of profits and services on them. Balancing company profitability with human rights and interests is a moral responsibility of marketers. Companies that have no ethics code or socially responsible policies—as well as those that do have these, but do not enforce them—increase the personal pressure, pain, and liability of individual professionals. Such tensions can lead to unethical and illegal activities.

R&D Engineering Professionals and Managers as Stakeholders

R&D managers and engineers are responsible for the safety and reliability of product design. Faulty products can mean public outcry, which can result in unwanted media exposure and possibly (perhaps justifiably) lawsuits. R&D managers must work and communicate effectively and conscientiously with professionals in manufacturing, marketing, and information systems; senior managers; contractors; and government representatives, to name a few of their stakeholders. As studies and reports on the Challenger space shuttle disaster illustrate, engineers and managers at the National Aeronautics and Space Administration (NASA) and the cooperating company, Thiokol, had different priorities, perceptions, and technical judgments regarding the "go, no-go" decision of that space launch. Lack of individual responsibility and critical judgment contributed to the miscommunication and resulting disaster.

Moral dilemmas can arise for R&D engineers whose technical judgments and risk assessments conflict with administrative managers seeking profit and time-to-market deadlines. R&D managers also can benefit from doing a stakeholder analysis, before disasters like the failed Challenger launch occurred. The discussion of the "levels of business ethics" in Chapter 1 also provides professionals with a way of examining their individual ethics and moral responsibilities.

Public Relations Managers as Stakeholders

Public relations (PR) managers must constantly interact with outside groups and corporate executives, especially in an age when communications media, external relations, and public scrutiny play such vital roles. PR managers are responsible for transmitting, receiving, and interpreting information about employees, products, services, and the company. A firm's public credibility and image depend on how PR professionals manage stakeholders because PR personnel must often negotiate the boundaries between corporate loyalty and credibility with external groups. These groups often use different criteria than corporate executives do for measuring success and responsibility, especially during crises. Moral dilemmas can arise when PR managers must defend company actions that have possible or known harmful effects on the public or stakeholders. A stakeholder analysis can prepare PR managers and inform them about the situation, the stakes, and the strategies they must address.

Human Resource Managers as Stakeholders

Human resource managers (HRMs) are on the front line of helping other managers recruit, hire, fire, promote, evaluate, reward, discipline, transfer, and counsel employees. They negotiate union settlements and assist the government with enforcing Equal Employment Opportunity Commission (EEOC) standards. Human resource management professionals must translate employee rights and laws into practice. They also research, write, and maintain company policies on employee affairs. They face constant ethical pressures and uncertainties over issues about invasion of privacy and violations of employees' rights. Stakeholders of HRMs include employees, other managers and bosses, unions, community groups, government officials, lobbyists, and competitors.

Moral dilemmas can arise for these managers when affirmative action policies are threatened in favor of corporate decisions to hide biases or protect profits. HRMs also straddle the fine line between the individual rights of employees and corporate self-interests, especially when reductions in force (RIFs) and other hiring or firing decisions are involved. As industries restructure, merge, downsize, outsource, and expand internationally, the HRMs' work becomes even more complicated.

Summary of Managerial Moral Responsibilities

Expert and functional area managers are confronted with balancing operational profit goals with corporate moral obligations toward stakeholders. These pressures are considered "part of the job." Unfortunately, clear corporate directions for resolving dilemmas that involve conflicts between individuals' rights and corporate economic interests generally are not available. Using a stakeholder analysis is "like walking in the shoes of another professional." You get a sense of his or her pressures. Using a stakeholder analysis is a step toward clarifying the issues involved in resolving ethical dilemmas. Chapter 3 presents moral decision-making principles that can help individuals think through these issues and take responsible action.

2.7 ISSUES MANAGEMENT, STAKEHOLDER APPROACH, AND ETHICS: INTEGRATING FRAMEWORKS

Issues management methods complement the stakeholder management approach. It may be helpful to begin by identifying and analyzing major issues before doing a stakeholder analysis. Many reputable large companies use issues managers and methods for identifying, tracking, and responding to trends that offer potential opportunities, as well as threats to companies.[37] Before discussing ways of integrating stakeholder management (and analysis) to issues management, issues management is defined.

"Think of an issue as a gap between your actions and stakeholder expectations. Second, think of issue management as the process used to close that gap."[38] The gap can be closed in a number of ways, using several strategies. A primary method is using an accommodating policy. Providing public education, community dialogue, and changing expectations through communication are some accommodating strategies used in issues management. Solving complicated issues may sometimes require radical actions, like replacing members from the board of directors and the senior management team.[39]

Issues management is also a formal process used to anticipate and take appropriate action to respond to emerging trends, concerns, or issues that can affect an organization and its stakeholders.

> Issues management is a . . . genuine and ethical long-term commitment by the organization to a two-way, inclusive standard of corporate responsibility toward stakeholders. Issues management involves connectivity with, rather than control of, others. Issues managers help identify and close gaps between expectation, performance, communication, and accountability. Issues management blends "many faces" within the entity into "one voice." Like the issues themselves, the process is multi-faceted and is enhanced by the strategic facilitation and integration of diverse viewpoints and skills.[40]

Many national and international business-related controversies develop around the exposure of a single issue that evolves into more serious and costly issues. Enron's problems in the beginning surfaced as an issue of overstated revenue. After months of investigation, members of the highest executive team were found to have been involved in deception, fraud, and theft.

Another issue still evolving is that of obesity in the United States. Once considered a personal lifestyle problem, obesity is now seen as a public health disease in the United States, which will be treated and paid for by one's health insurance. Still another set of evolving issues was seen in the Ford Explorer and Bridgestone/Firestone tire crisis that started with what appeared to be faulty tires. The issue escalated to questions about the design of the Ford vehicle itself, then to questions about many international deaths and accidents over a number of years. The CEO of Ford eventually lost his job.

TV programs like *60 Minutes, Dateline, Frontline,* and *Now* introduce breaking news that focuses on events, crises, and innovative practices that are being faced and addressed. Stakeholder and issues management frameworks can be used to understand the evolution of these issues in order to responsibly manage or change their effects.

Stakeholder and Issues Management: "Connecting the Dots"   Issues and stakeholder management are used interchangeably by scholars and corporate practitioners, as the two following quotes illustrate:

> For many societal predicaments, stakeholders and issues represent two complementary sides of the same coin.[41]

> Stakeholders tend to organize around "hot" issues, and issues are typically associated with certain vocal stakeholder groups. Issues management scholars can therefore explore how issues management requires stakeholder prioritization, and how stakeholder management gets facilitated when managers have deep knowledge of stakeholders' issue agendas. Earlier research also suggests that whether or not stakeholders decide to get involved with certain issues has a profound influence on issue evolution, and so do the timing and extent of their involvement.[42]

Applying stakeholder and issues management approaches should not be mechanical. Moral creativity and objectivity help, as discussed in Chapter 1. A general first step is to ask, "What is the issue, opportunity, or precipitating event that an organization is facing or has experienced? How did the issue emerge?" Generally there are several issues that are discovered. A process begins by analyzing and then framing which issues are the most urgent and have (or may have) the greatest impact on the organization. At this point, you can begin to ask *who* was involved in starting or addressing the issue? This triggers the beginning of a stakeholder analysis and the steps discussed earlier in the chapter. Depending on how the issue evolved into other issues—or whether there was a crisis at the beginning, middle, or end of the issue evolution—you will know which issues management framework from the following section is most relevant to analyze the situation.

Actually, stakeholder analysis questions help "connect the dots" in understanding and closing the gaps of issues management. Why? Stakeholder questions help discover the "who did what to whom to influence which results, and at what costs and outcomes?" A major purpose in analyzing and effectively managing issues and stakeholders is to create environments that enable high-performing people to achieve productive and ethical results.

Moral Dimensions of Stakeholder and Issues Management

Some studies argue that moral reasoning is "issue-dependent," that "people generally behave better when the moral issue is important."[43] Questions regarding issue recognition include: To what extent do people actually recognize moral issues? Is it by the magnitude of the potential consequences or the actual consequences of the issue? Is it by the social consensus regarding how important the issue is? Is it by how likely it is that the effects of the issue will be felt or how quickly the issue will occur?[44] Ethical reasoning and behavior are an important part of managing stakeholders and issues because ethics is the energy that motivates people to respond to issues. When ethical motives are absent from leaders' and professionals' thinking and feeling, activities can occur that cost all stakeholders. Learning to detect and prevent unethical and illegal actions by using these methods is an aim of this section.

Companies face issues every day. Some issues lead to serious consequences—oil spills, the loss of millions of lives to the effects of tobacco, violence from use of firearms, or the theft of pensions from ordinary employees who worked a lifetime to accrue them. Other issues evolve in a way that leads to spectacular outcomes: the invention and commercialization of the Internet, information technology that provides wireless access to anyone at any time in any place, and the capability to network customers, businesses, suppliers, and vendors. Learning to identify and change issues for the good of the organization and for the common and public good is another goal of the stakeholder management approach.

Introduction to Three Issue Management Frameworks

This section presents three general issues frameworks for mapping and managing issues before and after they become crises. All these frameworks can be used with the stakeholder management approach. Using a stakeholder analysis (which is part of the general stakeholder management approach) explains the "who, what, where, why, what happened" to affect an issue. After you have read the first three issues management approaches shown in Figures 2.8, 2.9,

FIGURE 2.8   6-Step Issue Management Process

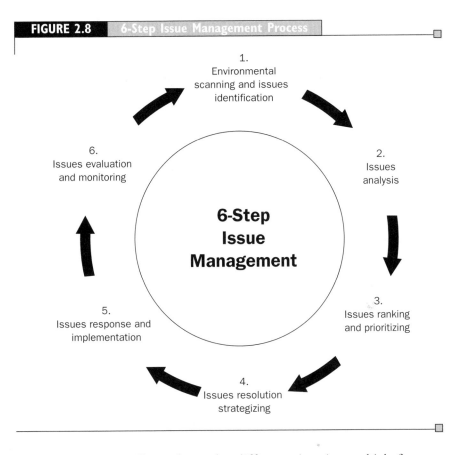

1.
Environmental
scanning and issues
identification

6.
Issues evaluation
and monitoring

2.
Issues
analysis

6-Step
Issue
Management

5.
Issues response and
implementation

3.
Issues ranking
and prioritizing

4.
Issues resolution
strategizing

and 2.10, you will see from the different situations which framework is relevant.

For example, Figure 2.8 is a straightforward framework that can be used for anticipating and thinking through issues that may have already affected an organization. Senior officers and staff would probably use this framework in their strategizing and "what-if" scenarios. If you are analyzing a case, you can also use this framework to show what steps the organization actually took to manage issues under investigation and what it *should* or *could* have done to manage the issues more responsibly and effectively. You can also use a stakeholder analysis at any point in this model.

Figure 2.9 is more specific and focuses on the evolution of an issue from inception to resolution. This framework, which is not organization-specific as is Figure 2.8, is most likely to be used by analysts and scholars studying issues, like outsourcing. In some cases, a stakeholder analysis can show why strategies and actions of particular stakeholders short-circuited the issue's evolution through all the stages in this figure.

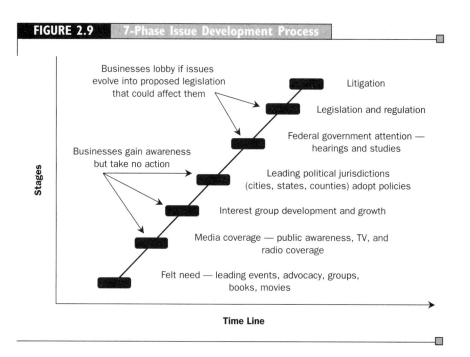

FIGURE 2.9   7-Phase Issue Development Process

Figure 2.10 is an abbreviated form of Figure 2.9. The framework in Figure 2.10 may be helpful if an organization does not respond to each of the stages in Figure 2.9. Figure 2.10 provides a more general set of stages: social, political, legislative, and social control. The complementary stakeholder analysis adds the rich detail of "who did what to whom, why, and with what outcome."

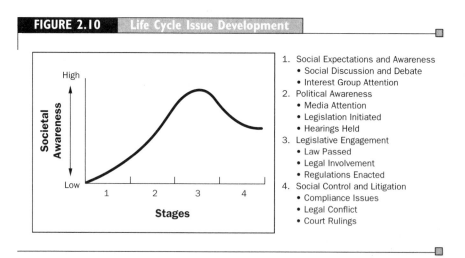

FIGURE 2.10   Life Cycle Issue Development

First Approach: 6-Step Issue Management Process   The first of the three methods is the most straightforward. This approach is most appropriate for companies or groups trying to understand and manage their internal environments. A third-party observer could also use this approach to describe how a group acted in retrospect or could act in the future. The process involves the following steps, illustrated in Figure 2.8.[45]

1. Environmental scanning and issues identification

2. Issues analysis

3. Issues ranking and prioritizing

4. Issues resolution strategizing

5. Issues response and implementation

6. Issues evaluation and monitoring

These steps are part of a firm's corporate planning process. In the strategic issues management process, a firm uses a selected team to work on emerging trends as they relate to the industry and company. As Heath (2002) noted, "The objective of issues management is to make a smart, proactive, and even more respected organization. This sort of organization is one that understands and responds to its stake-seekers and stakeholders."[46]

This framework is a basic approach for proactively mapping, strategizing, and responding to issues that affect an organization. For example, with regard to Microsoft's decision to outsource, Steve Ballmer, Microsoft's CEO, announced in July 2003 in an annual e-mail to the firm's 56,000 employees that the company wished to introduce $1 billion in cost-saving actions. Ballmer did not announce that part of the company's new global sourcing strategy would include contracting through outsourcers in India.[47] Ballmer had, no doubt, executed step 1 in the model.

If you, as an objective third-party observer, were analyzing Microsoft's strategy to outsource work, what issues could you identify that might affect the company? As you identify each issue (step 1), you might also begin to analyze the impact of the issue on the organization and other stakeholders (step 2). For example, cost savings might be a reason to outsource, but the following issue could emerge, "Have all the overhead costs, not just the labor hours worked, been calculated into the savings?" When analyzing outsourcing issues, you may question possible lack of quality, satisfaction with results, and problems to be anticipated in communicating complex tasks between U.S. and international programmers. As you move through the other steps of this model, this process should inform you of the "bigger picture" of costs and benefits of specific outsourcing strategies. Ethical issues are also likely to emerge, like the possible loss of consumers' privacy if databases are transferred or created internationally.

This 6-step process also enables you to advise upper-level managers and directors in the company regarding precautions to take to avoid the illegal and unethical consequences of an issue. This model sharpens your ability to see the effects of issues on organizations from conception to response and monitoring.

Second Approach: 7-Phase Issue Development Process

Issues are believed to follow a developmental life cycle. Views differ on the stages and time involved in the life cycle. Steven Fink's method of analyzing an eight-year issue's life is illustrated in Figure 2.9. It is instructive to understand some of the life-cycle stages suggested for tracking an issue.[48]

1. A felt need arises (from emerging events, advocacy groups, books, movies).

2. Media coverage is developed (television segments, such as on *60 Minutes* and *20/20,* and radio announcements).

3. Interest group development gains momentum and grows.

4. Policies are adopted by leading political jurisdictions (cities, states, counties).

5. The federal government gives attention to the issue (hearings and studies).

6. Issues and policies evolve into legislation and regulation.

7. Issues and policies enter litigation.

The outsourcing debate in general would be an interesting topic to analyze using this second issues framework. Christopher Clott's article, "Perspectives on Global Outsourcing and the Changing Nature of Work,"[49] provides excellent background information for such an assignment. Other industries that are outsourcing are facing consumer and watchdog organizations' scrutiny as ethical issues surface. For example, the accounting industry is being watched as issues evolve over the outsourcing of confidential client information. Steven Mintz (2004) observes,

> Outsourcing the preparation of income tax returns overseas raises significant ethical issues. Reports of the scope and size of the outsourcing market vary greatly, but the largest outsourcing companies claim that thousands of returns were processed during the 2003 tax season. SurePrep claims to have processed 6,000 returns last year and expects to process

as many as 30,000 by April 2004. SurePrep electronically transmits tax information to preparers in India. Four rules in the AICPA Code of Professional Conduct are of particular relevance to tax outsourcing: Rule 102, Integrity and Objectivity; Rule 201, General Standards; Rule 202, Compliance with Standards; and Rule 301, Confidential Client Information. The outsourcing of tax services continues a disturbing trend in the accounting profession of placing pecuniary interests ahead of the public interest.[50]

Stakeholder management methods are helpful with this issue's approach in identifying who moved an issue from one stage to another, how, and by what means this was done. Usually different stakeholder groups compete with one another, using different political and economic sources of power.

Third Approach: 4-Stage Issue Life Cycle A broader issues management approach is that of Thomas Marx,[51] who offered a 4-stage issue life cycle. Marx observed that issues evolve from social expectations to social control through the following steps (Figure 2.10).

1. Social expectations

2. Political issues

3. Legislation

4. Social control

Marx illustrated his framework with the automobile safety belt issue. The four stages of this case, according to Marx, were reflected by the following events.

1. Ralph Nader's now-classic book, *Unsafe at Any Speed,* published in 1965, created a social expectation regarding the safe manufacturing of automobiles. The Chevrolet Corvair, later pulled off the market, was the focus of Nader's astute legal and public advocacy work in exposing manufacturing defects.

2. The National Traffic and Motor Vehicle Safety Act and the resulting safety hearings in 1966 moved this expectation into the political arena.

3. In 1966, the Motor Vehicle Safety Act was passed, and four states began requiring the use of seat belts in 1984.

4. Social control was established in 1967, when all cars were required to have seat belts. Driver fines and penalties, recalls of products, and litigation concerning defective equipment further reinforced the control stage.

Nader's pioneering consumer advocacy and legal work with regard to U.S. automobile manufacturing set an enduring precedent for watchdog congressional and voluntary advocacy groups.

Selecting an issue in the news and tracing its evolution through these different stages provides a window into the processes of society. Issues are not static or predetermined commodities. Stakeholder' interests move or impede an issue's development. To understand how an issue develops or dies is to understand how power works in a political system.

QUICK ASSESSMENT

You are the president of a manufacturing company with 550 employees that has an excellent reputation in the small town in which you work. A newspaper reporter has discovered that two members of your top-level management team have been involved in buying illegal drugs on two occasions. Both employees have been with the company for more than seven years, and both have excellent work records and reputations in the community. You cannot afford to lose them.

The reporter has written a devastating story revealing all the details, has called on you to fire them immediately, and has given the story to the local television station. You have already received a call from the mayor to act responsibly with regard to the matter. More than 100 of your loyal and conscientious employees have e-mailed you, asking that you *not* fire the two employees and that, if you did fire them, they too would consider leaving the company.

Write out your response to this scenario. Describe what you *would* do (not what you would hope to or like to do) in the situation, and explain why.

Meet in small groups in your classroom and share your responses. Then make your report to the class. Observe the reasoning used and how the responses corresponded to any of the crisis management sections in the chapter.

What did you learn from the exercise? Explain.

2.8 TWO CRISIS-MANAGEMENT APPROACHES

In 1989, a British Midland Airways Boeing 737 crashed on the M1 motorway in Leicestershire, England, killing 47 people. British Midland chairman Sir Michael Bishop lost no time going to the scene and telling the press that as the head of the company, he was responsible. There was no hiding behind official inquiries or obfuscation. His crisis leadership technique was clear, sympathetic, positive, and transparent. The person in charge was visible, coherent, and reassuring. Bishop always kept the press informed of the inquiry and what British Midland was going to do next.

Consequently, his lead during a time of intense crisis is noted as a good example of crisis management from the top. Despite an enormous tragedy caused by technical and human failings, the company remains a profitable enterprise.[52]

"Crisis management" methods evolved from the study of how corporations and leaders responded (and should have responded) to crises. Using crisis management with stakeholder methods is essential for understanding and possibly preventing future fiascos because crises continue to occur in a number of areas: consumer products (Ford/Firestone tires), financial systems (Enron, the dot-com crash), and government projects (Challenger shuttle launch). Sir Michael Bishop's response to the crisis he faced in the previous scenario is a success story. Unfortunately, most corporate leaders have not responded so courageously.

Steven Fink (1986) states that a crisis is a "turning point for better or worse," a "decisive moment" or "crucial time," or "a situation that has reached a critical phase." He goes on to say that crisis management "is the art of removing much of the risk and uncertainty to allow you to achieve more control over your destiny."[53] Crises, from a corporation's point of view, can deteriorate if the situation escalates in intensity, comes under closer governmental scrutiny, interferes with normal operations, jeopardizes the positive image of the company or its officers, and damages a firm's bottom line. A turn for the worse also could occur if any of the firm's stakeholders were seriously harmed or if the environment was damaged. The following two approaches describe ways that organizations can respond to crises. You may turn to Chapter 4 to review some of the classic corporate crises that have occurred over the past few decades. Having such examples as the Exxon Valdez, the Ford Pinto disaster, and other crises in mind would be informative as you read how to examine and respond to a crisis from a stakeholder management perspective.

First Approach: Precrisis through Resolution

In 2000, a small fire at the Philips semiconductor plant in Albuquerque, New Mexico, blazed for only 10 minutes, but far away in Scandinavia the fire sparked a corporate crisis that shifted the balance of power between two of Europe's biggest mobile phone companies, Nokia and Ericsson. Both organizations were heavily dependent on microchips from Albuquerque, but only Nokia immediately spotted a glitch in the supply chain. Without actually knowing what was wrong and not settling for reassuring words from the Philips factory, Nokia made rapid crisis management decisions that resulted in company representatives flying to Albuquerque and giving the factory owners a series of "non-negotiable" instructions to follow if they wanted Nokia to remain a customer. Nokia also secured chips from just about every other producing company in Europe and so maintained supplies at the time of the mobile phone boom. Ericsson, on the other hand, was too late to react and paid the ultimate price.[54]

FIGURE 2.11   Four Crisis Management Stages

Stage 1	Stage 2	Stage 3	Stage 4
Precrisis	**Crisis occurs**	**Lingering**	**Health restored**
PRODROMAL STAGE	ACUTE STAGE	CHRONIC STAGE	CONFLICT RESOLUTION STAGE
Warning; symptoms	Point of no return	Self-doubt, self-analysis	Return to normalcy

According to this model, a crisis consists of four stages: (1) prodromal (precrisis), (2) acute, (3) chronic, and (4) resolved. Judgment and observation are required to manage these stages (Figure 2.11). This approach differs from the second one in that a "precrisis stage" is shown.[55]

The *prodromal stage* is the warning stage. If this stage is not recognized or does not actually occur, the second stage (acute crisis) can rush in, requiring damage control. Clues in the prodromal stage must be carefully observed. For example, a clue could be verbal, such as a union leader telling upper management that a strike may occur if certain contract conditions are not signed. Could the outsourcing phenomenon possibly be a warning signal for the exporting of mid- and upper-level jobs that will also affect the existence of a middle class in the United States? Or, is this phenomenon just another industry turnover cycle like the disappearance of the old textile industry, transistors, and stagecoaches? In the previous scenario, Nokia took the clues at the prodromal stage seriously; the result paid off.

In the second stage, *acute crisis,* damage has been done. The point here is to control as much of the damage as possible. This is often the shortest of the stages.

The third stage, *chronic crisis,* is the clean-up phase. This is a period of recovery, self-analysis, self-doubt, and healing. Congressional investigations, audits, and interviews occur during this stage, which can linger indefinitely, according to Fink. A survey of *Fortune* 500 CEOs reported that companies that did not have a crisis management plan stayed in this stage two and a half times longer than those who had plans. Did Microsoft experience a chronic crisis stage?

The final stage, *crisis resolution,* is the crisis management goal. The key question here is: What can and should an organization's leaders do to speed up this phase and resolve a crisis once and for all?

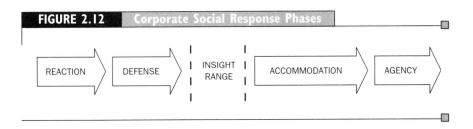

FIGURE 2.12   Corporate Social Response Phases

REACTION → DEFENSE → | INSIGHT RANGE | ACCOMMODATION → AGENCY

Second Approach: Reaction through Accommodation

Matthews, Goodpaster, and Nash[56] have suggested five phases of corporate social response to crises related to product crisis management. This model is based on the authors' study of how corporations have responded to serious crises. The phases, illustrated in Figure 2.12, are (1) reaction, (2) defense, (3) insight, (4) accommodation, and (5) agency. Before you continue here, read the Tylenol case at the end of this chapter and apply this crisis management method as you continue reading.

Not all executives involved in unsafe product crises respond the same way. This approach can be used to examine and evaluate the moral responsibilities of corporate responses to crises. These authors studied the classic product crises as well as more recent cases. It is interesting to observe how some executives continue to deny or avoid responsibility in crises that become disastrous. Knowledge of these stages certainly would be a first step toward corporate awareness. Let's look more closely at each stage.

The *reaction stage* is the first phase when a crisis has occurred. Management lacks complete information and time to analyze the event thoroughly. A reaction made publicly that responds to allegations is required. This stage is important to corporations, because the public, the media, and the stakeholders involved see for the first time who the firm selects as its spokesperson, how the firm responds, and what the message is.

The second stage, *defense,* signals that the company is overwhelmed by public attention. The firm's image is at stake. This stage usually involves the company's recoiling under media pressure. But this does not always have to be a negative or reactive situation.

The third stage, *insight,* is the most agonizing time for the firm in the controversy. The stakes are substantial. The firm's existence may be questioned. The company must come to grips with the situation under circumstances that have been generated externally. During this stage, the executives realize and confirm from evidence whether their company is at fault in the safety issues of the product in question.

In the fourth stage, *accommodation,* the company either acts to remove the product from the market or refutes the charges against product safety. Addressing public pressure and anxiety is the task in this stage.

During the last stage, *agency,* the company attempts to understand the causes of the safety issue and develop an education program for the public.

How did the leaders in the Tylenol case perform according to this method of crisis management? To use this approach for analysis, observe newspaper and media reports of industrial crises. Apply this model and compare how company executives and spokespersons handle crises. Take special note of how companies respond morally to their stakeholders. Observe the relative amount of attention companies give to consumers, the media, and government stakeholders. Use the frameworks in this chapter to help inform your observations and judgments. Develop a timeline as the crisis unfolds. Notice who the company chooses as its spokesperson. Determine how and why the company is assuming or avoiding responsibility.

Crisis Management Recommendations   A number of suggestions that corporations can follow to respond more effectively to crises are briefly summarized here. More in-depth strategies and tactics can be found in several sources.[57]

- Face the problem: Don't avoid or minimize it. Tell the truth.
- Take your "lumps" in one big news story rather than in bits and pieces. "No comment" implies guilt.
- Recognize that, in the age of instant news, there is no such thing as a private crisis.
- Stage "war games" to observe how your crisis plan holds up under pressure. Train executives to practice press conferences, and train teams to respond to crises that may affect other functional areas or divisions.
- Use the firm's philosophy, motto, or mission statement to respond to a crisis. For example, "We believe in our customer. Service is our business."
- Use the firm's closeness to customers and end users for early feedback on the crisis and to evaluate your effectiveness in responding to the events.

The following tactical recommendations are also helpful crisis prevention and management techniques:

- Understand your entire business and dependencies.

  Understanding your business provides the basis upon which all subsequent policies and processes are based and, therefore, should not be rushed.

- Carry out a business impact assessment.

  Having identified the mission critical processes, it is important to determine what the impact would be if a crisis happened. This process should assess the quantities (such as financial and service levels) and the qualitative (such as operational, reputation, legal and regulatory) impacts that might result from a crisis and the minimum level of resource for recovery.

- Complete a 360-degree risk assessment.

  This is used to determine the internal and external threats that could cause disruption and their likelihood of occurrence. Utilizing recognized risk techniques, a score can be achieved, such as high-medium-low, one to 10, or unacceptable/acceptable risk.

- Develop a feasible, relevant, and attractive response.

  There are two parts to this stage: developing the detailed response to an incident and the formulation of the business crisis plan that supports that response.

- Plan exercising, maintenance, and auditing.

  A business crisis plan cannot be considered reliable until it has been tested. Exercising the plan is of considerable importance, as a plan untested becomes a plan untrusted.[58]

Finally, issues and crisis management methods and preventive techniques are only effective in corporations if:

- Top management is supportive and participates.
- Involvement is cross-departmental.
- The issues management unit fits with the firm's culture.
- Output, instead of process, is the focus.[59]

SUMMARY

Organizations and businesses in the twenty-first century are more complex and networked than in any previous historical period. Because of the numerous transactions of corporations, methods are required to understand an organization's moral obligations and relationships to its constituencies.

The stakeholder management approach provides an analytical method for determining how various constituencies affect and are affected by business activities. The stakeholder approach also provides a means for assessing the power, legitimacy, and moral responsibility of managers' strategies in terms of how they meet the needs and obligations of stakeholders.

A stakeholder analysis is a strategic management tool that allows firms to manage relationships with constituents in any situation. An individual or group is said to have a "stake" in a corporation if it possesses an interest in the outcome of that corporation. A "stakeholder" is defined as an individual or group who can affect or be affected by the actions or policies of the organization.

Recent studies have indicated that profits and stockholder approval may not be the most important driving forces behind management objectives.[60] Job enrichment, concern for employees, and personal well-being are also important objectives. These studies reinforce the importance of the stakeholder management approach as a motivating part of an organization's social responsibility system.

The implementation of a stakeholder analysis involves a series of steps designed to help a corporation understand the complex factors involved in its obligations toward constituencies.

The moral dimensions of managerial roles also have a stakeholder perspective. The stakeholder approach can assist managers in resolving conflicts over individual rights and corporate objectives. This approach can help managers think through and chart morally responsible decisions in their work.

The use of the stakeholder analysis by a third party is a means for understanding social responsibility issues between a firm and its constituencies. Ethical reasoning can also be analyzed relative to the stakeholder approach.

Preventing and effectively negotiating disputes is a vital part of a professional's and leader's work. We discussed several alternative dispute resolution (ADR) methods in the chapter, emphasizing consensual, relational, and integrative methods that seek "win-win" approaches. The full range of dispute resolution methods is important to learn because conflict is part of ongoing organizational change.

Issues and crisis management frameworks complement the stakeholder analysis as social responsibility methods. Understanding what the central issues are for a company and how the issues evolved over time can help effectively and responsibly manage changes in a company's direction and operations. Crisis frameworks help to predict, prevent, and respond to emergencies. Issues and stakeholder management methods used together provide an overall approach to leading and managing organizational change responsibly and ethically.

Consultants Split on Bridgestone's Crisis Management

Crisis management experts criticized Bridgestone/Firestone for minimizing their tires' problems during the week of August 11, 2000. The experts gave the company mixed reviews on its handling of the recall of 6.5 million tires that were responsible for 174 deaths and more than 300 incidents involving tires that allegedly shredded on the highway in 1999. The tiremaker spokespersons claimed the poor tread on the tires was caused by underinflation, improper maintenance, and poor road conditions.

Mark Braverman, principal of CMG Associates, a crisis-management firm in Newton, Massachusetts, noted that the company blamed the victim and that Bridgestone/Firestone lacked a visible leader for its crisis-management effort. "The CEO should be out there, not executive vice presidents."

Steve Fink, another crisis-management expert, noted, "After they [Bridgestone/Firestone] announced the recall, they were not prepared to deal with it. They were telling consumers they will have to wait up to a year to get tires. And things like busy telephone call lines and overloaded Web sites—these are things that can be anticipated. That's basic crisis management."

Stephen Greyser, professor of marketing and communications at Harvard Business School, stated, "It's about what they didn't do up to now. The fact that the company [Bridgestone/Firestone] is just stepping up to bat tells me they've never really had the consumer as the principal focus of their thinking."

Defending the way Bridgestone/Firestone handled the crisis was Dennis Gioia, professor of organizational behavior at Smeal College of Business Administration at Pennsylvania State University: "With hindsight, you can always accuse a company of being too slow, given the history of automotive recalls. Sometimes you can't take hasty action or you would be acting on every hint there's a problem. It can create hysteria."

Discussion Question

Who do you agree or disagree with among these crisis-management consultants? Explain.

Source: "Consultants Split on Bridgestone's Crisis Management," *Wall Street Journal,* **11 August 2000, A6.**

QUESTIONS

1. Describe advantages of using stakeholder analysis to understand a complex business situation.

2. Would the Enron disaster have occurred had employees in that organization understood the illegal and unethical issues that were happening before the scandal was revealed? Explain.

3. How have the corporate scandals increased public awareness of activities that top-level stakeholders are capable of under the guise of innovating business models and creating wealth for shareholders? Does having an awareness of stakeholder and issues management methods increase your own power of observing what all players in a company are doing or might do? Explain.

4. Briefly describe a situation in which you were a major stakeholder involved in a dispute. How was the situation resolved (or not resolved)? What methods were used to resolve the situation? Looking back now, what methods could or should have been used to resolve that situation? For example, what would you now recommend happen to effectively resolve it fairly?

5. What are some of the types of power that stakeholders can use to support their positions? Briefly explain these.

6. Which roles and responsibilities in this chapter have you assumed in an organization? What pressures did you experience in that role that presented ethical dilemmas or issues for you? Explain.

7. What are the reasons for encouraging managers to use the stakeholder approach? Would these reasons apply to teams?

8. Give a recent example of a corporation that had to publicly manage a crisis. Did the company spokesperson respond effectively to stakeholders regarding the crisis? What should the company have done differently in its handling of the crisis?

9. Describe how you would feel and what actions you would take if you worked in a company and saw a potential crisis emerging at the "prodromal" or precrisis stage. What would you say, to whom, and why?

EXERCISES

1. Describe a situation in which you were a stakeholder. What was the issue? What were the stakes? Who were the other stakeholders? What was the outcome? Did you have a win-win resolution? If not, who won, who lost, and why?

2. Recall your personal work history. Who were your manager's most important stakeholders? What, in general, were your manager's major stakes in his or her particular position?

3. In your company, or one in which you have worked, what is the industry? The major external environments? Your product or service? Describe the major influences of each environment on your company (for example, on its competitiveness and ability to survive). Evaluate how well your company is managing its environments strategically, operationally, and technologically, as well as in relation to products and public reputation.

4. Choose one type of functional area manager described in the chapter. Describe a dilemma involving this manager, taken from a recent media report. Discuss how a stakeholder analysis could have helped or would help that manager work effectively with stakeholders.

5. Describe a complex issue that is evolving in the news or media. Explain how the issue has evolved into other issues. Which issues management framework would help track the evolution of this issue? Explain.

6. Describe a recent crisis that involved a product. Which crisis management model best explains the response? Explain, using that model.

Ethical Dilemma — Who Is Responsible to Whom?

Last year, I worked as a marketing manager in Belgium for a mid-sized engineering company. Total revenues for the company were $120 million. The company had recently gone public and, in two public offerings, had raised more than $60 million dollars. The firm was organized into four distinct strategic business units, based on products. The group that I worked in was responsible for more than $40 million in sales. We had manufacturing plants in four countries.

Our plant in Belgium manufactured a component that was used in several products, which produced $15 million in revenue. However, these products were old technology and were slowly being replaced in the industry. The overhead associated with the plant in Belgium was hurting the company financially, so they decided to sell the facility. The unions in Belgium are very strong and had approved the final sale agreement. After this sale, the work force was going to be reduced by half. Those who were laid off were not going to receive full severance pay, which, in Belgium, could take several years, and then workers would receive only 80% of total payment—a drastic change from what is offered in the United States. I was surprised that our executives in the United States had stated that the sales agreement was more than fair—contrary to the union's position. A strike was imminent; the materials manager was told to stock 10 weeks of product.

My ethical dilemma started after the strike began. Originally, the company thought the strike would not last longer than a couple of days. Instead of causing a panic among our customers, management decided to withhold information on the strike from our customers and sales force. I could understand the delay in telling our customers, but to withhold information from our sales force was, I believed, unconscionable. Inevitably, our inside sales representatives became suspicious when they called the Belgium plant to get the status of an order, and nobody answered. They called me, and I ignored the corporate request and informed them of the strike. When it became obvious that the strike was going to be longer than anticipated, I asked the vice presidents of marketing and sales about our strategy for informing the affected customers. They looked at me quizzically and told me to keep things quiet ("don't open a can of worms") because the strike should be over soon. In addition, they dictated that customer service should not inform customers of the strike and excuses should be developed for late shipments.

The strike lasted longer than 12 weeks. In this time, we managed to shut down a production line at Lucent Technologies (a $5-million customer) with only a couple of days' notice and alienated countless other valuable and loyal customers. I did not adhere to the company policy: I informed customers about the strike when they inquired about their order status. I also told customer service to direct any customer calls to me when we were going to miss shipments. This absolved them of the responsibility to tell the customer.

We did not take a proactive stance until 11 weeks into the strike, when the vice president of sales sent a letter informing our customers about the strike—too little and much too late to be of any help. The materials manager was fired because he only stocked 10 weeks of product even though management thought he should have been conservative with his estimates. Halfway through this ordeal, I updated my resume and started a search for a new job. It was clear that management was more concerned about their year-end bonus than doing the right thing for the long-term prospects of the company and its customers.

Questions

1. Do you agree with the writer's decision to inform customers about the strike? Explain.

2. Did management have the right to withhold this information from customers? Explain.

3. Explain what you would have done and why, if had you been in the writer's situation.

4. What should management have done in this case? When? Why?

CASE 3

THE TYLENOL CRISIS: HOW EFFECTIVE PUBLIC RELATIONS SAVED JOHNSON & JOHNSON

Source

Kaplan, T., Pennsylvania State University
    www.personal.psu.edu/users/w/x/wxk116/tylenol/crisis.html

"Public relations is the management function that establishes and maintains mutually beneficial relationships between an organization and the public on whom its success or failure depends."[61] In the fall of 1982, McNeil Consumer Products, a subsidiary of Johnson & Johnson, was confronted with a crisis when seven people on Chicago's West Side died mysteriously. Authorities determined that each of the people who died had ingested an Extra Strength Tylenol capsule laced with cyanide. The news of this incident traveled quickly and was the cause of nationwide panic. These poisonings made it necessary for Johnson & Johnson to launch a public relations program immediately, in order to save the integrity of both their product and their corporation.

The Story of the Tylenol Poisonings

When 12-year-old Mary Kellerman of Elk Grove Village, Illinois, awoke at dawn with cold symptoms, her parents gave her one Extra Strength Tylenol and sent her back to bed. Little did they know, they would wake up at 7:00 a.m. to find their daughter dying on the bathroom floor.[62]

That same morning, Adam Janus, 27, of Arlington Heights, Illinois, took Extra Strength Tylenol for a minor chest pain. An hour later, Janus suffered a cardiopulmonary collapse and died. That very evening, when relatives gathered at Janus' home, Adam's brother Stanley, 25, and his wife Theresa, 19, took Tylenol from the same bottle that had killed their loved one. They were both pronounced dead within the next 48 hours.[63]

Mary Reiner, 27, of the neighboring suburb Winfield, died after taking two Tylenol capsules the next day. Reiner, who was dead within hours at the local hospital, had just recently given birth to her fourth child. Paula Prince, 35, a United Airlines stewardess, was found dead in her Chicago apartment with an open bottle of Extra Strength Tylenol nearby. Mary McFarland, 31, of Elmhurst, Illinois, was the seventh victim of the poisoned Tylenol capsules.[64,65]

The cause of these strange and sudden deaths did not remain a mystery for long. The connection to Tylenol was discovered within days with the help of two off-duty firemen who were at home listening to their police radios. The two men were exchanging information about the deaths when they realized that Tylenol was mentioned in two of the reports. The men made some assumptions and told their superiors that there was a possibility that the over-the-counter drug was the mysterious killer.[66]

The Extra Strength Tylenol capsules in question were each found to contain 65 milligrams of cyanide. The amount of cyanide necessary to kill a human is five to seven micrograms, which means that the person who tampered with the pills used 10,000 times more poison than was needed to kill someone. Dr. Thomas Kim, chief of the Northwest Community Hospital at the time of the poisonings, said, "The victims never had a chance. Death was certain within minutes."[67,68]

The nation was warned about the danger of Tylenol as soon as a connection could be made. Police drove through Chicago announcing the warning over loudspeakers, while all three national television networks reported the deaths from the contaminated drug on their evening news broadcasts. A day later, the Food and Drug Administration advised consumers to avoid the Tylenol capsules "until the series of deaths in the Chicago area can be clarified."[69]

Officials at McNeil Consumer Products made clear that the tampering had not taken place at either of its plants, even though cyanide was available on the premises. A spokesman for Johnson & Johnson told the media of the company's strict quality control, and said that the poisonings could not have been performed in the plants. Because the cyanide-laced Tylenol had been discovered in shipments from both of the company's plants and had only been found in the Chicago area, authorities concluded that any tampering must have occurred once the Tylenol reached Illinois.[70]

The tainted Tylenol capsules were from four different manufacturing lots. Evidence suggested that the pills were taken from different stores over a period of weeks or months. The bottles, some of which had five or fewer cyanide-laced capsules and one which had 10, were tampered with and then placed back on the shelves of five different stores in the Chicago area.[71]

The publicity about the cyanide-laced capsules immediately caused a nationwide panic. A hospital in Chicago received 700 telephone calls about Tylenol in one day. People in cities across the country were admitted to hospitals on suspicion of poisoning by cyanide.[72]

Along with a nationwide scare, the poisoned capsules inspired copycats, who attempted to simulate the tampering in Chicago. In the first month after the Tylenol-related deaths, the Food and Drug Administration counted 270 incidents of suspected product tampering. However, the FDA thinks this number may have been inflated by the hysteria of consumers who blame any type of headache or nausea on food and medicine they think may have been poisoned. The FDA estimated that only about 36 of the cases were "true tamperings."[73]

After this crisis, Johnson & Johnson was faced with a dilemma. They needed to find the best way to deal with the tampering without destroying the reputation of their company and their most profitable product. Many marketing experts thought that Tylenol would be doomed by the public's doubts that the product was safe. "I don't think they can ever sell another product under that name," advertising genius Jerry Della Femina told the *New York Times* in the first days following the crisis. "There may be an advertising person who thinks he can solve this, and if they find him, I want to hire him because then I want him to turn our water cooler into a wine cooler."[74]

What Did Johnson & Johnson Do?   Della Femina was wrong in assuming that Tylenol would never sell again. Not only is Tylenol still one of the top selling over-the-counter drugs in this country, but it took very little time for the product to return to the market. Johnson & Johnson's handling of the Tylenol tampering crisis is considered by public relations experts to be one of the best in the history of public relations.

The public relations decisions made as a result of the Tylenol crisis arrived in two phases. The first phase was the actual handling of the crisis. The comeback of both Johnson & Johnson and Tylenol was the second phase in the public relations plan. The planning for phase two began almost as soon as phase one was being implemented.

Phase one of Johnson & Johnson's public relations campaign was executed immediately following the discovery that the deaths in Chicago were caused by Extra Strength Tylenol capsules. Johnson & Johnson's top management put customer safety first, before they worried about their company's profit.

The company immediately alerted consumers across the nation, via the media, not to consume any type of Tylenol product. They told consumers not to resume using the product until the extent of the tampering could be determined. Johnson & Johnson stopped the production and advertising of Tylenol and recalled all Tylenol capsules from the market. The recall included approximately 31 million bottles of Tylenol, with a retail value of more than $100 million.[75]

This was unusual for a large corporation facing a crisis. For example, when traces of benzene were found in Source Perrier's bottled water, instead of holding themselves accountable for the incident, Source Perrier claimed that the contamination resulted from an isolated incident. They recalled only a limited number of Perrier bottles in North America.[76]

When benzene was found in Perrier bottled water in Europe, an embarrassed Source Perrier had to announce a worldwide recall of the bottled water. Apparently, consumers around the world had been drinking contaminated water for months. Source Perrier was criticized by the media for having little integrity and for disregarding public safety.[77]

Johnson & Johnson, on the other hand, was praised by the media for their socially responsible actions. Along with the nationwide alert and recall, Johnson & Johnson established relations with the Chicago Police, the FBI, and the Food and Drug Administration. This way the company could have a part in searching for the person who laced the Tylenol capsules, and they could help prevent further tampering.[78,79]

An article by Jerry Knight, published in the *Washington Post* on October 11, 1982, said, "Johnson & Johnson has effectively demonstrated how a major business ought to handle a disaster." The article stated that, "This is no Three Mile Island accident in which the company's response did more damage than the original incident." They applauded Johnson & Johnson for being honest with the public.

The *Washington Post* article stressed that it must have been difficult for the company to withstand the temptation to disclaim any possible link between Tylenol and the seven sudden deaths in the Chicago area. They added that the company never attempted to do anything but try to get to the bottom of the deaths.

According to the article, "What Johnson & Johnson executives have done is communicate the message that the company is candid, contrite, and compassionate, committed to solving the murders and protecting the public." The *Washington Post* also mentioned that Johnson & Johnson almost immediately put up a reward of $100,000 for the killer.

The *Kansas City Times* published an article on November 12, 1982, by Rick Atkinson, that was composed of interviews with top executives at Johnson & Johnson shortly after the Tylenol crisis. James E. Burke, chairman of the board of the corporation at the time of the tampering, said that the poisonings shocked everyone at Johnson & Johnson. However, he did say that some of the initial public relations decisions pertaining to this case were easy to make.

Burke said that the decisions to pull advertising for Tylenol, recall all of the bottles from the lots that were laced with cyanide, and send warnings to health professionals were made with no hesitation. Although it seemed almost impossible that Johnson & Johnson could be held responsible for any of the tampering, the corporation had a hard decision to make: Should they implement a nationwide recall on the product?

There was a great deal of discussion about recalling Tylenol on a national level. Some executives worried about the panic that could result in the industry over such a widespread recall. There were arguments over which Tylenol products to pull and whether recalling $100 million in Tylenol would humor the killer and spur him to poison other products. The executives held off on the huge recall through the first weekend after the deaths.

That Saturday, three of the victims of the poisoned capsules were buried. There was coverage of the burials that night on television. Johnson & Johnson executives wept not only out of grief, but some out of guilt. One top executive said, "It was like lending someone your car and seeing them killed in a traffic accident." That weekend, opposition to the national recall all but vanished, and it was announced that 31 million bottles of Extra Strength Tylenol capsules would be pulled off merchants' shelves.

As a final step in this phase of Johnson & Johnson's public relations plan, the company offered to exchange all Tylenol capsules that had already been purchased for Tylenol tablets. It was estimated that millions of bottles of Tylenol capsules were in consumers' homes at the time. Although this proposition cost Johnson & Johnson millions more, and there may not have been a single drop of cyanide in any of the capsules they replaced, the company made this choice in order to preserve their reputation.[80]

Tylenol's Comeback   The planning for phase two of Johnson & Johnson's public relations plan, or the "comeback" phase, was already in the works by the time the first phase had been completed. Tylenol, which had a massive advertising budget prior to the poisonings, had become the number one alternative to aspirin in the nation. The product had 37% of the market for over-the-counter painkillers.[81] Because Tylenol was such a huge money-maker for Johnson & Johnson, the company unleashed an extensive marketing and promotional program to bring Tylenol back to its former status.[82]

Chairman of the Board James E. Burke said, in regard to the comeback, "It will take time, it will take money, and it will be very difficult, but we consider it a moral imperative, as well as good business, to restore Tylenol to its preeminent position."[83]

Less than six weeks after the nation learned of the sudden deaths in Chicago, McNeil Consumer Products revealed its public relations plan for the recovery of Tylenol at their sales conference in New Brunswick, New Jersey. There were five main components of the McNeil/Johnson & Johnson comeback crusade.[84]

Tylenol capsules were reintroduced bearing new triple-seal tamper-resistant packaging. The new packaging made McNeil Consumer Products the first company in the pharmaceutical industry to react to the Food and Drug Administration's new regulations and the national mandate for tamper-resistant packaging.[85]

To encourage the use of Tylenol by customers who may have strayed from the brand as a result of the tampering, McNeil Consumer Products provided $2.50-off coupons that were good toward the purchase of any Tylenol product.[86]

Salespeople at McNeil planned to recover former stock and shelf-facing levels for Tylenol by putting a new pricing program into effect. This new program gave consumers discounts as high as 25%. Also, a totally new advertising campaign was put in the works.[87]

Finally, more than 2,250 salespeople from Johnson & Johnson domestic affiliates were asked to make presentations to people in the medical community. These presentations were made by the millions to promote support for the reintroduction of Tylenol. The Tylenol comeback was a great success. Many executives attribute the success to the quick action of the corporation at the onset of the crisis. If Johnson & Johnson had not been so direct in protecting the public interest, Tylenol capsules would not have reemerged so easily.[88]

An article by Howard Goodman, published in the *Kansas City Times* on November 12, 1982, covering a press conference where James E. Burke launched Johnson & Johnson's national campaign for the comeback of Tylenol, applauded the corporation's efforts. The article, in a sense, provided free advertising for Tylenol's new packaging, stating, "the package has glued flaps on the outer box, which must be forcibly opened. Inside, a tight plastic seal surrounds the cap and an inner foil seal wraps over the mouth of the bottle. The label carries the warning: 'Do not use if safety seals are broken.'" This article was just the type of coverage that Johnson & Johnson needed to promote their recovery.

The *New York Times* published an article by Tamar Lewin on December 24, 1982, that announced to consumers that Tylenol had, in a short period of time, gained back much of the market that it lost to the cyanide deaths. The article stated that at that time Tylenol had 24% of the market for pain relievers, not much less than the 37% of the market that the product held before the crisis. This article continued the media trend of publicizing Tylenol's comeback in a positive light.

How Did Johnson & Johnson Make These Decisions?

The public relations decisions made in light of the Tylenol crisis must have come from somewhere. This basis for decision making became a bit more clear in 1983, when the *New Jersey Bell Journal* published an article written by Lawrence G. Foster. Foster, corporate vice president of Johnson & Johnson at the time of the Tylenol poisonings, joined the company in 1957 and helped the company build its first public relations department. In this article he explains that Johnson & Johnson simply turned to their corporate business philosophy, which they call "Our Credo," when determining how to handle the Tylenol situation.

Foster discusses that although corporate planning groups were including crisis management in their preparations for a healthy business environment, no crisis management plan would have been appropriate to tackle the Tylenol poisonings. This is because no management could ever be prepared for a tragedy of this scale. So, Johnson & Johnson turned to the Credo for help. "It was the Credo that prompted the decisions that enabled us to make the right early decisions that eventually led to the comeback phase," said David R. Clare, president of Johnson & Johnson at the time.[89]

The Credo was written in the mid-1940s by Robert Wood Johnson, the company's leader for 50 years. Little did Johnson know, he was writing an outstanding public relations plan. Johnson saw business as having responsibilities to society that went beyond the usual sales and profit incentives. In this respect, Foster explained, Johnson outlined his company's responsibilities to "consumers and medical professionals using its products, employees, the communities where its people work and live, and its stockholders." Johnson believed that if his company stayed true to these responsibilities, his business would flourish in the long run. He felt that the Credo was not only moral, but profitable as well.

As the Tylenol crisis became more serious as the hours went by, Johnson & Johnson top management turned to the Credo for guidance. As the Credo stressed, it was important for Johnson & Johnson to be responsible in working for the public interest.

The first important decision that put Johnson & Johnson's public relations program in the right direction was made immediately by the public relations department with complete support from the management. This decision was for the company to cooperate fully with all types of news media. It was crucial because the press, radio, and television were imperative to warning the public of the danger. Without the help of the media, Johnson & Johnson's program would have been completely ineffective.[90]

From this point on, the media did much of the company's work. Queries from the press about the Tylenol crisis were beyond 2,500. Two news clipping services found more than 125,000 pieces on the

Tylenol story. One of the services claimed that this story had been given the widest U.S. news coverage since the assassination of President John F. Kennedy. The television and news coverage on the crisis was just as extensive.[91]

By creating a public relations program that both protected the public interest and was given full support by media institutions, Johnson & Johnson was able to recover quickly and painlessly from possibly the greatest crisis ever to hit the pharmaceutical industry.

CASE 4

THE PLUNDERING OF ADELPHIA COMMUNICATIONS: THE SAGA OF THE RIGAS FAMILY

The Devil Is in the Details   The saying "the devil is in the details" may have held special meaning for Timothy Rigas, chief financial officer (CFO) of Adelphia Communications Corp., on March 27, 2002. A footnote on the last page of Adelphia's quarterly earnings press release revealed that the company was liable for $2.3 billion in off-balance-sheet loans to the Rigas family. In a conference call that day, Timothy Rigas disclosed, under pressure from analysts, that the loans were primarily used to finance Rigas family purchases of company stock. He was unconvincing in assuring the analysts that the Rigas family had enough resources to cover the debt. The information in that footnote was the beginning of the end for the Rigas family and its connection to Adelphia.

Adelphia's stock price fell 35% in the following three days. On May 14, 2002, NASDAQ suspended trading in Adelphia stock, and the next day the company missed $44.7 million in interest payments. Investigations of Adelphia were underway by the Securities and Exchange Commission (SEC) as well as by grand juries in Pennsylvania and New York. On May 23, 2002, John Rigas, Adelphia's founder, and his three sons, Timothy, Michael, and James, resigned as officers and directors of Adelphia. The company filed for Chapter 11 bankruptcy protection on June 25, 2002. A month later, on July 24, John, Michael, and Timothy Rigas, along with James Brown, who had been Adelphia's vice president of finance, and Michael Mulcahey, Adelphia's assistant treasurer, were arrested. They were subsequently indicted on 23 federal counts of conspiracy, securities fraud, wire fraud, and bank fraud. In November 2002, James Brown pled guilty to conspiracy, securities fraud, and wire fraud; he also agreed to become a witness for the prosecution.

After a four-month trial from early March to early July of 2004 and eight days of jury deliberations, John and Timothy Rigas were found guilty of 18 charges of conspiracy and fraud. Michael Mulcahey was found not guilty on all counts. Michael Rigas was found not guilty on one count of conspiracy and five counts of wire fraud, but the jury was deadlocked on 15 counts of securities fraud and two counts of bank fraud, and he is awaiting retrial.

What is the story behind the dramatic fall of the Rigas family?

The Founding and Growth of Adelphia   John Rigas, the son of a Greek immigrant who ran a hot dog restaurant in a nearby community, purchased the rural Coudersport, Pennsylvania, cable television franchise in 1952 for $300. Rigas was an ambitious and energetic businessman who played "fast and loose" with finances. He overdrew his bank account to get the $300 he used to purchase the franchise. In subsequent years Rigas borrowed heavily to acquire other rural cable systems in Pennsylvania and New York. Rigas barely stayed ahead of creditors by moving money from one bank account to another, and some people encountered considerable difficulty when they tried to collect the money Rigas owed them. Rigas' sons, Timothy and Michael, joined him in the family business after getting their college degrees. Another son, James, joined the business after college, law school, and a short stint with a company in San Francisco.

In the subsequent years, Adelphia grew rapidly. In 1985 the company had grown to 122,500 subscribers, mainly through acquisitions. In 1986, when Adelphia offered its stock for sale to the public, the company was negotiating deals that would increase its subscriber base to slightly over a quarter million and its number of employees to 370. By early 2002 the Rigas family had built Adelphia into the sixth largest cable television provider in the United States with $3.6 billion in annual revenue.

In becoming a publicly traded company, Adelphia's ownership structure enabled the Rigas family to continue to operate the company as their own personal empire. "Adelphia issued class A shares with one vote each to the public, but the Rigases retained all of the class B stock with ten votes per share. Therefore they got to pick the board of directors." Rigas, his three sons, and his son-in-law held five of the nine seats on the board. The other four seats were filled with John's friends and business associates.

Moreover, the Rigas family dominated the top management. John Rigas was chairman of the board of directors, president, and chief executive officer (CEO). Timothy Rigas was executive vice president, chief financial officer, chief accounting officer, treasurer of the company, and chairman of the board's audit committee. Michael Rigas was executive vice president for operations and secretary. James Rigas was executive vice president of strategic planning and headed Adelphia Business Solutions, a telephone services subsidiary of the parent company.

Even as a multibillion-dollar company, Adelphia remained headquartered in rural Coudersport, Pennsylvania, where it had been founded. Adelphia and the Rigas family prospered, and John Rigas became the town's biggest benefactor. He contributed to all types of community causes and regularly helped Coudersport's residents in a variety of ways. Many locals praised Rigas as a principled man who generously contributed to the community; believed in strong families, hard work, and church on Sunday; and refused to allow pornography channels on his cable systems.

The Plundering of Adelphia

According to U.S. Attorney James B. Comey, the Rigas family "looted Adelphia on a massive scale, using the company as the Rigas family's personal piggy bank." The Rigas family was accused of using "hundreds of millions of dollars in company funds for their own purposes and falsified accounting records to make it appear that Adelphia had more cable television subscribers than it really did and to disguise the amount of the company's debt." The Rigas family did not disclose its activities to non-family members of the board of directors or to the public.

The Rigas family charged all sorts of expenses—large and small—to Adelphia. According to SEC and Department of Justice filings, "company funds were used for everything from buying luxury condominiums for the Rigas family in Colorado, New York, and Mexico to financing John Rigas' daughter's film-production ventures, including the movie *Songcatcher*. Included among the plethora of expenses charged to Adelphia were $13 million for a partially completed private golf course and $700,000 for golf club memberships. Moreover, John, Timothy, and Michael Rigas never paid for $1.5 billion in company stock that they were issued. On a less massive scale, Adelphia paid $10,000 for two trips by a company-owned jet to deliver Christmas trees from Coudersport to Ellen Rigas, John's daughter who lived in New York. Adelphia also paid for Timothy's purchase of 100 pairs of bedroom slippers.

The Impacts of Adelphia's Implosion

In the weeks after Adelphia's monumental accounting irregularities were disclosed, Adelphia's stock lost significant value. It last traded at $6.13 a share on the day NASDAQ suspended trading. Adelphia's implosion significantly affected suppliers of technology and programming as well. Companies likely to suffer losses from Adelphia contracts were "gearing up to ask the courts to put them at the front of the line by declaring them 'critical vendors,' meaning Adelphia couldn't stay in business without them." Adelphia owed some technology suppliers large sums of money; Scientific-Atlanta Inc., for instance, was owed $83.8 million for equipment it had supplied. Programming vendors that stood to lose significant sums of money included ESPN from Walt Disney Co. and Fox News, FX, and other channels from News Corp. In addition to the impact on suppliers, Adelphia's problems left investors and rating agencies cautious about other debt-heavy cable companies like Charter Communications Inc., Cablevision Systems Corp., and Comcast Corp. The stock prices of these rival companies, as well as of the suppliers, fell because of investors' worried reactions.

Adelphia filed for Chapter 11 bankruptcy protection and began working toward reorganization. In January 2003, Bill Schleyer and Ron Cooper, two former AT&T Broadband executives, were hired to fill the top two management positions at Adelphia. The company headquarters was moved from Coudersport to a suburb of Denver, Colorado. In March 2003, Vanessa Wittman, who had helped 360 networks successfully work through a bankruptcy, was hired as Adelphia's CFO. In June 2003, in response to a shareholder lawsuit, the four non-family "board members appointed during the Rigas era finally agreed that they would step down when the company emerges from bankruptcy."

Questions for Discussion

1. Rigas family members were convicted of numerous counts of conspiracy and fraud. Putting yourself in their position, how would you explain/justify their unethical behavior?

2. How would an ethical person likely react to the justifying arguments that you discussed in responding to the previous question?

3. What dangers are associated with an ownership structure that allows a small group of individuals to exercise undue control over a publicly traded company?

4. Discuss the effects that unethical decisions and actions can have on an organization's stakeholders.

Sources

This case was developed from material contained in the following sources:

Beauprez, J. (January 18, 2003). Two AT&T Broadband veterans will lead bankrupt Adelphia Communications. *The Denver Post*, http://web14.epnet.com, accessed January 14, 2005.

DeKok, D. (August 4, 2002). Coudersport, Pa., residents upset by treatment of Adelphia. *The Patriot-News*, http://web14.epnet.com, accessed on January 14, 2005.

Farrell, M. (July 12, 2004). Rigas, son guilty; Mulcahey acquitted; acquittal, mistrial for Michael Rigas. *Multichannel News*, 1, 66-67.

Grover, R. (July 8, 2002). Adelphia's fall will bruise a crowd. *Business Week*, p. 44.

Leonard, D., Harrington, A., Burke, D., et al. (August 12, 2002). The Adelphia story. *Fortune*, http://web14.epnet.com, accessed on January 14, 2005.

McCafferty, J., Leone, M., Schneider, C. (December 2003). Adelphia comes clean. *CFO*, http://web14.epnet.com, accessed on January 14, 2005.

Neikirk, W. (July 24, 2002). Adelphia founder, 2 sons charged with looting funds for themselves. *Chicago Tribune*, http://web14.epnet.com, accessed on January 14, 2005.

Stern, C. (March 2, 2004). Fraud trial begins for Adelphia's founding family. *The Washington Post*, http://web14.epnet.com, accessed on January 14, 2005.

Tanaka, W., Fish, L. (July 24, 2002). Founders of Adelphia charged with "massive looting." *The Philadelphia Inquirer*, http://web14.epnet.com, accessed on January 14, 2005.

CASE 5

ACCOUNTING IRREGULARITIES AT WORLDCOM

Bernie Ebbers: The Believer   Bernard J. (Bernie) Ebbers was a man who believed in himself and his company. Ebbers, a former milk-man and bar bouncer in Edmonton, Alberta, Canada, became known as the "telecom cowboy" for amassing a fortune while building the second-largest telecommunications company in the United States. Headquartered in Clinton, Mississippi, WorldCom, at its zenith, had acquired more than 70 telecom companies and reported $3.8 billion in profits before taxes and other charges.

As Ebbers oversaw the explosive growth of WorldCom, he bor-rowed heavily to finance his own purchase of company stock. He even used his stock as collateral for other loans, some of which ostensibly were used to purchase additional stock. Ebbers apparently believed WorldCom would ride a wave of success for a long time because he locked himself into a personal financial "position that works only if the stock is going to rise and that is financially fatal if it declines."

The Origin and Growth of WorldCom   Ebbers moved from Edmonton, Alberta to Jackson, Mississippi to attend a small Baptist col-lege on a basketball scholarship. After college he remained in Mississippi, working as a basketball coach and hotel owner. In 1983, Ebbers "met a group of investors who had come to technologically-deprived central Mississippi to cash in on the federally mandated breakup of AT&T." The group formed Long-Distance Discount Services (LDDS) and des-ignated Ebbers as the leader. Ebbers believed that the road to success in telecommunications was to expand the communication networks, thereby increasing economies of scale. By 1995, many of America's largest cor-porations were customers of the LDDS voice and data network. LDDS renamed itself WorldCom and continued to acquire telecom companies.

During the 1990s, Ebbers used WorldCom's soaring stock value to make 60 acquisitions. The most notable acquisition was the hostile takeover of MCI Communications, which was the nation's second-largest long-distance company. By 2000, Ebbers had acquired "a grab bag of telecom companies, many of which were operating pretty much separately and without the efficiencies he had promised." Indeed, due to the failure to integrate and develop uniformity in billings, WorldCom at one time had 40 different billing systems. In total, Ebbers acquired more than 70 companies in building WorldCom into the second-largest telecommunications firm in the United States. In making these acquisitions, Ebbers relied heavily on the advice of Scott Sullivan,

WorldCom's master merger strategist and chief financial officer. Sullivan was known for his very aggressive financial practices.

Just as WorldCom was experiencing explosive growth, competition in the telecommunications industry began to drive down data-service fees, and WorldCom's annual revenue growth dropped from 19 percent in the late 1990s to nothing in 2002. WorldCom's stock reached a high of $64.50 per share in mid-1999 but had fallen to 83 cents per share in early July of 2002. WorldCom was sinking under $28 billion in debt.

Meanwhile, Ebbers was forced out of WorldCom by the company's board of directors. Previously WorldCom's board had decided "to loan Ebbers $366 million to pay off margin debt so that he wouldn't have to sell his 17 million shares of WorldCom stock." The existence of this loan triggered an investigation by the United States Securities and Exchange Commission (SEC) and led to Ebbers being pressured by WorldCom's board of directors to resign as CEO.

What brought about this precipitous decline in the fortunes of Bernie Ebbers and WorldCom?

Ethical Shenanigans and Accounting Irregularities   In March 2002, the United States Securities and Exchange Commission (SEC) launched an investigation into WorldCom's $366 million loan to Ebbers. Soon thereafter, Ebbers resigned under board pressure. When Ebbers resigned, the CFO, Scott Sullivan, was the only person who fully understood WorldCom's finances.

John W. Sidgmore, who was vice chairman during 2001, replaced Ebbers as CEO. Sidgmore ordered an assessment of all of World-Com's businesses. In the process of conducting this assessment, extraordinary accounting irregularities were discovered that enabled WorldCom to appear profitable when it wasn't. The accounting irregularities were extraordinary in that they were "mind-numbingly simple" accounting transactions rather than some exceptionally sophisticated shell game.

"How, exactly, did WorldCom cook its books? By treating routine expenses as capital investments. Normal operating expenses must be subtracted from a company's revenues in the year they occur. But capital expenditures can be subtracted from revenues a little at a time over many years. In the short term, that lets money flow to the bottom line and boosts financial results. It's the oldest trick in the book, and mind-numbingly simple. . . . Yet WorldCom's auditor—Arthur Andersen, the firm convicted of obstructing justice in the Enron case—somehow missed it." Over a period of 15 months, more than $3.8 billion of WorldCom's daily operating expenses were recorded as the purchase of assets, such as equipment or real estate. This made WorldCom's profits before taxes and other charges appear to be $3.8 billion higher than they actually were.

On June 25, 2002, WorldCom disclosed that it had improperly accounted for $3.8 billion in expenses. By August 2002, the amount of improperly treated expenses had risen to $7.1 billion. Eventually the amount of improperly stated expenses would rise to $11 billion. On June 25, WorldCom also disclosed that Scott Sullivan had been fired and that David Myers, the controller, had resigned. WorldCom turned its findings over to the SEC.

According to a September 23, 2002, report in *Business Week,* then-current as well as former employees of WorldCom revealed a variety of tricks the company used to manipulate its financial results. One routine practice was to double-count revenue from a single customer. Another practice was to keep delinquent accounts on the books long after the customer stopped paying, thereby enabling the company to count it as revenue instead of a liability. Another practice was to not close dead accounts. "Pressure to inflate revenues and cloak expenses appears to have been widespread at the company." People who refused to transfer operating expenses to the capital budget ran the risk of being terminated.

The Aftermath of Disclosing the Accounting Irregularities
In late July 2002, WorldCom filed for Chapter 11 bankruptcy protection. On August 1, 2002, Scott Sullivan, WorldCom's former CFO, and David Meyers, WorldCom's former controller, were arrested to face charges of securities fraud, conspiracy, and making false statements. In a statement issued through his attorneys, Bernie Ebbers "said he knew nothing of the accounting moves and called Sullivan and Myers 'competent, ethical, and loyal employees, devoted to the welfare of WorldCom.'" WorldCom's stock closed at 15 cents per share on the same day.

Although investigators tried to connect Ebbers to the fraud, they had been unable to do so at the time that Sullivan and Myers were arrested. Investigators were stymied by the lack of a paper trail implicating Ebbers. He did not use e-mail, and he rarely disclosed the company's full financial picture—even to top-level executives.

In March 2004, Sullivan entered a guilty plea for his role in the WorldCom fraud and turned state's witness. With Sullivan's cooperation in the investigation, the federal government moved quickly to indict Ebbers, alleging many connections between Ebbers and Sullivan in "cooking the company's books." According to the indictment, both Ebbers and Sullivan instructed the staff to make close-the-gap accounting adjustments (i.e., cooking the books to meet stock market expectations).

Moreover, Ebbers was alleged to have met with Sullivan "in October 2000, March 2001 and at other times to discuss how to cook the books."

Ebbers' trial got underway on January 18, 2005. He faced nine counts of conspiracy, securities fraud, and making false filings with the SEC. If convicted on all counts, he faced up to 85 years in prison. During the trial, prosecutors alleged "that Ebbers signed off on a multi-billion dollar accounting fraud to inflate WorldCom's publicly reported earnings and revenue numbers and prop up its stock price, in an effort to protect his personal fortune." According to Assistant U.S. Attorney William Johnson, "Money, power, and pressure corrupted Bernard J. Ebbers and motivated him to commit fraud." Ebbers testified that he was "unschooled in accounting and finance," and his attorney, Reid Weingarten, argued that "Ebber's crucial mistake was in delegating financial responsibility to the wrong man—former Chief Financial Officer Scott Sullivan." Jurors received the case for deliberation on March 4, 2005, just as this case was being completed.

Questions for Discussion

1. What are the potential ethical implications of pursuing a corporate strategy of rapid growth?

2. When a company lends one of its key executives a substantial sum of money, is a wise business decision being made? Why or why not?

3. How did WorldCom cook its books? What made these accounting irregularities so extraordinary?

Sources

This case was developed from material contained in the following sources:

"Bernie's Turn." (March 6, 2004). *Economist*, accessed from Corporate ResourceNet database at http://web14.epnet.com on January 14, 2005.

Colvin, G. (November 25, 2002). Bernie Ebber's foolish faith. *Fortune*, from Corporate ResourceNet database at http://web14.epnet.com, accessed on January 14, 2005.

Haddad, C., Rosenbush, S. (May 6, 2002). Woe is WorldCom. *Business Week*, from Business Source Premier database at http://web14.epnet.com, accessed on January 14, 2005.

Haddad, C., Foust, D., Rosenbush, S. (July 8, 2002). WorldCom's sorry legacy. *Business Week*, from Business Source Premier database at http://web14.epnet.com, accessed on January 14, 2005.

Haddad, C., Borrus, A. (September 23, 2002). What did Bernie know? *Business Week*, from Business Source Premier database at http://web14.epnet.com, accessed on January 14, 2005.

Howe, P.J. (August 2, 2002). FBI arrests two top former WorldCom financial executives. *The Boston Globe*, from Newspaper Source database at http://web14.epnet.com, accessed on January 14, 2005.

Kadlec, D., Fonda, D., and Parker, C. (July 8, 2002) WorldCom. *Time*, from Corporate ResourceNet database at http://web14.epnet.com, accessed on January 14, 2005.

Nuzum, C. (March 3, 2005). Ebbers was "big-picture" delegator, defense tells jury. *The Wall Street Journal Online*, http://online.wsj.com/article/0,,BT_CO_20050303_005962,00.html. Accessed March 5, 2005.

Nuzum, C. (March 2, 2005). Federal prosecutor: "corrupted" Ebbers hid WorldCom fraud. *The Wall Street Journal Online*, http://online.wsj.com/article/0,,BT_CO_20050302_005220,00.html. Accessed March 5, 2005.

Padget, T., Baughn, A.J. (May 13, 2002). The rise and fall of Bernie Ebbers. *Time*, from Corporate ResourceNet database at http://web14.epnet.com, accessed on January 14, 2005.

Playing defense. (March 4, 2005). *The Wall Street Journal Online*, http://online.wsj.com/article/0,,SB110960690974865933,00.html. Accessed March 5, 2005.

CASE 6

ARTHUR ANDERSEN . . . NO MORE: WHAT WENT WRONG?

A Mission of Destruction   Four days before the high-flying, energy-trading giant Enron disclosed a $618 million loss for the third quarter of 2001, an attorney for Arthur Andersen, the accounting firm that audited Enron's books, wrote a memo to Andersen employees directing them to do something extraordinary. They were ordered to destroy all audit material related to the Enron account except for the most basic work papers. They were directed to delete thousands of e-mail messages and other electronic files and to shred thousands of documents. As the destruction directive was being fulfilled, the U. S. Securities and Exchange Commission (SEC) initiated a probe of Enron's business activities. In order to secure needed accounting documents and information, the SEC issued subpoenas to Enron's auditor on November 8, 2001. "Supervisors at Arthur Andersen repeatedly reminded their employees of the document-destruction memo" in the two weeks preceding the issuance of these subpoenas. According to a January 21, 2002, report in *Time* magazine, Andersen declined "to rule out the possibility that some destruction continued even after" the subpoenas were issued. Of course, any destruction of documents after the issuance of a subpoena would be clearly illegal.

The Enron/Andersen accounting scandal unfolded at warp speed—particularly for the accounting firm. Very quickly, Enron fell into bankruptcy, and its stock became virtually worthless. Given the widespread, immediate, and dramatic impact of Enron's collapse on employees, stockholders, and the economy, no fewer than eight Congressional committees conducted hearings to determine how and why Enron failed. On January 15, 2002, David B. Duncan, Andersen's lead partner on the Enron account, was fired for directing the document-destruction binge. Andersen also put three partners in their Houston office on leave and relieved four other partners of all management responsibilities. On March 14, 2002, federal authorities indicted Andersen for obstruction of justice. In June 2002, Andersen was convicted of obstruction of justice for shredding documents and deleting e-mail messages and electronic files.

A seemingly unending stream of clients jettisoned Andersen as their auditing firm. In a few short months, Andersen's business was torn to shreds—much like the Enron documents! *Crain's Chicago Business* characterized Andersen's actions as "Andersen's ultimate train wreck." It wiped out 85,000 jobs—approximately 5,300 of them in Chicago—

and provided "fresh testament to the fragility of organizations that have only their reputations to sell."

How could Arthur Andersen, once a venerable accounting firm, end up having its reputation and very existence ripped to shreds?

Loose Controls and Cozy Relationships   Internal Arthur Andersen documents show that deletion of e-mails and electronic files and document shredding was but the tip of the iceberg of flawed operations. Andersen's "unusually loose controls and close ties to Enron undermined its role as auditor" and fostered the perhaps inevitable development of ethical problems.

Andersen, like other large accounting firms, had a team of experts known as the Professional Standards Group (PSG) "at its headquarters and elsewhere to review and pass judgment on knotty accounting, auditing, and tax issues facing its local offices." However, unlike other large accounting firms, Andersen allowed "regional partners—the front-line executives closest to the companies they audit—to overrule the experts." There were "repeated conflicts between Andersen's expert accountants and the Enron audit team." Members of Andersen's PSG objected strongly to Enron's accounting practices. However, David B. Duncan and key members of his audit team overruled the PSG's concerns "on at least four occasions, siding instead with Enron on controversial accounting that hid debt and pumped up earnings." Duncan's audit team also "wrote memos in which they falsely stated that PSG partners had signed off on Enron's inventive bookkeeping." Moreover, Enron executives insisted that Carl E. Bass, one of the PSG's primary skeptics of Enron's accounting practices, be barred from advising on Enron issues. Duncan prevailed upon Andersen's Chicago headquarters to remove Bass from membership in the PSG.

Local control over accounting, auditing, and tax decisions was a selling point to Andersen's clients. The people who brought in the clients were given the power to overrule the PSG, which created the potential for developing "very cozy relationships." As one federal investigator observed: "Who's most likely to say 'no' to the client—the national office or the local partner who works with the client all of the time?" Enron actually housed more than 150 people from Andersen's Houston office on its premises. "Andersen's Enron team became a power unto itself, worrying more about preserving its standing with the client than heeding qualms inside Andersen about its objectivity."

Andersen vigorously pursued business opportunities with Enron beyond its auditing activities. A client service team, working out of Andersen's marketing department, met regularly with Duncan to figure out what new tax advice or risk-management product they could sell to the energy giant. Capitalizing on its association with Enron, Andersen came to be regarded as the leading auditing firm for the oil and gas industry. Before both companies imploded, the association with Enron enhanced Andersen's reputation.

Further evidence of the Houston office's cozy relationship with Enron was found in the placement of former Andersen partners and staffers on Enron's management team. Enron's chief accounting officer and several other top Enron executives had come from Andersen. Moreover, "Andersen even cut a deal to handle some of the 'internal' auditing work for Enron along with vetting its public reports for the trading firm's audit committee."

The Enron account paid Andersen's Houston office more than $50 million annually. As one observer noted, "Andersen ended up being dominated by its most lucrative clients largely because it lacked leaders who could—or had the will to—jeopardize the gravy train by standing up to chief financial officers like Enron's Andrew Fastow."

A Pattern of Accounting Transgressions   The Enron debacle was not the first time that Andersen's local partners had been caught with their hands in the "accounting cookie jar." Two notable accounting transgressions occurred not too long before the Enron implosion.

In March 2001, the SEC charged that Waste Management Inc., based in Oak Brook, Illinois, awarded Andersen "a $3.7 million consulting project—later described by a former board member as a 'boondoggle'—after auditors knowingly approved inflated projections of how long the trash hauler's trucks would last." The inflated numbers increased Waste Management's pretax income by over $1 billion from 1992 to 1996. Houston-based USA Waste Services Inc. discovered this accounting scheme in 1998 when it acquired Waste Management and had to restate earnings by $1.7 billion. As a consequence of its involvement in the Waste Management accounting scheme, Andersen settled shareholder lawsuits in 1998 for $75 million and was fined $7 million by the SEC in 2001. Andersen did not admit to or deny the SEC's charges but did agree to the SEC's mandate that "future violations would carry stiffer sanctions."

In May 2001, Andersen "paid $110 million to settle a shareholder lawsuit stemming from its audit of Sunbeam," the Florida-based appliance manufacturer. According to the SEC, Sunbeam was forced to restate earnings due to a "fraudulent scheme to create the illusion of a successful restructuring of Sunbeam and thus facilitate a sale of the company at an inflated price." Commenting about the Sunbeam settlement on the heels of the Waste Management settlement, one Andersen competitor sarcastically observed that "settling a fraud case seems to be good for attracting business from other firms that want a soft touch for an auditor."

According to former SEC chairman Arthur Levitt, Andersen's violation of the Waste Management consent decree was "one of the main reasons for indicting the entire firm, instead of just the individual Andersen partners involved in the Enron audits." The U.S. Department of Justice won a conviction against Andersen for obstruction of justice. Andersen "instantly withered to almost nothing, tens of thousands of innocent employees lost their jobs, and thousands of partners who knew nothing about the crime . . . lost nest eggs they'd been building for years." In the summer of 2004, a federal appellate court unanimously denied Andersen's appeal of the conviction.

Questions for Discussion

1. Would you destroy electronic or paper records within a firm for which you worked to eliminate evidence that might be used against you? Why or why not?

2. Explain how Andersen's loose internal controls created the potential for ethical failures, such as the one at Enron.

3. Why are "arm's length relationships" crucial for ethical integrity in auditing? How did Andersen fail to maintain an "arm's length relationship" with Enron?

4. What is the logic of indicting an entire company for ethical failures rather than indicting only the responsible individuals?

5. Do you think the destruction of Andersen as a company was justified?

Sources

This case was developed from material contained in the following sources:

Colvin, G. (June 9, 2003). Spare the rod and save the company. *Fortune*, from Corporate ResourceNet database on http://web14.epnet.com, accessed on January 14, 2005.

"Judge Sides with KPMG; Andersen Conviction Upheld." (August 2004). *Practical Accountant*, p. 8.

McNamee, M., Borrus, A., and Palmeri, C. (March 29, 2002). Out of control at Andersen. *Business Week Online*, from Business Source Premier database on http://web14.epnet. com, accessed on January 14, 2005.

Strahler, S.R. (October 7, 2002). An icon crumbles. *Crain's Chicago Business*, from Corporate ResourceNet database on http://web14.epnet.com, accessed on January 14, 2005.

Weber, J., Palmeri, C., Lavelle, L., Byrnes, N., et al. (January 28, 2002). Can Andersen survive? *Business Week*, from Business Source Premier database on http://web14.epnet. com, accessed on January 14, 2005.

Weisskopf, M., Zagorin, A., Carney, J., et al. (January 21, 2002). Who's accountable? *Time*, from Corporate ResourceNet database on http://web14.epnet.com, accessed on January 14, 2005.

Notes

1. Lohr, S. (June 16, 2004). Evidence of high skill work going abroad. *New York Times,* C2.
2. Ibid.
3. Ibid.
4. The author recognizes the research in this section of Tom Kotarakos and Jeff Maranian, Master of Science Accounting graduate students at Bentley College.
5. Dubie, D. (July 28, 2003). Heavyweights tip scales for offshore outsourcing. *Network World,* http://www.nwfusion.com/news/2003/0728/offshore.html.
6. Ibid. For a list of American firms outsourcing jobs, see Lou Dobbs' Web site, www.cnn.com/CNN/Programs/lou.dobbs.tonight.
7. Clott, C. (Summer 2004). Perspectives on global outsourcing and the changing nature of work. *Business and Society Review, 109(2),* 153–170.
8. Berman, S., Wicks, A., Otha, S., Jones, T. (1999). Does stakeholder orientation matter? The relationship between stakeholder management models and firm financial perform-ance. *Academy of Management Journal, 42,* 488–506; Ogden, S., Watson, R. (1999). Corporate performance and stakeholder management: Balancing shareholder and customer interests in the U.K. privatized water industry. *Academy of Management Journal, 42,* 526–538.
9. Freeman, F. (1999). Divergent stakeholder theory. *Academy of Management Review, 24,* 191–205.
10. Key, S. (1999). Toward a new theory of the firm: A critique of stakeholder "theory." *Management Decision, 37(4),* 319.
11. Preston, L., Sapienza, H. (1990). Stakeholder management and corporate perform-ance. *Journal of Behavioral Economics, (19)4,* 373. See also, Evan, W., Freeman, R. (1988). A stakeholder theory of the modern corporation: Kantian capitalism. In Beauchamp, T. L., Bowie, N. E. *Ethical Theory and Business,* 3rd ed. Englewood Cliffs, NJ: Prentice Hall.
12. For a critique of the stakeholder theory, see Reed, D. (1999). Stakeholder management theory: A critical theory perspective. *Business Ethics Quarterly, 9(3),* 453–483.
13. Heugens, P., Van Den Bosch, F., Van Riel, C. (March 2002). Stakeholder integration. *Business & Society, 41(1),* 36.
14. Key.
15. Mitchell, R. B., Agle, B. R., Wood, D. (1997). Toward a theory of stakeholder identi-fication and salience: Defining the principle of who and what really counts. *Academy of Management Review, 22(4),* 853–886. See also Key.
16. Bowie, N., Duska, R. (1991). *Business ethics,* 2nd ed. Englewood Cliffs, NJ: Prentice Hall; Frederick, W. (1994). From CSR1 To CSR2: *The maturing of business and society thought. Business & Society, 3(2),* 150–166; Bowen, H. (1953). Social Responsibilities of Businessmen. New York: Harper.
17. More gain than pain. (July 15, 2004). *The Economist, 372,* 64.
18. U.S. lobbyists fighting against outsourcing. (June 3, 2003). *Rediff.com,* http://www.rediff.com/money/2003/jun/03outsource.htm.
19. Dobbs, L. (March 10, 2004). Exporting America: False choices. *CNN.com,* http://money.cnn.com/2004/03/09/commentary/dobbs/dobbs.
20. Jones, T. (April 1995). Instrumental stakeholder theory: A synthesis of ethics and economics. *Academy of Management Review, 20(2),* 404.
21. Clarkson, M. (Ed.) (1998). *The Corporation and Its Stakeholders: Classic and Contemporary Readings.* Toronto: University of Toronto Press.
22. Freeman, R. E. (1984). *Strategic Management: A Stakeholder Approach,* 25. Boston: Pitman.
23. Lohr, C2.
24. Frederick, W., et al. (1988). *Business and Society: Corporate Strategy, Public Policy, Ethics,* 6th ed. New York: McGraw-Hill.
25. Freeman, R. E. (1984). *Strategic Management: A Stakeholder Approach.* Boston: Pitman.
26. Savage, G., Nix, T., Whitehead, C., Blair, J. (1991). Strategies for assessing and man-aging organizational stakeholders. *The Executive, 5(2),* 61–75.
27. Andriof, J., Waddock, S. (2002). *Unfolding Stakeholder Thinking: Theory, Responsibility and Engagement.* Andriof, J., Waddock, S., Husted, B., Rahman, S., eds. Sheffield, U.K.: Greenleaf Publishing Ltd.

28. Barnes-Slater, C., Ford, J. Measuring conflict: Both the hidden costs and the benefits of conflict management interventions. *LawMemo.com Inc.*, http://www.lawmemo. com/emp/articles/measuring.htm; Lynch, D. (May 1997). Unresolved conflicts affect the bottom line–Effects of conflicts on productivity. *HR Magazine,* http://www.findarticles.com/p/articles/mi_m3495/is_n5_v42/ai_19569995.
29. American Arbitration Association. About AAA's eCommerce services. http://www.adr.org/index2.1.jsp?JSPssid=16235&JSPsrc=upload/livesite/focusArea/eCommerce/Services.htm.
30. New York State Unified Court System. Alternate dispute resolution. http://www.courts.state.ny.us/ip/adr/What_Is_ADR.shtml.
31. Barr, S. (June 16, 2004). Congress tackles outsourcing issues at Defense, IRS, Homeland Security. *Washington Post,* B2, http://www.washingtonpost.com/wp-dyn/articles/A44620-2004Jun15.html.
32. Morris, C. (May 2002). Definitions in the field of dispute resolution and conflict transformation. *Peacemakers Trust,* http://www.peacemakers.ca/publications/ADRdefinitions.html.
33. Ibid.
34. Ibid.
35. Fisher, R., Ury, W., Patton, B. (1991). *Getting to Yes: Negotiating Agreement Without Giving In,* 2nd ed. New York: Penguin Books, 11.
36. It is beyond the scope of this chapter to go into further detail on these methods. Recommended reading is suggested: Bush, R., Folger, J. (1994). *The Promise of Mediation: Responding to Conflict Through Empowerment and Recognition.* San Francisco, CA: Jossey-Bass Publishers; Cobb, S. (1994). A narrative perspective on mediation: Toward the materialization of the "storytelling" metaphor. In Cobb, S. *New Directions in Mediation: Communication Research.* Thousand Oaks, CA: Sage, 48–63; Cormick G. et al. (1997). *Building Consensus for a Sustainable Future: Putting Principles into Practice.* Ottawa, ON: National Round Table on the Environment and Economy; Fisher, R., Ury, W., Patton, B. (1991). *Getting to Yes: Negotiating Agreement Without Giving In,* 2nd ed. New York: Penguin Books; Folger, J., Bush, R. (2001). *Designing Mediation: Approaches to Training and Practice Within a Transformative Framework.* New York: The Institute for the Study of Conflict Transformation.
37. Wartick, S., Heugens, P. (Spring 2003). Guest editorial, future directions of issues management. *Corporate Reputation Review, 6(1),* 7–18.
38. Issue Management Council. What is issues management? Excerpted from a speech by Teresa Yancey Crane, founder of the Issue Management Council. http://www.issuemanagement.org/documents/im_details.html.
39. Wartick and Heugens, 15.
40. Ibid.
41. Who's on first–Issues or stakeholder management? (2002). In Windsor, D., Welcomer, S., eds. *Proceedings of the Thirteenth Annual Meeting of the International Association for Business and Society.* Oronto, ME: International Association for Business and Society, 1955–1988.
42. Bigelow, B., Fahey, L., Mahon, J. (1991). Political strategy and issues evolution: A framework for analysis and action. In Paul, K. ed. *Contemporary Issues in Business Ethics and Politics.* Lewiston, NY: Edwin Mellen, 1–26.
43. Jones, T. (1991). Ethical decision making by individuals in organizations: An issue-contingent model. *Academy of Management Review, 16(2),* 366–395.
44. Ibid.
45. King, W. (1987). Strategic issue management. In King, W., Cleland, D., eds. *Strategic Planning and Management Handbook,* 256. New York: Van Nostrand Reinhold; Buchholz, R. (1982). Education for public issues management: Key insights from a survey of top practitioners. *Public Affairs Review, 3,* 65–76; Brown, J. (1979). This Business of Issues: Coping with the Company's Environment. New York: Conference Board. Also see Carroll, A. B. (1989, 1983). *Business and Society: Ethics and Stakeholder Management,* 1st, 3rd eds. Cincinnati: South-Western.
46. Heath, R. (November 2002). Issues management: Its past, present and future. *Journal of Public Affairs, 2(4),* 209.
47. Offshore Outsourcing World Staff. (July 29, 2004). Budget conscious Microsoft sneaks overseas. *Offshore Outsourcing World,* http://www.enterblog.com/200407291752.html.

49. Clott.
50. Mintz, S. (March 2004). The ethical dilemmas of outsourcing. *The CPA Journal, 74(3)*, 6–10, http://www.nysscpa.org/cpajournal/2004/304/perspectives/nv1.htm.
51. Marx, T. (Fall 1986). Integrating public affairs and strategic planning. *California Management Review, 145.*
52. Power, P. (August 16, 2004). Calm in a crisis. *The Lawyer,* http://www.thelawyer.com/cgi-bin/item.cgi?id=111565&d=pndpr&h=pnhpr&f=pnfpr.
53. See Marx.
54. Ibid.
55. Fink, 20.
56. Matthews, J. B., Goodpaster, K., Nash, L. (1985). *Policies and Persons: A Casebook in Business Ethics.* New York: McGraw-Hill.
57. Mitroff, I., Shrivastava, P., Firdaus, U. (1987). Effective crisis management. *Academy of Management Executive, 1(7)*, 283–92.
58. Power.
59. Wartick, S., Rude, R. (Fall 1986). Issues management: Fad or function? California *Management Review,* 134–40.
60. Key.
61. Broom, G., Center, A., Cutlip, S. (1994). *Effective Public Relations,* 7th ed. Englewood Cliffs, NJ: Prentice Hall, 1.
62. Beck, M., Hagar, M., LaBreque, R., Monroe, S., Prout, L. (October 11, 1982). The Tylenol scare. *Newsweek,* 32.
63. Tifft, S. (October 11, 1982). Poison madness in the Midwest. *Time,* 18.
64. Beck et. al, 32.
65. Tifft, 18.
66. Ibid.
67. Ibid.
68. Kowalski, W. The Tylenol murders, http://www.personal.psu.edu/users/w/x/wxk116/tylenol.
69. Tifft, 18.
70. Beck et al, 33.
71. Kowalski.
72. Tifft, 18.
73. Church, G. (November 8, 1982). Copycats are on the prowl. *Time,* 27.
74. Knight, J. (October 11, 1982). Tylenol's maker shows how to respond to crisis. *Washington Post,* 2.
75. Broom et al., 381.
76. Broom et al., 59, 381.
77. Broom et al., 59.
78. Atkinson, R. (November 12, 1982). The Tylenol nightmare: How a corporate giant fought back. *Kansas City Times,* 2.
79. Broom et al., 381.
80. Knight, 2.
81. Ibid.
82. Johnson & Johnson. (1982). The comeback–A special report from the editors of worldwide publication of Johnson & Johnson corporate public relations.
83. Ibid.
84. Ibid.
85. Ibid.
86. Ibid.
87. Ibid.
88. Ibid.
89. Foster, L. (1983). The Johnson & Johnson Credo and the Tylenol crisis. *New Jersey Bell Journal, 6(1)*, 2.
90. Foster, 3.
91. Ibid.

3

Ethical Principles, Quick Tests, and Decision-Making Guidelines

Louise Simms, newly graduated with a master of business administration (MBA) degree, was hired by a prestigious multinational firm based in the United States. With minimal training, she was sent to join a company partner to negotiate with a high-ranking Middle Eastern government official. The partner informed Simms that he would introduce her to the government contact and then leave her to "get the job done." Her assignment was to "do whatever it takes to win the contract: it's worth millions to us." The contract would enable Simms' firm to select and manage technology companies that would install a multi-million-dollar computer system for that government. While in the country, Simms was told by the official that Simms' firm had "an excellent chance to get the contract" if the official's nephew, who owned and operated a computer company in that country, could be assured "a good piece of the action."

On two different occasions, while discussing details, the official attempted unwelcome advances toward Simms. He backed off both times when he observed her subtle negative responses. Simms was told that "the deal" would remain a confidential matter and the official closed by saying, "That's how we do business here; take it or leave it." Simms was frustrated about the terms of the deal and about the advances toward her. She called her superior in Chicago and urged him not to accept these conditions because of the questionable arrangements and also because of the disrespect shown toward her, which she said reflected on the company as well. Simms' supervisor responded, "Take the deal! And don't let your emotions get involved. You're in another culture. Go with the flow. Accept the offer and get the contract groundwork started. Use your best judgment on how to handle the details."

Simms couldn't sleep that night. She now had doubts about her supervisor's and the government administrator's ethics. She felt that she had conflicting priorities. This was her first job and a significant opportunity. At the same time, she had to live with herself.

3.1 DECISION CRITERIA, MORAL CREATIVITY, AND ETHICAL REASONING

Ethical dilemmas in business situations usually involve tough choices that must be made between competing interests. Although ethical reasoning has been defined, in part, by acting on "principled thinking," it is also true that moral creativity, negotiating skills, and knowing your values also help solve tough "real world" situations. Should Louise Simms move to close the lucrative deal or not? Is the official offering her a bribe? What other personal, as well as professional, obligations would she be committing herself to if she accepted? Is the official's request legal? Is it ethical? Is this a setup? If so, who is setting her up? Would Louise be held individually responsible if something went wrong? Who is going to protect her if legal complications arise? How is she supposed to negotiate such a deal? What message is she sending about herself as well as her company? What if she is asked to return and work with these people if the contract is signed? What does Louise stand to win and lose if she does or does not accept the official's offer?

Finally, what *should* Louise do to act morally responsible in this situation? Is she acting only on behalf of her company or also from her own integrity and beliefs? These are the kinds of questions and issues this chapter addresses. No easy answers may exist, but understanding principles, sharing ethical dilemmas and outcomes, discussing ethical experiences in depth, and using role play to analyze situations can help you identify, think, and feel through the issues that underlie ethical dilemmas. Louise might refer to the "My Ethical Motives" assessment in the box on page 115 to gauge her own motives.

The Louise Simms scenario may be complicated by the international context. This is a good starting point for a chapter on ethics, because business transactions now increasingly involve international players and different "rules of engagement." Chapter 7, on the global environment and stakeholder issues peculiar to multinational corporations, offers additional guidelines for solving dilemmas in international contexts. Deciding what is right and wrong in an international context also involves understanding laws and customs, and level of economic, social, and technological development of the nation or region involved. For example, do European and U.S. standards of doing business in other countries carry certain biases? Would these biases result in consequences that are beneficial or harmful to those in the local culture? On the other hand, we should not easily accept stereotypical descriptions of how to do business by means of what may be considered "local customs."

My Ethical Motives

Complete the following steps:

Step 1

Describe an ethical dilemma that you recently experienced. Be detailed: What was the situation? Who did it involve? Why? What happened? What did you do? What did you *not* do? Describe your reasoning process in taking or not taking action. What did others do to you? What was the result?

Step 2

Read the descriptions of relativism, utilitarianism, universalism, rights, justice, and moral decision making in this chapter. Explain which principle best describes your reasoning and your action(s) in the dilemma you presented in Step 1.

Step 3

Were you conscious that you were reasoning and acting on these (or other) ethical principles before, during, and after your ethical dilemma? Explain.

Step 4

After reading this chapter, would you have acted any differently in your dilemma than you did? Explain.

Moral Creativity   What begins as a business-as-usual decision can evolve into a dilemma or even a "defining moment" in one's life.[1]

An ethical decision typically involves choosing between two options: one we know to be right and another we know to be wrong. A defining moment, however, challenges us in a deeper way by asking us to choose between two or more ideals in which we deeply believe. Such challenges rarely have a "correct" response. Rather, they are situations created by circumstance that ask us to step forward and, in the words of the American philosopher John Dewey, "form, reveal, and test" ourselves. We form our character when we commit to irreversible courses of action that shape our personal and professional identities. We reveal something new about us to ourselves and others because defining moments uncover something that had been hidden or crystallize something that had been only partially known. And we test ourselves because we discover whether we will live up to our personal ideals or only pay them lip service.[2]

Joseph Badaracco at Harvard University offers three key questions with creative probes for individuals, work group managers, and company executives to address before acting in a "defining moment." For individuals, the key question is "*Who am I?*" This question requires individuals to:

1. Identify their feelings and intuitions that are emphasized in the situation

2. Identify their deepest values in conflict brought up by the situation

3. Identify the best course of action to understand the right thing to do[3]

Work group managers can ask, "*Who are we?*" They can also address these three dimensions of the team and situation:

1. What strong views and understanding of the situation do others have?

2. Which position or view would most likely win over others?

3. Can I coordinate a process that will reveal the values I care about in this organization?

Company executives can ask, "*Who is the company?*" Three questions they can consider are:

1. Have I strengthened my position and the organization to the best of my ability?

2. Have I considered my organization's role vis-à-vis society and shareholders boldly and creatively?

3. How can I transform my vision into action, combining creativity, courage, and shrewdness?

All professionals should ask the three sets of questions to help articulate a morally creative response to ethical dilemmas and "defining moments." What would have happened differently had the following CEOs reflected on these three sets of questions: Enron's Jeffrey Skilling and Ken Lay, Tyco's Dennis Kozlowski, Sam Waksal at ImClone, Gary Winnick at Global Crossing, and Martha Stewart at Martha Stewart Living Omnimedia?

The aim of this chapter is to present a range of decision-making resources that can help you evaluate moral responsibilities when resolving ethical dilemmas (Figure 3.1). Change begins with having an

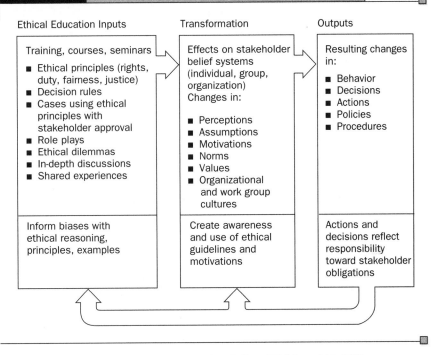

| **FIGURE 3.1** | **Intended Effects of Business Ethics Education on Stakeholder Belief Systems and Decisions** |

Ethical Education Inputs   Transformation   Outputs

Training, courses, seminars
- Ethical principles (rights, duty, fairness, justice)
- Decision rules
- Cases using ethical principles with stakeholder approval
- Role plays
- Ethical dilemmas
- In-depth discussions
- Shared experiences

Effects on stakeholder belief systems (individual, group, organization)
Changes in:
- Perceptions
- Assumptions
- Motivations
- Norms
- Values
- Organizational and work group cultures

Resulting changes in:
- Behavior
- Decisions
- Actions
- Policies
- Procedures

Inform biases with ethical reasoning, principles, examples

Create awareness and use of ethical guidelines and motivations

Actions and decisions reflect responsibility toward stakeholder obligations

Source: Copyright Joseph W. Weiss, Bentley College, Waltham, MA, 2005.

awareness that can help build confidence by perceiving dilemmas before they are played out and assisting you in negotiating solutions with a moral dimension.

12 Questions to Get Started   A first step in addressing ethical dilemmas is to identify the problem. This is particularly necessary for a stakeholder approach, because the problems depend on who the stakeholders are and what their stakes entail. Before specific ethical principles are discussed, let's begin by considering important decision criteria for ethical reasoning. How would you apply the criteria to Louise Simms' situation?

Twelve questions, developed by Laura Nash,[4] to ask yourself during the decision-making period are:

1. Have you defined the problem accurately?

2. How would you define the problem if you stood on the other side of the fence?

3. How did the situation occur?

4. To whom and to what do you give your loyalty as a person and as a member of the corporation?

5. What is your intention in making this decision?

6. How does this intention compare with the probable results?

7. Who could your decision injure?

8. Can you discuss the problem with the affected parties before you make your decision?

9. Are you confident that your decision will be valid over a long period?

10. Could you disclose, without qualm, your decision?

11. What is the symbolic potential of your action if understood? If misunderstood?

12. Under what conditions would you allow exceptions?

These 12 questions can help individuals openly discuss the responsibilities necessary to solve ethical problems. Sharing these questions can facilitate group discussions, build consensus around shared points, serve as an information source, uncover ethical inconsistencies in a company's values, help a CEO see how senior managers think, and increase the nature and range of choices. The discussion process is cathartic.

To return briefly to the opening case, if Louise Simms considered the first question, she might, for example, define the problem she faces from different perspectives (as discussed in Chapter 1). At the *organizational* level, her firm stands to win a sizable contract if she accepts the government official's conditions. Yet her firm's reputation could be jeopardized in the United States if this deal turned out to be a scandal. At the *societal* level, the issues are complicated. In this Middle Eastern country, this type of bargaining might be acceptable. In the United States, however, Louise could have problems with the Foreign Corrupt Practices Act. At the *individual* level, she must decide if her conscience can tolerate the actions and consequences this deal involves. As a woman, she may be at risk because advances were made toward her. Her self-esteem and integrity have also been damaged. She must consider the costs and benefits that she will incur from her company if she decides to accept or reject this assignment. As you can see, these questions can help Louise clarify her goal of making a decision and determine the price she is willing to pay for that decision.

Three Criteria in Ethical Reasoning   The following criteria can be used in ethical reasoning. They help to systematize and structure our arguments[5]:

1. Moral reasoning must be logical. Assumptions and premises, both factual and inferred, used to make judgments should be known and made explicit.

2. Factual evidence cited to support a person's judgment should be accurate, relevant, and complete.

3. Ethical standards used in reasoning should be consistent. When inconsistencies are discovered in a person's ethical standards in a decision, one or more of the standards must be modified.

If Louise Simms were to use these three criteria, she would articulate the assumptions underlying her decision. If she chose to accept the official's offer, she might reason that she assumed it was not a bribe, that if it were a bribe she assumed she would not get caught, and that even if she or her company did get caught, she would be willing to incur any penalty individually, including the loss of her job. Moreover, Louise would want to obtain as many facts as she could about the U.S. laws and the Middle Eastern country's laws on negotiating practices. She would gather information from her employer and check the accuracy of the information against her decision.

She would have to be consistent in her standards. If she chooses to accept the foreign official's conditions, she must be willing to accept additional contingencies consistent with those conditions. She could not suddenly decide that her actions were "unethical" and then back out midway through helping the official's nephew obtain part of the contract. She must think through these contingencies *before* she makes a decision.

Finally, a simple but powerful question can be used throughout your decision-making process: "What is my motivation for choosing a course of action?" Examining individual motives and separating these from the known motivations of others provides clarity and perspective. Louise, for example, might ask, "Why did I agree to negotiate with the official on his terms? Was it for money? To keep my job? To impress my boss? For adventure?" She also might ask whether her stated motivation from the outset would carry her commitments through the entire contracting process.

Moral Responsibility   A major aim of ethical reasoning is to gain a clear focus on problems to facilitate acting in morally responsible ways. Individuals are morally responsible for the harmful effects of their actions when (1) *they knowingly and freely acted or caused the act to happen and knew that the act was morally wrong or hurtful to others,* and (2) *they knowingly and freely failed to act or prevent a harmful* *act, and they knew it would be morally wrong for a person do this.*[6] Although no universal definition of what constitutes a morally wrong act exists, an act and the consequences of an act can be defined as morally wrong if physical or emotional harm is done to another as a result of the act.

Two conditions that eliminate a person's moral responsibility for causing injury or harm are *ignorance* and *inability*.[7] However, persons who intentionally prevent themselves from knowing that a harmful action will occur are still responsible. Persons who negligently fail to inform themselves about a potentially harmful matter may still be responsible for the resultant action. Of course, some mitigating circumstances can excuse or lessen a person's moral responsibility in a situation. These include circumstances that show: (1) *a low level of or lack of seriousness to cause harm,* (2) *uncertainty about knowledge of wrongdoing,* and (3) *the degree to which a harmful injury was caused or averted.* As we know from court trials, proving intent for an alleged illegal act is not an easy matter. Similarly, the extent to which a person is morally irresponsible can be difficult to determine. For example, should Bill Gates and Steve Ballmer consider that outsourcing work might hurt U.S. based employees? Are tobacco executives morally responsible for the deaths cigarette smoking causes? Did DuPont know that a certain chemical used in Teflon is dangerous to consumers' health? What principles and standards can we use to establish moral responsibility for ourselves and others?

In the following sections, five fundamental ethical principles that can be used in ethical reasoning are discussed (Figure 3.2). The principles are: (1) utilitarianism, (2) universalism, (3) rights, and (4) justice, (5) virtue. In addition, four social responsibility modes and four individual styles of ethical reasoning are presented. Finally, some "quick ethical tests" are provided, which you may use to clarify ethical dilemmas.

3.2 Utilitarianism: A Consequentialist (Results-Based) Approach

Jeremy Bentham (1748–1832) and John Stuart Mill (1806–1873) are acknowledged as founders of the concept of *utilitarianism*. Although various interpretations of the concept exist, the basic utilitarian view holds that an action is judged as right or good on the basis of its consequences. The ends of an action justify the means taken to reach those ends. As a *consequentialist principle,* the moral authority that drives utilitarianism is the calculated *consequences,* or results, of an action, regardless of other principles that determine the means or motivations for taking the action. Utilitarianism also includes the following tenets[8]:

FIGURE 3.2	Summary of Five Ethical Decision-Making Principles and Stakeholder Analysis

Belief Systems	Source of Moral Activity	Stakeholder Analysis Issues
Utilitarianism (Calculation of Costs and Benefits)	Moral authority is determined by the consequences of an act: An act is morally right if the net benefits over costs are greatest for the majority. Also, the greatest good for the greatest number must result from this act.	1. Consider collective as well as particular interests. 2. Formulate alternatives based on the greatest good for all parties involved. 3. Estimate costs and benefits of alternatives for groups affected.
Universalism (Duty)	Moral authority is determined by the extent the intention of an act treats all persons with respect. Includes the requirement that everyone would act this way in the same circumstances.	1. Identify individuals whose needs and welfare are at risk with a given policy or decision. 2. Identify the use or misuse of manipulation, force, coercion, or deceit that may be harmful to individuals. 3. Identify duties to individuals affected by the decision. 4. Determine if the desired action or policy would be acceptable to individuals if the decision were implemented.
Rights (Individual Entitlement)	Moral authority is determined by individual rights guaranteed to all in their pursuit of freedom of speech, choice, happiness, and self-respect.	1. Identify individuals and their rights that may be violated by a particular action. 2. Determine the legal and moral basis of these individual rights. 3. Determine the moral justification from utilitarian principles if individuals' rights are violated.
Justice (Fairness and Equity)	Moral authority is determined by the extent opportunities, wealth, and burdens are fairly distributed among all.	1. If a particular action is chosen, how equally will costs and benefits be distributed to stakeholders? 2. How clear and fair are the procedures for distributing the costs and benefits of the decision? 3. How can those who are unfairly affected by the action be compensated?
Ethical Virtue (Character-Based Ethic) Perspective	Moral authority is determined by individual or cultural self-interests, customs, and religious principles. An act is morally right if it serves one's self-interests and needs.	1. What are the moral beliefs and principles of the individual(s)? 2. If a particular action or policy is chosen, to what extent will ethical principles clash? 3. While seeking a mutually desirable outcome, how can conflicting moral beliefs and principles be avoided or negotiated?

Source: Copyright Joseph W. Weiss, Bentley College, Waltham, MA, 2005.

1. An action is morally right if it produces the greatest good for the greatest number of people.

2. An action is morally right if the net benefits over costs are greatest for all affected compared with the net benefits of all other possible choices.

3. An action is morally right if its benefits are greatest for each individual and if these benefits outweigh the costs and benefits of the alternatives.

There are also two types of criteria used in utilitarianism: *rule* based[9] and *act* based.[10] Rule-based utilitarianism argues that general principles are used as criteria for deciding the greatest benefit to be achieved from acting a certain way. The act itself is not the basis used for examining whether the greatest good can be gained. For example, "stealing is not acceptable" could be a principle that rule-based utilitarians would follow to gain the greatest utility from acting a certain way. "Stealing is not acceptable" is not an absolute principle that rule-based utilitarians would follow in every situation. Rule-based utilitarians might choose another principle over "stealing is not acceptable" if the other principle provided a greater good. *Act*-based utilitarians, on the other hand, analyze a particular action or behavior to determine whether the greatest utility or good can be achieved. Act-based utilitarians might also choose an action over a principle if the greatest utility could be gained. For example, an employee might reason that illegally removing an untested chemical substance from company storage would save the lives of hundreds of infants in a less-advantaged country because that chemical is being used in an infant formula manufactured in that country. The employee could lose his job if caught; still he calculates that stealing the chemical in this situation provides the greatest utility.

Utilitarian concepts are widely practiced by government policy makers, economists, and business professionals. Utilitarianism is a useful principle for conducting a stakeholder analysis, because it forces decision makers to (1) consider collective as well as particular interests, (2) formulate alternatives based on the greatest good for all parties involved in a decision, and (3) estimate the costs and benefits of alternatives for the affected groups.[11]

Louise Simms would use utilitarian principles in her decision making by identifying each of the stakeholders who would be affected by her decision. She would then calculate the costs and benefits of her decision as they affect each group. Finally, she would decide on a course of action based on the greatest good for the greatest number. For example, after identifying all the stakeholders in her decision, including her own interests, Simms might believe that her firm's capabilities were not competitive and that rejecting the offer would produce the greatest good for the people of the country where the contract would be negotiated, because obtaining bids from the most technically qualified companies would best serve the interests of those receiving the services.

Problems with utilitarianism include the following:

1. No agreement exists about the definition of "good" for all concerned. Is it truth, health, peace, profits, pleasure, cost reductions, or national security?[12]

2. No agreement exists about who decides. Who decides what is good for whom? Whose interests are primary in the decisions?

3. The actions are not judged, but rather their consequences. What if some actions are simply wrong? Should decision makers proceed to take those actions based only on their consequences?

4. How are the costs and benefits of nonmonetary stakes, such as health, safety, and public welfare, measured? Should a monetary value be assigned to nonmarketed benefits and costs?[13] What if the actual or even potentially harmful effects of an action cannot be measured in the short term, but the action is believed to have potentially long-term effects, say in 20 or 30 years? Should that action be chosen?

5. Utilitarianism does not consider the individual. It is the collective for whom the greatest good is estimated. Do instances exist when individuals and their interests should be valued in a decision?

6. The principles of justice and rights are ignored in utilitarianism. The principle of justice is concerned with the distribution of good, not the amount of total good in a decision. The principle of rights is concerned with individual entitlements, regardless of the collective calculated benefits.

Even given these problems, the principle of utilitarianism is still valuable under some conditions: when resources are fixed or scarce; when priorities are in conflict; when no clear choice fulfills everyone's needs; and when large or diverse collectives are involved in a zero-sum decision, i.e., when a gain for some corresponds to a loss for others.[14]

Utilitarianism and Stakeholder Analysis   Because businesses use utilitarian principles when conducting a stakeholder analysis, you, as a decision maker, should:

1. Define how costs and benefits will be measured in selecting one course of action over another—including social,

economic, and monetary costs and benefits as well as long-term and short-term costs and benefits. What principle, if any, would you use to base your utilitarian analysis?

2. Define what information you will need to determine the costs and benefits for comparisons.

3. Identify the procedures and policies you will use to explain and justify your cost-benefit analysis.

4. State your assumptions when defining and justifying your analysis and conclusions.

5. Ask yourself what moral obligations you have toward each of your stakeholders after the costs and benefits have been estimated.

3.3 Universalism: A Deonotological (Duty-Based) Approach

Immanuel Kant (1724–1804) is considered one of the leading founders of the principle of *universalism*. Universalism, which is also called "deontological ethics," holds that the ends do not justify the means of an action—the right thing must always be done, even if doing the wrong thing would do the most good for the most people. Universalism, therefore, is also referred to as a *nonconsequentialist* ethic. The term "deontology" is derived from the Greek word *deon,* or duty. Regardless of consequences, this approach is based on universal principles, such as justice, rights, fairness, honesty, and respect.[15]

Kant's principle of the *categorical imperative,* unlike utilitarianism, places the moral authority for taking action on an individual's duty toward other individuals and "humanity." The categorical imperative consists of two parts. The first part states that *a person should choose to act if and only if she or he would be willing to have every person on earth, in that same situation, act exactly that way.* This principle is absolute and allows for no qualifications across situations or circumstances. The second part of the categorical imperative states that, in an ethical dilemma, *a person should act in a way that respects and treats all others involved as ends as well as means to an end.*[16]

Kant's categorical imperative forces decision makers to take into account their duty to act responsibly and respectfully toward all individuals in a situation. Individual human welfare is a primary stake in any decision. Decision makers must also consider formulating their justifications as principles to be applied to everyone.

In Louise Simms' situation, if she followed deontological principles of universalism, she might ask, "If I accept the official's offer, could I justify that anyone anywhere would act the same way?" Or, "Since I value my own self-respect and believe my duty is to uphold self-respect for others, I will not accept this assignment because my self-respect has been and may again be violated."

The major weaknesses of universalism and Kant's categorical imperative include these criticisms: First, these principles are imprecise and lack practical utility. It is difficult to think of all humanity each time one must make a decision in an ethical dilemma. Second, it is hard to resolve conflicts of interest when using a criterion that states that all individuals must be treated equally. Degrees of differences in stakeholders' interests and relative power exist. However, Kant would remind us that the human being and his or her humanity must be considered above the stakes, power bases, or consequences of our actions. Still, it is often impractical not to consider other elements in a dilemma. Finally, what if a decision-maker's duties conflict in an ethical dilemma? The categorical imperative does not allow for prioritizing. A primary purpose of the stakeholder analysis is to prioritize conflicting duties. It is, again, difficult to take absolute positions when limited resources and time and conflicting values are factors.

Universalism and Stakeholder Analysis   The logic underlying universalism and the categorical imperative can be helpful for applying a stakeholder analysis. Even though we may not be able to employ Kant's principles absolutely, we can consider the following as guidelines for using his ethics:

1. Take into account the welfare and risks of all parties when considering policy decisions and outcomes.

2. Identify the needs of individuals involved in a decision, the choices they have, and the information they need to protect their welfare.

3. Identify any manipulation, force, coercion, or deceit that might harm individuals involved in a decision.

4. Recognize the duties of respecting and responding to individuals affected by particular decisions before adopting policies and actions that affect them.

5. Ask if the desired action would be acceptable to the individuals involved. Under what conditions would they accept the decision?

6. Ask if individuals in a similar situation would repeat the designated action or policy as a principle. If not, why not? And would they continue to employ the designated action?

3.4 RIGHTS: A MORAL AND LEGAL ENTITLEMENT-BASED APPROACH

Rights are based on several sources of authority.[17] Legal rights are entitlements that are limited to a particular legal system and jurisdiction. In the United States, the Constitution and Declaration of Independence are the basis for citizens' legal rights—e.g. the right to life, liberty, and the pursuit of happiness, and the right to freedom of speech. *Moral* (and *human*) *rights*, on the other hand, are universal and based on norms in every society—e.g. the right not to be enslaved and the right to work.

Moral and legal rights are linked to individuals, and in some cases, groups, not to societies, as is the case with a utilitarian ethic. Moral rights are also connected with duties, i.e. my moral rights imply that others have a duty toward me to not violate those rights, and vice versa. Moral rights also provide the freedom to pursue one's interests, as long as those interests do not violate others' rights. Moral rights also allow individuals to justify their actions and seek protection from others in doing so.

There are also special rights and duties, or *contractual rights*. Contracts provide individuals with mutually binding duties that are based on a legal system with defined transactions and boundaries. Moral rules that apply to contracts include: (1) the contract should not commit the parties to unethical or immoral conduct; (2) both parties should freely and without force enter the contractual agreement; (3) neither individual should misrepresent or misinterpret facts in the contract; (4) both individuals should have complete knowledge of the nature of the contract and its terms before they are bound by it.[18]

Finally, the concept of *negative* and *positive* rights defines yet another dimension of ethical principles.[19] A *negative right* refers to the duty others have to not interfere with actions related to a person's rights. For example, if you have the right to freedom of speech, others—including your employer—have the duty not to interfere with that right. Of course there are circumstances that constrain "free speech" as we will discuss in Chapter 4. A *positive right* imposes a duty on others to provide for your needs to achieve your goals, not just protect your right to pursue them. Some of these rights may be part of national, state, or local legislation. For example, you may have the right to equal educational opportunities for your child if you are a parent. This implies that you have the right to send your child to a public school that has the same standards as any other school in your community.

Positive rights were given attention in the twentieth century. National legislation that promoted different group's rights and the United Nations' Universal Declaration of Human Rights served as sources for positive rights. Negative rights were emphasized in the seventeenth and eighteenth centuries and were based on the Bill of Rights in the

Declaration of Independence. Currently, American political parties and advocates who are either politically to the "left" or to the "right" debate on whether certain moral rights are "negative" or "positive" and to what extent taxpayers' dollars and government funds should support these rights. For example, "conservative" writers like Milton Friedman[20] have endorsed government support of negative rights (like protecting property, and enforcing law and order) and argued against public spending on positive rights (like medical assistance, job training, and housing). As you can see, the concept of rights has several sources of moral authority. Understanding and applying the concept of rights to stakeholders in business situations adds another dimension of ethical discovery to your analysis.

Louise Simms might ask what her rights are in her situation. If she believes that her constitutional and moral rights would be violated by accepting the offer, she would consider refusing to negotiate on the foreign official's terms.

The limitations of the principle of rights include:

1. The justification that individuals are entitled to rights can be used to disguise and manipulate selfish, unjust political claims and interests.

2. Protection of rights can exaggerate certain entitlements in society at the expense of others. Fairness and equity issues may be raised when the rights of an individual or group take precedence over the rights of others. Issues of reverse discrimination, for example, have arisen from this reasoning.

3. The limits of rights come into question. To what extent should practices that may benefit society, but threaten certain rights, be permitted?

Rights and Stakeholder Analysis   The principle of rights is particularly useful in stakeholder analysis when conflicting legal or moral rights of individuals occur or when rights may be violated if certain courses of action are pursued. The following are guidelines for observing this principle[21]:

1. Identify the individuals whose rights may be violated.

2. Determine the legal and moral bases of these individuals' rights. Does the decision violate these rights on such bases?

3. Determine to what extent the action has moral justification from utilitarian or other principles if individual rights may be violated. National crises and emergencies may warrant overriding individual rights for the public good.

3.5 Justice: Procedures, Compensation, and Retribution

The principle of *justice* deals with fairness and equality. Here, the moral authority that decides what is right and wrong concerns the fair distribution of opportunities, as well as hardships, to all. The principle of justice also pertains to punishment for wrong done to the undeserving. John Rawls (1971), a contemporary philosopher, offers two principles of fairness that are widely recognized as representative of the principle of justice[22]:

1. Each person has an equal right to the most extensive basic liberties that are compatible with similar liberties for others.

2. Social and economic inequalities are arranged so that they are both (a) reasonably expected to be to everyone's advantage and (b) attached to positions and offices open to all.

The first principle states that all individuals should be treated equally. The second principle states that justice is served when all persons have equal opportunities and advantages (through their positions and offices) to society's opportunities and burdens. Equal opportunity or access to opportunity does not guarantee equal distribution of wealth. Society's disadvantaged may not be justly treated, some critics claim, when *only* equal opportunity is offered. The principle of justice also addresses the unfair distribution of wealth and the infliction of harm.

Richard DeGeorge identifies four types of justice[23]:

1. *Compensatory justice* concerns compensating someone for a past harm or injustice. For example, affirmative action programs, discussed in Chapter 6, are justified, in part, as compensation for decades of injustice that minorities have suffered.

2. *Retributive justice* means serving punishment to someone who has inflicted harm on another. A criterion for applying this justice principle is: "Does the punishment fit the crime?"

3. *Distributive justice* refers to the fair distribution of benefits and burdens. Have certain stakeholders received an unfair share of costs accompanying a policy or action? Have others unfairly profited from a policy?

4. *Procedural justice* designates fair decision practices, procedures, and agreements among parties. This criterion asks, "Have the rules and processes that govern the distribution of rewards, punishments, benefits, and costs been fair?"

These four types of justice are part of the larger principle of justice. How they are formulated and applied varies with societies and governmental systems.

Following the principle of justice, Louise Simms might ask whether accepting the government official's offer would provide a fair distribution of goods and services to the recipients of the new technological system. Also, are the conditions demanded by the government administrator fair for all parties concerned? If Simms determined that justice would not be served by enabling her company to be awarded the contract without a fair bidding process, she might well recommend that her firm reject the offer.

The obvious practical problems of using the principle of justice include the following: Outside the jurisdiction of the state and its judicial systems, where ethical dilemmas are solved by procedure and law, who decides who is right and who is wrong? Who has the moral authority to punish whom? Can opportunities and burdens be fairly distributed to all when it is not in the interest of those in power to do so?

Even with these shortcomings, the principle of justice adds an essential contribution to the other ethical principles discussed so far. Beyond the utilitarian calculation of moral responsibility based on consequences, beyond the universalist absolute duty to treat everyone as a means and not an end, and beyond the principle of rights, which values unquestionable claims, the principle of justice forces us to ask how fairly benefits and costs are distributed, regardless of power, position, wealth.

Rights, Power, and "Transforming Justice"

Justice, rights, and power are really intertwined. Rights plus power equals "transforming justice." T. McMahon states, "While natural rights are the basis for justice, rights cannot be realized nor justice become operative without power"[24]: Judges and juries exercise power when two opposing parties, both of whom are "right," seek justice from the courts.

Power generally is defined and exercised through inheritance, authority, contracts, competition, manipulation, and force. Power exercised through manipulation cannot be used to obtain justice legitimately. The two steps in exercising "transforming justice" are:

1. Be aware of your rights and power. McMahon states, "It is important to determine what rights and how much legitimate power are necessary to exercise these rights without trampling on other rights. For example, an employer might have the right and the power to fire an insolent employee, but she or he might not have enough to challenge union regulations."[25]

2. Establish legitimate power as a means for obtaining and establishing rights. According to McMahon, "If the legitimacy of transforming justice cannot be established, its exercise may then be reduced to spurious power plays to get what someone wants, rather than a means of fulfilling fights."[26]

This interrelationship of rights, justice, and power is particularly helpful in studying stakeholder management relationships. Since stakeholders exercise power to implement their interests, the concept of "rights plus power equals transforming justice" adds value in determining justice (procedural, compensatory, and retributive). The question of justice in complex, competitive situations becomes not only "Whose rights are more right?" but also "By what means and to what end was power exercised?"

Justice and Stakeholder Analysis   In a stakeholder analysis, the principle of justice can be applied with these questions:

1. How equitable will the distribution of benefits and costs, pleasure and pain, and reward and punishment be among stakeholders if you pursue a particular course of action? Would all stakeholders' self-respect be acknowledged?

2. How clearly have the procedures for distributing the costs and benefits of a course of action or policy been defined and communicated? How fair are these procedures to all affected?

3. What provisions can be made to compensate those who will be unfairly affected by the costs of the decision? What provisions can we make to redistribute benefits among those who have been unfairly or overly compensated by the decision?

3.6 VIRTUE ETHICS: CHARACTER-BASED VIRTUES

Plato and Aristotle are recognized as founders of virtue ethics, which also has roots in ancient Chinese and Greek philosophy. Virtue ethics emphasizes moral character in contrast to moral rules (deontology) or consequences of actions (consequentialism).[27]

Virtue ethics is grounded in "character traits," that is, "...a disposition which is well entrenched in its possessor, something that, as we say 'goes all the way down', unlike a habit such as being a tea-drinker—but the disposition in question, far from being a single track disposition to do honest actions, or even honest actions for certain reasons, is multi-track. It is concerned with many other actions as well, with emotions and emotional reactions, choices, values, desires, perceptions, attitudes, interests, expectations and sensibilities. To possess a virtue is to be a certain sort of person with a certain complex mindset. (Hence the extreme recklessness of attributing a virtue on the basis of a single action.)"[28]

The concepts of virtue ethics derived from ancient Greek philosophy are the following: virtue, practical wisdom, and eudaimonia (or happiness, flourishing, and well-being). Virtue ethics focuses on the type of person we ought to be, not on specific actions that should be taken. It is grounded in good character, motives, and core values. Virtue ethics argue that the possessor of good character is and acts moral, feels good, is happy, and flourishes. Practical wisdom, however, is often required to be virtuous. Adults can be culpable in their intentions and actions by being "thoughtless, insensitive, reckless, impulsive, shortsighted, and by assuming that what suits them will suit everyone instead of taking a more objective viewpoint. They are also, importantly, culpable if their understanding of what is beneficial and harmful is mistaken. It is part of practical wisdom to know how to secure real benefits effectively; those who have practical wisdom will not make the mistake of concealing the hurtful truth from the person who really needs to know it in the belief that they are benefiting him."[29]

Critiques of virtue ethics include the following major arguments: "First, virtue ethics fails to adequately address dilemmas which arise in applied ethics, such as abortion. For, virtue theory is not designed to offer precise guidelines of obligation. Second, virtue theory cannot correctly assess the occasional tragic actions of virtuous people. . . . Since virtue theory focuses on the general notion of a good person, it has little to say about particular tragic acts. Third, some acts are so intolerable, such as murder, that we must devise a special list of offenses which are prohibited. Virtue theory does not provide such a list. Fourth, character traits change, and unless we stay in practice, we risk losing our proficiency in these areas. This suggests a need for a more character-free way of assessing our conduct. Finally, there is the problem of moral backsliding. Since virtue theory emphasizes long-term characteristics, this runs the risk of overlooking particular lies, or acts of selfishness, on the grounds that such acts are temporary aberrations."[30] These same criticisms also apply to other ethical principles and schools of thought.

Virtue Ethics and Stakeholder Analysis   Virtue ethics adds an important dimension to rules and consequentialist ethics by contributing a different perspective for understanding and executing stakeholder management. Examining the motives and character of stakeholders can be helpful in discovering underlying motivations of strategies, actions, and outcomes in complex business and corporate transactions.

With regard to corporate scandals, virtue ethics can explain some of the motives of several corporate officers' actions that center on greed, extravagant habits, irrational thinking, and egotistical character traits.

Virtue ethics also adds a practical perspective. Beauchamp and Childress state, "A practical consequence of this view is that the education of, for example medical doctors, should include the cultivation of virtues such as compassion, discernment, trustworthiness, integrity, conscientiousness as well as benevolence (desire to help) and nonmalevolence (desire to avoid harm)."[31] These authors also note that "persons of 'good character' can certainly formulate 'bad policy' or make a 'poor choice'—we need to evaluate those policies and choices according to moral principles."

3.7 Ethical Relativism: A Self-Interest Approach

Ethical relativism holds that no universal standards or rules can be used to guide or evaluate the morality of an act. This view argues that people set their own moral standards for judging their actions. Only the individual's self-interest and values are relevant for judging his or her behavior. This form of relativism is also referred to as *naive relativism.*

If Louise Simms were to adopt the principle of ethical relativism for her decision making, she might choose to accept the government official's offer to promote her own standing in his firm. She might reason that her self-interest would be served best by making any deal that would push her career ahead. But Simms could also use ethical relativism to justify her rejection of the offer. She might say that any possible form of such a questionable negotiation is against her beliefs. The point behind this principle is that individual standards are the basis of moral authority.

The logic of ethical relativism also extends to cultures. *Cultural relativism* argues that "when in Rome, do as the Romans do." What is morally right for one society or culture may be wrong for another. Moral standards vary from one culture to another. Cultural relativists would argue that firms and business professionals doing business in a country are obliged to follow that country's laws and moral codes. A criterion that relativists would use to justify their actions would be: "Are my beliefs, moral standards, and customs satisfied with this action or outcome?"

The benefit of ethical and cultural relativism is that they recognize the distinction between individual and social values and customs.

These views take seriously the different belief systems of individuals and societies. Social norms and mores are seen in a cultural context.

However, relativism can lead to several problems. (It can be argued that this perspective is actually not ethical.) First, these views imply an underlying laziness.[32] Individuals who justify their morality only from their personal beliefs, without taking into consideration other ethical principles, may use the logic of relativism as an excuse for not having or developing moral standards. Second, this view contradicts everyday experience. Moral reasoning is developed from conversation, interaction, and argument. What I believe or perceive as "facts" in a situation may or may not be accurate. How can I validate or disprove my ethical reasoning if I do not communicate, share, and remain open to changing my own standards?

Ethical relativism can create absolutists—individuals who claim their moral standards are right regardless of whether others view the standards as right or wrong. For example, what if my beliefs conflict with yours? Whose relativism is right then? Who decides and on what grounds? In practice, ethical relativism does not effectively or efficiently solve complicated conflicts that involve many parties because these situations require tolerating doubts and permitting our observations and beliefs to be informed.

Cultural relativism embodies the same problems as ethical relativism. Although the values and moral customs of all cultures should be observed and respected, especially because business professionals are increasingly operating across national boundaries, we must not be blindly absolute or divorce ourselves from rigorous moral reasoning or laws aimed at protecting individual rights and justice. For example, R. Edward Freeman and Daniel Gilbert Jr. ask, "Must American managers in Saudi Arabia treat women as the Saudis treat them? Must American managers in South Africa treat blacks as white South Africans treat them? Must white South Africans treat blacks in the U.S. as U.S. managers treat them? Must Saudis in the U.S. treat women as U.S. managers treat them?"[33] They continue, "It makes sense to question whether the norms of the Nazi society were in fact morally correct."[34] Using rigorous ethical reasoning to solve moral dilemmas is important across cultures.

However, this does not suggest that flexibility, sensitivity, and awareness of individual and cultural moral differences are not necessary. It does mean that upholding principles of rights, justice, and freedom in some situations may conflict with the other person's or culture's belief system. Depending on the actions taken and decisions made based on a person's moral standards, a price may be paid for maintaining them. Often, negotiation agreements and understanding can be reached without overt conflict when different ethical principles or cultural standards clash.

Finally, it could be argued that cultural relativism does provide an argument against cultural imperialism. Why should American laws, customs, and values that are embedded in a U.S. firm's policies be enforced in another country that has differing laws and values regarding the activities in question?

Figure 3.2 summarizes the ethical principles presented here. This figure can be used as a reference for applying these principles individually and in a stakeholder analysis with groups.

Ethical Relativism and Stakeholder Analysis When considering the perspectives of relativism in a stakeholder analysis, ask the following questions:

1. What are the major moral beliefs and principles at issue for each stakeholder affected by this decision?

2. What are my moral beliefs and principles in this decision?

3. To what extent will my ethical principles clash if a particular course of action is taken? Why?

4. How can conflicting moral beliefs be avoided or resolved in seeking a desirable outcome?

An example of an ethical relativist is Sam Waksal who resigned as CEO of ImClone (a manufacturer of drugs for cancer and other treatment therapies) on May 22, 2002. He was arrested for securities fraud and perjury and was indicted for bank fraud, securities fraud, and perjury. He pleaded guilty to all of the counts in the indictment. (He also implicated his daughter and father in his insider trading schemes.) In addition, he pleaded guilty to tax evasion for not paying New York state sales tax on pieces of art that he purchased. He was sentenced to 87 months in prison and was ordered to pay a $3 million fine and $1.2 million in restitution to the New York State Sales Tax Commission. He began serving his prison sentence on July 23, 2003. Martha Stewart, an ImClone stockholder, was sentenced to five months in prison and five months of house arrest for being involved in using insider trading knowledge to sell shares of ImClone stock. She was also ordered to pay $30,000 in fines and court fees. Her broker, Peter Bacanovic, was given the same sentence, but a lower fine of $4,000. Bacanovic's assistant, Douglas Faneuil, was spared prison time and fined $2,000.[35] Waksal later said in an interview when asked how he got into this "mess": "It certainly wasn't because I thought about it carefully ahead of time. I think I was arrogant enough at the time to believe that I could cut corners, not care about details that were going on, and not think about consequences."[36]

3.8 Immoral, Amoral, and Moral Management

It is possible for owners, managers, and individual stakeholders to relate to their constituencies from three broad orientations: immorality, amorality, and morality.

Immoral treatment of constituencies signifies a minimally ethical or unethical approach, such as laying off employees without fair notice or compensation, offering upper-level management undeserved salary increases and perks, and giving "golden parachutes" (attractive payments or settlement contracts to selected employees) when a change in company control is negotiated. (Such payments are often made at the expense of shareholders' dividends without their knowledge or consent.) Managing immorally means intentionally going against the ethical principles of justice and fair and equitable treatment of other stakeholders.

Amoral management happens when owners, supervisors, and managers treat shareholders, outside stakeholders, and employees without concern or care for the consequences of their actions. No willful wrong may be intended, but neither is thought given to moral behavior or outcomes. Minimal action is taken while setting policies that are solely profit-oriented, production-centered, or short-term. Employees and other stakeholders are viewed as instruments for executing the economic interests of the firm. Strategies, control systems, leadership style, and interactions in such organizations also reflect an amoral, minimalist approach toward stakeholders. Nevertheless, the harmful consequences of amoral actions are real for the persons affected.

Moral management places value on fair treatment of shareholders, employees, customers, and other stakeholders. Ethics codes are established, communicated, and included in training; employee rights are built into visible policies that are enforced; and employees and other stakeholders are treated with respect and trust. The firm's corporate strategy, control and incentive systems, leadership style, and interactions reflect a morally managed organization. Moral management is the preferred mode of acting toward stakeholders, since respect and fairness are considered in decisions.

It is helpful to consider these three orientations while observing managers, owners, employees, and coworkers. Have you seen amoral policies, procedures, and decisions in organizations? The next section summarizes four social responsibility roles (Figure 3.3) that business executives view as moral for decision makers. The model presented complements the five ethical principles by providing a broad framework for describing ethical orientations toward business decisions. You may want to use the following framework to characterize your own moral and responsible roles,

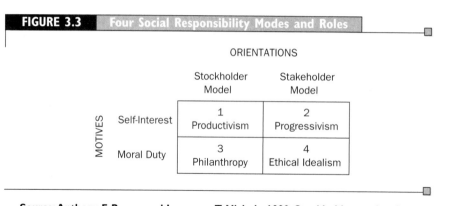

FIGURE 3.3   Four Social Responsibility Modes and Roles

Source: Anthony F. Buono and Lawrence T. Nichols. 1990. Stockholders and stakeholder interpretations of business' social rule. In *Business Ethics: Readings and Cases in Corporate Morality,* 2d ed., edited by Michael Hoffman and Jennifer Moore. New York: McGraw-Hill, 172. Reproduced with permission of Anthony F. Buono.

those of your boss and colleagues, and even those of contemporary international figures in government or business.

3.9 FOUR SOCIAL RESPONSIBILITY ROLES

What social obligations do businesses and their executives have toward their stockholders and society? The traditional view that the responsibility of corporate owners and managers was to serve only, or primarily, their stockholders' interests has been challenged and modified—but not abandoned—since the turn of this century. The debate continues about whether the roles of businesses and managers include serving social stakeholders along with economic stockholders. Because of changing demographic and educational characteristics of the workplace and the advent of laws, policies, and procedures that recognize greater awareness of employee and other stakeholders' rights, distinctions have been made about the responsibility of the business to its employees and to the larger society.

Four ethical interpretations of the social roles and modes of decision making are discussed and illustrated in Figure 3.3. The four social responsibility modes reflect business roles toward stockholders and a wider audience of stakeholders.[37]

Figure 3.3 illustrates two distinct social responsibility orientations of businesses and managers toward society: the *stockholder model* (the primary responsibility of the corporation to its economic stockholders) and the *stakeholder model* (the responsibility of the corporation to its social stakeholders outside the corporation). The two sets of motives underlying these two orientations are "self-interest" and "moral duty."

The stockholder self-interest (box 1 in Figure 3.3) and moral duty (box 3) orientations are discussed first, followed by the stakeholder self-interest (box 2) and moral duty (box 4) orientations. The two stockholder orientations are *productivism* and *philanthropy.*

Productivists (who hold a free-market ethic) view the corporation's social responsibility in terms of rational self-interest and the direct fulfillment of stockholder interests. The free market values the basis of rewards and punishments in the organization. This ethic drives internal and external vision, mission, values, policies, and decisions—including salaries, promotion, and demotions. Productivists believe the major—and, some would say, only—mission of business is to obtain profit. The free market is the best guarantee of moral corporate conduct in this view. Supply-side economists as productivists, for example, argue that the private sector is the vehicle for social improvement. Tax reduction and economic incentives that boost private industry are policies that productivists advocate as socially responsible. Ronald Reagan's "trickle-down" economic policies (seeking social benefits from private-sector wealth) are a recent example of this view.

Although all the ethical principles discussed earlier could be used by organizational leaders within each of these responsibility modes, productivists might advocate the use of *negative rights* to promote policies that protect shareholders' interests over *positive rights* that would cost taxpayers and use government resources to assist those more economically dependent on government services—who, productivists would argue, add an economic burden to the free market system.

A free-market-based ethic is widely used by owners and managers who must make tough workplace decisions such as: (1) How many and which people are to be laid off because of a market downturn and significantly lower profits? (2) What constitutes fair notice and compensation to employees who are to be terminated from employment? (3) How can employees be disciplined fairly in situations in which people's rights have been violated? A company is entitled to private property rights and responsibilities to shareholders. Robert Nozick, a Libertarian philosopher, is an advocate of a market-based ethic. He makes his case for a market-based principle of justice and entitlement in his book *Anarchy, State, and Utopia* (New York: Basic Books, 1974). Opponents to the market-based ethic argue that the rights of less-advantaged people also count, that property rights are not absolute in all situations, that there are times when the state can be justified in protecting the rights of others in disputes against property owners, and that the distribution of justice depends on the conditions of a situation—if war, illegal entry, fraud, or theft occur, some form of redistribution of wealth can be justified.[38]

Philanthropists, who also have a stockholder view of the corporation, hold that social responsibility is justified in terms of a moral duty toward helping less-advantaged members of society through organized, tax-deductible charity and *stewardship.* Proponents of this view believe that the primary social role of the corporation is still to obtain profits. However, moral duty drives their motives instead of self-interest (the productivist view). Advocates of this view are stewards and believe that those who have wealth ought to share it with disadvantaged people. As stockholder stewards, philanthropists share profits primarily through their tax-deductible activities. Ted Turner, the philanthropist, has contributed $1 billion to the United Nations to offer medical assistance to children internationally. The Bill and Melinda Gates foundation contributes millions of dollars to eradicate diseases around the globe.

Philanthropists might argue from principles of utilitarianism, duty, and universalism to justify their giving. Corporate philanthropy, generally speaking, is based primarily on the profit motive. Corporate philanthropists' sense of stewardship is contingent on their available and calculated use of wealth to help the less economically advantaged.

Progressivism and *ethical idealism* are the two social responsibility modes in the stakeholder model, the other dominant orientation. *Progressivists* believe corporate behavior is motivated by self-interest, but they also hold that corporations should take a broader view of responsibility toward social change. Enlightened self-interest is a value that characterizes progressivists. Rheinhold Niebuhr, the Christian theologian, was a modern example of a progressivist who argued for the involvement of the church in politics to bring about reasoned, orderly reform. He also worked with unions and other groups to improve workers' job conditions and wages. Progressivists support policies such as affirmative action, environmental protection, employee stock option programs (ESOPs), and energy conservation. Did ice cream maker Ben and Jerry's follow a progressivist philosophy for their formerly independent company?

Finally, *ethical idealists* believe that social responsibility is justified when corporate behavior directly supports stakeholder interests. Ethical idealists, such as Ralph Nader earlier in his career, hold that, to be fully responsible, corporate activity should help transform businesses into institutions where workers can realize their full potential. Employee ownership, cooperatives, and community-based and owned service industries are examples of the type of corporate transformation that ethical idealists advocate. The boundaries between business and society are fluid for ethical idealists. Corporate profits are to be shared for humanitarian purposes—to help bring about a more humane society.

Of course, as noted previously, a spectrum of beliefs exists for each of these four modes. For example, ethical idealists profess different visions regarding the obligations of business to society. Progressivists and ethical idealists generally tend to base their moral authority on legal and moral rights, justice, and universalism. Organizational leaders and professionals are obviously concerned with the operational solvency and even profitability (especially for-profit firms) of their companies. Still, they tend to believe that stakeholder interests and welfare are necessary parts of the economic system's effectiveness and success.

Which orientation best characterizes your current beliefs of business responsibility toward society: productivism, philanthropy, progressivism, or ethical idealism?

3.10 INDIVIDUAL ETHICAL DECISION-MAKING STYLES

In addition to the four social responsibility modes, researchers have defined ethical styles. Stanley Krolick developed a survey that interprets individual primary and secondary ethical decision-making styles.[39] The four styles he found are (1) individualism, (2) altruism, (3) pragmatism, and (4) idealism. These four styles are summarized here to complement the social responsibility modes and the ethical principles we have discussed. Caution must be used when considering any of these schemes to avoid stereotyping. These categories are guides for further reflection, discussion, and study.

Individualists are driven by natural reason, personal survival, and preservation. The self is the source and justification of all actions and decisions. Individualists believe that "If I don't take care of my own needs, I will never be able to address the concerns of others."[40] The moral authority of individualists is their own reasoning process, based on self-interest. Individualism is related to the principle of naive ethical relativism and to productivism.

Altruists are concerned primarily with other people. Altruists relinquish their own personal security for the good of others. They would, as an extreme, like to ensure the future of the human race. The altruist's moral authority and motivation is to produce the greatest good for the largest number of people. Unlike utilitarians, altruists would not diligently calculate and measure costs and benefits. Providing benefits is their major concern. Altruists justify their actions by upholding the integrity of the community. They enter relationships from a desire to contribute to the common good and to humankind. Altruists are akin to universalists and philanthropists.

Pragmatists are concerned primarily with the situation at hand, not with the self or the other. The pragmatist's bases for moral authority and motivation are the perceived needs of the moment and the potential consequences of a decision in a specific context. The needs of the moment dictate the importance of self-interest, concern for others, rules, and values. Facts and situational information are justifications for the pragmatist's actions. Pragmatists may abandon significant principles and values to produce certain results. They are closest philosophically to utilitarians. Although this style may seem the most objective and appealing, the shifting ethics of pragmatism make this orientation (and the person who espouses it) difficult and unpredictable in a business environment.

The Organization Game

Instructions: Read the following description of the game. Write out your working agreement. Then address the questions.

Assume that you are self-interested in the sense that you are interested in your own welfare, although not necessarily to the exclusion of interest in the welfare of others. Assume that you do not know your age, race, nationality, religion, abilities, or educational background. Assume that you do know that you are not presently employed but will be employed by an entirely new organization that designs, produces, and markets some high-tech product. You also know certain "goods" that you hope to achieve through your employment at the firm. These include security, adequate compensation, safe working conditions, and opportunity for advancement and personal growth. Your task is to devise a working agreement with others in the same circumstances about how the organization will handle:

1. *Purpose.* What is the ultimate purpose of the organization? To maximize profit? Provide customer satisfaction? Provide for the needs of the employees? Something else?

2. *Conflict.* What will be done in the event of disagreement between persons or groups within the organization?

3. *Authority.* Who, if anyone, has authority in the organization, how much are they to have, and how is it controlled?

4. *Change.* How can the rules you devise be changed, or can they be changed?

Falling under one or more of the previous agreements are some more specific areas of agreement you may want to consider. They largely concern distribution of burdens and benefits and include:

1. Employment: How will you decide who will be employed, the terms of employment, and in what capacity they will be employed?

2. Termination: What are the grounds and procedures for terminating an employee?

3. Promotion: Under what conditions will someone be promoted and how should the decision be made?

4. Compensation: How will pay rates be established? Will there bonuses, and on what grounds will they be awarded? What benefits will be available, if any?

5. Retirement: What retirement policies will be in place?

QUESTIONS

1. Evaluate your working agreement (including the specifics in it) using the ethical principles in this chapter (rights, justice, universalism, relativism, duty, others). Consider the employer and the employees as you evaluate the ethical terms of your agreement. What parts of your agreement distribute burden or benefits to the employer? To employees? Why?

2. How "just" is your agreement overall? (Discuss different theories of justice with this exercise.)

3. After sharing your agreement and these questions with the class, what did you learn about your theory of justice in the workplace?

Idealists are driven by principles and rules. Reason, relationships, or the desired consequences of an action do not substitute for the idealist's adherence to principles. Duties are absolute. Idealists' moral authority and motivation are commitment to principles and consistency. Values and rules of conduct are the justification that idealists use to explain their actions. Seen as people with high moral standards, idealists can also be rigid and inflexible. Stanley Krolick states, "This absolute adherence to principles may blind the idealist to the potential consequences of a decision for oneself, others, or the situation."[41] This style is related to the social responsibility mode of ethical idealism and to the principle of universalism.

Which of the four styles best characterizes your ethical orientation? The orientation of your colleagues? Your supervisor or boss?

Communicating and Negotiating across Ethical Styles

When working or communicating with an ethical style, you also must observe *the other person's ethical style.* According to Krolick, the first step is to "concede that the other person's values and priorities have their own validity in their own terms and try to keep those values in mind to facilitate the process of reaching an agreement.[42] The following guidelines can help when communicating, negotiating, or working with one of the four ethical styles:

- *Individualist:* Point out the benefits to the other person's self-interest.

- *Altruist:* Focus on the benefits for the various constituencies involved.

- *Pragmatist:* Emphasize the facts and potential consequences of an action.

- *Idealist:* Concentrate on the principles or duties at stake.

Learning to recognize and communicate with people who have other ethical styles and being flexible in accommodating your ethical style, without sacrificing your own, are important skills for working effectively with others.

3.11 QUICK ETHICAL TESTS

In addition to knowing the ethical principles, social responsibility modes, and ethical styles presented in this chapter, businesspeople can take short "ethical tests" before making decisions. Many of these rules reflect the principles discussed in this chapter. These "checkpoints," if observed, could change the actions you would automatically take in ethical dilemmas.

The Center for Business Ethics at Bentley College articulated six simple questions for the "practical philosopher." Before making a decision or acting, ask the following:

1. Is it right?

2. Is it fair?

3. Who gets hurt?

4. Would you be comfortable if the details of your decision were reported on the front page of your local newspaper?

5. What would you tell your child to do?

6. How does it smell? (How does it feel?)

Other quick ethical tests, some of which are classic, include:

- *The Golden Rule:* "Do unto others as you would have them do unto you." This includes not knowingly doing harm to others.

- *The Intuition Ethic:* We know apart from reason what is right. We have a moral sense about what is right and wrong. We should follow our "gut feeling" about what is right.

- *The Means-Ends Ethic:* We may choose unscrupulous but efficient means to reach an end if the ends are really worthwhile and significant. Be sure the ends are not the means.

- *The Test of Common Sense:* "Does the action I am getting ready to take really make sense?" Think before acting.

- *The Test of One's Best Self:* "Is this action or decision I'm getting ready to take compatible with my concept of myself at my best?"

- *The Test of Ventilation:* Do not isolate yourself with your dilemma. Get others' feedback before acting or deciding.

- *The Test of the Purified Idea:* "Am I thinking this action or decision is right just because someone with authority or knowledge says it is right?" You may still be held responsible for taking the action.[43]

Use these principles and guidelines for examining the motivations of stakeholders' strategies, policies, and actions. Why do stakeholders act and talk as they do? What principles drive these actions?

3.12 CONCLUDING COMMENTS

Individual stakeholders have a wide range of ethical principles, orientations, and "quick tests" to draw on before solving an ethical dilemma. Using moral reflection and creativity is also important when deciding between two "right" or "wrong" choices. Reflecting on one's core values combined with a sense of moral courage and shrewdness are also a recommended part of this decision-making process. When there are multiple stakeholders in a dilemma, the moral dimension of the stakeholder approach can be helpful by identifying the "ground rules" or "implicit morality" of institutional members. As R. Edward Freeman and Daniel Gilbert Jr. state:

> Think of the implicit morality of an institution as the rules that must be followed if the institution is to be a good one. The rules are often implicit, because the explicit rules of an institution may be the reason that the institution functions badly. Another way to think of the implicit morality of an institution is as the internal logic of the institution. Once this internal logic is clearly understood, we can evaluate its required behaviors against external standards.[44]

Back to Louise Simms . . . Let's return to the scenario in which Louise Simms is trying to decide what to do. Put yourself in Louise's situation. Identify your ethical decision-making style. Are you primarily an idealist, pragmatist, altruist, or individualist? What are some of your blind spots? Consider the three questions regarding a "defining moment" at the beginning of the chapter: "Who am I?" "Who are we?" "Who is the company?" What courses of action are available after reviewing your responses to these questions? Then, describe the ethical principles you usually follow in your life. Describe Louise's organization. Is it characterized as productivist (i.e., market ethics)? Progressive? Philanthropic? Idealist? What is your moral responsibility to yourself, your family and friends, your colleagues and work team, and to the company? Now make Louise's decision and share your decision with your classmates and consider their responses. Do you think you made the right decision?

SUMMARY

Complex ethical dilemmas in business situations involve making tough choices between conflicting interests. This chapter begins with questions for addressing dilemmas and "defining moments" creatively, boldly, and shrewdly. Twelve questions and three decision criteria that can assist individuals in determining the most suitable course of action are presented.

Individuals can gain a clear perspective of their own motivations and actions by distinguishing them from those of others. This perspective can be useful for guiding your own decision-making process. Understanding the criteria from this chapter can enable you to reason more critically when examining other stakeholders' ethical reasoning.

A primary goal of ethical reasoning is to help individuals act in morally responsible ways. Ignorance and bias are two conditions that cloud moral awareness. Five principles of ethical reasoning are presented to expose you to methods of ethical decision making. Each principle is discussed in terms of the utility and drawbacks characteristic of it. Guidelines for thinking through and applying each principle in a stakeholder analysis are provided. These principles are not mechanical recipes for selecting a course of action. They are filters or screens to use for clarifying dilemmas.

Three ethical orientations, moral, amoral, and immoral, can be used to evaluate ethics. Moral and immoral orientations are more discernible than amoral motives. Amoral orientations include lack of concern for others' interests and well-being. Although no intentional harm or motive may be observed, harmful consequences from ignorance or neglect reflect amoral styles of operating.

Four social responsibility roles or business modes are productivism and philanthropy (influenced by stockholder concerns) and progressivism and ethical idealism (driven by stockholder concerns but also influenced by external stakeholders).

Individuals also have ethical decision-making styles. Four different (but not exclusive) styles are individualism, altruism, pragmatism, and idealism.

Another person's ethical decision-making style must be understood when engaging in communication and negotiation. These styles are a starting point for identifying predominant decision-making characteristics.

The final section offers quick "ethical tests" that can be used to provide insight into your decision-making process and actions.

QUESTIONS

1. Do you believe ethical dilemmas can be prevented and solved morally without the use of principles? Explain.

2. Why are creativity and moral imagination oftentimes necessary in preventing and resolving ethical dilemmas and "defining moments" of conflict in one's workplace? Offer an example of an ethically questionable situation in which you had to creatively improvise to "do the right thing."

3. What is a first step for addressing ethical dilemmas? What parts of this chapter would and could you use to complement or change your own decision-making methods?

4. What are three criteria that can be used in ethical reasoning to help structure thinking and arguments?

5. What single question is the most powerful for solving ethical dilemmas?

6. What are two conditions that eliminate a person's moral responsibility?

7. Briefly explain five fundamental principles that can be used in ethical reasoning.

8. What are some of the problems characteristic of cultural relativism? Offer an example in the news of a company that has acted unethically according to the perspective of cultural relativism.

9. Why is utilitarianism useful for conducting a stakeholder analysis? What are some of the problems with using this principle? Give an example when you used utilitarianism to justify an ethically questionable action.

10. Briefly explain the categorical imperative. What does it force you, as a decision maker, to do when choosing an action in a moral dilemma?

11. Explain the difference between the principles of rights and justice. What are some of the strengths and weaknesses of each principle?

12. Which of the four social responsibility modes most accurately characterizes your college/university and place of work? Explain. Do your ethics and moral values agree with these organizations? Explain.

13. Briefly explain your ethical decision-making style as presented in the chapter.

14. Explain what ethical logic and actions people generally take to persuade you to do something that is ethically questionable. Refer to the ethical decision styles in the chapter.

15. Which of the ethical "quick tests" do you prefer? Why?

EXERCISES

1. Describe a serious ethical dilemma you have experienced. Use the 12 questions developed by Laura Nash to offer a resolution to the problem, even if your resolution is different from the original experience. Did you initially use any of the questions? Would any of these questions have helped you? How? What would you have done differently? Why?

2. Identify an instance when you thought ignorance absolved a person or group from moral responsibility. Then identify an example of a person or group failing to become fully informed about a moral situation. Under what conditions do you think individuals are morally responsible for their actions? Why?

3. With which of the four social responsibility business modes in the chapter do you most identify? Why? Name a company that reflects this orientation. Would you want to work for this company? Would you want to be part of the management team? Explain.

4. Select a corporate leader in the news who acted legally but immorally and one who acted illegally but morally. Explain the differences of the actions and behaviors in each of the two examples. What lessons do you take from your examples?

Ethical Dilemma   Now What Should I Do?

I was employed as a certified public accountant (CPA) for a regional accounting firm that specialized in audits of financial institutions and had many local clients. My responsibilities included supervising staff, collecting evidence to support financial statement assertions, and compiling work papers for managers and partners to review. During the audit of a publicly traded bank, I discovered that senior bank executives were under investigation by the FDIC for removing funds from the bank. They were also believed to be using bank funds to pay corporate credit card bills for gas and spouses' expenses. The last allegation noted that the executives were issuing loans to relatives without proper collateral.

After reviewing the work papers, I found two checks made payable to one executive of the bank that were selected during a cash count from two tellers. There was no indication based on our sampling that expenses were being paid for spouses. My audit manager and the chief financial officer (CFO) of my firm were aware of these problems.

After the fieldwork for the audit was completed, I was called into the CEO's office. The CEO and the chief operating officer (COO) stated that the FDIC examiners wanted to interview the audit manager, two staff accountants, and me. The CEO then asked the following question: "If you were asked by the FDIC about a check or checks made payable to bank executives, how would you answer?" I told them that I would answer the FDIC examiners by stating that, during our audit, we made copies of two checks made payable to an executive of the bank for $8,000 each.

The COO stated that during his review of the audit work papers he had not found any copies of checks made payable to executives. He also stated that a better response to the question regarding the checks would be, "I was not aware of reviewing any checks specifically made payable to the executive in question." The COO then said that the examiners would be in the following day to speak with the audit staff. I was dismissed from the meeting.

Neither the CEO nor the COO asked me if the suggested "better" response was the response I would give, and I did not volunteer the information. During the interview, the FDIC investigators never asked me whether I knew about the checks. Should I have volunteered this information?

Questions

1. What would you have done? Volunteered the information or stayed silent? Explain your decision.
2. Was anything unethical going on in this case? Explain.
3. Describe the "ethics" of the officers of the firm in this case.
4. What, if anything, should the officers have done, and why?
5. What lessons, if any, can you take from this case, as an employee working under company officials who have more power than you do?

CASE 7

SAMUEL WAKSAL AND IMCLONE

Seeking Approval for Erbitux   For several years, ImClone, a biotechnology company, was a "darling" of Wall Street. Its stock price rose from less than $1 per share in 1994 to $72 a share in November 2001. "The whole time it was producing nothing for sale. It did generate some revenue through licensing agreements with other drug companies—signs that the pharmaceutical industry did think ImClone was on to something." ImClone focused on developing a cancer treatment drug called Erbitux. Erbitux is intended to make cancer treatment more effective by "targeting a protein called epidermal growth factor receptor (EGFR), which exists on the surface of cancer cells and plays a role in their proliferation."

In its 10-K Annual Report for the fiscal year ending December 31, 2001, ImClone described Erbitux as the company's "lead product candidate" and indicated that Erbitux had been shown in early stage clinical trials to cause tumor reduction in certain cases. ImClone had planned to market the drug in the United States and Canada with its development partner, Bristol-Myers Squibb. On September 19, 2001, ImClone announced that Bristol-Myers Squibb had paid $2 billion for the marketing rights to Erbitux and would co-develop and co-promote Erbitux with ImClone.

ImClone was one of at least five pharmaceutical companies with EGFR drugs in mid- to late-stage testing. The winners at commercialization of a new drug class—such as EGFR—are the "companies that beat their rivals to market, since doctors tend to embrace the initial entries." Under this pressure, ImClone took a testing shortcut, using what is known as a single-armed study—one which is conducted without a control group. ImClone's use of the single-armed study failed to meet the United States Food and Drug Administration's (FDA) rigorous criteria for using the methodology.

Samuel Waksal, ImClone's co-founder and chief executive officer at the time, was directly involved in coordinating and publicizing ImClone's efforts to develop Erbitux and to obtain FDA approval for it. On June 28, 2001, ImClone began the process of submitting a rolling application—called a Biologics License Application (BLA)—seeking FDA approval for Erbitux. On October 31, 2001, ImClone submitted to the FDA the final substantial portion of its BLA. The FDA had a 60-day period within which a decision had to be made concerning whether to accept the BLA for filing. The FDA had three options: (1) accept ImClone's BLA for filing; (2) accept the BLA for filing, but simultaneously issue a disciplinary review letter notifying ImClone that the BLA still had serious deficiencies that would need to be corrected before the BLA could be approved; or (3) refuse to approve the drug by issuing a Refusal to File letter (RTF). When the FDA issues a RTF, the applicant must file a new BLA to start the process over.

Samuel Waksal's Reaction to the Impending Refusal to File

On December 25, 2001, Bristol-Myers Squibb learned from a source at the FDA that the FDA would issue a RTF letter on December 28, 2001. On the evening of December 26, 2001, Waksal learned of the FDA's decision and attempted to sell 79,797 shares of ImClone stock that were held in his brokerage account with Merrill Lynch. He initially told his agent to transfer the shares to his daughter's account. The following morning he instructed his agent to sell the shares. When Waksal's agent called Merrill Lynch in order to sell the shares, the agent was told that the shares were restricted and could not be sold without the approval of ImClone's legal counsel. When Merrill Lynch refused to conduct the transaction, Waksal ordered his agent to transfer the shares to Bank of America and then sell them. Bank of America also refused to conduct the transaction, and the shares were never sold.

On December 26, 2001, Waksal contacted his father, Jack Waksal, informing him of the impending RTF. The next morning, Jack Waksal placed an order to sell 110,000 shares of ImClone stock. Jack Waksal also called Prudential Securities and placed an order to sell 1,336 shares of ImClone stock from the account of Patti Waksal. On December 28, Jack Waksal sold another 25,000 shares of ImClone stock. When questioned by the staff of the Securities and Exchange Commission (SEC), Jack Waksal provided false and misleading explanations for these trades.

Also on the morning of December 27, 2001, before the stock market opened, Samuel Waksal had a telephone conversation with his daughter Aliza. At that time, Waksal was Aliza's only means of support, and he had control of her bank and brokerage accounts. During their conversation, he directed her to sell all of her ImClone shares. Immediately after talking to her father, Aliza placed an order at 9 a.m. to sell 39,472 shares of ImClone stock. By selling her shares at that moment in time, she avoided $630,295 in trading losses.

On December 28, 2001, Waksal purchased 210 ImClone put option contracts, buying them through an account at Discount Bank and Trust AG in Switzerland. He sold all 210 put option contracts on January 4, 2002, which resulted in a profit of $130,130. Waksal also failed to file a statement disclosing a change of ownership of his ImClone securities as required by Section 16(a) of the Exchange Act and Rule 16a-3.

According to the SEC, Waksal violated several sections of the Securities Act when he attempted to sell his own ImClone Stock, when he illegally tipped his father about the FDA decision, when he caused Aliza to sell her shares of ImClone stock, and when he purchased ImClone put option contracts.

The Outcome for Samuel Waksal and ImClone   Waksal resigned as ImClone's CEO on May 21, 2002. On June 12, 2002, he was arrested for securities fraud and perjury, and then two months later he was indicted for bank fraud, securities fraud, and perjury. On October 15, 2002, Waksal pled guilty to all of the counts in the indictment except those counts based on allegations that he passed material, nonpublic information to his father, Jack Waksal. On March 3, 2003, he also pled guilty to tax evasion charges for failing to pay New York State sales tax on pieces of art he had purchased. On June 10, 2003, Waksal was sentenced to 87 months in prison and was ordered to pay a $3 million fine and $1.2 million in restitution to the New York State Sales Tax Commission. Waksal began serving his prison sentence on July 23, 2003.

Unlike Waksal, ImClone appears to have survived the scandal. Under the leadership of Daniel Lynch, ImClone's former chief financial officer and its current chief executive officer, the company has staged a remarkable turnaround. Most of ImClone's 440 employees stayed with the company and helped Lynch revive it. Lynch says the employees stayed for one overpowering reason—they believed in Erbitux. As for himself, Lynch asserted that "What motivated me to get up in the morning was knowing that if I could get this drug approved, it would improve the lives of patients with cancer." Based on a clinical trial by Merck KGaA, ImClone's European marketing partner, the FDA, on February 12, 2004, "approved Erbitux for treating patients with advanced colon cancer that has spread to other parts of the body." Thus, Erbitux became ImClone's first commercial product.

Questions for Discussion

1. What might motivate an individual or a company to short-cut drug testing that is crucial for FDA approval?

2. Why did Samuel Waksal react as he did pursuant to learning that the FDA would not approve Erbitux?

3. Why were Samuel Waksal's actions unethical?

Sources

This case was developed from material contained in the following sources:

Ackman, D. (October 11, 2002). A child's guide to ImClone. *Forbes.com,* http://www.forbes.com/2002/10/11/1011topnews.html, accessed January 12, 2005.

Herper, M. (May 23, 2002). ImClone CEO leaves, problems remain. *Forbes.com,* http://www.forbes.com/2002/05/23/0523imclone.html, accessed January 12, 2005.

Herper, M. (June 10, 2003). Samuel Waksal sentenced. *Forbes.com,* http://www.forbes.com/2003/06/10/cx_mh_0610waksal.html, accessed January 12, 2005.

Reuters News Service. (February 12, 2004). FDA approves ImClone's Erbitux: Drug at center of insider-trading scandal involving Waksal, Stewart. *MSNBC.com,* http://msnbc.msn.com/ID/4251347, accessed January 12, 2005.

Shook, D. (February 14, 2002). Lessons from ImClone's trial—and error. *Business Week Online,* http://www.businessweek.com, accessed January 12, 2005.

Tischler, L. (September 2004). The trials of ImClone. *Fast Company,* http://pf.fastcompany.com/magazine/86/imclone.html, accessed January 12, 2005.

U.S. Securities and Exchange Commission. *SEC v. Samuel D. Waksal.* Wayne M. Carlin (WC-2114), Attorney for the SEC. Case 02 Civ. 4407 (NRB). Accessed at http://www.sec.gov/litigation/complaints/comp18026.htm on January 12, 2005.

U.S. Securities and Exchange Commission. *SEC v. Samuel D. Waksal, Jack Waksal and Patti Waksal.* Barry W. Rashover (BR-6413), Attorney for the SEC. Case 02 Civ. 4407 (NRB). Accessed at http://www.sec.gov/litigation/complaints/comp18408.htm on January 12, 2005.

Case 8

Aaron Feuerstein and Malden Mills: How Values Guide Actions in a Post-Crisis Situation

Malden Mills: A Burning Crisis   On the night of December 11, 1995, Aaron Feuerstein was celebrating his seventieth birthday but soon would face major challenges, both personally and professionally. Late that night, Feuerstein raced from the festivities and socializing to the site of a horrible inferno, where he saw three of four nineteenth-century factory buildings burn to the ground. The buildings housed Malden Mills, a textile business that had been in the Feuerstein family for three generations. Located in Lawrence, Massachusetts, the company was founded by Feuerstein's grandfather in 1906. The company's most notable product at the time of the fire was Polartec, an outerwear fabric manufactured from recycled plastic bottles. Companies like L.L. Bean, Patagonia, and Lands' End used Polartec in their winter clothing lines.

Michael Lavallee, one of many employees who rushed to the site, stood alongside Aaron Feuerstein, watching the buildings burn as 60 mile per hour winds fanned the flames. Lavallee lamented, "It's done. It's done. It's gone." Feuerstein saw it differently. "This is not the end," he declared.

The day after the fire, Feuerstein met with many of the company's 3,000 employees in the local high school gymnasium. "They thought they knew what he was going to say, that he was going to take millions of dollars in insurance payments, retire, and close what was left of the factory . . . or he was going to move his operation to Mexico or Asia." Feuerstein's employees were in for a major surprise. The employees listened in stunned silence as Feuerstein "told them that he had every intention of rebuilding his factory right there in Lawrence, and what's more, everyone would continue to receive full salary and benefits during construction." When he announced his intentions, almost all the workers who were present cheered—and some of them wept.

The only building that did not burn to the ground was a warehouse that contained the Polartec finishing operation. The warehouse also stored new equipment awaiting installation. Malden Mills' employees set up the equipment in the warehouse and resumed production within 10 days. After a few weeks, output reached 230,000 yards per week, which was 100,000 more yards per week than before the fire. The increased production was attributed to the employees' creativity in doing their jobs and their commitment to Feuerstein. Not all employees were back at work immediately, but no one was laid off. Feuerstein kept all 3,000 employees on the payroll "for 90 days at a cost of $1.5 million per week while the factories were being rebuilt."

Feuerstein received widespread acclaim for his decision to rebuild Malden Mills and his commitment to the company's employees and their communities. Some people viewed Feuerstein as a "saint." After all, didn't he act in the best interests of the employees and the community rather than in his own self-interest?

Aaron Feuerstein: A Man of Values

Feuerstein says that his decision to rebuild was simply about "doing the right thing." He believes that every decision has to be a good business decision as well as a good ethical decision. "We believe that when you make a business decision, it should not be based exclusively on how to make the bottom line look better so that the shareholders can have an immediate benefit," says Feuerstein. "It should be balanced. It should take into consideration what's right and wrong, as well as profit." Feuerstein maintains that "doing the right thing adds to the profitability of the corporation" in the long term.

Feuerstein displayed three sets of interrelated behaviors and associated attitudes in the aftermath of the 1995 fire that "may be judged as praiseworthy, post-crisis virtues." These virtues are (a) leader sensitivity and responsiveness to the high levels of uncertainty faced by stakeholders, (b) deep-rooted feelings of support and value for employees, and (c) a commitment to rebuilding and renewal.

Feuerstein's management philosophy, which is based on early experiences with his family and on his religious beliefs, includes being sensitive to people, assuming responsibility for all organization members, and fulfilling responsibilities to the community. When Feuerstein was growing up, he was frequently exposed to conversations between his father and grandfather about running Malden Mills. Business fairness, openness, loyalty, mutual trust, and cooperation were central to these conversations and to young Aaron's development.

Feuerstein relies on the *Torah*, the book of Jewish law, for guidance in his managerial decisions and actions. Drawing on the *Torah*, Feuerstein, a practitioner of Orthodox Judaism, observes, "You are not permitted to oppress the working man, because he's poor and he's needy, amongst your brethren and amongst the non-Jew in your community." Feuerstein often quotes a Jewish proverb that says, "When all is moral chaos, this is the time to be a 'mensch.'" Mensch is a Yiddish word that describes a righteous man, a man with a heart. Known as the "Mensch of Malden Mills," Feuerstein is perceived as a businessman who cares more about his workers than about his financial net worth.

Feuerstein's Critics   While acknowledging the widespread acclaim Feuerstein received for his post-crisis actions, some observers point out contradictions in his managerial and leadership behavior. Katarzyna Moreno, writing in *Forbes* magazine, cites investigations by the Occupational Safety and Health Administration, the office of the Massachusetts state fire marshal, and Malden Mills' insurance company that assert, "Malden repeatedly put its employees in harm's way and should have known about unsafe working conditions—which may have contributed to the fire—but didn't do enough to fix them and, instead lobbied regulators to back off."

Moreover, some of Feuerstein's critics say his actions were those of a fool. "They think he should have pocketed the insurance proceeds, closed the business, and walked away. Or else they think he should have grabbed the chance to move the company to some state or country with lower labor costs."

Thomas Teal, a writer for *Fortune* magazine, however, argued that Feuerstein is neither fool—nor saint. Rather, Teal maintains he is a businessman who "is as tough-minded as he is righteous." In supporting this assertion, Teal notes that although Feuerstein believes in downsizing, he seeks "to keep growing fast enough to give new jobs to the people that technology displaces, to weed out unnecessary jobs 'without crushing the spirit of the work force.'" Teal also cites Feuerstein's belief that simply seeking lower-cost labor by moving the company out of Lawrence, Massachusetts, might compromise Malden Mills' true competitive advantage—product quality.

Pushed into Bankruptcy Protection   In the years after rebuilding the factory, Malden Mills fell upon some difficult times. For the fiscal year ending October 31, 2001, operating income, projected at the beginning of the year to be $45 million, actually came in at $1.5 million. This resulted from warm weather that produced a drastic drop in sales of Polartec and "a tide of fleece knockoffs that flooded the market." Malden Mills became so mired in debt that it filed for Chapter 11 bankruptcy protection on November 29, 2001. At the time of the bankruptcy filing, the company's annual interest on its debt was $19 million, its liabilities totaled $180 million, and its depreciated assets were valued at $190 million.

As the 2001 fiscal year came to a close, Malden Mills' creditors brought in Frank Budetti and David Orlofsky, turnaround specialists from Kroll Zolfo Cooper Inc., to help run Malden Mills on a day-to-day basis. Aaron Feuerstein's role in running Malden Mills diminished significantly. GE Capital, Malden Mills' major creditor and its largest shareholder, along with other creditors, took control of the company following its bankruptcy filing.

When Malden Mills emerged from bankruptcy in the spring of 2003, Feuerstein retained his positions as president and chairman but only owned a minority stake—about 5%—in the company. Malden Mill's creditors held the majority interest. Feuerstein was granted the option of buying back the company for $157 million within the following three years, or for $92 million if the cash could be raised by July 31, 2003. Feuerstein obtained commitments for a significant portion of the $92 million repurchase price; some accounts indicate he raised all but about $10 million. The federal bankruptcy court extended the deadline to August 21, but Feuerstein missed it.

In June 2004, Aaron Feuerstein relinquished his positions as president and chairman of Malden Mills. On July 26, 2004, the major creditors appointed Michael Spillane president and chief executive officer of Malden Mills. In late October 2004, Aaron Feuerstein made another bid to buy back Malden Mills; the company's board of directors rejected the bid. James Harde, spokesman for Malden Mills' creditor-installed management team, observed, "Feuerstein is guaranteed the right to buy back control of the company if he can come up with $125 million—an amount that has risen over time." He added, "Mr. Feuerstein's offer was nowhere near the contractual option price. If he were to make an offer at the option price, then the company would accept it." As 2005 began, Feuerstein was still seeking to put together a repurchase deal.

In reaction to the board's rejection of the repurchase bid, Aaron's son, Daniel Feuerstein, emphasized his father's commitment to keeping manufacturing jobs in the United States rather than offshoring them, as he suspects will be done if the Feuerstein family does not regain control of Malden Mills. Regarding his father, Daniel Feuerstein says, "He doesn't make false claims about community responsibility in one sentence and then surreptitiously offshore the jobs to the Pacific rim."

A Retrospective Look by a Man of Values   In reflecting on the rebuilding decision, Feuerstein asserted that if he had to do it over, he would still make the same decision. He observed that Malden Mills' problems were "not a direct result of having acted fairly with workers and having treated them with respect." Rather, the problems resulted from a lack of adequate insurance to rebuild the factory with state-of-the-art equipment that would have enabled the company to continue producing the best quality in the marketplace. To cover the insurance shortage, Malden Mills borrowed heavily. Feuerstein commented, "Had I replaced the factory exactly as it was before the fire, I would have had enough insurance. But I wanted everything to be the absolute latest and best. As a result, we spent millions over what we were insured for." Feuerstein says, "I was proud of the family business and I wanted to keep that alive, and I wanted that to survive. But I also felt the responsibility for all my employees, to take care of them, to give them jobs." In pondering his own mortality, Aaron Feuerstein says that he wants to be remembered for not giving up and for trying to do the right thing.

Questions for Discussion

1. Evaluate Aaron Feuerstein's decision to rebuild Malden Mills after the fire and to keep all employees on the payroll in terms of being a good business decision as well as an ethical decision. Explain your answer.

2. Describe Aaron Feuerstein as a "man of values."

3. What guidance can Aaron's Feuerstein's values provide for your future behavior?

4. What challenges does seeking bankruptcy protection provide for a business owner who seems to care more about his workers than about his financial net worth?

Sources

This case was developed from material contained in the following sources:

Bailey, S. (December 3, 2003). Time for a miracle. *Boston.com*, http://www.boston.com/business/globe/articles, accessed January 7, 2005.

Boulay, A. (October 1996). Malden Mills: A study in leadership. *Quality Monitor Newsletter*, http://www.opi-inc.com/malden.htm, accessed January 7, 2005.

Brill, E.B. (January 31, 1997). Ethics is the bottom line: To Aaron Feuerstein, good Judaism makes good business sense. *Jewish News of Greater Phoenix*, http://www.jewishaz.com/jewishnews/970131/ethics.html, accessed January 7, 2005.

Gerloff, P. (December 2002). After the fire: An interview with Aaron Feuerstein. *More Than Money*, http://www.morethanmoney.org/articles/mtm31_after.htm, accessed January 11, 2005.

Jewell, M. (August 8, 2004). Malden Mills CEO has tough act to follow. *Business Custom Wire*, accessed from Regional Business News database on http://search.epnet.com on January 10, 2005.

Kerber, R. (January 29, 2003). Lawrence, Mass., fabric company strikes preliminary deal with creditors. *The Boston Globe*, accessed from Newspaper Source database on http://search.epnet.com on January 10, 2005.

Kerber, R. (January 29, 2004). Longtime leader seeks to regain control of Lawrence, Mass.-based Malden Mills. *The Boston Globe*, accessed from Newspaper Source database on http://search.epnet.com on January 10, 2005.

Meisler, A. (July 2003). Nice guy not quite finished. *Workforce*, accessed from ABI/INFORM Research database on http://proquest.umi.com on January 27, 2005.

"The mensch of Malden Mills." (July 3, 2003). *CBSNews.com*, http://www.cbsnews.com/stories/2003/07/03/60minutes/main56156.shtml on January 27, 2005.

Moreno, K. (April 14, 2003). Trial by fire. *Forbes*, accessed from ABI/INFORM Research database on http://proquest.umi.com on January 27, 2005.

Murray, A. (October 27, 2004). Feuerstein's buyback try is rejected. *Eagle-Tribune,*
http://www.eagletribuen.com/news/stories/20041027/FP_002.htm, accessed
January 27, 2005.

Pacelle, M. (May 9, 2003). Through the mill: Can Mr. Feuerstein save his business one
last time?—Textile owner overcame fire and changes in fashion; Creditors may be
tougher—Needed: $92 million by July 31. *Wall Street Journal,* accessed from
ABI/INFORM Research database on http://proquest.umi.com on January 27, 2005.

Pollak, S. (December 8, 2001). Firms should put people over profits. *The Daily Star,*
http://www.thedailystar.com/cgi-bin/starsafe.pl, accessed January 11, 2005.

Secretan, L. (November 16, 1998). Spirit at work: Do the right thing. *Industryweek
Midmarket,* http://www.industryweek.com/IWGC/columns.asp?ColumnId=225,
accessed January 7, 2005.

Seeger, M.W., Ulmer, R.R. (January 2001). Virtuous responses to organizational
crisis: Aaron Feuerstein and Milt Cole. *Journal of Business Ethics,* accessed from
ABI/INFORM Research database on http://proquest.umi.com on January 27, 2005.

Shafran, A. (June 30, 2002). Aaron Feuerstein: Bankrupt & wealthy. *Society Today,*
http://aish.com/societyWork/work/Aaron_Feuerstein_Bankrupt_and_Wealthy.asp,
accessed January 7, 2005.

Stone, J. (March 1, 2002). Looming problems; Corporate kindness might cost Aaron
Feuerstein his family's mill. *Fortune,* http://www.fortune.com, accessed January 10,
2005.

Teal, T. (November 11, 1996). Not a fool, not a saint. *Fortune,* http://www.fortune.com,
accessed January 10, 2005.

Case 9

Ford's Pinto Fires: The Retrospective View of Ford's Field Recall Coordinator

Brief Overview of the Ford Pinto Fires   Ford Motor Company, determined to compete with fuel-efficient Volkswagen and Japanese imports, introduced the subcompact Pinto in the 1971 model year. Lee Iacocca, Ford's president at the time, insisted that the Pinto weigh no more than 2,000 pounds and cost no more than $2,000. Even with these restrictions, the Pinto met federal safety standards, although some people have argued that strict adherence to the restrictions led Ford engineers to compromise safety. Some two million units were sold during the 10-year life of the Pinto.

The Pinto's major design flaw—a fuel tank prone to rupturing with moderate-speed rear-end collisions—surfaced not too long after the Pinto's entrance to the market. In April 1974, the Center for Auto Safety petitioned the National Highway Traffic Safety Administration (NHTSA) to recall Ford Pintos due to the fuel tank design defect. The Center for Auto Safety's petition was based on reports from attorneys of three deaths and four serious injuries in moderate-speed rear-end collisions involving Pintos. The NHTSA did not act on this petition until 1977.

As a result of tests performed for the NHTSA, as well as the extraordinary amount of publicity generated by the problem, Ford Motor Company agreed, on June 9, 1978, to recall 1.5 million 1971–1976 Ford Pintos and 30,000 1975–1976 Mercury Bobcat sedan and hatchback models for modifications to the fuel tank. Recall notices were mailed to the affected Pinto and Bobcat owners in September 1978. Repair parts were to be delivered to all dealers by September 15, 1978.

Unfortunately, the recall was initiated too late for six people. Between June 9, 1978 and September 15, 1978, six people died in Pinto fires after a rear impact. Three of these people were teenage girls killed in Indiana in August 1978 when their 1973 Pinto burst into flames after being rear-ended by a van. The fiery deaths of the Indiana teenagers led to criminal prosecution of the Ford Motor Company on charges of reckless homicide, marking the first time that an American corporation was prosecuted on criminal charges. In the trial, which commenced on January 15, 1980, "Indiana state prosecutors alleged that Ford knew Pinto gasoline tanks were prone to catch fire during rear-end collisions but failed to warn the public or fix the problem out of concern for profits." On March 13, 1980, a jury found Ford innocent of the charges. Production of the Pinto was discontinued in the fall of 1980.

Enter Ford's Field Recall Coordinator Dennis A. Gioia, currently a professor in the Department of Management and Organization at Pennsylvania State University, was the field recall coordinator at Ford Motor Company as the Pinto fuel tank defect began unfolding. Gioia's responsibilities included the operational coordination of all the current recall campaigns, tracking incoming information to identify developing problems, and reviewing field reports of alleged component failure that led to accidents. Gioia left Ford in 1975. Subsequently, "reports of Pinto fires escalated, attracting increasing media attention." The remainder of this case, written in Gioia's own words in the early 1990s, is his personal reflection on lessons learned from his experiences involving the Pinto fuel tank problem.

Why Revisit Decisions from the Early 1970s?

I take this case very personally, even though my name seldom comes up in its many recountings. I was one of those "faceless bureaucrats" who is often portrayed as making decisions without accountability and then walking away from them—even decisions with life-and-death implications. That characterization is, of course, far too stark and superficial. I certainly don't consider myself faceless, and I have always chafed at the label of bureaucrat as applied to me, even though I have found myself unfairly applying it to others. Furthermore, I have been unable to walk away from my decisions in this case. They have a tendency to haunt—especially when they have had such public airings as those involved in the Pinto fires debacle have had.

But why revisit 20-year-old decisions, and why take them so personally? Here's why: because I was in a position to do something about a serious problem . . . and didn't. That simple observation gives me pause for personal reflection and also makes me think about the many difficulties people face in trying to be ethical decision makers in organizations. It also helps me to keep in mind the features of modern business and organizational life that would influence someone like me (me of all people, who purposely set out to be an ethical decision maker!) to overlook basic moral issues in arriving at decisions that, when viewed retrospectively, look absurdly easy to make. But they are not easy to make, and that is perhaps the most important lesson of all.

The Personal Aspect

I would like to reflect on my own experience mainly to emphasize the personal dimensions involved in ethical decision making. Although I recognize that there are strong organizational influences at work as well, I would like to keep the critical lens focused for a moment on me (and you) as individuals. I believe that there are insights and lessons from my experience that can help you think about your own likely involvement in issues with ethical overtones.

First, however, a little personal background. In the late 1960s and early 1970s, I was an engineering/MBA student; I also was an "activist," engaged in protests of social injustice and the social irresponsibility of business, among other things. I held some pretty strong values, and I thought they would stand up to virtually any challenge and enable me to "do the right thing" when I took a career job. I suspect that most of you feel that you also have developed a strongly held value system that will enable you to resist organizational inducements to do something unethical. Perhaps. Unfortunately, the challenges do not often come in overt forms that shout the need for resistance or ethical righteousness. They are much more subtle than that, and thus doubly difficult to deal with because they do not make it easy to see that a situation you are confronting might actually involve an ethical dilemma.

After school, I got the job of my dreams with Ford and, predictably enough, ended up on the fast track to promotion. That fast track enabled me to progress quickly into positions of some notable responsibility. Within two years I became Ford's field recall coordinator, with first-level responsibility for tracking field safety problems. It was the most intense, information-overloaded job you can imagine, frequently dealing with some of the most serious problems in the company. Disasters were a phone call away, and action was the hallmark of the office where I worked. We all knew we were engaged in serious business, and we all took the job seriously. There were no irresponsible bureaucratic ogres there, contrary to popular portrayal.

In this context, I first encountered the neophyte Pinto fires problem—in the form of infrequent reports of cars erupting into horrendous fireballs in very low-speed crashes and the shuddering personal experience of inspecting a car that had burned, killing its trapped occupants. Over the space of a year, I had two distinct opportunities to initiate recall activities concerning the fuel tank problems, but on both occasions, I voted not to recall, despite my activist history and advocacy of business social responsibility.

The key question is how, after two short years, could I have engaged in a decision process that appeared to violate my own strong values—a decision process whose subsequent manifestations continue to be cited by many observers as a supposedly definitive study of corporate unethical behavior? I tend to discount the obvious accusations: that my values weren't really strongly held; that I had turned my back on my values in the interest of loyalty to Ford; that I was somehow intimidated into making decisions in the best interest of the company; that despite my principled statements, I had not actually achieved a high stage of moral development; and so on. Instead, I believe a more plausible explanation for my own actions looks to the foibles of normal human information processing.

I would argue that the complexity and intensity of the recall coordinator's job required that I develop cognitive strategies for simplifying the overwhelming amount of information I had to deal with. The best way to do that is to structure the information into cognitive "schemas," or more specifically "script schemas," that guide understanding and action when facing common or repetitive situations. Scripts offer marvelous cognitive shortcuts because they allow you to act virtually unconsciously and automatically, and thus permit you to handle complicated situations without being paralyzed by needing to think consciously about every little thing. Such scripts enabled me to discern the characteristic hallmarks of problem cases likely to result in recall and to execute a complicated series of steps required to initiate a recall.

All of us structure information all of the time; we could hardly get through the workday without doing so. But there is a penalty to be paid for this wonderful cognitive efficiency: we do not give sufficient attention to important information that requires special treatment because the general information pattern has surface appearances that indicate that automatic processing will suffice. That, I think, is what happened to me. The beginning stages of the Pinto case looked for all the world like a normal sort of problem.

Lurking beneath the cognitive veneer, however, was a nasty set of circumstances waiting to conspire into a dangerous situation. Despite the awful nature of the accidents, the Pinto problem did not fit an existing script; the accidents were relatively rare by recall standards, and the accidents were not initially traceable to a specific component failure. Even when a failure mode suggesting a design flaw was identified, the cars did not perform significantly worse in crash tests than competitor vehicles. One might easily argue that I should have been jolted out of my script by the unusual nature of the accidents (very low speed, otherwise unharmed passengers trapped in a horrific fire), but those facts did not penetrate a script cued for other features. (It also is difficult to convey to the lay person that bad accidents are not a particularly unusual feature of the recall coordinator's information field. Accident severity is not necessarily a recall cue; frequently repeated patterns and identifiable causes are.)

The Corporate Milieu

In addition to the personalized scripting of information processing, there is another important influence on the decisions that led to the Pinto fires mess: the fact that decisions are made by individuals working within a corporate context. It has escaped almost no one's notice that the decisions made by corporate employees tend to be in the best interest of the corporation, even by people who mean to do better. Why? Because the socialization process and the overriding influence of organizational culture provide a strong, if generally subtle, context for defining appropriate ways of seeing and understanding. Because organizational culture can be viewed as a collection of scripts, scripted information processing relates even to organizational-level considerations. Scripts are context bound; they are not free-floating general cognitive structures that apply universally. They are tailored to specific contexts. And there are few more potent contexts than organizational settings.

There is no question that my perspective changed after joining Ford. In retrospect, I would be very surprised if it hadn't. In my former incarnation as a social activist, I had internalized values for doing what was right—as I understood righteousness in grand terms, but I had not internalized a script for applying my values in a pragmatic business context. Ford and the recall coordinator role provided a powerful context for developing scripts—scripts that were inevitably and undeniably oriented toward ways of making sense that were influenced by the corporate and industry culture.

I wanted to do a good job, and I wanted to do what was right. Those are not mutually exclusive desires, but the corporate context affects their synthesis. I came to accept the idea that it was not feasible to fix everything that someone might construe as a problem. I therefore shifted to a value of wanting to do the greatest good for the greatest number (an ethical value tempered by the practical constraints of an economic enterprise). Doing the greatest good for the greatest number meant working with intensity and responsibility on those problems that would spare the most people from injury. It also meant developing scripts that responded to typical problems, not odd patterns like those presented by the Pinto.

Another way of noting how the organizational context so strongly affects individuals is to recognize that one's personal identity becomes heavily influenced by corporate identity. As a student, my identity centered on being a "good person" (with a certain dose of moral righteousness associated with it). As recall coordinator, my identity shifted to a more corporate definition.

This is an extraordinarily important point, especially for students who have not yet held a permanent job role, and I would like to emphasize it. Before assuming your career role, identity derives mainly from social relationships. Upon putting on the mantle of a profession or a responsible position, identity begins to align with your role. And information processing perspective follows from the identity.

I remember accepting the portrayal of the auto industry and Ford as "under attack" from many quarters (oil crises, burgeoning government regulation, inflation, litigious customers, etc.). As we know, groups under assault develop into more cohesive communities that emphasize commonalities and shared identities. I was by then an insider in the industry and the company, sharing some of their beleaguered perceptions that there were significant forces arrayed against us and that the well-being of the company might be threatened.

What happened to the original perception that Ford was a socially irresponsible giant that needed a comeuppance? Well, it looks different from the inside. Over time, a responsible value for action against corporate dominance became tempered by another reasonable value that corporations serve social needs and are not automatically the villains of society. I saw a need for balance among multiple values, and as a result, my identity shifted in degrees toward a more corporate identity.

The Torch Passes to You

So, given my experiences, what would I recommend to you, as a budding organizational decision maker? I have some strong opinions. First, develop your ethical base now! Too many people do not give serious attention to assessing and articulating their own values. People simply do not know what they stand for because they haven't thought about it seriously. Even the ethical scenarios presented in classes or executive programs are treated as interesting little games without apparent implications for deciding how you intend to think or act. These exercises should be used to develop a principled, personal code that you will try to live by. Consciously decide your values. If you don't decide your values now, you are easy prey for others who will gladly decide them for you or influence you implicitly to accept theirs.

Second, recognize that everyone, including you, is an unwitting victim of his or her cognitive structuring. Many people are surprised and fascinated to learn that they use schemas and scripts to understand and act in the organizational world. The idea that we automatically process so much information so much of the time intrigues us. Indeed, we would all turn into blithering idiots if we did not structure information and expectations, but that very structuring hides information that might be important—information that could require you to confront your values. We get lulled into thinking that automatic information processing is great stuff that obviates the necessity for trying to resolve so many frustrating decisional dilemmas.

Actually, I think too much ethical training focuses on supplying standards for contemplating dilemmas. The far greater problem, as I see it, is recognizing that a dilemma exists in the first place. The insidious problem of people not being aware that they are dealing with a situation that might have ethical overtones is another consequence of schema usage. I would venture that scripted routines seldom include ethical dimensions. Is a person behaving unethically if the situation is not even construed as having ethical implications?

People are not necessarily stupid, ill-intentioned, or Machiavellian, but they are often unaware. They do indeed spend much of their time cruising on automatic, but the true hallmark of human information processing is the ability to switch from automatic to controlled information processing. What we really need to do is to encourage people to recognize cues that build a "Now Think!" step into their scripts—waving red flags at yourself, so to speak—even though you are engaged in essentially automatic cognition and action.

Third, because scripts are context bound and organizations are potent contexts, be aware of how strongly, yet how subtly, your job role and your organizational culture affect the ways you interpret and make sense of information (and thus affect the ways you develop the scripts that will guide you in unguarded moments). Organizational culture has a much greater effect on individual cognition than you would ever suspect.

Last, be prepared to face critical responsibility at a relatively young age, as I did. You need to know what your values are and you need to know how you think so that you can know how to make a good decision. Before you can do that, you need to articulate and affirm your values now, before you enter the fray. I wasn't really ready. Are you?

Questions for Discussion

1. The Ford Pinto met federal safety standards, yet it had a design flaw that resulted in serious injuries and deaths. Is simply meeting safety standards a sufficient product design goal of ethical companies?

2. Gioia uses the notion of script schemas to help explain why he voted to not initiate a recall of the Ford Pinto. In your opinion, is this a justifiable explanation?

3. How can organizational context influence the decisions made by organizational members?

4. If you had been in Dennis Gioia's position, what would you have done? Why?

5. Describe the four key decision-making lessons that Dennis Gioia identifies for neophyte decision makers. Discuss how you expect or intend to use these four lessons in your own career.

Sources

The background information of this case was developed from material contained in the following sources:

"Ford Pinto Fuel-Fed Fires." *The Center for Auto Safety,* http://www.autosafety.org/article.php?scid=145&did=522, accessed January 20, 2005.

"Ford Pinto Reckless Homicide Trial." *The History Channel.com,* http://www.historychannel.com/speeches/archive/speech_465.html, accessed January 20, 2005.

Gioia, D.A. (May 1992). Pinto fires and personal ethics: A script analysis of missed opportunities. *Journal of Business Ethics, 11(5, 6),* 379–390.

Notes

1. Badaracco, Jr., J. (1998). A guide to defining moments, the discipline of building character. *Harvard Business Review 76 (2)*, 114.
2. Ibid., 114–115.
3. Ibid., 114–121.
4. Nash, L. (Nov./Dec. 1981). Ethics without the sermon. *Harvard Business Review*, 88.
5. Velasquez, M. G. (1998). *Business Ethics: Concepts and Cases*, 4th ed. Englewood Cliffs, NJ: Prentice Hall.
6. Ibid.
7. Ibid.
8. Mill, J. S. (1957). *Utilitarianism*. Indianapolis: Bobbs-Merrill; Carroll, A. (1993). *Business and Society: Ethics and Stakeholder Management*, 2nd ed. Cincinnati: South-Western; Valesquez, M. G. (1992). *Business Ethics: Concepts and Cases*, 3rd ed. Englewood Cliffs, NJ: Prentice Hall.
9. Brandt, R. (1959). *Ethical Theory*, 253–254. Englewood Cliffs, NJ: Prentice Hall.
10. Smart, J., Williams, B. (1973). *Utilitarianism: For and Against*, 4. Cambridge, England: Cambridge University Press.
11. Delong, J. V., et al. (March/April 1981). Defending cost-benefit analysis: Replies to Steven Kelman. *AEI Journal on Government and Society*, 39–43.
12. Hoffman, W. M., Moore, J. (1990). *Business Ethics: Readings and Cases in Corporate Morality*, 2nd ed. New York: McGraw-Hill.
13. Kelman, S. (January/February 1981). Cost-benefit analysis: An ethical critique. *AEI Journal on Government and Society*, 33–40.
14. Freeman and Gilbert.
15. Kant, I. *Groundwork of the Metaphysics of Morals*. Translated by H. Paton. (1964). New York: Harper & Row.
16. Feldman, F. (1978). *Introductory Ethics*, 119–128. Englewood Cliffs, NJ: Prentice Hall.
17. Tuck, R. (1979). *Natural Rights Theories: Their Origin and Development*. New York: Cambridge University Press; Stoljar, S. (1984). *An Analysis of Rights*. New York: St. Martin's Press; Shue, H. (1981). *Basic Rights*. Princeton, NJ: Princeton University Press; McCloskey, H. (1965). Rights. *The Philosophical Quarterly 15*, 115–127; Wasserstrom, R. (October 29, 1964). Rights, human rights, and racial discrimination. *The Journal of Philosophy 61*, 628–641; Singer, P. (1978). Rights and the market. In Arthur, J., Shaw, W. eds. *Justice and Economic Distribution*, 207–221. Englewood Cliffs, NJ: Prentice Hall; Hart, H. (April 1955). Are there any natural rights? *Philosophical Review 64*, 185; Valesquez, M. (2002). *Business Ethics*, 5th ed. Upper Saddle River, NJ: Prentice Hall.
18. Garrett, T. (1986). *Business Ethics*, 2nd ed., 88–91. Englewood Cliffs, NJ: Prentice Hall.
19. Feinberg, J. (1973). *Social Philosophy*. Englewood Cliffs, NJ: Prentice Hall.
20. Friedman, M. (1962). *Capitalism and Freedom*, 22–36. Chicago, IL: The University of Chicago Press.
21. Ibid.
22. Rawls, J. (1971). *A Theory of Justice*. Cambridge, MA: Harvard University Press.
23. DeGeorge, R. T. (1990). *Business Ethics*, 3rd ed. New York: Macmillan.
24. McMahon, T. (1999). Transforming justice: a conceptualization. *Business Ethics Quarterly, 9(4)*, 593–602.
25. Ibid., 600.
26. McMahon.
27. Hursthouse, R., Zalta, E.N. (ed.). (July 18, 2003), Virtue Ethics. *The Stanford Encyclopedia of Philosophy*, (Fall 2003), http://plato.stanford.edu/archives/fall2003/entries/ethics-virtue/.
28. Ibid.
29. Ibid.
30. Anonymous. Virtue Theory. *The Internet Encyclopedia of Philosophy*, www.worldnewsstand.net/gov/virtue.htm#Louden's%20Critique. This quote is taken from the section "Loudon's Critique," based on Robert Louden's "On some Vices of Virtue Ethics," *American Philosophical Quarterly 21*, 1984.
31. Beauchamp, T., Childress, J. (2002). *Principles of Biomedical Ethics*, 5th ed., Oxford University Press.

32. Steiner, G. A., Steiner, J. F. (2000). *Business, Government, and Society: A Managerial Perspective*, 9th ed. Boston: McGraw-Hill.
33. Freeman, R. E., Gilbert, Jr., D. (1988). *Corporate Strategy and the Search for Ethics*, 36. Englewood Cliffs, NJ: Prentice Hall.
34. Ibid., 39.
35. Based on the ImClone research of Amy Venskus, Master degree student at Bentley College, Waltham, MA, 2004.
36. CBS 60 Minutes. (June 27, 2004). Sam Waskal: I was arrogant. *CBSNews.com*, http://www.cbsnews.com/stories/2003/10/02/60minutes/main576328.shtml.
37. Buono, A. F., Nichols, L. T. (1990). Stockholder and stakeholder interpretations of business' social role. In Hoffman, W. M., Moore, J. *Business Ethics: Readings and Cases in Corporate Morality*, 2nd ed. New York: McGraw-Hill.
38. L. Davis. (1976). Comments on Nozick's entitlement theory. *The Journal of Philosophy*, 73, 839–842.
39. Krolick, S. (1987). *Ethical Decision-Making Style: Survey and Interpretive Notes.* Beverly, MA: Addison-Wesley.
40. Ibid.
41. Krolick, 18.
42. Krolick, 20.
43. Steiner and Steiner; Freeman and Gilbert; Mill; Carroll; Valesquez (1992). Based on Steiner and Steiner, and Carroll.
44. Freeman and Gilbert.

4

The Corporation and External Stakeholders
Managing Moral Responsibility: From the Boardroom to the Marketplace

"100 Best Corporate Citizens for 2004: Companies that Serve a Variety of Stakeholders Well"[1]

Business Ethics, a publishing company, researches and ranks the 100 best corporate citizens each year (beginning in 1999) according to corporations' service to seven stakeholder groups: stockholders, community, minorities and women, employees, environment, non-U.S. stakeholders, and customers. The list is not, as the publishers note, "a certification of flawlessness." In 2004, sixteen firms were pulled from the list because of significant controversies. The top ten socially responsible and ethical companies for 2004 included, in order:

1. Fannie Mae

2. Proctor & Gamble

3. Intel Corporation

4. St. Paul Companies

5. Green Mountain Coffee Roasters Inc.

6. Deere & Company

7. Avon Products, Inc.

8. Hewlett Packard

9. Agilent Technologies

10. Ecolab Inc.

Twenty-nine firms made the list every year from 1999 through 2004. Among those, the following are included in 2004: Intel (No. 3), Avon Products (No. 7), Herman Miller (No. 14), Timberland (No. 17), Cisco Systems (No. 19), Southwest Airlines (No. 22), AT&T (No. 43), Starbucks Coffee (No. 45), Merck (No. 48), and Medtronic (No. 57). Procter & Gamble (headquartered in Cincinnati, Ohio since 1837) has been the most consistent performer, ranking in the top five for five years. Hewlett-Packard has ranked in the top 10 all five years (No. 8 in 2004).

Two other examples of high ranking ethical firms include Ecolab and Deere & Company. Al Schuman, CEO of Ecolab of St. Paul, Minnesota, stated, "We ramped up quickly in response to the Anthrax scare with our Vortexx product, a fungicide, not to make a buck, but because it was the right thing to do." Robert W. Lane, chairman and CEO of Deere & Company said their slogan is, "'No smoke, no mirrors, no tricks: just right down the middle of the field.' That's John Deere."

4.1 MANAGING CORPORATE RESPONSIBILITY: FROM THE BOARDROOM TO THE MARKETPLACE

Managing legal and moral responsibility in the marketplace should begin with the board of directors for public companies and can be a significant part of a corporation's activities. Companies must manage new product risks and potential liabilities as well as successes with their customers—who are also consumers. When products seriously injure consumers, the company is at risk for sizable lawsuits and product boycotts and damage to its image, reputation, name brand loyalty, competitiveness, and even survival.

Managing products and services responsibly requires effective corporate governance and leadership that respects stakeholders' interests. Figure 4.1 illustrates a corporation's major external stakeholders, stakes, and responsibilities. A major stake for corporations is obviously profit. Brand name and reputation are also related dimensions of profitability. It is in a company's long-term interest to create and sustain customer trust by offering safe products, truthfully informing consumers about product content and use, and treating stakeholders ethically, as the lead-in excerpt indicates.

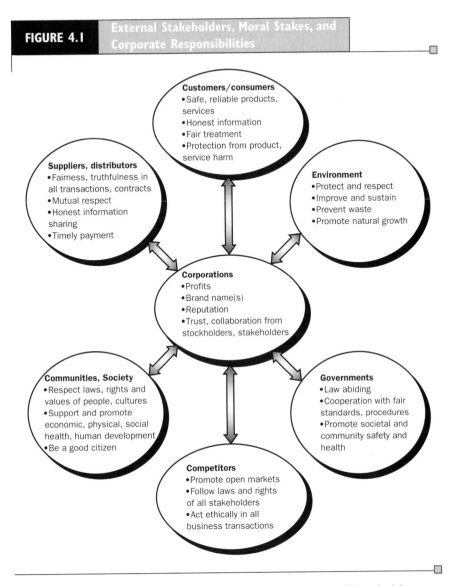

FIGURE 4.1   External Stakeholders, Moral Stakes, and Corporate Responsibilities

Customers/consumers
•Safe, reliable products, services
•Honest information
•Fair treatment
•Protection from product, service harm

Suppliers, distributors
•Fairness, truthfulness in all transactions, contracts
•Mutual respect
•Honest information sharing
•Timely payment

Environment
•Protect and respect
•Improve and sustain
•Prevent waste
•Promote natural growth

Corporations
•Profits
•Brand name(s)
•Reputation
•Trust, collaboration from stockholders, stakeholders

Communities, Society
•Respect laws, rights and values of people, cultures
•Support and promote economic, physical, social health, human development
•Be a good citizen

Governments
•Law abiding
•Cooperation with fair standards, procedures
•Promote societal and community safety and health

Competitors
•Promote open markets
•Follow laws and rights of all stakeholders
•Act ethically in all business transactions

Source: Based on the Caux Round Table's Principles for Business. The principles are printed in *Business Ethics* magazine, 52 S. 10th St. #110, Minneapolis, MN 55403.

Managing Stakeholders Profitably and Responsibly

There are incentives and legal sanctions that guide and constrain corporate leaders and their organizations to act ethically toward shareholders and stakeholders. The Sarbanes-Oxley Act and the revised 1991 Federal Sentencing Guidelines, combined with enforcement of corporate wrongdoers, stabilized a chaotic environment created by Enron and other scandals.[2]

Globalization, the ongoing diffusion of information technology, and the threat of other Enrons also continue to pressure corporate

Who Wants to Work for an Ethical Company?

Are salary, benefits, and career promotion worth more to you than working in an ethical company for responsible leaders and managers with stimulating intellectual opportunities?

A survey conducted by David Montgomery of Stanford and Catherine Ramus of UC Santa Barbara of more than 800 MBAs from 11 major North American and European schools by reported that "the financial package was only 80% as important as intellectual challenge." "Reputation for ethics and caring about employees" was almost 77% as important as the top criterion of "intellectual challenge." More than 97% reported that they would forego important financial benefits to work for an organization that had a better reputation for corporate social responsibility and ethics. MBAs reported a willingness to give up to 14% of their expected income for a company's reputation for ethics and social responsibility.

Career management professionals in 26 countries reported that 82% said corporate leadership ethics was significantly important to job seekers.

QUESTIONS

1. Do you agree or disagree with the results of the MBA survey? Explain.

2. How would you rank the following in order of importance (1 = most important; 4 = least important)?

___ Financial package

___ Ethical reputation of organization

___ Intellectual stimulation of the job

___ Care for employees of leaders and managers

3. Explain your ranking.

Source: Stanford Graduate School of Business Press Release. (July 26, 2004). Stanford Business School study finds MBA graduates want to work for caring and ethical employers.
Ethical Corporation Online,
http://www.csrwire.com/ethicalcorporation/article.cgi/2910.html.

---

competition, along with increasing wider shareholder activism. "The result is that many employees, investors, and consumers are seeking assurances that the goods and services they are producing, financing, or purchasing are not damaging to workers, the environment, or communities by whom and where they are made."[3] There is, consequently, renewed interest in the area of Corporate Social Responsibility (CSR)—i.e., how a business respects and ethically promotes the welfare of its stakeholders and society.[4]

Most executives and professionals are interested in their stakeholders and are law abiding. There is evidence that socially responsible corporations have a competitive advantage in the following areas:

1. Reputation[5]
2. Successful social investment portfolios[6]
3. Ability to attract quality employees[7]

As illustrated in the opening section, the organization Business Ethics ranks the top 100 socially responsible corporations in terms of citizenship, using its own collected data including the Domini 400 Social Index (which also tracks, measures, and publishes information on companies that act socially responsible). The Standard & Poor 500 plus 150 publicly owned companies are ranked on a scale that measures stakeholder ratings. Harris Interactive Inc. and Reputation Institute, a New York-based research group, conducted an online nationwide survey of 10,830 people to identify the companies with the best corporate reputations among Americans at the turn of the millennium.[8] The Reputation Quotient (RQ) is a standardized instrument that measures a company's reputation by examining how the public perceives companies based on 20 positive attributes. For example, emotional appeal; social responsibility; good citizenship in its dealings with communities, employees, and the environment; the quality, innovation, value, and reliability of its products and services; how well the company is managed; how much the company demonstrates a clear vision and strong leadership; and profitability, prospects, and risk.

The executive director of the Reputation Institute noted, "Reputation is much more than an abstract concept; it's a corporate asset that is a magnet to attract customers, employees, and investors."[9] You can score your own company's reputation in the "Rank Your Organization's Reputation" feature.

Rank Your Organization's Reputation

Score a company, college, or university at which you worked or studied on the following characteristics. Be objective. Answer each question based on your experience and what you objectively know about the company (college or university).

1 = very low; 2 = somewhat low; 3 = average; 4 = very good; 5 = excellent

- Emotional appeal of the organization for me _____
- The social responsibility of the organization _____
- The organization's treatment of employees, community, and environment _____

- The quality, innovation, value, and reliability of the organization's products and/or services _____

- The clarity of vision and strength of the organization's leadership _____

- The organization's profitability, prospects in its market, and handling of risks _____

- Total your score _____

Interpretation: Consider 30 a perfect score; 24 very good; 18 average; 12 low; and 6 very low.

1. How did your company do on the ranking? Explain.

2. Explain your scoring on each item; that is, give the specific reasons that led you to score your company on each item as you did.

3. Suggest specific actions your organization could take to increase its Reputation Quotient.

4.2 MANAGING CORPORATE RESPONSIBILITY WITH EXTERNAL STAKEHOLDERS

The Corporation as Social and Economic Stakeholder   The stakeholder management approach views the corporation as a legal entity and also as a collective of individuals and groups. The CEO and top-level managers are hired to maximize profits for the owners and shareholders. The board of directors is responsible for overseeing the direction, strategy, and accountability of the officers and the firm. To accomplish this, corporations must respond to a variety of stakeholders' needs, rights, and legitimate demands. From this perspective, the corporation has primary obligations to the economic mandates of its owners; however, to survive and succeed, it must also respond to legal, social, political, and environmental claims from stakeholders.

One study argued that "Using corporate resources for social issues not related to primary stakeholders may not create value for shareholders."[10] This finding does not suggest that corporations refrain from philanthropic activities; rather, "The emphasis on shareholder value creation today should not be construed as coming at the expense of the interests of other primary stakeholders."[11] Corporations are economic and social stakeholders. This is not a contradiction but a leadership choice that requires balancing economic and moral priorities.

The Social Contract   The stakeholder management approach of the corporation is grounded in the concept of a social contract. Developed by early political philosophers, a social contract is a set of rules and assumptions about behavior patterns among the various elements of society. Much of the social contract is embedded in the customs of society. Some of the "contract provisions" result from practices between parties. Like a legal contract, the social contract often involves a quid pro quo (something for something) exchange. Although globalization, massive downsizing, and related corporate practices continue to pressure many employer–employee relationships, the underlying principles of the social contract, like mutual trust and collaboration, remain essential.

The social contract between a corporation and its stakeholders is often based on implicit as well as explicit agreements. For example, it is argued that the success of many businesses is directly related to the public's confidence in those businesses. A loss of public confidence can be detrimental to the firm and to its investors. One way to retain and to reinforce public confidence is by acting in an ethical manner, a manner that shows a concern for the investing public and the customers of the firm.[12]

Balance between Ethical Motivation and Compliance

Ethics programs, as part of the social contract, are essential motivators in organizations. Studies suggest that ethics programs matter more than compliance programs on several dimensions of ethics: e.g., awareness of issues, search for advice, reporting violations, decision-making, and commitment to the firm.[13] Business relationships based on mutual trust and ethical principles combined with regulation result in long-term economic gains for organizations, shareholders, and stakeholders.[14] If corporate leaders and their firms commit illegal acts, taxpayers end up paying these costs. Corporate leaders and their stakeholders therefore have an interest in supporting their implicit social contract as well as their legally binding obligations.

There is a balance to be maintained between external regulation and self-regulation based on the public's trust in corporations. An *ABC News/Washington Post* poll found among those surveyed that 63% believe regulation of companies "is necessary to protect the public" (up 10 points from their 2000 survey). Thirty percent reported that regulation "does more harm than good," down 10 points from the 2000 survey. The poll also found that "From Enron to WorldCom, it's been broadly assumed that the recent scandals have shaken confidence in corporate America. In fact such confidence, although low, is no lower than usual. Only 23% of Americans express confidence in business corporations; 75% don't. That's about the same as it was 10 and even 20 years ago."[15]

Covenantal Ethic   The *covenantal ethic* concept is related to the social contract and is also central to a stakeholder management approach.

The covenantal ethic focuses on the importance of *relationships*—social as well as economic—between businesses, customers, and stakeholders. Relationships and social contracts (or covenants) between corporate managers and customers embody a "seller must care" attitude, not only "buyer beware."[16] A manager's understanding of problems is measured not only over the short term, in view of concrete products, specific cost reductions, or even balance sheets (though obviously important to a company's results), but also over the long term, in view of the quality of relationships that are created and sustained by business activity.[17]

The Moral Basis and Social Power of Corporations as Stakeholders

Keith Davis argues that the social responsibility of corporations is based on social power, and that "if a business has the power, then a just relationship demands that business also bear responsibility for its actions in these areas." He termed this view the "iron law of responsibility." "[I]n the long run, those who do not use power in a manner in which society considers responsible will tend to lose it." Davis discusses five broad guidelines or obligations business professionals should follow to be socially responsible:

1. Businesses have a social role of "trustee for society's resources." Since society entrusts businesses with its resources, businesses must wisely serve the interests of all their stakeholders, not just those of owners, consumers, or labor.

2. Business shall operate as a two-way open system with open receipt of inputs from society and open disclosure of its operations to the public.

3. "Social costs as well as benefits of an activity, product, or service shall be thoroughly calculated and considered in order to decide whether to proceed with it." Technical and economic criteria must be supplemented with the social effects of business activities, goods, or services before a company proceeds.

4. The social costs of each activity, product, or service shall be priced into it so that the consumer (user) pays for the effects of his consumption on society.

5. Business institutions as citizens have responsibilities for social involvement in areas of their competence where major social needs exist.[18]

These five guidelines provide a foundation for creating and reviewing the moral bases of corporate stakeholder relationships. The public is intolerant of corporations that abuse this mutual trust as recent surveys show. For example,

- 91% of the public surveyed would consider doing business with another company.
- 85% would tell family and friends about the company.
- 83% would not purchase that company's stock.
- 80% would not be employed at the company.
- 76% would boycott the company's services and products.
- 68% would not be as loyal to a job or employment at the company.[19]

Corporate Philanthropy   A corporation's social responsibility also includes philanthropic responsibilities in addition to its economic, legal, and ethical obligations. Corporate philanthropy is an important part of a company's role as "good citizen" at the global, national, and local levels. The public expects, but does not require, corporations to contribute and "give back" to the communities that support their operations. Procter & Gamble's reputation has been enhanced by its global contributions. Some of the largest corporate philanthropists include Ted Turner of Time Warner, who has given $1 billion to the United Nations; Bill Gates of Microsoft has provided $100 million to control AIDS/HIV in India; Kathryn Albertson of Albertson's Grocery has contributed in excess of $600 million to support public education in Idaho; and George Soros, the preeminent global investor, has donated more than $525 million to assist Russian health and education programs and U.S. drug and education programs.[20] Although corporate social responsibility and values-based, principled leadership are necessary elements for sustaining ethical stakeholder business relationships, effective regulation and strong corporate governance are also required.

4.3 MANAGING THE LEGAL ENVIRONMENT: CORPORATE GOVERNANCE AND REGULATION

Reforming Corporate Boards of Directors

Even though a majority of Enron's board was made up of "outside" directors—meaning directors not in Enron's management—a stunning 10 of the 15 outside directors had conflicts of interest including contracts with Enron, common bonds to charities, and memberships on the boards of other companies doing business with Enron.

The flagrant failure of Enron's board of directors is a warning we must heed. The more than 100 million people whom we call the new investor class, those middle-class Americans who entered the market in the 1990s, were shaken by the scandals. Investors are asking: If the distinguished Enron board failed so utterly in this case, how many other boards might be negligent?[21]

Corporations effectively govern themselves, to a large extent, through their own control systems and stakeholder relationships. A public corporation's federal and state charter provide the legal basis for its board of directors, stockholders, and officers to govern and operate the company.[22] As Enron and other corporate scandals demonstrated, self-governance does not always work well. A question often repeated from the scandals was, "Where were the boards of directors when the widespread fraud, deception, and abuse of power occurred?"

There are a number of reasons cited why many of the larger, prominent corporate boards of directors did not execute their mandated legal and ethical responsibilities including lack of independence, insider roles and relationships, conflicts of interest, overlapping memberships of board members with other boards, decision-by-committees, well-paid members with few responsibilities, and lack of financial expertise and knowledge about how companies really operate.[23]

A *Forbes* magazine study ranked 194 companies in stock performance over the past six years relative to their industry averages and ranked "best and worst" performing companies. The study also identified average corporate board director pay at the "best and worst" ranked companies. (See Figure 4.2 on board ranking by company.) Outside directors from the five worst ranked boards earned 1.6 times what outside directors did at the five highest ranked companies—average board pay was $69,887. One conclusion from the study was that highly paid board members were less likely to challenge the CEO who hired them. Less well-paid board members were more likely to be bolder in their roles and legal assignments, "which is to make demands on the chief executive and fire him if he doesn't deliver."[24]

The Sarbanes-Oxley Act of 2002 defines several reforms aimed at improving many of the problems of boards discussed previously. There are other "best practices" guidelines for boards, including:

1. Separating the role of chairman of the board when the CEO is also a board member

2. Setting tenure rules for board members

3. Regularly evaluating itself and the CEO's performance

4. Prohibiting directors from serving as consultants to the companies which they serve

5. Compensating directors with both cash and stock

FIGURE 4.2	Best and Worst Performing CEO's Company Boards	
Best-Performing CEO's Boards	**Number of Outside Directors**	
Amazon.com	6	
New York Community Bancorp	6	
L-3 Communications	6	
Commerce Bancorp	10	
Paccar	7	
Worst Performing CEO's Boards		
Masco	6	
Hilton Hotels	11	
Walt Disney	10	
Eli Lilly	10	
Textron	14	

Source: Neil Weinberg, "Blame the Board," *Forbes Magazine,* May 10, 2004, http://www.forbes.com/free_forbes/2004/0510/120.html.

6. Prohibiting retired CEOs from continuing board membership

7. Assigning independent directors to the majority of members who meet periodically without the CEO[25]

Roles and responsibilities of CEOs and organizational leaders are discussed in the following chapter.

Corporate Oversight and Regulation

Government at the federal, state, and local levels also regulates corporations through laws, administrative procedures, enforcement agencies, and courts. Regulation by the government is necessary in part because of failures in the free-market system. There are also power imbalances between corporations, individual consumers, and citizens. Individual citizens and groups in society need a higher authority to represent and protect their interests and the public good.[26]

The role of laws and the legal regulatory system governing business serves five purposes:

1. Regulate competition

2. Protect consumers

3. Promote equity and safety

4. Protect the natural environment

5. Ethics and compliance programs to deter and provide for enforcement against misconduct[27]

Corporate Scandals

Corporate scandals exemplify a failure of internal corporate governance and self-regulation by all parties involved and can be caused by individual leaders' greed, ineffective boards, all of which are part of the free-market system. Corporate scandals also cannot be initiated and sustained without the direct or indirect assistance and/or negligence from the SEC (Security Exchange Commission), banks, investment traders and managers, media, Wall Street, federal legislators, and other players.[28] Starting with Enron and followed by WorldCom, Qwest, Tyco, HealthSouth, and others, more than $7 trillion in stock market losses were accrued. These losses also cost American employees and families more than 30% of their retirement savings.[29] A quick summary illustrates the aftermath of some of the major scandals.

- Enron Corporation: Former chairman and CEO Ken Lay pleaded not guilty to charges that he was involved in a plan to deceive the public, company shareholders, and government regulators. Jeffrey Skilling, a former executive, pleaded not guilty to fraud, conspiracy, insider trading, and other federal counts. The former CFO, Andrew Fastow, pleaded guilty to two counts of conspiracy and agreed to cooperate with prosecutors.

- WorldCom Inc.: Bernard Ebbers, former CEO, pleaded not guilty to fraud and conspiracy charges for allegedly leading an accounting fraud estimated at more than $11 billion. Scott Sullivan, former CFO, pleaded guilty to fraud charges and will testify against Ebbers.

- Tyco International Ltd.: Former CEO Dennis Kozlowski and CFO Mark Swartz were accused of stealing $600 million from the company. A New York state judge declared a mistrial in the case because of pressure on a jury member. A retrial is scheduled in 2005. Larceny charges are being considered against Mark Belnick, the former Tyco lawyer.

- Adelphia Communications Corporation: Founder John Rigas and his son Timothy were convicted of conspiracy and bank and securities fraud. Rigas' other son Michael was acquitted of conspiracy charges.

- Credit Suisse First Boston: Frank Quattrone, former investment banking executive, was convicted of obstruction of justice. His first trial in 2003 ended in a hung jury. Quattrone, who made millions helping Internet companies go public during the dot-com boom, may be sentenced to a year or more prison time.

- HealthSouth Corporation: Former CEO Richard Scrushy was federally charged with leading a multibillion-dollar scheme that inflated HealthSouth earnings to show the company was meeting Wall Street forecasts. Sixteen former HealthSouth executives were charged as part of a conspiracy to inflate company earnings. Scrushy is the only executive who has not pleaded guilty and is not cooperating with investigators.

- Martha Stewart, founder of Martha Stewart Living Omnimedia, was convicted of conspiracy, obstruction of justice, and lying about her personal sale of ImClone Systems shares. She was refused a new trial on perjury charges against a government witness. Stewart was sentenced to five months in prison. Her broker, Peter Bacanovic, was fined $2,000.

- Qwest Communications International Inc.: Denver Federal prosecutors did not win a conviction against any of four former mid-level executives accused of scheming to deceptively book $34 million in revenue for the company. Grant Graham, former chief financial officer for Qwest's global business unit; Bryan Treadway, a former assistant controller; Thomas Hall, a former senior vice president; and John Walker, a former vice president, each faced 11 charges of conspiracy, securities fraud, wire fraud, and making false statements to auditors.[30]

The "Carrot" or "Stick" Approach: Which Works Best?

Which is more effective at influencing legal and ethical behavior in organizations, the carrot (voluntary corporate ethics programs) or the stick (legal compliance programs)? Studies show that a combination of external regulations, compliance standards, and a company's ethics programs can be effective in preventing and deterring immoral and illegal activities.[31] The 2002 Sarbanes-Oxley Act, however, was a direct regulatory response by Congress to corporate scandals. (PricewaterhouseCoopers called this law the most important legislation affecting corporate governance, financial disclosure, and public accounting practice since the 1930s.)[32] A summary of the Sarbanes-Oxley Act shows that federal provisions were established to provide oversight, accountability, and enforcement of truthful and accurate financial reporting in public firms.

Sarbanes-Oxley Act   Following is a summary of key sections of the Sarbanes-Oxley Act:

- Establishes an independent public company accounting board to oversee audits of public companies

- Requires one member of the audit committee to be an expert in finance

- Requires full disclosure to stockholders of complex financial transactions

- Requires CEOs and CFOs to certify in writing the validity of their companies' financial statements. If they knowingly certify false statements, they can go to prison for 20 years and be fined $5 million.

- Prohibits accounting firms from offering other services, like consulting, while also performing audits. This constitutes a conflict of interest.

- Requires ethics codes, registered with the Securities and Exchange Commission (SEC), for financial officers

- Provides a 10-year penalty for wire and mail fraud

- Requires mutual fund professionals to disclose their vote on shareholder proxies, enabling investors to know how their stocks influence decisions

- Provides whistle-blower protection for individuals who report wrongful activities to authorities

- Requires attorneys of companies to disclose wrongdoing to senior officers and to the board of directors, if necessary; attorneys should stop working for the companies if senior managers ignore reports of wrongdoing.[33]

Pros and Cons of Implementing the Sarbanes-Oxley Act

Critics of Sarbanes-Oxley argue against the implementation and maintenance of the law for the following reasons:

1. **It is too costly.** One estimate from a survey by Financial Executives International stated that firms with $5 billion in revenue could expect to spend on average $4.7 million implementing the internal controls required, then $1.5 million annually to maintain compliance.[34]

2. **It impacts negatively on a firm's global competitiveness.** This argument is also based on the costs of keeping internal operations compliant with the act. Critics argue that other companies around the globe do not have this expense, so why should U.S. public firms?

3. **Government costs also increase to regulate the law.** The SEC receives tips about possible violations of securities laws through its e-mail complaint service (http://www.sec.

gov/complaint.shtml). Complaints jumped from 77,000 in 2001 to 180,000 in 2003. "The SEC received nearly 250,000 complaints this year. More than 1,300 e-mail complaints arrive each day," John Stark of the SEC's enforcement division said. The majority tend to be tips about accounting problems at public companies.[35]

4. **CFOs are overburdened and pressured by having to enforce and assume accountability required by the law.** A survey by *CFO* magazine found that since 2001, "one-fifth of financial executives said they felt more pressure to use tricky accounting methods to 'make results appear more favorable.' Half felt there was the exact same amount of pressure as there was three years ago, before regulators supposedly cracked down."[36]

5. **An exodus will occur of public companies returning to private ownership.** Critics claim that implementing Sarbanes-Oxley requirements throughout an organization is too costly and wasteful for small and mid-sized firms wishing to go public.

Paul Volcker and Arthur Levitt, two widely respected experts from the SEC and Federal Reserve respectively, offered the following counterclaims to some of the previous criticisms[37]:

1. **The costs of implementing Sarbanes-Oxley are minimal compared to the costs of not having it**—recall the $7 trillion in stock losses alone, not counting the damage done to employee families and effects on the economy at large.

2. **The changes required to implement this law are difficult;** however, a recent *Corporate Board Member* magazine survey that found more than 60% of 153 directors of corporate boards of directors believe the effect of Sarbanes-Oxley has been positive for their firms, and that more than 70% viewed the law as also positive for their boards.[38]

3. **The data does not support the argument that this law presents a competitive disadvantage to global firms.** The NASDAQ stock exchange has added six international listings in the second quarter of 2004. A recent survey by Broadgate Capital Advisors and the Value Alliance found that only 8% of 143 foreign companies that issue stocks that trade in the United States claimed that Sarbanes-Oxley would cause them to rethink entering the U.S. market.[39]

4. If a company uses the Sarbanes-Oxley Act as a reason to not go public, **the firm should not go public or use**

investors' funds. U.S. markets are among the most admired in the world because they are the best regulated.

5. **Financial officers who complain about the require-ments of Sarbanes-Oxley may in fact be suffering from the lack of internal controls they had before.** In 2003, 57 companies of all sizes said they had material weaknesses in their controls, after their auditors, who were paid to test financial controls, were terminated. These same auditors decreased their testing of internal controls because they faced pressures to cut their fees.

The costs and benefits of implementing Sarbanes-Oxley continue to be debated. Still, Paul Volcker and Arthur Levitt argue that, "While there are direct money costs involved in compliance, we believe that an investment in good corporate governance, professional integrity, and transparency will pay dividends in the form of investor confidence, more efficient markets, and more market participation for years to come."[40]

Revised 1991 Federal Sentencing Guidelines   Before the 2002 Sarbanes-Oxley Act, the 1991 Federal Sentencing Guidelines were passed to help federal judges set and mitigate sentences and fines in companies that had a few "bad apples" who had committed serious crimes. The guidelines were also designed to alleviate sentences on companies that had ethics and compliance programs. Under these guidelines, a corporation (large or small) receives a lighter sentence and/or fine—or perhaps no sentence or probation—if convicted of a federal crime, provided that the firm's ethics and compliance programs were judged to be "effective." The guidelines changed the view of cor-porations as entities that were legally liable and punishable for criminal acts committed within their boundaries to the view of the corporation as a moral agent responsible for the behavior of its employees. As a moral agent, the corporation could be evaluated and judged on how effective the leaders, culture, and ethics training programs were toward preventing misconduct and crime.[41]

1991 Original Seven Criteria of the Revised Guidelines

Companies that acted to prevent unethical and criminal acts would, under the guidelines, be given special consideration by judges when being fined or sentenced. A point system was established to help mitigate the fine and/or sentence if the company displayed the fol-lowing seven criteria:

1. Established standards and procedures capable of reducing the chances of criminal conduct

2. Appointment of compliance officer(s) to oversee plans

3. Took due care not to delegate substantial discretionary authority to individuals who are likely to engage in criminal conduct

4. Established steps to effectively communicate the organization's standards and procedures to all employees

5. Took steps to ensure compliance through monitoring and auditing

6. Employed consistent disciplinary mechanisms

7. When an offense was detected, took steps to prevent future offenses, including modifying the compliance plan, if appropriate.[42]

The guidelines have been revised to reflect the post-Enron corporate environment. The revisions add specificity to the 1991 version, include top-level officers' accountability, and attempt to increase the effectiveness and integration of a company's ethics and compliance programs with its culture and operations. Ed Petry, Director of the Ethics Officer Association (EOA), served on the federal committee that revised the guidelines. Petry summarized some of the prominent revisions to the guidelines as follows[43]:

- Compliance and Ethics Programs (C&EP) are now described in a stand-alone guideline.

- The connection between effective compliance and ethical conduct is stressed.

- Organizations are required to "promote an organizational culture that encourages ethical conduct and a commitment to compliance with the law."

Together, the Sarbanes-Oxley Act of 2002 and the 2004 Revised Federal Sentencing Guidelines serve as constraints and deterrents to immoral and criminal corporate conduct that ultimately affects stakeholders and stockholders.

In the next section, we examine how well corporations have managed corporate crises in the past. A number of questions are addressed:

4.4 MANAGING EXTERNAL ISSUES, CONFLICTS, AND CRISES

Companies have made serious mistakes as the result of poor self-regulation. As several of the now-classic environmental and product- and consumer-related crises illustrate, corporations have responded and reacted slowly and many times insensitively to customers and other stakeholders. The Internet may decrease the time executives have to respond to potential and actual crises.[44]

It is important to review some of the major crises from the 1970s to the present, since several of these are only now being resolved. Also, these cases serve to remind corporate leaders and the public that there is a balance between legal regulation and corporate self-regulation. When corporations fail to regulate themselves and to provide just and fair corrective actions to their failures, government assistance is needed.

We noted in Chapter 2 that issues and crisis management should be part of a company's management strategy and planning process. Failure to effectively anticipate and respond to serious issues that erupt into crises has been as damaging to companies as the crises. The Exxon Valdez oil spill and the Manville Corporation's asbestos crisis are summarized in the feature boxes on the following pages. The insightful reflections and lessons of Dennis Gioia, Ford's vehicle recall coordinator during the infamous Ford Pinto disaster, is presented at the end of Chapter 3. A sample of other crises includes the following[45]:

- In June 2001, Katsuhiko Kawasoe, Mitsubishi Motor Company's president, apologized for that firm's 20-year cover-up of consumer safety complaints. (The company also agreed in 1998 to pay $34 million to settle 300 sexual harassment lawsuits filed by women in its Normal, Illinois plant. This is one of the largest sexual harassment settlements in U.S. history.)

- By the end of 2001, the American Home Products Corporation paid more than $11.2 billion to settle about 50,000 consumer lawsuits related to the fen-phen diet drug combination. In addition, the company put aside $1 billion to cover future medical checkups for former fen-phen users and $2.35 billion to settle individual suits.

- Between 1971 and 1974, more than 5,000 product liability lawsuits were filed by women who had suffered severe gynecological damage from A. H. Robins Company's Dalkon Shield, an intrauterine contraceptive device. Although the company never recalled its product, it paid more than $314 million to settle 8,300 lawsuits. It also established a $1.75 billion trust to settle ongoing claims. The firm avoided its responsibility toward its customers by not considering a recall for nine years after the problem was known.

- Procter & Gamble's Rely tampon was pulled from the market in 1980 after 25 deaths were allegedly associated with toxic shock syndrome caused by tampon use.

- Firestone's problems first came to light in 1978, when the Center for Auto Safety said it had reports that Firestone's steel-belted radial TPC 500 tire was responsible for 15 deaths and 12 injuries.

In October 1978, after attacking the publicity this product received, Firestone executives recalled 10 million of the 500-series tires. Firestone recently paid $7.5 million in addition to $350,000 to settle the first case in the Bridgestone/Firestone-Ford Explorer crisis. Two hundred injury and death suits have been settled since the recall, and $50 million is estimated to settle the lawsuits.

- A federal bankruptcy judge approved Dow Corning Corporation's $4.5 billion reorganization plan, with $3.2 billion to be used to settle claims from recipients of the company's silicone gel breast implants and the other $1.3 billion to be paid to its commercial creditors. A jury had already awarded $7.3 million to one woman whose implant burst, causing her illness. The company is alleged to have rushed the product to market in 1975 without completing proper safety tests and to have misled plastic surgeons about the potential for silicone to leak out of the surgically implanted devices. More than 600,000 implants were subsequently performed.

Johns-Manville Corporation: Asbestos Legacy

"'They'll be following in our footsteps,' said Robert A. Falise, chairman of the Manville Personal Injury Settlement Trust, which was created by the bankruptcy court to ensure a steady source of money to pay claims filed against Johns-Manville by workers exposed to asbestos in their workplaces."[1] The company will be responding to outstanding claims by asbestos victims and their families for several decades. In June 2000, the company was sold to Warren Buffett for $1.9 billion in cash and the assumption of $300 million in debt. The asbestos-related trust, created to pay claimants, received $1.5 billion. As of March 2001, the trust had paid more than $2.5 billion to 350,000 beneficiaries. There are still more than a half million claimants and another half million expected to file. Looking backward, reviews of Manville's social responsibility management of the complex web of issues surrounding its asbestos production are mixed.

Asbestosis, mesothelioma, and lung cancer—all life-threatening diseases—share a common cause: inhalation of microscopic particles of asbestos over an extended period of time. The link between these diseases and enough inhaled asbestos particles is a medical fact. Manville Corporation is a multinational mining and forest product manufacturer, and it was a leading commercial producer of asbestos. As of March 1977, 271 asbestos-related damages suits were filed against the firm by workers. The victims claimed the company did not warn them of the life-threatening dangers of asbestos. Since 1968, Manville has paid more than $2.5 billion in such claims. And since the 1950s, Manville has faced hundreds of lawsuits from workers: Their estimated value is more than $1 billion. By 1982, Manville faced more than 500 new asbestos lawsuits filed each month. Consequently, in August 1982, Manville filed for Chapter 11 bankruptcy in order to reorganize and remain solvent in the face of the lawsuits; the firm was losing more than half the cases that reached trial. The reorganization was approved, and Manville set up a $2.5 billion trust fund to pay asbestos claimants. Shareholders surrendered half their value in stock, and it was agreed that projected earnings over 25 years would be reduced to support the trust.

Manville devised a settlement that gave the Manville Personal Injury Settlement Trust enough cash to continue meeting claims filed by asbestos victims. Under the settlement, the building products division stated it would give the trust 20% of Manville's stock and would pay a special $772 million dividend in exchange for the trust's releasing its right to receive 20% of Manville's profits. After the transaction, the trust would own 80% of Manville and have $1.2 billion in cash and marketable securities, plus $2.3 billion in assets. This transaction enabled Manville to rectify its balance sheet. Also, it changed its name to Schuller Corporation.

After Manville spent several years operating under Chapter 11 of the U.S. Bankruptcy Code, the company emerged with $850 million in cash, 50% of its common stock, a claim on 20% of the company's consolidated profits, and bonds with a face value of $1.3 billion. The trust is expected to pay 10% of an estimated $18 billion in present and future asbestos claims to 275,000 victims who already have filed claims.[2]

The extent of Manville's social responsibility toward its workers, the litigants, the communities it serves, and society has, at best, been uneven. Manville, since 1972, has been active and cooperative with the U.S. Department of Labor and the AFL/CIO in developing standards to protect asbestos workers. However, Dr. Kenneth Smith—the medical director of one of the firm's plants in Canada—refused in the 1970s to inform Manville workers that they had asbestosis.

There is also the complication and confusion of evolving and changing legislation on asbestos. The U.S. Supreme Court, as stakeholder, has not taken a stand on who is liable in these situations: Are insurance firms liable when workers are initially exposed to asbestos and later develop cancer, or are they liable 20 years later? Also, right-to-know laws are not definitive in state legislatures. Does that leave Manville and other corporations liable for government's legal indecision?

Of the original 16,500 personal injury plaintiffs, 2,000 have died since the reorganization in 1982. With Warren Buffet's purchase of the company and the asbestos trust solidified, the management of this issue for the company is over.

Note that companies continue to settle asbestos lawsuits. The *Mesothelioma Reporter* Web site (http://www.mesotheliomareporter. org/lawsuits/) tracks and reports these settlements. For example, a recent settlement was reported for Pfizer, subsidiary Quigley Co., and others who were defendants at a trial "that alleged that they caused personal injury by exposure to asbestos. The asbestos sometimes caused mesothelioma." That Web site reported that *ABC News* stated that "Pfizer will establish a trust for the payment of pending claims as well as any future claims. It will contribute $405 million to the trust over 40 years through a note, and about $100 million in insurance. Pfizer will also forgive a $30 million loan to Quigley."[3] As with other corporate crises, the aftermath continues.

Notes

1. Gross, D. (April 29, 2001). Recovery lessons from an industrial phoenix. *New York Times*, 3, 4.
2. Tejada, C. (1996). Manville settlement gives trust enough cash for asbestos claims. *Wall Street Journal*.
3. Pfizer to pay $430 million to settle asbestos claims. (September 3, 2004), *The Mesothelioma Reporter*.

QUESTIONS

1. Should asbestos victims' claims be the liability of Manville or of the decision makers who authorized the work policies and orders?

2. Who was or is to blame for the asbestos-related deaths and injuries in the Manville case?

3. Is the declaration of Chapter 11 bankruptcy and the creation of a trust the best or only solution in this case? Who wins and who loses with this type of settlement? Why?

4. What ethical principle(s) did Manville's owners and officers use regarding this type of settlement? What principle(s) do you believe they should have used? Explain.

Exxon Valdez: Worst Oil Spill in United States History

"A year after the Exxon Valdez ripped open its bottom on Bligh Reef [off the Alaskan coast] and dumped 11 million gallons of crude oil, the nation's worst oil spill is not over. Like major spills in the past, this unnatural disaster sparked a frenzy of reactions: congressional hearings, state and federal legislative proposals for new preventive measures, dozens of studies, and innumerable lawsuits."[1] The grounding of the tanker on March 24, 1989, spread oil over more than 700 miles. Oil covered 1,300 miles of coastline and killed 250,000 birds, 2,800 sea otters, 300 seals, 250 bald eagles, and billions of salmon and herring eggs, according to the Exxon Valdez Oil Spill Trustee Council, which manages Exxon settlement money.

More controversial was Exxon's failure to pay the $5 billion in assessed damages.[2] A grand jury indicted Exxon in February 1990. At that time, the firm faced fines totaling more than $600 million if convicted on the felony counts. More than 150 lawsuits and 30,000 damage claims were reportedly filed against Exxon, and most were not settled by July 1991, when Exxon made a secret agreement with seven Seattle fish processors. Under the arrangement, Exxon agreed to pay $70 million to settle the processors' oil-spill claims against Exxon. However, in return for the relatively quick settlement of those claims, the processors agreed to return to Exxon most of any punitive damages they might be awarded in later Exxon spill-related cases. Exxon paid about $300 million in damages claims in the first few years after the spill. However, "lawyers for people who had been harmed called that a mere down payment on losses that averaged more than $200,000 per fisherman from 1990 to 1994."[3]

The charge that the captain of the Valdez, Joseph Hazelwood, had a blood-alcohol content above 0.04 percent was dropped, but he was convicted of negligently discharging oil and ordered to pay $50,000 as restitution to the state of Alaska and to serve 1,000 hours cleaning up the beaches over five years.[4] Exxon executives and stockholders have been embroiled with courts, environmental groups, the media, and public groups over the crisis. Exxon has paid $300 million to date in nonpunitive damages to 10,000 commercial fishers, business owners, and native Alaskan villages.

In 1996, a grand jury ordered Exxon to pay $5 billion in punitive damages to the victims of the 1989 oil spill. At the time the fish processors had entered the secret agreement with Exxon, they did not know the Alaskan jury would slap the company with the $5 billion punitive damages award. One of the judges claimed that had the jury known about this secret agreement, it would have charged Exxon even more punitive damages.[5] As of 2001, Exxon has not paid any of these damages. It is also estimated that with Exxon's reported rate of return on its investments, it makes $800 million every year on the $5 billion it does not pay. By 2002, the company will make back the $5 billion it refuses to pay with accrued interest.[6] Brian O'Neill, the Minneapolis lawyer who represents 60,000 plaintiffs in the suit against Exxon, stated,

"I have had thousands of clients that have gone bankrupt, got divorced, died, or been down on their financial luck" while waiting for the settlement.[7] In the meantime, Captain Hazelwood continues to pick up trash on Alaska state lands. And the November 2001 federal appeals court ruling opens the way for a judge to reduce the $5 billion punitive verdict. (However, the 1994 jury award of $287 million to compensate commercial fishers was not reduced.)[8]

Recently, the Environmental News Network (ENN) reported that local residents and several government scientists are still at odds on "whether Exxon Mobil Corporation should be forced to pay an additional civil penalty for the spill." The sources continue, "The landmark $900 million civil settlement Exxon signed in 1991 to resolve federal and state environmental claims included a $100 million re-opener clause for damages that 'could not reasonably have been known' or anticipated. Under the settlement terms, the re-opener may be asserted until 2006."[9]

Hosmer, a noted ethicist, stated:

The most basic lesson in accident prevention that can be drawn from the wreck of the Exxon Valdez is that management is much more than just looking at revenues, costs, and profits. Management requires the imagination to understand the full mixture of potential benefits and harms generated by the operations of the firm, the empathy to consider the full range of legitimate interests represented by the constituencies of the firm, and the courage to act when some of the harms are not certain and many of the constituencies are not powerful. The lack of imagination, empathy, and courage at the most senior levels of the company was the true cause of the wreck of the Exxon Valdez.[10]

Notes

1. Dumanoski, D. (April 2, 1990). One year later—The lessons of Valdez. *Boston Globe*, 29.

2. Allen, S. (March 7, 1999). Deep problems 10 years after Exxon Valdez/Worst oil spill in US has lingering effects for Alaska, industries. *Wall Street Journal*, A1.

3. Ibid.

4. See the following website for resources regarding the aftermath and information on the Exxon Valdez crisis: http://library.thinkquest.org/10867/research/online-sources.shtml.

5. McCoy, C. (June 13, 1996). Exxon's secret Valdez deals anger judge. *Wall Street Journal*, A3.

6. Rawkins, R. (Feb. 28, 1990). U.S. indicts Exxon in oil spill. *Miami Herald*, 5.

7. See note 4 above.

8. Associated Press. Exxon Valdez fine excessive, court says. (Nov. 8, 2001). *USA Today*, 6A.

9. Rosen, Y. (March 24, 2004). Exxon penalties could rise as Valdez oil lingers. *Environmental News Network* online web resource.

10. Hosmer, L. (1998). Lessons from the wreck of the Exxon Valdez: The need for imagination, empathy, and courage. *Business Ethics Quarterly*, 122.

QUESTIONS

1. Should Exxon's officers and lawyers pay the $5 billion in punitive damages to settle this case? Why or why not?

2. Should Captain Hazelwood have been convicted of criminal drunkenness in this case? If so, how would that have changed the outcome of the settlement? If not, why?

3. Has Captain Hazelwood settled his "debt" in this case by agreeing to serve 1,000 hours in cleanup time in Alaska? Explain.

4. Describe Exxon's ethics toward this disaster.

5. What should be done now, if anything, and who should do it to settle this case?

6. Respond to Hosmer's statement. Do you believe this sentiment applies to all responsibilities of senior executives in corporations; that is, do they need to show imagination, empathy, and courage toward all their constituencies? Explain your answer.

4.5 CORPORATE RESPONSIBILITY TOWARD CONSUMER STAKEHOLDERS

Consumers may be the most important stakeholders of a business. If consumers do not buy, commercial businesses cease to exist. Consumer confidence and spending also are important indicators of economic activity as well as of business prosperity. Consumer interests should be foremost when businesses are designing, delivering, and servicing products. Unfortunately, this often is not the case. As the classic crises illustrate, many companies have manufactured or distributed unreliable products, placing consumers at risk. Many advertisers continue to make false and misleading claims about products. What, then, is the nature of corporate responsibility toward consumers as stakeholders?

U.S., French, and German Consumers   One study contrasted consumers' views on the social responsibility of organizations in the cultures of their three countries.[46] American individualism was compared to German and French communitarian social values. German consumers were more willing to support businesses that were identified as socially responsible than were U.S. consumers. Germans placed a higher priority on social responsibility attributed to businesses than did Americans. U.S. consumers highly valued the economic aspects of corporations first and the legal responsibilities second, although French and German consumers were more concerned about businesses conforming to legal and ethical standards. The French consumer sample considered ethical responsibilities second in importance to corporations' legal duties. German consumers were most interested in businesses conforming to social norms and less so in corporate economic performance. The study, admittedly based on small sample sizes, indicates regional differences in consumers' expectations of corporations' social responsibility and "points to the difficulty of implementing uniform communication programs about social responsibility across borders."[47] The results also indicate cultural differences in consumers' expectations about corporate responsibility. Are there corporate values and responsibilities toward consumers that should not be limited by geographies and cultural boundaries?

Corporate Responsibilities and Consumer Rights

Corporations have certain responsibilities and duties toward their customers and consumers in society:

- *The duty to inform* consumers truthfully and fully of a product or service's content, purpose, and use

- *The duty not to misrepresent or withhold information* about a product or service that would hinder consumers' free choice

- *The duty not to force or take undue advantage* of consumer buying and product selection through fear or stress or by other means that constrain rational choice

- *The duty to take "due care" to prevent any foreseeable injuries* or mishaps a product (in its design and production or in its use) may inflict on consumers[48]

While these responsibilities seem reasonable, there are several problems with the last responsibility, known as "due care" theory. First, there is no straightforward method for determining when "due care" has been given. What should a firm do to ensure the safety of its products? How far should it go? A utilitarian principle has been suggested, but problems arise when use of this method adds costs to products. Also, what health risks should be measured and how? How serious must an injury be? The second problem is that "due care" theory assumes that a manufacturer can know its products' risks before injuries occur. Certainly, testing is done for most high-risk products; but for most products, *use* generally determines product defects. Who pays the costs for injuries resulting from product defects unknown beforehand by consumer and manufacturer? Should the manufacturer be the party that determines what is safe and unsafe for consumers? Or is this a form of paternalism? In a free market, who should be able to determine what products will be used at what cost and risk?[49]

Related rights consumers have in their social contract with corporations include:

- *The right to safety*—to be protected from harmful commodities
- *The right to free and rational choice*—to be able to select between alternative products
- *The right to know*—to have easy access to truthful information that can help in product selection
- *The right to be heard*—to have available a party who will acknowledge and act on reliable complaints about injustices regarding products and business transactions
- *The right to be compensated*—to have a means to receive compensation for harm done to a person because of faulty products or for damage done in the business transaction[50]

These rights are also constrained by free-market principles and conditions. For example, "products must be as represented: Producers must live up to the terms of the sales agreement; and advertising and other information about products must not be deceptive. Except for these restrictions, however, producers are free, according to free-market theory, to operate pretty much as they please."[51]

The "buyer beware" principle plays well according to free-market theory, because this doctrine underlies the topic of corporate responsibility in advertising, product safety, and liability.

Free-Market Theory: Relationship between Consumers and Corporations

Free-market theory holds that the primary aim of business is to make a profit. As far as business obligations toward consumers, this view assumes an equal balance of power, knowledge, and sophistication of choice in the buying and selling of products and services. If businesses deliver what customers want, customers buy. Customers have the freedom and wisdom to select what they want and to reject what they do not want. Faulty or undesirable products should not sell. If businesses do not sell their products or services, it is their own fault. The marketplace is an arena of arbitration. Consumers and corporations are protected and regulated, according to this view, by Adam Smith's "invisible hand."

Several scholars argue that Adam Smith's "invisible hand" view is not completely oriented toward stockholders. For example, Szwajkowski argued that "Smith's viewpoint is most accurately positioned squarely between those who contend firms should act out of self-interest and those who believe corporations should be do-gooders. This middle ground is actually the stakeholder perspective. That is, stakeholders are in essence the market in all its forms. They determine what is a fair price, what is a successful product, what is an unacceptable strategy, what is intolerable discrimination. The mechanisms for these determinations include purchase transactions, supplier contracts, government regulation, and public pressure."[52] The author continues, "Our own empirical research has clearly shown that employee relations and product quality and safety are the most significant and reliable predictors of corporate reputation."[53]

Free markets require certain conditions for business activity to help society. These conditions include (1) minimal moral restraints to enable businesses to operate and prevent illegal activities such as theft, fraud, and blackmail; (2) full competitiveness with entry and exit; (3) relevant information needed to transact business available to everyone; and (4) accurate reflection of all production costs in the prices that consumers and firms pay (including the costs of job-related accidents, injuries from unsafe products, and externalities, which are spillover costs that are not paid by manufacturers or companies, but that consumers and taxpayers often pay, e.g., pollution costs). Legal and ethical problems arise when some or all of these conditions are violated, as the corporate crises illustrated at the beginning of this chapter.

Problems with the Free-Market Theory   Although the free-market theory is currently popular and has validity, controversy also exists regarding its assumptions about consumer-business relationships. For example, consider these arguments:

1. Most businesses are not on an equal footing with consumers at large. Large firms spend sizable amounts on research aimed at analyzing, creating, and—some argue—manipulating the demand of targeted buyers. Children, for example, are not aware of the effects of advertising on their buying choices.

2. Whether many firms' advertising activities truthfully inform consumers about product reliability, possible product dangers, and proper product use is questioned. A thin line exists between deceit and artistic exaggeration in advertising.

3. The "invisible hand" is often nonexistent for consumers in need of protection against questionable advertising and poorly manufactured products released to market. One reason a stakeholder view has become a useful approach for determining moral, legal, and economic responsibility is that the issues surrounding product safety, for example, are

complex and controversial. Who is right or wrong and who is innocent or liable must be examined before informed judgments are made. The question then arises, what are realistic company obligations toward consumers in market-place relationships and exchanges?

Another important argument against free-market theory is based on what economists refer to as *imperfect markets,* that is, markets in which competition "is flawed by the ability of one or more parties to influence prices."[54] An example of an imperfect market and skewed market power occurs in Africa, "where a few pharmaceutical companies effectively control the availability of several key drugs. In effect, they are beyond the financial means of millions of Africans or their governments. When a few dominating companies cut the prices of several key ingredients of the AIDS cocktail, they demonstrated this power. But this also revealed a further imperfection in the real market, where only rickety systems, if any, exist to deliver the drugs to patients requiring sophisticated and continuous follow-up care."[55]

Mixed Market Economies   The debate regarding free markets, imperfect markets, and other forms of social organization is interesting but not always helpful in describing how these systems actually work in the marketplace. The free-market system has been more accurately described by economist Paul Samuelson as a "mixed economy."[56] Mixed economies include a balance between private property systems and the government laws, policies, and regulations that protect consumers and citizens. In mixed economies, ethics becomes part of legal and business debates. Principles of justice, rights, and duty coexist with utilitarian and market principles.

Consumer Protection Agencies and Law   Because of imperfect markets and market failures, consumers are protected to some extent by federal and state laws in the United States. Five goals of government policymakers toward consumers include:

1. Providing consumers with reliable information about purchases

2. Providing legislation to protect consumers against hazardous products

3. Providing laws to encourage competitive pricing

4. Providing laws to promote consumer choice

5. Protecting consumers' privacy[57]

Some of the most notable U.S. consumer protection agencies include:

1. *The Federal Trade Commission (FTC)* deals with online privacy, deceptive trade practices, and competitive pricing

2. *The Food and Drug Administration (FDA)* regulates and enforces the safety of drugs, foods, and food additives, and sets standards for toxic chemical research

3. *The National Highway Traffic Safety Administration (NHTSA)* deals with motor vehicle safety standards

4. *The National Transportation Safety Board (NTSB)* handles airline safety

5. *The Consumer Product Safety Commission* sets and enforces safety standards for consumer products

6. *The Department of Justice (DOJ)* enforces consumer civil rights and fair competition

Governmental and international agencies also work to protect consumers' legal rights. The European Union (EU) has the health and consumer protection directorate general that overseas initiatives on health, safety, economic, and public health.[58] Consumer's World's Web site (http://www.consumerworld.org/pages/agencies.htm) has an extensive list of consumer protection agencies that includes both the United States and international countries, including India, Estonia, Hong Kong, Korea, Mexico, and Canada, as well as other European countries.

4.6 CORPORATE RESPONSIBILITY IN ADVERTISING, PRODUCT SAFETY, AND LIABILITY

Advertising is big business. Total worldwide advertising in 2004 was estimated at $495.9 billion.[59] In 1991, $126.7 billion was spent on advertising; by 1994, the total estimate was $150 billion.[60] The extent to which advertising is effective is debatable, but because consumers are so frequently exposed to ads, it is an important topic of study in business ethics. The purpose of advertising is to inform customers about products and services and to persuade them to purchase them. Deceptive advertising is against the law. A corporation's ethical responsibility in advertising is to inform and persuade consumer stakeholders in ways that are not deceitful. This does not always happen, as the tobacco, diet, and food industries, for example, have shown.

Ethics and Advertising   At issue, legally and ethically, for consumers is whether advertising is deceptive and creates or contributes to creating harm to consumers. Although advertising is supposed to provide information to consumers, a major aim is to sell products and services. As part of a selling process, both buyer and seller are involved. As discussed earlier, "buyer beware" imparts some responsibility to the buyer for believing and being susceptible to ads. Ethical issues arise whenever corporations target ads in manipulative, untruthful, subliminal, and coercive ways to vulnerable buyers such as children and minorities. Also, inserting harmful chemicals into products without informing the buyer is deceptive advertising. The tobacco industry's use of nicotine and addictive ingredients in cigarettes was deceptive advertising.

The American Association of Advertising (AAA) has a code of ethics that helps organizations monitor their ads. The code cautions against false, distorted, misleading, and exaggerated claims and statements as well as pictures that are offensive to the public and minority groups.

The FTC and Advertising   The Federal Trade Commission (FTC) and the Department of Labor (DOL) are the federal agencies in the United States appointed and funded to monitor and eliminate false and misleading advertising when corporate self-regulation is not used or fails. Following is a sample of the FTC's guidelines:

> The Federal Trade Commission Act allows the FTC to act in the interest of all consumers to prevent deceptive and unfair practices. In interpreting Section 5 of the act, the Commission has determined that a representation, omission or practice is *deceptive* if it is likely to:
>
> • mislead consumers
>
> • affect consumers' behavior or decisions about the product or service
>
> In addition, an act or practice is *unfair* if the injury it causes, or is likely to cause, is:
>
> • substantial
>
> • not outweighed by other benefits
>
> • reasonably avoidable

The FTC Act prohibits unfair or deceptive advertising in any medium. A claim can be misleading if relevant information is left out or if the claim implies something that's not true. For example, a lease advertisement for an automobile that promotes "$0 Down" may be misleading if significant and undisclosed charges are due at lease signing. In addition, claims must be *substantiated,* especially when they concern health, safety, or performance. The type of evidence may depend on the product, the claims, and what experts believe necessary. If your ad specifies a certain level of support for a claim—"*tests show X*"—you must have at least that level of support.

Sellers are responsible for claims they make about their products and services. Third parties—such as advertising agencies or Web site designers and catalog marketers—also may be liable for making or disseminating deceptive representations if they participate in the preparation or distribution of the advertising or know about the deceptive claims.[61]

Advertising and the Internet   Advertising on the Internet presents new opportunities and problems for consumers. Figure 4.3 indicates the ubiquity of Internet use, misuse, and possible criminal activities. The ubiquity of ads on the Web causes ethical problems, particularly for parents and those wishing to protect youth from a host of pop-up ads as well as exposure to Web sites and advertisements dealing with sex, pornography, violence, drinking, and tobacco.

Pop-up and pop-under ads (ads that open up in a separate, full browser window, underneath whatever site the user is viewing) are used on some of the most visited services.[62] In addition, marketers are turning to Web films to push their products through "byte-sized movies." In place of TV commercials that confront consumers with 30-second product introductions, the new "advertainment" shorts (also known as "commission content") present product or service information to the viewer through a story; Madonna starred in a BMW-funded film directed by her husband. "You're not using a product-based appeal, you're using an image-based appeal."[63]

At issue ethically is the unlimited availability of and exposure to explicit sexual, pornographic, and other questionable content on ads and Web sites, mixed with carefully crafted entertainment that is enhanced by new technologies. Should youth be able to log on from their computers, or from computers in libraries and cyber cafes, to Web sites showing explicit sexual and pornographic pictures and video? The issue centers on how much government protection through censorship the public wants. Although AOL and other servers offer controls for parents, as do private firms through products such as CyberPatrol, CYBERsitter, and WebTrack, the issue remains one of principle: How much regulation interferes with free speech for all? Moreover, the file-sharing technology made popular by Napster provides additional opportunities not only to see explicit material, but to also share the content instantly.

Another ethical issue introduced through the Internet and pioneered by Napster is the blurring of boundaries between advertising and product sampling, which enables people to steal copyrighted songs, movies, and other information on the Web. "What do you tell 40 million kids who know how to turn a product into data that they can trade freely?"[64] Responses to this question from technology chief executives included the following: "You teach them some values. You can walk into any store and steal something, and kids don't do it. We've got to bring up a generation that understands that if you steal a movie over the Net, that is stealing." Another executive: "You've got to make it easier to do something legally than it is to do it illegally."[65] Although Napster was forced to change its online copyright violation practices, the ethical questions the technology and practice presented remain relevant areas of ethical inquiry. For example, Coles, Harris, and Davis (2004) state that,

> While music piracy is an ongoing, endemic problem for the 'big 5,' it is not yet clear whether MP3 users buy more or less music as a result of their online searches. In fact it has been suggested that there is some bad news for the industry in respect of its heavy-handed attempts to control music online with legal and technical measures, in the form of consumer resistance.[66] More recently then, questions have been raised as to how the Internet will develop now that music has become an integral part of online activities. The advent of portable MP3 players and their growing popularity, despite the early legal challenge, has encouraged a new wave of organizing CD collections and compiling personal playlists, while the popularity of Web radio is growing.[67]

Again, the FTC has regulatory guidelines for online advertising, dot-com disclosures, and information sharing. The following is a sample from the FTC's Web site:

> "Dot-Com Disclosures: Information About Online Advertising," an FTC staff paper, provides additional information for online advertisers. The paper discusses the factors used to evaluate the clarity and conspicuousness of required disclosures in online ads. It also discusses how FTC rules and guides that use terms like "writing" or "printed" apply to Internet activities and how technologies such as e-mail may be used to comply with certain rules and guides.
>
> Protecting Consumer's Privacy Online
>
> The US Dept. of Justice, FTC, and other agencies announced an international crackdown on phishing, Nigerian "419," and other fraud schemes that have become commonplace on the Internet. The Center for Democracy and Technology (CDT) has urged federal agencies to take this kind of action, but stresses that further large scale investigations will be necessary if current law is to actually serve as a deterrent to online fraud.[68]

The Children's Online Privacy Protection Act (COPPA) and the FTC's implementing rule took effect April 21, 2000. Commercial Web sites directed to children less than thirteen years old or general audience sites that are collecting information from a child must obtain parental permission before collecting such information. The FTC also launched a special site at http://www.ftc.gov/kidzprivacy to help children, parents, and the operators understand the provisions of COPPA and how the law will affect them.[69]

The U.S. House of Representatives Judiciary Committee also passed the Internet Spyware Prevention Act of 2004 predicting that the problem

FIGURE 4.3	**How Serious, Really, is Internet Spam, Spyware, & Crime?**

–There were 600 million Internet users in 2002 worldwide, double the 1999 number.

–In Germany, Internet crimes account for 1.3 percent of all recorded crimes, "but for 57%—or $8.3 billion—of the material damage caused by crime."

–A fast-rising crime worldwide is "phishing," e-mails that appear to be from banks and other financial institutions asking consumers for their credit card details.

–A 2004 survey of 494 U.S. corporations found 20% had been subject to "attempts of computer sabotage and extortion, among others through denial of service attacks."

–Web sites promoting racism, hatred and violence have risen by 300% since 2004. Most are hosted in the United States, but many may originate in Europe.

–Child pornography on the Internet is an industry worth approximately $20 billion this year. "Surveys in 2003 suggest that child pornography accounts for 24% of image searches in peer-to-peer applications."

–Organized crime is well established in cyberspace, using the Internet for human trafficking and committing economic crimes. In March, German police confiscated 19 Internet servers, 200 computers, 40,000 compact discs, and 38 terabytes of private videos and software that was for sale through the Internet. In April, searches across Europe netted illegal software, CDs, and DVDs valued at $61.3 million.

Source: Robert Wielaard, "Europe Council Looks to Fight Cybercrime," *BizReport,* **September 15, 2004, http://www.bizreport.com/news/7981.**

of spyware would be solved. Personal and organizational computers have been seriously disrupted by spyware software. This act carries penalties of up to five years in prison for using spyware that has also led to identity theft and gave the DOJ $10 million to find ways to fight spyware and phishing, which is "the act of sending an e-mail to a user falsely claiming to be an established legitimate enterprise in an attempt to scam the user into surrendering private information that will be used for identity theft,"[70] without making phishing illegal.[71]

The debate continues over whether or not congressional legislation and laws can stop Internet spyware and spam. Critics of congressional action alone argue that both industries and government must work to end spam and spyware.[72] Europe, also involved in solving cybercrime, takes a wider stakeholder involvement approach that includes legal, enforcement, industry, and consumers. The European Cybercrime Convention, sponsored by the Council of Europe, provides a treaty for combating global cybercrime. The 2001 cybercrime convention was approved by 30 countries, including Canada, Japan, South Africa, and the United States, and has been ratified by eight countries.[73]

Paternalism or Manipulation?   Moral responsibility for consumers in advertising can be viewed along a continuum. At one end of the spectrum is the criticism regarding *paternalism;* that is, "Big Brother" (the government, in most cases) regulates the free market as well as what consumers can hear and see. Too much protection can lead to too much control over free choice. This is not desirable in a democratic market economy. At the other extreme of the continuum is the illusion of free choice, which is another type of control; that is, corporations manipulate consumers' free choice through cleverly researched ads aimed at deception. This is also undesirable, since it limits consumer choice and knowledge. Ideally, corporations should seek to inform consumers truthfully while using nonmanipulative, persuasive techniques to sell their products.

Enforcement of advertising can also be viewed along this continuum. Outright bans on ads can result in court decisions that rule that consumer free choice has been violated and that a party was or could be harmed. At the other end, companies and industry groups can police themselves, as has been the case in the alcohol industry, with the U.S. Brewers Association issuing guidelines against beer ads that promote overindulgence. Where moral and legal disputes over specific ads occur on the continuum is a matter of perception and judgment. Therefore, the general debate over the pros and cons of what constitutes ethical advertising continues.

Arguments for Advertising   Arguments that justify advertising and the tactics of puffery and exaggeration include:

1. Advertising introduces people to and influences them to buy goods and services. Without advertising, consumers would be uninformed about products.

2. Advertising enables companies to be competitive with other firms in domestic and international markets. Firms across the globe use advertisements as competitive weapons.

3. Advertising helps a nation maintain a prosperous economy. Advertising increases consumption and spending, which in turn creates economic growth and jobs, which in turn benefits all. "A rising tide lifts all ships."

4. Advertising helps a nation's balance of trade and debt payments, especially in large industries, such as the food, automobile, alcoholic beverage, and computer technology, whose exports help the country's economy.

5. Customers' lives are enriched by the images and metaphors advertising creates. Customers pay for the illusions as well as the products advertisements promote.

6. Consumers are not ignorant. Buyers know the differences between lying, manipulation, and colorful hyperbole aimed

at attracting attention. Consumers have freedom of choice. Ads try to influence desires already present in people's minds. Companies have a constitutional right to advertise in free and democratic societies.[74]

Arguments against (Questionable) Advertising   Critics of questionable advertising practices argue that advertising can be harmful for the following reasons. First, advertisements often cross that thin line that exists between puffery and deception. For example, unsophisticated buyers, especially youth, are targeted by companies. David Kessler, former commissioner of the FDA, referred to smoking as a pediatric disease, since 90% of lifelong smokers started when they were 18 and half began by the age of 14.[75]

Another argument is that advertisements tell half-truths, conceal facts, and intentionally deceive with profit, not consumer welfare, in mind. For example, the $300 billion to $400 billion food industry is increasingly being watched by the FDA for printing misleading labels that use terms such as "cholesterol free," "lite," and "all natural" are under attack, with an added push from the Nutritional Education and Labeling Act of 1990. Consumers need understandable information quickly on how much fat (a significant factor in heart disease) is in food, on standard serving sizes, and on the exact nutritional contents of foods.[76] At stake in the short term for food companies is an outlay of between $100 million and $600 million for relabeling. In the long term, product sales could be at risk.

> One of the great paradoxes of Americans today is that we are obsessed with diet and health and yet have one of the worst diets in the world. 54% of adults are considered overweight. Only 2% of children eat the recommended variety of foods daily. Food industry executives blame the customers, saying they ask for low-fat food but rarely buy it. For many Americans, the problem isn't just that they are consuming so much fat, it is that they don't know what they are eating. To put this in perspective, consider nutrition guidelines that suggest the 30-year-old male eat a maximum of 2,900 calories and 97 grams of fat per day, and the average 30-year-old female eat no more that 1,900 calories and 73 grams of fat, according to the Center for Science in the Public Interest (CSPI). Many Americans far exceed those recommendations, in part because of their increasing reliance on restaurant food.[77]

Fast Food Nation   Eric Schlosser's book *Fast Food Nation* explores a topic related to advertising and nutrition. Schlosser argues that there is a dark side of the fast food industry, where the best and worst of American marketing and capitalism connect, as manifested in the transformation of fast food production globally; the reliance on low-paid, unskilled labor; and alarming health trends. McDonald's has 28,700 outlets in 120 countries. Fast food chains are driving independent restaurants out of business. Almost a quarter of the adult population in the United States eats at a fast food restaurant daily. More than $110 billion was spent in fast food restaurants in 2000 compared with $6 billion in 1970. In 1960, the average American ate 4 pounds of frozen french fries a year; in 2001, that amount was more than 30 pounds. Chicken McNuggets have twice as much fat per ounce as hamburgers. The typical soda has the equivalent of 10 tablespoons of sugar.[78]

Schlosser traces the growth of the fast food restaurant industry to American marketing gurus Ray Kroc, who led the franchising of McDonald's, and Carl Karcher, who set up hot dog stands that grew into a fast food empire. Although these businessmen were geniuses in creating advertising innovations and linking them to build franchising empires, the results of the products for consumers are more questionable. Schlosser describes worst-case scenarios such as the slaughterhouses where beef is prepared for fast food chains, where conditions give rise to food-borne diseases. (About 14 people die in the United States each day from Listeria and E. coli.) Schlosser's historical arguments and exposé are reminiscent of Upton Sinclair's classic research-based book, *The Jungle*, in which he described Chicago's slaughterhouses and the working conditions for immigrant employees in the early 1900s.

Although *Fast Food Nation* is criticized for its negative bias toward the fast food industry, some of Schlosser's critics agree that his research is "impressive and comprehensive, even if his conclusions are somewhat overstated."[79] The book has signaled a trend that is here: obesity.

Obesity: Myth or National Health Problem?

Obesity is no longer only an adult problem. Matthew Grimm states, "Ever-increasing obesity rates among children mired the overall state of U.S. youth in 2002, sending it 15 points lower than it was in 1975 as measured by Duke University's Child-Welfare Index (CWI), an aggregate of nearly three dozen factors such as crime, safety, community and family environments, as well as suicide rates. The latest index, released by the sponsoring Foundation for Child Development, corroborates last year's alarm by the Centers for Disease Control (CDC) that obesity rates in children, up to 15.6% in 2002 from 6.1% in 1974, stands at "epidemic" proportions."[80] Marketers have targeted children (as early as seven years), youth, and schools for advertising and selling fatty foods.

The seriousness of obesity in the United States became even more evident when in July 2004, the federal Medicare program recognized obesity as a disease, which opens the door for those who qualify to obtain treatment and coverage for weight-loss therapies.[81] Critics of health insurance payment for obesity treatments claim that declaring obesity a disease is exaggerated. Obesity should, critics claim, be a matter of individual responsibility. "It's not just a bad idea, it's completely unscientific," said University of Colorado law professor Paul Campos, author of *The Obesity Myth.* "We're in the grip of a kind of out-of-control cultural hysteria on this issue that leads to really irrational social decisions, such as making obesity a disease among the elderly."[82]

On the other hand, "An estimated 300,000 Americans die each year from obesity-related causes, and we spent $117 billion in obesity-related economic costs just last year," U.S. Surgeon General David Satcher reported.[83] Obesity is one of the most serious public health problems in the United States. As a disease, it rivals smoking and is related to others diseases like type 2 diabetes, heart disease, and some types of cancer.[84]

Tobacco and Alcohol Advertising   Critics argue that tobacco and alcohol companies, in particular, continue to promote products that are dangerously unhealthy and that have effects that endanger others. "The World Health Organization (WHO), estimates the number of smokers in the world today at 1.3 million, and predicts that will rise to 1.7 million by 2025."[85] The tobacco industry spent approximately $8.2 billion in 1999 for traditional magazine direct-to-consumer advertising. Cigarette companies reportedly are targeting ads at low-income women and minorities and focusing less on college-educated consumers. Three thousand new teenagers and youth begin smoking each day. One out of three is predicted to die from tobacco-related illnesses—several when they are middle-aged.[86]

R.J. Reynolds's "trend-influence marketing" and Brown & Williamson's "relationship marketing" have the goal of connecting with customers on a personal level. For example, the "Lucky Strike Force," teams of attractive twentysomethings, promotes the brand while offering smokers roses and coffee. R.J. Reynolds hosted 700 parties for smokers in 70 U.S. cities. Philip Morris hosted 117 events that featured musicians like Smash Mouth, Violent Femmes, and Afghan Whigs.[87]

The Philip Morris tobacco company told the Czech government that smoking is not a public health menace because the premature deaths save the country money on elder care. The company calculated that in 1999 "the premature demise of smokers saved the Czech government between $24 million and $30 million on health care, housing, and pensions." The company stated that "weighing the costs and benefits," the Czech government actually made $147 million from its smoking policies when considering the care it paid for smokers who were still living and for victims of secondhand smoke.[88] The company later stated, "We're not trying to suggest that there would be a bene-fit to society from the diseases related to smoking."

The U.S. Supreme Court ruled unanimously in June 2001 that states have no right to restrict outdoor tobacco advertising near schools and public parks. The ruling, a victory for tobacco companies, followed a Massachusetts case that prohibited tobacco ads within 1,000 feet of public parks, playgrounds, and schools.[89] The 2001 ruling raised questions regarding the topic of advertising and free speech, e.g., "Does a cor-poration have the same free speech rights under the First Amendment to purchase advertising as people have to air political, social, and artistic views? For most of the nation's history, the Supreme Court has said that commercial speech (offering a product for sale) does not deserve the same protection as political speech. But in a series of recent cases, the Rehnquist Court is giving businesses powerful new First Amendment rights to advertise hazardous products."[90]

U.S. Government versus Tobacco Industry: Racketeering

The tobacco controversy took yet another turn in 2004 when the DOJ brought the largest civil action against the tobacco industry, alleging that the industry defrauded and misled the public for 50 years regard-ing health risks of cigarette smoking. The DOJ requested $280 billion from the industry to repay its "ill-gotten" profits.[91]

William Schultz, a former Justice Department lawyer, who helped develop the case, stated that "What the government will argue is that the tobacco industry had a strategy to create doubt over health risks that make smokers more hesitant to quit, and those not smoking more likely to start. The fraud is that the companies knew about the health risks but created doubt and controversy about them to maintain their sales."[92] The lawsuit "has the potential to significantly transform the industry—forcing it to increase cigarette prices sharply, to change how it markets and promotes its product, and to spend billions for stop-smoking programs."[93]

Alcohol Ads   Alcohol is a form of substance abuse. Alcohol abuse is the third leading cause of preventable death in America, taking $186 billion from the national economy annually. For every 1,000 employ-ees there are an estimated 44 problem drinkers; 127 employee family members who are problem drinkers; 34 lost work days from sickness, injury and problem drinking annually; 219 work days of decreased productivity from alcohol use; 43 extra nights spent in the hospital by employees and their family members each year, and 32 extra emer-gency room visits by employees and their families each year.[94] Almost three million children have serious alcohol problems but less than 20% get the needed treatment.

Alcohol ads also raise problems for consumers. Critics of alcohol ads argue that youth, in particular, are targeted—enticed by suggestive messages linking drinking to popularity and success. The Marlboro man, the infamous and now defunct Old Joe Camel, and other cigarette brands linked adventure, fun, social acceptance, being "cool," and risk taking to smoking. Several popular movie stars are paid by cigarette companies to smoke in films. Consumers, public lobbying groups such as Mothers Against Drunk Driving (MADD), and state attorneys general have protested the use of such ads in places that attract teens and youth to smoking and drinking.

"Are Minors (Individuals under the Legal Drinking Age) Personally Responsible for their Voluntary Choices? Should Minors Be Punished as Adults?"

On November 13, Ayman Hakki filed a lawsuit in Washington, D.C., against several alcohol producers. The suit claims that in an effort to create brand loyalty in the young, the defendants have deliberately targeted their television and magazine advertising campaigns at consumers under the legal drinking age for more than two decades.

Hakki asks for damages including all of the profits the defendants have earned since 1982 from the sale of alcohol to minors. He is also seeking class-action status for his suit. The plaintiff class would consist of all parents whose underage children purchased alcohol in the last 21 years."[1]

QUESTION

1. What is your opinion regarding the following quote:

"Suits against tobacco and alcohol companies for targeting youthful purchasers reflect a particular philosophy regarding people under the legal drinking or smoking age: they are too immature to take full responsibility for their actions. This philosophy is in serious tension with the approach that has increasingly come to dominate our society's approach to juvenile criminal justice: when minors commit crimes, they ought to be held accountable and punished as adults."[2]

Notes

1. Colb, S. (December 3, 2003). A lawsuit against "big alcohol" for advertising to underage drinkers. *FindLaw*, http://writ.news.findlaw.com/colb/20031203.html.
2. Ibid.

Ethical Questions and Advertising   Advertising issues related to what is legal or illegal, moral or immoral, are matters of judgment, values, and changing societal standards. Most of these types of issues are argued in and out of courts on a case-by-case basis. Still, corporations and consumers can use the following questions to address the moral responsibility of advertisements:

1. Is the consumer being treated as a means to an end or as an end? What and whose end?

2. Whose rights are being protected or violated intentionally and inadvertently? At what and whose costs?

3. Are consumers being justly and fairly treated?

4. Are the public welfare and good taken into consideration for the effects as well as the intention of advertisements?

5. Has anyone been harmed, and can this harm be proven?

Advertising and Free Speech   In commercial speech cases, there is no First Amendment protection if it can be proven that information was false or misleading. In other types of free speech cases, people who file suit must prove either negligence or actual malice.[95]

Should certain ads by corporations be banned or restricted by courts? For example, should children be protected from accessing pornography ads on the Internet? Should companies that intentionally mislead the public when selling their products be denied protection by the court?[96] The U.S. Supreme Court has differentiated commercial speech from pure speech in the context of the First Amendment. (See *Central Hudson Gas and Electric Corporation* v. *Public Service Commission*, 1980, and *Posadas de Puerto Rico Associates* v. *Tourism Company of Puerto Rico*, 54 LW 4960). Pure speech is more generalized, relating to political, scientific, and artistic expression in marketplace dealings. Commercial speech refers to language in ads and business dealings. The Supreme Court has balanced these concepts against the general principle that freedom of speech must be weighed against the public's general welfare. The four-step test developed by Justice Lewis F. Powell Jr. and used to determine whether commercial speech in advertisements could be banned or restricted follows:

1. Is the ad accurate, and does it promote a lawful product?

2. Is the government's interest in banning or restricting the commercial speech important, nontrivial, and substantial?

3. Does the proposed restriction of commercial speech assist the government in obtaining a public policy goal?

4. Is the proposed restriction of commercial speech limited only to achieving the government's purpose?[97]

For example, do you agree or disagree with the argument that the conservative plurality on the U.S. Supreme Court has argued in the tobacco smoking controversy to give more free speech rights to tobacco companies? (As suggested by Lawrence Gostin, "The [U.S. Supreme] court has held that the FDA lacks jurisdiction to regulate cigarettes. The court observed that Congress, despite having many opportunities, has repeatedly refused to permit agency regulation of the product. Thus, Congress has systematically declined to regulate tobacco but has also preempted state regulation. Moreover, the Supreme Court's recent assertion of free speech rights for corporations prevents both Congress and the states from meaningfully regulating advertising. To the extent that commercial speech becomes assimilated into traditional political and social speech, it could become a potent engine for government deregulation. And, perhaps, that is the agenda of the court's conservative plurality."

Source: "Corporate Speech and the Constitution: The Deregulation of Tobacco Advertising," *American Journal of Public Health,* **March, 2002, Vol. 92 Issue 3, 352–6.**

The commercial speech doctrine remains controversial. The Supreme Court has turned to the First Amendment to protect commercial speech (which is supposedly based on informational content). Public discourse is protected to ensure the participation and open debate needed to sustain democratic traditions and legitimacy. The Supreme Court has ultimate jurisdiction over decisions regarding the extent to what commercial speech, in particular, ads, and cases meets the previous four standards.

Recent judicial decisions regarding a number of areas (including consumer privacy, spam, obesity, telemarketing, tobacco ads, casino gambling advertising, and dietary supplement labeling [see *Greater New Orleans Broadcasting Association Inc.* v. *United States* and *Pearson* v. *Shalala*]), have sent a message that "[T]he government's heretofore generally accepted power to regulate commercial speech in sensitive areas has been restricted." Regulators have prohibited certain advertisements and product claims based on the government's authority to protect public safety and the common good. The courts have sent the government (namely, the FDA) "back to the drawing board" to write disclaimers for claims it had argued to be inconclusive. The FDA's regulatory power has currently been curtailed.[98]

The following section explores corporations' responsibility toward consumer stakeholders with regard to the manufacture, distribution, and sale of products.

Product Safety and Liability
Managing product safety should be priority number one for corporations. A sign in one engineering

facility reads, "Get it right the first time or everyone pays!" Product quality, safety, and liability are interrelated topics, especially when products fail in the marketplace. As new technologies are used in product development, risks increase for users.

How Safe Is Safe? The Ethics of Product Safety
Each year thousands of people die and millions are injured from the effects of smoking cigarettes, using diet drugs, suffering from silicone breast implants, and using consumer products such as toys, lawn mowers, appliances, power tools, and household chemicals, according to the Consumer Product Safety Commission. But how safe is safe? Few, if any, products are 100 percent safe. Adding the manufacturing costs to the sales price to bolster safety features would, in many instances, discourage price-sensitive consumers. Just as companies use utilitarian principles when developing products for markets, consumers use this logic when shopping. Risks are calculated by both manufacturer and consumer. However, enough serious instances of questionable product quality and lack of manufacturing precautions taken occur to warrant more than a simple utilitarian ethic for preventing and determining product safety for the consuming public. This is especially the case for commercial products such as air-, sea-, and spacecrafts, over which consumers have little, if any, control.

Are cigarettes safe products? "Cigarette smoking remains the leading cause of death and illness among Americans. Every year, roughly 430,000 Americans die from illnesses caused by tobacco use, accounting for one-fifth of all deaths. Tobacco use costs the nation about $100 billion each year in direct medical expense and lost productivity."[99]

Are other types of drugs safer than nicotine and additives in cigarettes? A "meta-analysis" (i.e., "the first comprehensive scientific review of both published studies and unpublished data that pharmaceutical companies have said they own and have the right to withhold") by the British medical journal *The Lancet* found that "most antidepressants are ineffective and may actually be unsafe for children and adolescents."[100] The study reported that youth, ages 5-18, should avoid the antidepressants—Paxil, Zoloft, Effexor, and Celexa—because of the risk of suicidal behavior with no benefit from taking the drug. Prozac was found an effective drug for depressed children and had no increased suicide risk.[101] In 2002, the study stated that U.S. psychiatrists, pediatricians, and family practitioners, prescribed almost 11 million serotonin mood enhancers and other antidepressant prescriptions for youth ages 1 to 17. It is interesting to note that the British government recommended against the use of most antidepressants for children, except for Prozac. The EU regulators recommended against Paxil being given to children. And the U.S. FDA requested drug manufacturers warn more strongly on their labels about possible links between the drugs taken by adolescents and "suicidal thoughts and behaviors." Also, a Columbia University expert committee was asked to review "drug-company data and to create a definition of what is suicidal thinking and suicidal behavior."[102]

Consumers also value safety and will pay for safe products up to the point where, in their own estimation, the product's *marginal value equals its marginal cost;* that is, people put a price on their lives whether they are rollerblading, sunning, skydiving, drinking, overeating, or driving to work.[103]

Product Safety Criteria: What Is the Value of a Human Life?

The National Commission on Product Safety (NCPS) notes that product risks should be reasonable. Unreasonable risks are those that could be prevented or that consumers would pay to prevent if they had the knowledge and choice, according to the NCPS. Three steps that firms can use to assess product safety from an ethical perspective follow[104]:

1. How much safety is technically attainable, and how can it be specifically obtained for this product or service?

2. What is the acceptable risk level for society, the consumer, and the government regarding this product?

3. Does the product meet societal and consumer standards?

These steps, of course, will not be the same for commercial aircraft as for tennis shoes.

Estimates regarding the monetary value of human life vary. As Figure 4.4 illustrates, these "expert" estimates range from $3 million to $5 million.

Regulating Product Safety

Because of the number of product-related casualties and injuries annually and because of the growth of the consumer movement in the 1960s and 1970s, Congress passed the 1972 Consumer Product Safety Act, which created the Consumer Product Safety Commission (http://www.cpsc.gov). This is the federal agency empowered to protect the public from unreasonable risks of injury and death related to consumer product use. The five members of the commission are appointed by the president. The commission has regional offices across the country. It develops uniform safety standards for consumer products; assists industries in developing safety standards; researches possible product hazards; educates consumers about comparative product safety standards; encourages competitive pricing; and works to recall, repair, and ban dangerous products.

FIGURE 4.4   The Price of a Human Life?

Assume it would cost $500 per car to put antiskid brakes in each of 10 million cars sold this year—a total of $5 billion. Then assume that installing gadgets on this year's fleet ultimately would save 5,000 lives, or $1 million per life. Next assume that, on average, individuals value their lives at $5 million. Since the $1 million cost of saving a life is less than the $5 million value of life, the safety feature might be worth buying.

If seat belts cost, say, $50 per car and equipping 1 million cars with seat belts will save 1,000 lives, then regulators must assume lives are worth at least $50,000 a piece. Take another example. If smoke detectors cost $20 each and are widely seen as reducing the risk of a death by 1 chance in 10,000, then buyers surely would value their lives for at least 20 times $10,000, or $200,000. Again, if it takes an extra $100,000 in lifetime earnings to persuade miners to cope with 1 extra chance in 100 of premature death underground, then miners implicitly must value their lives at no more than 100 times $100,000, or $10 million.

The following table has estimates of the minimum value of a human life found in a sampling of governmental regulations. The figures take into account the medical and hospital costs avoided if calculated lives are saved, but these figures ignore other benefits of regulations, such as prevention of property damage and injuries that do not result in death. The estimates are based on risk experts' calculations of what a human life is worth considering all costs of installing various lifesaving gadgets. For example, if the government spent $110 million annually on a B-58 bomber ejection system and 5 lives would be saved, then each life is estimated at $22 million ($110 million divided by 5).

Automobiles	Child restraint in cars	$1,221.3	million
	Dual master cylinders for car brakes	$7.8	million
Ejection System	For the B-58 bomber	$22.0	million
Flashing Lights	For railroad crossings	$0.73	million
Sea Walls	For protection against 100-year-storm surges	$96.0	million
Asbestos	Banned in brake linings	$0.23	million
	Banned in automatic transmission parts	$1,200.0	million
Radiation	Safety standards for X-ray equipment	$0.4	million
	Safety standards for uranium mine tailings	$190.0	million

Source: Harvard Center for Risk Analysis.

Who is to say a life is worth $5 million rather than $500 million? Numerous studies calculate the value of life. But these studies do not produce uniform answers, nor do risk analysts claim this. People have very different estimates for risk. But researchers are still willing to generalize. Most middle-income U.S. citizens usually act as if their lives were worth $3 million to $5 million, based on what individuals demand in extra pay for dangerous jobs and what they spend for safety devices.

Source: "How Much for a Life? Try $3 Million to $5 Million" by Peter Passell from The New York Times, January 29, 1995, p. F3. Copyright © 1995 by The New York Times Co. Reprinted by permission.

Each year the commission targets potentially hazardous products and publishes a list with consumer warnings. It recently targeted Cosco for the faulty product design of children's products. The death of an 11-month-old in July 1988 in a Cosco-designed crib was never reported by the company even though the company began to redesign the product.

Cosco was forced to pay a record $1.3 million in civil penalties to settle charges that it violated federal law by failing to report hundreds of injuries and the death.[105]

The CPSC is constrained in part by its enormous mission, limited resources, and critics who argue that the costs for maintaining the agency exceed the results and benefits it produces.

Consumer Affairs Departments and Product Recalls.

Many companies actively and responsibly monitor their customers' satisfaction and safety concerns. Companies set up and coordinate consumer affairs departments (CADs) to ensure customer confidence and corporate responsiveness. Procter & Gamble, General Electric, Shell Oil, Federal Express, and Pepsi Co., to name only a few, have established such departments. One survey estimated that 80% of the 500 largest companies have Web sites that enable customers to ask questions and post comments.[106]

Many companies aggressively and voluntarily recall defective products and parts when they discover or are informed about them. When unsafe products are not voluntarily recalled, the EPA, NHTSA, FDA, and CPSC have the authority to enforce recalls of known or suspected unsafe products. Recalled products are usually repaired. If not, the product or parts can be replaced or even taken out of service. American autos are frequently recalled for replacement and adjustment of defective parts.

Amitai Etzioni, a noted business ethicist, argues that,

> There is, of course, no precise way of measuring how much more the public is willing to pay for a safer, healthier life via higher prices or taxes, or by indirect drag on economic growth and loss of jobs. In part this is because most Americans prefer to deal with these matters one at a time rather than get entangled with highly complex, emotion-laden general guidelines. In part it is also because the answer depends on changing economic conditions. Obviously, people are willing to buy more safety in prosperity than in recession.[107]

Product Liability Doctrines

Who should pay for the effects of unsafe products, and how much should they pay? Who determines who is liable? What are the punitive and compensatory limits of product liability? The payout in 2001 in litigation and settlements in diet pill cases alone totaled $7 billion.[108] Also, 26 major companies have filed for bankruptcy court protection, and several others claim they have paid more than $10 billion to settle asbestos liability-related lawsuits from products used in the 1970s.[109] The doctrine of product liability has evolved in the court system since 1916, when the dominant principle of *privity* was used. Until the decision in *Macpherson* v. *Buick*

Motor Company, consumers injured by faulty products could sue and receive damages from a manufacturer if the manufacturer was judged to be negligent. Manufacturers were not held responsible if consumers purchased a hazardous product from a retailer or wholesaler.[110] In the *Macpherson* case, the defendant was ruled liable for harm done to Mr. Macpherson. A wheel on the car had cracked. Although Macpherson had bought the car from a retailer and although Buick had bought the wheel from a different manufacturer, Buick was charged with negligence. Even though Buick did not intend to deceive the client, the court ruled the company responsible for the finished product (the car) because—the jury claimed—it should have tested its component parts.[111] The doctrine of *negligence* in the area of product liability was thus established. The negligence doctrine means that all parties, including the manufacturer, wholesaler, distributor, and sales professionals, can be held liable if reasonable care is not observed in producing and selling a product.

The doctrine of *strict liability* is an extension of the negligence standard. Strict liability holds that the manufacturer is liable for a person's injury or death if a product with a known or knowable defect goes to market. A consumer has to prove three things to win the suit: (1) an injury happened, (2) the injury resulted from a product defect, and (3) the defective product was delivered by the manufacturer being sued.[112]

Absolute liability is a further extension of the strict liability doctrine. Absolute liability was used in 1982 in the *Beshada* v. *Johns-Manville Corporation* case. Employees sued Manville for exposure to asbestos. The court ruled the manufacturer liable for not warning of product danger even though the danger was scientifically unknown at the time of the production and sale of the product.[113] Medical and chemical companies, in particular, whose products could produce harmful but unknowable side effects years later would be held liable under this doctrine.

Legal and Moral Limits of Product Liability

Product liability lawsuits have two broad purposes: First, they provide a level of compensation for injured parties, and second, they act to deter large corporations from negligently marketing dangerous products.[114] When a California jury recently awarded Richard Boeken, a smoker who had lung cancer, a record $3 billion in a suit filed against Philip Morris, it may have overstepped the boundaries of rationality regarding the nature of product liability law. The legal and moral limits of product liability suits evolve historically and are, to a large degree, determined by political as well as legal stakeholder negotiations and settlements. Consumer advocates and stakeholders (for example, the Consumer Federation of America, the National Conference of State

Legislators, the Conference of State Supreme Court Justices, and activist groups) lobby for strong liability doctrines and laws to protect consumers against powerful firms that seek profits over consumer safety. In contrast, advocates of product liability law reform (for example, corporate stockholders, Washington lobbyists for businesses and manufacturers, and the President's Council on Competitiveness) argue that liability laws in the United States have become too costly, routine, and arbitrary. They claim liability laws can inhibit companies' competitiveness and willingness to innovate. Also, insurance companies claim that all insurance-paying citizens are hurt by excessive liability laws that allow juries to award hundreds of millions of dollars in punitive damages because as a result, insurance rates rise.

However, a two-year study of product liability cases concluded that punitive damages are rarely awarded, more rarely paid, and often reduced after the trial.[115] The study, partly funded by the Roscoe Pound Foundation in Washington, D.C., is the most comprehensive effort to date to show the patterns of punitive damages awards in product liability cases over the past 25 years. The results of the study follow:

1. Only 355 punitive damages verdicts were handed down by state and federal court juries during this period. One-fourth of those awards involved a single product—asbestos.

2. In the majority of the 276 cases with complete post-trial information available, punitive damages awards were abandoned or reduced by the judge or the appeals court.

3. The median punitive damages award for all product liability cases paid since 1965 was $625,000—a little above the median compensatory damages award of $500,100. Punitive damages awards were significantly larger than compensatory damages awards in only 25% of the cases.

4. The factors that led to significant awards—those that lawyers most frequently cited when interviewed or surveyed—were failure to reduce risk of a known danger and failure to warn consumers of those risks. A Cornell study reported similar findings.[116]

Also, an earlier federal study of product liability suits in five states showed that plaintiffs won less than 50% of the cases; a Rand Corporation study that surveyed 26,000 households nationwide found that only 1 in 10 of an estimated 23 million people injured each year thinks about suing; and the National Center for State Courts surveyed 13 state court systems from 1984 to 1989 and found that the 1991 increase in civil caseloads was for real-property rights cases, not suits involving accidents and injuries.[117]

Contrary to some expectations, another study found that "judges are more than three times as likely as juries to award punitive damages in the cases they hear." Plaintiffs' lawyers apparently mistakenly believe that juries are a soft touch, and "they route their worst cases to juries. But in the end, plaintiffs do no better before juries than they would have before a judge." The study also found that the median punitive damages award made by judges ($75,000) was nearly three times the median award made by juries ($27,000).[118]

Federal Activity   One of the most debated issues regarding product and professional liability is medical malpractice suits. The full House of Representatives met and passed a bill that will "federalize medical malpractice liability, including nursing homes and medical devices on March 13, 2003. One of President Bush's major campaign issues was tort reform." A major feature of the bill is capping malpractice claims to $250,000 for noneconomic damages and limiting punitive damages to $250,000 (or twice the economic damages or whichever is larger).[119] Stakeholders line up on different sides of this issue. Trial lawyers argue noneconomic damages caps on lawsuits would be unfair to injured patients, like stay-at-home mothers and those who would not receive large awards from juries in the economic portion of the lawsuit. "'It's not reform to take away the rights of the American family,' said Carlton Carl, spokesman for the Association of Trial Lawyers of America. "It is not fair to those who have been injured by the negligence of others."[120] On the other side of the issue are physicians and insurers who argue that tort reform is necessary to keep insurance rates reasonable and physicians in business.[121] If physicians lose their jobs, patients also lose.

Proactive Action by States   Thirty-three states have laws in the making to limit liability and reduce damages awards. Seven states have already limited the amount of punitive damages that can be awarded.[122] Several states have also introduced reforms to cap punitive damages.[123]

Product liability litigation may change dramatically in the coming years, moving liability back to the injured consumer. Tort reform legislation is predicted to reduce liability to negligence by redefining defective product design to protect manufacturers and by limiting the discovery and disclosure of defectiveness by excluding expert witnesses.[124]

E-Commerce and Product Liability   Product liability law is largely an undeveloped area in e-commerce. As such, "Advertisers are advised to assume that what they sow on the Web with intent to sell may generate a presumption of reliance by injured consumers.

Advertisers must assume that any express warranty is vulnerable to claims by a range of people who have specifically relied on it. If anything, the vastness of the Web environment will expand this field of liability."[125] E-marketers should avoid unqualified safety language, including variations of the word "safe." They should also avoid broad warranty-guarantee language unless such claims can be backed up. It is advised that e-marketers use caution and common sense and seek counsel's advice on the breadth and limits of selling language.

Product liability laws in the United States are influenced by the political process at the federal and the state levels. Different stakeholders redraw battle lines on product liability laws depending on a number of factors, including industry interests, power, and political access. As a result, tort reform continues to evolve. As discussed in Chapter 2, alternative dispute resolution (ADR) offers approaches to negotiating product liability differences without going to court. Trained mediators assist both sides of disputes in negotiating settlements. Since ADR offers cost savings in terms of time, court expenditures, and dissatisfied outcomes, this process could help companies, industries, and individuals resolve what appeared to be irreconcilable conflicts.

4.7 CORPORATE RESPONSIBILITY AND THE ENVIRONMENT

A time existed when corporations used the environment as a free and unlimited resource. That time is ending, in terms of international public awareness and increasing legislative control. The magnitude of environmental abuse, not only by industries but also by human activities and nature's processes, has awakened an international awareness of the need to protect the environment. At risk is the most valuable stakeholder, the earth itself. The depletion and destruction of air, water, and land are at stake. Consider the destruction of the rain forests in Brazil; the thinning of the ozone layer; climatic warming changes from carbon dioxide accumulations; the smog in Mexico City, Los Angeles, and New York City; the pollution of the seas, lakes, rivers, and groundwater as a result of toxic dumping; and the destruction of Florida's Everglades National Park. At the human level, environmental pollution and damage cause heart and respiratory diseases and skin cancer. Registered voters have stated that the most important environmental problems facing the nation are air pollution (26%), unsafe drinking water (11%), water pollution (11%), and toxic/hazardous waste (10%).[126]

Most Significant Environmental Problems

Toxic Air Pollution   More people are killed, it is estimated, by air pollution (automobile exhaust and smokestack emissions) than by traffic crashes. The so-called greenhouse gases are composed of the pollutants carbon monoxide, ozone, and ultrafine particles called particulates. These pollutants are produced by the combustion of coal, gasoline, and fossil fuels in cars. In 2001, the American Lung Association ranked the following U.S. metropolitan areas the worst in terms of ozone and greenhouse pollution: Los Angeles and three other California sites, the Houston-Galveston area of Texas, and Atlanta. Another study stated that by adopting greenhouse gas abatement technologies that are currently available, 64,000 lives could be saved in Sao Paulo, Brazil; Mexico City, Mexico; Santiago, Chile; and New York City alone in the next 20 years. The same study estimated that 65,000 cases of chronic bronchitis could be avoided and almost 37 million days of lost work saved.[127]

Air pollution and greenhouse gases are linked to global warming, as evidenced in

- The 5 degree increase in Arctic air temperatures, as the earth becomes warmer today than at any time in the past 125,000 years.

- The snowmelt in northern Alaska, which comes 40 days earlier than it did 40 years ago.

- The sea-level rise, which, coupled with the increased frequency and intensity of storms, could inundate coastal areas, raising groundwater salinity.

- The atmospheric CO_2 levels, which are 31% higher than preindustrial levels 250 years ago.[128]

Nationally, carbon dioxide emissions are a major source of air pollution. "America's Top Five Warming Polluters (by Carbon Dioxide Emissions from Company-Owned or Operated Power Plants)" are listed in Figure 4.5. These companies had estimated annual CO_2 emissions of 70 million tons and reported 2003 revenue of $4.4 billion.[129] Internationally, greenhouse gas emission statistics show that Spain had the largest increase in emissions, followed by Ireland, the United States, Japan, the Netherlands, Italy, and Denmark. The EU, Britain, and Germany had emission decreases during this period (Figure 4.6).

To stabilize the climate, global carbon emissions must be cut in half, from the current six billion tons a year to under three billion tons a year. This reduction can be accomplished by producing more efficient cars and power plants, using mass transit and alternative energy, and improving

FIGURE 4.5	America's Top Five Global Warming Polluters: By Carbon Dioxide Emissions from Company-Owned or Operated Power Plants

#1: American Electric Power Company, Inc. (AEP)/American Electric Power Service Corp.
        Estimated annual CO_2 emissions: 226 million tons
        2003 reported revenue: $15.6 billion
#2: The Southern Company (SO)
        Estimated annual CO_2 emissions: 171 million tons
        2003 reported revenue: $11.28 billion
#3: Tennessee Valley Authority
        Estimated annual CO_2 emissions: 110 million tons
        2003 reported revenue: $6.95 billion
#4: Xcel Energy Inc. (XEL)
        Estimated annual CO_2 emissions: 75 million tons
        2003 reported revenue: $7.9 billion
#5: Cinergy Corp. (CIN)
        Estimated annual CO_2 emissions: 70 million tons
        2003 reported revenue: $4.4 billion

Source: U.S. Embassy in Tokyo, "U.S. Releases Reports on Technologies to Reduce Greenhouse Gases," December 3, 2003, http://japan.usembassy.gov/e/p/ tp-20031204-01.html.

FIGURE 4.6	Greenhouse Gas Emissions: United States, Japan, and Selected EU Countries

	Reduction Target Increases by 2008–2012*	Emission Change 1990–1999
Spain	15%	23.2%
Ireland	13.0	22.1
United States	−7.0	16.0
Japan	−6.0	7.8
Netherlands	−6.0	6.1
Italy	−6.5	4.4
Denmark	−21.0	4.0
European Union	−8.0	−4.0
Britain	−12.5	−14.0
Germany	−21.0	−18.7

*Kyoto Protocol and E.U. burden sharing

Source: European Commission: European Climate Network. Adapted from G. Winestock, "EU Wrestles with Business over Emissions," *Wall Street Journal*, July 13, 2001, A9.

building and appliance standards. These changes would also help alleviate energy crises as well as global warming and air pollution.[130]

A *New York Times* article noted that, "In a striking shift in the way the administration of President George W. Bush has portrayed the science of climate change, a report (found on http://www.climatescience.gov/) to Congress focuses on federal research indicating that emissions of carbon dioxide and other heat-trapping gases are the only likely explanation for global warming over the last three decades."[131] Attached to the report was a letter signed by Bush's secretaries of energy and commerce and by his science adviser.

Water Pollution and the Threat of Scarcity

"Approximately 1.1 billion people worldwide lack access to improved water sources, and 2.4 billion people lack access to any type of improved sanitation. This lack of access comes with a heavy price. Some 1.7 million deaths a year worldwide are attributable to unsafe water and to poor sanitation and hygiene, mainly through infectious diarrhea. Most of the deaths (90%) occur in children, and virtually all occur in developing countries. Every year, more than one million people die of malaria, a disease closely linked to the poor management of water resources, and about 6% of the global burden of disease is water related. Much of the morbidity and mortality could be mitigated by providing adequate sanitation services, a safe water supply, and hygiene education. These are effective interventions that studies suggest could reduce mortality from diarrheal disease by an average of 65% and related morbidity by 26%."[132]

Water pollution is a result of industrial waste dumping, sewage drainage, and runoff of the agricultural chemicals. The combined effects of global water pollution are causing a noticeable scarcity. Water reserves in major aquifers are decreasing by an estimated 200 trillion cubic meters each year. The problem stems from the depletion and pollution of the world's groundwater. "In Bangladesh, for instance, perhaps half the country's population is drinking groundwater containing unsafe levels of arsenic. By inadvertently poisoning groundwater, we may turn what is essentially a renewable resource into one that cannot be recharged or purified within human scales, rendering it unusable."[133] It is estimated that the United States will have to spend $1 trillion over the next 30 years to begin to purify thousands of sites of polluted groundwater. An EPA report estimated that it could cost $900 million to $4.3 billion dollars annually to implement one of the tools under the Clean Water Act for cleaning up the nation's waters.[134] It will require an integrated global effort of public and private groups, of individuals and corporations to begin planning and implementing massive recycling, including agricultural, chemical, and other pollution controls to address water protection and control. Many companies have already begun conservation efforts. Xerox has halved its use of dichloromethane, a solvent used to make photoreceptors. The firm also reuses 97% of the solvent and will replace it with a nontoxic solvent. The Netherlands has a national goal of cutting wastes between 70 and 90%.

Causes of Environmental Pollution   Some of the most pervasive factors that have contributed to the depletion of resources and damage to the environment are as follows:

1. *Consumer affluence.* Increased wealth—as measured by personal per capita income—has led to increased spending, consumption, and waste.

2. *Materialistic cultural values.* Values have evolved to emphasize consumption over conservation—a mentality that believes in "bigger is better," "me first," and a throwaway ethic.

3. *Urbanization.* Concentrations of people in cities increase pollution, as illustrated by Los Angeles, New York City, Mexico City, Sao Paulo, and Santiago to name a few.

4. *Population explosion.* Population growth means more industrialization, product use, waste, and pollution.

5. *New and uncontrolled technologies.* Technologies are produced by firms that prioritize profits, convenience, and consumption over environmental protection. Although this belief system is changing, the environmental protection viewpoint is still not mainstream.

6. *Industrial activities.* Industrial activities that, as stated earlier, have emphasized depletion of natural resources and destructive uses of the environment for economic reasons have caused significant environmental decay.[135]

Enforcement of Environmental Laws   A number of governmental regulatory agencies have been created to develop and enforce policies and laws to protect the general and workplace environments. The Occupational Safety and Health Administration (OSHA), the Consumer Product Safety Commission, the Environmental Protection Agency, and the Council on Environmental Quality (CEQ) are among the more active agencies that regulate environmental standards. The EPA, in particular, has been a leading organization in regulating environmental abuses by industrial firms.

In 1970, the EPA's mission and activities concentrated on controlling and decreasing toxic substances, radiation, air pollution, water pollution, solid waste (trash), and pesticides. The EPA has since used its regulatory powers to enforce several important environmental laws such as:

- *The Clean Air Act of 1970, 1977, 1989, and 1990:* The latest revision of this law includes provisions for regulating urban smog, greenhouse gas emissions, and acid rain and for slowing ozone reduction. Alternative fuels were promoted and companies were authorized to sell or transfer their right to pollute within same-state boundaries—before, pollution rights could be bought, sold, managed, and brokered like securities.

- *The Federal Water Pollution Control Act of 1972:* Revised in 1977, this law controls the discharge of toxic pollutants into the water.

- *The Safe Drinking Water Act of 1974 and 1996:* It established national standards for drinking water.

- *The Toxic Substances Control Act of 1976:* It created a national policy on regulating, controlling, and banning toxic chemicals where necessary.

- *The Resource Conservation and Recovery Act (RCRA) of 1976:* This legislation provides guidelines for the identification, control, and regulation of hazardous wastes by companies and state governments. The $1.6 billion Superfund was created by Congress in 1980. It provides for the cleanup of chemical spills and toxic waste dumps. Chemical, petroleum, and oil firms' taxes help keep the Superfund going, along with U.S. Treasury funds and fees collected from pollution control. One in four U.S. residents lives within four miles of a Superfund site. It is estimated that 10,000 sites still need cleaning, and it may cost $1 trillion and take 50 years to complete this work.[136]

- *Chemical Safety Information, Site Security, and Fuels Regulatory Relief Act of 1999:* It created standards for storing flammable fuels and chemicals.

The Ethics of Ecology

Advocates of a new environmentalism argue that when the stakes approach the damage of the earth itself and human health and survival, the utilitarian ethic alone is an insufficient logic to justify continuing negligence and abuse of the earth. For example, Sagoff argues that cost-benefit analysis can measure only desires, not beliefs. In support of corporate environmental policies, he asks:

> Why should we think economic efficiency is an important goal? Why should we take wants and preferences more seriously than beliefs and opinions? Why should we base public policy on the model of a market transaction rather

than the model of a political debate? Economists as a rule do not recognize one other value, namely, justice or equality, and they speak, therefore, of a "trade-off" between efficiency and our aesthetic and moral values. What about the trade-off between efficiency and dignity, efficiency and self-respect, efficiency and the magnificence of our natural heritage, efficiency, and the quality of life?[137]

This line of reasoning raises questions such as these: What is human life worth? What is a "fair market" price or replacement value for Lake Erie? The Atlantic Ocean? The Brazilian rain forests? The stratosphere?

Five arguments from those who advocate corporate social responsibility from an ecology-based organizational ethic include the following:

1. Organizations' responsibilities go beyond the production of goods and services at a profit.

2. These responsibilities involve helping to solve important social problems, especially those they have helped create.

3. Corporations have a broader constituency than stockholders alone.

4. Corporations have impacts that go beyond simple marketplace transactions.

5. Corporations serve a wider range of human values than just economics.[138]

Although these guidelines serve as an ethical basis for understanding corporate responsibility for the environment, utilitarian logic and cost-benefit methods will continue to play key roles in corporate decisions regarding their uses of the environment. Also, judges, courts, and juries will use cost-benefit analysis in trying to decide who should pay and how much when settling case-by-case environmental disputes. Some experts and industry spokespersons argue that the costs of further controlling pollutants such as smog outweigh the benefits. For example, it is estimated that the cost of controlling pollution in the United States has exceeded $160 billion.[139] A World Health Organization study has estimated that air pollution will cause 8 million deaths worldwide by 2020. How many lives would justify spending $160 billion annually? Although some benefits of controlling pollution have been identified, such as the drop in emissions, improvement of air and water quality, cleanup of many waste sites, and growth of industries and jobs related to pollution control (environmental products, tourism, fishing, and boating), it is not clear whether these benefits outweigh the costs.[140] One question sometimes asked regarding this issue is, Would the environment be better off *without* the environmental laws and protection agencies paid by tax dollars?

Green Marketing, Environmental Justice, and Industrial Ecology

An innovative trend in new ecology ethical thinking is linking the concepts of green marketing, environmental justice, and industrial ecology.[141] Green marketing is the practice of "adopting resource conserving and environmentally-friendly strategies in all stages of the value chain."[142] The green market was estimated at 52 million households in the United States in 1995. One study identified trends among consumers who would switch products to green brands: 88% of consumers surveyed in Germany said they would switch, as would 84% in Italy and 82% in Spain.[143] Companies are adopting green marketing as a competitive advantage and are also using green marketing in their operations: for example, packaging materials that are recyclable, pollution-free production processes, pesticide-free farming, and natural fertilizers.

Environmental justice is "the pursuit without discrimination based on race, ethnicity, and/or socioeconomic status concerning both the enforcement of existing environmental laws and regulations and the reformation of public health policy."[144] Linking environmental justice to green marketing involves identifying companies that would qualify for visible, prestigious awards—such as the Edison Award—for producing the best green products. To win the award, companies would demonstrate that they had, for example, (1) produced new products and product extensions that represented an important achievement in reducing environmental impact, (2) indicated where and how they had disposed of industrial and toxic materials, and (3) incorporated recycling and use of less toxic materials in their strategies and processes.

The green marketing and environmental justice link to industrial ecology is made in the long-range vision and practice of companies' integrating environmental justice into sustainable operational practices on an industrywide basis. Industrial ecology is based on the principle of operating within nature's domain—that is, nothing is wasted; everything is recycled.

Rights of Future Generations and Right to a Livable Environment

The ethical principles of rights and duties regarding the treatment of the environment and multiple stakeholders are (1) the rights of future generations and (2) the right to a livable environment. These rights are based on the responsibility that the present generation should bear regarding the preservation of the environment for future generations. In other words, how much of the environment can a present generation use or destroy to advance its own economic welfare? According to ethicist John Rawls, "Justice requires that we hand over to our immediate successors a world that is not in worse condition than the one we received from our ancestors."[145]

The right to a livable environment is an issue advanced by Blackstone.[146] The logic is that each human being has a moral and legal right to a decent, livable environment. This "environmental right" supersedes individuals' legal property rights and is based on the belief that human life is not possible without a livable environment. Therefore, laws must enforce the protection of the environment based on human survival. Several landmark laws have been passed, as noted earlier, that are based more on the logic related to Blackstone's "environmental right" than on a utilitarian ethic.

Recommendations to Managers   Boards of directors, business leaders, managers, and professionals should ask four questions regarding their actual operations and responsibility toward the environment:

1. How much is your company really worth? (This question refers to the contingent liability a firm may have to assume depending on its practices.)

2. Have you made environmental risk analysis an integral part of your strategic planning process?

3. Does your information system "look out for" environmental problems?

4. Have you made it clear to your officers and employees that strict adherence to environmental safeguarding and sustainability requirements are a fundamental tenet of company policy?[147]

Using the answers to these questions, an organization can determine its stage on the corporate environmental responsibility profile (see Figure 4.7).

The stages range from Beginner (who shows no involvement and minimal resource commitment to responsible environmental management) to Proactivist (who is actively committed and involved in funding environmental management).

Finally, managers and professionals can determine whether their company's environmental values are reflected in these three ethical principles, quoted from the article "Toward a Life Centered Ethic for Business."[148]

The Principle of Connectedness. Human life is biologically dependent on other forms of life, and on ecosystems as a whole, including the non-living aspects of ecosystems. Therefore, humans must establish some connection with life and respect that it exists because living things exist in some state of cooperation and coexistence.

FIGURE 4.7   5 Stages of Environmental Corporate Commitment

Stage	Manager Mindset	Resource Commitment	Top-Level Support & Involvement
1. Beginner	Environmental management unnecessary	Minimal resource commitment	No involvement
2. Firefighter	Environmental issues addressed when necessary	Budgets for problems as they occur	Piecemeal involvement
3. Concerned citizen	Environmental management is a worthwhile function	Consistent yet minimal budget	Commitment in theory
4. Pragmatist	Environmental management is an important business function	Generally sufficient funding	Aware and moderately involved
5. Proactivist	Environmental management is a priority item	Open-ended funding	Actively involved

Source: Reprinted from "Proactive Environmental Management: Avoiding the Toxic Trap" by Christoper B. Hunt and Ellen R. Auster, *MIT Sloan Management Review,* Winter, 1990, p. 9, by permission of publisher. © 1990 by Massachusetts Institute of Technology. All rights reserved.

The Principle of Ecologizing Values. Life exists in part because of the ecologizing values of linkage, diversity, homeostatic succession, and community. There is a presumption that these values are primary goods to be conserved.

The Principle of Limited Competition. "You may compete (with other living beings) to the full extent of your abilities, but you may not hunt down your competitors or destroy their food or deny them access to food. You may compete but may not wage war."[149] [We would add to the last sentence, "without just cause."]

SUMMARY

Managing corporate social responsibility from the corporate board of directors to the marketplace requires commitment, significant time, effort, and resources from organizations. At stake is a company's reputation and even survival. A profile of several of the "100 Best Corporate Citizens" companies illustrated firms that operate ethically in the marketplace.

The corporation as social and economic stakeholder was presented from the perspectives of the social contract and covenantal ethic. Corporate social responsibility was also discussed from legal, ethical, philanthropic, and pragmatic views. Managing and balancing legal compliance with ethical motivation was illustrated by the Sarbanes-Oxley Act and the revised Federal Sentencing Guidelines. A summary of events from corporate scandals was shown by explaining the need for legal compliance in corporations. Arguments were offered to explain that legal compliance legislation and programs alone are necessary but not sufficient to motivate ethical and legal behavior in organizations.

Corporate responsibility toward consumers was presented by explaining these corporate duties: (1) the duty to inform consumers truthfully, (2) the duty not to misrepresent or withhold information, (3) the duty not to unreasonably force consumer choice or take undue advantage of consumers through fear or stress, and (4) the duty to take "due care" to prevent any foreseeable injuries. The use of a utilitarian ethic was discussed to show the problems in holding corporations accountable for product risks and injuries beyond their control.

The free-market theory of Adam Smith was summarized by way of explaining the market context governing the exchange of producers and buyers. Several limits of the free market were offered—namely, imperfect markets exist, the power between buyers and sellers is not symmetrical, and the line between telling the truth and lying about products is very thin. Economist Paul Samuelson's "mixed-economy" was introduced to offer a more balanced view of free-market theory and of the unrealistic demands often placed on corporations in marketing new products.

Nevertheless, businesses have legal and moral obligations to provide their consumers with safe products without using false advertising and without doing harm to the environment. The complexities and controversies with respect to this obligation stem from attempts to define "safety," "truth in advertising," and levels of "harm" caused to the environment. The Federal Trade Commission's guidelines for online marketing show that this agency has considerable power and legitimacy in informing the public about ads; it also serves as a useful watchdog on corporate advertising and product regulation. Arguments for and against advertising were presented, with problematic examples of false advertising from the food and tobacco industries highlighted.

Product safety and liability were discussed through the doctrines of negligence, strict liability, and absolute liability. The Johns-Manville asbestos crisis was presented as an example. The legal and moral limits of product liability were summarized. Presently, states are moving to limit punitive damages in product liability cases, and tort reform is predicted to change the direction of product liability litigation toward more protection for manufacturers than for injured consumers.

Corporate responsibility toward the environment was presented by showing how air, water, and land pollution is a serious, long-term problem. Federal laws aimed at protecting the environment were summarized. Increasing concern over the destruction of the ozone layer, the destruction of the rain forests, and other environmental issues has presented firms with another area where economic and social responsibilities must be balanced. Innovative concepts and corporate attitude changes were discussed. Green marketing, environmental justice, and industrial ecology principles are being practiced by a growing number corporations, particularly in Europe—especially since green products and clean manufacturing processes (and certifications) offer a competitive advantage. An innovative move by some corporations is to include environmental safety practices in the strategic, enterprise, and supply chain dimensions of industrial activities and practices. A diagnostic (Figure 4.6) enables a company to identify its stage of social responsibility toward the environment.

QUESTIONS

1. Identify three companies in the news or which you are familiar with that operate ethically. What are the reasons these companies/organizations are ethical?

2. Do you believe that the Sarbanes-Oxley Act is *not* needed? Explain or offer a different argument.

3. Are the revised 1991 Federal Sentencing Guidelines, in your opinion, helpful to organizational leaders and boards of directors in promoting more ethical behavior? Explain. What other actions, policies, or procedures would you recommend?

4. Which of the corporate crises summarized in the chapter were you unfamiliar with? Do you believe these crises represent business as usual or serious breakdowns in a company's system? Why?

5. After reading the Johns-Manville and Exxon Valdez summaries, identify some ways these crises could have been (1) avoided and (2) managed more responsibly after they occurred.

6. What was your score on the Rank Your Organization's Reputation quiz in the chapter? After reading previous chapters in this book, how would you describe the "ethics" of your organization, university, or college toward its customers and stakeholders? Explain.

7. Do you believe the covenantal ethic and social contract views are realistic with large organizations like ExxonMobil and Citibank or federal agencies like the FTC and the Department of Defense? Why or why not? Explain.

8. Are there ethical principles of advertising that apply to consumers in all cultures and countries? Explain.

9. What is the free-market theory of corporate responsibility for consumers, and what are some of the problems associated with this view? Compare this view with the social contract and stakeholder perspectives of corporate social responsibility.

10. Describe an advertisement in the media that you believe is unethical. Explain your argument.

11. What constitutes "unreasonable risk" concerning the safety of a product? Identify considerations that define the safety of a product from an ethical perspective.

12. Do you believe the environment is in trouble from human pollution, or do you believe this is "hype" from the press and scientists? Explain.

EXERCISES

1. Identify a recent example of a corporation accused of false or deceitful advertising. How did it justify the claims made in its ad? Do you agree or disagree with the claims? Explain.

2. In a paragraph, explain your opinion of whether the advertising industry requires regulation.

3. Outline some steps you would recommend for preventing future corporate scandals like Enron.

4. Can you think of an instance when you or someone you know was affected by corporate negligence in terms of product safety standards? If so, did you or the person communicate the problem to the company?

5. Do you believe cigarette, cigar, and pipe smoking should be banned from all public places where passive smoking can affect nonsmokers? Explain. Use the following (or other) Web sites to argue your position: http://www.cdc.gov; http://www.tobacco.org; http://www.thetruth.com; http://www.trytostop.org; http://www.cancer.org; http://www.getoutraged.com.

6. Find a recent article discussing environmental damage caused by a corporation's activities. Recommend methods the firm in the article should employ to reduce harmful effects on the environment.

7. Find a recent article discussing an innovative way in which a corporation is helping the environment. Explain why the method is innovative and whether you believe the method will really help the environment or will only help the company promote its image as a good citizen.

Ethical Dilemma   Ethical Practice or Entrapment?

My job requires that I lie every day I go to work. I work for a private investigation agency called XRT. Most of the work I do involves undercover operations, mobile surveillances, and groundwork searches to determine the whereabouts of manufacturers that produce counterfeit merchandise.

Each assignment I take requires some deception on my part. Recently I have become very conscious of the fact that I frequently have to lie to obtain concrete evidence for a client. I sometimes dig myself so deeply into a lie that I naturally take it to the next level without ever accomplishing the core purpose of the investigation.

Working for an investigative agency engages me in assignments that vary on a day-to-day basis. I choose to work for XRT because it is not a routine 9 to 5 desk job. But to continue working for the agency means I will constantly be developing new untruthful stories. And the longer I decide to stay at XRT, the more involved the assignments will be. To leave would probably force me into a job photocopying and filing paperwork once I graduate from college.

Recently I was given an assignment which I believed would lead me to entrap a subject to obtain evidence for a client. The subject had filed for disability on workers' compensation after being hit by a truck. Because the subject refused to partake in any strenuous activity because of the accident, I was instructed to fake a flat tire and videotape the subject changing it for me. Although I did not feel comfortable engaging in this type of act, my supervisors assured me that it was ethical practice and not entrapment. Coworkers and other supervisors assured me that this was a standard "industry practice," that we would go out of business if we didn't "fudge" the facts once in a while. I was told, "Do you think every business does its work and makes profits in a purely ethical way? Get real. I don't know what they're teaching you in college, but this is the real world." It was either do the assignment or find myself on the street—in an economy with no jobs.

QUESTIONS

1. What is the dilemma here, or is there one?

2. What would you have done in the writer's situation? Explain.

3. React to the comment, "Do you think every business does its work and makes profits in a purely ethical way? Get real. I don't know what they're teaching you in college, but this is the real world." Do you agree or disagree? Why?

4. Describe the ethics of this company.

5. Compare and contrast your personal ethics with the company ethics revealed here.

CASE 10

NAPSTER: FROM ILLEGAL WEAPON TO KILLER APPLICATION

Napster and other Internet companies opened the proverbial Pandora's box when they introduced peer-to-peer (P2P) networks. P2P applications changed the way people used the Internet by creating an environment where millions of users could share various types of files, including files that hold a copyright, such as digital music files called MP3s. Napster rapidly became one of the most popular P2P applications, amassing a file-sharing community that originally had over 38 million registered accounts. Research firm Media Metrix discovered the application on almost 10% of American computers connected to the Internet. Another research firm, NetRatings, found Napster on slightly more than 6% of Internet-connected computers in the United Kingdom and Germany.

Napster.com originally provided its services and interface programs to make the exchange of MP3s more straightforward and convenient. This convenience fomented a controversy over the legality of using music without permission from the owner. The Napster P2P application, in conjunction with the continuous improvement of Internet connectivity and speed, enabled users to have unrestricted access and to copy limitless files for free.

The Technology Behind the P2P Application

The P2P application created a marketplace where users select and exchange files directly and promptly without the dependence of a centralized mediator. P2P file-sharing technology eliminates the need for accessing a large centralized marketplace where information is gathered, stored, and controlled by one party. Although there are several variations of P2P applications, Napster.com originally provided a directory of MP3s where users could download music from another user's PC without charge.

The P2P application utilizes various file-sharing protocols. TCP/IP, which stands for transmission control protocol/Internet protocol, is the most widely used Internet protocol for the transmission of data. Data are first broken down into many packets of information and then transferred along a medium to its destination. Each client/server, while connected to the Internet, begins the transfer of data by calling upon a file transfer protocol (FTP). FTP is used in conjunction with TCP/IP to communicate with the destination client/server and, in this manner, transfers data at speeds equal to the slowest connection. The communication link between each client and server is typically a modem connection, which is relatively slow. Faster connection speeds like T3, T1, DSL, and broadband connections download files considerably faster than the 56-kbps connections of modems. Connection speeds are the backbone of the file-sharing phenomenon—the faster the Internet connection, the faster files are downloaded. Without these speeds, time would be consumed in downloading files.

Brief History of the Development of P2P Applications

The P2P application—first called file transfer protocol (FTP)—was developed at MIT in 1971. This early program, however, was limited in usefulness because it required the user to know the exact file name before the file could be found. Several incremental changes were made throughout the 1970s and 1980s, and then, in 1990, Alan Emtage at McGill University in Montreal developed a program called "Archie." Archie worked like a search engine as it regularly downloaded indexes of public FTP host computers and file names. Archie was limited to querying file names containing key words. In October 1993, Archie evolved into Aliweb, which allowed webmasters to include an index of URL keywords, thereby permitting more than just the file name to be queried.

The next generation of P2P programs was much more advanced and user friendly. Shawn Fanning, a 19-year-old college student at the time, developed the most recognizable P2P—Napster, which had the music recording industry pursuing regulation for copyrighted files. Another P2P application, Docster, used a technology similar to Napster. However, instead of the MP3s being queried, specific text documents were targeted and exchanged, with the site working like a virtual library. Another start-up, Lightshare Inc., used the P2P application to directly connect users who wanted to buy and sell merchandise through an auction format similar to eBay. Justin Frankel and his fellow programmers at Nullsoft, an AOL company, created a file-sharing protocol—Gnutella—that utilized limitless P2P exchanges of all file types. Gnutella users shared MP3s as well as pictures, documents, and proprietary software—for example, Windows 2000.

Users of P2P Applications

Users of P2P applications are anyone and everyone connected to the Internet who wants to search for information, songs, and documents. A key question that originally surrounded the security of P2P applications was, "Should I be worried about the potential hazards of giving anyone access to my computer?" Users were—and are—more reluctant to join the file-sharing phenomenon if speeds are too slow. At many colleges with newer and faster Internet and networking hardware, students flocked to join the frenzy caused by P2P networks. Consequently, the bandwidth of college networking systems was inundated with file sharing and exchanging—so much that "[t]hirty-four percent of 50 U.S. colleges and universities have banned students from using Napster Inc.'s song-swap service on their campuses." Despite ongoing P2P concerns regarding security and legality, a majority of college students used Napster on a regular basis. Users of P2P applications also originally had concerns about paying a price to share files over the Internet. P2P companies like Napster eventually changed their freewheeling practices and accommodated copyright holders to avoid legal issues.

Napster's Fall from Glory   The file-sharing technology developed by Napster and other companies impacted several groups in society, most notably the music industry. Dr. Dre, a concerned music artist, summed up his feelings toward Napster this way: "I'm in the business to make money, and Napster is ____ing that up!" British Music Rights—an organization for composers, songwriters, and publishers—asked society to "[r]espect the value of music." Both popular artists and lesser known songwriters and composers rely upon music sales for their livelihoods, and they were affected negatively by the file-sharing technology.

The corporations that provided financial and marketing support to recording artists and songwriters were also affected by file-sharing technology. Warner Brothers Music, Sony, Bertelsmann Music Group (BMG), Universal, and EMI Group Plc, all members of the Recording Industry Association of America (RIAA), settled lawsuits with MP3.com for distributing copyrighted materials without their consent over the Internet. Hillary Rosen, president of RIAA, said the recording industry lawsuit against MP3.com was "never about stifling the technology or putting this company out of business, but rather about protecting the copyright owners' and artists' rights to be compensated for their works."

After the settlement with MP3.com, the focus was no longer on who would distribute the music over the Internet, but rather how. The same plaintiffs that filed lawsuits against MP3.com also filed lawsuits against Napster, claiming that the company's music-sharing application encouraged copyright infringement by facilitating the exchange of songs over the Internet for free. In the ensuing legal battles, Napster had both its supporters and detractors.

Limp Bizkit was one of the first musical groups to adopt Napster and its file-sharing service. The band's lead singer, Fred Durst, publicly supported Napster, saying the file-sharing service "provides an amazing way to market and promote music to a massive audience." He also went on to say that Napster provided a great forum for fans to sample an album before buying it. Courtney Love, another recording artist and Napster supporter, said, "Stealing our copyright provisions in the dead of night when no one is looking is piracy. It's not piracy when kids swap music over the Internet using Napster. There were one billion downloads last year, but music sales are way up, so how is Napster hurting the music industry? It's not. The only people who are scared of Napster are the people who have filler on their albums and are scared that if people hear more than one single they're not going to buy the album."

Lars Ulrich, the drummer for the popular rock band Metallica, on the other hand, sued Napster for copyright infringement. He claimed Napster's service of sharing MP3s was "trafficking stolen goods." Ulrich, like most of the recording industry, was threatened by Napster's reach.

Technology—such as P2P or any other computer software applications—must be developed in accordance with the laws and acts associated with copyrights. Napster was accused of interrupting the process. At issue was the disruptive technology of Napster and other similar applications that impinged on others' property rights. The courts had to consider (1) how to address the fact that millions of users were in violation of copyright laws, (2) how to protect the intellectual property and rights of the copyright holders, and (3) how to harness this technical ability to freely and easily access and then share vast amounts of information without restraint.

Forrester, an Internet research group, predicted that by 2005 lost music sales worldwide would amount to $3 billion, and the free music services and file-swapping technologies would be responsible for a major part of the loss. A survey conducted by MSNBC asked users if they would be willing to pay to use Napster. Seventy percent of the 17,633 people who responded said they would not be willing to pay. Andrea Schmidt, president and chief executive of BMG's e-commerce group predicted that 80% of Napster's estimated 38 million users worldwide would pay about $15 per month to subscribe to Napster.

By mid-2001, Napster lost its court battles with the music industry, and its free music file-sharing service was shut down. Other services—like Kazaa, Aimster, and Napigator—stepped in to fill the Napster vacuum. In some ways, the Napster alternatives may be harder for the music industry to thwart. Of the nine alternative services that one research firm tracked, several used file-sharing formats similar to that used by Napster. Consequently, recording companies that have already filed lawsuits against two of the newer services may have a tough time keeping the music from flowing.

The Reincarnation of Napster   Napster's name, some intellectual property, and hardware were sold at auction to Roxio Inc., a software company that developed and sold CD burning applications. Roxio later sold its consumer software division and renamed itself Napster Inc.

The reincarnated Napster focused on online subscription sales of music, and at the end of 2004, it had 270,000 paid subscribers. While the customer base was miniscule in comparison to online music store rivals like Apple's iTunes Music Store and Microsoft's MSN Music Store, Napster—true to its previous incarnation—was nonetheless highly ambitious. On February 2, 2005, Napster Inc. "unveiled a portable version of its music subscription service, backed by a $30 million ad campaign that takes aim at rival Apple Computer Inc.'s popular iPod player." The ad campaign urges consumers to "compare the costs of spending $10,000 to buy and transfer 10,000 songs from Apple's iTunes store to an iPod, with the $15-per-month fee to carry songs from a catalog of over a million tracks on Napster-compatible players." Five existing MP3 players will support Napster's new service with at least an additional 14 players expected to support it by mid-2005.

Called Napster to Go, Chris Gorog, Napster's chairman and chief executive officer, asserted that the new service would "change the music industry forever." An industry observer, Matt Whipp, noted that a revolutionary change fostered by Napster to Go would certainly be interesting. Reflecting some skepticism about the Gorog's assertion, Whipp added, "The music industry's first response to illegal file-sharing—largely through Napster—was the provision of music services such as PressPlay and MusicNet. Yet it was Apple's a la carte iTunes service that broke the mold and made a success out of online music that was otherwise failing."

Apple was the dominant player in online music sales as 2005 began, but its dominance, coupled with the issue of music portability, created an opportunity for Napster. Anyone with a Mac or PC could purchase music from Apple's iTunes Music Store for 99 cents per download. However, Apple iPod owners could store only songs purchased from the Apple iTunes Music Store on their iPods. Critics of Apple's iPod ask, "[I]s it really fair that if you purchase an iTunes track for 99 cents that you must get an iPod to be able to carry it around with you?" This restricted portability created openings for Napster and others with stakes in the online music industry.

Music subscription providers indicate that Janus, the Digital Rights Management (DRM) software developed in 2004 by Microsoft, will solve the problem of users "not being able to take their music with them beyond their personal computers." However, the Windows DRM technology embedded into Napster's content may create problems for Napster's future growth. Because of the embedded DRM technology, any Napster customer who decides to try out the service and then discontinue it won't be able to play any of the music that has already been purchased. As a Reuters News Service article observed, "It will be interesting to see how much of a success Napster's new service will be, and whether or not they can damage Apple's current dominance in the portable music player . . . and online music downloading services."

A Parting Perspective

The Napster controversy set off an unprecedented flurry of publicity for a company that originally had no source of revenue. Napster showed that with a killer app and disruptive technology, there were few free lunches—especially when the stakes were so high. Napster's first incarnation failed to adequately consider all relevant stakeholders by not addressing the legitimate financial interests of artists and companies in the recording industry. The reincarnated Napster seems to have learned the stakeholder lesson regarding the financial interests of artists and recording companies, and perhaps it will become extraordinarily successful and continue to "change the music industry forever," as Chris Gorog asserted. At the very least, Napster now appears to be doing a better job of balancing the financial interests of the producers of music with the fair use rights of consumers. Moreover, any new online music company that uses P2P network technology must look at all stakeholders and issues surrounding its product before implementing a business model. Eventually, a P2P environment may exist where users feel comfortable trading files and copyright holders are fairly compensated.

Questions for Discussion

1. What are the major issues in this case?

2. Who are the key stakeholders, and how have they changed since Napster's beginning?

3. What were the stakes for the different constituencies associated with Napster's first and second incarnations?

4. Why did Napster not succeed in the marketplace with its original P2P application?

5. What is the appropriate balance between fair use rights of consumers and the financial interests of artists and the recording companies?

Sources

This case was developed from material contained in the following sources:

Brevetti, F. (February 7, 2005) Apple's iTunes music service may be supreme—but for how long? *Inside Bay Area*, http://www.insidebayarea.com/businessnews/onthemove/ci_2557889, accessed February 10, 2005.

Caney, D. (November 14, 2000) MP3.com, Universal settle for 53.4. *Reuters*, http://www.zdnet.com.

Chudnov, D. (August 1, 2000) Docster: The future of document delivery, *Library Journal, 125(13)*, 60.

Gartner Group Inc. (August 30, 2000) Napster banned at 34% of colleges. *Reuters,* http://msnbc.com/news/453430.asp.

Goodman, D. (April 25, 2000) Limp Bizkit backs Napster. *Reuters,* http://www.zdnet.com.

http://duke.usak.ca/~reeves/prog/geo314/archie.html.

http://gnutella.wego.com/go/wego.pages.page2?groupId=116705&view=page&pageId=18401&folder ID=118398&pan-elId=119597&action=view.

(June 29, 2000) http://www.Napster.com/speakout/artists.html.

Kover, A. (June 26, 2000) Napster: The hot idea of the year. *Fortune,* http://library.notherlight.com.

Kueffner, S. (November 28, 2000) Bertlesmann is poised to unveil Napster plans. http://interactive.wsj.com.

Learmonth, M. (October 32, 2000) Let the music play: Bertlesmann and Napster come together. http://www.thestandard.com.

Musicians fight "free" net music. (November 27, 2000) *Reuters,* http://msnbc.com/news.

Napster. (July 29, 2004) *Wikipedia,* http://en.wikipedia.org/wiki/Napster.

Napster takes aim at the iPod. (February 3, 2005) *Afterdawn.com,* http://www.afterdawn.com/news/archive/6029.cfm, accessed February 10, 2005.

Napster University: File swapping and the future of entertainment. (December 9, 2000) http://research.webnoize.com/item.rs?ID=9155.

Postel, J., and J. Reynolds. (October 1985) RFC959. http://www.landfield.com/rfcs/rfc959.html.

Stelin, S. (October 15, 2001) Napster's many successors. *New York Times,* 13.

Whipp, M. (February 3, 2005) Napster debuts a premium version of its music subscription service. *PC Pro,* http://www.pcpro.co.uk/news/69015/napster-debuts-a-premium-version-of-its-music-subscription-service.html, accessed February 10, 2005.

Zeidler, S. (February 3, 2005) Napster unveils portable service, anti-iPod campaign. *Reuters News,* http://story.news.yahoo.com/news?tmpl=story2&u=/nm/20050203/wr_nm/media_napster_dc, accessed February 10, 2005.

CASE 11

APPLE COMPUTER'S ONLINE MUSIC VENTURE

On April 28, 2003, Apple Computer, Inc. introduced a new version of iTunes, the company's innovative digital music jukebox software. This fourth major revision of iTunes included a surprising new feature, the iTunes Music Store—a vast collection of digitally encoded song files from all the major U.S. record companies, available for download at a price of 99 cents each. Customers could choose to download complete albums, usually priced at $9.99. The iTunes Music Store sold over one million songs in the first week, despite it being exclusively available to Macintosh users—roughly 5% of the personal computer market. This marked a major shift in power and distribution of songs within the music industry, and brought issues of copyright and "fair use" to the foreground of major media outlets.

Background and Industry Overview

MP3s   By the middle of 1995, MP3s—highly compressed digital audio files—became commonly available over the Internet and were small enough to be easily downloaded by users, even using the relatively slow modems of the day. The file format was the result of several audio encoding and psycho-acoustics projects funded by the European Union, culminating in the Moving Picture Experts Group (MPEG) specification "MPEG-1 Audio Layer 3." The roughly 10:1 compression rate allowed by MP3 encoding resulted in song files typically in the range of 3 to 4 megabytes, or about 1MB per minute of audio.

Mass storage capacity grew rapidly while the cost per unit of storage dropped at an exponential rate. Late in 1998, the cost of storing a complete music album on a hard drive equaled the cost of buying the same album on CD. This key figure, along with growing networks on college and university campuses and consumer broadband services, proved to be the tipping point for MP3 popularity.

Napster   By 1999, MP3 had become a household word on campus networks and personal computers. However, music lovers who were seeking MP3s experienced difficulty in finding the files. Software such as Nullsoft's WinAmp and Panic's Audion allowed users to create—or "rip"—their own MP3s from audio CDs, and many MP3 players existed, but no one had developed a good way of finding the millions of MP3s that existed on the Internet. Then, in the fall of 1999, Shawn Fanning—a then-19-year-old freshman at Northeastern University—released Napster to the world as a free download. The software—a type of peer-to-peer (P2P) network application—specialized in finding

MP3s by storing a list of all users' MP3s on a central server, and then allowing any connected user to search and download those files directly from other computers online.

The software's popularity grew quickly and made file trading so easy that by December of 1999 several major record companies in the U.S., claiming copyright infringement, filed lawsuits against Napster. The record companies sought to disable Napster's service despite the fact that the company's servers did not actually host any of the copyrighted material in question. By the second half of 2001, Napster had lost its court battles and was effectively shut down. The remaining assets—the name, some intellectual property, and hardware—were sold to Roxio Inc., a software company known for its CD burning applications. Subsequently, Roxio sold its consumer software division and renamed itself Napster Inc.

The RIAA Fights On   Even before the Recording Industry Association of America's (RIAA) lawyers succeeded in shutting down the Napster P2P network, many similar applications began appearing on the Internet as free downloads. One popular Napster clone, Kazaa—owned by Sharman Networks—gained the most notoriety from its legal battles around the world. Despite some affirmation from U.S. federal courts that similar P2P software had substantial non-infringing uses, Sharman Networks saw nearly continuous litigation after purchasing the rights to Kazaa.

A major factor that swayed consumers away from networks of copyrighted music files was the RIAA's increasingly public campaign of dissuasion by way of lawsuits and threatening letters. In one infamous case, the RIAA brought suit against 12-year-old Brianna LaHara, who was living with her mother in a low-income Housing Authority apartment. Fearing a public backlash, the RIAA lawyers quickly settled out of court for only $2,000, substantially less than the $150,000 per song in damages they normally sought. Since a federal appeals court ruling in December 2003, the RIAA has been unable to force Internet service providers (ISPs) into divulging the names of specific users thought to be violating copyright laws. Still, the RIAA continues to send out threatening letters and to file lawsuits against "John Doe," specified by Internet addresses.

Reinventing the Wheel

iMac   After Steve Jobs' highly publicized return to the computer company he co-founded in 1976, he set about reviving the languishing Macintosh computer line. By first cutting the number of products offered and then stressing the importance of innovation, Jobs managed to turn around the Macintosh unit, which launched the all-new iMac personal computer to great fanfare and accolades in mid-1998. By the beginning of 2001, the iMac computer line had become very successful, and the design had been refined to include a CD-RW drive—an optical drive capable of both *reading* and *writing* to inexpensive CD media. By October 2001, all of Apple's computers featured CD-RW drives, allowing users to backup valuable data or to burn their own music CDs.

iTunes   On January 9, 2001, Steve Jobs announced the availability of iTunes, then Apple's newest software, free for any Macintosh user to download. iTunes was touted as the "World's Best and Easiest to Use Jukebox Software." Macintosh users downloaded almost 300,000 copies of the digital music jukebox software within the first week. The copies were widely regarded as the first user-friendly solution to issues related to creating MP3s, like playing, organizing, and even burning them to blank CDs. iTunes also showed how wonderfully simple and elegant a well written program could be on the Macintosh platform. One of the most important features of iTunes, overlooked by many at first, was the ability to transfer songs from the computer to one of many popular portable MP3 players. MP3 players were quite popular digital music players; they were incredibly small and light, but could only hold one or two albums of MP3s at a time.

iPod   Eight months after the first release of iTunes, Apple announced the iPod, a portable digital music player based around a tiny new hard drive technology that enabled the device to store 5 gigabytes (5GB) of data—roughly 1,000 songs—at a time. Many PC users admired the simplicity of the iPod's design, which used a simple scroll wheel for all navigation, and its tight integration with iTunes software. However, many people also complained that the $399 price tag would guarantee the failure of the Mac-only device, even though it had many advanced features not found on competing devices and was much more compact than any other device that offered 5GB capacity. Subsequent events proved these naysayers wrong.

In less than a year, Apple introduced a Windows-compatible iPod— essentially identical to the Mac versions, but with MusicMatch software instead of iTunes. By July 2003, sales of both Mac and Windows iPods reached 1,000,000 units. After July 2003, sales increased sharply, as Apple sold 1 million iPods roughly every four and half to five months. Apple quickly developed additional iPod devices, having four distinct offerings in the iPod product line by early 2005. The iPod holds up to 10,000 songs, coming in 20GB and 40GB models, whereas the iPod Mini holds 1,000 songs. The iPod Shuffle comes in

512MB or 1GB models and plays up to 240 songs in random order. The iPod Photo comes in 40GB or 60GB models holding up to 15,000 songs or 25,000 photos. All of the devices can be used with Mac OS X or Windows 2000/XP computer operating systems. Moreover, music can be imported in a variety of formats, including MP3, Advanced Audio Coding (AAC), and Apple Lossless Encoder. As of early 2005, Apple has sold over 10 million iPods.

iTunes Music Store   The iTunes Music Store was launched on April 28, 2003. It initially featured over 200,000 songs from all of the major record labels and allowed users to download either individual songs or complete albums, for 99 cents and $9.99 respectively. It was originally only available to Macintosh users, as the iTunes software had not been released for Windows computers. Some people doubted Apple's ability to make any headway in the market, because of the limited user-base, and the fact that Apple was not the first company to try a legal download service for music. Despite these issues, Apple managed to sell over one million songs within the first week. The opportunity for additional, potentially substantial sales growth occurred with Apple's release, on October 16, 2003, of the first version of iTunes to support Windows-based PCs. Apple also announced that it would fully support the iTunes Music Store and all versions of iPods.

Since late 2003, the iTunes Music Store has enjoyed significant expansion. Via the Internet, the iTunes Music Store is open 24/7 for music downloads and, as of early 2005, has sold more than 230 million songs. With more than one million songs available for downloading, iTunes Music Store has "hundreds of thousands of songs from major music companies, including EMI, Sony/BMG, Universal, and Warner Bros . . . [and] more than 100,000 new tracks from independent artists and record labels." According to the Apple Web site, the iTunes Music Store allows users to quickly find, purchase, and download music. Users can burn individual songs on an unlimited number of CDs, listen to songs on an unlimited number of iPods, and play songs on up to five Macintosh computers or Windows PCs.

Digital Rights Management   Apple's successes with the iTunes software, iPod music player line, and iTunes Music Store did not occur without grappling with the thorny issue of Digital Rights Management (DRM). By the spring of 2002, DRM was an important concern for music lovers, music content owners, and technology companies. "DRM doesn't mean just basic copy-protection of digital content (like e-books, MP3s, or DivX videos), but it basically means full protection for digital content, ranging from delivery to end user's ways to use the content." In terms of music, "companies wish to develop a product which would allow record labels to sell copy-protected audio tracks over the Internet, so that only the buyer could be allowed to listen to the tracks." This desire on the part of music companies runs counter to national laws that traditionally have required record labels to grant "fair use" rights for their products. Fair use means that a customer must be allowed to make personal copies of the purchased music for use in a car, in a portable digital audio player, on a desktop or laptop computer, and so on. Typically, this problem has been solved by permitting the user to make a specified number of copies of the original file but disallowing additional copying of the files.

Apple's implementation of DRM technology—the code that permits (or limits) uses of copyrighted material in the digital world—represents a compromise of fair personal use and property rights for the users and copyright holders. Originally, in order to get all the major record labels to agree to Apple selling music online, Apple proposed a system that would limit the uses of the downloaded material, but only enough to inconvenience the true "pirates" of copyrighted music. The system allowed a customer to copy each music file an unlimited number of times in order to backup the file or move it from one home computer to another. The only limitation was that no more than three computers could be "enabled" to play the song at a time. In addition, the system allowed users on a network to stream their entire music library to any number of friends or strangers. Streaming enabled network users to listen but not copy, much like listening to the radio. Finally, the system allowed users to burn as many as 10 copies of a full downloaded album, after which point the user could continue to burn those songs as parts of a mix, but not as an original album.

iTunes users soon discovered that they could stream music from other users across the entire Internet. Web sites such as ShareiTunes.com and iTunesdb.com offered free services that let users browse all the available streams of users online, effectively letting anyone with iTunes listen—free of charge—to any song available. Apple responded by releasing a new version of iTunes that partially crippled the network streaming abilities, as well as reworking the structure of other DRM codes. As a result, users could freely stream from any other iTunes user on their network segment—typically each floor of a dorm or each household—but not across the Internet. Also, each copyrighted album could only be burned to a CD seven times—down from 10 times. In the users' favor, however, Apple increased the number of "enabled" computers from three to five. All songs could still be loaded onto and played from an unlimited number of iPods, allowing friends with extra capacity on their iPods to share complete music libraries.

Matthew Haughey of the Creative Commons—a group dedicated to the protection of public domain and fair use rights—reported on

DRM technology in a May 2003 interview of actor, writer, and technology guru Wiley Wiggins. Wiggins offered the following observation on DRM technology and Apple's application of it in the iTunes Music Store:

> Well, for all the flack it might get on Slashdot, I think Apple's Music Store is a pretty open and moderate use of DRM that keeps both nervous companies and users fairly happy. I'll support it in the hopes that the music selection grows, and because I think Apple has one of the more benevolent attitudes towards sharing information of the big media/computer conglomerates. . . . I can only hope that these technologies are used more in this style, as opposed to silly, broken formats that won't let you burn CDs or copy music off more than one computer. Unlimited [burns of] CDs and [use in] iPods is a step in the right direction.

The Future of DRM and Apple   Major questions remain regarding the future of consumers' fair use rights, the long-term impact of DRM software, and Apple's role in both. Many in the music industry have applauded Apple's pioneering of digital music and its moderate use of DRM, thereby maintaining consumer rights on some level. However, Apple's model of consumer rights has already changed once, and its terms of use and end user licenses dictate that the company has the right to change its model in the future, retroactively modifying consumers' rights to previously purchased music.

Considering growing competition in the marketplace, the interests of the big four record companies, and the advantage of online music providers with the record companies, the future of DRM is far from certain. As the market for digital devices has evolved, "most music players either have no DRM protection at all or have a proprietary method as with Sony and Apple devices." People who have "an iPod device can use only the music in the format delivered by iTunes," yet the music in iTunes Music Store is available to anyone with a Mac or a PC. Moreover, consumers can buy music online "from a variety of different platforms and retailers supported by Windows media. For instance, liquid.com, Napster, Wal-Mart, MusicMatch and so many others, many of which are selling their songs for less than 99 cents."

In 2004, Microsoft instituted a DRM program named Janus that allows "consumers to buy content directly over the Internet for their handheld devices without going through their PCs in order to connect to their music stores. Apple does not have a hand-held device that communicates that way." In addition, Janus includes the delivery of audio, video, and text—something that Apple indicates is not in its plans. "Microsoft's attempt to establish a standard with Windows Media Player has been greeted with suspicion by the consumer electronics business." In late January 2005, the four largest consumer electronics companies announced an agreement to adopt a common DRM method that would enable "copy-protected music and video to play across devices from any manufacturer."

In February 2005, John Borland, a columnist writing about technology and the music business, commented, "Today, online music purchasers have to make sure they are buying from a store that's compatible with their MP3 player. Music from Microsoft's MSN Music Store cannot be played directly on the iPod, for example." Also in February 2005, Michael Robertson, who helped create "the early digital music wars with his MP3.com site," announced his intention to establish an online music store that provides music without any copyright protection. Robertson indicated he would open the service with hundreds of thousands of songs from independent and unsigned artists. The price per download will be 88 cents—11 cents less than from iTunes Music Store. Robertson intends to approach the major music labels as well, even though they have adamantly opposed selling any songs online that are not wrapped in DRM technology.

Apple has certainly created a name for itself in the digital age of music, from the first user-friendly solution to building, managing, and sharing a music library, to the now ubiquitous white headphones of the iPod digital music player. Even though Apple may have struck a delicate balance of consumer rights versus copyrights, that balance may only be temporary as the competitive pressures of the marketplace continue to unfold.

Questions for Discussion

1. How do (a) the technological configuration of the iPod product line and (b) usage applications of the iTunes Music Store serve consumers and, at the same time, restrict their freedom?

2. What are the ethical implications of Apple's marketing of the iPod product line and sale of music through the iTunes Music Store?

3. What is "Digital Rights Management," and what ethical issues does it raise for Apple Computer and other providers of online music?

4. In your view, how will the battle over Digital Rights Management likely unfold in the future?

Sources

This case was developed from material contained in the following sources:

Ante, S. E. (May 15, 2000) The e-biz 25. *Business Week Online*, http://www.businessweek.com/2000/00_20/b3681001.htm.

Apple introduces iTunes. (January 9, 2001). *Apple Press Release Archive*, http://www.apple.com/pr/library/2001/jan/09itunes.html.

Apple iPod. *Apple Web Site*, http://www.apple.com/ipod, accessed February 10, 2005.

Apple iTunes. *Apple Web Site*, http://www.apple.com/itunes, accessed February 10, 2005.

Borland, J. (February 2, 2005) MP3.com founder returns to music biz. *CNET News.com*, http://www.news.com.com/2102-1027_3-5561133.html, accessed February 10, 2005.

Brevetti, F. (February 7, 2005) Apple's iTunes music service may be supreme—but for how long? *Inside Bay Area*, http://www.insidebayarea.com/businessnews/onthemove/ci_2557889, accessed February 10, 2005.

DRM. *Afterdawn.com*, http://www.afterdawn.com/glossary/terms/drm.cfm, accessed February 10, 2005.

Haughey, M. (May 2003). Wiley Wiggins: Interview by Matthew Haughey. *The Creative Commons*, http://creativecommons.org/getcontent/features/wiggins.

iTunes downloads top 275,000 in first week. (January 16, 2001). *Apple Press Release Archive*, http://www.apple.com/pr/library/2001/jan/16itunes.html.

iTunes music store sells over one million songs in first week. (April 28, 2003) *Apple Press Release Archive*, http://www.apple.com/pr/library/2003/may/05musicstore.html.

Horowitz, J., Lloyd, D. (June 26, 2004) Instant expert: A brief history of iPod. *IPodlounge*, http://www.ipodlounge.com/articles_more.php?id=4280_0_8_0_C.

Malone, S. (January 20, 2005) Consumer electronics giants agree on digital rights management. *PC Pro*, http://www.pcpro.co.uk/news/68389/consumer-electronics-giants-agree-on-digital-rights-management.html, accessed February 10, 2005.

MP3Tunes: A DRM-less music store. (February 2, 2005) *Afterdawn.com*, http://www.afterdawn.com/news/archive/6026.cfm, accessed February 10, 2005.

MP3. (July 29, 2004) *Wikipedia*, http://en.wikipedia.org/wiki/Mp3.

Napster. (July 29, 2004) *Wikipedia*, http://en.wikipedia.org/wiki/Napster.

The #1 music download store. *Apple Web Site*, http://www.apple.com/itunes/store, accessed February 10, 2005.

Roberts, P. (May 15, 2003) Piracy worries end iTunes streaming. *PCWorld Magazine*, http://www.pcworld.com/news/article/0,aid,110755,00.asp.

Sanford, G. (October, 2001) Apple-history. http://www.apple-history.com.

Schultz, J. (April 29, 2004) Meet the new iTunes, less than the old iTunes? *LawGeek*, http://lawgeek.typepad.com/lawgeek/2004/04/meet_the_new_it.html.

Timeline of RIAA lawsuits. (July 22, 2004) *Wikipedia*, http://en.wikipedia.org/wiki/RIAA.

US court ruling in favor of P2P application providers. (April, 2003). *Key Corporate Milestones: Sharman Networks*, http://www.sharmannetworks.com/content/view/full/130.

Zeidler, S. (February 3, 2005) Napster unveils portable service, anti-iPod campaign. *Reuters News*, http://story.news.yahoo.com/news?tmpl=story2&u=/nm/20050203/wr_nm/media_napster_dc, accessed February 10, 2005.

CASE 12

DOW CORNING AND THE SILICONE BREAST IMPLANT CONTROVERSY

On May 15, 1995, after years of controversy surrounding silicone breast implants and in the face of thousands of individual lawsuits, Dow Corning Corporation (DCC)—a 50-50 joint venture of Dow Chemical Company and Corning Inc.—filed for Chapter 11 bankruptcy protection. Richard Hazelton, the CEO of DCC, explained the decision, "It became clear to Dow Corning that to continue our current course ultimately would make it impossible to either resolve this controversy responsibly or remain a healthy company. A Chapter 11 reorganization will bring closure and preserve underlying business."

Background: Market Opportunities, Competitive Pressures, Internal Company Questions   Dow Corning Corporation was a start-up venture between Dow Chemical Company and Corning Inc. in 1943. As an incubator, the goal of DCC was to create and market a new material—silicone. Although the company later proved successful, with almost 10,000 employees and revenues in excess of $2 billion, it did so with the support of Dow Chemical and Corning, both looking for promising profits from the new venture.

The first silicone gel breast implant took place in 1964. Between that time and the mid-1990s, "about two million women nationwide have received breast implants, most of them for cosmetic reasons." Although the majority of these women were satisfied with the implants, "a small minority of recipients in both Canada and the United States have complained that the implants have ruptured, allowing gel to leak into the breast cavity and migrate to other parts of the body. Some women maintain that implant problems cause pain in the chest, arms, and back, as well as debilitating autoimmune diseases such as rheumatoid arthritis. Some also complain that scar tissue formed around the implants, causing a hardening of the breasts."

Although the silicone gel breast implants were believed by scientists at DCC to be safe for humans, internal memos suggest that DCC succumbed to competitive pressures, did not pay attention to some animal tests, and ignored employees' complaints about safety issues. By 1975 competitors had already cut DCC's market share in this area by a third. To counter the competition, DCC wanted to rush its new product—Flo-gel—to market by June 15, 1975. Projected annual sales were 50,000 units. An internal memo pertaining to market urgency, dated January 31, 1975, stated, "17 weeks, 121 days, 2,904 hours, 174,240 minutes."

The Flo-gel product suffered from "gel-bleed"—the seepage of silicone molecules through the plastic container that housed the liquid gel. Because of gel-bleed, the implants had a noticeably greasy, even oily, sensation when handled. In an internal memo dated May 2, 1975, sales managers stated that the implants on display at a trade show "were bleeding on the velvet in the showcase." Even members of a task force that had been established by Dow Corning in January 1975 expressed concern that gel-bleed might cause problems in humans.

Animal studies conducted on rabbits in February 1975 revealed inflammation, and a test on dogs revealed gel leakage. Thomas Talcott, a product engineer with the implant team, argued for more study because of his concern that a ruptured implant sac in a human could cause health risks. When his arguments were ignored, he resigned. Flo-gel went to market in the fall of 1975. A disgruntled and angry sales force started fielding complaints from plastic surgeons over gel-bleed, leaking gel, and ruptured implants. An internal memo from one sales professional to his superior stated, "To put a questionable lot of mammaries on the market is inexcusable. I don't know who is responsible for this decision, but it has to rank right up there with the Pinto gas tank."

The Controversy   Women who have had medical problems with their implants alleged, with their doctors' support, that the following medical disorders were present: autoimmune disease, breast cancer, arthritis, abnormal tissue growth, scleroderma, lupus erythematosus, fatigue, and nerve damage. Still, DCC has maintained the safety of the implants, stating the women "claim that whatever injury, disease, or illness from which they suffer is causally related to their implants."

Numerous studies, including a Mayo Clinic Study, a University of Southern California Study, and a French International Study, reported similar results regarding the safety of breast implants. The French Ministry said that an analysis of international research "showed that the risk of contracting autoimmune diseases and cancer after the implantation of silicone breast implants was no greater than in the general public." Scientists involved "noted that no study could completely dismiss the possibility that breast implants contributed to medical disorders." The degree of safety may never be completely known, but as of 1995, "about 5% of the two million American women with silicone implants have demanded compensation for side effects."

A Historical Perspective   In 1976, the federal government passed an amendment to the Food, Drug, and Cosmetic Act that provided stricter reporting and inspection standards for all new medical devices.

At that time, there were 1,700 types of devices on the market, many of them containing silicone. Through a grandfather clause, these devices were allowed to remain on the market with minimal Food and Drug Administration (FDA) review. A manufacturer simply filed a "510(k)" form informing the FDA of the new product and its similarity to an existing product already on the market. In 1996, the FDA acknowledged that there were 58,000 medical devices, many containing solid silicone, that entered the market through this 510(k) process.

It was almost 12 years before further government attention was given to the breast implant controversy. Dr. Sydney Wolfe, a physician and director of the Public Citizen Health Research Group in Washington, said in a petition, "an increasingly larger pool of women is being created who may, in the prime of their lives, ultimately develop chronic illness, disfigurement, and disability because of the implants (silicone)." Dr. Wolfe began to publicly attack manufacturers and plastic surgeons for downplaying the potential health risks. Opponents of Dr. Wolfe agreed with Bruce Hansel, a biochemist and bioengineer at the Emergency Care Research Institute (ECRI), a watchdog group that had been tracking silicone-containing medical devices. Hansel stated, "You can nit-pick anything to death. There will never be a perfect biomaterial, but I would say that silicone in my view is probably the biomaterial of the 20th century. It is the best biomaterial we have going for us now." "Manufacturers continue to deny a link between such illnesses of the human immune system and breast implants, but various doctors have concluded that such causation exists."

As a result of conflicting expert medical data and opinions, the FDA once again became involved in the breast implant controversy. The agency announced, in November of 1988, that although manufacturers could continue to produce breast implants, they would have to provide more detailed information on the safety concern for a 1991 investigation. Unfortunately, the 1991 investigation proved uneventful. Although the FDA panel cited the overall lack of safety data, it did not move to ban the sale of breast implants. The panel noted testimony from breast cancer patients (and their psychological benefits from the implants) as an integral part of their decision.

By 1991, "the FDA had received 2,500 reports of illnesses or injuries associated with the implants, which have been used in one million women. But the degree of risk was unclear because extensive research had not been done." As pressures mounted regarding the product's safety, DCC adamantly "denied any link between the implants and illness." Moreover, "rather than wait for results from the [FDA] research, Dow undertook to determine the safety of silicone gel implants." The Dow Corning study of silicone implants in March 1993 "reported that the silicone gel in the implants altered the immune systems of laboratory rats . . . but [rats] are more susceptible to inflammatory reactions than humans."

The Right to Know   Another issue associated with the breast implant controversy is the patients' right to know. "Dow Corning has actively covered this issue up," said Dr. Wolfe, the director of the Public Citizen Health Research Group. "They are reckless and they have a reckless attitude about women." Wolfe continued, "DCC was only thinking of themselves when they 'repeatedly assured women and their doctors that the implants were safe' while keeping 'guard over hundreds of internal memos that suggested that some of Dow Corning's own employees have long been dissatisfied with the scientific data on implants.'"

The release of these internal memos suggests that Dow had long known of major problems with the silicone implants that it has marketed since 1975. The following are highlights from a sample of the memos to and from Dow scientists:

Jan. 28, 1975: Memo from Arthur H. Rathjen, chairman of the Dow implant task force, as Dow rushed a new implant to market: "A question not yet answered is whether or not there is excessive bleed [leakage] of the gel through the envelope. We must address ourselves to this question immediately. . . . The stakes are too high if a wrong decision is made."

Sept. 15, 1983: Memo from Bill Boley: "Only inferential data exists to substantiate the long-term safety of these gels for human implant applications."

April 10, 1987: Memo to Rathjen and others suggesting that Dow was considering a study to review 1,250 implant recipients: "The cost of this data is expected to be minimal, less than $10 million." The study never took place.

In response to disclosure of these memos, Dow Corning stepped up an ad campaign that it had started in the fall of 1991. In newspapers across the country, DCC urged women with questions about implants to call a company hotline. The ads said that instead of "half-truths," callers would receive information based on 30 years of valid scientific research. But when some women called, they were told that the implants were "100 percent safe." Shortly afterward, the FDA warned Dow Corning that some of the information on its hotline was "false or used in a confusing or misleading context."

While the question regarding whether the implants cause harm to patients was being contested, also at issue was DCC's failure to inform stakeholders and clients that some DCC employees expressed concern about the implant's safety. Failure to accurately inform consumers of questionable products in a timely manner violated the right of these women to know. "If you do not have data on the range of risks and problems, you are not free to choose, you are free to be ignorant. Informed consent requires both information and choice. Since the companies have not supplied the information, this is a dubious choice."

The Legal Onslaught   One of the first lawsuits filed was by a woman who claimed that a silicone breast implant manufactured by Dow Corning caused her to contract a disabling immune-system disorder. The case, brought in 1989 by Mariann Hopkins, resulted in a 1991 federal jury verdict ordering Dow Corning to pay Hopkins $840,000 in compensatory damages and $6.5 million in punitive damages. Dow Corning claimed that this award "triggered the explosion of breast-implant litigation. . . . State and federal courts have been inundated with cases . . . against all manufacturers of mammary prostheses in which plaintiffs claim whatever injury, disease, or illness from which they suffer is causally related to their implants."

The explosion of lawsuits revealed a variety of health problems being attributed to faulty silicone breast implants and varying degrees of legal passion in pursuit of settlements. "Among the women involved, there was a wide range of consequences and varying degrees of certainty about the link between implants and subsequent medical difficulties. The intensity of the pursuit varied from lawyer to lawyer, and the willingness of parties to settle changed with time, making patterns of settlement difficult to establish." Two Houston attorneys in particular campaigned through public ads to solicit women who had experienced problems with gel implants. These attorneys wanted to keep their clients away from any class action suit in order to have each person appear before the manufacturer, a judge, and a jury. The lawyers won $25 million in their first trial against Bristol-Myers Squibb. These attorneys at one point had over 2,000 individual cases lined up for adjudication. They were obtaining settlements of $1 million per case with fees of 40% per settlement.

In response to the explosion of litigation, Dow Corning and two other producers of silicone breast implants, Bristol-Myers Squibb Co., and Baxter Health Care Corp., attempted to bundle the individual suits together in a class action suit. As a result, all of the individual lawsuits were consolidated into a class action suit in 1992. In 1994, Federal District Judge Sam C. Pointer approved a proposed settlement, in which these companies agreed to pay $4.25 billion to women who contended that implants caused illness. The settlement was designed to provide women with net payments ranging from $105,000 to $1.4 million, depending on their physical condition and age. These amounts could be reduced if an unexpected number of women registered to participate and if the companies refused to pay more. Women would have an opportunity to leave the settlement if payments were reduced, although such actions possibly could have jeopardized the entire settlement idea. "The settlement contributions would be based on each manufacturer's market share, litigation exposure, and ability to defend the claims, with Dow Corning paying $2 billion, Bristol-Meyers Squibb $1.5 billion, and Baxter $556 million." The manufacturers also had the ability "to drop out if a certain number of victims chose not to participate. Each manufacturer would be left to their own discretion to determine if the number of participants was significant."

In June 1994 Dow Corning announced that it might have to declare bankruptcy if too many women opted out of the $4.25 billion settlement. These comments led some financial analysts to suggest that Dow Corning was "trying to 'scare' women into joining the settlement, which could potentially save the company millions of dollars in litigation fees." Critics argued that Dow Corning and the other implant manufacturers were attempting to make the settlement appear generous, but that it was not a generous solution. "In reality, the payout to each woman would depend on the total number of claims filed and could decrease dramatically as the number of plaintiffs climbs. And the rights of women to drop out of the plan and seek their own settlements would actually be sharply curtailed." As the legal onslaught continued, David Bernick, lead counsel for Dow Corning, said, "[t]he volume of cases grew so quickly there was no way to keep up with it. . . . Dow went Chapter 11 because it could not fight all these claims." Dow Corning filed for bankruptcy protection on May 15, 1995.

Many people feel DCC threatened bankruptcy early on to scare women into opting to join the class action suit. The various methods used by manufacturers to get women to join the suit were not completely successful, however, as "more than 11,300 women rejected the $4.25 billion settlement. Those women have reserved their right to sue implant manufacturers individually." These individual lawsuits, coupled with the difficulties DCC experienced in coming to agreement with so many other women, led to DCC's filing for Chapter 11.

DCC provides a compelling modern-day example of the close relationship that has developed between product liability suits and Chapter 11 filings, an issue that Congress must finally address. "If bankruptcy is now the ultimate limit on liability, what figure short of that can Congress agree on to avoid the danger implicit in Dow Corning's case: that an otherwise viable business, and the jobs that go with it, might go down the drain of tort practice."

Aftermath and Final Resolution   "As the 1990s wore on, one study after another failed to establish a connection between implants and illness. The studies in turn emboldened judges to bar much of the plaintiffs' more speculative expert testimony under new 'gatekeeping' guidelines laid down by the U.S. Supreme Court." In August 1996, Judge Sam Pointer "appointed an independent national science panel that included experts in the fields of immunology, epidemiology, toxicology, and rheumatology . . . to review and criticize the scientific literature concerning a possible causal link between silicone breast implants and connective tissue diseases and related signs and symptoms, as well as immune system dysfunction." On December 1, 1998, Pointer's science panel issued its report "presenting no evidence linking silicone breast implants to systemic conditions such as connective tissue disease." In June 1999, the Institute of Medicine, a part of the National Academy of Sciences, issued a 400-page report prepared by an independent committee of 13 scientists which "concluded that, although silicone breast implants may be responsible for localized problems such as hardening or scarring of breast tissue, implants do not cause any major diseases such as lupus or rheumatoid arthritis." As one analyst observed, "[t]he cumulative weight of the scientific evidence . . . forced the endgame. Plaintiffs began to lose in court, and settlement values plummeted."

In July 1998, Dow Corning made an offer of $3.2 billion to settle all of the claims against it. In December 1999, Judge Arthur Spectors approved Dow Corning's $4.5-billion reorganization plan, including $3.2 billion to settle claims brought by silicone gel breast implant recipients. The remaining $1.3 billion was to be paid to commercial creditors, in part through a $900 million to $1 billion bond issue. However, Dow Corning would not emerge from bankruptcy until June 2004.

On June 1, 2004, Dow Corning officially emerged from bankruptcy, and the company said it would begin paying the silicone breast implant recipients who has settled for $3.2 billion in 1998. The settlement plan covers more than 300,000 women who had received implants before 1994. Each recipient will receive between $2,000 and $250,000 depending on her medical condition. Women who received implants after 1994 are not included in the settlement because they "presumably understood the potential health risks."

Both the plaintiffs and defendant claim to have been victimized. The plaintiffs claim to have been victimized "by an inadequately tested medical device that frequently ruptured and leaked poisonous goo." Dow Corning claims to have been victimized "by a tort system that allowed a few lawyers to extort billions of dollars using a dollop of junk science."

In reflecting on the nine-year struggle to settle the claims of the breast implant recipients, Gary Anderson, Dow Corning's current chairman, observes: "Although breast implants have never represented more than one percent of our business, our company is often identified with them. We are confident that the science shows a clear picture today—through more than 30 independent studies, government and court-appointed panels, and court decisions—that breast implants are not associated with disease. Nevertheless, we are pleased to put this issue behind us."

Final Thoughts　DCC's silicone breast implant troubles occurred in a free-market, capitalist society. A free market encourages innovation, but it can also lead to corporate manipulation and to the introduction of dangerous products into the market. Marcia Angell, a physician and executive editor of *The New England Journal of Medicine*, concluded in her book *Science on Trial: The Clash of Medical Evidence and the Law in the Breast Implant Case* that "[o]nly by relying on scientific evidence can we hope to curb the greed, fear, and self-indulgence that too often govern such disputes. This is the lesson of the breast implant story." Charles Rosenberg, Professor of History and Sociology of Science at the University of Pennsylvania, argued in a *New York Times* review of Dr. Angell's book that "it is difficult to share her hope that scientific evidence can or will translate easily or naturally into social policy. She is dismayed, for example, that regulations 'should be influenced by political and social considerations.' Yet this is the way our system works. In most policy matters, scientific evidence is only one among a complex assortment of factors that interact to produce particular decisions." A careful reading of the events, stakeholders, and outcomes in the silicone breast implant controversy reveals the social, economic, legal, political, and scientific factors involved "the practice of Federal regulation, the relationship between science and courts, the lack of consistently enforced professional standards in law, medicine and journalism." A major lesson from this case also involves the role of the plaintiffs. The Houston lawyers' relentless pressure with inconclusive medical facts on Dow Corning, along with their courtroom successes, demonstrates that "facts" alone are insufficient factors in determining truth.

Questions for Discussion

1. Identify the major stakeholders and stakes in this case. Who gained and lost in this case?

2. Was the Dow Corning Corporation justified in considering bankruptcy? Why or why not?

3. What are the ethical issues and principles involved in this case?

4. Who has acted the most responsibly in this case? The least? Explain.

5. Who in this case was at fault? Support your answer.

6. In writing about the disputes regarding the silicone breast implants, Marcia Angell concluded that "[o]nly by relying on scientific evidence can we hope to curb the greed, fear and self-indulgence that too often govern such disputes. This is the lesson of the breast implant story." Do you agree or disagree? Is this the major or the only lesson from this case? Explain.

Sources

This case was developed from material contained in the following sources:

Associated Press. (April 12, 1994). 5 firms join implant settlement. *Boston Globe*, 44.

Associated Press. (July 21, 1994). Firms may face thousands of suits. *Boston Globe*, 19.

Associated Press. (August 5, 1994). FDA is petitioned to outlaw saline-filled implants. *Boston Globe*, 17.

Associated Press. (September 2, 1994). Judge finalizes $4.25B settlement from breast implant maker. *Boston Globe*, 3.

Associated Press. (September 16, 1994). Women rejecting implant award. *Boston Globe*, 79.

Associated Press. (February 15, 1995). Couple wins $5.2M in breast implant case: Dow Chemical faulted. *Boston Globe*, 88.

Associated Press. (March 29, 1995). Dow freed from suit. *Boston Globe*, 14.

Associated Press. (April 26, 1995). Company reinstated in implant lawsuit. *Boston Globe*, 7.

Associated Press. (May 11, 1995). Jury selection is halted over an implant and Dow Corning denies trying to influence liability. *Boston Globe*, 14.

Byrne, J. (March 9, 1992). The best-laid ethics programs. *Business Week*, 67–69.

Carelli, R. (January 10, 1995). Justices uphold breast implant award. *Boston Globe*, 10.

Dow Chemical loses breast implant suit. (March 2, 1995). *Facts on File*, 154.

Dow Chemical not liable in implant case. (March 30, 1995). *Facts on File*, Medicine and Health, 233.

Dow Corning announces medical silicone resins. (May 30, 1994). *Chemical & Engineering News*, 9.

Dow Corning down for the count: A new high flier for Boeing. (May 21, 1995). *Boston Globe*, 48.

Foreman, J. (January 25, 1992). Safety of solid silicone at issue. *Boston Globe*, 1.

Foreman, J. (May 15, 1992). Lawyers fight over limits of implant trials. *Boston Globe*, 25.

Foreman, J. (June 17, 1994). Breast implant study criticized timing, funding of report at issue. *Boston Globe*, 4.

Foreman, J. (November 20, 1994). Dec. 1 deadline to join implant lawsuit. *Boston Globe*, 6.

Gilbert, E. (March 7, 1994). Breast implant makers prepare $4B settlement. *National Underwriter*, 6.

Grimmer, L. (November 3, 1992). Silicone-gel implant records altered, company admits. *Boston Globe*, 3.

Haney, D. Q. (December 21, 1994). Harvard doctors quit implant study, citing conflict. *Boston Globe*, 35.

Homsy, C.A. (July 2003). How FDA regulations and injury litigation cripple the medical device industry. *USA Today Magazine*, accessed from Academic Search Elite database on http://web8.epnet.com on January 29, 2005.

Wojcik, J. (February 21, 1994). Implant makers near a deal. *Business Insurance*, 1, 51.

Kever, J. (June 13, 2004). Long legal battle over silicone implants yields cash but few answers. *Houston Chronicle*, accessed from Newspaper Source database on http://web8.epnet.com on January 29, 2005.

Lehr, D. (September 10, 1993). 4.75B accord eyed on breast implant plaintiffs, manufacturers agree on compensation fund. *Boston Globe*, 1.

McCarthy, M. (April 2, 1994). U.S. breast implant agreement. *Lancet*, 7.

Neuffer, E. (March 20, 1992). Maker quits implant market: Dow Corning cites drop in sales, sets up fund. *Boston Globe*, 1.

Reisch, M. (June 20, 1994). Dow Corning mulls over filing for bankruptcy. *Chemical & Engineering News*, 8.

Rosenberg, C. (July 14, 1996). The silicon papers. *New York Times Book Review*, 10.

Sissel, K. (June 9, 2004). Dow Corning emerges from bankruptcy. *Chemical Week*, accessed from Academic Search Elite database on http://web8.epnet.com on January 29, 2005.

Tolson, M. (November 2, 2003). Silicone implants on way back to market, but safety debate still alive. *Houston Chronicle*, accessed from Newspaper Source database on http://web8.epnet.com on January 29, 2005.

Warrick, E.L. (1990). *Forty Years of Firsts: The Recollections of a Dow Corning Pioneer*. New York: McGraw-Hill.

CASE 13

COLT AND THE GUN CONTROL CONTROVERSY

On December 7, 1999, the Clinton administration announced its intention to join settlement negotiations between the gun industry and local cities and counties. The aim was to limit the flow of handguns to youths and criminals. In addition, the Clinton administration announced that if no visible progress was observed in the negotiations, it would file a nationwide class action lawsuit against the industry on behalf of the Department of Housing and Urban Development seeking compensation for lack of security and other costs associated with gun violence. How did the gun industry arrive at this predicament? Founded on the U.S. Constitution's Second Amendment right to bear arms, the gun industry has long served the public in supplying firearms. Now, the same industry is defending itself against criticism from some of its past supporters.

Colt has a long history as one of the largest and most innovative suppliers of firearms. Its varying success as well as longevity continue to be intertwined with the social and political life of the nation and the world. Both Colt's and the gun industry's survival and future success hinge, at least in part, on the resolution of the social and political controversy regarding gun control.

Colt's Evolution as a Major Player in the Gun Industry

In 1836, Sam Colt received a U.S. patent for a firearm equipped with a revolving cylinder containing five or six bullets. Prior to Sam Colt's invention, only one- and two-barrel flintlock pistols were available. Colt's invention, which applied to both long arms and side arms, was remarkably simple. However, the idea was not an instant success because many people still preferred the traditional flintlock musket or pistol. Sam Colt built his first plant, the Patent Arms Manufacturing Co., in Patterson, New Jersey. He soon developed new products based on the basic principle of loading gunpowder and bullets into a revolving cylinder. The products generally performed very well, but sales were disappointing despite the fact that the U.S. government purchased small quantities of the Colt ring lever rifle and Colt 1839 carbine. In 1842, because of the sluggish sales, the Patterson, New Jersey, plant was closed, much of its equipment was auctioned, and bankruptcy proceedings were initiated.

Meanwhile, units in the U.S. Dragoon force and Texas Rangers "credited their use of Colt firearms for their great success in defeating Indian forces." At the outbreak of the Mexican War in 1846, U.S. Army Captain Samuel Walker collaborated with Sam Colt on the design of a new, more powerful revolver. This proved to be a critical rejuvenation point for Sam Colt's gun manufacturing business. Subsequently in 1855, with an initial issuance of 10,000 shares of stock, the firm was incorporated in Connecticut as the Colt's Patent Fire Arms Mfg. Co. The company produced 150 weapons a day and gained a reputation for exceptional quality, workmanship, and design. The company continued supplying arms to the military as well as to private citizens, and soon opened a plant England to penetrate the international arms market.

Before the official declaration of the U.S. Civil War, Colt supplied arms to both the North and the South. After war was declared, Colt supplied only Union forces. Colt was a major producer and supplier of firearms during both World Wars and in subsequent U.S. military actions. After World War II, Colt was almost entirely dependent on government orders; as a result, sales fluctuated greatly. The Korean War temporarily boosted its earnings until 1952, but after the United States withdrew, Colt was in financial trouble.

In 1955, Leopold Silberstein, head of Penn-Texas Corporation, purchased the Colt Firearms Company and organized it as a wholly owned subsidiary. Four years later a group of investors took control of the company away from the Silberstein family and changed the company's name to Fairbanks Whitney. In 1964, the parent company decided to reorganize under the name of Colt Industries and changed the firearms subsidiary's name to Colt's Inc., Firearms Division. Through the 1970s and 1980s, Colt continued to expand its product line. However, Colt received a major setback when the U.S. government decided to replace the Colt .45 as the official sidearm of the armed forces. In 1990, the company was sold again to a coalition of private investors, the state of Connecticut, and union employees. The company was renamed Colt Manufacturing Company, and it brought some new products to market. Colt was forced to enter into Chapter 11 bankruptcy in 1992, and in 1994 it emerged from bankruptcy under the ownership of still another group of investors.

In the mid-1990s, Colt embarked on a joint research and development program with the National Institute of Justice that thrust it into the limelight of the gun control controversy as much as any other arms manufacturer. Indeed, Colt may have started a new era of weapons technology when it began work with the National Institute of Justice on the "Smart Gun." This is a significant advancement in light of all the controversy surrounding recent gun violence, especially in high schools.

In the late 1990s, the market prospects of the Colt Manufacturing Company looked promising. The company introduced several new commercial products, as well as winning back its contract with the government to provide more than 32,000 M-16 rifles and to update 88,000 M16A1 rifles for the U.S. Air Force. Colt also acquired Saco Defense, which specialized in automatic weapons for the military.

In addition, the company had orders extending through 2010 for exclusive production of the M-4 carbine for the U.S. military.

Framing the Gun Control Controversy   After World War I, events unfolded that would create a controversy affecting Colt and the entire gun industry for the rest of the century. The St. Valentine's Day massacre of 1929 brought the death toll in Chicago's underworld turf wars to 135 as gangsters battled over the profits from bootleg liquor during Prohibition. Realizing just how dangerous firearms could be in the hands of criminals, Americans started demanding the first national gun-control laws. But Congress moved cautiously, caught in the cross-fire of a Second Amendment argument over the right of gun owner-ship. It was the 1933 assassination attempt on President Franklin D. Roosevelt that prompted Washington to restrict the sale of sawed-off shotguns, machine guns, and automatic weapons. The National Firearms Act of 1934 aimed to cut down on ownership of machine guns and sawed-off shotguns by slapping a $200 tax on their purchase.

Violence from firearms is without question a major problem in United States. "Guns kill nearly 30,000 people each year in the United States and injure many more. . . . As everyone knows, that has played into one of the signature controversies of U.S. political life. On the one hand, there are the gun control advocates—supporters of the Brady Handgun Act of 1993 and of required registration for gun pur-chases. On the other hand, there are the supporters of the right to bear arms even when concealed." The proponents and opponents of gun control are deeply divided. As one observer noted, "Few issues divide the American polity as dramatically as gun control. Framed by assassinations, mass shootings, and violent crime, the gun debate feeds on our deepest national anxieties."

A fundamental question of the gun control controversy is, "Do guns make society more or less safe?" Gun control advocates maintain that "the ready availability of guns diminishes public safety by facili-tating violent crimes and accidental shootings." They "emphasize the risk that insufficient regulation will make citizens vulnerable to delib-erate or accidental shootings, while opponents stress the risk that excessive regulation will leave citizens unable to defend themselves against violent predation." Gun control opponents believe that the availability of guns "enhances public safety by enabling potential crime victims to ward off violent predation."

The mindsets of gun control proponents and opponents differ dra-matically. This is perhaps best captured with the observation that, "For those who fear guns, the historical reference points are not the American Revolution or the settling of the frontier, but the post-bellum period, in which the privilege of owning guns in the South was reserved to whites, and the 1960s, when gun-wielding assassins killed Medgar Evers, John and Robert Kennedy, and Martin Luther King, Jr." Contrast this with the primary argument of gun control opponents (or the guns rights advocates), which states, "The right of self-defense is an important right. A firearms prohibition would be a significant violation of the right to self-defense. Therefore, a firearms prohibition would be a serious rights violation."

Perhaps the profound division between gun control opponents and proponents can be better understood by examining the social and political meanings associated with guns and gun ownership. Guns are not just weapons or sporting equipment; they are also symbols that are positively or negatively associated with a variety of political and sociological events. "[H]ow an individual feels about gun control will depend a lot on the social meanings that [he or] she thinks guns and gun control express, and not just on the consequences [he or] she believes they impose." Gun control proponents are *egalitarian* (i.e., favoring collective action to equalize power, status, and wealth) in their value orientation, whereas gun control opponents are *individualistic* (i.e., favoring individual autonomy and resenting collective interference).

Legislative Initiatives Regarding Gun Control   The Gun Control Act of 1968 was passed following the assassinations of Martin Luther King Jr. and Robert Kennedy. Congress rushed to ban the sale of mail order guns and placed minimum safety standards on imported guns to raise their purchase price. No standards were adopted for guns manufactured in the United States, however; and the law helped spawn a huge domestic gun industry that turned out cheap handguns, now known as "junk guns" and "Saturday night specials." This did not have much impact on Colt as most of its business still came from government contracts.

The Brady Handgun Act of 1993 mandated a five-day waiting period and background check for persons buying handguns from retailers. The law followed the shooting of President Ronald Reagan and Press Secretary Jim Brady in 1981. Hundreds of thousands of felons, fugitives, and others have been denied handguns since the law was enacted, but the country also witnessed an exponential growth in gun purchases at gun shows and flea markets, where background checks are not required.

Since the 1929 St. Valentine's Day massacre, it has been estimated that the United States has been inundated with more than 20,000 gun laws on the state and federal books. The most significant of the federal laws have always followed in the wake of high-profile shootings. One of the more recent was the April 1999 high school massacre in Littleton, Colorado, which left 15 people dead. History repeated itself, and the Senate passed legislation in response to the shootings.

However, Paul Blackman, who tracks gun legislation for the National Rifle Association (NRA), believes that "as far as crime is concerned, gun-control laws as a group are a total failure in affecting violence." On the other hand, David Bernstein of the Center to Prevent Handgun Violence claims, "We think that the Brady Law was a major factor in reducing violence." Legislation such as the 1993 Brady Handgun Act prevented 250,000 felons and fugitives from purchasing handguns over the following five years.

Litigation Regarding Gun Control   On October 30, 1998, New Orleans became the first city in the nation to file suit against the gun industry. Two weeks later, Chicago followed with a second lawsuit against the industry. The lawsuits claimed the industry failed to incorporate adequate safety systems into guns that would prevent widespread firearm misuse by unauthorized users. These lawsuits closely resemble the lawsuits brought against the tobacco industry. At first, the public considered tobacco-related diseases to be a result of choice made by the smoker. Little responsibility was attributed to the tobacco industry. After the deluge of state and city lawsuits against the tobacco industry, public views changed. Litigation caused a shift in public opinion and forced the tobacco industry to the bargaining table, where its executives finally acknowledged cigarette smoking was dangerous to one's health. Guns may become society's next tobacco controversy.

The litigation in the gun control controversy focused on four choices that the firearms industry was alleged to have consciously made. First, the lawsuits alleged that the industry focused all its design innovation efforts on making smaller and/or more powerful guns, while it had blocked installation of feasible safety devices that would prevent thousands of unintentional shootings. Second, the industry's distribution system was being attacked because it allegedly had no controls, and the industry may have consciously targeted criminal markets, making it easy for criminals to obtain guns from the legal marketplace. Third, the suits alleged that some gun manufacturers made high-firepower assault weapons that had no real sporting or self-defense use but were more suited for criminals. Finally, the suits claimed that the industry erroneously advertised that guns increased home safety, when evidence contradicted this message.

A federal appeals court determined on October 16, 2001, that the Second Amendment gives individual citizens a right to own firearms. This ruling is expected to be influential in the continuing legal battle over the issue in the courts. "Some legal experts who argue that the Second Amendment provides an individual right to firearms said the ruling was one of the most important ever on the issue. Eugene Volokh, a law professor at the University of California at Los Angeles, said the opinion would lay the groundwork for many other decisions that will analyze when gun control is permitted and when it is not."

Firearm Companies and Insurers   As an increasing number of cities and counties brought lawsuits against the firearms industry, the gun companies' own insurers notified their clients that they would not pay any large legal bills or any judgments associated with the lawsuits. Without the insurers, the firearms firms would be forced to defend themselves and therefore could be more likely to require bankruptcy protection or discontinue their business. In response to this threat, many gun companies sued their insurers. Some of these lawsuits, such as *The National Shooting Sports Foundation* v. *Nationwide Mutual Insurance* in New Orleans, have been successful.

The consequences of the insurance issue are more expensive insurance for gun companies. Some gun-control advocates see this as another motivation to encourage companies to avoid litigation and make positive changes to their industry. According to Josh Horowitz, director of the Firearms Litigation Clearinghouse, the insurance problem is "one more thing to bring them to the settlement table."

The Impact on the Gun Industry and Colt   The gun industry has fought back and is not without its supporters. Industry representatives are claiming the U. S. government has no grounds for an anti-gun suit. According to industry lawyer James P. Dorr, "[T]o sue someone they have authorized to sell those products has no basis in law." Also, the Second Amendment Foundation is accusing the cities and states of trying to make firearms unavailable or unaffordable and has sued on these grounds. It is their position that anti-gun litigation is like "blaming the National Weather Service for storm damage."

Colt has been portrayed by the media as discontinuing the handgun portion of its business in 1999 due to the financial implications of these and other pending lawsuits. Countering this allegation, William Keys, CEO of Colt, observed, "The lawsuits did not force us into this decision." Keys maintained that the reality was that Colt discontinued seven lines of handguns simply because they had not been selling. However, in December of 1999, Colt contradicted this assertion in a letter to its shareholders that claimed, "We have had to face the harsh reality of the significant impact which our litigation defense costs are having on our ability to operate competitively in the marketplace."

With all the actual and potential litigation, Colt, as well as the rest of the gun industry, may indeed be in a fight for survival. Colt does not have pockets as deep as those of the tobacco industry; therefore, it will need to be creative to forge reasonable settlements. Undoubtedly, some gun manufacturers will be driven out of business by the gun-control controversy. However, with its history and established reputation for supplying innovative firearms to the U.S. government, Colt just may have a chance to navigate its way through the minefield of lawsuits, especially while the Bush administration remains in the White House.

The Gun Control Controversy: Still Unresolved   In March 2004, the United States Senate, in a vote of 90 to 8, rejected a bill highly favored by the NRA; this bill would have given gun manufacturers protection from lawsuits. "The NRA wanted the bill because gun manufacturers face some 30 significant lawsuits. Judges in Washington, Ohio, and California have ruled that gun manufactures can be sued for civil penalties when criminals use their products." The NRA withdrew its support and lobbied senators to kill the bill when a bipartisan coalition managed to pass two amendments to the bill. One amendment would renew a 10-year ban on military-style assault weapons, and the other would require background checks of prospective gun purchasers at gun shows. The NRA's vigorous lobbying for the original bill and against the amendments to it "demonstrates the NRA's absolute opposition to sensible gun legislation," observed Senator Dianne Feinstein, the author of the original 1994 legislation banning assault weapons. Police chiefs from around the nation lobbied senators to pass both amendments.

The law banning assault weapons expired in September 2004 without much more than token political opposition expressed at press conferences held by a "few anti-gun diehards, such as Senators Charles Schumer and Dianne Feinstein." A quote from former President Bill Clinton's memoirs, *My Life*, is instructive about the social and political volatility of gun control legislation. Clinton writes, "After the [1994] election, I had to face the fact that the law-enforcement groups and other supporters of responsible gun legislation, though they represented the majority of Americans, simply could not protect their friends in Congress from the NRA. The gun lobby outspent, out-organized, outfought, and out-demagogued them." In this context, reasonable people can legitimately wonder: "Will the gun control controversy ever be resolved?"

Questions for Discussion

1. What is the controversy regarding gun control in the United States? Are you for or against gun control? Explain.

2. Who is "winning" (stands to gain) and who is "losing" (more likely to suffer) in this controversy?

3. Looking at the evolution of laws and litigation on gun control, what insights do you gain?

4. Are guns (firearms) a "dangerous" product like cigarettes? Explain.

5. Explain your position on private citizens being able to buy and use firearms.

Sources

This case was developed from material contained in the following sources:

Bloom, D. (December 7, 1999). White House takes aim at gun makers. *MSNBC News.*

Chatterjee, S. (March 3, 2004). Senate defeats bill to protect gun makers from lawsuits. *Knight Ridder Tribune Washington Bureau.*

Colt History. Official company Web site, http://www.colt.com/law/history.asp, accessed on March 6, 2005.

Colt refutes *Newsweek* article. (October 11, 1999). http://www.colt.com/colt/html/n_news2.

Crowley, M. (September 27, 2004). Muzzled. *New Republic, 231(13),* 11–13.

Glaberson, W. (October 17, 2001). Court says individuals have a right to firearms. *New York Times,* 14.

Huemer, M. (April 2003). Is there a right to own a gun? *Social Theory and Practice, 29(2),* 297–324.

Kahan, D.M., Braman, D. (April 2003). More statistics, less persuasion: A cultural theory of gun-risk perceptions. *University of Pennsylvania Law Review, 151(4),* 1291–1327.

Kennedy, D. (April 18, 2003). Research fraud and public policy. *Science, 300(5618),* 393.

Levin, M., Rubin, A. (December 8, 1999). US to join legal fray against gun makers. *Los Angeles Times.*

Phinney, D. (June 11, 1999). When laws take aim at guns. *ABC News.*

Siebel, B. (1999). City lawsuits against the gun industry: A roadmap for reforming gun industry misconduct. *St. Louis University Public Law Review* 18(1):247–290.

Walsh, S. (November 26, 1999). Insurers are bailing out on the gun industry. *Washington Post,* A01.

CASE 14

WAL-MART: PROBLEMS IN PARADISE?

Wal-Mart by the Numbers   Wal-Mart, the largest corporation and retailer in the world, employs over 1.4 million people. As of January 31, 2005, the company had 3,702 stores in the United States—1,353 Wal-Mart stores, 1,713 Supercenters, 551 Sam's Clubs, and 85 Neighborhood Markets—and another 1,603 stores in other parts of the world. In fiscal year 2003, ending January 31, 2004, Wal-Mart racked up sales of over $256 billion. Through the first three quarters of fiscal 2004, ending October 31, 2004, Wal-Mart had sales of $213 billion, which was on pace to exceed fiscal 2003 sales by a significant amount. To put Wal-Mart in perspective domestically, its stores account for over 30% of sales of all household staples (toothpaste, shampoo, paper towels) and 20% of all Hollywood distribution (CDs, videos, DVDs). Wal-Mart is also the third largest pharmacy operator in United States behind Walgreens and CVS, and its 1,400 Supercenters make it the nation's largest grocer.

Sam Walton launched his first Wal-Mart in 1962 in Rogers, Arkansas. The banner that hung across the first store summed up one of Walton's underlying philosophies—it read, "We Sell for Less." As a discounter, Walton defined his business by volume, not by individual products. In articulating this philosophy, Walton said, "by cutting your price, you can boost your sales to a point where you earn far more at the cheaper retail than you would have by selling the item at the higher price." With its low-price philosophy, Wal-Mart has become an influential force in the U.S. economy, employing more people than any other company. Enjoying a favorable reputation among the business community, Wal-Mart ranked at the top of *Fortune* magazine's list of "Most Admired Companies in America" in 2003 and 2004.

The Employment Status of Women at Wal-Mart   Wal-Mart's corporate Web site asserts that, "Wal-Mart will not tolerate discrimination in employment on the basis of race, color, age, sex, sexual orientation, religion, disability, ethnicity, national origin, martial status, veteran status, or any other legally-protected status." This statement is also part of the company's code of conduct. Also emphasized are the three basic beliefs upon which Sam Walton built the Company. One of these beliefs is *Respect for the Individual*, which, according to one retired senior Wal-Mart executive, signifies that the slogan "'[o]ur people make the difference' is not a meaningless slogan—it's a reality at Wal-Mart. We are a group of dedicated, hardworking, ordinary people who have teamed together to accomplish extraordinary things. We have very different backgrounds, different colors, and different beliefs, but we do believe that every individual deserves to be treated with respect and dignity."

Against this backdrop of professed commitment to equal opportunity, Wal-Mart has been facing discrimination lawsuits for many years. Most prominent among these suits is the class action suit *Dukes* v. *Wal-Mart Stores, Inc.*, filed on June 19, 2001 in United States District Court for the Northern District of California. According to data supplied by statistical consultant Richard Drogin on behalf of the plaintiffs, Wal-Mart has an established pattern of discrimination against women. Drogin's data indicated that:

- Wal-Mart employed fewer women in management in 2001 than its competitors did in 1975.

- 65% of the company's hourly employees were women, but women only made up one-third of the company's management.

- In individual stores, men hold 86% of store manager positions and close to two-thirds of all store management positions.

- Woman on average scored higher on performance evaluations, but it took 4.38 years for a woman to be promoted to assistant manager while it took only 2.86 years for men.

- Female employees working hourly jobs on average made $1,100 less than their male counterparts.

- A female regional vice president's average salary of $279,772 was 46% less than that of an average male regional vice president.

Allegations of Sex Discrimination at Wal-Mart In recent years Wal-Mart found itself subjected to a tremendous amount of scrutiny regarding its treatment of female employees. The public scrutiny began in 1998 when Stephanie Odle filed an Equal Employment Opportunity Commission (EEOC) complaint against Wal-Mart that led to the filing of the class action suit against Wal-Mart for sex discrimination. The lead plaintiff on this case is Betty Dukes, who alleges that she tried unsuccessfully for nine years to be promoted from her position of cashier at Wal-Mart. In the complaint, Dukes, five other plaintiffs, and the class they represent, charged that "Wal-Mart discriminates against its female employees by advancing male employees more quickly than female employees, by denying female employees equal job assignments, promotions, training, and compensation, and by retaliating against those who oppose its unlawful practices." In addition, the plaintiffs sought to end Wal-Mart's discriminatory practices, to receive relief for the class, and to secure punitive damages. *Dukes* v. *Wal-Mart Stores, Inc.* also alleged that Wal-Mart's underlying culture and policies contributed to the discrimination that the plain-tiffs experienced.

The named plaintiffs in the June 19, 2001 filing were all women, but they came from different geographic areas of the United States; all but one were former employees of Wal-Mart Stores, Inc. Former employ-ees include Patricia Surgeson, a resident of Solano County, California; Sandra Stevenson, a resident of Lake County, Illinois; Stephanie Odle, a resident of Norman, Oklahoma; Kimberly Miller, a resident of Marion County, Florida; and Micki Earwood, a resident of Springfield, Ohio. The plaintiffs were employed by Wal-Mart Stores, Inc. from just under five years to almost twelve years. Betty Dukes, a resident of Contra Costa County, California, was the only named plaintiff who was employed by Wal-Mart at the time of the filing. The stories of Betty Dukes, Stephanie Odle, and Micki Earwood provide insight into the ways in which sex discrimination allegedly took place at Wal-Mart.

Betty Dukes, a 52-year-old African-American woman working at Wal-Mart in Pittsburg, California, had been with the company for almost 10 years. When Dukes joined the Pittsburg Wal-Mart store she had high aspirations. She had a vision in mind and thought that Wal-Mart would allow her to realize her goals. During her time with Wal-Mart, Dukes applied for numerous promotions. Though qualified and having excellent performance reviews, she was passed over each time as men filled these positions. The men filling these positions had less seniority than Dukes and were often less qualified. On one occasion when she applied for a position in the "male" hardware department she was instead asked to sell baby clothes in the children's department. Reflecting on this period of time, Dukes observed, "I was denied the training I requested to obtain promotions within the company. When I complained about unfair treatment, I was unfairly disciplined, demoted, and forced to accept a pay cut. Moreover, I observed men receive promotions to positions over and over again." On another occasion Dukes observed, "I was always told to wait, that my time would come, that there were no openings available, that I didn't have enough experience to move on. But on a number of occasions men with less experience than me were put in jobs that I desperately wanted and know I could have done well."

In 2000, frustrated by the lack of opportunities for women at Wal-Mart, Dukes contacted the Impact Fund, an anti-discrimination organ-ization based in Berkeley, California. The Impact Fund was already in the midst of investigating similar claims from other female employees of Wal-Mart, and Dukes' account of her work experience at Wal-Mart was not unique. The Impact Fund had 110 similar voluntary declara-tions from Wal-Mart's female employees. Based on their investigation in 2001, the Impact Fund stated in the sex discrimination claim that "our research discovered that women doing the same jobs as men were being paid less. This was not in one store, or one region; it was a consistent pattern right across the country."

In 1996, while working as an assistant manager in a Sam's Club store, *Stephanie Odle* became outraged when she discovered that a male co-worker with the same job responsibilities made approximately $10,000 more than she did. Odle complained to her supervisors and claims she was told that her co-worker made more money because he had "a wife and kids to support." Odle continued to complain, was told to present a personal budget, and was then given a raise equivalent to $2,000 for the year. With the raise she still made significantly less money than her male co-worker. In another instance, Odle says she made a suggestion that was disregarded, but when a male co-worker made the same suggestion a month later, it was executed. She confronted her co-worker, and he responded with "I guess it's a man thing." Odle was eventually fired from Sam's Club and brought a complaint to the EEOC. She claimed that she was fired for speaking up.

Micki Earwood worked at Wal-Mart in Ohio for 10 years. During this time she held positions ranging from associate to department manager, but she says she was never accepted into Wal-Mart's management training program. She claimed she was fired when she complained to her superiors about gender-based pay discrepancies.

The sex discrimination case against Wal-Mart has grown to include the sworn testimony of more than 100 women. One unnamed female employee declares that when she asked to be transferred to the hardware department she was told, "You're a girl. Why do you want to be in hardware?" *Kathleen MacDonald* claims that when she asked why she did not get a promotion, her manager explained, "God created Adam first, and, therefore, women always came second." MacDonald complained often about the unequal pay structure between men and women. She says she went as far as complaining to the regional personnel manager and did not know what to do after that. Eventually she did get a raise; however, she still was not making as much as her male co-workers. *Mary Crawford* was not promoted, and the position was given to a man with less experience. When she asked why she did not receive the promotion, she remembers hearing, "[t]he man would always get the job." When she did end up getting promoted, she still did not earn as much as male co-workers in the same position.

Gretchen Adams did get promoted to running the deli in her store. In fact, she was so good at her job that she traveled all over the country to train other employees. She discovered that a man she was training was getting paid $3,500 more than she was. When *Claudia Renati* was seeking a promotion to marketing manager, she was told that in order to get the position she would have to move to Alaska.

The man eventually hired for the position was her manager's neighbor, who worked in construction and had no management experience. When the position re-opened, Renati was once again told she would have to travel to get the position. In this case, the man hired did not have to travel and was another neighbor of her manager.

Mary Alice Cox worked for Wal-Mart for seven years as a cashier and never made even seven dollars an hour; a male co-worker told her he was making over eight dollars an hour.

Sex Discrimination, Class Action, and the Law   The Civil Rights Act of 1964 forbade gender-based discrimination in the employment arena. Section 703 of this act specified that:

- It shall be an unlawful employment practice for an employer to fail or refuse to hire or to discharge any individual, or otherwise to discriminate against any individual with respect to his compensation, terms, conditions, or privileges of employment, because of such individual's race, color, religion, sex, or national origin.

- It shall be an unlawful employment practice for an employer to limit, segregate, or classify his employees in any way, which would deprive or tend to deprive any individual of employment opportunities or otherwise adversely affect his status as an employee, because of such individual's race, color, religion, sex, or national origin.

The class action filing of *Dukes* v. *Wal-Mart Stores, Inc.* is also affected by Rule 23 of the Federal Rules of Civil Procedure, which prescribes the conditions under which class action suits may be brought in the federal courts. Rule 23(a) outlines the prerequisites for a class action. They are: "(1) the class is so numerous that joinder of all members is impracticable; (2) there are questions of law or fact common to the class; (3) the claims or defenses of the representative parties are typical of the claims or defenses of the class; and (4) the representative parties will fairly and adequately protect the interests of the class."

In addition to meeting these prerequisites, an action may only be maintained as a class action if one of the following three conditions outlined in Rule 23(b) are met:

1. The prosecution of separate actions by or against individual members of the class would create a risk of either inconsistent or varying adjudications with respect to individual members of the class which would establish incompatible standards of conduct for the party opposing the class, or adjudications with respect to individual members of the class which would, as a practical matter, be dispositive of the

interests of the other members not parties to the adjudications or substantially impair or impede their ability to protect their interests.

2. The party opposing the class has acted or refused to act on grounds generally applicable to the class, thereby making appropriate final injunctive or corresponding declaratory relief with respect to the class as a whole.

3. The court finds that the questions of law or fact common to the members of the class predominate over any questions affecting only individual members, and that a class action is superior to other available methods for the fair and efficient adjudication of the controversy.

Class Action or Not?   A very contentious issue in the *Dukes* v. *Wal-Mart Stores, Inc.* case has been whether a class action is warranted. Wal-Mart challenged the legal validity of the class action, arguing in a September 24, 2003 hearing before U.S. District Judge Martin Jenkins that the lawsuit should be broken into separate class actions against each of the 3,473 stores across the United States because decisions about pay and promotions are largely made at the store level. The company contended that the outlets "operate with so much autonomy that they are like independent businesses with different management styles that affect the way women are paid and promoted." Wal-Mart attorneys argued "that a class of potentially 1.6 million women would be too unwieldy to manage," and the experiences of a few women cannot be representative of a class as large as 1.6 million. Further, Wal-Mart contended that the suit ignored the thousands of women who earn more than their male counterparts, and that the allegations were flawed due to ignoring factors that cause one job to pay more than another. Nancy Abell, a Wal-Mart attorney, observed that "if Wal-Mart faces a single class-action spanning the entire country, the company will seek testimony from 4,000 store managers, resulting in a trial that would last 13 years."

Attorneys for the plaintiffs argue that even though the case focuses on the experiences of only a few named women, thousands of women with similar experiences have contacted them. The plaintiff's attorneys further argue that the gender disparities were caused by Wal-Mart's culture. Although the company promoted from within, those who received promotions were usually men. "[R]ather than posting job openings for management positions so that anyone could apply for them, the company often kept information about new openings quiet, simply tapping the shoulders of those it wanted to promote," the plaintiffs said. Brad Seligman, a lawyer for the plaintiffs, vigorously countered Wal-Mart's contention that each unit was very autonomous. "Wal-Mart stores are virtually identical in structure and job duties," according to Seligman. "There is a high emphasis on a common culture, which is the glue that holds the company together."

On June 22, 2004, U.S. District Court Judge Martin Jenkins ruled that six current and former Wal-Mart employees from California may represent all female employees of Wal-Mart who worked at its U.S. stores any time since December 26, 1998. "In certifying the case as the largest civil rights class action ever certified against a private employer, the judge described the case as 'historic in nature, dwarfing other employment discrimination cases that came before it.'" In his findings Judge Jenkins went on to say that the evidence presented by the plaintiffs "raises an inference that Wal-Mart engages in discriminatory practices in compensation and promotion that affect all plaintiffs in a common manner." Judge Jenkin's ruling suggests that Wal-Mart committed sexual discrimination in violation of Title VII of the Civil Rights Act of 1964.

Wal-Mart has denied the gender discrimination of women put forth in *Dukes* v. *Wal-Mart Stores, Inc.* and has appealed Judge Jenkins' class-action ruling. On December 8, 2004, the Washington Legal Foundation (WLF), in support of Wal-Mart's appeal, filed an amicus curiae brief in the U.S. Court of Appeals for the 9th Circuit in San Francisco, urging the court to overturn Jenkins' class action certification decision. In the amicus curiae brief, the WLF argued the plaintiffs failed to demonstrate (a) that "the case could manageably be tried as a class action," and (b) that "common issues of fact and law predominate over individual issues—an absolute prerequisite for certification of a class action." The WLF also was particularly critical of Judge Jenkin's decision to rely on the testimony of the plaintiffs' expert witness. The WLF argued that "[t]he plaintiffs do not allege that Wal-Mart has a company policy of discriminating against female employees. Rather, they allege that Wal-Mart maintains an amorphous 'corporate culture' that can 'perpetuate gender stereotypes' and lead to differences in pay and promotion between men and women. WLF argued that class treatment of such vague claims is never appropriate; rather, WLF argued that every case of alleged discrimination must stand or fall on its own merits."

Implications of *Dukes* v. *Wal-Mart Stores, Inc.*   *Dukes* v. *Wal-Mart Stores, Inc.* is but one of a long string of sex discrimination suits brought against Wal-Mart over a number of years. What sets the Dukes' claim apart is its size. If Wal-Mart loses *Dukes*, the monetary implications could be staggering. Analysts have estimated the settlement costs at upwards of $8 billion. Although the potential monetary settlement is enormous, Wal-Mart is the largest company in the world,

and with profits of $9 billion for the 2003 fiscal year, it is unlikely that even an $8 billion dollar settlement would significantly harm Wal-Mart. Interestingly, the plaintiffs in *Dukes* v. *Wal-Mart* are looking for more. They want to see Wal-Mart's culture change. As Brad Seligman, a lawyer at the Impact Fund and the plaintiffs' lead attorney, emphasized, "[t]he plaintiffs won't be satisfied with back pay and punitive damages. We want to change the way the company does business."

Wal-Mart's reaction to the discrimination complaints has been that they are a natural offshoot of success. Coleman Peterson, Wal-Mart's head of human resources, observes the any organization the size and status of Wal-Mart is going to have some people allege discrimination. Peterson characterizes this as a "bump in the night" and says that anyone who thinks such bumps won't occur is being unrealistic. Although Wal-Mart might view the sex discrimination allegations as a "bump in the night," the company has recently initiated numerous changes to its labor practices. Among these are:

- The creation of a 40-person compliance team to ensure labor laws and new corporate diversity goals are met.

- Reduction in bonuses if the company fails to promote women and minorities in proportion to the number who apply for management positions.

- A new job and wage structure that increases the number of job classifications from four to seven.

- A change in future pay scales to reflect increases based on knowledge, problem solving skills, and accountability requirements, as well as by market rates.

The decision whether the *Dukes* v. *Wal-Mart Stores, Inc.* case merits class action status is a pivotal one for Wal-Mart, its employees (particularly women), other employers, and American society at large. "If the suit becomes a national class action, it would give lawyers for the women tremendous leverage against Wal-Mart as they pursue punitive damages, as well as back pay. Without the muscle provided by a class action . . . Wal-Mart's women workers who believe they have been discriminated against probably won't be able to find attorneys to pursue a case against the nation's largest company."

Questions for Discussion

1. Based on the stated human resources philosophy of Wal-Mart, would it be likely that the company would discriminate based on gender differences? Explain.

2. Put yourself in the role of the plaintiffs. What ethical arguments would you offer in support of their allegations?

3. Put yourself in the role of Wal-Mart. What ethical arguments would you offer to counter the plaintiffs' allegations?

4. What do you think the plaintiffs meant by their allegation that Wal-Mart's culture is a significant contributor to gender discrimination?

5. Is a class action against Wal-Mart justified? Explain your position.

6. Explain how the outcome of *Dukes* v. *Wal-Mart Stores, Inc.* (regardless of how it is resolved) is important for major stakeholders in the case, including the American society.

Sources

This case was developed from material contained in the following sources:

Armour, S. (June 24, 2004) Rife with discrimination. *USA Today*, 03b.

Burns, G. (September 24, 2003). Class action no bargain for Wal-Mart: 1.5 million could be added to bias suit by women. *Chicago Tribune*, http://www.againstthewal.com/new_page_4.htm#Claa_action_no_bargain_for_Wal-Mart__, accessed March 31, 2005.

Class action complaint. (June 19, 2001). http://www.cmht.com/pdfs/walmart-cmpl.pdf, accessed February 5, 2005.

Cullen, L. (July 5, 2004). Wal-Mart's gender gap. *Time, 164(1)*, 44.

Daniels, C. (July 12, 2004). Wal-Mart's women problem. *Fortune*, 28.

Daniels, C. (July 21, 2003). Women vs. Wal-Mart. *Fortune*, 79.

Donegan, L. (June 27, 2004). The woman who is taking on Wal-Mart. *Guardian Unlimited*, http://www.guardian.co.uk/usa/story/0,12271,1248350.00.html, accessed July 31, 2004.

Dukes v. *Wal-Mart Stores, Inc.* (June 19, 2001). http://news.findlaw.com/hdocs/docs/walmart/dukeswalmart61901.pdf, accessed June 30, 2004.

Featherstone, L. (December 16, 2002). Wal-Mart values. *The Nation*, http://www.thenation.com/doc.mhtml?i=20021216&s=featherstone, accessed July 27, 2004.

Federal judge orders Wal-Mart Stores, Inc., the nation's largest private employer, to stand trial for company-wide sex discrimination. (June 22, 2004). *Equal Rights Advocates*, http://www.equalrights.org/media/walmart062204.asp, accessed February 5, 2005.

Girion, L. (April 28, 2003). Brief details claims at Wal-Mart. *Los Angeles Times.*

Hirsh, S. (June 27, 2004). Wal-Mart case highlights problem of sexual discrimination in the workplace. *Knight Ridder Tribune Business News*, 1.

Hoover's Inc. (November 4, 2003). Wal-Mart Stores Inc. *Hoover's Company Profiles.*

House Report 108-144. Class Action Fairness Act of 2003. Rule 23 class action requirements. Committee Reports for the 108th Congress. http://www.congress.gov/cgi-bin/cpquery/?&dbname=cp108&&r_n=hr144.108&sel=TOC_34194&, accessed June 30, 2004.

Kollars, D. (July 24, 2004). Lincoln, Calif., woman joins sex-discrimination suit against Wal-Mart. *Knight Ridder Tribune Business News*, 1.

Law Library of Congress. Civil rights. Civil Rights Act of 1964, http://memory.loc.gov/ammem/awhhtml/awlaw3/civil.html, accessed June 30, 2004

Liedtke, M. (September 25, 2003). Wal-Mart asks judge to break up lawsuit. *Associated Press*, http://www.cmht.com/casewatch/cases/walmart/Welcome%20to%20AJC!htm, accessed February 5, 2005.

Meadows, B., Atlas, D., Barnes, S., Goulding, S., Harrington, M. (July 12, 2004). Taking on a giant. *People, 62(2),* 75.

Moss, D. (July 2, 2004). Women in Wal-Mart suit forcing change. *USA Today,* A15.

Phillips, N. (July 4, 2004). Women workers in South Carolina join bias against Wal-Mart. *Knight Ridder Tribune Business News,* 1.

Press Release: Media Advisory. (June 22, 2004). Federal Judge Martin Jenkins certifies class. *Wal-Mart Class Website,* http://walmartclass.com/walmartclass94.pl?wsi=0&websys_screen+all_press_release_view&websys_id=14, accessed June 30, 2004.

Rosen, R. (June 30, 2003). Women and Wal-Mart. *San Francisco Chronicle,* http://www.sfgate.com/cgi-bin/article.cgi?file=/chronicle/archive/2003/06/30/ED143046.DTL, accessed July 25, 2004.

Wal-Mart: Pricing Philosophy. http://www.walmartstores.com/wmstore/wmstores/Mainabout.jsp?pagetype=about&template=ContentWithImages.jsp&categotyOID=-8278&catID=-8242, accessed June 30, 2004.

Wal-Mart Stores, Inc., the nation's largest private employer, sued for company-wide sex discrimination. (June 19, 2001). *Case Watch—Wal-Mart Stores Inc.,* http://www.cmht.com/cases_cwwalmart1.php, accessed February 5, 2005.

Washington Legal Foundation. (December 9, 2004). Court urged to decertify massive class action suit (*Dukes* v. *Wal-Mart Stores, Inc*). http://www.wlf.org/upload/120904RS.pdf, accessed February 5, 2005.

Washington Legal Fund. (December 8, 2004). Case detail: *Dukes* v. *Wal-Mart Stores, Inc.* http://www.wlf.org/Litigating/casedetail.asp?detail=319, accessed February 5, 2005.

Wilson, C., Takeuchi, L. (July 5, 2004). Wal-Mart's gender gap. *Time,* 44.

Wolverton, T. (September 25, 2003). Wal-Mart waits for a high stakes ruling. *TheStreet.com, Inc.,* http://www.cmht.com/cases_cwwalmart6.php, accessed February 5, 2005.

Zellner, W. (March 3, 2003). No way to treat a lady? As a sex discrimination suit unfolds, studies of Wal-Mart practices show a big gap in the status of men and women. *Business Week,* 63.

CASE 15

NIKE'S RESPONSES TO SWEATSHOP CHARGES:
PROTECTED OR UNPROTECTED SPEECH?

Imagine that every day you go to work you are exposed to toxic chemicals without having any protective clothing or safety training and that the workplace has poor ventilation and fire safety. Suppose that you are subjected to physical and verbal abuse at the hands of your employer and that there is a lack of drinking water in the workplace. Suppose further that you are paid only a couple of dollars per day and forced to work excessive overtime hours. Would these be satisfactory working conditions—for anyone, anywhere in the world?

These are the types of conditions found in businesses commonly known as sweatshops. A sweatshop is typically characterized by poor working conditions, including health and safety hazards; extreme exploitation, including the absence of a living wage or benefits; and arbitrary discipline, such as physical and psychological abuse.

According to CorpWatch, sweatshops exist throughout the world and in a variety of manufacturing industries, including apparel, shoes, toys, and electronics. Nearly 70% of immigrant garment workers in Los Angeles receive less than the legal minimum wage. Women workers in some Central American countries are often forced to undergo pregnancy testing or take contraception. Workers in many Asian countries are exposed to dangerous chemicals while making shoes.

Sweatshop Accusations and Nike's Responses Nike began encountering criticism in the early 1990s for the sweatshop conditions that existed in its contractors' factories. Nike responded by becoming one of the first American companies to establish and publish a code of conduct for the contract manufacturers in its supply chain. According to Nike officials, the company's Code of Conduct was an initial step in a conscious strategy to improve working conditions at its contract factories. Drafted in 1991, the Code of Conduct was distributed to the contract factories in 1992 and was intended to guide decisions in those production facilities.

In June 1996, Bob Herbert, a columnist for the *New York Times*, wrote two articles accusing Nike of exploiting workers in Asian sweatshops. Herbert charged that laborers earning $2.20 per day in Indonesia or $30 per month in Vietnam were manufacturing Nike's athletic shoes. Herbert contrasted these miniscule wages with "the $20 million a year Nike was then paying basketball legend Michael Jordan to promote its products and to [Nike CEO Phil] Knight's own $1.6 million salary and bonus for fiscal 1995." Knight responded with a letter to the editor, which the *New York Times* promptly published. Knight maintained that "Nike has paid, on average, double the minimum wage as defined in countries where its products are produced under contract. History shows that the best way out of poverty for such countries is through exports of light manufactured goods that provide the base for more skilled production."

In January 1997, the accounting firm Ernst & Young, hired by Nike, conducted a labor and environmental audit of several Nike contract factories in Vietnam. Ernst & Young uncovered sweatshop conditions in numerous factories. Nike did not publicly disclose the audit report. Nike also hired Andrew Young, the former U.N. ambassador, to evaluate 12 factories that made its athletic footwear, most in Asia. Young, who had access to the secret Ernst & Young document, issued a favorable report in June 1997, and Nike issued press releases about his findings. Nike also "wrote letters to colleges faced with anti-sweatshop activists who were urging the schools to boycott Nike products. The company emphasized its code of conduct requiring contractors to adhere to decent labor standards."

A worker at Tae Kwang Vina Industrial Co. (TKV), one of the factories covered in the secret Ernst & Young audit report, leaked the document to Dara O'Rourke, a consultant with the United Nations Industrial Development Organization in Vietnam and a research associate with Transnational Resource and Action Center (TRAC). In November 1997, TRAC—now known as CorpWatch—released the leaked Nike document. O'Rourke's independent assessment of the factory and photos from inside it made front-page news in the *New York Times*. TRAC asserted that its "release of the Ernst & Young report significantly increased the pressure on Nike to improve conditions in its overseas factories." TRAC also cited an editorial in the *Multinational Monitor*, which argued that "for a whole year, Nike denied that its contractors in Asia abused and mistreated workers. The company said that the information was being sent out by fringe activists on the Internet. . . . With the leak of an Ernst & Young report, the fringe became mainstream."

Enter Marc Kasky In April 1998, Marc Kasky, a community activist living in San Francisco, sued Nike, alleging that Nike CEO Knight's letter to the editor violated California's consumer protection laws against deceptive advertising and unfair business practices. Kasky's suit also "alleged that Nike officials had made false or misleading claims on at least eight other occasions in the course of responding to criticisms of its Asian labor practices: in five press releases, two personal letters to critics, and one form letter sent to scores of athletic directors at colleges and universities."

Nike maintained that its campaign was designed to explain working conditions at factories of their overseas contractors. Nike further maintained "that its statements concerned labor practices, not products, and therefore should be considered protected political speech." Kasky countered that Nike's campaign was indeed commercial speech—it was intended to protect the company's image and sell more sneakers. This set the stage for a legal battle over commercial speech and its First Amendment protection.

Commercial Speech   In 1942, the U.S. Supreme Court ruled that business-related speech, in contrast to ordinary speech, did not enjoy First Amendment protection. At that time, commercial speech was narrowly construed as speech that does "no more than propose a commercial transaction." By 1976, the U.S. Supreme Court altered its position somewhat, indicating that some forms of commercial speech should receive First Amendment protection. "The increased protection for commercial speech was intended not to serve the interests of faceless businesses but to ensure the public's right to receive information from commercial sources." Courts began to recognize that commercial speech could include claims about the social responsibility of manufacturers.

Over the years the boundaries between commercial speech and ordinary speech (sometimes referred to as political speech) became extremely murky as different courts and regulatory agencies—usually the Federal Trade Commission (FTC)—dealt with specific cases. Some advertising claims that seemed very similar to public discourse were treated as regulated commercial speech. "To make matters even more confusing, courts also acknowledged that commercial speech was not necessarily limited to paid advertisements, nor, conversely, did messages in paid advertisements necessarily amount to paid commercial speech."

A company can be sued if someone thinks its commercial speech is false or misleading, and the consumer protection laws don't require that malice be intended. Moreover, under California's extremely broad consumer protection laws, anyone can sue on behalf of the general public. Consequently, a person who brings suit in California need not have experienced any harm or damages from a company's alleged false or misleading commercial speech, which was the case with Marc Kasky.

The Legal Battle over Nike's Speech   *Kasky* v. *Nike* alleged that Nike's commercial speech contained false and misleading statements. Nike argued that the various communications in question were not commercial speech, but rather protected political speech. Nike requested that the trial court dismiss the suit. The California Superior

Court sided with Nike, with the dismissal being subsequently affirmed by the California Court of Appeal. Kasky appealed to the California Supreme Court, and on May 2, 2002, the lower court decision was reversed by a 4-3 vote. In ruling against Nike, the California Supreme Court stated, "[B]ecause a company's public statements about its operations might persuade consumers to buy its products, those statements must be treated as run-of-the-mill commercial speech, thereby warranting severely limited constitutional protection." The California Supreme Court ruling also "indicated that such speech could be restricted even when those statements appear in news stories, op-eds, press releases, or on Web sites published anywhere in the world, just as long as the statements reach residents of California."

Nike appealed the California Supreme Court ruling to the U.S. Supreme Court. Nike asked the U.S. Supreme Court to declare unconstitutional the California law under which Kasky brought his original lawsuit. The issue before the Supreme Court was whether Nike could be held liable for its misrepresentations under false advertising laws or whether its various public documents and letters to the press and others were constitutionally protected speech. Nike argued that responsible corporate communication "benefits consumers by ensuring that they receive information that is both complete and accurate." In its legal brief, Nike maintained that the California court ruling was having a "chilling effect" on its activities. Nike said the prospect of being sued in California made it too risky for the company to release its annual corporate responsibility report, participate in the Dow Jones Sustainability Index, participate in media interviews, or accept invitations to speak at business and academics forums.

Nike's appeal received support from many different organizations and entities. The United States Government, the American Civil Liberties Union, the U.S. Chamber of Commerce, organized labor, numerous media organizations, many European entities, and trade associations filed amicus curiae or "friend of the court" briefs after the U.S. Supreme Court decided to hear Nike's appeal. An amicus brief filed by a group of 40 media organizations including CBS, CNN, the New York Times Company, and the Washington Post Company, argued that "[t]his chilling effect will deprive the public of access to important news stories and the clash of competing viewpoints that undergirds the First Amendment."

Just as some interested parties filed amicus briefs on behalf of Nike, other interested parties filed amicus briefs supporting Kasky. As a member of the socially responsible investing (SRI) community, Domini Social Investments LLC filed an amicus brief with the U.S. Supreme Court in support of Marc Kasky. The brief argued that, "The SRI community depends upon the accurate flow of corporate social

and environmental performance data. All investors depend on government regulators to ensure that information from corporations is provided on a timely and accurate basis. If any of this information is
deemed to be 'political speech,' it will severely undercut these regulatory efforts. Nike's definition of political speech—any commercial
speech that also touches upon matters of public concern—is alarm-
ingly broad, potentially affecting nearly every aspect of a corporation's
business, from treatment of stock options to compliance with environmental regulations." The attorney for Domini also emphasized
that "[i]t is important to note that this case has no bearing on Nike's
actual practices regarding its overseas contractors, or whether its statements were in fact false or misleading. It addresses only the constitutional question of whether companies like Nike can claim full First
Amendment protection for public statements regarding their own
business practices that also touch upon matters of public concern."

ReclaimDemocracy.org and the National Voting Rights Institute
jointly filed an amicus brief in support of Kasky. This brief asserted
"[t]he claim that corporations possess a right to intentionally deceive
the public has no basis in the U.S. Constitution. Incorporation is a
privilege granted by the people's representatives in state governments,
and corporations must remain subordinate to our democratic institutions. The discredited judicial creations of 'corporate personhood' and
corporate 'political rights' should be unequivocally rejected by the
Court."

On April 23, 2003, the U.S. Supreme Court heard oral arguments
in the case of *Nike* v. *Kasky*. Nike's lead counsel, Harvard Law
Professor Laurence Tribe, urged the Supreme Court "to reaffirm the
First Amendment right to free and open debate and to overturn an
unprecedented California state court ruling that severely restricts the
ability of business and other organizations to speak out on matters of
public importance." Tribe asserted that Nike was not selling anything
when it defended itself against accusations about its overseas contractors running sweatshops. He further stated, "[i]t was a lively political
debate that included letters to the editor and other public statements
that were intended to set the record straight." An attorney representing Kasky countered that, "Nike's statements amounted to misleading
efforts to sell its products. He said Nike's defense included specific
statements about work conditions and other labor issues, and were
intended to reassure potential consumers."

On June 26, 2003, the U.S. Supreme Court announced its 6-3
decision declining to rule on the First Amendment issue and sending
the case back to California for trial. The next day Kasky told the
Associated Press, "[w]e now have the opportunity to go to trial to
determine if Nike's comments were true or not."

National and international reaction to the case's return to California for trial suggested that resolution of the case in the court system could set three international precedents. First, Nike's contractors might have to open their business practices to unwanted public scrutiny. Second, companies would need to exercise much greater caution about claims made not only in advertising, but also in public relations and all other public statements that might be construed as advertising. Third, companies with sweatshop practices or conditions would encounter additional public scrutiny.

On September 12, 2003, Nike and Marc Kasky jointly announced a settlement of the case brought by Kasky. "The two parties mutually agreed that investments designed to strengthen workplace monitoring and factory worker programs are more desirable than prolonged litigation." Nike agreed to contribute $1.5 million over a three-year period to the Fair Labor Association (FLA) to help fund workplace-related programs. The $1.5 million figure was in addition to Nike's other FLA expenditures on monitoring and related activities. Nike also agreed to maintain a $500,000 funding commitment over two years to the after-hours worker education program in its footwear facilities and to its Micro Enterprise program. The Micro Enterprise program provides small business loans to poor people in developing nations, especially in rural areas where the people do not have access to commercial banks.

No court ever addressed the truth or falsity of any statement made by Nike. Nike admitted no liability in the settlement.

Nike's Activities since the Settlement   Nike's Code of Conduct has been revised and updated over the years. In 2002, Nike instituted Code Leadership Standards (CLS) that included "23 safety standards, 13 standards for management concerns (including labor issues), 9 standards for environmental regulations, and 6 health standards." The CLS provided guidance for the company's supply chain. As of early 2005, Nike's supply chain consisted of more than 900 contract factories with more than 660,000 contract workers—predominately women, aged 19 to 25—in more than 50 countries including the United States.

Through its independent external monitoring (IEM), the Fair Labor Association's verifies Nike's and other participating companies' compliance in their contract factories. The FLA conducts unannounced, independent, external monitoring visits in a company's contract factories and reports all noncompliance findings in those factories. In preparing its 2004 report, the FLA conducted 40 IEM visits to Nike contractors. There were no noncompliance findings of employment of underage workers or forced or bonded labor in facilities producing for Nike. Some noncompliance existed regarding health and safety as well as wages and hours. The noncompliance findings regarding health and safety issues usually related to inadequate postings and evacuation procedures, safety equipment, and personal protective equipment. Noncompliance involving wage and hour issues primarily concerned overtime limitations, overtime compensation, and worker awareness of their wages and benefits. In all instances, Nike initiated appropriate remediation, either independently or in conjunction with other FLA participating companies.

Nike has made substantial progress in dealing with sweatshop issues in its supply chain, but more remains to be done. All of the sweatshop issues probably will never be resolved. Of equal importance is the failure to resolve the issues raised by all the legal maneuvering between Marc Kasky and Nike. Perhaps one day, companies and consumers will know which business communications are commercial and which are not.

Questions for Discussion

1. Why are sweatshops viewed with disgust and abhorrence? Does a sweatshop accomplish anything positive?

2. Is it ethically appropriate to expect a company that operates beyond California's boundaries to essentially conform all of it communications to California's legal standards?

3. The U.S. Supreme Court declined to rule on the First Amendment issue regarding whether Nike was using commercial speech or protected political speech; consequently, it remains unresolved. In your judgment, was Nike using commercial speech or political speech? Explain your answer.

4. No court ever addressed the truth or falsity of any statement made by Nike. In your viewpoint, did Nike make false and misleading statements? Explain your position.

5. Considering all of the costs associated with Kasky's lawsuit and Nike's defense as well as the end result, was this a wise use of resources? What good, if any, did this do for people working in sweatshop conditions?

Sources

This case was developed from material contained in the following sources:

Bachman, S.L. (June 27, 2003) Nike v. sweatshop critic: Back to California. *Global Policy Forum*, http://www.globalpolicy.org/globaliz/econ/2003/0630nike.htm, accessed February 17, 2005.

Code of Conduct. *Nikebiz.com*, http://www.nike.com/nikebiz/nikebiz.jhtml?page=25&cate=code, accessed February 17, 2005.

Exposing sweatshops. (June 11, 2003) *CorpWatch*, http://www.corpwatch.org/article.php?id=11304, accessed February 20, 2005.

Global giving. *Nikebiz.com*, http://www.nike.com/nikebiz/nikebiz.jhtml?page=26&item=globalization, accessed February 17, 2005.

Hammond, K. (November 7, 1997) Leaked audit: Nike factory violated worker laws. *MotherJones.com*, http://www.motherjones.com/news/feature/1997/11/nike.html, accessed February 20, 2005.

Henderson, S. (April 24, 2003) Supreme Court hears Nike case. *Knight Ridder Tribune Washington Bureau*, from Newspaper Source database at http://search.epnet.com/login.aspx?direct=true&db=nfh&an=2W61647916701, accessed February 17, 2005.

Herman, E. (June 27, 2003) Supreme Court sends false-advertising lawsuit against Nike back to California. *New York Daily News*, from Newspaper Source database at http://search.epnet.com/login.aspx?direct=true&db=nfh&an=2W63885868202, accessed February 17, 2005.

Holmes, S. (April 28, 2003) Free speech or false advertising? *Business Week*, from Business Source Premier database at http://search.epnet.com/login.aspx?direct=true&db=buh&an=9586203, accessed February 17, 2005.

McCaffrey, S. (January 11, 2003) Supreme Court to decide if Nike can stretch the truth in its defense. *Knight Ridder Tribune Washington Bureau*, from Newspaper Source database at http://search.epnet.com/login.aspx?direct=true&db=nfh&an=2W60092923630, accessed February 17, 2005.

Nike, Inc. and Kasky announce settlement of *Kasky* v. *Nike* First Amendment case. *Nikebiz.com: Press Release*, http://www.nike.com/nikebiz/news/pressrelease.jhtml?year=2003&month=09&letter=f, accessed February 17, 2005.

Nike Inc.—FLA independent external monitoring in Nike's applicable facilities. (2004) *Fair Labor Association 2004 Annual Report*, http://www.fairlabor.org/2004report/companies/participating/factoryData_nike.html, accessed February 20, 2005.

Nike urges U.S. Supreme Court to reaffirm First Amendment right to free and open debate. (April 23, 2003) *Nikebiz.com: Press Release*, http://www.nike.com/nikebiz/news/pressrelease.jhtml?year=2003&month=04&letter=c, accessed February 17, 2005.

Nike vs. Kasky: Corporations are not persons. (June 11, 2003) *CorpWatch*, http://www.corpwatch.org/article.php?id=1710, accessed February 20, 2005.

Our business model & its challenges. *Nikebiz.com*, http://www.nike.com/nikebiz/nikebiz.jhtml?page=25&cate=businessmodel, accessed February 17, 2005.

Parloff, R. (August 11, 2002) Can we talk? A shocking First Amendment ruling against Nike radically reduces the rights of corporations to speak their minds. Will the Supreme Court let it stand? *Fortune*, http://www.fortune.com/fortune/subs/print/0,15935,367780,00.html, accessed February 17, 2005.

Socially conscious investors file amicus brief with Supreme Court in *Nike* v. *Kasky*. (April 7, 2003) *CorpWatch*, http://www.corpwatch.org/article.php?id=6313, accessed February 20, 2005.

Notes

1. Asmus, P. (Spring 2004). 100 best corporate citizens for 2004. *Business Ethics*, http://www.business-ethics.com/100best.htm.
2. Valenti, C. (August 7, 2004). Crime and punishment. *ABC News*, http://abcnews.go.com/sections/business/DailyNews/corporatepunishment_020807.html.
3. Viewpoint: beyond compliance: Social accountability can protect companies and profits. (April 13, 2001). *Asiaweek*, 1.

4. Carroll, A. (1991). The pyramid of corporate social responsibility: Toward the moral management of organizational stakeholders. *Business Horizons, 34(4),* 39–48; Corporate social responsibility has gained credibility as important as operational effectiveness. The IISD, International Institute for Sustainable Development, is considering the creation of ISO standards for corporation social responsibility, see "ISO CSR Standards: What should an ISO standard on social responsibility look like?" *International Institute for Sustainable Development,* http://www.iisd.org/standards/csr.asp.

5. Albinger, H., Freeman, S. (2000). Corporate social performance and attractiveness as an employer to different job seeking populations. *Journal of Business Ethics, 28(3),* 243–253; Fombrun, C., Shanley, M. (1990). What's in a name? Reputation building and corporate strategy. *Academy of Management Journal, 33,* 233–258. See current articles on corporate reputation at *Corporate Reputation Review,* http://www.ingenta.com/journals/browse/hsp/crr?mode=direct.

6. See the Current Trends Report at the Social Investment Forum's home page, http://www.socialinvest.org.

7. Turban, D., Greening, D. (1997). Corporate social performance and organizational attractiveness to prospective employees. *Academy of Management Journal, 40,* 648–672. Also see Orlitzky, M. et al. (May–June 2003). Corporate social and financial performance: A meta-analysis. *Organizational Studies, 24,* 403–442.

8. Alsop, R. (2001). Corporate reputations are earned with trust, reliability, study shows. *Wall Street Journal,* http://www.reputations.com.

9. Ibid.

10. Hillman, A., Keim, G. (2001). Shareholder value, stakeholder management, and social issues: What's the bottom line? *Strategic Management Journal, 22,* 125.

11. Ibid., 136.

12. Torabzadeh, K., et al. (1989). The effect of the recent insider-trading scandal on stock prices of securities firms. *Journal of Business Ethics, 8,* 303.

13. Thomas, T., Schermerhorn, J., Jr., Dienhart, J. (2004). Strategic leadership of ethical behavior in business. *Academy of Management Executive, 18(2),* 56–66; Trevino, L., et al. (1999). Managing ethics and legal compliance: What works and what hurts. *California Management Review, 41(2),* 131–151.

14. Trevino.

15. Langer, G. (July 1, 2004). Confidence in business: Was low and still is. *ABC News,* http://abcnews.go.com/sections/business/DailyNews/corporatetrust_poll020701.html.

16. Nash, L. (1990). *Good Intentions Aside: A Manager's Guide to Resolving Ethical Problems,* 101. Boston: Harvard Business School.

17. Ibid., 104.

18. Davis, K., Blomstrom, R. (1966). *Business and Its Environment.* New York: McGraw-Hill.

19. Thomas, et al., 60. Also see 2002 Cone Corporate Citizenship Study. *Cone, Inc.,* http://www.coneinc.com/Pages/pr_13.html.

20. Faircloth, A., Bollinger, C. (February 2, 1998). *Fortune's* 40 most generous Americans. *Fortune,* 88; William H. Gates: Chairman and Chief Software Architect: Microsoft Corporation. (August 2004). *Microsoft Corporation,* http://www.microsoft.com/billgates/bio.asp.

21. Permanent Subcommittee of Investigations of the Committee on Governmental Affairs, United States Senate. (July 8, 2002). The role of the Board of Director's in Enron's collapse. http://www.auditcommittee.ch/board_role_in_enron_collapse.pdf.

22. Jennings, M. (2000). *NYT The Board of Directors.* New York: Lebhar-Friedman Books.

23. Krantz, M. (November 24, 2002). Web of board members ties together corporate America. *USA Today,* http://www.usatoday.com/money/companies/management/2002-11-24-interlock_x.htm; Corporate Board Member Resource Center. *Corporate Board Member Magazine,* http://www.boardmember.com/network/index.pl?section=1024&show=index; Dallas, L. (Winter 1997). Proposals for reform of corporate board of directors: The dual board and board ombudsperson. *Washington and Lee Law Review, 54(1),* 91–148; Daily, C., Dalton, D. (2003). Conflicts of interest: A corporate governance pitfall. *The Journal of Business Strategy, 24(4),* 7.

24. Weinberg, N. (May 10, 2004). Blame the board. *Forbes*, http://www.forbes.com/free_forbes/2004/0510/120.html.
25. Ending the Wall Street walk: Why corporate governance now? (1996). *Corporate Governance*, http://www.corpgov.net/forums/commentary/ending.html cited in Steiner, G., Steiner, J. (2003). *Business, Government, and Society*, 10th ed. New York: McGraw-Hill, 675.
26. Carroll, A., Buchholtz, A. (2003). *Business and Society*, 5th ed. Mason, OH: South-Western/Thomson, 320.
27. Ferrell, O., Fraedrich, J., Ferrell, L. (2005). *Business Ethics*, 6th ed. Boston, MA: Houghton-Mifflin Company, 54.
28. See *Frontline* and the *PBS* (Public Broadcasting Service) film, "Bigger Than Enron," http://www.pbs.org/whbh/pages/frontline/shows/regulation.
29. Caruso, K. (Spring 2004). Restoring public trust in corporate America: A legislative or a principled solution? *Southern New Hampshire University Journal*, 36–51, http://www.snhu.edu/img/assets/3670/caruso.pdf; Heffes, E.M. (June 2003). Restoring corporate integrity and public trust. *Financial Executive*, 18–20.
30. Associated Press. (July 8, 2004). Status of high-profile corporate scandals. *Forbes*, http://www.forbes.com/associatedpress/feeds/ap/2004/07/08/ap1449008.html; Cook, D. (April 19, 2004). Qwest prosecutors end up empty-handed. *CFO.com*, http://www.cfo.com/article.cfm/3013277?f=TodayInFinance_Inside.
31. Trevino.
32. The Sarbanes-Oxley Act of 2002. *Pricewaterhouse Coopers*, http://www.pwc.com/extweb/newcoatwork.nsf/docid/D0D7F79003C6D644852 56CF30074D66C.
33. Summary of Sarbanes-Oxley Act of 2002. *The American Institute of Certified Public Accountants*, http://www.aicpa.org/info/sarbanes_oxley_summary.htm; *The Sarbanes-Oxley Act Community Forum*, http://www.sarbanes-oxley-forum.com; *Sarbanes-Oxley*, http://www.sarbanes-oxley.com; Spotlight on: Sarbanes-Oxley rule-making and reports. *U.S. Securities and Exchange Commission*, http://www.sec.gov/spotlight/sarbanes-oxley.htm; Lawrence, A., et al. (2005). *Business and Society*, 11th ed. Boston: McGraw-Hill, 305; Ferrell, O., et al. (2005). *Business Ethics*, 6th ed. Boston: Houghton Mifflin Company.
34. Volcker, P., Levitt, A., Jr. (June 14, 2004). In defense of Sarbanes-Oxley. *The Wall Street Journal*, A16.
35. Farrell, G. (August 15, 2004). Accounting leads rise, making boards edgy. *USA Today*, http://www.usatoday.com/printededition/money/20040729/1b_whistleblowergreg29.art.htm.
36. Demos, T. (June 28, 2004). CFO pressure cooker. *Fortune*, http://www.fortune.com/fortune/investing/articles/0,15114,650833,00.html.
37. Volcker and Levitt, Jr.
38. Ibid.
39. Ibid.
40. Ibid.
41. United States Sentencing Commission. (January 2003). Increased penalties under the Sarbanes-Oxley Act of 2002. http://www.ussc.gov/r_congress/S-Oreport.pdf; Lies, M., II. Create a corporate compliance program. *George S. May International Company*, http://law.georgesmay.com/1.htm; Hartman, L. (2004). *Perspectives in Business Ethics*, 3rd ed. Boston: McGraw-Hill; Ferrell, O., et al. (2005). *Business Ethics*, 6th ed. Boston: Houghton Mifflin Company, 172.
42. Lies, II.
43. Petry, E. (June 2004). Effective compliance and ethics programs, 2004 amendments to the U.S. sentencing guidelines for organizations. *DII Signatory Workshop/Best Practices Forum*.
44. See Belsie, L. (September 13, 2000). The rise of corporate apology: Bridgestone/Firestone's crisis reveals quickening cycle of accountability in era of Web and instant communication. *Christian Science Monitor*, 1; Gaines-Ross, L., et al. (November 17, 2003). Using the Web to communicate in a crisis. *IR Web Report*, http://www.irwebreport.com/features/031101-1.htm.
45. The following excerpts are based on these sources: Geyelin, M. (Aug. 27, 2001). For Firestone, tire trial is mixed victory. *Wall Street Journal*, A3; Belsie, 1; Sissell, K. (Dec. 8, 1999). Judge approves Dow Corning bankruptcy plan. *Chemical Week*, 21;

Bloomberg News. (May 17, 2001). Payout in 2001 in diet cases to be $7 billion. *New York Times*, C.7; Donaldson, T., Werhane, P. (1988). *Ethical Issues in Business: A Philosophical Approach*, 89–100, 414–414. Englewood Cliffs, NJ: Prentice-Hall; Barett. (April 3, 1985). Dalkon Shield maker concedes possible user injuries. *Dallas Times Herald*, A8; Buchholz, R. A. (1989). *Fundamental Concepts and Problems in Business Ethics*. Englewood Cliffs, NJ: Prentice Hall; Geyelin, M. (Nov. 12, 1991). Dalkon Shield trust lawyers draw fire. *Wall Street Journal*, B5; Matthews, J., Goodpaster, K., Nash, L. (1991). *Policies and Persons: A Casebook in Business Ethics*, 2d ed. New York: McGraw-Hill.

46. Maignan, I. (2001). Consumers' perceptions of corporate social responsibilities: A cross-cultural comparison. *Journal of Business Ethics*, 30(1), 57–72.

47. Ibid., 69.

48. Velasquez, M. (1988, 1998). *Business Ethics Concepts and Cases*, 2d and 4th eds. Englewood Cliffs: Prentice Hall.

49. Velasquez, M. (2001). The ethics of consumer protection. In Hoffman, W., Frederick, R., Schwartz, M., eds. *Business Ethics*, 4th ed., 424. Boston: McGraw-Hill.

50. Buchholz, R. (July/Aug. 1991). Corporate responsibility and the good society: From economics to ecology. *Business Horizons*, 24; Holloway and Hancock. (1973). *Marketing in a Changing Environment*, 2d ed. New York: John Wiley and Sons.

51. Boatright, J. (1999). *Ethics and the Conduct of Business*, 3d ed., 273. Englewood Cliffs, NJ: Prentice Hall.

52. Szwajkowski, E. (Dec. 2000). Simplifying the principles of stakeholder management: The three most important principles. *Business and Society, 39(4)*, 381. Other advocates of this interpretation of Smith's views include Bishop, J. (1995). Adam Smith's invisible hand argument. *Journal of Business Ethics, 14*, 165; Rothchild, E. (1994). Adam Smith and the invisible hand. *AEA Papers and Proceedings, 8(2)*, 312–322; Winch, D. (1997). Adam Smith's problems and ours. *Scottish Journal of Political Economy*, 44, 384–402.

53. Szwajkowski, 381.

54. Bell, C. (April 3, 2001). Testing reliance on free market. *Boston Globe*, C4.

55. Ibid.

56. Samuelson, P. (1973). *Economics*, 9th ed., 345. New York: McGraw-Hill. This discussion is also based on Velasquez, 1998, 166–200.

57. Lawrence, et al., 316–317.

58. Ferrell, et al., 203.

59. Coen, R. (June 2003). Robert Coen presentation on advertising expenditures. *Universal McCann's Insider Report*, http://www.interpublic.com/aboutUs/advertlO/Coen%20Insider's%Report%20-%20June%202003.pdf.

60. Wright, J. (1996). *General Editory*, The Universal Almanac, 270. Kansas City: Andrews and McMeel.

61. http://www.ftc.gov/bcp/online/pubs/buspubs/ruleroad.htm (Sept. 2000).

62. Hansell, S. (July 23, 2001). Pop-up Web ads pose a measurement puzzle. *New York Times*, C1.

63. Evangelista, B. (July 23, 2001). Byte-size movies. *New York Times*, E1.

64. Dobrzynski, J. (July 29, 2001). So, technology pros, what comes after the fall? *New York Times*, B1, B11.

65. Ibid.

66. Best, J. (January 24, 2001). Why technology can't stop music piracy. *ZDNet*, http://reviews-zdnet.com.com/4520-6033_16-4205494.html.

67. Coles, A., Harris, L., Davis, R. (2004). Is the party over? Innovation and music on the Web. *Information, Communication & Ethics in Society*, 2, 25, http://www.troubador.co.uk/image/journals/2-1-3-Harris4410.pdf.

68. US takes action against online frauders. (August 26, 2004). *Center for Democracy & Technology*, http://www.cdt.org/privacy.

69. http://www.ftc.gov/bcp/online/pubs/buspubs/ruleroad.htm (Sept. 2000).

70. Phishing definition. *Webopedia*, http://sbc.webopedia.com/TERM/p/phishing.html.

71. Davis, Z. (September 15, 2004). Congress can't stop spyware. *Yahoo! News*, http://news.yahoo.com/news?tmpl=story&u=/zd/20040915/tc_zd/135410.

72. Thompson, R. (August 9, 2004). We must beat spyware. *EWeek Enterprise News and Reviews*, http://www.eweek.com/article2/0,1759,1630837,00.asp.

73. Wielaard, R. (September 15, 2004). Europe council looks to fight cybercrime. *BizReport*, http://www.bizreport.com/news/7981.

74. Velasquez (1998), 343–349.

75. Post, J., Lawrence, A., Weber, J. (1999). *Business and Society*, 9th ed., 464. Boston: Irwin McGraw-Hill.

76. Noble, B. (Oct. 27, 1991). After terms of deregulation, a new push to inform the public. *New York Times*, F5.

77. Kranish, M. (July 29, 2001). Fat chance. *Boston Globe*, D1.

78. Schlosser, E. (2001). *Fast Food Nation*. New York: Houghton Mifflin.

79. Nagorski, A. (Feb. 26, 2001). Hold the French fries: A reasoned attack on the fast-food culture. *Newsweek*, 50; Schrader, M. (March 12, 2001). Survey of fast food in America presents one-sided, dark view. *Nation's Restaurant News*, 84; Schlosser, E. (March 2001). Fast food nation: The dark side of the all-American meal. *Food Management*, 13.

80. Grimm, M. (April 5, 2004). Is marketing to kids ethical? *Brandweek*, *45(14)*, 4.

81. Stein, R., Connolly, C. (July 16, 2004). Medicare changes its stance, classifies obesity as a disease: Coverage expected for weight-loss treatments. *San Francisco Chronicle*, A3, http://www.sfgate.com/cgi-bin/article.cgi?file=/c/a/2004/07/16/MNGFA7MOSN1.DTL.

82. Ibid.

83. Sealey, G. (January 22, 2002). Whose fault is fat? *ABC News*, http://abcnews.go.com/sections/us/DailyNews/obesityblame020122.html.

84. Ibid.

85. Dean, T. (June 8, 2004). Smoking chokes progress on U.N. millennium goals. *Inter Press Service News Agency*, http://www.ipsnews.net/africa/interna.asp?idnews=24101.

86. Post, Lawrence, and Weber.

87. http://www.msnbc.com/news/615678.asp?cp1=1, p. 2.

88. Jackson, D. (July 25, 2001). When death is the bottom line. *Boston Globe*, A19.

89. Supreme Court rules against Massachusetts in tobacco case. (June 28, 2001). *CNN.com*, http://www.cnn.com/2001/LAW/06/28/scotus.tobacco.ads.

90. Gostin, L. (March 2002). Corporate speech and the Constitution: The deregulation of tobacco advertising. *American Journal of Public Health*, *92(3)*, 352–356.

91. Kaufman, M. (September 19, 2004). U.S. racketeering trial against tobacco industry is set to start. *The Washington Post*, A14, http://www.washingtonpost.com/wp-dyn/articles/A32031-2004Sep18.html.

92. Ibid.

93. Ibid.

94. See The National Council on Alcoholism and Drug Dependence's Web site for fact sheets on alcohol and drug use (http://www.ncadd.org/facts/index.html).

95. Associated Press. (January 11, 2003). Supreme Court to take up Nike free-speech case. *The Olympian*, http://www.theolympian.com/home/news/20030111/business/6112.shtml.

96. Biskupic, J. (June 29, 2004). High Court upholds block of Web porn law. *USA Today*, http://www.usatoday.com/news/washington/2004-06-29-sc-porn_x.htm.

97. See Steiner, Steiner. (2000). *Business, Government, and Society*, 9th ed., 596. Boston: McGraw-Hill.

98. Cava, A. (Spring 2000). Commercial speech 1999: Significant developments. *Academy of Marketing Science Journal*, *28(2)*, 316–317. For more detail and discussion on these issues and recent Court cases see Emord, J. (Spring 2000). *Pearson v. Shalala*: The beginning of the end for FDA speech suppression. *Journal of Public Policy & Marketing*, *19(1)*, 139–143; 2003 year-end summary and hot topics in 2004. *Loeb & Loeb*, http://www.loeb.com/CM/Alerts/Jan2004YearEndSummary.pdf.

99. Cigarette smoking overview. *eMedicine.com*, http://www.emedicinehealth.com/articles/20785-1.asp.

100. Schleicher, A. (April 26, 2004). Most antidepressants deemed unsafe for children. *PBS Online NewsHour*, http://www.pbs.org/newshour/extra/features/jan-june04/depressed_4-26.html.

101. Ibid.

102. Ibid.

103. Lee, D. (Dec. 2000). How government prevents us from buying safety. *Ideas on Liberty, 50(12)*, 32–33.
104. DeGeorge. (1990). *Business Ethics*, 3d ed., 182, 183. New York: Macmillan.
105. O'Donnell, J. (April 4, 2001). Cosco's history reads like a recipe for recalls/Company kept quiet. *USA Today*, B1.
106. Simplest e-mail queries confound companies. (Oct. 21, 1996). *Wall Street Journal*, B1, B9. See Post, Lawrence, and Weber, chapter 14, for a discussion of consumer affairs departments.
107. Etzioni, A. (1978). The need to put a price on life. *The Communitarian Network*, http://www.gwu.edu/~ccps/etzioni/B113.html. Originally printed in *The Washington Post* (October 29, 1978). Reprinted in the *Journal of Physical Education and Recreation*, (June 1979), *(50)6*, 39–40; as "How Much is a Life Worth?" in the *Detroit News Magazine* (December 3, 1978) and *Social Policy*, (March–April 1979) *(9)5*, 4–8.
108. Payout in 2001 in diet cases to be $7 billion. (May 17, 2001). *New York Times*, C7.
109. Sook Kim, Q. (Feb. 7, 2001). Asbestos claims continue to mount—Did broker of settlements unwittingly encourage more plaintiffs' suits? *Wall Street Journal*, B1.
110. Des Jardins, J., McCall, T., eds. (1990). *Contemporary Issues in Business Ethics*, 255. Belmont, CA: Wadsworth.
111. See Posch, R. (1988). *The Complete Guide to Marketing and the Law*, 3. Englewood Cliffs, NJ: Prentice Hall; Sturdivant, F., Vernon-Wortzel, H. (1991). *Business and Society: A Managerial Approach*, 4th ed., 305. Homewood, IL: Irwin.
112. Carroll, 258; Des Jardins and McCall, 255.
113. Carroll, 259.
114. Editor. (June 19, 2001). Maljustice in the courts. *Boston Globe*, A14.
115. Geyelin, M. (Jan. 6, 1992). Law: Product suits yield few punitive awards. *Wall Street Journal*, B1.
116. Felsenthal, E. (June 17, 1996). Punitive awards are called modest, rare. *Wall Street Journal*, B4.
117. Geyelin, B1.
118. Bravin, J. (June 12, 2000). Surprise: Judges hand out most punitive awards. *Wall Street Journal*, B1.
119. Burke, T. (April 2003). A status report on tort reform. *Product Liability, 4(2)*, http://www.hklaw.com/Publications/Newsletters.asp?IssueID=3618&Article=2013.
120. Albert, T. (February 23, 2004). Tort reform wouldn't dent health spending. CBO report. *American Medical News*, http://www.ama-assn.org/amednews/2004/02/23/prsa0223.htm.
121. Ibid.
122. Geyelin, B1.
123. Morrow, D. (Nov. 9, 1997). Transporting lawsuits across state lines. *New York Times.*
124. Ollanik, S. (November 2000). Products cases: An uphill battle for plaintiffs. *Trial*, 20–28. See The effects of tort reform: Evidence from the states. (June 2004). *Congressional Budget Office*, http://www.cbo.gov/showdoc.cfm?index=5549&sequence=0 for updates on states activities in tort reforms.
125. Shapo, M. Reeg, K. (Winter 2001). E-commerce and products liability: A primer on exposure at the speed of light. *Federation of Insurance & Corporate Counsel Quarterly* (Iowa City, Iowa), 73–98.
126. Pollution is top environmental concern. (Aug. 29, 2000). *USA Today*, D1.
127. Seabrook, C. (Aug. 17, 2001). Air pollution labeled a killer/Direct link to deaths, study claims. *Atlanta Constitution*, A3.
128. Steiner, R. (July 19, 2001). Does global warming really matter? *USA Today*, A15.
129. Office of New York State Attorney General Eliot Spitzer: Press Release. (July 21, 2004). Eight states & NYC sue top five U.S. global warming polluters. http://www.oag.state.ny.us/press/2004/jul/jul21a_04.html.
130. Steiner, A15.
131. Andrew C. Revkin, *New York Times* (August 26, 2004). U.S. report on warming puts blame on humans White House shifts view on the causes of greenhouse gases. *San Francisco Chronicle*, http://www.sfgate.com/cgi-bin/article.cgi?file=/c/a/2004/08/26/MNGAD8EJNK1.DTL.
132. World Water Day 2004: Water and disasters. *World Health Organization*, http://www.who.int/water_sanitation_health/wwd2004fs/en.

133. Sampat, P. (July 2001). The hidden threat of groundwater pollution. *USA Today*, 28–31.
134. Woods, R. (Aug. 3, 2001). EPA estimates costs of clean water TMDL program. *Environmental News*, EPA Headquarters press release, 1.
135. Based on Steiner, Steiner. (1991). *Business, Government, and Society*, 3d ed., 591; and Steiner and Steiner (2000), 484–485.
136. Post, J., Lawrence, A., Weber, J. (2002). *Business and Society*, 10th ed., 266. New York: McGraw-Hill.
137. Sagoff, M., ed. Des Jardins, J., McCall, J. (1990). *Economic Theory and Environmental Law in Contemporary Issues in Business Ethics*, 360–364. Belmont, CA: Wadsworth.
138. Buchholz (1991), 19.
139. Environmental Protection Agency. (1990). *Environmental Investments: The Cost of a Clean Environment*. Washington, DC: EPA.
140. Post, Lawrence, and Weber (2001), 272.
141. This section is based on Oyewole, P. (Feb. 2001). Social costs of environmental justice associated with the practice of green marketing. *Journal of Business Ethics, 29(3)*, 239–251.
142. Johri, L., Sahasakmontri, K. Green marketing of cosmetics and toiletries in Thailand. *Journal of Consumer Marketing, 15(3)*.
143. See Oyewole, 239.
144. Ibid., 240.
145. Velasquez, 1998, 292.
146. Blackstone, W. (1974). Ethics and ecology. In Blackstone, W., ed. *Philosophy and Environmental Crisis*. Athens: University of Georgia Press.
147. Bloom, G., Morton, M. (Summer 1991). Hazardous waste is every manager's problem. *Sloan Management Review, 83*.
148. Freeman, R., Reichart, J. (2000). Toward a life centered ethic for business. *Society for Business Ethics, The Ruffin Series No. 2*, 154. Reprinted with permission of the publisher.
149. Quinn, D. (1992). *Ishmael*, 129. New York: Bantam Books.

5

The Corporation and Internal Stakeholders
Values-Based Moral Leadership, Culture, Strategy, and Self-Regulation

> What we call courage is a strong emotional commitment—and the keyword is emotional—to some ideas. Those ideas could be called a vision for where we're trying to drive the enterprise. They could be called values for what we think is important in life. They could be called principles of what is right and wrong. When people don't just have an intellectual sense that these are logically good, but are deeply committed to them, they're developing courage. When you run up against barriers that keep you from those ideals, the stronger your commitment, the more likely you are to take action consistent with those ideals. Even if it's against your short-term best interests . . . The bigger the context, the greater the barriers, the more the snake pits . . . the more there will be times for courageous acts.[1] John Kotter, Harvard University

5.1 LEADER AND STAKEHOLDER MANAGEMENT

Leadership requires involvement in stakeholder relationships. Business relationships involve transactions that often lead to choices requiring ethical decisions and, many times, moral courage. Layoffs, consumer lawsuits, environmental crises, and effects of harmful products are a few examples of situations that involve both business and ethical decisions. Leaders are responsible for the economic success of their enterprises and for the rights of those served inside and outside their boundaries. Leaders are not only CEOs, but also individuals with responsibilities throughout an organization. Research on leadership demonstrates that moral values, courage, and credibility are essential leadership capabilities.[2] James Collins' five-year research project on "good to great" companies found that leaders who moved from "good to great" showed what he called "Level 5" leadership. These leaders "channel their ego needs away from themselves and into the larger goal of building a great company. It's not that Level 5 leaders have no ego or self-interest. Indeed, they are incredibly ambitious—*but their ambition is first and foremost for the institution, not themselves.*"[3]

Collins also concluded that Level 5 leaders build "enduring greatness through a paradoxical blend of personal humility and professional will."[4]

This chapter focuses on the challenges that values-based leaders face while managing internal stakeholders, strategy, and culture in organizations. From a stakeholder management approach, an organization's leaders are responsible for initiating and sustaining an ethical, principled, and collaborative orientation toward those served by the firm.[5] Leaders model and enforce the values they wish their companies to embody with stakeholders.[6] One of an organization's most prized assets is its reputation, as noted earlier in the text. Reputations are built through productive and conscientious relationships with stockholders and stakeholders.[7]

A stakeholder, values-based approach determines whether the leaders and culture:

- Are integrated *or* fragmented
- Tolerate *or* build relationships
- Protect the organization *or* create mutual benefits and opportunities
- Develop and sustain short-term *or* long-term goals and relationships
- Encourage idiosyncratic dependent implementation based on division, function, business structure, and personal interest and style *or* encourage coherent approaches, driven by enterprise, visions, missions, values, and strategies.[8]

Defining Purpose, Mission, and Values   Leading an organization begins by identifying and enacting purpose and ethical values that are central to internal alignment, external market effectiveness, and responsibility toward stakeholders. As Figure 5.1 shows, key questions executives must answer before identifying a strategy and leading their

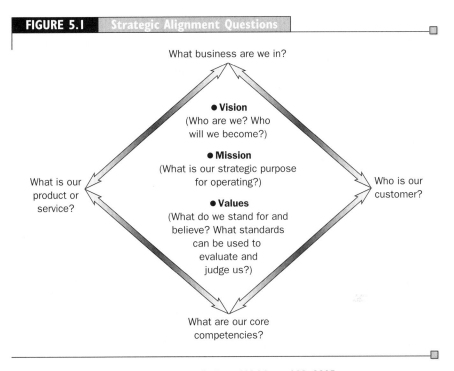

| FIGURE 5.1 | Strategic Alignment Questions |

What business are we in?

● **Vision**
(Who are we? Who
will we become?)

● **Mission**
(What is our strategic purpose
for operating?)

What is our
product or
service?

● **Values**
(What do we stand for and
believe? What standards
can be used to
evaluate and
judge us?)

Who is our
customer?

What are our core
competencies?

Copyright Joseph W. Weiss, Bentley College, Waltham, MA, 2005.

firm are centered on defining the organization's vision, mission, and values. Once those dimensions are in place, then the other questions (What business are we in? What is our product or service? Who are our customers? What are out core competencies?) can be addressed.

A values-based leadership approach is exemplified by Chester Barnard, who wrote in 1939 that effective leaders and managers "inspire cooperative personal decisions by creating faith in common understanding, faith in the probability of success, faith in the ultimate satisfaction of personal motives, and faith in the integrity of common purpose."[9] In the classic book *Built to Last*,[10] authors James Collins and Jerry Porras state, "Purpose is the set of fundamental reasons for a company's existence beyond just making money. Visionary companies get at purpose by asking questions similar to those posed by David Packard [cofounder of Hewlett-Packard] . . . 'I want to discuss *why* a company exists in the first place . . . why are we here? I think many people assume, wrongly, that a company exists simply to make money. While this is an important result of a company's existence, we have to go deeper and find the real reasons for our being.'"

JetBlue's CEO, David Neeleman, said,

> For our company's core values, we came up with five words: safety, caring,
> fun, integrity, and passion. We guide our company by them. But from my
> experience—and I've had a lot of life experiences that were deep religious
> experiences—I feel that everyone is equal in the way they should be treated
> and the way they should be respected. I think that I try to conduct myself in
> that way. I treat everyone the same: I don't give anyone more deference
> because of their position or their status. Then I just try to create trust with
> our crewmembers. I know if they trust me, if they know I'm trying to do the
> best things I think are in their long-term interest, then they'll be happier and
> they'll feel like this is a better place to work.[11]

Ethical companies may also include a "social mission" in their formal
mission and values statements. A social mission is a commitment by
the organization to give back to their community and external stakeholders who make the organization's existence possible. Ben and Jerry's,
Lands' End, Southwest Airlines, and many other companies commit to
serving their communities through different types of stewardship outreach, facility sharing (e.g., day care and tutoring programs), and
other service-related activities.

A starting point for identifying a leader's values is the vision and
mission statement of the company. Levi Strauss & Co.'s values and
vision statement, shown in Figure 5.2, exemplifies an inspirational
vision with ethical values.

The visionary, built-to-last companies "are premier institutions—
the crown jewels—in their industries, widely admired by their peers
and having a long track record of making a significant impact on the
world around them . . . a visionary company is an *organization*—an
institution . . . visionary *companies* prosper over long periods of time,
through multiple product life cycles and multiple generations of active
leaders."[12] Such companies include 3M, American Express, Boeing,
Citicorp, Ford, General Electric, Hewlett-Packard, IBM, Johnson &
Johnson, Marriott, Merck, Motorola, Nordstrom, Philip Morris, Procter
and Gamble, Sony, Wal-Mart, and Disney. These visionary companies,
Collins and Porras discovered, succeeded over their rivals by developing and following a "core ideology" that consisted of core values plus
purpose. Core values are "the organization's essential and enduring
tenets—a small set of general guiding principles; not to be confused
with specific cultural or operational practices; not to be compromised
for financial gain or short-term expediency." Purpose is "the organization's fundamental reasons for existence beyond just making money—
a perpetual guiding star on the horizon; not to be confused with
specific goods or business strategies."[13] Excerpts of core ideologies
from some of the visionary companies include[14]:

- Disney: "To bring happiness to millions and to celebrate, nur-
  ture, and promulgate wholesome American values."

FIGURE 5.2	Levi Strauss & Co. Values and Vision Statement

VALUES

Our values are fundamental to our success. They are the foundation of our company, define who we are and set us apart from the competition. They underlie our vision of the future, our business strategies and our decisions, actions and behaviors. We live by them. They endure.

Four core values are at the heart of Levi Strauss & Co.: Empathy, Originality, Integrity and Courage. These four values are linked. As we look at our history, we see a story of how our core values work together and are the source of our success.

Empathy—Walking in Other People's Shoes

Empathy begins with listening . . . paying close attention to the world around us . . . understanding, appreciating and meeting the needs of those we serve, including consumers, retail customers, shareholders and each other as employees.

Levi Strauss and Jacob Davis listened. Jacob was the tailor who in the 1870s first fashioned heavy cotton cloth, thread and metal rivets into sturdy "waist overalls" for miners seeking durable work pants. Levi in turn met Jacob's needs for patenting and mass production of the product, enthusiastically embracing the idea and bringing it to life. The rest is history: The two created what would become the most popular clothing in the world—blue jeans.

Our history is filled with relevant examples of paying attention to the world around us. We listened. We innovated. We responded.

- As early as 1926 in the United States, the company advertised in Spanish, Portuguese and Chinese, reaching out to specific groups of often-neglected consumers.
- In the 1930s, consumers complained that the metal rivets on the back pockets of our jeans tended to scratch furniture, saddles and car seats. So we redesigned the way the pockets were sewn, placing the rivets underneath the fabric.
- In 1982, a group of company employees asked senior management for help in increasing awareness of a new and deadly disease affecting their lives. We quickly became a business leader in promoting AIDS awareness and education.

We believe in empathetic marketing, which means that we walk in our consumers' shoes. In the company's early years, that meant making durable clothes for workers in the American West. Now, it means responding to the casual clothing needs of a broad range of consumers around the world. Understanding and appreciating needs—consumer insight—is central to our commercial success.

Being empathetic also means that we are inclusive. Levi Strauss' sturdy work pants are sold worldwide in more than 80 countries. Their popularity is based on their egalitarian appeal and originality. They transcend cultural boundaries. Levi's® jeans—the pants without pretense—are not just for any one part of society. Everyone wears them.

Inclusiveness underlies our consumer marketing beliefs and way of doing business. We bring our Levi's® and Dockers® brands to consumers of all ages and lifestyles around the world. We reflect the diverse world we serve through the range and relevancy of our products and the way we market them.

Likewise, our company workforce mirrors the marketplace in its diversity, helping us to understand and address differing consumer needs. We value ethnic, cultural and lifestyle diversity. And we depend and draw upon the varying backgrounds, knowledge, points of view and talents of each other.

As colleagues, we also are committed to helping one another succeed. We are sensitive to each other's goals and interests, and we strive to ensure our mutual success through exceptional leadership, career development and supportive workplace practices.

Empathy also means engagement and compassion. Giving back to the people we serve and the communities we operate in is a big part of who we are. Levi Strauss was both a merchant and a philanthropist—a civic-minded leader who believed deeply in community service. His way lives on. The company's long-standing traditions of philanthropy, community involvement and employee volunteerism continue today and contribute to our commercial success.

Originality—Being Authentic and Innovative

Levi Strauss started it and forever earned a place in history. Today, the Levi's® brand is an authentic American icon, known the world over.

Rooted in the rugged American West, Levi's® jeans embody freedom and individuality. They are young at heart. Strong and adaptable, they have been worn by generations of individuals who have made them their own. They are a symbol of frontier independence, democratic idealism, social change and fun. Levi's® jeans are both a work pant and a fashion statement—at once ordinary and extraordinary. Collectively, these attributes and values make the Levi's® brand unlike any other.

Innovation is the hallmark of our history. It started with Levi's® jeans, but that pioneering spirit permeates all aspects of our business—innovation in product and marketing, workplace practices and corporate citizenship. Creating trends. Setting new standards. Continuously improving through change. For example:

- We were the first U.S. apparel company to use radio and television to market our products.
- With the introduction of the Dockers® brand in 1986, we created an entirely new category of casual clothing in the United States, bridging the gap between suits and jeans. A year later,

(Continued)

FIGURE 5.2   Continued

Dockers® khakis had become the fastest growing apparel brand in history. Throughout the 1990s, we were instrumental in changing what office workers wear on the job.

■ Our European Levi's® brand team reinvented classic five-pocket jeans in 1999. Inspired by the shape and movement of the human body, Levi's® Engineered Jeans™ were the first ergonomically designed jeans.

Now, more than ever, constant and meaningful innovation is critical to our commercial success. The worldwide business environment is fiercely competitive. Global trade, instantaneous communications and the ease of market entry are among the forces putting greater pressure on product and brand differentiation. To be successful, it is imperative that we change, competing in new and different ways that are relevant to the shifting times.

As the "makers and keepers" of Levi Strauss' legacy, we must look at the world with fresh eyes and use the power of ideas to improve everything we do across all dimensions of our business, from modest improvements to total re-inventions. We must create product news that comes from the core qualities of our brands—comfort, style, value and the freedom of self-expression—attributes that consumers love and prefer.

Integrity—Doing the Right Thing

Ethical conduct and social responsibility characterize our way of doing business. We are honest and trustworthy. We do what we say we are going to do.

Integrity includes a willingness to do the right thing for our employees, brands, the company and society as a whole, even when personal, professional and social risks or economic pressures confront us. This principle of responsible commercial success is embedded in the company's experience. It continues to anchor our beliefs and behaviors today, and is one of the reasons consumers trust our brands. Our shareholders expect us to manage the company this way. It strengthens brand equity and drives sustained, profitable growth and superior return on investment. In fact, our experience has shown that our "profits through principles" approach to business is a point of competitive advantage.

This values-based way of working results in innovation:

■ Our commitment to equal employment opportunity and diversity predates the U.S. Civil Rights movement and federally mandated desegregation by two decades. We opened integrated factories in California in the 1940s. In the 1950s, we combined our need for more production and our desire to open manufacturing plants in the American South into an opportunity to make change: We led our industry by sending a strong message that we would not locate new plants in Southern towns that imposed segregation. Our approach changed attitudes and helped to open the way for integration in other companies and industries.

■ In 1991, we were the first multinational company to develop a comprehensive code of conduct to ensure that individuals making our products anywhere in the world would do so in safe and healthy working conditions and be treated with dignity and respect. Our Terms of Engagement are good for the people working on our behalf and good for the long-term reputation of our brands.

Trust is the most important value of a brand. Consumers feel more comfortable with brands they can trust. Increasingly, they are holding corporations accountable not only for their products but also for how they are made and marketed. Our brands are honest, dependable and trusted, a direct result of how we run our business.

Integrity is woven deeply into the fabric of our company. We have long believed that "Quality Never Goes Out of Style®" Our products are guaranteed to perform. We make them that way. But quality goes beyond products: We put quality in everything we do.

Courage—Standing Up for What We Believe

It takes courage to be great. Courage is the willingness to challenge hierarchy, accepted practices and conventional wisdom. Courage includes truth telling and acting resolutely on our beliefs. It means standing by our convictions. For example:

■ It took courage to transform the company in the late 1940s. That was when we made the tough decision to shift from dry goods wholesaling, which represented the majority of our business at the time, and to focus instead on making and selling jeans, jean jackets, shirts and Western wear. It was a foresighted—though risky—decision that enabled us to develop and prosper.

■ In the 1980s, we took a similar, bold step to expand our U.S. channels of distribution to include two national retail chains, Sears and JCPenney. We wanted to provide consumers with greater access to our products. The move resulted in lost business in the short term because of a backlash from some important retail customers, but it set the stage for substantial growth.

■ We also demonstrated courage in our workplace practices. In 1992, Levi Strauss & Co. became the first Fortune 500 company to extend full medical benefits to domestic partners of employees. While controversial at the time, this action foreshadowed the widespread acceptance of this benefit and positioned us as a progressive employer with prospective talent.

With courage and dedication, we act on our insights and beliefs, addressing the needs of those we serve in relevant and significant ways. We do this with an unwavering commitment to excellence. We hold ourselves accountable for attaining the high performance standards and results that are inherent in our goals. We learn from our mistakes. We change. This is how we build our brands and business. This is how we determine our own destiny and achieve our vision of the future.

* * *

The story of Levi Strauss & Co. and our brands is filled with examples of the key role our values have played in meeting consumer needs. Likewise, our brands embody many of the core values that our consumers live by. This is why our brands have stood the test of time.

Generations of people have worn our products as a symbol of freedom and self-expression in the face of adversity, challenge and social change. They forged a new territory called the American West. They fought in wars for peace. They instigated counterculture revolutions. They tore down the Berlin Wall. Reverent, irreverent—they all took a stand.

Indeed, it is this special relationship between our values, our consumers and our brands that is the basis of our success and drives our core purpose. It is the foundation of who we are and what we want to become:

VISION
People love our clothes and trust our company.
We will market the most appealing and widely worn casual clothing in the world.
We will clothe the world.

Source: Levi Strauss & Co. Reprinted by permission.

- Wal-Mart: "We exist to provide value to our customers—to make their lives better via lower prices and greater selection; all else is secondary . . . Be in partnership with employees."

- Sony: "Respecting and encouraging each individual's ability and creativity."

- Motorola: "To honorably serve the community by providing products and services of superior quality at a fair price."

Built-to-last companies "more thoroughly indoctrinate employees into a core ideology than their comparison companies (i.e., those companies in Collins' and Porras' study that did not last), creating cultures so strong that they are almost cult-like around the ideology."[15] Visionary companies also select and support senior management on the basis of fit with the core ideology. These best-in-class companies also attain more consistent goals, strategy, and organizational structure alignment with their core ideology than do comparison companies in Collins and Porras's study.[16]

Your Moral Leadership Profile

Using actual situations in which you served in a leadership role, score the following statements with regard to how each statement characterizes your leadership style:

1 = Very little, 2 = Somewhat, 3 = Moderately, 4 = A lot, 5 = Most of the time

1. I follow ethical principles even if I would not be taken seriously.

1 2 3 4 5

2. I would not "cave in" to pressure from bullies or pushy people.

1 2 3 4 5

3. I let everyone know when something is not fair or just.   1 2 3 4 5

4. I do not get tense or anxious under pressure.   1 2 3 4 5

5. I speak out and let everyone know the truth, regardless of possible consequences.   1 2 3 4 5

6. I don't follow the majority opinion, seeking approval of a group's views if those views are unjust.   1 2 3 4 5

7. I follow ethical values in my decisions and actions, rarely making decisions randomly.   1 2 3 4 5

8. I am not afraid to say "no" and disagree even though I might lose personal stature.   1 2 3 4 5

9. I take risks to support my beliefs even if I become unpopular with the group.   1 2 3 4 5

10. I would follow the mission of the project even if I lose personal face and approval.   1 2 3 4 5

Your Scores and Interpretation   Add up your scores. Total of 10 statements = ____. If you received 40 or higher, you are considered a courageous leader. A score of 20 or below indicates you avoid conflict and difficult situations that challenge your moral leadership. Examine the items in which you scored highest and lowest. Do these scores and items reflect your moral courage in tough situations generally? Why or why not? What do you need to do to improve or change your moral courage? How do your scores compare to other students?

Source: From *The Leadership Experience*, 3rd edition by Daft. © 2005. Reprinted with permission of South-Western, a division of Thomson Learning: www.thomsonrights.com. Fax 800-730-2215.

Leadership Stakeholder Competencies   Core competencies of responsible leaders include the ability to:

1. Define and lead the social, ethical, and competitive mission of organizations. This includes community-based, social, and environmental stewardship goals that promote being a global corporate citizen.[17]

2. Build and sustain accountable relationships with stakeholders.[18]

3. Dialogue and negotiate with stakeholders, respecting their interests and needs beyond economic and utilitarian dimensions.[19]

4. Demonstrate collaboration and trust in shared decision making and strategy sessions.

FIGURE 5.3	Johnson & Johnson Credo

We believe our first responsibility is to the doctors, nurses, and patients; to mothers and
   fathers; and all others who use our product and services. In meeting their needs,
   everything we do must be of high quality.
We must constantly strive to reduce our costs in order to maintain reasonable prices.
Customers' orders must be serviced promptly and accurately.
Our suppliers and distributors must have an opportunity to make a fair profit.

We are responsible to our employees, the men and women who work with us throughout
   the world.
Everyone must be considered as an individual. We must respect their dignity and
   recognize their merit.
They must have a sense of security in their jobs.
Compensation must be fair and adequate, and working conditions clean, orderly, and safe.
We must be mindful of ways to help our employees fulfill their family responsibilities.
Employees must feel free to make suggestions and complaints.
There must be equal opportunity for employment, development, and advancement for
   those qualified.
We must provide competent management, and their actions must be just and ethical.

We are responsible to the communities in which we work and to the world community as
   well.
We must be good citizens—support good works and charities and bear our fair share of
   taxes.
We must encourage civic improvements and better health and education.
We must maintain in good order the property we are privileged to use, protecting the
   environment and natural resources.

Our final responsibility is to our stockholders.
Business must make a sound profit.
We must experiment with new ideas.
Research must be carried on, innovative programs developed, and mistakes paid for.
New equipment must be purchased, new facilities provided, and new products launched.
Reserves must be created to provide for adverse times.
When we operate according to these principles, the stockholders should realize a fair return.

**Source: Johnson & Johnson. Used by permission of Johnson & Johnson, the
copyright owner.**

   5. Show awareness and concern for employees and other
      stakeholders in the policies and practices of the company.

   Effective ethical leaders develop a collaborative approach to setting
direction, leading top-level teams, and building relationships with partners and customers. For example, at Johnson & Johnson, one of the
seven principles of leadership development states: "People are an asset
of the corporation; leadership development is a collaborative, corporation-
wide process."[20] The company lives its leadership principles through
its Executive Development Program. Figure 5.3 shows Johnson &
Johnson's Credo. The now classic "Beliefs of Borg-Warner" Corporation

Credo is also shown in Figure 5.4 as another example of values companies should aspire to follow.

Organizational leaders are also ultimately responsible for the economic viability and profitability of a company. From a values-based, stakeholder management perspective, leaders must also oversee and implement the following in their organizations:

- Set the vision, mission, and direction.
- Create and sustain a legal and ethical culture throughout the organization.
- Articulate and guide the strategy and direction of the organization.
- Ensure the competitive and ethical alignment of organizational systems.
- Reward ethical conduct.[21]

Herb Kelleher cofounded Southwest Airlines in 1966 on a personal $10,000 investment. He retired June 19, 2001, with a $200 million stake in the company. Kelleher's principles of management are straightforward and simple[22]:

- Employees come first, customers second.
- The team is important, not the individual.
- Hire for attitude, train for skills.
- Think like a small company.
- Eschew organizational hierarchy.
- Keep it simple.

Kelleher owned and operated Southwest Airlines on these principles. When asked how the company would survive once he stepped down, Kelleher responded, "The real answer is we have a very strong culture and it has a life of its own that is able to surmount a great deal. If we should, by happenstance, have someone succeed me who is not interested in the culture, I don't think they would last a long time. The place would just rise up."[23] Kelleher's message is printed in white letters on the black elevator glass in the lobby of Southwest's corporate headquarters:

> The people of Southwest Airlines are the creators of what we have become—and what we will be. Our people transformed an idea into a legend. That legend will continue to grow only so long as it is nourished—by our people's indomitable spirit, boundless energy, immense goodwill, and burning desire to excel. Our thanks—and our love—to the people of Southwest Airlines for creating a marvelous family and a wondrous airline.[24]

FIGURE 5.4	The Beliefs of Borg-Warner: To Reach Beyond the Minimal

Any business is a member of a social system, entitled to the rights and bound by the responsibilities of that membership. Its freedom to pursue economic goals is constrained by law and channeled by the forces of a free market. But these demands are minimal, requiring only that a business provide wanted goods and services, compete fairly, and cause no obvious harm. For some companies, that is enough. It is not enough for Borg-Warner. We impose upon ourselves an obligation to reach beyond the minimal. We do so convinced that by making a larger contribution to the society that sustains us, we best assure not only its future vitality, but our own.

This is what we believe.

We Believe in the Dignity of the Individual.

However large and complex a business may be, its work is still done by dealing with people. Each person involved is a unique human being, with pride, needs, values, and innate personal worth. For Borg-Warner to succeed, we must operate in a climate of openness and trust, in which each of us freely grants others the same respect, cooperation, and decency we seek for ourselves.

We Believe in Our Responsibility to the Common Good.

Because Borg-Warner is both an economic and social force, our responsibilities to the public are large. The spur of competition and the sanctions of the law give strong guidance to our behavior, but alone do not inspire our best. For that we must heed the voice of our natural concern for others. Our challenge is to supply goods and services that are of superior value to those who use them; to create jobs that provide meaning for those who do them; to honor and enhance human life; and to offer our talents and our wealth to help improve the world we share.

We Believe in the Endless Quest for Excellence.

Though we may be better today than we were yesterday, we are not as good as we must become. Borg-Warner chooses to be a leader—in serving our customers, advancing our technologies, and rewarding all who invest in us their time, money, and trust. None of us can settle for doing less than our best, and we can never stop trying to surpass what already has been achieved.

We Believe in Continuous Renewal.

A corporation endures and prospers only by moving forward. The past has given us the present to build on. But to follow our visions to the future, we must see the difference between traditions that give us continuity and strength and conventions that no longer serve us—and have the courage to act on that knowledge. Most can adapt after change has occurred; we must be among the few who anticipate change, shape it to our purpose, and act as its agents.

We Believe in the Commonwealth of Borg-Warner and Its People.

Borg-Warner is both a federation of businesses and a community of people. Our goal is to preserve the freedom each of us needs to find personal satisfaction while building the strength that comes from unity. True unity is more than a melding of self-interests; it results when values and ideals also are shared. Some of ours are spelled out in these statements of belief. Others include faith in our political, economic, and spiritual heritage; pride in our work and our company; the knowledge that loyalty must flow in many directions; and a conviction that power is strongest when shared. We look to the unifying force of these beliefs as a source of energy to brighten the future of our company and all who depend on it.

Source: Borg-Warner Corp. The beliefs of Borg Warner: To reach beyond the minimal. Reprinted with permission of the Borg-Warner Corporation.

Leaders who dare to be different through stretch-goals while maintaining a moral, values-based approach:

- Seek to revolutionize every strategy and process for optimal results while maintaining the organization's integrity.[25]

- Empower everyone to perform beyond stated standards, while maintaining balance of life and personal values.

- Understand and serve customers as they would themselves.

- Create and reward a culture obsessed with fairness and goodwill toward everyone.

- Act with compassion and forgiveness in every decision toward every person and group.

- Do unto their stockholders and stakeholders as they would have them do to their company.

- Treat the environment as their home.

Spiritual Dimension of Leadership   An emerging body of literature describes leadership from a deeper spiritual perspective.[26] Spirituality, broadly defined, is the search for "ultimate meaning and purpose in one's life."[27] This dimension of leadership is inherently linked to ethics in that leaders as stewards and servants[28] do "the right thing" for their followers, communities, and society. The following characteristics illustrate leadership from a spiritual perspective[29]:

- Understand and practice reflective "being" as well as "doing"; genuine spirituality must be the willingness to enter into the process of dialogue with oneself and with others, and to try to stay with it over a period of time. "Being is the only reality with integrity; obeying one's conscience brings one into communion with this 'integrity of Being.'"[30]

- Use discernment, prayer, and patience in strategic decision making. Decisions are analyzed within the context of communities.

- See the leadership role as a calling that reveals its presence by the enjoyment and sense of renewed energy in the practice and results yielded.

- Seek to *connect* with people and connect people to people with *meaning* and in meaningful ways.

- Create communities, environments, and safe havens for empowerment, mobilization, development, spiritual growth, and nourishment.

- Lead with reflection, choice, passion, reason, compassion, humility, vulnerability, and prayer, as well as courage, boldness, and vision.

Aaron Feuerstein of Malden Mills Industries, Inc., Jeffrey Swartz of The Timberland Company, David Steward of World Wide Technology, Inc., and Krishan Kalra of BioGenex Laboratories, Inc. are a few of a growing number of executives who have used their spiritual beliefs in their professional lives to create and promote strategies and policies involving employees, customers, suppliers, vendors, their communities, and other stakeholders. JetBlue's David Neeleman also admits that his Mormon background and "missionary" responsibilities as a youth influenced his continuing values and practices toward his employees and stakeholders.[31]

The study by Ian Mitroff and Elizabeth Denton[32] interviewed 215 executive officers and managers. A surprising finding in the study was that the leaders desired a way to express their spiritual selves while at work, rather than to "park it at the office door." Leaders and organizations enable the expression of spirituality in different ways: from the *religious firm,* where religious teachings are openly articulated, modeled, and included in business practices, to the *values-based company* (like Ben & Jerry's), where secular values (awareness, consciousness, dignity, honesty, openness, and trust) are guides in the firm. In these types of firms, the Golden Rule is the major business principle and "the whole person comes to work" and "causes no embarrassment by expressing 'deeply felt emotions' such as love and grieving."[33]

Failure of Ethical Leadership Corporate leaders can and do fail when their decisions lack moral courage. In addition to examples and cases in this text regarding U.S. corporate scandals, there are also classic scenarios of leaders who violated their legal and ethical responsibilities to stockholders and stakeholders. Micky Monus, former CEO of the Phar-Mor company (a failed discount retail drugstore chain that attempted to take on Wal-Mart), was sentenced to 20 years in prison and fined $1 million on December 12, 1995, when he was "convicted on all counts of a 109-count indictment that charged him with conspiracy to commit mail fraud, wire fraud, bank fraud, and transportation of funds obtained by theft or fraud." Monus was hailed as a community hero in Youngstown, Ohio, when he led Phar-Mor to historical growth. His charismatic, entrepreneurial personality and leadership had a dark side—greed, deceit, and theft. His influence also led his young finance management team into the massive theft, fraud, and cover-up.[34]

There was also "Chainsaw Al" Dunlap, former CEO of Sunbeam, who was fired following a Securities and Exchange Commission investigation of accounting fraud under his watch. Dunlap was known for his ability to achieve profits. To meet Sunbeam's profit projections and appease Wall Street analysts, Dunlap devised a method of selling Sunbeam spare parts (used to fix broken blenders and grills) for $11 million to a company that warehoused the parts. That company valued the parts at $2 million. Dunlap and company pressured the warehouse firm to sign a contract to buy the parts at $11 million, booking $8 million in profit. (The parts were never sold). He was instrumental in laying off large numbers of employees and cutting back organizational operations to achieve profitability.[35] Dunlap described his other approaches to doing business in his book *Mean Business: How I Save Bad Companies and Make Good Companies Great.*[36]

Seven symptoms of the failure of ethical leadership provide a practical lens to examine a leader's shortsightedness.[37]

1. Ethical blindness: They do not perceive ethical issues due to inattention or inability.

2. Ethical muteness: They do not have or use ethical language or principles. They "talk the talk" but do not "walk the talk" on values.

3. Ethical incoherence: They are not able to see inconsistencies among values they say they follow; e.g., they say they value responsibility, but reward performance based only on numbers.

4. Ethical paralysis: They are unable to act on their values from lack of knowledge or fear of the consequences of their actions.

5. Ethical hypocrisy: They are not committed to their espoused values. They delegate things they are unwilling to or cannot do themselves.

6. Ethical schizophrenia: They do not have a set of coherent values; they act at work one way, at home another way.

7. Ethical complacency: They believe they can do no wrong because of who they are. They believe they are immune to being unethical.

Ethical Dimensions of Leadership Styles   Every leadership style has an ethical dimension. The following spectrum of styles is illustrated here because it reflects some of the ethical principles discussed in Chapter 3. An organizational leader's (as well as your own) moral decision-making style can also be evaluated using the following continuum, shown in Figure 5.5.[38]

FIGURE 5.5 Moral Leadership Styles

LESS ETHICAL   MORE ETHICAL

← ——+————————+——————————+——————————+ →

Manipulator   Bureaucratic   Professional   Transforming
(end-justifies-   administrator   manager   leader
means ethic)   (rule ethic)   (social contract   (personal ethic)
                                              ethic)

The *manipulator* leadership style is based on a Machiavellian principle that views leadership amorally. That is, the end result justifies the means taken to reach it. Power is the driving force behind a manipulator's motives. This is an egotistically and essentially economically motivated moral leadership style. Leaders who lack trust and interest in relationship building and are oriented toward the short term may also be manipulators. Although the motives underlying this style may be amoral, the consequences could prove immoral. Have you ever worked under someone who used this style?

The *bureaucratic* administrator is a rule-based moral leadership style. Based on the theories of German sociologist Max Weber,[39] the bureaucratic administrator acts on the rational principles embodied in an ideal organizational bureaucracy, i.e., fixed rules that explain the purpose and functions of the organization; a hierarchy that shows the chain-of-command; well-defined job descriptions; professional managers who communicate and enforce the rules; and technically qualified employees who are promoted by expertise and rewarded by rank and tenure. The driving force behind this style is *efficiency* ("doing things right," functioning in the least wasteful manner) more than effectiveness (producing the intended result or aim, "doing the right things"). Although this leadership style has an admirable aim of basing decisions only on objective, rational criteria, the moral problem with it lies in the "sin of omission." That is, a leader may follow all the rules exactly but hurt someone unintentionally by not attending to legitimate human needs because the option to do so was not included in the rules.

For example, a military captain may follow remote orders of a general by sending a regiment into a battle zone that he knows will lead to disaster based on available "on the ground" conditions. Nevertheless, rather than risk disobeying orders and the formal consequences, he proceeds. Another captain who has a different moral leadership style may choose to risk disobeying orders to save the troops. Rules for overly bureaucratic leaders can become ends in themselves.

Rules cannot address all problems and needs in what we know are imperfect and political organizations. The well-intentioned bureaucratic administrator may try to act amorally, but his or her efforts could result in immoral and irresponsible consequences. Do you recognize this moral leadership style? Have you ever worked for someone who used it?

The *professional* manager aims at effectiveness and "doing things right." This style is grounded in Peter Drucker's[40] view of managers as professionals who have the expertise and tools for accomplishing work effectively through others. Based on a social contract, this management style relies—like the previous two styles—on amorality for getting work done. For example, professional career managers use rational objectives and their training to accomplish the organization's work. The organization's corporate culture and the social contract—implicit and explicit agreements—made between managers and organizational executives set the ground rules that govern the manager's behavior. However, social contracts are not always ethical.

An ethical problem with this leadership style lies in the real possibility that the collective corporate culture and the dominant governing group may think and act amorally or immorally. *Groupthink* (consensus-dominated decision making, based on uncritical, biased thinking) may occur.[41] The collective may lead itself astray. Professional managers by training are still prone to unethical behavior. Do you recognize managers or leaders who act amorally or immorally as "professionals"?

Finally, the *transforming* leadership style, based on James Burns'[42] theory, is grounded on a personal ethic. The transformational leader bases his or her effectiveness on relationships with followers. Also, this style focuses on the charisma, energy, and excitement the leader brings to relationships. The transformational leader is involved in the growth and self-actualization of others and views others according to their potential. This type of leader identifies and elevates the values of others. He or she empowers, coaches, and helps promote other leaders. This leadership style is moral because "it raises the level of human conduct and aspirations of both leaders and led, and thus has a transforming effect on both."[43]

William Hitt[44] moved the continuum of moral leadership one step beyond the transformational leader to what he termed an "encompassing approach to leadership," or "the effective leader–manager." The *encompassing* leader learns from the shortcomings of each of the four leadership styles on the continuum and uses all of their strengths.

For example, manipulative leadership does value the effective use of power. However, this style's deceptive and dysfunctional use of power should be avoided. The bureaucratic administrator values the effective use of rules; however, these should not become ends rather than means. The professional manager values results; however, human concerns should be valued more highly than physical and fiscal results.

The transformational leader values human empowerment; however, even this characteristic is not the complete job of management.

Socially and morally responsible leaders should observe their obligations to all stakeholders, including their own conscience, and observe in their dealings the ethical principles of rights, justice, and duty—in addition to utilitarian logic.

How Should CEOs as Leaders Be Evaluated and Rewarded?

CEO Pay: Excessive or Earned?   Pay and compensation are not the only ways organizational leaders, CEOs in particular, are compensated. There are also intrinsic as well as extrinsic rewards that motivate leaders, especially those who follow the servant and stewardship models. However, many CEOs of large, publicly traded firms are selected and evaluated based on their level of pay and compensation. And although many have increased the revenue and market value of their firms many times over, there are a large number of CEOs whose pay and compensation drastically exceeds their firm's performance.

Lucian Bebchuk, Harvard law professor and co-author of the book *Pay Without Performance, the Unfulfilled Promise of Executive Compensation* stated that "Executive compensation is a good proxy for the level of accountability in the system. The interests of executives here are very strong. Making concession on compensation is much more painful than concessions on other dimensions. They still remain insufficiently accountable."[45] Consider these facts, "CEO salaries are up 4.1% to a median $908,000 at companies with fiscal years that ended in the first half of 2004, according to Equilar Inc., a compensation analysis firm. Bonuses in this group have risen by a third from last year to a median $975,000."[46] The base salary plus bonus median of CEOs increased to $1.9 million in cash from $1.65 million in 2003, in a study of 68 of Standard & Poor's (S&P) 500 companies. Stock-option grants, incentive plan payouts, and stock awards (long-term pay) increased 10% to a median $5.1 million from $4.7 million in 2003. "Over the longer term, CEOs earned a median salary of $821,000 five years ago, according to data from Mercer, the consulting unit of Marsh & McLennan Cos. (MMC). Overall pay in 1999, which adds in value of bonus, equity-based and long-term rewards, was nearly $5 million." By 2003, that amount increased by $1.2 million to $6.2 million.[47]

Several issues are at stake here. First, after the corporate scandals, many investors and the public are more skeptical of CEO pay and performance. Second, many CEOs who have been with the same company most of their careers are looking toward retirement and do not need bonuses or perks that they could well afford on their own. Third, the salary increases, stock options, and perks are offered even when the company's performance is suboptimal and layoffs are occurring. Fourth, the CEO's pay can be 20, 30, or 50 times higher than the salaries of some first-line managers and supervisors. However, a difference of more than a factor of seven is considered sizable for an average CEO position. Finally, although CEOs certainly bear greater responsibility, risk, and blame for a company's successes and failures, one question remains: Are employees and managers rewarded and punished more unfairly for their individual shortcomings and contributions than CEOs and other company officers? Should such comparisons be made at all?

CEO Evaluations   The board of directors of a company is technically responsible for disciplining and rewarding the CEO. A Korn/Ferry survey of board members found that 72% of the largest U.S. companies do a formal CEO evaluation.[48] Evidence shows that "CEO appraisals require a special commitment from the CEO and from the board members" in order for the process to work well and the results to be meaningful.[49] However, in many instances, it is the CEO who is also president of the company and chairperson of the board.

Two forces influence the popularity of boards of directors evaluating CEOs. The first is the increased recognition of the critical roles CEOs play and the increased compensation levels received for those roles. The second influential force is pressure from the investment community, which dates back to the beginning of shareholder awareness in the 1980s, when corporate acquisitions and restructuring activities were questioned with regard to the effectiveness of CEOs and their boards, due diligence, and management practices. Still, not all CEOs are formally evaluated with their top-level team members and other employees. For publicly traded companies, such as those listed on the New York Stock Exchange, NASDAQ, and other trading companies, industry analysts constantly score and keep pressure on the performance of CEOs and chief financial officers (CFOs)—by the numbers. Market performance is a major evaluator of these officers' effectiveness. Annual reports and financial audits available to stockholders are another form of assessing leaders.

CEOs are also evaluated by assessing gaps between their stated and enacted strategies and by using customer and employee surveys. Assessments of the organization's systems are also reflections of the leader's overall effectiveness in directing, aligning, and implementing strategy. Finally, leaders must balance and align stakeholder interests with the dominant mission and values of the company. Certainly not all CEOs are overpaid. Still, many critics argue that CEO pay and compensation in the larger, publicly traded companies is not in line with the performance of their firms, especially over the last decade.

FIGURE 5.6 Contingency Alignment Model

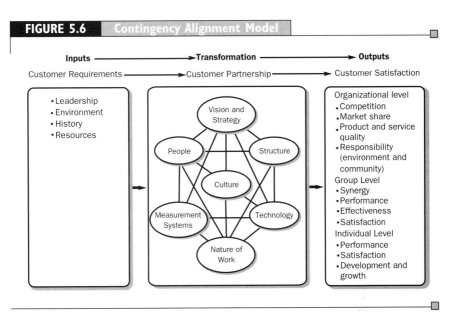

Copyright Joseph W. Weiss, Bentley College, Waltham, MA, 2005.

5.2 ORGANIZATIONAL CULTURE AND STAKEHOLDER MANAGEMENT

Coupled with leadership, organizational culture is central to a firm's overall effectiveness and operating efficiency. As Figure 5.6 illustrates, culture is the "glue" that holds the other organizational dimensions (strategy, structure, people, systems) together. Organizational leaders are only as effective as the cultures they model, build, and sustain.

Organizational Culture Defined   A corporation's culture is the shared values and meanings its members hold in common, which are articulated and practiced by an organization's leaders. Purpose, embodied in corporate culture, defines organizations.

Corporate culture is transmitted through: (1) the values and leadership styles that the leaders espouse and practice, (2) the heroes and heroines that the company rewards and holds up as models, (3) the rites and symbols that organizations value, and (4) the way that organizational executives and members communicate among themselves and with their stakeholders.

Heroes and heroines in corporations set the moral tone and direction by their present and past examples. They are the role models; they define what is successful and attainable; they symbolize the company to outsiders and insiders; and they preserve the valued qualities of the firm, set standards of excellence, and motivate people. Enduring corporate and organizational cultural heroes include Herb Kelleher at Southwest Airlines, Sam Walton at Wal-Mart, Ben Cohen and Jerry Greenfield at Ben & Jerry's, Mary Kay at Mary Kay, David Packard at Hewlett-Packard, and Bill Gates at Microsoft. Jimmy Carter, an unpopular president during his term, now has higher popularity ratings than when he was in office and will probably be remembered as a highly ethical president and person. Carter still works on housing and inner-city projects to assist the poor and economically disadvantaged. Who are the heroes and heroines in your organization? By what qualities and characteristics are they remembered? Are they moral, immoral, or amoral leaders?

Rituals in companies help define corporate culture and its moral nature. Corporately sanctioned rituals that bring people together, foster openness, and promote communication can lower stress and encourage moral behavior. Social gatherings, picnics, recognition ceremonies, and other company outings where corporate leaders are present and values, stories, problems, accomplishments, and aspirations are shared can lead to cultures that value people and the company's aims. Does ethics matter for an organization's survival and market effectiveness? The "good management hypothesis" suggests that there is a positive relationship between a corporation's performance and how it treats its stakeholders. Studies confirm this hypothesis.[50]

Observing Organizational Culture   Organizational cultures are both visible and invisible, formal and informal. They can be studied by observation, by listening to and interacting with people in the culture, and in the following ways:

- Studying the physical setting
- Reading what the company says about its own culture
- Observing and testing how the company greets strangers
- Watching how people spend time
- Understanding career path progressions
- Noting the length of tenure in jobs, especially for middle managers
- Observing anecdotes and stories

How would you describe your organizational or company culture using these methods?

Traits and Values of Strong Corporate Cultures   Strong corporate cultures: (1) have a widely shared philosophy, (2) value the importance of people, (3) have heroes (presidents and products) that symbolize the success of the company, and (4) celebrate rituals, which provide opportunities for caring and sharing, for developing a spirit of "oneness" and "we-ness."[51] From a stakeholder management view, organizational systems are aligned along the purpose, ethical values, and mission of the company. Also, individuals and teams in ethical cultures demonstrate a tolerance and respect for individual differences, compassion, ability for forgiveness and acceptance, and freedom and courage to do the right thing in questionable situations.

Corporate values statements serve as the economic, political, social, and ethical compasses for employees, stakeholders, and systems. Two classic benchmark values statements are those of Johnson & Johnson (Figure 5.3) and Borg-Warner (Figure 5.4). Seattle-based Boeing Corporation's values were first articulated by its former CEO William Allen. These values still serve as an outstanding example at the individual level. They are[52]:

- Be considerate of my associates' views.
- Don't talk too much . . . let others talk.
- Don't be afraid to admit that you don't know.
- Don't get immersed in detail.
- Make contacts with other people in industry.
- Try to improve feeling around Seattle toward the company.
- Make a sincere effort to understand labor's viewpoint.
- Be definite, don't vacillate.
- Act—get things done—move forward.

High-Ethics Companies   What would a highly effective values-based organizational culture look like? Mark Pastin studied 25 "high-ethics, high-profit" firms, which at the time included Motorola, 3M, Cadbury Schweppes, Arco, Hilby Wilson, Northern Chemical, and Apple Computer. Although the list of high-ethics firms—like "built-to-last" firms—may change, the four principles that Pastin used to describe such firms serve as a benchmark for understanding ethically effective organizations:

> *Principle 1*: High-ethics firms are at ease interacting with diverse internal and external stakeholder groups. The ground rules of these firms make the good of these stakeholder groups part of the firm's own good.

> *Principle 2*: High-ethics firms are obsessed with fairness. Their ground rules emphasize that the other person's interests count as much as their own.

Principle 3: In high-ethics firms, responsibility is individual rather than collective; individuals assume responsibility for the firm's actions. The ground rules mandate that individuals are responsible to themselves.

Principle 4: The high-ethics firm sees its activities as having a purpose, a way of operating that members of the firm value. And purpose ties the firm to its environment.[53]

Cultures in Trouble   What about companies that are not ethical? Companies that reinforce secrecy, hidden agendas, and physical settings that isolate executives from managers and employees and emphasize status over human concern often are cultures in trouble. Troubled corporate and organizational cultures can breed and encourage unethical activities, as illustrated by Enron, WorldCom, Adelphia, Arthur Andersen, and so many other firms involved in corporate scandals.

Organizations that also over-stress hypercompetition, profit-at-any cost, and singular economic or introverted self-interest over stakeholder obligations and that have no moral direction often have cultures in trouble. Signs of cultures in trouble, or weak cultures, include the following[54]:

- An inward focus
- A short-term focus
- Morale and motivational problems
- Emotional outbursts
- Fragmentation and inconsistency (in dress, speech, physical settings, or work habits)
- Clashes among subcultures
- Ingrown subcultures
- Dominance of subculture values over shared company values
- No clear values or beliefs about how to succeed in business
- Many beliefs, with no priorities about which are important
- Different beliefs throughout the company
- Destructive or disruptive cultural heroes, rather than builders of common understanding about what is important
- Disorganized or disruptive daily rituals

Malcolm S. Salter, Harvard Business School professor, described Enron's culture the following way:

> Enron is a case about how a team of executives, led by Ken Lay, created an extreme performance-oriented culture that both institutionalized and tolerated deviant behavior. It's a story about a group of executives who created a

world that they could not understand and therefore could not control. It's a story about the delinquent society—and I use that phrase intentionally—that grew up around the company, and here I'm referring to the collusion of Enron's various advisors and financial intermediaries. And most importantly, Enron is a story about how fraud is often preceded by gross incompetence: where the primary source of that incompetence is inexperience, naiveté, an ends-justify-the-means attitude toward life, and so on. And most importantly, an inability to face reality when painful problems arise.[55]

A values-based stakeholder management approach would assess an organization's values with these questions: Do the leaders and culture embody "high-ethic" or "in trouble" characteristics in their values, actions, and policies? Are the values written down? Do others know the values? Do the values reflect a concern for and obligation toward the organization's stakeholders? Do the values reflect a utilitarian, just, dutiful, or egotistical ethic? Are the values taken at "face value" only, or are they practiced and implemented by employees? Do the values and communication patterns promote moral, immoral, or amoral behavior?

5.3 LEADING AND MANAGING STRATEGY AND STRUCTURE

If culture is the glue that holds organizations together, strategy maps the direction. The moral dimensions of strategy are also based on ethics. People are motivated to implement strategies that they believe in, are able to enact, and that produce results. Strategy and the strategy development process are the domain of organizational leaders. Gary Hamel, a contemporary strategy guru, calls for a "revolution" in leading the strategy innovation process. He states that "you need a set of values that will set you apart from the courtiers and wannabes." Those values include "honesty, compassion, humility, pragmatism, and fearlessness."[56] The strategy-making process also involves stakeholder management. A corporation's strategy is propelled and supported by its people, stakeholders, culture, and moral contributions to its communities, customers, and society. Strategic thinking has evolved from a mechanistic process to a more holistic process, which emphasizes innovation, generation of value for stakeholders and stockholders, involvement and learning with stakeholders, and building customer partnerships and relationships.[57] This section and the next discuss the relationships between corporate strategy, structure, culture, systems, and moral responsibility. How do strategy and structure influence the moral behavior of employees?

Corporate leaders are responsible for orchestrating the development and execution of strategy. An organization's strategy influences legality, morality, innovation, and competitiveness in the following ways:

1. Strategy sets the overall direction of business activities. Enterprise strategy, for example, can emphasize revenue and growth over customer satisfaction or product quality. It can drive technical concern over professional development. Corporate strategy can also direct a firm's activities toward social issues, employee rights, and other stakeholder obligations. It can include or exclude stakeholders and employees. It can innovate recklessly for the short term or in long-term ways that benefit society as well as a few market niches.

2. Strategy reflects what management values and prioritizes. It mirrors management's ethics and morality. It is the message to the messengers. Strategy says: "We care and value your feedback, safety, and concerns," or "we only want your money and participation in our profits."

3. Strategy sets the tone of business transactions inside the organization. Reward and control systems reflect the values of the larger strategic direction. An emphasis on profit at the expense of employee development is usually reflected as rigid and unrealistic incentive and revenue quota systems. Growth and expansion can be made a priority at the expense of talent development and contribution.

Marianne Broadbent, a leading scholar in information technology, offers the following insights about strategy.

> When creating a strategy, I see a number of steps: the aspiration, the big business principles or maxims, then having a number of scenarios or options which are based on a set of strategic assumptions that you constantly, constantly pick to see if they are in sync. And then you use that information to shift and change. At a tactical level, that means rolling out products and services in a very careful, risk-managed way so that you can sense and respond to the marketplace.
>
> Strategy is very much about synchronizing the enterprise with its external environment as much as possible. Think about how increasingly interconnected economies, markets, technology and political situations are. September 11 is a great example of how quickly things can change and how interdependent logistics, for example, is with strategy, with customer service, with the politics of what's going on at the moment. I look at strategy more as synchronization, and that which focuses much more on what we call the market inputs rather than the outputs.[58]

Enterprise strategy also sets and affects corporate expectations, ways of doing business, rewards, motivations, and performance. Strategy influences the types of control systems that govern business activities and the pressures that lead to moral or immoral behavior. All stakeholders have an interest in the strategies and strategy building processes of organizations.

Four Levels of Strategy Corporations formulate at least four levels of strategy: *enterprise, corporate, business,* and *functional.*[59] The enterprise strategy, the broadest level, identifies the corporation's role in society, decides how the firm will be perceived by stakeholders, defines its principles and values, and shows the firm's standards. The corporate strategy identifies goals, objectives, and business areas on which the firm's policies and plans are based. Business strategy translates the corporate strategy into more detailed goals and objectives for specific business activities. Functional strategy takes business strategy into even more detail in marketing, research and development, production, sales, and other functional areas.

At the enterprise strategic level, the CEO and upper-level managers state their social responsibility and stakeholder commitments. Corporate strategy also should reflect ethical considerations. For example, R. Edward Freeman and Daniel Gilbert Jr. argued that we must understand the multiple and competing values underlying stakeholders' actions in order to understand the choices corporations make.[60]

From a values-based stakeholder management approach, the strategy development and implementation process should reflect the vision and mission of the organization. As with the Levi Strauss values and vision statement in Figure 5.2, the strategy would be reviewed from these statements: "*Integrity—Doing the Right Thing.* Ethical conduct and social responsibility characterize our way of doing business. We are honest and trustworthy. We do what we say we are going to do. Integrity includes a willingness to do the right thing for our employees, brands, the company and society as a whole, even when personal, professional and social risks or economic pressures confront us. This principle of responsible commercial success is embedded in the company's experience. It continues to anchor our beliefs and behaviors today and is one of the reasons consumers trust our brands. Our shareholders expect us to manage the company this way. It strengthens brand equity and drives sustained, profitable growth and superior return on investment. In fact, our experience has shown that our 'profits through principles' approach to business is a point of competitive advantage."

From a stakeholder perspective, a firm should identify issues that affect its stakeholder obligations and relationships while developing strategies. From a social and moral perspective, managers should be concerned about fulfilling their internal stakeholder obligations through these strategies. Responsible corporations must be prepared to equitably and justly enable the workforce with new technical skills and integrate aging employees, dual-career families, and new immigrants. Flexible work times, health care programs, and flexible management styles must be implemented to manage this changing workforce responsibly.

Organizational Structure   Structure is another organizational dimension, shown in Figure 5.6, along with strategy and culture, that is part of an organization's infrastructural makeup. Ask to see almost any organization's structure and you will be handed a hierarchical set of boxes connected by lines. This so-called pyramid, or functional structure, is one of the oldest forms of depicting arrangements in companies.

Regardless of the specific type of structure, from an ethical, values-based stakeholder management perspective, key concerns and questions regarding any structure are:

- How centralized or decentralized are the authority, responsibility, communication, and information flow?
- How organic (less structured) or mechanistic (more structured) are the systems?
- How tall (more layers of bureaucracy) or flat are the reporting systems?
- How formal or informal are procedures, rules, and regulations?
- How much autonomy, freedom, and discretion do internal stakeholders and decision makers have?
- How flexible, adaptable, and responsive are systems and professionals to responding to internal and external threats, opportunities, and potential crises?

Although there are no absolute guidelines regarding which structure is more immune to or leads to ethical problems, the following overview provides some evidence how structure relates to ethical behavior. Functionally *centralized* structures can encourage lack of communication, coordination, and increased conflict because each area is typically separated by its own boundaries, managers, and systems. Infighting over budgets, "turf," and power increase the likelihood of unethical, and even illegal, activities. For example, post-September 11, 2001, reports show the overly centralized CIA and FBI communicated poorly with each other, with the White House, and with other systems of government.

On the other hand, highly supervised employees in bureaucratic firms may also act more ethically than employees in entrepreneurial, laissez-faire firms because employees tend to think through the risk of getting caught in firms with more supervised structures. A study conducted by John Cullen, Bart Victor, and Carrol Stephens[61] reported that a subunit's location in the organizational structure affects its ethical climate: At a savings and loan association and also at a manufacturing plant, the employees at the home offices reported less emphasis on laws, codes, and rules than did the employees at the branch offices.

Perhaps control by formal mechanisms becomes more necessary when direct supervision by top management is not feasible.

There is evidence that *decentralized* structures can encourage more unethical behavior among employees than more supervised, controlled structures. Citicorp's credit card processing division illustrated the relationships among organizational structure, competitive pressures, and immoral and illegal behavior. The bank fired the president and 11 senior executives of that division because they fraudulently overstated revenue by $23 million for two years. The inflating of revenue by division employees may have been related to the fact that employee bonuses were tied to unrealistic revenue targets. Citicorp centralized its organizational functions. In this case, the decentralized structure left the bank susceptible to potential abuse by employees. On the other hand, some decentralized structures may enable individually responsible and ethical professionals to communicate their beliefs and report errors faster up and down a more fluid chain of command.

Pressures from upper-level managers who overemphasize unrealistic quarterly revenue objectives and who give unclear policies and procedures to guide ethical decision making may also contribute to immoral behavior in more decentralized structures. There is evidence to support the argument that middle- and lower-level managers, in particular, feel pressured to compromise their personal moral standards to meet corporate expectations.[62] Managers in large firms may compromise their personal ethics to meet corporate expectations for several reasons, which include:

1. Decentralized structures with little or no coordination with central policy and procedures encourage a climate for immoral activities when pressures for profit-making increase.

2. Unrealistic short-term and bottom-line profit quotas add pressure on employees to commit unethical actions.

3. Overemphasis on numbers-driven financial incentives encourages shortcuts.

4. Amoral organizational and work-unit cultures can create an environment that condones illegal and immoral actions.

Boundaryless and Networked Organizations   The decentralization of organizations has been accelerated by information technology and the re-engineering of business processes. Software applications and Web-enabled intranets and extranets allow the boundaries within organizations and between customers and companies to become more transparent and fluid.[63] Dell Computer has eliminated middle layers of its company, supply chain, and industry by enabling individual customers to design, order, and purchase—and even receive, in the case of software—their own customized computer products online. These changes are not easy, nor are they isolated from the larger context of the organization. An organizational expert[64] noted that the main reason implementation of major technology changes fails is that "the technology was seen as the solution, without taking into account the complex dynamic of the organization and people. It doesn't matter in which area, whether it's knowledge management or B2B. You can't forget that organizations are made of people and technology, and both people and technology will define the success of an organization."

From both an ethics and efficiency perspective, care should be taken by companies implementing digital networks because one study[65] reported that digital networks generate both opportunities for and threats to worker autonomy. Major opportunities include increased communication capabilities, "informedness," and "teleworking." Threats to worker autonomy are electronic monitoring, dependence on third-party operators and managers, and task prestructuring, which can reduce individual responsibility and control. These opportunities and problems depend, in part, on the type of organizational structure in place: how open and responsive it is or how closed and vulnerable if may be to unethical activities.

5.4 LEADING AND BALANCING INTERNAL STAKEHOLDER VALUES IN THE ORGANIZATION

The other internal dimensions of organizations, illustrated in Figure 5.6, should also be aligned in order for the organization to succeed in meeting its goals.

In practice, aligning an organization's values and mission with its internal stakeholders, while treating external groups and organizations ethically, is difficult because of competing values of internal stakeholders. The following quote from Anderson[66] illustrates the diversity among stakeholder values:

> An organization in almost all its phases is a reflection of competing value choices. Owners want a return on their investment. Employees want secure jobs and career development. Managers want growth and industry leadership. Government regulators want minimal pollution, safety, work opportunities for a wide variety of groups, and tax revenues. For top managers, this competition comes to a head because they must unravel complex problems whose solutions benefit some groups but have negative consequences for

FIGURE 5.7	A Functional Profile of Internal Organizational Stakeholders: Professional Orientations

Professional Stakeholders

Orientations	Marketing & Sales	Research & Development (R&D)	Production	Finance & Accounting	Information Systems
Background	Liberal arts; social sciences; entrepreneurial; technical	Electrical engineering; technical	Mechanical engineering; operations	Finance; accounting; auditing; tax	Software "engineers;" data management; programming
Goals and "Stakes"	High product mix; revenue and market competitiveness; customer satisfaction	Market dominance, innovation, competitiveness	Product yield; quality control	Low-cost capital; efficient borrowing; accountability	Problem solving; organizational integration; systems functioning
Focus and Rewards	Product or service leadership; creative autonomy; bonuses; equity; career mobility	Next "killer" application; resources to innovate; prestige	Product lifecycle stability; peace with R&D job security; bonuses	Low costs; high yields; data access; accuracy; cooperation; career advancement	Satisfied users; state-of-art technology; career advancement; new skill development
Time Horizon	Short to medium time frame	Medium to long time frame	Short to continuous time frame	Continuous time frame	Continuous time frame

Copyright Joseph W. Weiss, Bentley College, Waltham, MA, 2005.

others. Framing these decisions inevitably leads to some crucial dilemmas for managers, who must answer the broad question, "What is a convincing balance among competing value choices?"

Balancing internal stakeholder interests can be difficult because of the diversity of professional and functional backgrounds, training, goals, time horizons, and reward systems. These differences are further influenced by organizational politics, the constraints and pressures of other internal systems, and changing roles and assignments. Figure 5.7 is an example of an organization's internal stakeholders and competing professional value orientations.

Function orientations such as marketing, research and development, production, information systems, and finance have built-in competing values, especially when employees who are under pressure must design, deliver, and service complex products and services for demanding customers. Marketing and sales professionals' work with short- to medium-term time horizons and are rewarded on the basis of their results. Sales professionals, in particular, have a very short time horizon and depend on the success of individual and team selling ability to satisfy, retain, and attract customers. Research and development (R&D) professionals generally have a longer time horizon and are rewarded for their innovations.

Contrast, for example, marketing and sales professionals with R&D professionals, as shown in Figure 5.7, and you can see how value differences and role conflicts can occur within cross-functional teams. Competition and conflict can lead to higher productivity and also to unethical decisions and practices such as producing unsafe products or lying to customers to make a sale.

From a stakeholder management perspective, it is the role of an organization's leaders, with the support of each professional, to ensure that the internal integrity and market effectiveness of a company is based on the types of relationships and values that embody trust, collaboration, and a "win–win" goal for stakeholders and stockholders. Amorally and unethically led and managed organizations with conflicting internal values can, and sometimes do, lead to illegal situations. Interpersonal communication skills, conflict resolution, and collaborative negotiation methods (as exemplified in Chapter 2) are also needed to help integrate these functional area differences.

Value and innovation are created when the collaborative efforts of an organization's systems create synergy. The organization's vision, values, and mission, which are reinforced by the culture and example of the leaders, are the cornerstone for integrating structures and systems. Following this logic, W. Chan Kim and Renee Mauborgne[67] posed the following research question: "What type of organization best unlocks the ideas and creativity of its employees to achieve this end?" They discovered that "when putting value innovation strategies into action, structural conditions create only the potential for individuals to share their best ideas and knowledge. To actualize this potential, a company must cultivate a corporate culture conducive to willing collaboration."[68]

These authors describe "the positively reinforcing cycle of fair process" as one which creates innovative outcomes for companies. They describe this process as follows: For each success a group has in implementing a "general value innovation strategy" based on fair process, the result strengthens the group's cohesiveness and their belief in the process. This, in turn, sustains the collaboration and creativity inherent to value innovation. The four components of that process include[69]:

1. Engagement, explanation, expectation, clarity
2. Idea sharing and voluntary cooperation

3. Value innovation plans and rapid execution

4. Organizational confidence in and respect for colleagues' intellectual and emotional worth

5.5 CORPORATE SELF-REGULATION AND ETHICS PROGRAMS: CHALLENGES AND ISSUES

A values-based stakeholder management approach assumes that corporations (owners and management) *ought* to intrinsically value all stakeholders' interests.[70] In practice, this is not always the case.[71] Responsible self-regulation in companies can enhance entrepreneurship and reduce unnecessary costs of too much bureaucratic control (e.g., it is estimated that Sarbanes-Oxley costs large public companies $16 million to implement). Complete your company's "ethical weather report" (Figure 5.8) to identify your point of view regarding how ethical your company is.

Establishing codes of ethical and legal conduct, implementing stakeholder management assessments, and enacting ethics programs can help a company financially and morally, as the following discussion indicates. The federal sentencing guidelines were established in 1984 by the Congress, which passed a crime bill that instituted the U.S. Sentencing Commission. This commission, made up of federal judges, was empowered with sentencing those found in violation of the guidelines. In 1987, uniform guidelines were created for sentencing *individuals* in the federal courts. Some federal judges quit the bench in protest of the strictness of the guidelines and the sentences they were required to hand down. In 1991, the commission shifted the emphasis from individual wrongdoers to *organizations* that might be found guilty for the illegal actions of their employees. The 1991 guidelines threaten fines of up to $290 million to companies found guilty of violating the federal guidelines. However, those fines can be substantially reduced if an organization implements an "effective program to prevent and detect violations of law." Corporate interest and participation in ethics programs flourished.[72] (The recently revised guidelines were discussed in Chapter 4).

Corporate self-regulation does not seem to work to prevent illegal and unethical activities—even with the federal sentencing guidelines—without active leadership involvement and support from other organizational systems.[73] The corporate scandals proved this to be true. Moreover, agreement on and commitment to "best practices" also enhance effective self-regulation with regard to company and industry.[74]

FIGURE 5.8   Ethical Weather Report

Step 1: Complete the following questionnaire using the organization in which you are working or one in which you have worked. Beside each statement, write the number from the scale that accurately reflects your knowledge and experience with the company.

Completely False	Mostly False	Somewhat False	Somewhat True	Mostly True	Completely True
0	1	2	3	4	5

_____ 1. In this company, people are expected to follow their own personal and moral beliefs.

_____ 2. People are expected to do anything to further the company's interests.

_____ 3. In this company, people look out for each other's good.

_____ 4. It is very important here to follow strictly the company's rules and procedures.

_____ 5. In this company, people protect their own interests above other considerations.

_____ 6. The first consideration is whether a decision violates any law.

_____ 7. Everyone is expected to stick by company rules and procedures.

_____ 8. The most efficient way is always the right way in this company.

_____ 9. Our major consideration is what is best for everyone in the company.

_____ 10. In this company, the law or ethical code of the profession is the major consideration.

_____ 11. It is expected at this company that employees will always do what is right for the customer and the public.

Step 2: Score your answers by adding up your responses to 1, 3, 6, 9, 10, and 11. Write the sum under Subtotal 1 below. Now reverse the scores on questions 2, 4, 5, 7, and 8 (5 = 0, 4 = 1, 3 = 2, 2 = 3, 1 = 4, 0 = 5). Add these reverse scores (i.e., number value) and write the sum in Subtotal number 2. Now add Subtotal 1 with Subtotal 2 for your overall score. The total score ranges between 0 and 55. The higher the score, the more the organization supports ethical behavior.

Subtotal 1 _____ + Subtotal 2 _____ = Overall Score _____

Step 3: Write a paragraph explaining your organization's ethical profile: Why is it the way it is? Offer specific steps you would recommend in your organization's cultural dimensions, leadership, policies, or procedures that would either enhance its already ethical climate or help change the climate.

Source: Reprinted from Organizational Dynamics, Autumn/1989, J.B. Cullen, B. Victor, C. Stephens, An Ethical Weather Report Assessing the Organization's Ethical Climate, © 1989, with permission from Elsevier.

Ethics Codes   Ethics codes are value statements that define an organization. Johnson & Johnson's Credo (Figure 5.3) is an outstanding example. Major purposes of ethics codes include[75]:

- To state corporate leaders' dominant values and beliefs, which are the foundation of the corporate culture

- To define the moral identity of the company inside and outside the firm

- To set the moral tone of the work environment

- To provide a more stable, permanent set of guidelines for right and wrong actions

- To control erratic and autocratic power or whims of employees

- To serve business interests (because unethical practices invite outside government, law enforcement, and media intervention)

- To provide an instructional and motivational basis for training employees regarding ethical guidelines and for integrating ethics into operational policies, procedures, and problems

- To constitute a legitimate source of support for professionals who face improper demands on their skills or well-being

- To offer a basis for adjudicating disputes among professionals inside the firm and between those inside and outside the firm

- To provide an added means of socializing professionals, not only in specialized knowledge, but also in beliefs and practices the company values or rejects

One survey of U.S. corporate ethics codes found that the most important topics to include were general statements about ethics and philosophy; conflicts of interest; compliance with applicable laws; political contributions; payments to government officials or political parties; inside information; gifts, favors, and entertainment; false entries in books and records; and customer and supplier relations.[76] Notable firms go further in detailing corporate obligations. The examples of Johnson & Johnson and Borg-Warner (Figures 5.3 and 5.4) define their obligations to various stakeholders. Other exemplary codes include those of General Electric, Boeing, General Mills, GTE, Hewlett-Packard, McDonnell Douglas, Xerox, Norton, Chemical Bank, and Champion International.

Companies looking to buy (acquirers) other companies (targets) perform *preacquisition due diligence* on the management, finance, technology, services and products, legality, and ethics of the targets. That is, companies looking to buy other companies need to perform analyses to discover if the targets are telling the truth about their products, finances, and legal records. "Where does one start in uncovering the ethical vulnerability of a target?" The following basic questions are suggested as a starting point[77]:

1. Does the target have a written code of conduct or code of ethics?

2. Does the company provide ethics training or ethics awareness-building programs for management and company employees?

3. Are avenues, such as an ethics office or hotline, available for employees to ask questions about ethical issues?

The problems with corporate ethics codes in general are the following[78]:

1. Most codes are too vague to be meaningful, i.e., the codes do not inform employees about how to prioritize conflicting interests of distributors, customers, and the company. What does being a "good citizen" really mean in practice?

2. Codes do not prioritize beliefs, values, and norms. Should profit always supersede concern for customers or employees?

3. Codes are not enforced in firms.

4. Not all employees are informed of codes.

Ethics codes are a necessary but insufficient means of assisting or influencing professionals with managing moral conduct in companies. One study[79] showed that companies that had corporate ethics codes had "less wrongdoing and higher levels of employee commitment." However, the authors explained that "formal ethical codes are one component of a milieu that encourages and supports high standards of ethical behavior; that is, these organizations have formal and informal mechanisms to ensure that ethical conduct becomes 'a way of life.'" Also, employee behavior was not as influenced by the ethics codes because the codes "are not part of the organizational environment." Part of the message here may also be that implementing several organizationally supported and integrated values-based stakeholder management and ethics programs has a better chance of meeting intended goals than does reliance on brochures and printed documents.

Ombudspersons and Peer Review Programs   Ombudspersons and peer review programs are methods that corporations use to manage the legal and moral aspects of potentially problematic activities in the workplace. The ombudsperson approach provides employees with a means of having their grievances heard, reviewed, and resolved. Originating in Sweden, this concept was first tried at Xerox in 1972 and later at General Electric and Boeing. Ombudspersons are third parties inside the corporation to whom employees can take their grievances. At Xerox, employees are encouraged to solve their problems through the chain of command before seeking out the ombudsperson. However, if that process fails, the employee can go to the ombudsperson, who acts as an intermediary. The ombudsperson, with the employee's approval, can go to the employee's manager to discuss the grievance. The ombudsperson can continue through the chain of command, all the way to the president of the corporation, if the problem has not been satisfactorily resolved for the employee. Ombudspersons have no power themselves to solve disputes or override managers' decisions. Complaints usually center on salary disputes, job performance appraisals, layoffs, benefits, and job mobility. At General Electric, ombudspersons report that they handle 150 cases every year.

An example of an effective ombudsperson program is that of the International Franchise Association (IFA). Its board of directors adopted a comprehensive self-regulation program that has a clearly, strongly stated ethics code, an investor awareness and education program, a franchise education compliance and training program, a code enforcement mechanism, and an ombudsperson program, which is described as follows: "The ombudsperson program is designed to enable franchisors and franchisees to identify disputes early and to assist them in taking preventative measures . . . facilitating dispute resolution . . . recommending non-legal methods and approaches to resolving disputes, encourage [both parties] to work together to resolve disputes, provide confidentiality throughout the process, and provide objective and unbiased advice and guidance to all the participants."[80]

A problem with the ombudsperson approach is that managers may feel their authority is threatened. Employees who seek out ombudspersons also might worry about their managers retaliating against them from fear or spite. Confidentiality also has to be observed on the part of ombudspersons. The ombudsperson is as effective as the support of the program by stakeholders allows it to be. An ombudsperson's success is measured by the trust, confidence, and confidentiality he or she can create and sustain with the stakeholders. Finally, the ombudsperson's effectiveness depends on the acceptance by managers and employees of the solutions adopted to resolve problems.

Ombudsperson programs have, for example, been successful at IBM, Xerox, General Electric, the U.S. Department of Education, Boeing, and several major U.S. newspaper organizations.[81]

The *peer review panel* is another program that more than 100 large companies have used to enable employees to express and solve grievances, thus relieving stress that could lead to immoral activities. Employees initially use the chain of command whenever a problem exists. If the supervisors or executives do not resolve the problem, the employee can request a peer review panel to help find a solution. Two randomly selected workers in the same job classification are chosen for the panel along with an executive from another work unit. The selection must be reviewed in reference to company policy. Peer review panels work when top management supports such due process procedures and when these mechanisms are perceived as long-term, permanent programs.

Peer review programs have received positive reviews and have had good results, particularly in the health care and accounting industries. More than 50% of the U.S. state boards of accountancy require certified public accountants to participate in a peer review program to obtain a license to practice.[82] Congress has mandated the use of the Medicare Peer Review Organization since 1982.[83] In England, peer review accreditation programs have evolved as external voluntary mechanisms that also provide organizational development of health care providers.[84] Ombudsperson and peer review programs serve as popular mechanisms not only for solving disputes among stakeholders, but also for integrating the interests of diverse stakeholders.

Ethics Programs   Ethics departments provide another method for handling moral questions and concerns in the workplace. Among the largest corporations having such departments are Verizon, Johnson & Johnson, Texas Instruments, and General Dynamics. Many large companies have organized ethics programs in response to public scandals, potentially harmful misconduct, and competitors' programs.[85]

Ethics programs serve several purposes. Telephone hotlines are the first step toward opening lines of communication in the organization. Professional staff in ethics departments handle grievances, coordinate problem resolution across functional and staff areas, and create, update, and help enforce ethics codes. At General Dynamics, for example, more than 30,000 contacts with ethics officers since 1985 have resulted in 1,419 sanctions, 165 terminations, 58 cases of financial reimbursement, 26 demotions, and 10 referrals to lawyers for civil lawsuits or to public prosecutors for criminal proceedings.

Some critics of these programs doubt that a full-time ethics department is really necessary. They cite examples of companies, such as IBM and Johnson & Johnson, that have cultivated records of positive ethical conduct by using less formal alternatives. Despite the skepticism about their effectiveness, ethics programs will most likely continue to be created for two reasons: (1) according to federal sentencing guidelines that went into effect November 1, 1991, judges are asked to look more favorably on firms that can provide evidence of a substantial investment in programs and procedures designed to facilitate ethical behavior; and (2) the demise of several of the large Wall Street investment firms has awakened companies to the fact that the unethical conduct of a few employees can have detrimental effects on the entire organization.

Financial concerns factor into the decision of whether or not to set up an ethics program. Many companies, such as Verizon, are investing in these programs in response to a public scandal or known misconduct. Others, such as Texas Instruments (TI), have seen competitors struggling with issues of ethical conduct and have implemented ethics programs to reinforce their previously written company code of ethics. According to Carl Skoogland, TI's first ethics director, "We have had a written code for over 30 years but we wanted a formal focal point for reinforcing what we felt was an already strong culture." Whatever the motivation, ethics programs appear to be an effective means of handling a variety of personnel and moral issues in the workplace.

We conclude this chapter by summarizing a "Readiness Checklist" organizations can use to determine whether or not their executives and professionals use a values-based stakeholder management approach to create and sustain integrity in the organization. If not, they may review their vision, mission, values statements as well as their ethics and codes of conduct. You may consider applying the checklist to your organization or institution.

Is the Organization Ready to Implement a Values-Based Stakeholder Approach? A Readiness Checklist   A values-based stakeholder readiness checklist can inform and educate (even interest and mobilize) top level leaders to evaluate the ethics of their business practices and relationships. The following readiness checklist is an example that can be modified and used as a preliminary questionnaire for this purpose:

1. Do the top leaders believe that key stakeholder and stockholder relationship building is important to the company's financial and bottom-line success?

2. What percentage of the CEO's activities is spent in building new and sustaining existing relationships with key stakeholders?

3. Can employees identify the organization's key stakeholders?

4. What percentage of employee activities is spent in building productive stakeholder relationships?

5. Do the organization's vision, mission, and value statements identify stakeholder collaboration and service? If so, do leaders and employees "walk the talk" of these statements?

6. Does the corporate culture value and support participation and open and shared decision making and collaboration across structures and functions?

7. Does the corporate culture treat its employees fairly, openly, and with trust and respect? Are policies employee-friendly? Are training programs on diversity, ethics, and professional development available and used by employees?

8. Is there collaboration and open communication across the organization? Are openness, collaboration, and innovation rewarded?

9. Is there a defined process for employees to report complaints and illegal or unethical company practices without risking their jobs or facing retribution?

10. Does the strategy of the company encourage or discourage stakeholder respect and fair treatment? Is the strategy oriented toward the long or short term?

11. Does the structure of the company facilitate or hinder information sharing and shared problem solving?

12. Are the systems aligned along a common purpose or are they separate and isolated?

13. Do senior managers and employees know what customers want, and does the organization meet customer needs and expectations?

If answers to these questions are mostly affirmative, the internal organization most likely reflects ethical leadership, culture, and practices. If responses are mostly negative, legal and ethical problems may be imminent.

SUMMARY

A stakeholder management, values-based approach is central to organizing and aligning internal systems to respond to all stakeholders. "Built-to-last" and "good to great" companies have a fundamental purpose and a set of core values that form a foundation for competitive long-term achievement.

Leaders define and model the moral character of organizations. Leaders guide the identification of a vision, mission, and values and then serve as ethical role models in their stakeholder and business relationships. Figure 5.1 illustrates a strategic alignment model that leaders can use to guide their strategy development process. James Collins' "Level 5" leader profile was used as an example of successful leaders. A values-based stakeholder management approach was summarized and argued that organizations can be economically successful by being socially responsible and ethical with their stakeholders.

Leadership in organizations can be defined from a values-based approach: Leaders define and model the social and ethical as well as the competitive mission of companies. They build and sustain relationships with stakeholders while demonstrating collaboration and trust. Stakeholder management is the basis for strategic alliances.

Former president of Southwest Airlines Herb Kelleher, Aaron Feuerstein of Malden Mills, and Jeffrey Swartz of The Timberland Company are a few examples of successful competitive industry leaders who lead ethically and spiritually.

Failure of ethical leadership is evidenced by seven symptoms: ethical blindness, muteness, incoherence, paralysis, hypocrisy, schizophrenia, and complacency. Micky Monus, former CEO of the Phar-Mor company, failed to lead ethically and was sentenced to 20 years in prison for mail fraud, wire fraud, bank fraud, and theft. "Chainsaw Al" Dunlap, former CEO of Sunbeam, was fired after the SEC found fraudulent activities during his tenure.

The reasonableness of CEO pay and performance was questioned and discussed: Are CEOs paid too much considering the performance (or lack thereof) of their firms? Critics say yes—not for all CEOs, but certainly for enough to question CEO pay. CEO evaluations by boards of directors can be a way to curb and address unfair pay practices.

Figure 5.6 summarizes an alignment contingency model for understanding the "big picture" of leaders' tasks in defining and implementing effective and ethical strategies, cultures, and structures. Strategies, cultures, structures, and systems are aligned along a vision, mission, and core values. This approach is compatible with the "built-to-last" and "good to great" studies of successful organizations. Customers as key stakeholders are central to an organization's alignment since they are essential to a firm's success.

Strategy must be aligned with markets, values, culture, leadership style, and structure to be effective. Strategy serves both a revolutionary role (to be innovatively competitive) and a more classical role at four levels: enterprise, corporate, business, and function. Strategies influence ethics by the expectations, pressures, motivation, and rewards they create. Overly aggressive strategies, which may also be unrealistic, can create implementation pressures that lead to unethical activities.

Culture, structure, and other systems are internal dimensions that enable leaders and professionals to implement strategy. "High-ethics" company cultures can serve as a benchmark for other organizations' cultures. Such cultures are grounded in well-defined purposes that drive operations. These cultures are also modeled by leaders who are devoted to fairness, interaction with all stakeholders, concern for stakeholder interests, and individual responsibility.

Organizational structures that are overly centralized or decentralized may foster ethical problems. Although there is not a "one best way" to structure a company, there are advantages and disadvantages to each type of structure. For example, centralized functional structures discourage open communication and sharing and must be integrated.

Decentralized structures, such as networks and project teams with little or no coordination, may create a climate for unethical activities, such as fraud, theft, and unfair pressure of customers and alliance partners. Having leaders who rely on mission-driven ethical values that are communicated, reflected in the culture, and enforced throughout a firm is a necessary part of structural alignment.

Figure 5.7 illustrates the challenge of balancing internal organizational and professional stakeholders' values. Professional stakeholders in marketing, R&D, sales, finance, and production often function within four boundaries: rewards, time horizons, training backgrounds, and resource constraints. A critical task of organizational leaders is to guide internal professionals and focus them on the mission and values of the company.

An overview of self-regulated ethics programs was presented. Ethics codes, ombudspersons, peer review, and ethics officers programs are ways in which corporations can attempt to regulate themselves. Johnson & Johnson's "Credo" in Figure 5.4 is an example of an outstanding ethics code.

A readiness checklist for assessing a values-based, stakeholder readiness perspective was offered that enables firms to address the extent to which they use a values-based stakeholder approach in their business practices.

QUESTIONS

1. Describe the most ethical leader for whom you have worked. Now describe the least ethical leader. Which leader did you learn valuable lessons from and enjoy working with the most? The least? Why? What role did ethics play in your answers? Explain.

2. Do you believe leaders in large Fortune 500 companies follow and model their stated visions, missions, and values in everyday business dealings? Explain. Identify a Fortune 500 company and CEO in the news that demonstrates ethical behavior. Is there any evidence that his or her company's performance is related to ethical leadership behavior? Explain.

3. Do companies have to operate ethically to be financially successful? Explain.

4. Identify some characteristics of a values-based stakeholder approach to leading and running a company. Do you agree or disagree with these characteristics? Explain.

5. Which of the 13 values-based readiness checklist steps would you expect are least practiced in most companies? Which steps on the list do you believe the organization for which you work(ed) practiced least? Why?

6. Do you believe most CEOs in U.S. companies are overpaid and under-perform? Explain. What pay or performance criteria do you believe should be used for top-level officers in publicly traded companies?

7. Offer one difference a values-based, ethical stakeholder approach could make in the formulation and implementation of an organization's strategy? Explain.

8. Suggest three differences a values-based, ethical stakeholder perspective could make in forming and building a new organizational culture? Explain.

9. What clues would you look for in identifying ethical and unethical activities by evaluating an organization's structure? Explain.

10. If you were to evaluate the alignment of an organization's strategy, structure, and culture from a values-based stakeholder approach, suggest three criteria you would use and some questions you would ask.

11. Which is most effective for organizational stakeholders: internal self-regulation or government regulation? Defend your points.

12. Explain the strengths and weaknesses of organizational (a) ethics codes, (b) ombudsperson and peer review programs, and (c) ethics departments.

EXERCISES

1. Assume you are an ombudsperson or an ethics officer for a large organization. What problems do you believe you would experience? Why? What contributions do you think you could make in this role? Why?

2. Describe the type of training you would need and list specific competencies that would help you in the role of ombudsperson or ethics officer.

3. Draft a brief values statement (or list some major values) of the ideal company for which you would like to work. Compare your list with other students' lists. What similarities and differences did you find? Compare your list to the examples in this chapter. What are the similarities or differences?

4. Briefly describe the leader of an organization in which you work or have worked. Evaluate the moral, amoral, or immoral characteristics of the leader. Refer to the "ethics of leadership styles" and the "seven symptoms of the failure—or success—of leadership" in the chapter.

5. Return to question 4. Suggest specific ways that your leader could improve his or her leadership competency and ethical style.

6. Briefly describe the culture of an organization in which you work or have worked. Explain how the culture affected a specific business practice. How ethical or unethical were the effects of the culture on that business practice? Explain.

7. Return to question 6. Suggest a few ways in which that organization's culture could be strengthened or changed. Offer a suggestion for the way the strategy formulation or implementation could be changed. Offer a way in which one of the practices or management methods of the system could be changed for improvement.

Ethical Dilemma   **Values and Leadership at Z (Insurance) Corp.**

"What Would You Do?"   I graduated from the University of New England on a beautiful day in May of 2002. Graduating cum laude, with a job in my back pocket, I thought that my future was as bright as the sun was that day. However, unlike that beautiful day, blue skies did not lie ahead for me professionally.

During the spring of my senior year, I was busy interviewing for full-time positions after graduation. At one particular campus career fair, I came across the Z Insurance Corp. booth. As a business student, I had a keen interest in financial services. I believed and still believe that it is a noble profession, which helps to give hard working people the power to be financially stable, save money for retirement, or put their children through college. Because of these interests, I was very curious to see what Z Corp. had to offer in the realm of financial services.

Looking back (with 20/20 hindsight), I believe that I was duped from the beginning. I'll tell you why in the following two actual scenarios.

Scenario One: "How I Learned to Lie to the Elderly"

My grandmother is one of the most caring and wonderful people I know. Recently, my grandfather passed away and left my grandmother with a considerable amount of money, and little financial experience to manage it. She guarded the money very carefully, since it was earned by her best friend and loving husband. Back to Z Corp.

The new "recruits" at Z Corp. have a two-week long orientation before they can begin their work. During the first couple of days of this orientation we watched films that illustrated how we would be helping senior citizens protect their life savings. These films had positive messages about America's senior citizens including how to communicate with them in a respectful manner, cherish their money as if it was ours, and take each question they had with the utmost care. Although I was still a bit shocked by the fact that I was now an insurance salesperson, I was excited by the prospect of making a difference in the lives of America's senior citizens. I was picturing folks, similar to my grandmother, who would trust us to help them protect their life's hard earned money.

These utopian ideals were soon transformed into harsh realities. Daily, I became increasingly aware of the games that this company was playing with us as well as the people that we were to "help." On one particular day, we were discussing how we were going to "entice" our customers on the phones so that they would listen to our message about long-term care insurance. Again, we didn't know that we going to be involved in "cold calling," which was yet another surprise to us. During this meeting, we were given our "communication," which was to be followed very closely, not deviating from any of the scripts. While I was reading over the "communication," something struck me as peculiar. The following is a rough sample of our "communication":

> Z Corp. Rep: "Hello, my name is Lea Stern from Z Corp. I am a financial advisor. I am calling in regards to literature that you received in the mail from us. Do you recall receiving this information?"
>
> (Usually the response was "No, I don't remember seeing anything from Z Corp.")
>
> Z Corp. Rep: (chuckling) "Oh, I am sure you may not have. We all receive so much in the mail these days that you may have thrown it away or may have not read it yet."

After I read this script, I asked the sales manager whether or not these folks actually received something from Z Corp. regarding to long-term care insurance. What he said in response to my question still rings clear in my head. So clear, in fact, that I am going to quote it. "These folks are old and confused. Most likely they received something in the mail about 'financial planning.' We are banking on the fact that they will not remember or realize who it was from and will take our word that it was from us."

"Old and confused" is how the sales manager described my loving grandmother. Because of the values that I grew up with and still hold, I could not imagine taking advantage of hard working seniors in such a twisted, immoral way. With this one statement, I decided that I did not respect my manager or Z Corp. My attitude changed immediately. I knew from that moment that I would find it very hard to work for Z Corp. and almost impossible to work for that manager.

Scenario Two: "Reading the Fine Print"   I have been blessed with a wonderful family who surrounded me with caring people who would never try to take advantage of me. Maybe I am trusting and a bit naïve, but I'm not stupid! With the experience I described previously at Z Corp., I learned that this trust could be a double-edged sword. I lived 21 years not realizing how twisted company policies and practices could be; it took only one week at Z Corp. for me to wake up to "corporate realities"—at least in an insurance sales setting.

At the career fair at the University of New England, I had a wonderful conversation with a sales manager at Z Corp. We discussed the virtues of being a financial advisor such as recommending appropriate mutual funds based on financial needs, careful investments, and the merits of having Series 6 and 7 licenses. I enjoyed the fact that Z Corp. seemed to be a company that helped folks invest in diversified ways. Never once were insurance sales, cold calling, or no pay for four months mentioned; not during the first, second, or final interview. Only when I signed on and was in training did I find out the truth about this shifty company.

During each of the lunches on that first week of our orientation, the "recruits" discussed what we called the "footnote." We used this term because we felt there was another footnote regarding pay, customer contact, or office supplies. I felt as if I was employed at a different company, with a completely different position than the one for which I originally interviewed. Some of this may have been my fault. For example, I never asked what the values of this company were or what its mission was. However, important points such as job function and company mission, as well as reimbursement, should be communicated truthfully. I felt as if the people at Z Corp. did not communicate effectively with us at all. A communication channel was not established between the managers and me at Z Corp. Without proper communication, I was taken advantage of and didn't feel comfortable being in the follower role. I didn't know what the company stood for, and most importantly I didn't know what I stood for!

QUESTIONS

1. What are your general reactions to the two scenarios?

2. Would you react similarly or differently than the writer? Explain.

3. Do you believe the writer is naïve and that these scenarios represent the "real world" from which she has been sheltered? Or, do you think this company is a single "rotten apple" among the more honest companies in this industry and the writer should react as she did? Explain.

4. Are there any illegal or unethical tactics the company sales manager/rep is using? Explain.

Ethical Dilemma	Whose Values? Whose Decision?

Jim Howard is a sales manager at a software company that produces a search interface for databases with indexed information. The company is an established vendor and has a good reputation in the market for its high quality products, fast and personal customer support, and strong loyalty to its customers. Part of the values statement of the company includes, "We will treat our customers with respect and dignity."

In his first year with the company, Jim noticed that the sales force was having difficulty acquiring new customers and retaining existing ones. The problem was complex: a shrinking market with continuously increasing buying power, increasing competition, and the emergence of free alternatives from the Internet. These problems started to significantly affect the company's revenue. The company's reaction was to drastically decrease the cost of its products, bundle databases into packages, and start to alter product introductions by including several value-added services that were new to the market.

Jim Howard's boss suggested that Jim take over the responsibility for the yearly renewals of customer subscriptions from the company's secretary, which previously had been regarded as an easy clerical procedure. When he started to check the old accounts and follow up with renewals, he faced a problem that he thought would never have occurred: unfair treatment of old customers in comparison to new customers in terms of the product pricing. Existing customers were offered renewal at triple the price of the same package and renewals offered to new customers.

When he asked his boss whether he should inform the old customer that the price had changed and whether the old customer could now benefit from the lowered price, the answer was, "Why don't we try to get this price? If the customer refuses to pay it, then we'll negotiate." An additional difficulty was that, in the last few months, information had been disseminated to all customers that made the company's new pricing strategy visible to customers. Jim shared the fact that this information was already available to customers with his boss and pointed out the contradiction. His boss remained insistent, to the point of shouting, that Jim follow his previous instructions with the sales force.

Jim felt he was betraying the company, the customer, his sales force, and his own professional values. He didn't want to lose his job, and he didn't want to lose any more customer accounts.

QUESTIONS

1. If you were Jim, what would you do in this situation?

2. What are the issues here? For whom?

3. Who stands to be hurt the most from following the advice of Jim's boss?

4. What would a values-based stakeholder management approach suggest that you do, if you were Jim? Lay out an action plan and be ready to role-play your suggested approach.

5. Compare what your answer to question 1 to your approach in question 5. Any differences? If so, could you still follow what you said in question 4?

CASE 16

FORTUNE'S GLOBAL MOST ADMIRED COMPANIES: DO VALUES MAKE A DIFFERENCE?

Which companies do you admire most, and why do you admire them? *Fortune* magazine conducts an annual survey of business analysts, executives, and directors to determine, among the world's largest companies, which ones are most admired. The annual survey results, published in the magazine and available to subscribers on the *Fortune* Web site, typically appear in late February or early March. The same fundamental procedure is used for each year's survey.

For *Fortune's* 2005 survey, 357 companies—213 of which were headquartered outside the United States—were divided into 30 industry groups. Each company had at least $8 billion in revenue for 2003 or was a former industry leader. The Hay Group, which conducts the survey for *Fortune* magazine, sent a questionnaire to more than 10,000 analysts, executives, and directors during the fourth quarter of 2004. The respondents were asked to use a scale, ranging from one to ten, to rank the *other companies in their industry* with respect to nine categories (or reputational attributes). These reputational criteria are: innovation; social responsibility; financial soundness; ability to attract, develop, and retain employee talent; use of corporate assets; quality of management; globalness (i.e., global business acumen); long-term investment value; and quality of products and services. *Fortune* maintains that the industry rankings are especially meaningful because companies are being graded by their competitors.

When we look at all 357 companies included in the 2005 global survey, which company is at the top of the list on each of *Fortune's* reputational criteria, and which companies appear most frequently in the top 10 on the reputational attributes?

Which Companies Top the Lists?   As shown in the following table, Berkshire Hathaway is the top-rated company on three of the reputational attributes—use of corporate assets, quality of management, and long-term investment value. No other company appears at the top of a 2005 list more than once. However, four of these companies—FedEx, United Parcel Service (UPS), General Electric (GE), and Alcoa, are among the companies that appear most frequently on the nine attribute lists.

Which Companies Appear Most Frequently?   The following table identifies the frequency with which companies appeared on

Reputational Attribute	Company with the Highest Ranking
Innovation	FedEx
Social Responsibility	United Parcel Service
Financial Soundness	Intel
Ability to Attract, Develop, and Retain Employee Talent	General Electric
Use of Corporate Assets	Berkshire Hathaway
Quality of Management	Berkshire Hathaway
Globalness	Alcoa
Long-Term Investment Value	Berkshire Hathaway
Quality of Products/Services	Texas Instruments

Source: The material in this table was developed from the list of the top 10 companies on each reputational attribute at *Fortune.com*.

the top 10 lists for the nine reputational attributes. Procter & Gamble (P&G) was in the top 10 on all nine attributes. Interestingly, P&G did not occupy the number one spot on any list. The next most frequent rate of appearance was Alcoa and FedEx with seven of nine attributes in the top 10. Both Alcoa and FedEx missed the top 10 list on financial soundness. Alcoa also placed out of the top 10 on employee talent, and FedEx missed the top 10 for use of corporate assets. Berkshire Hathaway, GE, and UPS appeared in the top 10 on six of nine lists. Berkshire Hathaway did not make the top 10 for social

Companies	Number of Times Appearing in Top Ten
Procter & Gamble	9
————————————	8
Alcoa, FedEx	7
Berkshire Hathaway, General Electric, United Parcel Service	6
Anheuser-Busch, Texas Instruments, Walgreen	5
BP	4
Continental Airlines, Exxon Mobil, Intel, PepsiCo, Toyota Motor	3
Caterpillar, Tesco	2
American Electric Power, BASF, Best Buy, Cisco Systems, Johnson & Johnson, L.M. Ericsson, Nestlé, RWE, Verizon Communications, Wal-Mart Stores, Weyerhaeuser	1

Source: The material in this table was developed from the list of the top 10 companies on each reputational attribute at *Fortune.com*.

responsibility, globalness, or quality of products/services. GE missed the top 10 on innovation, social responsibility, and quality of products/services. UPS fell short of the top 10 on innovation, quality of management, and globalness.

The 2005 *Fortune* Global Most Admired Companies survey results clearly indicate that Alcoa, Berkshire Hathaway, FedEx, GE, P&G, and UPS are companies worthy of the admiration of the business community. But why is this so? Perhaps the answer can be found by exploring the core values that each company uses to guide its activities.

Alcoa   Alcoa, with 131,000 employees in 43 countries, is the world's leading producer of primary aluminum, fabricated aluminum, and alumina. Alcoa serves the aerospace, automotive, packaging, building and construction, commercial transportation, and industrial markets. The company also produces vinyl siding, precision castings, fastening systems, and electrical distribution systems for cars and trucks.

According to Alcoa's Web site, excellence results from always keeping the company values in mind. Alcoa's core values are listed below.

- *Integrity*—Alcoa's foundation is our integrity. We are open, honest, and trustworthy in dealing with customers, suppliers, coworkers, shareholders and the communities where we have an impact.

- *Environment, Health, and Safety*—We work safely in a manner that protects and promotes the health and well-being of the individual and the environment.

- *Customer*—We support our customers' success by creating exceptional value through innovative product and service solutions.

- *Excellence*—We relentlessly pursue excellence in everything we do, everyday.

- *People*—We work in an inclusive environment that embraces change, new ideas, respect for the individual, and equal opportunity to succeed.

- *Profitability*—We earn sustainable financial results that enable profitable growth and superior shareholder value.

- *Accountability*—We are accountable, individually and in teams, for our behaviors, actions, and results.

Berkshire Hathaway   Berkshire Hathaway is a holding company for a number of diverse business activities, including property and casualty insurance businesses and several large businesses that manufacture products for building components and apparel and footwear markets, to name only a few. The company holds numerous retail, distribution, financial, and food services businesses. "Operating decisions for the various Berkshire businesses are made by managers of the business units. Investment decisions and all other capital allocation decisions are made for Berkshire and its subsidiaries by Warren E. Buffett, in consultation with Charles T. Munger." Buffett, a noted investment guru, is chairman, and Munger is vice chairman of Berkshire's board of directors.

Although Berkshire Hathaway does not succinctly identify any core values on its Web site, the company describes in detail 14 principles that guide its business activities. These principles, along with explanatory and amplifying text, are provided in the *Owner's Manual* that is provided to all Berkshire shareholders. Listed here are several of Berkshire's managerial principles regarding the businesses in which the company invests and relationships with its own shareholders.

- Although our form is corporate, our attitude is partnership. We do not view the company itself as the ultimate owner of our business assets but instead view the company as a conduit through which our shareholders own the assets.

- In line with Berkshire's owner-orientation, most of our directors have a major portion of their net worth invested in the company.

- Our preference would be to reach our goal by directly owning a diversified group of businesses that generate cash and consistently earn above-average returns on capital. Our second choice is to own parts of similar businesses, attained primarily through purchases of marketable common stocks by our insurance subsidiaries.

- We use debt sparingly and, when we do borrow, we attempt to structure our loans on a long-term fixed rate basis.

- A managerial "wish list" will not be filled at shareholder expense.

- We feel noble intentions should be checked periodically against results. We test the wisdom of retaining earnings by assessing whether retention, over time, delivers shareholders at least $1 of market value for each $1 retained.

- We will be candid in our reporting to you, emphasizing the pluses and minuses important in appraising business value. Our guideline is to tell you the business facts that we would want to know if our positions were reversed. We owe you no less. We also believe candor benefits us as managers: The CEO who misleads others in public may eventually mislead himself in private.

FedEx   FedEx is a worldwide network of companies that provides individuals and businesses with "flexible, specialized services that represent the broadest array of supply chain, transportation, business, and related information services." FedEx identifies six core values that guide its business activities: people, service, innovation, integrity, responsibility, and loyalty. FedEx articulates each value in a specific way.

- *People*—We value our people and promote diversity in our workplace and in our thinking.

- *Service*—Our absolutely, positively spirit puts our customers at the heart of everything we do.

- *Innovation*—We invent and inspire the services and technologies that improve the way we work and live.

- *Integrity*—We manage our operations, finances, and services with honesty, efficiency, and reliability.

- *Responsibility*—We champion safe and healthy environments for the communities in which we live and work.

- *Loyalty*—We earn the respect and confidence of our FedEx people, customers, and investors every day, in everything we do.

General Electric   GE is a conglomerate of 11 technology, services, and financial businesses employing more than 300,000 people in 160 countries around the world. Some of GE's diverse business interests involve appliances, automotive parts, aviation, consumer electronics, energy, financial services, home comfort and safety, lighting, and media and entertainment.

GE identifies its values as a major unifying force for the company. According to the GE Web site, the company's values are "[m]ore than just a set of words, these values embody the spirit of GE at its best. They reflect the energy and spirit of a company that has the solid foundation to lead change as business evolves. And they articulate a code of behavior that guides us through that change with integrity." GE's values focus on being passionate, curious, resourceful, accountable, team-oriented, committed, open, and energizing—each and every one always with unyielding integrity. The values "are a call to action that asks every GE employee to recommit to a common set of beliefs about how we work in our world today."

Procter & Gamble   P&G is a consumer products company with 98,000 people working in about 80 countries worldwide; its products and services are sold to consumers in 140 countries. P&G's product lines include *personal and beauty solutions* such as antiperspirants/ deodorants, cosmetics, and hair care and skin care products; *health and* *wellness solutions* such as oral care products and prescription drugs; *house and home solutions* such as household cleaners and laundry and paper products; *baby and family solutions* such as snacks, beverages, and baby care products; and *pet nutrition and care solutions*. Some of the company's major brands are Pampers, Tide, Ariel, Pantene, Bounty, Folgers, Pringles, Charmin, Downy, Crest, and Olay.

The P&G Web site states that the company lives by five core values. Each of the values is identified below along with a description of the meaning of each value.

- Leadership

  We are all leaders in our area of responsibility, with a deep commitment to deliver leadership results.

  We have a clear vision of where we are going.

  We focus our resources to achieve leadership objectives and strategies.

  We develop the capability to deliver our strategies and eliminate organizational barriers.

- Integrity

  We always try to do the right thing.

  We are honest and straightforward with each other.

  We operate within the letter and spirit of the law.

  We uphold the values and principles of P&G in every action and decision.

  We are data-based and intellectually honest in advocating proposals, including recognizing risks.

- Trust

  We respect our P&G colleagues, customers, and consumers and treat them as we want to be treated.

  We have confidence in each other's capabilities and intentions.

  We believe that people work best when there is a foundation of trust.

- Ownership

  We accept personal accountability to meet our business needs, improve our systems, and help others improve their effectiveness.

  We all act like owners, treating the Company's assets as our own and behaving with the Company's long-term success in mind.

- Passion for Winning

  We are determined to be the best at doing what matters most.

  We have a healthy dissatisfaction with the status quo.

We have a compelling desire to improve and to win in the marketplace.

United Parcel Service   UPS is "the world's largest package delivery company and a leading global provider of specialized trans- portation and logistics services." Every day, UPS manages "the flow of goods, funds, and information in more than 200 countries and terri- tories worldwide." Its business is guided by the following four endur- ing beliefs:

- We believe integrity and excellence are the core of all we do.

- We believe that attention to our customers' changing needs is central to the success of UPS.

- We believe that people do their best when they feel pride in their contributions, when they are treated with dignity, and when their talents are encouraged to flourish in an environ- ment that embraces diversity.

- We believe that innovation fortifies our organization through the discovery of new opportunities to serve our people and our customers.

What Do the Values Communicate about the Most Admired Companies?   Collectively, the values of Alcoa, Berkshire Hathaway, FedEx, GE, P&G, and UPS emphasize factors that are essential for sustainable business success. Whether they are customers, employees, investors, or suppliers, people are very impor- tant to these companies in terms of business operations and success. These companies value integrity and infuse it into their relationships with all stakeholders. These companies recognize that modern busi- nesses operate in an environment with resource constraints and that all resources must be used wisely. These companies are committed to excellence in all that they do. With values that emphasize crucial ele- ments of sustainable business success, is it any wonder that Alcoa, Berkshire Hathaway, FedEx, GE, P&G, and UPS are among the most admired companies in the world?

Questions for Discussion

1. Why is it important to work for a company with a favorable reputation?

2. Explain why the nine attributes in the *Fortune* survey are useful in assessing a company's reputation relative to its competitors and to firms in other industries.

3. What similarities and differences do you see in the core values (guiding principles) of Alcoa, Berkshire Hathaway, FedEx, GE, P&G, and UPS?

4. Referring to the similarities and differences in question 3, discuss how they might be related to the companies' reputational status as shown in the second table.

5. Of what use are core values in guiding the ethical decisions and actions of organization members?

Sources

This case was developed from material contained in the following sources:

Alcoa. *Alcoa at a Glance*. Alcoa Web site, http://www.alcoa.com/global/en/about_alcoa/overview.asp, accessed on March 15, 2005.

Alcoa. *Vision & Values*. Alcoa Web site, http://www.alcoa.com/global/en/about_alcoa/vision_and_values.asp, accessed on March 15, 2005.

Berkshire Hathaway. *Berkshire Hathaway 2004 Annual Report*. Berkshire Hathaway Web site, http://www.berkshirehathaway.com/2004ar/2004ar.pdf, accessed on March 15, 2005.

Buffet, Warren E. *Owner's Manual*. Berkshire Hathaway Web site, http://www.berkshirehathaway.com/ownman.pdf, accessed on March 15, 2005.

Global most admired companies—key attributes. (March 7, 2005). *Fortune.com*, http://www.fortune.com/fortune/globaladmired/subs/2005/keyattributes/, accessed on March 11, 2005.

FedEx. *Mission*. FedEx Web site, http://www.fedex.com/us/about/today/mission.html, accessed on March 15, 2005.

FedEx. *Our Companies*. FedEx Web site, http://www.fedex.com/us/about/today/companies/?link=4, accessed on March 15, 2005.

General Electric. *Products & Solutions*. General Electric Web site, http://www.ge.com/en/product, accessed on March 15, 2005.

General Electric. *Values*. General Electric Web site, http://www.ge.com/en/company/companyinfo/at_a_glance/ge_values.htm, accessed on March 15, 2005.

Proctor & Gamble. *Products*. Procter & Gamble Web site, http://www.pg.com/products/usa_product_facts.jhtml, accessed on March 15, 2005.

Proctor & Gamble. *Purpose, Values and Principles*. Procter & Gamble Web site, http://www.pg.com/company/who_we_are/ppv.jhtml, accessed on March 15, 2005.

Proctor & Gamble. *Who We Are*. Procter & Gamble Web site, http://www.pg.com/company/who_we_are/index.jhtml, accessed on March 15, 2005.

United Parcel Service. *About UPS*. United Parcel Service Web site, http://www.ups.com/content/us/en/about/index.html, accessed on March 15, 2005.

United Parcel Service. *The UPS Charter*. United Parcel Service Web site, http://www.pressroom.ups.com/mediakits/companyinfo, accessed on March 15, 2005.

Who's on top and who's not: The world's most admired companies. (March 7, 2005). *Fortune.com*, http://www.fortune.com, accessed on March 11, 2005.

CASE 17

WHAT'S WRITTEN VERSUS REALITY:
ETHICAL DILEMMAS IN A HI-TECH
PUBLIC RELATIONS FIRM

Industry and Company Overview The goal of public relations (PR) is to make desired targets aware of clients and products. Through relationships with the media—press, television, and Internet—as well as stock market analysts, client and product awareness are broadened. Articles in trade magazines and newspapers, television interviews, tradeshow bookings, promotional tours, and general market research on clients and their competitors are the stock and trade of this business. Consultative strategies on the launch of initial public offerings (IPOs), timing and marketplace, corporate branding, and crisis management, as well as C-level (CEO, CFO, CAO, CIO) media training sessions, are some higher-level offerings of PR agencies.

The nature of the PR industry is competitive, individualistic, and "catty." Agencies compete for clients and qualified staff and are quick to bad-mouth their competitors. Very little loyalty seems to exist in this industry. Staff members are quick to "agency hop"—leave for a competing agency offering them more money—and to "client hop"—leave the agency to work for a client. Title inflation and pay inflation flourish in this individualistic and egotistical culture. As mediocre staff hop up the corporate ladder, title and pay grow commensurately. Eventually, it is discovered that these people are overpaid and underqualified; then they are blackballed. Word spreads rapidly throughout the industry regarding these peoples' shortcomings, making it very difficult for them to progress further in their careers.

Additionally, agencies are eager to "client swap" or terminate their relationship with an existing client if a competitor offers the agency more money. The client with the biggest budget wins, regardless of contractual obligations.

The nature of the PR professional is not reported favorably. An article in *PRWeek*, a major PR trade publication, reported that 25% of all PR professionals admit lying in order to advance their careers or their client's business.

During the spring and summer of 2004 an ethical problem was unfolding in the Los Angeles office of the PR firm Fleishman-Hillard regarding false billing for services provided to the city of Los Angeles. The city canceled all contracts with PR agencies as a result of the false billing, implicitly calling into question the ethics of the entire industry. As Julia Hood, editor of *PRWeek* wrote in an editorial, "Is there any other industry where a unilateral ban on all service providers in a certain category would be enacted because of the actions of one firm?"

Concern about the use of video news releases and paid endorsements as PR tools also contributed to the negative perceptual indictment of the entire PR industry. Although both major industry groups— the Council of PR Firms and the Public Relations Society of America— have a general code of ethics, some PR professionals apparently violate the codes with some degree of frequency. Some PR professionals have criticized the Council of PR Firms and the industry asserting that "[a]s an industry, we need to be incredibly transparent."

Seven Common Ethical Dilemmas   This case focuses on seven common ethical dilemmas that PR professionals have faced in a real public relations agency. Public Relations, Inc. (PRI) is a disguised name for an actual, medium-to-large agency located in the northeastern United States that specializes in PR consulting for hi-tech companies. The seven recurring ethical dilemmas involve the following:

- Client noncompete agreements
- Client confidentiality with respect to insider information
- Integrity of client information
- Employee poaching
- Friends and family stock gifting
- Unrealistic financial forecasting
- Promised versus realized employee benefits

Several vice presidents and senior vice presidents at PRI were consulted to identify and validate these dilemmas and to discuss real-life outcomes when their own professional ethics are challenged.

Ethical Dilemmas: Up Close and Personal   Each of the ethical dilemmas that have occurred (and still occur) at PRI is identified with an example. First, the written "policy" regarding the practice is identified. Then, an example of the dilemma is given, followed by the result. Finally, comments and afterthoughts regarding the dilemma are offered.

Dilemma 1: Client Noncompete Agreements   Contracts between the agency and a client specifically state that the agency will not solicit or accept work from a competitor during the term of the contract. If the agency wants to pursue a competitor, it should end the relationship prior to making contact with the competitor. Of course, this is a gamble, so PR agencies rarely follow this clause if the competitor has more money to spend.

What's Written

- The noncompete clause in the contract: "PRI will not solicit or accept work from a competitor during the term of this contract."

Dilemma

- You have a long-standing relationship with Client G.
- This client is very demanding, and the staff members on the account are unhappy.
- One of your staff members has told you that he has a contact inside Client M, a more desirable client, but a competitor of Client G.

Reality: What Happened

- PRI contacted Client M, made the sales pitch, and won a contract. Upon Client M's contract signature, PRI notified Client G that the relationship would be terminated.

Comments and Afterthoughts   This is commonplace in the PR industry. The client with the biggest budget wins; there is little, if any, client loyalty. In turn, there is very little agency loyalty. A company may burn through three agencies in one year. There is a disincentive, or "hassle factor," as well as a cost factor in switching agencies. Bringing an agency "up to speed" on a company's business and strategy can be time consuming.

Dilemma 2: Confidentiality of Insider Information

Highly confidential client information is shared with PR agencies in an effort to place clients and their products in the best strategic position. Once the client–agency relationship is terminated, all documents containing confidential information are returned to the client. However, the staff cannot simply erase the information they absorbed while working for that client. Because PR professionals gain domain expertise by working with clients within the same industry, they are frequently asked to pitch to competitors of their current clients. Then, if the pitch is won, their current client is terminated, and the PR pro is assigned to the new competing client. Below is an example of a dilemma that occurred with the "Ford" and "Chevy" of hi-tech clients.

What's Written

- The clause in the contract: "PRI will keep confidential all client information for the term of this contract."

Dilemma

- Because you have industry-specific experience (you worked with Client G), you have been placed in charge of the Client M account.

- You know that Client G is developing a new product that could clobber Client M's product.

Reality: What Happened

- Client M was not told the confidential information.

- Due to the financial impact of the competition, Client M reduced its marketing budget.

Comments and Afterthoughts   We are not aware of any breach of confidentiality at PRI. However, that does not mean that it does not occur. The guideline for this decision is whether the client is so unscrupulous that it would appreciate this kind of information. Sharing this kind of information is a double-edged sword; the client may be concerned that the PR firm would share its trade secrets and pull the business. Therefore, the motivation for keeping information confidential is often not an ethical decision, but a financial decision.

Dilemma 3: Integrity of Client Information   PR professionals rely on client-supplied information. The information is then passed on to the media for broadcast or publication. It is not the responsibility of the PR agency to research the accuracy of client-supplied information. However, the blame can fall on the agency when things go wrong. What follows reflects information in a July 25, 2000, *PRWeek* article describing a PR agency that was blamed for publishing misinformation.

> Pitching a CEO's credentials in a rags-to-riches tale is a tried-and-true PR tactic. But what if a client's head honcho lied on his resume, approved a press-kit bio constructed around these falsehoods, then turned around and pinned the blame on the PR firm when the media uncovered the truth? That's exactly what happened to The Horn Group, which found itself in Bay Area headlines last week when the CEO of client Luna Information Systems tried to finger them for circulating "An Entrepreneur's Story"—press materials containing exaggerated and unfounded claims about his background and education.

The CEO told the Horn Group that he was a graduate of Harvard Business School and played professional soccer for eight years. All this was false. Still, how can a PR pro question a client on the truth or accuracy of information without offending the client in this egotistical industry?

What's Written

- As a PR professional, one is not required to check the accuracy of the information provided by the client.

Dilemma

- Client L is releasing a new product: *Printer 2005.*

- Your client has provided you with some product specifications that sound fabulous, almost "too good to be true."

- You have already lined up some great press opportunities and will lose them if you delay the release.

Reality: What Happened

- PRI questioned the information and gave up some of the press opportunities.

- The client was extremely offended and threatened to fire PRI.

- Client L's information was published and was wrong.

Comments and Afterthoughts   There is a balance among losing press arrangements, offending clients, and covering the agency's reputation. This is a judgment call.

Dilemma 4: Employee Poaching   Contracts between the agency and the client specifically state the client will not solicit any employees of the agency during the term of their contract. Knowing that this statement alone will not deter solicitation, the agency includes additional language: "If the client solicits and hires any employees from PRI, the client must pay 50% of the employees' current salary." Since headhunters charge fees up to 35%, the 50% charge acts as a disincentive. However, in a booming economy clients are willing to spend more to get the right person for the job. Paying the 50% fee for a known quantity is more efficient than paying 35% for an uncertain hire. Employees of the agency develop strong relationships with their clients as part of their jobs. If a client offers them a higher paying, more prestigious job, it is tough to pass up the opportunity.

What's Written

- Included in the client contract is this clause: "If Client L solicits and hires any employees from PRI, Client L must pay 50% of employees' current salary."

Dilemma

- You have a great relationship with your client, Client L, and have secretly contemplated working at Client L.

- Client L has mentioned that there is a position available that would be "perfect" for you . . . but that the 50% fee is a lot of money.

Reality: What Happened

- Together, the employee and Client L approached PRI's CEO.
- The 50% fee was waived in exchange for increased business for PRI.

Comments and Afterthoughts   This is a win–win situation—and is rare. There are three clients that currently owe PRI fees for employee recruitment. Since the client relationships have been terminated, PRI has little leverage for collection. Legal suits have been filed in these three cases.

Dilemma 5: Friends and Family Stock Gifting   The clients of PRI are dot-coms and hi-tech companies requiring assistance in their IPO launches and with general PR. Clients commonly offer friends and family (F&F) stock to the agency and its employees. To avoid conflicts of interest, PRI has a "Just Say No" policy to such stock offers. This policy is more to protect the firm from legal liability of conflicts than to act ethically. Clients not offering F&F stock may try to claim that they were not given the same level of service, interview opportunities, press coverage, and so on as clients that contributed stock.

What's Written

- PRI has a "Just Say No" policy to F&F stock.

Dilemma

- You have a long-standing relationship with Client I.
- This client is launching its IPO next month, which is expected to be very successful.
- Knowing your policy, Client I offers F&F stock for your spouse.

Reality: What Happened

- No stock was accepted.

Comments and Afterthoughts   We are only aware of this case because the employee informed PRI. There may be many cases of which PRI is unaware.

Dilemma 6: Unrealistic Financial Forecasting The senior management team is recognized and rewarded for business growth, organic growth of existing clients' accounts, and new clients. In order to appear successful, many of the senior managers are overly conservative—that is, they "sandbag" or low ball—their forecasts of clients' planned spending with the agency. Then when actual revenues are higher than originally planned, the senior manager looks like a hero and is awarded a bonus accordingly.

What's Written

- Forecasts should be accurate for the good of the company.

Dilemma

- Your bonus is based on increased activity from the annual forecast of the organic growth of existing clients (as well as new business).
- All your clients have increased their budgets for next year.
- If you claim this in the annual forecast, you will need to grow the business even more over the year to realize your bonus.

Reality: What Happened

- Sandbagging!

  Results: A scramble to hire more staff, inappropriate expense planning, and overall inaccurate information for decision making.

Comments and Afterthoughts The reward system needs to be changed to encourage behavior that is desired—namely, accurate forecasting.

Dilemma 7: Promised Versus Realized Employee Benefits This is a dilemma of cultural conflict. As in many companies, PRI has a "face-time" culture. The senior leaders paid their dues by working long hours and, consequently, expect their junior staff members to do the same. Although PRI presents itself as a results-oriented agency, the "face-time" culture dominates. Additionally, there are political battles among some of the senior leaders. This conflict filters down to middle management and below. How can a middle manager fairly lead his or her staff without limiting his or her own advancement?

What's Written

- PRI offers a new FlexTime Condensed Workweek available to all employees, with manager approval (created by Human Resources).

Dilemma
- Your boss does not support this plan and has an adversarial relationship with the head of Human Resources.
- A staff member has requested a condensed workweek.
- You know that approving this request may be a career-limiting move for both you and the staff person in this "face-time" culture.

Reality: What Happened
- The manager encouraged the staff person to wait 90 days and see how other staff members manage their workload on this plan.
- The manager suggested to the boss that the staff person participate in the FlexTime plan as a show of support for the CEO (self-promotion).
- The boss said, "NO!"

Comments and Afterthoughts   Employee participation in this FlexTime program is less than 5%. The corporate culture is contradictory to a traditional 40-hour week, much less a flexible 40-hour week. The regular week is 50 plus hours of face time.

PRI's Ethical Profile

Leadership   The managers at PRI seem to relate to their constituencies from an amoral orientation—although willful wrongdoing probably does not exist, little, if any consideration is given to the moral implications of decisions and actions. PRI managers often act without consideration of or concern for the consequences of their actions for other stakeholders; instead, they operate on the basis of the "ends justifies the means." The egotistical nature of the organizational culture feeds into this style of leadership. Motivations that drive managers' actions include power, ego, and economics. The leadership has a short-term focus and lacks trust or long-term relationship-building qualities.

Culture   The culture in this industry and at PRI is individualistic and egotistical. The industry is also very competitive. There is little loyalty, either between agencies and clients or between employees and their agencies. This culture does not encourage professionals to act in an ethical manner. As was mentioned earlier, 25% of all PR professionals admit to lying.

Structure   PRI has several locations throughout the world and is one branch of a larger network of PR firms worldwide. Consequently, the company has a divisional structure that operates in a fairly decentralized manner. Due to the looser control associated with decentralized structures, additional opportunities for engaging in unethical behavior can arise.

Control Systems   The contracts that exist between agencies and clients compose one system that is put in place to govern the behavior of the two parties. The contracts are typically prepared by the PR agency. Some clauses can be very specific and detailed when it is in the best interests of the agency, such as the employee poaching clause. In other cases, when there is not such a specific benefit to the agency, wording in the contract if often vague, as in the client confidentiality clause. In this example, nothing is said to indicate that the information should be kept confidential when the contract expires or is terminated. This, and other similarly vague clauses, leaves employees to face ethical dilemmas regarding appropriate behavior.

Although there are contracts governing the relationship between the agency and the client, there are no clear written policies for the employees. A clear set of guidelines could help employees understand the agency's expectations regarding the appropriate decisions when faced with common ethical dilemmas.

As the unrealistic financial forecasting dilemma described, there is a reward system in place for agency employees. Company reward systems can have a profound influence on employee behavior. Companies should evaluate their reward systems carefully to ensure that they reinforce desired behaviors. In this case, the structure of the reward system has negative consequences in that it encourages managers to make overly conservative forecasts. The result is the inability of the firm to gather accurate information for planning and decision making.

Impact of These Factors on Employee Behavior   The relationship among these factors at PRI influences the actions of employees. The decentralized structure and lack of clear policies encourage a climate that allows immoral activities, especially when there is strong pressure to increase profits. An incentive system driven by numbers encourages shortcuts around responsible decisions. The amoral orientation of the culture and leadership may inadvertently condone questionable, if not immoral, decisions and actions. Of course, PRI is not alone in facing these problems.

Closing Thoughts   PRI's leadership may not be able to overcome industry and company barriers to create a truly high-ethics environment. The owners and top managers do not appear to want their employees to act with any absolute sense of what is right and wrong. They do want employees to use a "reasonable person" approach to decision making when faced with ethical dilemmas. PRI's leaders would, in all likelihood, encourage entrepreneurial and competitive interpretations regarding what the "right decision" would be in a particular situation.

PRI can take certain actions to help employees resolve ethical dilemmas. A set of guidelines could be developed to help people do "the right things" in very gray areas—especially in addressing common ethical dilemmas faced in this industry. Top managers could lead by example and ensure that their behaviors are consistent with the behaviors they desire from employees. The reward system could be reevaluated to ensure that it rewards the desired results without creating other dilemmas for the agency. In summary, the agency should try to implement some measures that achieve the desired results—results that do not always clash with the highly competitive industry culture.

Questions for Discussion

1. How would you conduct yourself regarding each of the seven dilemmas if you were a PRI employee? Explain.

2. How would you "fit" at PRI as an employee? Do your "ethics" match the company's ethics? Explain.

3. What issues would *you* likely face as a leader (either CEO, CFO, or CIO) at PRI? Explain.

4. Do PRI's leaders face the same ethical tensions and consequences as its lower-level employees? Explain.

5. As an ethics consultant, what specifically, if anything, would you recommend to the PRI leadership regarding the ethical dilemmas it continually faces? Explain.

Sources

This case utilized material contained in the following sources:

Bess, A. (August 1, 2004). St. Louis PR giant Fleishman-Hillard takes steps to boost ethical guidelines. *St. Louis Post-Dispatch*, from Newspaper Source database at http://search.epnet.com/login.aspx?direct=true&db=nfh&an=2W60864225496 accessed on March 14, 2005.

Grove, A. (July 24, 2000). Client's counterfeit biography hurls Horn Group into the headlines. *PRWeek*.

Leyland, A. (May 1, 2000). One out of four pros admits to lying on job. *PRWeek*.

Van Der Pool, L. (January 17, 2005). PR execs call for closer look at tools of the trade. *Adweek, 46(3)*, 8.

CASE 18

SOTHEBY'S PRICE FIXING

About Sotheby's   Founded in 1744 in London, England, Sotheby's is one of the oldest and largest auction houses in the world. Although Sotheby's beginning was not as exalted as one would imagine for an auction house that has long catered to the extremely rich, it was still looked upon as a fashionable enterprise in eighteenth-century Britain. After the death of Sotheby's founder, Samuel Baker, in 1778, the company remained under the direction of the Sotheby family. For nearly a century the auction house focused on the sale of fine books but has since expanded into the sale of art and related items. By 1917, Sotheby's had grown sufficiently to require a new location. The firm moved the auction house from Wellington Street to New Bond Street in London. After the move, the firm embarked on a dramatic development process that enhanced its global image with several impressive art auctions. Sotheby's became associated with elegant auctions that brought in increasingly large amounts of revenue. One of the firm's most distinguished sales occurred in 1961, when Rembrandt's *Aristotle Contemplating the Bust of Homer* was sold for $2.3 million to The Metropolitan Museum of Art. In 1964, Sotheby's began its global expansion by acquiring the United States' largest auction house, Parke-Bernet. Since this initial acquisition, Sotheby's has continued to expand and now has sales rooms and offices in North America; the United Kingdom and Ireland; Europe and the Middle East; Asia, Africa, and the Pacific; and Latin America.

With the rapid growth of the firm, Sotheby's went public in 1977. The firm's shares were well received by investors, and their value doubled within two years of the public offering. Sotheby's experienced market troubles in the early 1980s and was subsequently bought by A. Alfred Taubman in 1983. Under Taubman's leadership, Sotheby's reverted to private ownership. Sotheby's thrived in the late 1980s; one example of the firm's success was the sale of the Duchess of Windsor's jewels in 1987, which made headlines as one of the largest international auctions ever. The sale brought in over $50 million. In 1988, Taubman decided to take the company public again.

Since the auction house's beginning over 250 years ago, Sotheby's has experienced numerous market swings that have caused the company to change the way it does business. In 2000, Sotheby's expanded its operations by offering online auctions via Sothebys.com. The online auctions began on a successful note, aided by the sale of a print of the Declaration of Independence as well as panels from the Boston Garden's parquet. Soon, however, the online auctions fizzled and the Web site became just an information tool for live auctions.

The Business Environment of Auction Houses   The world of auction houses includes two major players—Sotheby's and Christie's—and numerous second tier players such as Phillips. Sotheby's and Christie's control 80 to 90% of the $5 billion international art auction market. This 80 to 90% figure has remained remarkably consistent to this day.

Christie's remains Sotheby's prime competitor. Established by James Christie in 1766 in London, the firm is still headquartered there, although it has sales rooms and offices around the world, competing in essentially the same markets as Sotheby's. Christie's conducted some of the greatest auctions of the eighteenth and nineteenth centuries, including the sale of Sir Robert Walpole's collection of paintings, which would form the base of the Hermitage Museum Collection in St. Petersburg. As noted on Christie's Web site, "Christie's auctions became major attractions on London's social agenda." Today, Christie's focuses on auctions of art, books and manuscripts, collectibles, jewelry, motor cars, and vintage wines, among other property.

Auctions have long been viewed as fashionable events; maintaining this image is very costly. The major auction houses—Sotheby's and Christie's—spare no expense to market to extremely wealthy people. Both auction houses have renovated their locations to include grand multi-story lobbies and costly decorations. The appearances of the auction houses may give the impression that the firms are doing exceptionally well, but this wasn't always the truth. Both Christie's and Sotheby's cut staff members while attempting to maintain their affluent image.

Auction houses typically earn their income from clients who pay a certain fee or percentage to the auction house for the sale of their items. However, when the items are well known, the auction house may waive the fee in order to gain publicity from the sale. Sellers also have the option of having the auction houses bid against each other to get the lowest fee or no fee at all. With the reduced fees collected, the auction houses have to find ways to reduce behind-the-scenes expenses but still show prosperity. According to Holman W. Jenkins, a reporter for the *Wall Street Journal*, the auction houses' "costs are front-loaded: Each has to maintain a network of sumptuous offices and showrooms around the world. Each has to employ a staff replete with experts in art and finery who exude impeccable standards of personal snootiness." Clearly, catering to the clientele of auction houses is a costly venture.

Key Executives at Sotheby's and Christie's   In the early and mid-1990s, key executives at Sotheby's and Christie's engaged in a series of meetings that would eventually result in the firms being embroiled in a price fixing scandal.

Sotheby's Executive A. Alfred Taubman   A. Alfred Taubman purchased Sotheby's in 1983 and became chairman of the board of directors of the company; some people believe he purchased the company as a wedding present for his wife, a former Miss Israel. Before acquiring Sotheby's, Taubman had been a successful shopping-mall developer. He founded Taubman Centers in 1950 in Detroit, Michigan, and played a significant role in reshaping retail in the United States by building regional shopping malls. According to *Forbes* magazine, Taubman had accumulated a net worth of nearly $770 million.

In the years after Taubman acquired Sotheby's, the auction business suffered due to the economic downturn of the late 1980s. To generate needed cash and interest, Taubman took the company public in 1988, but he remained the principal stockholder. Many people credit the company's turnaround to Taubman's flair and business skills, which helped improve the popularity of the auction business for people who had not previously participated in auctions.

Sotheby's Executive Diana "DeDe" Brooks   Diana Brooks joined Sotheby's in 1979 after beginning her career in the banking industry as a lending officer at Citibank. Brooks caught the eye of Taubman soon after he bought the company, largely due to her strong business skills and aggressive style. In 1994, Taubman appointed Brooks president and CEO of Sotheby's. Brooks is credited with helping to improve the company's bottom line as well as relaxing the British company's fairly uptight culture. However, her aggressive style as a woman running a major company created many critics, although most of the time Brooks shrugged them off. During her time at the helm, Brooks helped lead many successful auctions that brought in new customers. Her first time running an auction at a podium was Jacqueline Kennedy Onassis's estate auction, which, at over $34 million, was one of Sotheby's largest and most notable sales.

Christie's Executives   Two of Christie's executives—Sir Anthony Tennant and Christopher Davidge—were key figures in the price fixing scandal. Tennant was "a British aristocrat who helped raise the fortunes of the Guinness company before becoming Christie's chairman." Davidge was the president and CEO of Christie's. He was a self-made millionaire who struggled to overcome his working class background and to achieve a position in high society.

The Price Fixing Scandal

After a long period of eroding commissions due to clients playing the auction houses against each other, top executives from both Sotheby's and Christie's decided that they needed to act to regain profits. Taubman and Tennant are said to have met nearly a dozen times from 1993 to 1996, at which the two allegedly agreed to fix commissions that would be charged to clients. In attempting to keep these meetings secret, Taubman scheduled the entries in his date book as meeting with "Sir A.," "Anthony," "Tony," or even "****."

Although these business leaders had their plan in place, they had to get other executives to carry out the plan. According to Brooks' testimony, Taubman "directed her to meet with her counterpart at Christie's to set up a joint schedule of higher prices and coordinate other business practices and that he congratulated her when the scheme was carried out." Davidge, who was Brooks's counterpart at Christie's, asserted that, "Tennant, after at least a dozen meetings with Taubman, instructed him to collude with Brooks." According to the U.S. Department of Justice, at these meetings, Brooks and Davidge agreed to raise and publicly release non-negotiable sellers' commission rates, exchange customer information to enforce the schedules, not to make interest-free loans to sellers, and not to raid employees from each other.

Christie's introduced the non-negotiable commissions in March of 1995, and Sotheby's followed suit in April of 1995. Because Christie's and Sotheby's combined had a vast majority of the auction business, clients didn't have any choice other than to pay the non-negotiable commission fees. After the new schedules went into effect, the clients had no leverage in playing the companies against one another to get a reduced commission rate. According to some estimates, the non-negotiable commission schedule added nearly $15 million per year in additional revenue for each company, with little additional cost. Becoming suspicious about the price hikes of Sotheby's and Christie's, "American authorities launched a somewhat half-hearted antitrust investigation."

Francois Pinault, a wealthy French executive, purchased Christie's in 1998. Subsequently, CEO Davidge negotiated a $7 million severance package before resigning. In January of 2000, soon after he resigned and just as the American government's investigation seemed to be fizzling out, Davidge delivered some 600 pages of documents to the Department of Justice in which he detailed the alleged price fixing scheme in return for amnesty. Soon afterwards, Christie's agreed to cooperate with the government, although by then numerous civil lawsuits had been filed; these suits were later combined into one class-action lawsuit. Taubman and Brooks were forced to relinquish their executive positions in February 2002 as the government probe rapidly progressed. After the evidence surfaced, Taubman blamed the price fixing on Brooks, saying that he was unaware of it, while Brooks contended that she was just following orders.

Impact of the Price Fixing Scandal   Christopher Davidge struck a deal to avoid prosecution. Anthony Tennant was indicted in the U.S. but could not be extradited because at the time collusion was a civil, not a criminal, charge in the United Kingdom. Thus, no one from Christie's went to jail. This was not the case with the Sotheby's executives. Diana Brooks pled guilty to price fixing and cooperated in the prosecution of Taubman. She did not serve any jail time and "received a relatively light sentence of six months of home detention, 1,000 hours of community service, and a $350,000 fine." In addition, she agreed to give back nearly $3 million in salary to the company to settle claims against her. Alfred Taubman was sentenced to one year in prison and paid a $7.5 million fine for conspiring with Christie's to set the commission prices. He also agreed to pay $156 million toward settlement of the civil lawsuits filed against Sotheby's. On June 13, 2003, Alfred Taubman completed 10 months of a one-year prison term for his role in the price fixing scandal. He served nine months at a federal prison in Rochester, Minnesota, and one month at a halfway house in Detroit, Michigan.

"Christie's, like Sotheby's, was forced to pay hundreds of millions of dollars to settle a class-action suit stemming from the case. In the aftermath of the conspiracy, many employees at both houses lost their jobs, and, at Sotheby's, numerous employees' stock-based retirement funds were wiped out as public shares in the company plummeted." Sotheby's and Christie's each paid $256 million toward the $512 million settlement of the class-action civil suit. In addition to the civil penalties, Sotheby's paid a $45 million fine to the government as a penalty for the price fixing.

Sotheby's and Taubman—Where Are They at Today?
During the last few years, Sotheby's and Christie's experienced a slump in art prices that may have been tied to a poor economy. However, Sotheby's has been able to recover from the price fixing scandal. Sotheby's stock price hit a five-year low in 2002 but has since begun to climb back to normal levels. When Taubman and Brooks

were forced to relinquish their executive positions in February 2002, William Ruprecht, a 25-year employee of Sotheby's took over as CEO. Although Sotheby's was drowning in debt, Ruprecht led the company's return to financial success. Sotheby's posted a substantial increase in commission revenues during 2004 and saw its operating margins return to the early-1990s levels of 20%. Bob Goldsborough, an analyst with Ariel Capital Management, observes, "Sotheby's isn't just surviving in the wake of the price fixing scandal; it's thriving." Taubman still owns 80% of Sotheby's class B shares, which gives him voting control of the company.

As a long-time avid supporter and promoter of Detroit, Michigan, Alfred Taubman returned to his philanthropic, civic, and nonprofit activities in that city subsequent to his release from prison. In late July of 2003, "[m]ore than 70 of metro Detroit's most accomplished leaders gathered . . . at the Detroit Athletic Club to celebrate their friendship with Taubman." Federal Appeals Judge Damon Keith observed, "The theme was one of friendship. We wanted Al Taubman to know that we support him, we appreciate all of his compassion and gifts that he has given to this city, state, and country." In early November 2003, after delivering a speech to the annual University of Michigan Real Estate Forum, Taubman told reporters, in reference to the price fixing scandal, that: "I still don't know what I did supposedly. I wouldn't break the law for anything in the world. I never have, and people who know me believe me."

Questions for Discussion

1. Why is price fixing unethical?

2. Why would the business community and civic and political leaders continue to openly support someone who has been convicted of collusion and price fixing?

3. How can you explain Alfred Taubman's assertion that "he didn't break the law and didn't know what he supposedly did," when he had, in fact, been convicted, served prison time, and paid substantial fines?

Sources

This case was developed from material contained in the following sources:

Ackman, D. (April 29, 2002). Sotheby's Brooks sent to her room, but no jail. *Forbes.com*, http://www.forbes.com/2002/04/29/0429brooks.html.

Ackman, D. (November 20, 2001). Taubman log: Taking ethics quite seriously. *Forbes.com*. http://www.forbes.com/2001/11/20/1120taubman.html.

Artful auctioneering. (March 11, 1995). *The Economist*, 334(7905), 83–84.

Blumenthal, R. (November 14, 2001). Taubman datebooks cited in Sotheby's collusion trial. *New York Times*, D3.

Blumenthal, R., Vogel, C. (November 20, 2001). Chief witness accuses former boss at Sotheby's. *New York Times*, A1.

Christie's history. http://www.Christies.com/history/overview/asp, accessed March 3, 2005.

Corporate information: History. Sotheby's Web site at http://search.sothebys.com/about/corporate/as_corphistory.html, accessed March 2, 2005.

Creswell, J. (September 20, 2004). Sotheby's is back in auction. *Fortune, 150(6)*, 50.

Ebony, D. (December 2004). Auction house follies, review of C. Mason's *The Art of the Steal: Inside the Sotheby's-Christie's Auction House Scandal. Art in America*, 43.

Former Sotheby's head convicted of price fixing scheme. (December 10, 2001) *Ethics Newsline, 4(49)*, 1.

Gallagher, J. (November 7, 2003). Freed mall developer looks back, forward at University of Michigan forum. *Detroit Free Press*, from Newspaper Source database at http://search.epnet.com/login.aspx?direct=true&db=nfh&an=2W63843341044, accessed on March 2, 2005.

Holman, W. J., Jr. (December 12, 2001). Business world: Silly trial, silly law. *The Wall Street Journal*, A19.

Rohleder, A. (November 14, 2001). Time line: The rise of Christie's and Sotheby's. *Forbes.com*, http://www.forbes.com/2001/11/14/1114timeline.html.

Rohleder, A. (November 14, 2001). Who's who in the Sotheby's price fixing trial. *Forbes.com*, http://www.forbes.com/2001/11/14/1114players.html.

Sellers, P. (August 5, 1996). Women, sex & power. *Fortune, 134(3)*, 42.

Snavely, B. and Ankeny, R. (July 28, 2003). Taubman eases back into local public eye. *Crain's Detroit Business*, from MasterFILE Premier database at http://search.epnet.com/login.aspx?direct=true&db=f5h&an=10479212, accessed on March 2, 2005.

Sotheby's and former top executive agree to plead guilty to price fixing on commissions charged to sellers at auctions. (October 5, 2000). *U.S. Department of Justice Press Release*, http://www.usdoj.gov/opa/pr/2000/October/591at.htm.

Sotheby's fined £13m for price fixing. (October 30, 2004). *BBC News Online*, http://news.bbc.co.uk/2/hi/entertainment/2375667.stm.

Sotheby's Home Page. http://search.sothebys.com/, accessed March 3, 2005.

What an art. (August 7, 2004). Review of C. Mason's *The Art of the Steal: Inside the Sotheby's-Christie's Auction House Scandal*, from Corporate ResourceNet database at http://search.epnet.com/login.aspx?direct=true&db=crh&an=14073890, accessed on March 2, 2005.

Notes

1. Stampatori, R. (September 2004). Everything you wanted to know about courage . . . but were afraid to ask. *Fast Company, 86*, 97–111, http://www.fastcompany.com/magazine/86/courage.html.
2. Kouzes, J., Posner, B. (2003). *Credibility: How Leaders Gain and Lose It, Why People Demand It, Revised Edition*. San Francisco: Jossey-Bass; Finkelstein, S. (2003). *Why Smart Executives Fail*. New York: Portfolio; Zauderer, D. (September 22, 1992). Integrity: An essential executive quality. *Business Forum*, 12–16.
3. Collins, J. (2001). *Good to Great*, 21. New York: HarperCollins.
4. Ibid. It should be noted that the companies and leaders Collins studied achieved their greatness over 15-year time periods that spanned the 1970s, 1980s, and some into the 1990s. Although many of the companies are not currently great, Collins' best practices and principles continue to be widely read and used by corporations.

5. Waddock, S., Smith, N. (2000). Relationships: The real challenge of corporate global citizenship. *Business and Society Review, 104(1),* 47–62; Clarkson, M. (1995). A stakeholder framework for analyzing and evaluating corporate social performance. *Academy of Management Review, 20,* 91–117; Liedtka, J. (1998). Constructing an ethic for business practice: Competing effectively and doing good. *Business and Society, 37(3),* 254–280.

6. For more on this perspective, see Svendsen, A. (1998). *The Stakeholder Strategy.* San Francisco: Berrett-Koehler; and also Quinn, D., Jones, T. (1995). An agent morality view of business policy. *Academy of Management Review, 20(1),* 22–42.

7. Waddock, S., Graves, S. (March/April 1997). Does it pay to be ethical? *Business Ethics,* 14; Waddock, S., Graves, S. (1997). The corporate social performance–financial performance link. *Strategic Management Journal, 18(4),* 303–319; Waddock, S., Graves, S. (1997). Quality of management and quality of stakeholder relations: Are they synonymous? *Business and Society Review, 36(3),* 250–279; Waddock, S., Graves, S. (2000). Beyond built to last . . . stakeholder relations in built-to-last companies. *Business and Society Review, 105(4),* 393–418.

8. Based on Svendsen, Table 1, 2.

9. Barnard, C. (1939). *The Functions of the Executive,* 259. Cambridge, MA: Harvard University Press; Selznick, P. (1983). *Leadership in Administration: A Sociological Interpretation.* Berkeley: University of California Press.

10. Collins, J., Porras, J. (1994). *Built to Last: Successful Habits of Visionary Companies,* 78. New York: Harper Collins.

11. Ford, R. (2004). David Neeleman, CEO of JetBlue Airways, on people + strategy = growth. *The Academy of Management Executive, 18(2),* 141.

12. Collins, *Built to Last,* 78.

13. Based on Svendsen, 1–2.

14. Based on Svendsen, 73.

15. Svendsen, 70.

16. Based on Svendsen, 70.

17. Greenleaf, R. (1977). *Servant Leadership: A Journey into the Nature of Legitimate Power and Greatness.* Mahwah, NJ: Paulist Press.

18. Svendsen, A., Boutilier, R. Stakeholder 360: Measuring the quality of stakeholder relationships. *The Centre for Innovation in Management,* http://www.cim.sfu.ca/folders/research/6-stakeholder-360.pdf.

19. Ibid.

20. Fulmer, R. (Winter 2001). Johnson & Johnson: Frameworks for leadership. *Organizational Dynamics, 29(3),* 219.

21. Trevino, L., Hartman, L., and Brown, M. (Summer 2000). Moral person and moral manager: How executives develop a reputation for ethical leadership. *California Management Review, 42(4),* 128–142.

22. Brelis, M. (November 5, 2000). Herb's way. *Boston Globe,* F1; O'Neill, M. (May 28, 2001). The chairman of the board looks back. *Fortune,* 63–76.

23. Brelis, F4.

24. Ibid.

25. Tichy, N., McGill, A. (2003). *The Ethical Challenge: How to Lead with Unyielding Integrity.* San Francisco: Jossey-Bass.

26. Vaill, P. (1998). *Spirited Leading and Learning: Process Wisdom for a New Age.* San Francisco: Jossey-Bass; Novak, M. (1996). *Business as a Calling: Work and the Examined Life.* New York: The Free Press; Conger, J. (1994). *Spirit at Work: Discovering the Spirituality in Leadership.* San Francisco: Jossey-Bass; Mitroff, I., Denton, E. (1999). *A Spiritual Audit of Corporate America: A Hard Look at Values in the Workplace.* San Francisco: Jossey-Bass/Pfeiffer; Weiss, J. (August 2000). New careers, leadership as calling and spirituality. Paper delivered at the Academy of Management annual meeting, Spirituality and Religion Interest Group, Toronto, Canada.

27. Frederick, W. (March, 2001). Review of Mitroff and Denton's *A Spiritual Audit of Corporate America: A Hard Look at Values in the Workplace. Religion and Society, 40(1),* 118.

28. Greenleaf, R. (1977). *Servant Leadership: A Journey into the Nature of Legitimate Power and Greatness.* Mahwah, NJ: Paulist Press; Block, P. (1993). *Stewardship: Choosing Service over Self-Interest.* San Francisco: Berrett-Koehler Publishers.

29. See Weiss (note 26) for sources and citations used here.

30. Havel, V. (1989). *Letters to Olga,* trans. P. Wilson, 232. New York: Henry Holt.

31. Ford, 139–143.
32. Mitroff and Denton.
33. Mitroff and Denton.
34. See http://www.law.emory.edu/6circuit/oct97a0311p.06.html, *United States of America, Plaintiff (Appellee)* v. *Michael I. Monus, Defendant (Appellant)*, No. 95–4316; appeal from the United States District Court for the Northern District of Ohio at Cleveland, No. 93–00034. George W. White, Chief District Judge. Argued September 8, 1997; decided and filed October 21, 1997.
35. For an account of the proceedings against Micky Monus, see http://www.emory .edu/6circuit/oct97a0311p.06.html; Byrne, J. (July 6, 1998). How Al Dunlap self-destructed. *Business Week*, 44–45; Norris, F. (May 18, 2001). They noticed the fraud but figured it was not important. *New York Times*, C1.
36. Dunlap, A.J., Andelman, B. (1996). *Mean Business: How I Save Bad Companies And Make Good Companies Great*. New York: Simon & Schuster.
37. Driscoll, D.M., Hoffman, W. (2000). *Ethics Matters*, 68. Waltham, MA: Center for Business Ethics.
38. Hitt, W. (1990). *Ethics and Leadership: Putting Theory into Practice*, 138–174. Columbus, OH: Batelle.
39. Gerth, H. (1946). *From Max Weber: Essays in Sociology*, trans. C. Wright Mills. Cambridge: Oxford University Press.
40. Drucker, P. (1978). *Management: Tasks, Responsibilities, Practices*. New York: Harper & Row.
41. Janis, I. (1972). *Groupthink: Psychological Studies of Policy Decisions and Fiascoes*. Boston: Houghton Mifflin.
42. Burns, J. (1978). *Leadership*. New York: Harper & Row; Hitt.
43. Hitt, 169.
44. Ibid.
45. Intindola, B. (December 4, 2004). CEO pay stays high, more disclosure seen. *MSN Money*, http://news.moneycentral.msn.com/breaking/breakingnewsarticle.asp?feed= OBR&Date=20041204&ID=4127373.
46. Ibid.
47. Ibid.
48. Conger, J., Lawler III, E., Benson, G., et al. (2000). CEO appraisal: Keys to effectiveness. *Global Focus, 12(2)*, 35–44.
49. Young, G. (March 2000). Boards of directors and the adoption of a CEO performance evaluation process. *Journal of Management Studies, 37(2)*, 277.
50. See note 7.
51. Deal, T., Kennedy, A. (1982). *Corporate Culture: The Rites and Rituals of Corporate Life*, 9–12. Reading, MA: Addison-Wesley.
52. Keogh, J., ed. (1988). *Corporate Ethics: A Prime Business Asset. A Report on Policy and Privacy in Company Conduct*. New York: The Business Roundtable.
53. Pastin, M. (1986). *The Hard Problems of Management: Gaining the Ethics Edge*, 218–228, San Francisco: Jossey-Bass.
54. Keogh, 45.
55. Lagace, M. (July 12, 2004). Enron's lessons for managers. *HBS Working Knowledge*, http://hbswk.hbs.edu/item.jhtml?id=4253&t=organizations&nl=y.
56. Hamel, G. (2000). *Leading the Revolution*, 204–205. Cambridge, MA: Harvard Business School Press.
57. Cusumano, M., Markides, C. (2001). *Strategic Thinking for the Next Economy*. San Francisco: Jossey-Bass.
58. Broadbent, M. (July 2002). Synchronizing the CIO. *CIO Insight, 15*, 32–35.
59. Hofer, C., Schendel, D. (1979). *Strategic Management: A New View of Business Policy and Planning*. Boston: Little, Brown.
60. Freeman, R. E., Gilbert Jr., D. (1988). *Corporate Strategy and the Search for Ethics*. Upper Saddle River: Prentice Hall.
61. Cullen, J., Victor, B., and Stephens, C. (1989). An ethical weather report: Assessing the organization's ethical climate. *Organizational Dynamics, 18*, 50–62.
62. Posner, B., Schmidt, W. (1984). Value and the American manager: An update. *California Management Review*, Spring, 202–216.
63. Ashkeas, R., Ulrich, D., Jick, T., et al. (1995). *The Boundaryless Organization*. San Francisco: Jossey-Bass.
64. Chan, K. (May 21, 2001). From top to bottom. *Wall Street Journal*, R12.

65. Brey, P. (1999). Worker autonomy and the drama of digital networks in organizations. *Journal of Business Ethics, 22(1),* 15–22.
66. Anderson, C. (1997). Values-based management. *Academy of Management Executive, 11(4),* 25.
67. Kim, W., Mauborgne, R. (2001). Strategy, value innovation, and the knowledge economy, 197–228. In Cusumano, M., and Markides, C. *Strategic Thinking for the Next Economy.* San Francisco: Jossey-Bass.
68. Ibid., 218.
69. Ibid., 222.
70. Donaldson, T., Preston, L. (1995). The stakeholder theory of the corporation: Concepts, evidence, and implications. *Academy of Management Review, 20,* 65–91.
71. Ansoff, H. (1965). *Corporate Strategy,* 38. New York: McGraw-Hill; Boatright, J. (1999). *Ethics and the Conduct of Business,* 3rd ed., Upper Saddle River: Prentice Hall.
72. Driscoll, D., Hoffman, W., Petry, E. (1995). *The Ethical Edge,* 120. New York: MasterMedia Ltd.
73. Weaver, G., Trevino, L., Cochran, P. (February, 1999). Corporate ethics practices in the mid–1990s: An empirical study of the Fortune 1000. *Journal of Business Ethics, 18(3),* 283–294.
74. Self-regulation future. (April 16, 2001). *Advertising Age, 72,* 16; Harker, D., Harker, M. (Dec., 2000). The role of codes of conduct in the advertising self-regulatory framework. *Journal of Macromarketing, 20(2),* 155–166.
75. Brooks, L. (1989). Corporate codes of ethics. *Journal of Business Ethics, 8,* 117–129; Bowie, N., Duska, R. (1990). *Business ethics.* 2nd ed. Upper Saddle River: Prentice Hall.
76. Frankel, M. (1989). Professional codes: Why, how, and with what impact? *Journal of Business Ethics, 8,* 109–115.
77. Harrison, J. (1999). Finding the ethics soft spots of a target. *Mergers and Acquisitions, 34(2),* 8.
78. Frankel.
79. Somers, M. (2001). Ethical codes of conduct and organizational context: A study of the relationship between codes of conduct, employee behavior, and organizational values. *Journal of Business Ethics, 30,* 194.
80. Franchise association launches ombudsman program as key self-regulation component. (April 2001). *Franchising World, 33,* 36.
81. Campbell, K. (July 6, 2000). This is a job for . . . ombudsman writer of wrongs! *Christian Science Monitor, 15,* 15; Burd, S. (Oct. 8, 1999). U.S. Education Department introduces ombudsmans and 6 other top managers. *Chronicle of Higher Education 46,* A46; Carbone, J. (Sept. 16, 1999). Ombudsman looks into supplier complaints. *Purchasing, 127,* 42.
82. Moriarity, S. (Dec. 2000). Trends in ethical sanctions within the accounting profession. *Accounting Horizons, 14,* 427–439.
83. Bhatia, A., Blackstock, S., Nelson, R., et al. (Fall 2000). Evolution of quality review programs for Medicare: Quality assurance to quality improvement. *Health Care Financing Review, 22,* 69–74.
84. Shaw, C. (April 7, 2001). External assessment of health care. *British Medical Journal, 322,* 851–854.
85. See http://www.eoa.org for information on ethics programs and the Ethics Officer Association.

6

Employee Stakeholders and the Corporation

A strong national economy depends, in part, on preparing workers to be qualified job candidates possessing skills that are relevant to the needs of today's employers. In addressing this challenge, the Department of Labor must work with a wide spectrum of job seekers, including those with special needs such as the disadvantaged, people with disabilities, veterans, disadvantaged youth, and those who have lost their jobs due to foreign competition. Addressing the job seekers' needs is further complicated by the dynamics of the changing workplace. New technologies, increased competition, and changing labor markets have prompted employers to downsize, change employment patterns, and seek alternative labor sources such as qualified foreign workers.[1]

Overall employment is somewhat high, but white-collar unemployment is only 2.9%! Also noteworthy is the quite extensive national survey last quarter that showed 70% of current employees are waiting for the economy to improve so that can leave their current situation. That's a remarkable figure of discontent, but also shows the grass is probably not any greener . . . Also, more than 25% of the working population will reach retirement age by 2010, resulting in a potential shortage of nearly 10,000,000 workers. One-fifth of this country's large, established companies will be losing 40% or more of their top-level talent in the next five years. Nearly all of the 24 million people who stop working in this decade will be experienced employees who are headed into retirement.[2]

This chapter begins by addressing the changing characteristics of the workforce in the United States. What is different about the workforce, and how does this affect the corporation's ethical responsibilities? What, if anything, binds employees to their companies? What is the changing nature of the employer–employee social and psychological contract? How has this contract changed historically? The rights and responsibilities of employers and employees are briefly discussed to offer a perspective on what each party can expect from the other. Information is also presented on due process, dating in the workplace, same-sex marriage, and other employee-related issues in organizations. Problems of discrimination in the workplace and affirmative action legislation are then examined. The text addresses the question: What is illegal and unethical regarding workplace discrimination? Sexual harassment and the law are defined. Recommendations for organizations and individuals for preventing and dealing with this problem are discussed. Finally, we address issues surrounding whistle-blowing versus loyalty to the firm. What are the boundaries of employee loyalty? When do employees have the right or obligation to "blow the whistle" on the company?

6.1 EMPLOYEE STAKEHOLDERS: THE WORKFORCE IN THE TWENTY-FIRST CENTURY

The forces and effects of globalization, terrorism, information technology, and the Internet continue to influence business practices and processes, as discussed in Chapter 1. Industries and companies are downsizing, restructuring, merging, and reinventing their businesses. Mid-level management layers are being pressured, many even diminishing. Functions are being outsourced, offshored, eliminated, and replaced by online automation, cheaper international labor, and networked infrastructures. Knowledge workers with technological and people skills must manage processes and themselves in cyberspace with speed, efficiency, and accuracy.

Within the context of the so-called "digital economy," the following changes with employees and professional stakeholders occur[3]:

- A shift to knowledge work, which increases the potential for satisfying work but heightened stress.
- The concept of "a job and career for life" is dead or dying. Professionals are changing careers five to eight times on average during their working lives.
- Compensation, income, and the social distribution of benefits are shifting. Decreases in income are occurring among middle- and low-level professionals, and the gap between upper- and mid-to-low-level income holders is widening.
- Quality of work life is not inherent or guaranteed in the workplace. In one worst-case scenario, Thomas Malone of MIT

stated that all work relationships could possibly be mediated by the market, with every employee functioning as a company in shifting alliances and ventures.[4]

What about Barbara?

I am 51, divorced, no children young enough to write off, but still young enough to support. I have one class left to obtain a Legal Secretary Certificate at a local Business College. Prior to school, I worked a second job. I cannot quit school until I move, because I would not be able to pay student loans back right now. In the last year I have cut every cost I can. I have only the most basic phone service, no cell phone, cable antenna only. There is no where else to cut. I go to a beauty school for hair services.

A large retail firm has something they call their B-10 policy. Once a year, get rid of 10% of the work force and the remaining employees will be motivated to work harder. (apparently they are unaware of positive reinforcement). I do not know if this applies to the entire company, but it does apply to my area. Being politically correct, employees are written up twice before they are let go. I was once written up for "doing work," honestly! The second write up was for an error I made while doing volunteer work while representing this firm. I had done a large amount of volunteer work for this company prior to the incident I was written up for. In reality, both write ups were for "not following directions." I went to supervisors, and was never let go, but I have not received a raise in over two years. I am the perfect employee! Great attendance, very strong work ethic, and I make nothing!

I am putting my house on the market in Jan. I cannot afford payments anymore. Must find something cheaper, not an easy task either. My real estate taxes and home owners insurance have gone up. I always vote for the tax levy for the school district, however. Our medical insurance costs have increased, the benefits have decreased. I take four pills per day that cost me over $100 per month.

We have middle management who intimidate us, want us to fear them, tell others to treat us in the same horrid way. The company believes that managers do not need to know the jobs, only how to manage. That may work in some departments, but not all. Bad policy. I have not worked in Corporate America since 1975. I worked with autistic children for eight years prior to starting with the retail firm. People tell me that this firm is just like the rest of Corporate America. If so, Corporate America really sucks!

I really should ask the President how I am to survive, shouldn't I?

QUESTIONS

1. What is your reaction to this e-mail? Explain.

2. Is Barbara's situation unique, or is she representative of other employees in the workforce?

3. What advice would you offer her?

Source: This is an e-mail sent to this author from Barbara. She was using this text and decided to share her honest thoughts. I asked and received her permission to publish the e-mail, disguising the name of her employing company.

The Changing Workforce   The workforce is aging; managerial leadership positions are more difficult to fill; women entrants are increasing in number, with a mix of advances but with continued salary inequality; workforce cultures are mixing, as are values and potential value conflicts; the education gap in the workforce continues; the level of education lags in the United States compared to other countries; the number of workers with disabilities is expanding; and gay couples, still denied legal marriage in all states but one, are denied family health care insurance in most companies. The ethical implications of these changes for corporations are discussed in this chapter after the major trends are summarized.[5]

The Aging Workforce   The workforce is aging. Between 2004 and 2020, the number of workers age 55 and over will increase by 80% to over 33 million.[6] In 2001, the number of workers who are age 40 and older surpassed the number of those who are younger than age 40 for the first time. At the same time, those aged 16 to 24—the babybusters (who were born after the boomers)—make up 16% of the workforce, a proportion that continues to decrease. The seniors, older than age 55, represent about 13% of the workforce. Japan was the first nation ever with a population in which the average age is 40. By 2020, 6 out of 10 Japanese workers will be retired.

One result of the population growth slowdown is that the number of managerial leadership positions will outstrip available talent. As baby boomers age and retire, the number of managerial positions required is predicted to increase by 20% from 2000 to 2010, while U.S. demographic projections indicate a drop of 15% in the number of workers aged 35 to 44 (the pool from which these positions are filled) during this period. Older workers will be needed for their skills and experience, and also because of the shortage of younger workers to replace them.[7]

Women in the Workforce   Women represented 46.5% of the U.S. workforce in 2002, with 50.5% in management and professional

FIGURE 6.1	Does Your Organization Capitalize on Gender Strength?

- What evidence demonstrates that women enjoy working in the organization, and how is this monitored?
- What training and development opportunities are there, and how well are these accessed?
- What mentoring and coaching opportunities exist for women? How are these implemented and monitored?
- Do women have real choices about work-life responsibilities?
- How is women's advancement supported through internal networks?
- Who are the women's visible role models in the organization and why?
- How does the organization actively attract and position themselves with women?
- What do the stats and trends show when it comes to attracting, retaining and developing women?
- How can women be assured of fair and transparent promotion processes, and accessible dispute mechanisms?
- How are equal pay for equal work, fair rewards and recognition for women monitored?
- What do the women think about the effectiveness of parental and care support options?
- What external awards and recognitions have the organization (and the female employees) received?

Source: Adapted from Aurora Gender Capital Management online service for women to research and compare organizations at www.wherewomenwanttowork. com.

specialty positions. This figure is projected to reach 47.5% in 2008 and 10 million by 2010.[8] Two thirds of the new entrants between 1985 and 2000 were women. Three fourths of all working women will be in their childbearing years. Women with children less than 6 years old represent the most rapidly increasing segment of the workforce. Women hold over half of managerial and professional specialty positions. Of members of boards of directors, 12.5% are women; 4.1% of top earners are women. Two women were *Fortune* 500 CEOs in 2000. Figure 6.1 suggests questions leaders and managers can ask to assess whether or not their organizations are capitalizing on it gender diversity.

Gay Marriages and Workforce Rights "Gay marriages are still not recognized under federal law, which defines marriage as a union between one man and one woman." This means that health care benefits offered to a same-sex spouse by a partner's employer are federally taxed. Also, no Social Security benefits can be passed on to surviving same-sex partners.[9]

In 2004 Massachusetts became the first state to grant gays and lesbians the right to marry. Whether or not other states will recognize

Massachusetts' same-sex unions is unresolved. How would the benefits be affected, for example, of a same-sex married Boston employee moved by an employer to another state that prohibits gay marriages?

On July 1, 2000, Vermont was the first state to grant, under the "civil unions" law, same-sex couples the similar rights and responsibilities as married couples. Denmark, Norway, Sweden, Germany, and France have similar systems. The Netherlands expanded its definition of marriage in 2001 to include both opposite-sex and same-sex couples. Belgium followed in 2003, along with Ontario, a Canadian province in Canada. Same-sex marriage became available in three Canadian provinces (British Columbia, Ontario, and Quebec) and in one territory (Yukon) in 2004. Lawsuits are ongoing in Manitoba and Nova Scotia. If these courts approve same-sex marriage, over 80% of Canadian same-sex couples can marry in their own province.[10]

Some political jurisdictions have special legislation that allows gay and lesbian couples to register their committed relationship and gain some benefits. However, they do not receive all of the advantages that opposite-gender couples automatically acquire when they marry. These areas include most of the Scandinavian nations, the state of Vermont in the U.S. (where the arrangement is called a civil union), a few other U.S. states, and a few provinces in Canada.[11]

Nearly 6,000 U.S. employers have offered medical benefits to over 125,000 of their employees in same-sex unions. At least 198 members of Fortune 500 firms extend such coverage. A Hewitt Associates 2000 survey showed that 600 companies (or 22%) offered partner benefits. Companies are motivated to do so to help recruiting, retention, and corporate reputations. This coverage adds only 1 to 2% to a firm's health care costs.[12]

The Increasing Cultural Mix   By 2080, people of color will make up more than 27% of the U.S. population and 15% of the U.S. workforce. Census figures from the year 2000 show that the Hispanic population grew 58% to 35.3 million people since 1990 and is now the largest minority. Hispanic Americans outnumber African Americans in Florida and make up one third of California's population. It is reported that Hispanics make up almost 25% of the U.S. populaton.[13] Also, for the first time, Americans had the option of identifying themselves as belonging to more than one race. Seven million people, 2.4% of the nation, described themselves as multiracial.[14] This cultural mix is becoming increasingly evident in the workforce.

Educational Weaknesses and Gaps   U.S. students finished in the bottom half on math skills according to a new OECD (Organization for Economic Cooperation and Development) international comparison shown for 15-year-olds. Students in Hong Kong, Finland, and South Korea excelled in mathematics from the 40 surveyed countries. The U.S. also had the poorest outcomes per dollar spent on education, ranking 28 of 40 countries in math and 18 in reading. "The gap between the best and worst performing countries has widened," said Andreas Schleicher, the official who directed the study and wrote the report.[15]

The survey also questioned students about their own views of themselves and their work, and it found that although good students were more likely to think they were good, countries that did well often had a large number of students who did not feel they were doing well. The study also reported that although girls typically did only a little worse than boys on the test, they consistently reported much lower interest in and enjoyment of mathematics and much higher levels of helplessness and stress in mathematics classes. The study concluded that "while spending on educational institutions is a necessary prerequisite for the provision of high-quality education, spending alone is not sufficient to achieve high levels of outcomes.[16]

Mainstreaming Disabled Workers   Hiring and mainstreaming qualified disabled workers is increasing in importance because of the combined effects of the shrinking and aging of the workforce. A survey by the International Center for the Disabled found that two thirds of the working-age disabled were not in the workforce, although a "large majority" said they preferred to work.[17] Disabilities affect a large percentage of the workforce. There are about 54 million individuals with a disability nationally. Disabilities are categorized as permanent (for example, physical disabilities), temporary (such as those resulting from injury or stress), and progressive (e.g., AIDS, alcohol and drug addiction, cancer). A 2004 assessment from the National Organization on Disability/Harris Survey of Americans with Disabilities concluded that disabled Americans are three times as likely to live in poverty as the general public, and are twice as likely to drop out of high school, and are also twice as likely to be constrained by transportation options, and three times as many individuals with disabilities have less health care as the general public. It is interesting to note that "everybody is just one car wreck away, a diagnosis away, a progressive condition away from joining the ranks of the disabled."[18] Employers who hire persons with disabilities report they are more likely to be loyal, appreciative to their employers, and able to think outside the box.

Issues and Implications of Workforce Changes   These trends in the workforce necessitate accommodation from managers and employees. Moral and legal conflict will likely increase in workplace situations if responsible and proactive leadership, policies, and training are not planned and implemented with regard to the following:

1. *Age discrimination:* Companies can respond to aging and younger employees with fairness by implementing programs to accommodate skill training and mentoring. "Reverse mentoring" is occurring in some companies, in which younger, more technically savvy employees mentor and train older professionals.

2. *Sexual harassment:* More women are speaking out under the protection of Title VII of the amended Civil Rights Act, which is discussed later in this chapter. Sexual harassment continues to be reported across industries, including in outstanding companies such as Wal-Mart. Moreover, men's sex harassment charges regarding male bosses are also being reported. Nearly 15% of sexual harassment complaints filed with the Equal Employment Opportunity Commission were filed by men in 2003, an increase from 9% in 1992.[19] Diversity training programs are now offered in many larger reputable U.S. firms.

3. *Health care provisions:* Companies must work with a range of stakeholders, including government, community, and employees, to deal with the increasing health care costs for aging baby boomers. These issues become more acute during strained economic cycles and in industries striving to maintain market competitiveness. The present trend with U.S. health care is employer cutbacks with employees having to bear more of the contributions.

4. *Educational challenges:* A major stake here is the competitiveness of the U.S. in the global economy. Deficiencies in the American educational system are recognized by federal and state governments. The need for knowledgeable workers who are competent in people skills is another major concern. Also, a gap exists in the workforce between highly and poorly educated professionals. Highly educated workers demand more involvement and autonomy, less supervisory control, more information, more career opportunities, and rewards commensurate with performance. Less-educated workers require more training, education, supervision, and structured opportunities to improve their productivity and increase their mobility. This educational mix strains personal, moral, and managerial-employee relationships unless training programs continue to be made available.

FIGURE 6.2   Evolution of Work and Family Life Systems Models

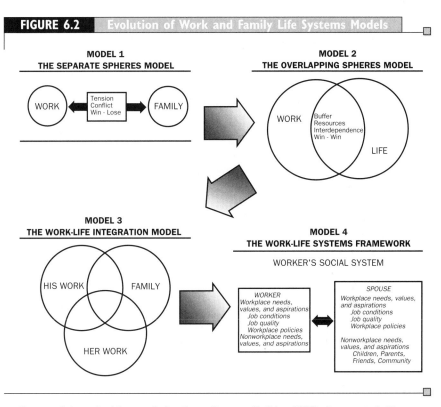

Source: Adapted with permission from Barnett, R. (Mar. 1999). A new work-life model for the twenty-first century. *Annals of the American Academy of Political and Social Science, 562,* 143–158.

5. *Paradigm shift toward a new "work-life" model:* As more dual-career and child-rearing couples enter the workforce, conflicts and problems evolve over roles and responsibilities as families cope with workplace demands. Working family models illustrating these tensions have evolved over decades. Four such models, which are summarized in Figure 6.2, include: (1) an early model depicting complete separation of work and family life and issues, in which men worked and women maintained the family; (2) an overlapping model of "work" and "family life" spheres in which the boundaries were still fuzzy, but roles were recognized as being interrelated; (3) a model that defined multiple roles and responsibilities, including "his work," "her work," and "family" obligations, which, like the previous two models, was based on scarcity and zero-sum assumptions (i.e., a fixed number

of resources that resulted in win–lose situations) regarding the allocation and use of resources and responsibilities at home and at work; and (4) the most recent work-life systems model, which assumes a systems perspective in which roles and responsibilities are not seen as competitive, isolated, or overlapping in undefined ways between family members, and the organization and community are built into individual and family responsibilities, which are shared to optimize the well-being of the entire system (company, employees, and families). In the fourth model, the emphasis also shifts from individual and family to include workplace needs, values, and aspirations; job conditions; and quality of life. Company policies are recognized as part of the work-life equation and include flextime and part-time arrangements.

The top 10 firms from a survey of the "100 Best Corporations for Working Mothers" included Bristol-Myers Squibb Company, Discovery Communications Inc., Eli Lilly and Company, IBM, Johnson & Johnson, JPMorgan Chase, PricewaterhouseCoopers LLP, Prudential Financial Inc., S. C. Johnson & Son, Inc., and Wachovia Corporation.[20]

Advancement of Women in the Workforce   Women accounted for 47% of the total labor force (male and female) in 2003. The labor-market participation rate of women, 25 to 44 years of age, rose over 75% with an earning exceeding $1 trillion annually. Of working married women, 48% of women provide half or more of a household's income. Women also own almost half (47%) of the stocks[21] and will acquire over 85% of the $12 trillion growth of U.S. private wealth between 1995 and 2010.[22,23] Catalyst, a New York-based working women's organization, surveyed 461 female top executives, with the title of vice president or higher, at the 1,000 largest U.S. companies to determine the three highest-ranking barriers to advancement for women. This study was noted as the first large-scale study of women in senior management.[24] The findings follow:

- 52% believed male stereotyping and preconceptions of women were primary factors in holding women back.
- 49% believed exclusion from informal networks of communication was a primary reason.
- 47% chose their own lack of general management or line experience as a primary barrier to advancement.[25]

In a parallel study of Fortune 500 and Service 500 chief executives, of whom 99% were men, only 25% of male chief executives cited male stereotyping and preconceptions of women as a top factor for holding women back. Fifteen percent believed that exclusion from informal networks was a primary barrier to women's advancement. Eighty-two percent said the most serious deterrent to women's advancement was lack of general management or line experience. The conclusion to the study pointed out the gender gaps in the male corporate culture and what female executives and companies must do to bridge this gap.

Next, we look at generational values as another way of understanding the workforce and its diversity. Place yourself into the designated generation where your age fits, and decide whether or not, and if so to what extent, your values and beliefs—especially as these surface in your workplace and working relationships—are influenced by generational factors.

Generational Value Differences in the Workplace
Generational analysis looks at differences among world views, attitudes, and values of generations of Americans. Large differences in the generations from World War II to the present in the U.S. population have had a substantial influence on government, corporate, and workplace policies. This information, although subjective, is used to develop workplace strategies and to evaluate ethical principles and beliefs of different groups in the workforce.[26] The following brief summary of five generations' dominant value orientations highlights some of these differences.

GI Generation (born 1901–1925)
This generation survived the Great Depression and served in World War II. Members of this generation are church-goers and belong to clubs and professional organizations. They express rugged individualism but are members of many groups. They tend to believe in upward mobility, civic virtue, and the American Dream.

Silent Generation (born 1926–1945)
This generation was too young to fight in World War II. They were influenced by the patriotism and self-sacrifice of the GI generation, from whom they did not wish to differentiate themselves. Their dominant principles are allegiance to law and order, patriotism, and faith. The Silent Generation likes memorabilia such as plaques, trophies, and pictures of themselves with important people.[27]

Baby Boomers (born 1945–1964)
This is currently the most powerful demographic generation, with 76 million members. They have led and set trends in society. They distinguish themselves from the former generations by assuming debt. Their "buy now, pay later" belief characterizes their instant gratification practices. They can be moralistic, but they question authority and the moral and ethical principles of

institutions. They do not "join" or sacrifice personal pleasure for the good of the group or collective. They mix and match religious traditions and avoid the dogma and teachings of single religions. Baby Boomers value health and wellness, personal growth, involvement, public recognition, status symbols, first class travel upgrades, visible roles such as speaking at an industry trade show, and any type of resort or retreat.[28]

Generation X (born 1965–1981)   Known as the "baby busters," this generation has 41 million members. Sandwiched between the two larger generations, they feel demographically overlooked. They came from a time of high national debt and bleak job markets, and were labeled as the "McJob" generation—a phrase referring to holders of low-level, entry-level jobs. This generation generally believes that they will get less materially than the boomers. Insecurity is a dominant theme for X-ers, who value close friends and virtual families more than material success. They, like the boomers, are also suspicious of institutions. They experience their journey through life as one that changes rapidly and continuously.

Generation Y (born 1982–2003)   The millennial generation (or "echo boomers") numbers about 80 million. It is the second largest generation since the boomers. They spend $170 billion a year of their parents' and their own money and comprise one third of the U.S. population. They have grown up with television, computers, instant messaging, and new technologies, just as the boomers grew up with the telephone. Y-ers don't want to be associated with X-ers, whom they believe are selfish and complaining and the least heroic generation—a bunch of slackers. Y-ers started growing up with a strong job market. They are ambitious, motivated, extremely impatient and demanding, and have a sense of entitlement.

Millennials (Generation Y) are also extremely practical, welcome clear rules and guidelines, display high levels of trust and optimism, are keenly aware of current events and sensitive to their surroundings, and define success in terms of team rather than individual achievement.[29] Generation Y are more positive than other employee groups and more likely to agree that "senior management communicates a clear vision of the future direction of my organization." They:

- have more favorable views on workplace issues, from work-life balance to performance reviews to having access to their immediate supervisor.
- value teamwork and fairness and were more critical than other age groups on issues of fairness and cooperation.
- want to be challenged at work.

- are motivated less by money and more by opportunities to advance and have a life outside of the office.

- are concerned about tuition reimbursement and flexible spending accounts for dependent care.

Over half of Generation Y-ers would leave their organization to work for an organization that offered better benefits.[30]

From a manager's viewpoint, Generation Y employees require "super-high maintenance," since they are "on fast forward with self-esteem." They often expect office cultures to adapt to them. With these attitudes, they generally require coaching, rigorous feedback, and smaller and more realistic goal setting, with deadlines and increasing responsibility.

From the employer's perspective, integrating individual and group differences in the workforce requires, as mentioned earlier, leadership, planning, new policies, and training. In larger, more complex organizations, providing education and training to integrate the workforce is a necessity.[31] With which of these values do you identify? What other values that are not listed here motivate you? Underlying individual values combined with other background factors influence perceptions, beliefs, behaviors, and ethical decisions.

The social contract between employers and employees continues to evolve. The following section looks at the changing historical and legal relationships, rights, and obligations between employee stakeholders and employers.

6.2 The Changing Social Contract between Corporations and Employees

The social contract that has historically defined the employee/employer relationship is known as *the employment-at-will (EAW) doctrine*. This doctrine remains the dominant view of the employment relationship in the U.S., although parts of the doctrine have eroded since its inception. This implied legal agreement has been in effect since 1884, when the *Payne v. Western A.R.R. Co.* judgment ruled that "all may dismiss their employees at will, be they many or few, for good cause, for no cause, or even for cause morally wrong without being thereby guilty of legal wrong."

Essentially, the EAW doctrine can be defined as "the right of an employer to fire an employee without giving a reason and the right of an employee to quit when he or she chooses."[32] If employees are unprotected by unions or other written contracts, they can be fired, according to this doctrine. As the insert from an actual company shown on page 375 ("Read Carefully Before Signing") illustrates, employees can be and are asked to acknowledge how tenuous their "contract" with a company can be.

The EAW doctrine evolved as part of the laissez-faire philosophy of the Industrial Revolution. Between the 1930s and 1960s, however, exceptions to the doctrine appeared. Federal legislation since the 1960s has been enacted to protect employees against racial discrimination and to provide rights to a minimum wage, to equal hiring and employment opportunities, and to participation in labor unions.

The vast majority of states have an at-will provision in their legislative laws. In California, it is easier to terminate an employee than it is in New York. Some states have other obligations that must be addressed by employers, like good faith or fair dealing practices.[33]

Since the 1970s, state court decisions have limited the EAW doctrine. Specifically, state courts have upheld employees' rights to use legal action against their employers if an employee termination violated "public policy" principles; examples include (1) if employees were pressured to commit perjury or fix prices, (2) if employees were not permitted to perform jury duty or file for workers' compensation, (3) if employees were terminated because they refused to support a merger, and (4) if employees reported alleged employer violations of statutory policy (whistle-blowing).

An important 1981 California Appeals Court decision, *Pugh* v. *See's Candies, Inc.*, ruled that, in a noncontractual employment arrangement, an implied promise from the employer existed. The employer could not act arbitrarily with its employees regarding termination decisions when considering the following factors: (1) duration of employment, (2) recommendations and promotions received, (3) lack of direct criticism of work, (4) assurances given, and (5) the employer's acknowledged policies.[34]

Although the EAW doctrine has undergone change, it remains the cornerstone of U.S. labor law, as is illustrated in Figure 6.3. States vary on the application of the EAW doctrine, but the U.S. Eighth Circuit Court of Appeals has favored employers. The federal court has stated that it will not act as a "superpersonnel board" of a company. Figure 6.3 is a copy of a contract an employee must sign before beginning work at this reputable company in Massachusetts. It is an example of a strongly worded EAW-oriented contract.

At issue in the EAW doctrine is the continuing debate over the nature of property and property rights. Each organization defines property rights and responsibilities offered to managers and employees, such as severance payments, pensions, stock options, access to resources, and golden parachutes. Employers also view employees' labor, time, and effort as part of their property. At issue in the EAW doctrine is whether an employee's education, skills, and other intangible assets are seen as the employee's "property," and if so, whether employees have certain

FIGURE 6.3	Employee Contract under the EAW Doctrine

READ CAREFULLY BEFORE SIGNING:

I understand that refusal to submit to the testing noted [elsewhere] or a positive drug screen result will eliminate any consideration for employment.

I also certify that the statements and information furnished by me in this application are true and correct. I understand that falsification of such statements and information is grounds for dismissal at any time the company becomes aware of the falsified notification. In consideration of my employment, I agree to conform to the rules and regulations of the company and acknowledge that my employment and compensation can be terminated, with or without cause, and with or without notice, at any time, at the option of either the company or myself. I further understand that no policy, benefit or procedure contained in any employee handbook creates an employment contract for any period of time and no terms or conditions of employment contrary to the foregoing should be relied upon, except for those made in writing by a designated officer of the Company.

I agree and hereby authorize XYZ, Inc. to conduct a background inquiry to verify the information on this application, other documentation that I have provided and other areas that may include prior employment, consumer credit, criminal convictions, motor vehicle and other reports. These reports may include information as to my character, work habits, performance, education and experience along with reasons for termination of employment from previous employers. Further, I understand that you may be requesting information from various Federal, State and other agencies which maintain records concerning my past activities relating to my driving, credit, criminal, civil and other experiences as well as claims involving me in the files of insurance companies. I authorize all previous employers or other persons who have knowledge of me, or my records, to release such information to XYZ, Inc. I hereby release any party or agency and XYZ, Inc. from all claims or liabilities whatever that may arise by such disclosures or such investigation.

_____   _____
Date of Application   Signature of Applicant

rights regarding these assets. Due process is one such right that accompanies the EAW doctrine.[35]

The debate will continue over whose "property" and rights take precedence and whose are violated and on what grounds between employer and employee, especially in disputed firings that do not involve clear legal violations of employee rights, such as blatant discrimination. One scholar has noted that:

> The present-day debate revolves mainly around utilitarian issues. To what extent is the welfare of society advanced by preserving or limiting the traditional prerogatives of employers? Employers typically favor employment at will not because they want to fire without cause but because they would rather avoid the need to account for their personnel decisions in court and face the possibility of stiff punitive awards. Even advocates of greater employee protection recognize the dangers of the courts becoming too deeply involved in business decision making.[36]

The next section presents employee rights and employer responsibilities and offers recommendations to managers for avoiding arbitrary termination decisions.

6.3 EMPLOYEE AND EMPLOYER RIGHTS AND RESPONSIBILITIES

The EAW doctrine was a transition from a feudal European governance context to a contemporary U.S. pluralistic setting. Employee rights in the workplace also continue to evolve. Changing social, political, legal, and technological forces present new issues, opportunities, and controversies between employee rights and corporate duties.

In a market economy, employer and employee rights and responsibilities are based on contrasting (sometimes conflicting) assumptions and values. Employers control private property and proprietary rights over their intellectual property, as noted earlier. Employees claim their constitutional rights to individual freedom, liberty, and control over their private lives. Employers try to maximize productivity and profits, to sustain financial growth and stability, to minimize costs, to improve quality, to increase market share, and to stabilize wages. Employees seek to increase their wages and benefits, to improve working conditions, to enhance mobility, and to ensure job security. No perfect boundary exists between employer and employee rights in a capitalist market economy.

Before discussing specific rights and responsibilities between employers and employees, this section begins by defining "rights" and two premises based on this definition. Then two organizing concepts that underlie employee rights are suggested: balance and governmental rights. The concept of balance is based on utilitarian ethical reasoning and that of moral entitlement is based on Kantian nonconsequentialist reasoning. Although these concepts are not mutually exclusive, it is helpful to understand the logic behind them in order to argue their merits and shortcomings as they apply to specific workplace controversies.

Moral Foundation of Employee Rights   The ideal relationship between employer and employees is one based on mutual respect and trust. Trust generally leads to open communication, which, in turn, provides an environment of collaboration and productivity. In many companies, this is, unfortunately, not the case. Power and authority relationships between employers and employees are, by definition, asymmetrical. Employees are generally, as stated by J. Rowan, in a "comparatively inferior bargaining position with respect to their employers. This inequity opens up possibilities for various sorts of exploitation, such as inadequate compensation, discrimination, and privacy invasions, all of which have been known to occur." Rowan also notes that "employee rights are complex, in that managers, as a prerequisite for making ethically sound decisions, must assess which alleged employee rights are legitimate . . . and must weigh them against the rights of those in other stakeholder groups."[37] From these observations, a definition of "rights" is offered.

A right can be understood as a "moral claim." A right is moral when it is not necessarily part of any conventional system, as are legal rights. A right is a claim because it corresponds with a duty on the part of the person against whom the right is held. For example, I claim that I have a right to be safe in my workplace. I hold this claim against my employer, because the employer has the duty to provide me with this safety. Under particular circumstances, my moral claim can be argued and disputed. It may not be an absolute claim.

The moral foundation for employee rights is based on the fact that employees are persons. One generic right that all persons have is a right to freedom, including the concept of negative freedom (i.e., the right not to be coerced or inhibited by external forces.) Regarding employees, this right to freedom is a claim "that when managers choose to hire employees, they must bear in mind that they are deal-ing with persons, and the (positive and negative) freedom of their employees is therefore to be respected."[38] The second generic right of employees is the right to well-being. This right follows from individu-als' having interests, which are preconditions for pursuing goals. Interests and the pursuit of goals are morally important because they are not satisfied when a person does not have well-being. When employ-ees cannot satisfy their job-related goals, interests, and requirements because of work-related conditions, an employee's right to well-being may have been violated. With regard to these arguments on the moral foundation of employee rights, Sanford Jacoby has noted, "Employees should at all times be treated in a way that respects them as persons."[39] We might add that the same observation holds true for employers; they also should be treated with respect as individuals.

The Principle of Balance in the Employee and Employer Social Contract and the Reality of Competitive Change

As common law and custom have evolved from the EAW doctrine to implied employee rights, employers have the opportunity to consider more than stockholder and financial interests when dealing with employee stakeholders. As argued in Chapter 5, a values-based stakeholder man-agement perspective views the employee–employer relationship from a "win–win" foundation. Both employers and employees act from a base of values. When the values of an organization align and draw on the values of employees, innovation, productivity, and individual, as well as corporate, development can occur.

In a highly competitive, globalizing environment in which intellectual skills, flexibility, and speed of work are emphasized, traditional views of company ownership and employee loyalty change. The evolving social contract between employers and employees still recognizes employers' power over their physical and material property, but the contractual relationship between employer and employee aims in principle at *balance,* mutual respect, integrity, and fairness. The employer's interest in operating the business as she or he determines can and should be balanced against the employee's welfare, interests, and willing contribution to add value. In the early twenty-first century, small and mid-size employers are also pressured to balance global economic demands and tighter profit margins with employee interests. Larger firms continue to reduce their workforce and cut costs through outsourcing and offshoring, as discussed earlier in the text. Although employers generally have more power than employees in the contractual relationship, employees in the United States, for example, are still citizens under the protection of the Constitution. Employees must also balance their self-interests and motivations with the needs of the organization to succeed, which is necessary for the organization provide employment.

It is interesting to note that the principle of balance in the employer–employee relationship has been historically prevalent in some of the developed Asian countries, such as Japan, South Korea, Singapore, and Taiwan. In Japan, in particular, the Confucian tradition of harmony has underscored the cooperative relationship between unions and companies.[40] European countries, including Germany and France, have also enacted laws that protect employee benefits and welfare. Some of these countries have traditions that include socialism and strong populist social policies. Some of these traditions and practices are also beginning to change under the competitive pressures of economic downturns, the use of information technology, and global competition. For example, lifelong employment in many Japanese companies is no longer guaranteed. Offshoring and outsourcing are now practiced at Sony, Matsushita, and Toshiba to mention a few firms.[41]

Rights from Government Legislation   Employee rights are based on principles determined by law. Certain *government rights* (federal, state, and local) of the employee are not negotiable in written or implied contracts: for example, rights related to the minimum wage; sexual harassment; discrimination based on race, creed, age, national origin, gender, or disability; and the right to assemble. Although employee rights based on certain legislation are not always negotiated according to employer–employee self-interests, these rights can be disputed, depending on circumstances. Reverse discrimination, to be discussed later, is one such example. Although private corporations are the property of the owners, certain employee legal rights are still within a corporation's boundaries. (Refer back to Chapter 3 for a discussion of different classifications of moral rights.)

Rights and Responsibilities between Employers and Employees

Employers and employees have rights and responsibilities each should honor with respect to the other. This section discusses these mutual responsibilities, some of which stem from each party's rights by law and legislation, while others are based on ethical principles. As discussed in Chapter 5, a values-based, stakeholder management approach views the employer–employee relationship as one grounded on mutual trust and reciprocal responsibility. Although laws and legislation serve the purpose of protection for both parties, without trust that is demonstrated in fair and equitable treatment of basic rights and responsibilities, one or both parties stand to lose. Nevertheless, not all employers or employees have a personal, professional, or organizational ethic that respects the other's rights in all situations. Historical attitudes, negative prejudices, and stereotypes sometimes surface in institutionally unjust practices toward individuals and groups. For these reasons, ethical and legal rights and responsibilities must be written, made part of employee training, and reinforced in company codes, leadership examples, and organizational best practices to be effective. When voluntary trust and mutual respect fail and harm is done to employers or employees, the legal system can be evoked.

Employer Responsibilities to Employees

Employers are obliged to pay employees fair wages for work performed and to provide safe working conditions. Take a look at and answer the questions in the box entitled, "Who Has Rights in this Situation?" After you have answered and discussed the questions, what, if anything, did you learn about your and other classmates' values and beliefs regarding employee-employer responsibilities and obligations?

Who Has Rights in this Situation?

Aparna Jairam [a high-tech employee in India] isn't trying to steal your job [you as a high-tech U.S. employee]. That's what she tells me, and I believe her. But if Jairam does end up taking it—and, let's face facts, she could do your $70,000-a-year (U.S.) job for the wages of a Taco Bell counter-jockey—she won't lose any sleep over your plight. When I ask what her advice is for a beleaguered American programmer afraid of being pulled under by the global tide that she represents, Jairam takes the high road, neither dismissing the concern nor offering soothing happy talk.

Instead, she recites a portion of the 2,000-year-old epic poem and Hindu holy book, the Bhagavad Gita: "Do what you're supposed to do. And don't worry about the fruits. They'll come on their own."

QUESTIONS

1. Do you agree with Aparna? Why or why not? Please explain.

2. On what, if any, ethical grounds could you either justify or reject her assessment? Explain.

Source: Pink, D. (February 2004). The new face of the silicon age. *Wired Magazine*, 12(2), http://www.wired.com/wired/archive/12.02/india.html.

Fair Wages   Fair wages are determined by factors such as what the public and society support and expect, conditions of the labor market, competitive industry wages in the specific location, the firm's profitability, the nature of the job and work, laws governing minimum wages, comparable salaries, and the fairness of the salary or wage negotiations.[42] As will be discussed in this chapter, fair wages for comparable jobs held by men and women are not always paid. Women earn 86 cents on every dollar earned by men, an increase over 65 cents in 1970. Women age 15 to 24 years took home 91 cents for every dollar earned by male counterparts. The wage gap is due to many reasons. But as one researcher noted, "Moving into male-dominated occupations in and of itself isn't the key to raising women's incomes. In none of the broad occupational categories do women make even 90% of what men make."[43]

Safe Working Environment   Employers also are obliged to provide workers with a safe working environment and safe working conditions. The Occupational Safety and Health Administration (OSHA) and federal laws and regulations provide safety standards and enforce employer institution of the company's own safety standards. The problems of employers providing—and of employees accepting—safe working environments stem from (1) lack of knowledge and of available, reliable information about levels of health risks; (2) lack of appropriate compensation proportional to the level of occupational risk; and (3) employees accepting known risks when the employer does not offer any safer alternatives.[44] When the option is employment versus no employment, workers, especially in low-income, noncompetitive employment regions, often choose jobs with hazardous risks to their health or life. Employees have a right to know about unsafe working conditions, as we also discuss later in the chapter.

Employers should pay competitive wages commensurate with the occupational risks associated with a profession, job, or work setting.

For example, race car drivers would not be expected to receive the same pay as college professors. Employers also are expected to provide full information on the risks and health hazards related to the work, products, and working environments to all employees exposed to those risks. Finally, employers also should offer health insurance programs and benefits to employees exposed to workplace hazards. Not all employers meet these obligations. For those who cannot provide health and protection of employees in high risk, potentially unsafe environments, employers should not be in that business.

Working Conditions that Empower Employees   Although employers are not required by law to offer employees working conditions that provide meaningful tasks and job satisfaction, doing so can lead to increased performance, job satisfaction, and productivity. Employees work most productively when they can participate in the control of their tasks, when they are given responsibility for and autonomy over their assignments, and when they are treated with respect.[45] Quality of work life (QWL) programs that provide employees with more autonomy, participation, satisfaction, and control in their work tasks have demonstrated positive results.[46] Many companies are organizing self-designing work teams, quality circles, and learning communities to tap into employee creativity and abilities. As noted in Chapter 5, there is an increase in companies offering opportunities for employees to practice their own religious and spiritual rituals during the work day. Employers and employees both gain when personal and organizational needs are met. Working environments that can provide conditions for this alignment are increasing.

Employee Responsibilities to Employers   Employees are responsible for fulfilling their contracted obligations to the corporation; for following the goals, procedural rules, and work plans of the organization; for offering competence commensurate with the work and job assignments; and for performing productively according to the required tasks. Other responsibilities include timeliness, avoiding absenteeism, acting legally and morally in the workplace and while on job assignments, and respecting the intellectual and private property rights of the employer.

Conflicts of Interest   Employee responsibilities to employers become complicated when conflicts of interest appear, that is, when an employee's private interests compete or are not aligned with the company's interests. More obvious conflicts of interest arise in a number of situations, such as taking or offering commercial or personal bribes, kickbacks, gifts, and insider information for personal gain.

The so-called gray areas are more problematic for determining whose interests are violated at the expense of others: for example, an employee quits a firm, joins a competitor, and then is accused by the former employer of stealing proprietary property (that is, passing on intellectual property, sharing trade secrets, or offering a competitive advantage by divulging confidential information). Whose interests are violated?[47] Some courts have used a "balancing model" based on utilitarian logic to resolve trade-secret-protection cases; that is, an employee's interest in mobility and opportunity is weighed against the employer's right to decide the extent of protection given to confidential information. For example, the following three criteria have been used to decide whether trade secrets have been divulged by employees:

1. True trade secrecy and established ownership must be shown.

2. A trade secret must have been disclosed by an employee, thus breaching a duty of confidentiality.

3. The employer's interest in keeping the secret must outweigh the employee's interest in using the secret to earn a living and the public's interest in having the secret transmitted.

Courts also use other considerations in these types of rulings (for example, contract obligations, promises made, truthfulness, confidentiality, and loyalty). The point here is that as technology and expertise become more sophisticated and as employee mobility—and downsizing—increase, workplace and courtroom criteria regarding the proof of conflict of interest also grow more complicated. Although a utilitarian model is used to help determine conflict-of-interest court cases, such as trade secrecy, ethical principles such as rights, duty, and justice also remain essential considerations for determining right and wrong; violations of loyalty, confidentiality, or truthfulness; and harm done to either employers or employees.

Employee Rights in the Workplace

Labor, along with money and materials, is considered capital in a free-market system. However, labor is not the same as materials and money; labor also means human beings who have general constitutional rights that should not be relinquished between working hours.[48] Yet, clashes of interests and of stakes between employee rights and management demands frequently occur. The boundary between an employer's private property and an employee's individual rights is often blurred in everyday experience. Understanding employee rights is part legal and part ethical because these rights must be viewed and interpreted within corporate policy, procedures, and particular circumstances. In some instances, there are clear violations of an employee's rights; other times there are "gray," or uncertain, areas. When employees and employers cannot agree on whose rights are seriously violated, third-party negotiation, arbitration, and even settlement may be required. This section presents major types of employee rights in the workplace:

- The right not to be terminated without just cause
- The right to due process
- The right to privacy
- The right to know
- The right to workplace health and safety
- The right to organize and strike
- Rights regarding plant closings

These rights become even more important in a society that rapidly transforms technological and scientific inventions into part of the human workplace environment.

Just Cause Termination   Employees have a right not to be terminated arbitrarily or without just cause, even in a free-market economy.[49] Under conditions of volatile economic downturns, mergers and acquisitions, new start-up failures (as with the "dot-com bubble burst"), and massive negative profit margin shifts in industries, it is often not difficult for employers to claim "just cause."

"Just Cause" Guideline

A basic principle in disciplinary cases is that the employer must have "just cause" for imposing the action. A test for determining whether there is "just cause" was developed by Arbitrator Daugherty in the celebrated *Enterprise Wire* case (46 LA 359, 1966 and 50 LA 83). An absolute "no" answer to any one or more questions in this guideline indicates that the employer's action was "arbitrary, capricious and/or discriminatory in one or more respects, thereby signifying an abuse of managerial discretion and allowing the arbitrator to substitute his judgment for that of the employer."

1. Was the employee adequately warned of the consequences of his conduct?

2. Was the employer's rule or order reasonably related to efficient and safe operations?

3. Did management investigate before administering the discipline?

4. Was the investigation fair and objective?

5. Did the investigation produce substantial evidence or proof of guilt?

6. Were the rules, orders, and penalties applied evenhandedly and without discrimination to all employees?

7. Was the penalty reasonably related to the seriousness of the offense and the past record?[50]

As a principle, it also has been argued that workers should have three rights regarding work to maintain self-respect:

- The right to employment
- The right to equal opportunity
- The right to participate in job-related decisions[51]

These rights are less entitlements than goals and depend on market conditions. Just cause termination is problematic when other forms of employer discrimination are determined, such as discrimination in age, gender, disability, race, national origin, and other Title VII areas. For example, an Ohio jury awarded a 68-year-old woman $30.6 million in an age discrimination lawsuit after a jury ruled that the company violated her rights by refusing to give her another job within the company when it terminated her from her management position.[52]

Due Process   Due process is one of the most important underlying rights employees have in the workplace because it affects most of their other rights. Due process refers to the right to have an impartial and fair hearing regarding employers' decisions, procedures, and rules that affect employees. As applied in the workplace, due process essentially refers to grievance procedures.

At a more general level, due process rights protect employees from arbitrary and illegitimate uses of power. These rights are based on the Fifth and Fourteenth Amendments of the Constitution, which state that no person shall be deprived of "life, liberty, or property, without the due process of law."

Patricia Werhane[53] states that the following corporate procedural mechanisms are needed to ensure employees' right to due process:

- Right to a public hearing
- Right to have peer evaluations
- Right to obtain external arbitration
- Right to an open, mutually approved grievance procedure

The right to due process applies to other employee rights, such as those involving privacy; safety and health; safe working environment;

holding meetings and gatherings; and hiring, firing, and other human resource decisions.

Right to Privacy Employees' right to privacy remains one of the most debated and controversial rights. It raises these questions: Where does the employer's control over employee behavior, space, time, and property begin and end? What freedoms and liberties do employees have with employer property rights? What rights do employers have to protect their private property, earnings, and costs from employees? The U.S. Constitution does not actually refer to a person's right to privacy; the working definition of employees' right to privacy has come to mean "to be left alone." Privacy in the workplace also can refer to employees' right to autonomy and to determine "when, how, and to what extent information about them is communicated to others."[54]

The extent of an employee's privacy in the workplace remains an unsettled area of controversy. The definition of what constitutes an employee's privacy is still somewhat problematic, including the notion of psychological privacy (involving an employee's inner life) and the notion of physical privacy (involving an employee's space and time).[55] In the 1965 *Griswold* v. *Connecticut* case, the Supreme Court ruled that the Constitution guarantees individuals a "zone of privacy" around them into which the government cannot intrude. Proponents of this definition argue that this zone includes personnel records and files and protection against polygraph and psychological testing and surveillance in the workplace. The ruling also is intended to protect employees in their after-work activities; their need for peace and quiet in the workplace; their dress, manners, and grooming; and their personal property in the workplace. Identifying this "zone of privacy" has proved complicated, especially in cyberspace and the use of technological surveillance.

Technology and Employee Privacy Although employee privacy rights remain largely undefined regarding uses and abuses of emerging technologies in the workplace, the following main types of court-upheld privacy violations and permissible employee privacy inquiries can serve as guidelines. Court-upheld privacy violations include:

1. Intrusion (locker room and bathroom surveillance)
2. Publication of private matters
3. Disclosure of medical records
4. Appropriation of an employee's name for commercial uses
5. Eavesdropping on employee conversations and retrieving or accessing employee e-mail (if unauthorized)

Permissible employee privacy inquiries include:

1. Criminal history inquiries
2. Credit history inquiries
3. Access to medical records[56]

Polygraph and Psychological Testing

Employers are particularly concerned about employee privacy rights regarding testing. Polygraph and psychological testing and other related techniques that many managers would like to use to prevent and detect crime in the workplace may constitute violation of employee rights. Workplace theft has been estimated by the U.S. Department of Commerce to cost in excess of $40 billion a year in the United States.[57] Here are some of the issues surrounding the use of polygraphs and psychological testing:

1. These tests are not reliable or valid; they are only indicators.
2. The tests, to some extent, can be manipulated and influenced by the operators.
3. The tests may include irrelevant questions (such as those pertaining to gender, lifestyle, religion, and after-work activities) that invade a person's privacy.
4. Employees do not have control over the test results or how the information is used.

Researchers in the field of honesty testing have concluded that only 1.7% (at worst) to 13.6% (at best) of such tests are accurate.[58]

Workplace Surveillance

Surveillance of employees at work (that is, employers using technology to spy on and invade workers' privacy) is also a subject of concern. Software programs are used to monitor workers who use computer terminals.[59] Employers can detect the speed of employees' work, number and length of phone calls made and received, breaks taken, when machines are in use, and so on. Although some form of work-related monitoring is certainly legal and even necessary, the ethical issues that the American Civil Liberties Union (ACLU) raises are the possible invasion of employee privacy and fair treatment. What type of information does an employer have a right to, and what effects do stress and anxiety from monitoring have on employee welfare? The Electronic Communications Privacy Act renders electronic eavesdropping through computer-to-computer transmissions, private videoconferences, and cellular phones illegal.

A study released by the Society for Human Resource Management, a trade association in Alexandria, Virginia, showed that 80% of the organizations in the study used e-mail. Only 36% of those groups had policies concerning e-mail use and only 32% had written privacy policies. The issue of individual employee privacy remains somewhat undefined in the workplace.[60, 61]

Internet Use in the Workplace   This is another undefined area regarding employee use of technology that requires the employer's development of "appropriate use policies," or AUPs. Millions of messages are estimated to pass through the Internet every hour. Instant Messengering (IM: real-time text conversation that takes place in private online chat areas) is growing in the workplace and causing companies problems. Fifty-three million adult Internet users traded instant messages in 2004, up 29% from 2000. Among users who are 18 to 27 years of age, 46% use IM more than e-mail. Employers are concerned about IM informal conversations that waste time.[62]

Jo Tucker, head of labor and employment practices at Morrison and Foerster, a law firm based in Irvine, California, stated that "if a worker is using a computer in a company office, on company time, privacy is what the employer says it is."[63] Without AUPs, Internet use in the workplace remains a guessing game between employer and employee. An employee Internet use policy depends on the company, its corporate culture, and the nature of its business. The policy must have the involvement and endorsement of top-level leadership. Monitoring capability, with employee awareness, must also accompany the policy. As J. Martin states, "A clear AUP policy effectively removes employee expectations of privacy on the Internet, eliminating potential lawsuits."[64] All use policies should also be spelled out clearly with no ambiguities and with simple, easy, enforceable rules. Part of such a policy involves the security of data for the entire company, because the reputation of the system and violations of it involve not only employees but also all stakeholders. A policy on Internet use can help companies in the following ways: (1) save employee work time, (2) prevent tying up phone lines and computer disk space that could be used for vital company business, (3) prevent exposing sensitive company data stored on computers to outside attack, and (4) prevent creations of conditions that enable employee harassment of each other and, ultimately, of the company.

Guidelines offered to employers regarding employee privacy include:

- Inform employees not to assume privacy in the workplace.
- Require employees to acknowledge the company's privacy policy in writing.
- Use private information only for legitimate purposes.

FIGURE 6.4   Quick Tips for Office Romance

1. Know your company's policy. Dating a co-worker is not illegal, but if it violates your office's policy, it could get you fired. Check with your human resources department or make some discreet inquiries.
2. Test the waters. Don't jump headfirst into an office fling. Take time to weigh all considerations and possible consequences.
3. Establish some ground rules. Talk to your partner early on about how you plan to handle the relationship and what you would do if things turn sour. Make sure you're both on the same page.
4. Be considerate and professional. Even if your co-workers are accepting of the relationship, no one wants to see public displays of affection. Blatant flirting or physical contact could make you fodder for gossip, too.
5. Stay focused on your job. Being in love is distracting. But don't let the relationship detract from your professional responsibilities.
6. Don't play favorites. Of course you want to protect your loved one's interests, but don't let your bias seep into the office. Consider avoiding tasks where a conflict of interest might develop.
7. Be honest. No matter how cautious you are, the secret's bound to get out. Be prepared to confirm the rumor and plan on telling your boss that you will keep your relationship professional at work.
8. Proceed with caution. Lawsuits and sexual harassment issues are always a possibility if the relationship creates a hostile work environment or causes discriminated or special treatment of any kind. Be extra cautious if you're considering a romantic relationship with a boss or a subordinate. Many company policies specifically forbid liaisons between upper- and lower-level employees.

Source: Minarcek, A. (June 29, 2004). Taboo on office romance fading. *Cox News Service*, http://www.azcentral.com/ent/dating/articles/0629officeromance29.html. Reprinted with permission.

- Limit access to private information about employees to only those with a need to know.

- Secure employee medical records separately from other personnel files.

- Obtain signed permission releases and waivers before using an employee's name or photograph in any commercial advertisement, promotional material, or training film.[65]

Dating in the Workplace   As employees spend more time in the workplace, it is not uncommon for attraction and dating to occur. A 2003 survey of 390 managers and executives by the AMA (American Management Association) found that 30% reported they had dated a co-worker, and two thirds said employees' dating in the workplace was not prohibited. "Of those 67%, 96% said it was okay to date co-workers, and 24% said it was okay for employees to date their bosses."[66] Issues arise whenever problems in the dating relationships occur. Gossip, accusations, even sexual harassment complaints can and do occur. Guidelines offered in Figure 6.4 can help protect both employers and employees.

Drug Testing and Privacy Rights   Privacy is also an issue in drug testing. Advocates for employee drug testing argue that company health costs and costs associated with sick and lost (nonproductive) days are affected when employees contract serious diseases, such as AIDS, or suffer from drug and alcohol addiction. Also, in industries (such as the airline industry or nuclear plant operations) where drug abuse can cost the lives of innocent people, screening drug abusers is viewed as in the public interest. Those who oppose forced employee drug testing argue that the practice violates employees' rights to due process and privacy.

The following guidelines can be used by companies for policy development in drug-testing programs[67]:

1. Tests should be administered only for jobs that have a clear and present potential to cause harm to others.

2. Procedural testing limitations should include previous notice to those being tested.

3. Employees tested should be notified of the results.

4. Employees tested should be informed that they are entitled to appeal the results.

5. The employer should demonstrate how the information will be kept confidential (or destroyed).

Four steps managers can take to develop corporate policy guidelines to prepare for privacy regulation in general are[68]:

1. *Prepare a "privacy impact statement."* This analysis of the potential privacy implications should be taken as part of all proposals for new and expanded systems.

2. *Construct a comprehensive privacy plan.* The privacy impact statement provides the input for planning; the plan specifies all that has to be achieved.

3. *Train employees who handle personal information.* Make employees aware of protecting privacy and of the particular policies and procedures that should be followed.

4. *Make privacy part of social responsibility programs.* Keep organizational members informed about company plans regarding privacy issues, with or without regulatory pressures.[69]

Genetic Discrimination   Should employers perform DNA testing on employees when several areas of discrimination could surface? Two examples are: (1) Employment based on a person's predisposition to a disease could negatively and unfairly affect hiring, firing, and benefits; and (2) insurance companies that could obtain an employee's

genetic information would also be able to deny a person certain benefits. One lawsuit, settled in April 2001, was filed against Burlington
Northern Santa Fe Railway Company in Fort Worth, Texas. The railroad agreed to stop genetic testing. Testing had been required for those
employees who filed claims for carpal tunnel syndrome. On the other
hand, if scientists can master stem cells to tailor-make organ or tissue
transplants to understand and eventually treat the underlying mechanisms of diseases, why shouldn't the federal government fund this
research and practice?

The Genetic Nondiscrimination in Health Insurance and Employment Act was introduced by Senator Thomas Daschle of South Dakota
and Congresswoman Louise Slaughter from New York in 2001. This Act
would prevent genetic testing of employees. President Bush's reported
interest regarding genetic discrimination has been on placing a cap on
damages that might arise from such lawsuits, although he did sign legislation in 1997, while he was governor of Texas, that prohibited genetic
discrimination in employment and group health plans.[70] The testing
and use of genetic information of employees remains to be fully defined
and enforced in the workplace and in legislation.[71]

The Right to Know and Workplace Health and Safety

Every employee is entitled to a safe, healthy workplace environment,
because one of ten employees in private industry suffers from an industrial accident or disease while working. Information about unsafe, hazardous workplace conditions and some form of protection from these
hazards are needed.[72] Employees have a right to know the nature and
extent of hazardous risks to which they are exposed and to be informed
and trained about and protected from those risks. Right-to-know laws
have been passed in 20 states since the mid-1980s.[73]

The Occupational Safety and Health Administration (OSHA) is the
federal agency responsible for researching, identifying, and determining workplace health hazards; setting safety and health standards; and
enforcing the standards. These remain major tasks. Critics of OSHA
claim they are too overwhelming for one agency to monitor and execute effectively. The missions and budgets of government regulatory
agencies—including OSHA—are also a function of the politics of the
governing administration and Congress.

Smoking in the Workplace: Whose Rights?

Legislation has,
or is projected to, ban smoking in public places including workplaces in several countries including the U.S.[74] Among stakeholders
who have argued and lobbied against smoking in the workplace are
the Environmental Protection Agency (EPA), OSHA, and ASH (Action

on Smoking and Health—the powerful national antismoking group). Pro-smoking advocates include the tobacco industry and its lobbying group, the Tobacco Institute, and the Bakery, Confectionery, and Tobacco Workers union. OSHA has not been able to place an absolute ban on smoking in all workplaces to date, even though tobacco has been shown to be one of the leading causes of death. The issue reflects societal habits and attitudes and the politics and economics of the industry.[75]

Consider these facts. It is estimated that 28% of Americans age 18 and over are smokers. Approximately 80% of workers are protected to some extent by a workplace policy, and nearly half of all indoor workers are employed in smoke-free workplaces. Twenty states and the District of Columbia have laws that restrict smoking in private-sector workplaces.[76] Almost 75% of 1,794 facility managers in a survey claim they ban or segregate smoking in their workplaces.[77] One of OSHA's strategies has been to link smoking in the workplace to indoor air-quality problems and pollution and to legislate against it. The Clean Air Act is one such move to further restrict indoor smoking in public facilities. Employers need to keep track of laws and regulations that affect employee rights regarding smoking in the workplace.

The Right to Organize and Form Unions

Workers have a right to organize, just as owners and managers do. Individuals, as workers and citizens, have the right of free association to seek common ends. This also means employees have a right to form unions. Although unions have a right to exist, they have no special rights beyond those due organizations with legal status.[78]

Plant Closings and Employee Rights

Companies have the right to relocate and transfer operations to any place they choose. If firms can find cheaper labor, raw materials, and transportation costs; lower taxes; no unions; and other business advantages for making a profit elsewhere, they often close plants and move. Companies also close plants because of loss of competitiveness, financial losses, and other legitimate economic reasons. The ethical questions posed to corporate managers regarding plant closings are: What rights do the employees who are affected by the closing have? What responsibilities does the company have toward the affected communities, and even toward the national economy?

Since August 1988, companies with more than 100 employees must by law give 60-day notice to workers before closing. Employees also have moral rights—to be treated fairly, equally, and with justice—when companies decide to relocate or close. Employees have the right to be compensated for the costs of retraining, transferring, and relocating; they have rights to severance pay and to outplacement and support programs that assist them in finding alternative employment; and they have the right to have their pension, health, and retirement plans honored.[79]

Employees also should be given the right to find a new owner for the plant and to explore the possibility of employee ownership of the plant before it is closed.[80] These rights extend beyond workers and include the welfare of the communities where the plant operated. Plant closings affect jobs, careers, families, and the local tax base and can even negatively affect the regional and national economies, when sizable operations are shut down or moved abroad.

Whatever the motivations for corporate closings or transfer of facilities, the rights of employees and local community groups stand, even though these rights are often negotiated against the utilitarian interests of corporations in specific economic contexts. As mentioned earlier, with globalization and increased pressures on corporate profits, plant closings have become almost commonplace. Responsible employers keep employees informed of planned facility closings.[81]

The Family and Medical Leave Act   The Family and Medical Leave Act (FMLA) was enacted into law in 1993, eight years after it was introduced in Congress by Christopher Dodd, William Clay, and Patricia Schroeder. The final rules were established in 1995. The FMLA entitles eligible employees to a maximum of 12 weeks of unpaid leave per year for the birth or adoption of a child, to care for a spouse or immediate family member with a serious health condition, or when an employee is unable to work because of personal illness. The 12 weeks need not be used consecutively because intermittent leave or reduced work schedules are allowed under the act. To be considered eligible, an employee must have been employed for a continuous 12-month period and for at least 1,250 hours during the year preceding the leave.

Companies that employ at least 50 people within a 75-mile radius are mandated to offer such leave. The employer is required to maintain any preexisting health coverage during the leave. Once the leave is concluded, the employee must be reinstated to the same position or an equivalent job. An equivalent position must have the same pay, benefits, working conditions, authority, and responsibilities.

Employers have the right to request a 30-day advance notice for foreseeable absences and may require employees to present evidence to support medically necessary leave. Employers may request employees to obtain a second medical opinion at the employer's expense.

Employers may deny reinstatement of employment to "key employees." Such employees must be among the 10% highest paid company employees, and their absence must have a serious economic impact on their organization. It is the duty of employers to inform employees of their status as "key employees" when they request a leave.

Major problems with the FMLA, from employees' experience, have been serious illnesses (e.g., *Price* v. *City of Fort Wayne*); from employers' perspective, rising health and company costs; and from government's viewpoint, administrative requirements (e.g., *Viereck* v. *City of Gloucester City*). Employers often unintentionally violate the sometimes confusing and contradictory FMLA.[82] The courts have also tended to rule in favor of employees who have less serious and even minor illnesses. Finally, based on a 7-year study of more than 7,500 adults, it was found that the burden of not having a national or state-by-state family paid leave policy falls heaviest on the middle class and the working poor. Although 40% of Americans in the top quartile of income lacked a sick leave policy at work, 54% of Americans in the second quartile, 63% in the third quartile, and 76% of workers in the bottom quartile lacked sick leave . . . Although 41% of working parents in the top quartile of income have 2 weeks or less of sick leave and vacation leave, 57% of parents in the second quartile, 68% in the third quartile, and an astounding 84% in the bottom quartile had 2 weeks or less of sick and vacation leave.[83, 84]

6.4 DISCRIMINATION, EQUAL EMPLOYMENT OPPORTUNITY, AND AFFIRMATIVE ACTION

It is difficult to imagine that throughout most of the 19th century, women in America could not vote, serve on juries, issue lawsuits in their own name, or initiate legal contracts if they lost their property to their husbands. In an 1873 Supreme Court decision, *Bradwell* v. *Illinois,* a woman had "no legal existence, separate from her husband, who was regarded as her head and representative in the social state."[85]

It is also difficult to imagine the legal status of black people in the United States in 1857. In the Dred Scott case, one of the opinions of the Supreme Court considered blacks as "beings of an inferior order . . . and so far inferior that they had no rights that the white man was bound to respect."[86]

More recently, discrimination has surfaced in a number of categories. Racial profiling remains an issue. Black individuals are more likely to be stopped and arrested by police than whites. Income disparities between whites and minorities continue to rise. The average income of a black family was 65% of a white family income; in 1994, that percentage was 63%.[87] The ratio of women's annual pay to men's for full-time employment was 83.8 cents on the dollar during the last decade. Women still make, on average, 76 cents on the dollar for comparable work compared with men.[88] It is against this background that the doctrines, laws, and policies of discrimination, equal opportunity, and affirmative action must be considered.

Discrimination   Discriminatory practices in employer–employee relationships include unequal or disparate treatment of individuals and groups.[89] Unequal or preferential treatment is based on irrelevant criteria, such as gender, race, color, religion, national origin, or disability. Systematic and systemic discrimination is based on historical and institutionally ingrained unequal and disparate treatment against minorities, the disadvantaged, and women.

Examples of contemporary and systemic discrimination in employer–employee relationships are found in practices such as recruitment, screening, promotion, termination, conditions of employment, and discharge.[90] These practices are attributed to closed employment systems and practices resulting from seniority systems, "old boy networks," and arbitrary job classifications. Recruiting procedures that are biased toward certain groups and that do not openly advertise to minority groups are discriminatory. Screening practices that exclude certain groups and that use biased tests or qualifications are discriminatory. Promotion procedures that have "glass ceilings" (i.e., invisible discriminatory barriers to advancement) for women and minority groups are discriminatory.[91] Seniority tracks that favor white males or other groups over minorities or women are discriminatory. Terminating employees on the basis of sex, age, race, or national origin is discriminatory. Since September 11, 2001, Middle Eastern individuals have faced greater discrimination in the U.S.

On October 26, 2001, President Bush signed the USA Patriot Act into law. The intent of the Act is to unite and strengthen America by "providing appropriate Tools required to intercept and obstruct terrorism." "While many of its provisions were designed to bolster domestic security, enhance surveillance procedures, etc., Title III of the Act, 'International Money Laundering Abatement and Anti-Terrorism Financing Act of 2001,' contains many new provisions and amendments to the Bank Secrecy Act and the Money Laundering Control Act of 1986. These will affect both financial and non-financial institutions in how they do business."[92]

The Act is constantly evolving, adding new requirements and compliance procedures. Provisions are intended to establish anti-money laundering compliance programs. "The legislation adds new crimes which are prerequisites to the crime of money laundering. These include terrorism, foreign corruption, certain export controls, certain foreign crimes and extraditable offenses."[93] The costs and complexity of implementing these laws has and is challenging many banks and other financial institutions to stretch beyond their original mission, means, and capabilities. Although the intent is praiseworthy, ethical questions remain, "To what extent will these laws protect or punish the innocent, including the business institutions who are the implementers?"

Equal Employment Opportunity and the Civil Rights Act

Title VII of the Civil Rights Act of 1964 makes discrimination on the basis of gender, race, color, religion, or national origin in any term, condition, or privilege of employment illegal. The law prohibits discrimination in hiring, classifying, referring, assigning, promoting, training, retraining, conducting apprenticeships, firing, and dispensing wages and fringe benefits. The Civil Rights Act also created the Equal Employment Opportunity Commission (EEOC) as the administrative and implementation agency to investigate complaints that individuals submit. The EEOC negotiates and works with the Justice Department regarding complaints; however, the EEOC cannot enforce the law except through grievances.

The Civil Rights Act of 1991 extended, for the first time, punitive damages to victims of employment discrimination. This law states that job bias on the basis of gender, disability, religion, or national origin will be punished as severely as job discrimination based on race. It also makes it easier for job-bias plaintiffs to win lawsuits. This legislation shifts the legal burden of proof to the employer, who must defend any intentional or unintentional employment bias, especially if the practice in question has a "disparate impact" on minorities or women. Under this law, the employer must demonstrate that the alleged discriminatory act is "job-related for the position in question and consistent with business necessity."[94] "Job-related" and "business necessity" are undefined and are determined by the courts. The act specifies that employers with more than 500 employees could be liable for up to $300,000 in compensatory and punitive damages. Smaller companies are liable for less, depending on the number of workers they employ.

The Equal Employment Opportunity Act of 1972 amended the 1964 act to empower the EEOC to enforce the law by filing grievances from individuals, job applicants, and employees in the courts. All private employers with 15 or more employees fall under the jurisdiction of the revised act, with the exception of bona fide tax-exempt private clubs. All private and public educational institutions and employment agencies are covered by the law. Labor unions (local, national, and international) with 15 or more members are included. Joint labor-management committees that administer apprenticeship, training, and retraining programs are also under this law's jurisdiction.

There were 58,124 charges filed through Title VII in 2000, which resulted in recovery of $149 million in monetary benefits to workers who had been discriminated against.[95]

Age and Discrimination in the Workplace The Age Discrimination in Employment Act (ADEA) of 1967, revised in 1978, prohibits employers from discriminating against individuals based on their age (between ages 40 and 70) in hiring, promotions, terminations, and other employment practices. In 1987, ADEA again was amended when Congress banned any fixed retirement age. The EEOC also issued a final rule in 2001 that aimed at prohibiting contracts requiring terminated employees to give back severance benefits if they challenged their terminations under the ADEA. "The new regulation takes effect at a time when several large corporations have announced significant layoffs. In recent years, companies have increasingly tried to tie severance deals during mass terminations to waivers of ADEA rights, as many employees who lose their jobs in such actions are over 40 and covered by the statute."[96]

Age discrimination also applies to younger individuals. Hanigan Consulting Group of New York surveyed 170 recent graduates, some scheduled to receive master's and doctoral degrees. The firm found that some applicants were asked questions that clearly violated antidiscrimination laws; for example: Do you intend to get married and have children? What will your boyfriend think of you working long hours? How old are you? Are you married? The basic guideline, according to a Boston attorney with Seyfarth, Shaw, is "if the question is not business-related and there is no legitimate business reason for asking it, then do not ask it."[97]

Comparable Worth and Equal Pay The Equal Pay Act of 1963, amended in 1972, prohibits discriminatory payment of wages and overtime pay based on gender. The law, in large part, is based on the doctrine of "comparable worth." This doctrine and the Equal Pay Act hold that women should be paid wages comparable to men who hold jobs that require equal skill, effort, and responsibility and that have the same working conditions. This law addresses this inequity and also applies to executive, professional, sales, and administrative positions. In 2000, President Clinton failed to get the Paycheck Fairness Act into legislation. That act would have enabled the EEOC to collect and monitor data on pay and compensation from employers based on gender, race, and national origin. Fines could have been levied against companies with unequal pay scales. The Republican-led Congress would not have likely passed the act had it been proposed by the Clinton Administration.[98] Although glass ceilings and lower wages for comparable work prevail in the U.S. workplace for women, other gains have been made, as previously discussed.

Affirmative Action   *Affirmative action* programs are a proactive attempt to recruit applicants from minority groups to create opportunities for those who, otherwise, because of past and present discriminatory employment practices, would be excluded from the job market. Affirmative action programs attempt to make employment practices blind to color, gender, national origin, disability, and age. Although the doctrine of equal opportunity states that everyone should have an equal chance at obtaining a job and a promotion, affirmative action goes further. For example, Richard DeGeorge stated, "Affirmative action implies a set of specific result-oriented procedures designed to achieve equal employment opportunity at a pace beyond that which would occur normally."[99]

Affirmative action programs were designed to set goals, quotas, and time frames for companies to hire and promote women and minorities in proportion to their numbers in the labor force and in the same or similar occupational categories within the company.

Courts have supported and eroded affirmative action approaches in the Civil Rights Act. Because of the changing social, political, and demographic landscape in the U.S., different membership on the Supreme Court, and evidence of reverse discrimination, changes in affirmative action law are occurring. Affirmative action remains a controversial topic and policy. Individuals' rights are violated when affirmation action programs seek to protect particular groups. Also, in a market economy where individual achievement based on merit is encouraged and rewarded, it seems unfair that arbitrary quotas should supersede those who do excel. On the other side of the controversy are advocates of affirmative action who claim that the playing field still is not level in U.S. corporate, educational, and other institutions whose officers select, hire, reward, and promote based on race, gender, national origin, ability, and other biases.

Four arguments that have been offered to explain and summarize affirmative action as it applies to hiring, promotions, and terminations are:

1. Affirmative action does not justify hiring unqualified minority group members over qualified white males. All individuals must be qualified for the positions in question.

2. Qualified women and minority members can be given preference morally, on the basis of gender or race, over equally qualified white males to achieve affirmative action goals.

3. Qualified women and minority members can be given preference morally over better-qualified white males, also, to achieve affirmative action goals.

4. Companies must make adequate progress toward achieving affirmative action goals even though preferential hiring is not mandatory.[100,101]

Ethics and Affirmative Action   The ethical principles behind affirmative action are often debated. Affirmative action as a doctrine is derived from several ethical principles that serve as bases for laws.

First, the *principle of justice* can be used to argue for affirmative action, by claiming that because white males have historically dominated and continue to unfairly dominate the highest paying, most prestigious employment positions in society, members of groups who have been excluded from comparable employment opportunities because of past and present discriminatory practices deserve to be compensated through affirmative action programs embodied in equal opportunity laws. Opponents of affirmative action argue that it is unfair and unjust that the distribution of benefits be based only on a few categories (race, sex, ethnicity) rather than on achievement or other criteria.

Second, a *utilitarian principle* can be used to support affirmative action by claiming that such programs help the majority of people in a society. Opponents argue that affirmative action cannot be shown or proven to work or that its benefits exceed its costs.

Finally, using a *rights principle*, proponents of affirmative action can argue that protected groups have a right to different treatment because these groups have not had equal or fair access to benefits as other groups have. In fact, the rights of minorities, women, and other underprivileged groups have been denied and violated regarding access to education, jobs, and other institutional opportunities. Opponents using the rights principle argue that the rights of all individuals are equal under the law. The controversy continues as the economic, social, political, and demographic environments change.

Reverse Discrimination: Arguments against Affirmative Action   Arguments against affirmative action are directed toward the doctrine itself and against its implementation of quotas. The doctrine has been criticized on the grounds that nondiscrimination requires discrimination (that is, reverse discrimination). Reverse discrimination is alleged to occur when an equally qualified woman or member of a minority group is given preference over a white male for a job or when less qualified members of an ethnic minority are given hiring preference over white males through a quota system. Affirmative action, opponents argue, discriminates against gender and race, that is, white males. Some even say affirmative action discriminates against age: white, middle-aged males.

Another major argument against affirmative action says that individuals are held responsible for injustices for which they were not and are not responsible. Why should all contemporary and future white males, as a group, have to compensate for discriminatory practices others in this demographic category once committed or now commit?

Although these claims have some validity, proponents of affirmative action argue that injustices from discrimination have been institutionalized against minority groups. It happens that white males continue to benefit from the competitive disadvantages that past and present discriminatory practices have created for others. To compensate and correct for these systemic disadvantages based on race, gender, and other irrelevant (i.e., not related to employment) characteristics, social affirmative action goals and programs must be implemented. Still, the law is not a perfect means to correct past or present injustices. People of all races will continue to be hurt by discrimination and reverse discrimination practices. In the meantime, the court system will continue to use civil rights laws, affirmative action guidelines, and moral reasoning to decide on a case-by-case basis the justice and fairness of employment practices.

The following discussion is a summary of four notable Supreme Court cases and one U.S. Circuit Court case that illustrates how affirmative action and discrimination issues have been addressed.

Supreme Court Rulings and Reverse Discrimination

The Bakke Case Allan Bakke, a white male, sued the Regents of the University of California at Davis because he was denied admission to the medical school in 1973. He sued on the basis of reverse discrimination. Bakke charged that the university gave preferential treatment to less qualified applicants who belonged to minority groups. Of 100 places in the entering class of 1973, 84 were open for competitive admission; 16 places were given preference to candidates who belonged to minority groups. In 1978, the Supreme Court ruled, in a five-to-four vote, in favor of Bakke. The decision argued against strict quotas but upheld the criterion of race as a consideration in admissions policies. The ruling sent the message that quotas based on race were illegal when no previous discrimination had been proved. However, quotas could be used to offset inequalities as part of settlements when previous discrimination was shown.[102]

The Weber Case   Brian Weber, a white male, sued his employer, Kaiser Aluminum and Chemical Corporation, and the Steelworkers Union because he had been discriminated against by his exclusion from a quota-regulated training program. Weber won the case at the lower District Court and at the Court of Appeals. However, in 1979, the Supreme Court, in a five-to-two vote, overturned these decisions *(Weber v. Kaiser Aluminum and Chemical Corporation)*. The Court ruled that blacks can be given special consideration for jobs that have been held predominantly by whites and that affirmative action programs rectify "manifest racial imbalances." The message the Supreme Court sent to employers was that reverse-discrimination charges should not prevent them from implementing affirmative action programs. In this case, white citizens were not displaced or hurt because of the quota-based training program.

The Stotts Case   Carl Stotts, a black district fire chief in Memphis, sued the Memphis Fire Department in a class-action suit in 1977, charging that the department discriminated against him and other black citizens in its policy of "last hired, first fired" (or LIFO, which is an acronym for "last in, first out"). The city announced layoffs in 1981 because of a budget deficit. It implemented the layoffs with a union-negotiated seniority policy. Stotts won at the District Court level but lost in an appeal by the city of Memphis and the labor union in the Supreme Court in 1984. The majority vote in the Supreme Court ruled that bona fide seniority systems are protected under the 1964 Civil Rights Act and could not be disrupted, especially during layoff periods. The ruling, in effect, sent a message to employers that bona fide seniority systems are blind to skin color.

The **Adarand Constructors v. Pena** *Case*   The Court's attitude on minority preference programs has begun to change. In 1995, its ruling in *Adarand Constructors v. Pena* effectively eliminated mandatory special consideration of contracts of minorities. The case questioned the legality of a federal mandate that required at least 10% of federally funded highway projects to go to businesses owned by minorities or women. The majority opinion, written by Justice Sandra Day O'Connor, states that all racial classifications must be held to rigorous judicial standards, whether passed by Congress or the states, and must be narrowly tailored to advance governmental interests. This overrules the previous 1990 decision that allowed Congress to mandate a program specifically designed to increase the number of minority broadcasters. In *Missouri v. Jenkins,* the Supreme Court reviewed a federally directed racial integration program that required the state of

Missouri to spend more than $200 million a year to improve inner-city schools. The Court ruling did not dismantle the program but questioned the methods used to measure its progress.

The Hopwood *v.* Texas *Case*

A U.S. Circuit Court ruled that the University of Texas could not use race as a determining factor for admissions. In this case, several white students sued the school when they were not admitted because of the school's policy to admit a certain number of nonwhite students. This ruling opened the door for other educational systems to re-evaluate their admission quotas. It also may have the potential to limit admission policies that consider the racial diversity of students. If this case affects other educational institutions, affirmative action policies could be questioned in business as well. Presently, it is not easy to predict the outcome. The issue remains: Is the playing field level or not in the U.S. regarding race?[103]

The Grutter *v.* University of Michigan Law School *Case*

A federal judge in Detroit ruled in March of 2001 that the race-conscious admissions system in the University of Michigan's law school is unconstitutional. "All racial distinctions are inherently suspect and presumptively invalid. Whatever solution the law school elects to pursue, it must be race-neutral," wrote Judge Bernard Friedman of the United States District Court in Detroit. This case represents a continuing push to ban the use of race in admissions policies, initiated in 1995 when the University of California Regents banned the asking for racial identity on admissions applications. That decision influenced a Federal Court of Appeals decision in 1996 to also ban the practice of asking for racial identity in Texas, Mississippi, and Louisiana. Since then, voters in California and Washington have not accepted affirmative action in state contracts and educational settings.[104]

Affirmative action has come under attack since 1991. The Supreme Court has moved toward a more conservative stance with the appointment of Clarence Thomas and David Souter in 1990. Although the Court has not ended affirmative action, it did establish a "strict scrutiny" standard, making it more difficult for current affirmative action programs to be enacted. Further evidence that the Supreme Court has moved toward more conservative positions was their 1997 refusal to hear an appeal by opponents of Proposition 209, the California ballot that amended the state's constitution to prohibit preferential treatment on the basis of race and color by state agencies.[105]

These laws certainly are not inclusive of all the equal-opportunity legislation or federal policy directives passed and amended from the 1960s through the 1990s, but they represent some of the prominent ones.

Laws alone cannot, nor perhaps should they, guarantee or equalize employment opportunities, fairness, and justice to members of groups that have been discriminated against historically and that experience bias currently. Stereotypes and biases can be manipulated through subtle, legal means, such as in the ways job descriptions and evaluations are written and carried out, by the types of qualifications included in job descriptions, in advertising methods for jobs, and by other exclusionary conditions and practices of employing and terminating people. Still, equal opportunity laws and their enforcement change and evolve in free-market systems and representative democracies. As the consensus opinions of voters and power blocs change, so do laws and policies. Laws set social goals. The pursuit or abandonment of those goals depends on their perceived value and utility by the majority of voters, or, in other instances, the courts. It is impossible to separate the politics and economics from the judicial and legislative processes in a capitalistic, representative democracy.

In June 2002, the Supreme Court upheld the equal protection clause of the 14th Amendment that guarantees equal treatment under the law by condoning the University of Michigan Law School's practice of using race to help integrate the institution's student body. The second Supreme Court opinion ruled that the admissions program in the university's undergraduate school violated the equal protection clause of the Constitution by giving minorities a bonus of 20 points in a 150-point system for race. "Two white students have sued the university claiming they were denied admission in favor of less-qualified minorities before the Supreme Court ruled. They want a federal judge to award damages to 30,000 white and Asian students who may have been illegally denied admission to make way for other minority students."[106]

UCLA Law Professor Richard H. Sander argues that affirmative-action programs are harmful for African-American law school students because high attrition rates resulting from admitting students who fail to do the work will, in turn, turn away African-American students from entering. Sander's opponents disagree with his methods and analysis. The debate over just and unfair affirmative action policies and procedures, especially in university admittance policies, continues.

6.5 SEXUAL HARASSMENT IN THE WORKPLACE

Sexual harassment was not a specific violation of federal law before 1981. It now may be difficult to imagine flagrant acts of sexual violation against women, but as recently as 20 years ago, when women worked in mines, they, like their male counterparts, were stripped and soaked in axle grease in a primitive hazing ritual, and then, unlike the male employees, the women were tied to wooden supports in spread-eagle positions.[107] The Senate hearings on sexual harassment charges against Supreme Court nominee Clarence Thomas awakened public and corporate concern about sexual harassment in society and the workplace. In addition, the overt sexual harassment of female U.S. Navy professionals also has brought attention to this issue. Although sexual harassment can be and is committed by both men and women, it is more often women who are the unwilling victims.

Sexual harassment remains among the most prominent civil rights issues in the workplace. There were 15,836 sexual harassment charges filed with the EEOC or state agencies in 2000 with $54.6 million paid in monetary benefits (not including monetary benefits obtained through litigation). TWA recently agreed to pay $2.6 million to settle a sexual harassment suit filed in 1998. The suit is one of the largest in New York State. The company will pay $1.5 million to nine women who worked in ground traffic control, passenger service, and maintenance. The *New York Times* reported that three women "accused three high-level managers of egregious sexual harassment that included groping and verbal abuse." Lawyers for the women said that the airline did nothing about repeated complaints taken to different levels of management before the suit was filed.[108]

What Is Sexual Harassment?   The Supreme Court ruled in 1986 that sexual harassment is illegal under Title VII of the 1964 Civil Rights Act and that when a "hostile environment" is created through sexual harassment in the workplace, thereby interfering with an employee's performance, the law is violated, regardless of whether economic harm is done or whether demands for sexual favors in exchange for raises, promotions, bonuses, and other employment-related opportunities are granted.[109]

Under Title VII, the EEOC guidelines (1980) define sexual harassment as follows:

Unwelcome sexual advances, requests for sexual favors, and other verbal or physical conduct of a sexual nature constitute sexual harassment when (1) submission to such conduct is made either explicitly or implicitly a term or condition of an individual's employment, (2) submission to or rejection of such conduct by an individual is used as the basis for employment decisions affecting such an individual, or (3) such conduct has the purpose or effect of unreasonably interfering with an individual's work performance or creating an intimidating, hostile, or offensive working environment.

The courts have defined sexual harassment as conduct ranging from blatant grabbing and touching to more subtle hints and suggestions about sex. Forms of sexual harassment include the following[110]:

- Unwelcome sexual advances
- Coercion
- Favoritism
- Indirect harassment
- Physical conduct
- Visual harassment (For example, courts have ruled that sexual harassment was committed when graffiti were written on men's bathroom walls about a female employee and when pornographic pictures were displayed in the workplace.)

Who Is Liable?   The EEOC guidelines place absolute liability on employers for actions and violations of the law by their managers and supervisors, whether or not the conduct was known, authorized, or forbidden by the employer. Employers also are liable for coworkers' conduct if the employer knew, or should have known, of the actions in question, unless the employer shows, after learning of the problem, that the company took immediate and appropriate action to correct the situation. Employers may be liable for harassment of nonemployees under the same conditions as those stated for coworkers.[111]

Moreover, under EEOC guidelines employers are responsible for establishing programs (and standards) that develop, train, and inform employees about sanctions and procedures for dealing with sexual harassment complaints (see Figure 6.5). It is in the employer's economic and moral interest to institute such programs, because courts mitigate damages against companies that have harassment prevention and training programs. Some of the leaders in establishing sexual harassment policies and programs are Nynex, AT&T, DuPont, Corning, and Honeywell, to mention only a few.

Tangible Employment Action and Vicarious Liability   A currently prominent feature of harassment cases is the concept of "tangible employment action," which Supreme Court Justice Anthony Kennedy described as "hiring, firing, failing to promote, reassignment with significantly different responsibilities or a decision causing a significant change in benefits."[112] An employer's defense against claims of harassment has been created in cases in which a hostile environment was evident but no tangible employment action occurred. In the

FIGURE 6.5	Sample Corporate Sexual Harassment Policy

1. Sexual harassment is a violation of the corporation's EEO policy. Abuse of anyone through sexist slurs or other objectionable conduct is offensive behavior.
2. Management must ensure that a credible program exists for handling sexual harassment problems. If complaints are filed, they should receive prompt consideration without fear of negative consequences.
3. When a supervisor is made aware of an allegation of sexual harassment, the following guidelines should be considered:
   a. Obtain information about the allegation through discussion with the complainant. Ask for and document facts about what was said, what was done, when and where it occurred, and what the complainant believes was the inappropriate behavior. In addition, find out if any other individuals observed the incident, or similar incidents, to the complainant's knowledge. This is an initial step. In no case does the supervisor handle the complaint process alone.
   b. If the complaint is from an hourly employee, a request for union representation at any point must be handled as described in the labor agreement.
   c. The immediate supervisor or the department head and the personnel department must be notified immediately. When a complaint is raised by, or concerns, an hourly employee, the local labor relations representative is to be advised. When a complaint is raised by or concerns a salaried employee, the personnel director is to be advised.
4. The personnel department must conduct a complete investigation of the complaint for hourly and salaried employees. The investigation is to be handled in a professional and confidential manner.

Source: Based on the General Motors corporate policy on sexual harassment.

Supreme Court decision in the case *Burlington Industries* v. *Ellerth,*

> Kimberly Ellerth's harasser threatened to take steps against her if she didn't comply with his wishes. Since he never carried out the threat, Ellerth's employment status was not negatively affected. However, her harassment was severe and pervasive, and Burlington was held liable for that instead.[113]

Severe and pervasive harassment that has no tangible employment action characterized another case, *Faragher* v. *City of Boca Raton.* In this case, it was determined that

> lifeguard Beth Faragher had been repeatedly harassed by two male supervisors for several years. She complained to other beach supervisors, but to no avail. Attorneys for the city argued that she had not complained to authorities at a high enough level. This defense laid the foundation for another key concept the Court stressed: "vicarious liability."[114]

Employers, under this concept, could be liable for harassment if it is committed by anyone present in the workplace and if it is brought to the attention of any manager or supervisor. Employers are liable for harassment by anyone who is present in the workplace (coworkers, customers, vendors), if the employers know or should have known about the harassment. Moreover, employers are liable for harassment by all supervisors, whether the employer knew about the harassment or not. This represents a significant change in sexual harassment liability.

Employer Guidelines with Extended Liability Rulings
Employers should:

- Exercise reasonable care to prevent and correct for any harassment. There should be an anti-harassment policy and a complaint procedure present, made known to every employee, readily available, and used in training. The EEOC enforcement guidelines provide an excellent source of training materials.
- Quickly and effectively address all harassment complaints.[115]

Individual Guidelines
Although sexual harassment often occurs as part of a power issue (i.e., people in more-powerful positions exert pressure over people in less-powerful posts), a frequent observation is that men and women tend to see sexual harassment differently. This certainly does not justify legally or morally unwelcome sexual advances. It does suggest, however, that employers need to provide adequate education, training, and role-playing between the sexes so that gender differences in perceptions and feelings on what constitutes sexual harassment can be understood. Some practical guidelines that employees (men, in this instance) can use to check their motives and behavior regarding sexual harassment include the following[116]:

- If you are unsure whether you have offended a woman, ask her. If you did offend her, apologize, and don't do it again.
- Talk over your behavior with noninvolved women and with men you can trust not to make a mockery of your concerns.
- Ask yourself how you would feel if a man behaved toward your daughter the way you feel you may be behaving toward women.
- Ask yourself also if you would act this way if the shoe were on the other foot, if the woman were your boss or if she were physically stronger or more powerful than you.
- Most of all, don't interpret a woman's silence as consent. Silence is, at least, a "red light." Through silence, a woman may be trying to send you a signal of discomfort. Be very certain that your comments or behaviors are welcome, and if they are not, stop them.

Sexual Harassment and Foreign Firms in the United States
Two foreign companies operating in the United States have reacted differently to sexual harassment charges; this is a perilous area where the law and societal norms are rapidly changing. These companies'

reactions have exposed them to increased liability. One of the firms, Astra, a Swedish pharmaceutical firm, fired its CEO of the U.S. subsidiary and two other top managers. The other company, Mitsubishi, has denied all charges, has maintained that EEOC is wrong, and has mounted a full-scale public relations campaign to discredit complainers. Both companies lacked one of the most basic requirements consultants recommend: a clear and strong written policy on sexual harassment.[117]

Companies have the obligation of training and supporting their employees who work and conduct business internationally on harassment and discrimination laws. "When in Rome, do as the Romans do" does not mean do nothing, act immorally, or act from your own intuition as an employee representing your company. As Figure 6.6 illustrates, many countries have specific laws on employment discrimination and sexual harassment. Some are not the same as in the U.S. For example, Venezuela, as of January 1, 1999, has a new employment discrimination statute that prohibits sexual harassment and punishes this crime by a prison term from 3 to 12 months. The offender must also pay the victim twice the amount of economic damage in regard to lack of access to positions, promotions, or job performance that resulted from the sexual harassment.[118] Louise Simms, the MBA student from the opening story in Chapter 3, may now have more information to research before approaching her employer and potential client.

6.6 WHISTLE-BLOWING VERSUS ORGANIZATIONAL LOYALTY

The decision to become a whistleblower frequently requires breaking with the very group that we have viewed as critical to our financial success if not our very survival. The decision entails destabilizing one's life and placing all of the essential underpinnings of our financial security and the security of those who depend on us at total risk. It is easy to understand that such a decision is accompanied by a good deal of anxiety and stress.[119]

Among all of the rights discussed in this chapter, one of the most valued by a U.S. citizen is the freedom of speech. But how far does this right extend into the corporation, especially if an employee observes an employer committing an illegal or immoral activity that could harm others? What are the obligations and limits of employee loyalty to the employer? Under what, if any, circumstances should employees blow the whistle on their supervisors, managers, or firms?

Whistle-blowing is "the attempt of an employee or former employee of an organization to disclose what he or she believes to be wrongdoing

| FIGURE 6.6 | Survey of Harassment and Discrimination Law |

Jurisdiction	Prohibitions on Employment Discrimination	Prohibitions on Sexual Harassment	Legal Basis
Argentina	Yes	Yes, by judicial ruling	Section 16, Argentine Constitution
Australia	Yes	Yes	Race, Sex, and Disability Acts
Belgium	Yes	Yes	Article 10, Belgian Constitution; Royal Decree of September 19, 1997
Brazil	Yes	No	Article 5, Brazilian Constitution; Section 461, Brazilian Labor Code
Canada	Yes	Yes	Human rights laws of each province
Chile	Yes	Yes	Article 19, Constitution; Article 2, Labor Code
Colombia	Yes	No	Article 53, Constitution; Article 10, Labor Code
Czech Republic	Yes, by judicial decision	No	Decision No. 13/94, Constitutional Court
Egypt	Yes	No, except by extension of Civil Code	Article 40, Constitution
France	No	Yes	Article L 122-46, French Labor Code; Article 27, Law of December 31, 1992
Germany	No	Yes	Section 2, Article 31, Constitution; Disability Act; Employee Protection Act
Hong Kong	Yes	Yes	Sex Discrimination Ordinance; Disability Discrimination Ordinance
Hungary	Yes	No	Article 5, Hungarian Labor Code
Ireland	Yes	Yes	Employment Equality Act
Italy	Yes	Yes, by judicial decision	Law No. 125 of April 10, 1991
Japan	Yes	Yes	Equal Employment Opportunity Act
Mexico	No	Yes	Section 153, Mexican Penal Code
Netherlands	Yes	Yes	Article 3, Dutch Labor Conditions Act; Article 7, Dutch Civil Code
People's Republic of China	Yes	No	Article 12, Labor Law of the PRC (1995)

Philippines	No	Yes	Republic Act 7877 (1995)
Poland	Yes	No	Articles 32 and 33, Constitution; Labor Code
Republic of South Africa	Yes	No	Act No. 66, South African Labor Reform Act of 1995
Russia	Yes	No	Russian Labor Law of 1995
Singapore	Yes; age only	No	Retirement Act
Spain	Yes	Yes	Articles 9, 14, and 35, Spanish Constitution; Section 34.3.95 of Spanish Employment Act
Sweden	Yes	Yes	The Act on Equal Opportunities at Work
Switzerland	No	Yes	Article 3, Law on Equal Treatment of Women and Men
Taiwan	No	Yes	Article 83, ROC Social Order Maintenance Act
Thailand	Yes	Yes	Constitution; Labor Protection Act
Ukraine	Yes	No	Article 42, Labor Code of the Ukraine
United Kingdom	Yes	Yes	Sex, Race, and Disability Discrimination Laws
Venezuela	No	Yes	Law on Violence Against Women and Family

Source: Adapted with permission from Gerald Maatman, Jr. "Harassment, discrimination laws go global." *National Underwriter,* **September 11, 2000, 3.**

in or by the organization."[120] Whistle-blowing can be internal (reported to an executive in the organization), external (reported to external public interest groups, the media, or enforcement agencies), personal (harm reportedly done only to the whistle-blower), and impersonal (harm observed as done to another).[121] Whistle-blowing goes against strong U.S. cultural norms of showing loyalty toward an employer and colleagues and avoiding the "snitch" label. However, strong cultural norms regarding fairness, justice, a sense of duty, and obedience to the law and to one's conscience also exist. A moral dilemma can occur when a loyal employee observes the employer committing or assisting in an illegal or immoral act and must decide what to do. The whistle-blower may not only lose his or her job but may also experience negative and damaging repercussions in his or her profession, marriage, and family life. Dr. Jeffrey Wigand, head of research at Brown and Williamson Tobacco Company from 1989 to 1993, testified that this company knew and controlled nicotine levels in its products. His testimony, along with that of others, helped the government initially win a substantial lawsuit against the tobacco industry. As the film *The Insider* accurately documented, Wigand paid an enormous personal price as a witness.[122] Karen Silkwood, the now classic example of one person's bold attempt to share inside information, may have been murdered for blowing the whistle on the Kerr-McGee plutonium company:

> Karen Silkwood was killed on November 12, 1974, at 28 years of age while driving to meet a reporter from the New York Times with documentation about plutonium fuel rod tampering at the Kerr-McGee uranium and plutonium plants in Cimarron, Oklahoma.[123]

The second edition of Richard Rashke's book, *The Killing of Karen Silkwood* (Cornell University Press, 2000), recounts the story in detail.

Not all whistle-blowers undergo such traumatic fates as the two examples offered here. Michael Haley, a Federal Bank Examiner, won $755,533 in backpay, future loss of income, and compensatory damages under the federal whistle-blower statute and another amended federal statute. He had worked as a bank examiner for the Office of Thrift Supervision (OTS), starting in 1977. He inspected OTS-regulated banks, evaluating the soundness of their operations. He was terminated after he reported violations in federal banking laws and regulations regarding a forced merger.[124]

Under what conditions is whistle-blowing morally justified? DeGeorge[125] discusses five conditions:

1. When the firm, through a product or policy, will commit serious and considerable harm to the public (as consumers or bystanders), the employee should report the firm.

2. When the employee identifies a serious threat of harm, he or she should report it and state his or her moral concern.

3. When the employee's immediate supervisor does not act, the employee should exhaust the internal procedures and chain of command to the board of directors.

4. The employee must have documented evidence that is convincing to a reasonable, impartial observer that his or her view of the situation is accurate and evidence that the firm's practice, product, or policy seriously threatens and puts in danger the public or product user.

5. The employee must have valid reasons to believe that revealing the wrongdoing to the public will result in the changes necessary to remedy the situation. The chance of succeeding must be equal to the risk and danger the employee takes to blow the whistle.

The risks to whistle-blowers can range from outright termination to more subtle pressures, such as strong and hidden criticisms, undesirable and burdensome work assignments, lost perks, and exclusion from communication loops and social invitations.[126] Although 21 states have laws protecting corporate and governmental whistle-blowers from reprisal, experience shows that the government's actual protection to whistle-blowers, even if after resigning or being fired they are reinstated with back pay and compensation for physical suffering, is weak because of the many subtle forms of retaliation, such as those just listed.[127]

When Whistle-Blowers Should Not Be Protected   The most obvious condition under which whistle-blowers should not be protected is when their accusations are false and their motivation is not justifiable or accurate.

The following instances show when whistle-blowers should not have freedom of speech against their employers:

- When divulging information about legal and ethical plans, practices, operations, inventions, and other matters that should remain confidential and that are necessary for the organization to perform its work efficiently

- When an employee's personal accusations or slurs are irrelevant to questions about policies and practices that appear illegal or irresponsible

- When an employee's accusations do not show a conviction that a wrongdoing is being committed and when such accusations disrupt or damage the organization's morale

- When employees complain against a manager's competence to make daily work decisions that are irrelevant to the legality, morality, or responsibility of management actions

- When employees object to their discharge, transfer, or demotion if management can show that unsatisfactory performance or violation of a code of conduct was the reason for the decision[128]

Factors to Consider before Blowing the Whistle   Whistle-blowing is a serious action with real consequences. It often involves a decision to be made among conflicting moral, legal, economic, personal, family, and career demands and choices. No single answer may appear. A stakeholder analysis and questions can help the potential whistle-blower identify the groups and individuals, stakes, priorities, and trade-offs when selecting among different strategies and courses of action.

The following 12 guidelines offer factors[129] that a person should consider when deciding whether to blow the whistle on an employer:

1. Make sure the situation warrants whistle-blowing. If serious trade secrets or confidential company property will be exposed, know the harm and calculated risks.

2. Examine your motives.

3. Verify and document your information. Can your information stand up in a hearing and in court?

4. Determine the type of wrongdoing and to whom it should be reported. Knowing this will assist in gathering the type of evidence to obtain.

5. State your allegations specifically and appropriately. Obtain and state the type of data that will substantiate your claim.

6. Stay with the facts. This minimizes retaliation and avoids irrelevant mudslinging, name-calling, and stereotyping.

7. Decide whether to report to internal contacts or external contacts. Select the internal channel first if that route has proven effective and less damaging to whistle-blowers. Otherwise, select the appropriate external contacts.

8. Decide whether to be open or anonymous. Should you choose to remain anonymous, document the wrongdoing and anticipate what you will do if your identity is revealed.

9. Decide whether current or alumni whistle-blowing is the best alternative. Should you blow the whistle while you are an employee or resign first? Resigning should not be an automatic option. If the wrongdoing affects others, your decision is not only a personal one, but also you are fulfilling moral obligations beyond your own welfare.

10. Follow proper guidelines in reporting the wrongdoing. Check forms, meeting deadlines, and other technicalities.

11. Consult a lawyer at every step of the way.

12. Anticipate and document retaliation. This assists your effectiveness with courts and regulatory agencies.

Managerial Steps to Prevent External Whistle-Blowing

Managers have a responsibility to listen to and respond to their employees, especially regarding the observations of and reporting of illegal and immoral acts. Chapter 5 discussed mechanisms such as "ethics offices," ombudsperson programs, and peer review programs. These are part of a corporation's responsibility to provide due process for employees to report personal grievances, to obtain effective and just resolution of them, and to report the wrongdoings of others, including the employers. Four straightforward and simple steps management can take to prevent external whistle-blowing are[130]:

1. Develop effective internal grievance procedures and processes that employees can use to report wrongdoings.

2. Reward people for using these channels.

3. Appoint senior executives and others whose primary responsibilities are to investigate and report wrongdoing.

4. Assess large fines for illegal actions. Include executives and professionals who file false or illegal reports, who knowingly market dangerous products, or who offer bribes or take kickbacks.

Preventing, reporting, and effectively and fairly correcting illegal and immoral actions, policies, and procedures are the responsibilities of employers and employees. Management cannot expect employees to be loyal to a company that promotes or allows wrongdoing to its stakeholders. Whistle-blowing should be a last resort. A more active goal is to hire, train, and promote morally and legally sensitive and responsive managers who communicate with and work for the welfare of all stakeholders.

SUMMARY

The demographics of the workforce at the beginning of the 21st century continue to change. These changes include the aging of employees, the "shrinking" of the workforce, an increasing number of women and minority entrants, the demand for work–life balance from singles and dual-career families, the gap in educational levels, and a greater demand for the skills of disabled workers. The changes in the composition of the workforce signal changes in work-related values and motivations. Corporations and managers can expect moral tensions to rise regarding issues such as age discrimination, health care needs, conflicting communication, generational differences, and requests for more balance and flexible work schedules. "One size fits all" management techniques do not work.

The social and psychological contract between corporations and employees is also changing. The original employment-at-will doctrine serves as the basis for employment between employer and employee; however, over the years, this doctrine has been complemented by the doctrine of implied employee rights. Most firms, large and small, use a mix of the two doctrines. Two underlying concepts of employee rights are balance and governmental rights.

The nature of legal and moral relationships between employers and employees is also changing. Employers rely on federal and state laws to guide their employee policies and procedures. However, many employers implement benefits and policies aimed at motivating and supporting employees' well being. Work–life resources and insurance coverage for employees' same-sex partners are such examples.

Recent court decisions have supported racial affirmative action practices at the university admittance level. Although EEOC policies and affirmative action practices remain a part of federal law, some states are showing less acceptance of these laws and procedures. Current and future issues related to sexual harassment and reverse discrimination will continue to shape legal and moral guidelines for corporations. Conflicts regarding due process, privacy, safety, drug testing, sexual harassment, technology monitoring, and other workplace topics will continue to be resolved through court cases and legislation; their resolution will influence corporate policies in the future.

Sexual harassment laws and guidelines for employers and employees and the moral dilemma of organizational loyalty versus personal ethics will always be important issues. The justification for whistle-blowing and guidelines for potential whistle-blowers must be considered by employees before blowing the whistle and by corporations to prevent external whistle-blowing.

QUESTIONS

1. Identify two major trends in the changing demographics of the workforce. Include a trend that you as a student or employee are now or could be affected by.

2. Identify moral tensions and/or conflicts that could lead to illegal and/or unethical behavior associated with the changes you gave in Question 1.

3. What are three major factors an employer should consider to avoid arbitrarily terminating an employee? What steps would you take if you were terminated by an employer who arbitrarily fired you?

4. What problems do you see occurring when employees date in a company? What additions or changes would you make to the tips and suggestions offered on dating in the chapter?

5. What does the term *legal and moral entitlement* mean to you as an employee or future employee? Give an example. Do you agree that employees have legal and moral entitlements in the workplace? Explain.

6. Do you believe dating should be permitted among employees in the workplace without formal policies setting boundaries and rules? Why or why not?

7. Do you believe managers and company officers should date lower level employees with less power and status? Why could this situation present ethical dilemmas?

8. What are some changes that have occurred as a result of the Civil Rights Act of 1991?

9. Do you believe there is now an "equal playing field" regarding access to educational institutions, jobs, and other employment opportunities for all individuals and groups in the United States? Explain. Do you believe women should still be a protected group under Title VII of the Civil Rights Act? Explain. Do you believe minorities of different races in the U.S. other than Caucasian should still be protected? If so, which group(s)? If not, explain why not.

10. What are some arguments for and against "reverse discrimination"? Is the "playing field" in U.S. corporations more level now?

11. Describe criteria used to determine whether verbal or physical actions constitute sexual harassment. What are some specific types of sexual harassment? Have you been sexually harassed in a work setting? Can you describe what happened and the outcome?

12. What should employees expect from their employers and their companies now in terms of rights and obligations? Explain. Is loyalty to an employer a "dead" or "dying" concept now? Why or why not?

13. Do you believe whistle-blowing is justifiable in corporations? Would, or could you, blow the whistle? Under what circumstances would you be compelled to blow the whistle as an employee in an organization? Offer an example.

14. Should corporate managers prevent whistle-blowing? Why or why not? Explain.

15. How can employers prevent whistle-blowing?

EXERCISES

1. Argue the pros and cons of eliminating standards such as test scores, grade point averages, and other objective criteria for admitting minorities and members of protected groups to universities and colleges. Do you believe such objective criteria should be eliminated by university and college admissions committees? Explain.

2. Select an employee right in the workplace from the chapter. Give an example, based on your own outside reading or experience, of a situation

involving this right. Was it violated? How? What was the outcome? What should the outcome have been? Why?

3. Identify an example from your own experience or someone you know of discrimination or sexual harassment. Did this experience influence your view of affirmative action or employee protection programs? If so, how?

4. Write a paragraph describing a situation from your experience in which you felt justified that you had cause to blow the whistle. Did you? Why or why not? Under what circumstances do you feel whistle-blowing is justified?

5. Think of three people you know from the different generations discussed in the chapter. From these people, who is and is not satisfied with their work and jobs? Explain why they are or are not satisfied. Refer back to the generational differences and values in the chapter. To what extent did "generational differences" have in your analysis of the individuals' work satisfaction? To what extent did "ethical reasons" affect their work satisfaction? Explain.

6. Create a "for" and "against" set of arguments regarding the "employment-at-will" doctrine in the present economic and demographic environment. After you make a complete set of arguments, which position do you support? Did your views change after this exercise? Why or why not?

Ethical Dilemma   Cheating or Leveling the Playing Field?

Part I   During one of last year's midterm examinations in my finance class, I was faced with my first ethical dilemma in college. My friend and I were studying for the exam when he explained that he was going to punch the formulas into his calculator. He said that he has attention deficit hyperactivity disorder (ADHD) and that it was very difficult for him to remember formulas. I shrugged off the suggestion in the hope that he would exclude me from his decision. A few days later, during the examination, I looked around and noticed that he was not the only one who had entered the formulas in their calculators. My first reaction was "damn, maybe I could have done the same thing." Then I remembered how the professor had told us that this was not allowed and that we had all signed onto the college's "honor code" system, which stated that we would not cheat and that we would report those who did. It was at that moment that I realized I was faced with a dilemma: to tell or not to tell. I violated the honor code if I kept silent; I violated my friend's trust if I told. After all, I thought, he did have ADHD. Shouldn't he be given a break? Also, I didn't want to tell on so many students. I'm not a police officer.

QUESTION

What would you have done in this situation and why? Answer this question before continuing.

Part II   I chose to continue taking the test without telling the professor that students were using their calculators to "remember" their formulas. When I arrived at class next week, the professor had a sad look on his face because the class average for the examination was only 72% correct. There was only one person who received an A. Surprise, I was the A student! I was one of the few who had not cheated, and I got the highest grade in the class. Not only did I get the highest grade, but I finished the semester with a grade well above the curve. At the semester's end, I reflected on the cheating incident. Had I chosen to tell the professor, one of two things could have happened: 1) The class would have had to take a make-up examination, or 2) several of my classmates would have received a 0, or have been punished in some way. (It's also possible that my A may not have counted because all the exams were trashed.) In fact, by my not telling, I ended up being able to capitalize on the other students' not studying. Had I blown the whistle, we may all have been required to take the test over, and, yes, I would have gotten an A; however, the curve would have been more narrow. This way, as I see it, I won and the others got their "just rewards," even though they cheated and I did, by default, violate the honors code.

QUESTIONS

1. Do you agree with this student's logic and ethical reasoning? Explain.

2. What do you believe should have happened (if anything) to the student in this situation? Explain.

3. What would you have done differently and why? Justify your answer.

CASE 19

SHERRON WATKINS—REVELATIONS OF A LETTER

Who Is Sherron Watkins?   Sherron Watkins gained fame as the so-called "whistle-blower" in the Enron accounting scandal.

"Enron hid billions of dollars in debts and operating losses inside private partnerships and dizzyingly complex accounting schemes that were intended to pump up the buzz about the company and support its inflated stock price." Watkins wrote two letters, one anonymously, to Enron's chairman, Kenneth Lay. In those letters she "exposed top officials—perhaps including Lay himself—who for months had been trying to hide a mountain of debt, and started a chain reaction of events that brought down the company."

Watkins had a "flair for numbers" and the training and expertise to recognize a "funny accounting scheme." She received an accounting degree from the University of Texas at Austin in 1981 and a master's degree in accounting in 1982, after which she went to work for Arthur Andersen's Houston office. Watkins transferred to Andersen's New York City office and then subsequently returned to Houston in the early 1990s to work for Enron. Eight years after joining Enron, Watkins had risen to the position of vice president for corporate development.

According to one retrospective account of the Enron scandal, Watkins "understood that something very bad was going on, something everyone else seemed to think was perfectly okay, and that public revelation would be disastrous." Somehow Watkins "was able to escape the group-think that ensnared her colleagues."

Nonetheless, she worried about the future—apparently both Enron's and her own. As she wrote in a six-page letter to Ken Lay, "I am incredibly nervous that we will implode in a wave of accounting scandals. My eight years of Enron work history will be worth nothing on my résumé, the business world will consider the past successes as nothing but an elaborate accounting hoax. Skilling[1] is resigning now for 'personal reasons' but I would think that he wasn't having fun, looked down the road and knew this stuff was unfixable and would rather abandon ship now than resign in shame in two years."

The Events Leading up to Watkins' Instant Fame   During the summer of 2001, Sherron Watkins worked for then chief financial officer Andrew Fastow, looking for assets to sell as Enron ran into financial trouble. She repeatedly uncovered "off-the-books arrangements

---

[1]Referring to Jeffrey Skilling, Enron's chief executive officer, before his abrupt resignation on August 14, 2001.

that no one could explain or seemed to want to investigate." She was uncomfortable approaching Fastow or then-CEO Jeffrey Skilling, not trusting either one. Fastow himself played a major role in the off-the-books partnerships she kept encountering. Watkins also knew that other executives who questioned such transactions had encountered Skilling's wrath, and she feared being fired if she approached Skilling directly. Consequently, Watkins debated for weeks regarding the course of action to take.

Her direction became clear when Jeff Skilling abruptly quit his job on August 14, 2001, and Kenneth Lay, Enron's chairman, called a company-wide meeting to take place on August 16, asking for employee comments and concerns beforehand. Watkins wrote an anonymous one-page letter expressing her concerns about the off-the-books arrangements and deposited it in the designated dropbox. Lay did not address Watkins' concerns during the company-wide meeting.

Subsequently, Watkins sought advice from a friend and former colleague at Arthur Andersen; that friend concurred with her concerns. Drawing on this advice, Watkins prepared a six-page letter describing her worries and presented the letter to Ken Lay in an August 22 meeting with him. Prior to delivering the letter to Lay, Watkins asked her mother, Shirley Klein Harrington, to review it. In a subsequent interview, Harrington commented, "There was no option about whether or not she was going to send it. She knew she had to say something. But all along she never imagined that she was going to be the *only* one."

Watkins' six-page letter was very revealing and filled with much angst. She observed that "Skilling's abrupt departure will raise suspicions of accounting improprieties and valuation issues. . . . It sure looks to the layman on the street that we are hiding losses in a related company and will compensate that company with Enron stock in the future." She went on to ask, "Is there any way our accounting gurus can unwind these deals now? . . . We are under too much scrutiny and there are probably one or two disgruntled 'redeployed' employees who know enough about the 'funny' accounting to get us into trouble." Watkins added, "I realize that we have had a lot of smart people looking at this and a lot of accountants including AA & Co.[2] have blessed the accounting treatment. None of that will protect Enron if these transactions are ever disclosed in the bright light of day."

Watkins believed that the probability of discovery of the "funny accounting" significantly increased after Skilling's departure. Consequently, she suggested in her letter to Ken Lay that he had two alternative courses of action: (a) "The probability of discovery is low

---

[2]AA & Co. refers to Arthur Andersen, the accounting firm that audited Enron's books.

enough and the estimated damage too great; therefore we find a way to quietly and quickly reverse, unwind, write down these positions/transactions" or (b) "The probability of discovery is too great, the estimated damages to the company too great; therefore we must quantify, develop damage containment plans and disclose." In short, the first solution linked a low probability of discovery with what some people might consider to be a cover-up of the problems of significant magnitude. The second suggestion advocated a more open and forthright approach to dealing with significant problems that surely would be discovered by the public. In her letter, Watkins said, "I firmly believe that the probability of discovery significantly increased with Skilling's shocking departure. Too many people are looking for a smoking gun."

Lay promised Watkins he would have a team of lawyers review the controversial deals discussed in Watkins' letter. Lay decided to use Enron's legal counsel, Vinson & Elkins, despite Watkins' concern regarding the conflict of interest involved in doing so. Vinson & Elkins provided advice on some of the questionable deals that Watkins discussed in her letter.

According to Watkins, "Enron's unspoken message was, 'Make the numbers, make the numbers, make the numbers—if you steal, if you cheat, just don't get caught. If you do, beg for a second chance, and you'll get one."

How Did Watkins Gain Instant Fame?

Watkins' letter to Lay was discovered in a box of Enron documents that had been seized pursuant to a Congressional investigation of the Enron collapse and associated accounting scandal. Investigators released—some observers say leaked—the letter, in its entirety, on January 15, 2002. Immediately, Watkins was dubbed a "hero whistle-blower." One account described Watkins as "the tough-talking Texas woman who had stood up to all of the good old boys in the corporate hierarchy, the men who had been making millions while their employees and shareholders watched some, or all, of their life savings evaporate." Another commentator observed that Watkins had enough courage "to send the boss a pull-no-punches, put-it-on-record letter telling him . . . that his company was more or less a Ponzi scheme, and it sounds like she knew she wasn't telling him anything he didn't already know." In commenting on reactions to the letter's release, still another columnist wrote, "what was once envisioned as a new kind of company resembled little more than a circular firing squad of executives, accountants, consultants, and lawyers, all fighting to stay in business or, at least, out of jail."

Although some of the news media characterized Watkins as the "Enron whistle-blower," others in the media pointed out that Watkins never really blew a whistle. One commentator observed,

"A whistle-blower would have written that letter to the *Houston Chronicle,* and long before August; Watkins wrote it to Ken Lay, and warned him of potential whistle-blowers lurking among them." Another commentator wrote, "A whistle-blower, literally speaking, is someone who spots a criminal robbing a bank and blows a whistle, alerting police. That's not Sherron Watkins. What the Enron vice president did was write a memo to the bank robber, suggesting he stop robbing the bank and offering ways to avoid getting caught. Then she met with the robber, who said he didn't believe he was robbing the bank, but said he'd investigate to find out for sure. . . . [A] whistle-blower is someone who alerts the public. She never did."

On Valentine's Day of 2002, appearing before a Congressional subcommittee, Watkins testified that Jeffrey Skilling, Andrew Fastow, and other Enron executives, as well as Arthur Andersen and Vinson & Elkins, duped Ken Lay and the board of directors. Some observers questioned Watkins' apparent continuing loyalty to Kenneth Lay. Some observers were surprised—perhaps even stunned—that Watkins expressed support for Ken Lay and Enron's board. Apparently, Watkins' sister, Julie Reagan, was not surprised. Reagan says, "She's a very loyal person—loyal to her friends and her family and even her job. So I think if she didn't care about Enron, she would have left without ever having bothered to correct what was going on. But what she wanted to do was make it right."

Dan Ackman, a writer for *Forbes* magazine, commented, "Many people were in a position to expose Enron's accounting. Each did nothing. Watkins did something. But not much." Watkins agrees. "My warnings were too little, too late," she says. "The question is, why weren't objections raised and addressed much earlier? . . . Most people do know right from wrong."

Watkins' Professional Life: Today and Tomorrow

Sherron Watkins resigned from Enron late in 2002. *Time* magazine named her "person of the year" in 2002. She co-wrote a book, *Power Failure* (Doubleday, 2003) about her experiences at Enron. She lectures on business ethics and the erosion of trust in corporations, receiving as much as $35,000 per appearance. Watkins also meets frequently with high-level executives to discuss her experiences and perspectives. Watkins admits to being a fan of ethics training programs and employee hotlines run by external, independent parties. But she does not believe that ethics training and employee hotlines are substitutes for a culture that rewards rather than punishes honesty.

In the future, Watkins plans to open a not-for-profit consulting firm that will help corporations do annual "board checkups," with an emphasis on spotting ethical and other problems before its too late. Reflecting back on the ordeal at Enron, Watkins concludes, "the company did not

put its money where its mouth was when it came to vision and values."
Some would say that Watkins is guilty of the same anomaly. "It is ironic,"
according to one critic, "that Watkins hopes to make a name for herself
in the boardroom, when she didn't choose to inform Enron's board of
the company's problems but instead went to Lay."

Questions for Discussion

1. What risks did Sherron Watkins take by writing the six-page letter to Kenneth Lay? Do you believe she should have written the letter? Why or why not?

2. Suppose that Sherron Watkins decided to do nothing with the knowledge she had regarding Enron's "funny accounting." What would have been the possible risks (or consequences) to her for failing to act?

3. Was Sherron Watkins a whistle-blower or not? Explain your position.

4. What responsibility does an employee have for reporting questionable or unethical activity that he/she uncovers while doing his/her job? Does this responsibility differ, depending on whether the individual is a lower, middle, or upper-level employee?

Sources

This case was developed from material contained in the following sources:

Ackman, D. (February 14, 2002). Sherron Watkins had whistle, but blew it. *Forbes*, http://www.forbes.com/2002/02/14/0214watkins.html, accessed February 4, 2005.

Colvin, G. (July 25, 2002). Wonder women of whistleblowing. *Fortune*, http://www.fortune.com/fortune/subs/print0,15935,369960,00.html, accessed February 4, 2005.

Duffy, M. (January 19, 2002). By the sign of the crooked E. *Time.com*, http://www.time.com/business/printout/0,8816,195268,00.html, accessed February 4, 2005.

Frey, J. (January 25, 2002). The woman who saw red: Enron whistle-blower Sherron Watkins warned of the trouble to come. *Washington Post*, http://www.washingtonpost.com/ac2/wp-dyn/A35005-2002Jan24?language=printer, accessed February 4, 2005.

The letter to Ken Lay. (January 16, 2002). *Fortune*, http://www.fortune.com/fortune/subs/print0,15935,369225,00.html, accessed February 4, 2005.

Mehta, S. (October 14, 2003). Employees are the best line of defense. *Fortune*, http://www.fortune.com/fortune/subs/print0,15935,518339,00.html, accessed February 4, 2005.

Pelligrini, F. (January 18, 2002). Person of the week: "Enron whistleblower" Sherron Watkins. *Time.com*, http://www.time.com/pow/printout/0,8816,194927,00.html, accessed February 4, 2005.

Reingold, J. (September 2003). The women of Enron: The best revenge. *Fast Company*, http://pf.fastcompany.com/magazine/74/enron_Watkins.html, accessed February 4, 2005.

CASE 20

WOMEN ON WALL STREET: FIGHTING FOR EQUALITY IN A MALE-DOMINATED INDUSTRY

Allison Schieffelin and Morgan Stanley   On June 12, 2004, Morgan Stanley agreed to pay $54 million to settle dozens of claims from women who alleged that the securities firm denied them pay increases and promotions due to their gender. The case, filed by the Equal Employment Opportunity Commission (EEOC) on September 10, 2001, resulted from repeated complaints by Allison Schieffelin, a 43-year-old former convertible-bond sales clerk who worked in the firm's institutional-stock division for 14 years. Schieffelin earned more than $1 million a year, making her one of the highest-paid and highest-ranking women on Wall Street to publicly challenge the industry's pay and promotion practices. Schieffelin claims that she was trapped under a glass ceiling and continuously denied promotion to managing director despite being the top performer in her department. The EEOC claims that in addition to being repeatedly denied promotions and pay raises, women employees in Schieffelin's division "endured coarse behavior and lewd comments from their male colleagues and supervisors." Moreover, firm-organized sales outings with clients to golf resorts and strip clubs excluded women.

Of the $54 million settlement, $12 million will be paid directly to Schieffelin. About $40 million will be used to settle complaints from an estimated 100 current and former female employees of the institutional-stock division. The remaining $2 million will be used to enhance anti-discrimination training at the firm. In addition to the monetary settlement, Morgan Stanley must also fund a program to have an appointed outsider monitor hiring, pay, and promotion practices for a three-year period. Although the settlement seems large, it is merely "pocket change" to a firm like Morgan Stanley; the $54 million represents approximately 2% of the $2.45 billion in profits the firm earned in the first half of fiscal 2004.

Background on the *Schieffelin et al.* v. *Morgan Stanley* Case   Allison Schieffelin first complained of Morgan Stanley's working environment in a 1995 written review of her boss stating, "He makes the convertible department and the firm by extension an uncomfortable place for women." During that same year, she also submitted an internal complaint about "unwelcome advances" from one of her male managing directors. At the time, she thought that management would be pleased with the tactful manner in which she handled the issues; however, today she feels management placed her on a "watch list" instead.

In December 1998, after three years of withstanding the men's locker-room type atmosphere in which the male employees openly "swapped off-color jokes and tales of sexual exploits and treated their female colleagues as inferior," Schieffelin took her harassment and discrimination complaints beyond the firm's executives to the EEOC. She hoped that the firm would see that she had been a dedicated employee throughout her entire career and that the issues with the firm's pay and promotion practices needed to be amended. Instead, she claims the firm "embarked on a campaign to get me to quit." She was fired in October 2001 for what the firm claims to be misconduct after a heated confrontation with her supervisor; however, both Schieffelin and the EEOC viewed her firing as illegal retaliation for her discrimination complaints. One year after Schieffelin complained, Morgan Stanley's New York convertibles department, the department in which Schieffelin worked, promoted Gay Ebers-Franckowiak to managing director—the first female managing director in that department; many people believe that this was no coincidence.

Morgan Stanley denied all discrimination charges and claimed that their female employees were and are treated equally. The EEOC planned to reveal evidence at the trial proving otherwise. The anticipated evidence indicated that some male employees of the firm ordered breast-shaped birthday cakes and hired strippers to entertain at office parties. The evidence supposedly provided statistics regarding the disparities between female and male promotion and pay within the firm. The trial was scheduled to begin July 12, 2004; however, a settlement was wrapped up mere minutes before opening arguments began. As part of the settlement, payroll statistics that showed whether or not there was a pattern of discrimination were sealed.

An Isolated Occurrence or an Industry-Wide Problem?

The allegations made against Morgan Stanley are not new to the securities industry. Several previous cases, in addition to statistics produced by the Securities Industry Association (SIA), indicate that sex discrimination is a persistent problem on Wall Street.

In April 2004, Merrill Lynch agreed to pay $2.2 million to Hydie Sumner as part of a class-action lawsuit brought by more than 900 women claiming the financial giant had a long history of gender discrimination. Sumner wanted her old job back; she also said that she wanted to be a Merrill Lynch manager in order to make changes at the firm. "I thought, one day, I'll be a manager and I'll have a choice, and I won't manage like him [Stephen McAnally, former manager of the Merrill Lynch San Antonio office]," said Sumner. As of early 2005, Merrill Lynch paid Sumner $1.9 million but was fighting the other

$300,000, indicating that this payment would "not be considered until the issues relating to Ms. Sumner's reinstatement at the firm are resolved."

In a more recent lawsuit, Stephanie Villalba, former head of Merrill Lynch's private client business in Europe, sued for $13 million on gender bias charges. She claimed that her male boss had difficulty accepting her in a senior position and as a result, she was "bullied, belittled, and undermined." In early 2005, an employment tribunal in the United Kingdom ruled in favor of "Villalba's claim of victimization on certain issues, that included bullying e-mails in connection with a contract, but found no evidence of a 'laddish culture' at the bank." Villalba intends to appeal the ruling.

In February 2004, Susanne Pesterfield, a former broker for Smith Barney, settled her case with the investment firm on the eve of an arbitration hearing. She alleged that during her seven years at the firm, she endured a "pattern of sexual harassment and a male-dominated culture that included trips to strip clubs." She described a working environment that was "hostile to women and in which women weren't given the same opportunities to succeed as men were given." She claimed that her male colleagues were better paid and received better leads for potential clients.

Pesterfield's accusations were not new to Smith Barney. A class-action lawsuit brought by female employees in 1996 led to a 1998 settlement in which the firm's parent company, Citigroup Inc., paid out close to $100 million. The infamous case has been referred to as the "Boom-Boom Room" in reference to the basement "party room" in the Garden City branch of what was then Shearson Lehman Brothers, wherein discrimination and sexual harassment occurred. Among other things, the conversations that took place among the male employees went beyond their accomplishments on the trading floor to include their latest accomplishments in the bedroom. Shearson's manager took a "boys will be boys" approach that encouraged obscene comments and lewd behavior.

In her book *Tales from the Boom-Boom Room*, Susan Antilla provides a detailed account of the workplace culture at Shearson. According to Antilla, "it was a time when men in branch offices of brokerage firms were encountering significant numbers of female colleagues for the first time. For some of them, it was unsettling." In the late 1990s, many well-educated women entered the financial services industry in hopes of finding great opportunities. Instead, they found an industry that continued to be dominated by white males and an environment that belittled and repressed women.

The acts of alleged sex discrimination abound; nearly 3,000 women filed claims in 1996 and 1997 against Smith Barney and Merrill Lynch.

Although most of the women settled, some did not, including Nancy Thomas, Sonia Ingram, Laura Zubulake, Deborah Paulhus, and Neill Sites. Perhaps most notable is the case of Nancy Thomas, a broker at Merrill Lynch for 18 years. Among the numerous allegations of sex discrimination made by Thomas, one is particularly salacious. Thomas alleges that in 1991 "someone left her a package in the mailroom with a dildo, lubricating cream, and an obscene poem." An arbitration hearing commenced in New York on September 13, 2004; arbitrators have scheduled an additional 18 hearing sessions through July 2005. Merrill Lynch maintains that none of the testimony given as of late November 2004 "supports even one of Thomas's allegations."

Wall Street's Glass Ceiling—The Numbers Tell the Story

The *2003 Report on Diversity Strategy, Development & Demographics* produced by the Securities Industry Association (SIA) presents data suggesting there has been little improvement in the advancement of women in the securities industry in recent years, and that biased pay and promotion practices are not just outdated. Even though Wall Street firms seem to be making attempts to improve the workplace environment for women, statistics prove that a strong glass ceiling still exists. There was a gradual decrease in the percentage of women in the industry between the years 1999 and 2003 (43% and 37%, respectively), and management positions in 2001 and 2003 continued to be dominated by white males. In 2003, white males held 85% of (branch) office manager positions, 76% of the managing director positions, and 79% of the executive management positions. This compares to 85%, 81%, and 75% for the three position categories in 2001. The same is true for line positions such as brokers (80% in 2001 versus 78% in 2003), investment bankers (77% versus 71%), and traders (71% versus 74%). On the other hand, "white women and men and women of color continue to comprise the majority (89%) of the staff and junior level positions."

These numbers become even more disturbing when one considers that women are not new to the profession. In 1974, women held 33.8% of all securities industry jobs with 6.5% being management positions. Muriel F. Siebert, chair of Muriel Siebert & Co. and the first woman with her own seat on the New York Stock Exchange, has worked on Wall Street since the 1950s. She claims that highly educated and successful women are consistently "dropping out" of the industry and changing careers because they feel they have no chance of reaching top management positions.

Catalyst, a nonprofit research organization working to advance women in business, conducted a study of female professionals in the securities industry. Published in 2001 as *Women in Financial Services:*

The Word on the Street, the results indicated the top three barriers to women's advancement were lack of mentoring opportunities, commitment to personal and family responsibilities, and exclusion from informal networks of communication. The survey also highlighted the differences in the viewpoints of male and female professionals with respect to the advancement of women. While 65% of women believed they had to work harder than men to get the same rewards, only 13% of men believed this to be true; 51% of women felt they were paid less than men for doing the same work, while only 8% of men agreed with this statement. In addition, 50% of men believed that women's opportunities to advance to senior leadership in their firms had increased greatly over the preceding five years, but only 18% of women agreed. Many of the women who file complaints, as well as their lawyers, maintain that the perceptual divide between genders is a serious issue. They argue that the men in charge at Wall Street firms do not recognize the existence of a problem, and therefore they fail to look at the statistics and to see the "big picture."

Mandatory Arbitration and Coercion Prevent Statistics from Appearing in Court   In 1986, the Supreme Court ruled that sexual harassment is illegal under Title VII of the 1964 Civil Rights Act. However, recent statistics and settlements in gender discrimination suits suggest that the glass ceiling, at least within the securities and investment banking businesses, still exists. What makes Wall Street such a laggard when it comes to the treatment and advancement of women? One factor could be that before 1999 any employee of a Wall Street firm was required to resolve all disputes in a "closed-door negotiation process" rather than in a public hearing. As the rest of corporate America was hit with discrimination lawsuits in the 1980s and 1990s, the problems occurring on Wall Street remained, for the most part, behind closed doors. After the Boom-Boom Room case and the Merrill Lynch suit in the late 1990s, the Securities and Exchange Commission removed the mandatory arbitration requirement for Wall Street employees who had civil-rights claims. As a result, "the National Association of Securities Dealers and the New York Stock Exchange changed their arbitration rules in a way that permitted employees to sue under federal discrimination statutes in federal court."

Why Should the Securities Industry Make Changes?   Sex discrimination lawsuits have been costly, in terms of money and negative publicity, for securities firms. Avoiding such costs in the future is a strong motivation for change, but not the only one. Another powerful reason is the increasingly influential role of women in business. In 1998, women owned close to 8 million U.S. businesses, which was

one-third of the total, and "more than 40% of households with assets of $600,000 or more [were] headed by women." In 2004, 10.6 million firms were at least 50% female-owned; 48% of all privately held firms were at least 50% female-owned.

Moreover, as more working women approach retirement age and younger women rise in the ranks, securities firms desire to increase their female clientele. As a result, there is an increasing demand for female brokers to serve the needs of this "new" client base. Women investors tend to prefer doing business with a friendly, trustworthy advisor rather than just a person with financial expertise, and thus they aim to establish a personal relationship with their brokers/advisors. To serve an increasingly diverse client base, investment firms must recognize that they will need a diverse group of employees who recognize and react appropriately to the needs of their clients.

Who Wins, Who Loses?   Richard Berman, the judge in the recent Morgan Stanley case, described the $54 million settlement as a "watershed event in protecting the rights of women on Wall Street." Many others, including Elizabeth Grossman, an EEOC lawyer on the case, hope that the settlement will act as a revelation for not only Morgan Stanley but other Wall Street firms as well. The settlement may cause other firms within the securities and investment banking industry to reevaluate their pay and promotion practices. Additional complaints may also surface because of the settlement.

Although some people view the settlement in a positive light, others see a negative side. As part of the settlement, claimants agreed not to disclose any of the statistics and facts that would have been presented in the case. Although the women who will share the $54 million settlement scored a big win, some people believe that Morgan Stanley and other securities firms "scored an even bigger win" by preventing embarrassing statistics from being revealed in the courtroom and to the public.

The securities and investment banking firms seem to have a "what the public doesn't know, won't hurt them" attitude. Unless the compensation and promotion statistics of those firms are exposed to the public, Wall Street businesses will continue operating within its current culture. In "Money Talks, Women Don't," an article about the Morgan Stanley settlement, Susan Antilla stated, "Ingrained cultural misconduct changes only when customers, colleagues, and the public get wind of the nasty facts and companies are embarrassed. Those who can afford to keep their problems quiet may never have to change."

Today on Wall Street   Some aspects of work on Wall Street have improved for women, but changing the culture of an entire industry cannot happen overnight, especially if firms are reluctant to admit that a problem exists. Antilla suggests that there has been reluctance to address the discrimination and harassment issues even after they were revealed in the Boom-Boom Room and Merrill Lynch lawsuits of the late 1990s. Antilla says, "When it came to acknowledging that there was still a problem to work on—violators to stop and biases to correct—Wall Street had become a little like the dysfunctional family hiding the crazy uncle in the attic. Everyone knew sexual harassment was there and indeed had put much energy into urgently and quietly negotiating the crises that resulted from it. But hardly anyone spoke openly about the problem—called the doctor, if you will—and started the real work of making things better."

Today, firms are more likely to have diversity programs and sexual harassment training. Many companies have altered their recruiting processes and several have established partnerships with support organizations that promote equal opportunities in professions for women and minorities. Some companies are working at changing the "tone at the top" by promoting women to top positions and challenging old attitudes within the companies. For example, in late 2002 Smith Barney hired its first woman chief executive, Sallie Krawcheck. Since then, the company has fired some of its most successful brokers for mistreating female co-workers, thereby sending a message that such behavior will not be tolerated—even in the most valued employees. Despite these efforts, the industry statistics and continual lawsuits suggest that women in the financial services industry are not playing on a level playing field quite yet.

Indeed, as one Wall Street observer, Dan Ackman, a columnist for *Forbes* magazine, noted, "beyond the numbers, nearly every woman on Wall Street will tell you there are, to this day, subtle and not-so-subtle double standards and a still pervasive atmosphere of harassment." As the business writer John Churchill reports, "Many complainants claim the firms have just become subtler in their discrimination, rigging teams, for instance, so that when men retire or change firms, the most lucrative accounts they leave behind get assigned to other members of the old-boy network, not to the most senior broker in the office." Consequently, the most important question with respect to sexual discrimination in the securities and investment banking industry may be, "What must happen in order for a true and pervasive cultural change to take place on Wall Street?"

Questions for Discussion

1. Is business ethics relevant to the topic and examples in this case or is this just business as usual? Explain.

2. What are the ethical implications of the one-time arbitration requirement that prevented Wall Street employees from seeking redress through the court system?

3. Why is the securities and investment banking business male-oriented and dominated?

4. Why does sex discrimination seem to persist on Wall Street in spite of the negative publicity of lawsuits and monetary costs of settlement?

5. What can or should be done to transform the persistent culture of sex discrimination on Wall Street?

6. Would you like working on Wall Street as a woman? Explain.

7. As a man or woman, what lessons would you take from this case if you accepted a professional job in a Wall Street firm?

Sources

This case was developed from material contained in the following sources:

Ackman, D. (July 14, 2004). How Schieffelin beat the street. *Forbes*, http://www.forbes.com/careers/2004/07/14/cx_da0714topnews.html, accessed February 13, 2005.

Allen, E. (April 24, 2004). San Antonio woman wins Merrill Lynch suit, becomes voice for discrimination. *Knight Ridder Tribune Business News*, 1.

Antilla, S. (August 9, 2004). In the companies of men: A rash of gender-discrimination suits suggests the Morgan Stanley payout may be only the beginning. *New York Magazine*, http://newyorkmetro.com/nymetro/news/people/columns/intelligencer/9580/, accessed February 13, 2005.

Antilla, S. (November 29, 2004). Merrill's woman problem—What men didn't know: Susan Antilla. Bloomberg Columnists, http://www.bloomberg.com/apps/news?pid=10000039&sid=aLk_r1Imn86Y&refer=columnist_antilla, accessed February 15, 2005.

Antilla, S. (July 21, 2004). Money talks, women don't. *New York Times*, A19.

Antilla, S. (2003). *Tales from the Boom-Boom Room*, New York: HarperCollins Publishers.

Appleson, G. (July 12, 2004). Morgan Stanley settles sex bias case. *ABC News* Web site, http://abcnews.go.com/wire/Business/reuters20040712.458.html.

Calian, S. (June 9, 2004). Merrill faces gender-bias suit. *The Wall Street Journal*, C15.

Catalyst. (2001). Fact sheet. *Women in Financial Services: The Word on the Street*, http://www.catalystwomen.org/press_room/factsheets/fact_women_in_financial_services.htm.

Churchill, J. (August 1, 2004). Where the women at? *Registered Rep*, http://registeredrep.com/mag/finance_women, accessed February 15, 2005.

Discrimination claim—Merrill bites back. (September 2, 2004) *Here Is the City News*, http://www.hereisthecitynews.com/news/business_news/3734.cntns, accessed February 15, 2005.

Kelly, K. and DeBaise, C. (July 13, 2004). Morgan Stanley settles bias suit for $54 million; Last-minute deal avoids sex-discrimination trial; $12 million for Ms. Schieffelin. *The Wall Street Journal*, A1.

Langton, J. (December 5, 2002). "The Boom-Boom Room" details travails of women on Wall Street. *Knight Ridder Tribune Business* News, 1.

Marsh, A. (September 21, 1998). Women are from Venus, men are from Wall Street. *Forbes*, 162(6), 94.

McGeehan, P. (July 14, 2004). Discrimination on Wall St.? The numbers tell the story. *New York Times*, 1.

McGeehan, P. (February 10, 2002). Wall Street highflier to outcast: A woman's story. *New York Times*, 3-1.

Millar, M. (February 3, 2005). Merrill Lynch faces appeal over sexual discrimination ruling. *PersonnelToday.com*, http://www.personneltoday.co.uk/Articles/2005/02/03/27792/Merrill+Lynch+faces+appeal+over+sexual+discrimination.htm, accessed February 15, 2005.

Mollenkamp, C. (February 23, 2004). Deals and deal makers: Former broker at Smith Barney settles sexual harassment case. *The Wall Street Journal*, C5.

Securities Industry Association, Inc. (2003). Key findings. *Report on Diversity Strategy, Development & Demographics*, 16–17.

Stephanie Villalba loses sex discrimination case. *Femalefirst.co.uk*, http://www.femalefirst.co.uk/business/182004.htm, accessed February 15, 2005.

Top facts about women-owned businesses. (2004). *Center for Women's Business Research*, http://www.nfwbo.org/topfacts.html, accessed February 15, 2005.

Notes

1. U.S. Department of Labor. DOL Annual Report, Fiscal Year 2004—Performance and Accountability Report. Strategic Goal 1: A Prepared Workforce. http://www.dol.gov/_sec/media/reports/annual2004/strat_goal1.pdf.
2. Data Dome, Inc. (March 2004). WorkForce Trends Newsletter. *WorkForce Trends, 3(1)*, http://www.datadome.com/worktrends/worktrends3_1.html.
3. Based on the discussion of Tapscott, D. (1996). *The Digital Economy*, 296–303. New York: McGraw-Hill; Washburn, E. (January/February 2000). Are you ready for generation X? *The Physician Executive, 26(1)*, 51–56; Heng, S. (June 17, 2002). Technology and work—the 21st century and its challenges. *Deutsche Bank Research*, http://www.euractiv.com/Article?tcmuri=tcm:29-110287-16&type=Analysis.
4. Tapscott, 301; Howe, N. (2000). *Millennials Rising*. New York: Vintage Books.
5. http://www.rand.org/pubs/monographs/2004/RAND-MG104.pdf.
6. SeniorNet. (Fall 2003). Technology trends: The changing workforce. http://www.seniornet.org/php/default.php?ClassOrgID=5403&PageID=7142.
7. Ibid.
8. U.S. Bureau of Labor Statistics. (1999). Employment and earning. January issues. Monthly labor review. At www.catalystwomen.org/press/factsheets/factscote00.html; Jamieson, D., O'Mara, J. (1991). *Managing Workforce 2000: Gaining the Diversity Advantage*. San Francisco: Jossey-Bass; American Federation of Labor–Congress of Industrial Organizations. Facts about working women. http://www.aflcio.org/issuespolitics/women/factsaboutworkingwomen.cfm.
9. Shuit, D. (June 2004). Gay marriages, benefits questions. *Workforce Management, 83(6)*, 1.
10. Robinson, B.A. (August 30, 2004). Same-sex marriages (SSM) & civil unions. *Ontario Consultants on Religious Tolerance*, http://www.religioustolerance.org/hom_marr.htm.
11. The Human Rights Campaign (HRC), a gay-positive civil rights agency working for equal treatment for persons of all sexual orientations, offers a Web site with links to descriptions of same-sex marriage and civil union laws in each U.S. state at http://www.hrc.org.
12. Kiger, P. (February 2004). A court decision isn't likely to spur changes in partner benefits. *Workforce Management, 83(2)*, 1–2.
13. U.S. Census Bureau Press Release. (September 8, 2004). Hispanic Heritage Month 2004: Sept. 15–Oct. 15. http://www.census.gov/Press-Release/www/releases/archives/facts_for_features_special_editions/002270.html.
14. Schmitt, E. (April 1, 2001). U.S. Now more diverse, ethnically and racially. *New York Times*, 18.
15. Norris, F. (December 7, 2004). U.S. students fare badly in international survey of math skills. *New York Times*, http://www.nytimes.com/2004/12/07/national/07student.html.
16. Ibid.
17. Arellano, K. (September 4, 2000). Employers look to the disabled: Labor shortage creates opportunity, *Denver Post*, F1.

18. Eckberg, J. (September 26, 2004). Disabled workers can solve shortfall. *The Cincinnati Enquirer,* http://www.enquirer.com/editions/2004/09/26/biz_dailygrind0926.html.
19. CNN/Money. (September 17, 2004). More men charging harassment. http://money.cnn.com/2004/09/17/news/economy/sexual_harassment/.
20. Working Mother Media, Inc. 100 best companies for working mothers 2004–2004 top 10 companies. http://www.workingmother.com/top10.html.
21. Peter Hart and NASD and the Investment Institute.
22. Barletta, M. (May 1, 2000). Pink parasols and a kinky princess. *Trendsight Group,* http://www.trendsight.com/resources/articles/pinkparasols.html.
23. Data Dome, Inc. (August 2004). WorkForce Trends Newsletter. *WorkForce Trends, 3(3),* http://www.datadome.com/worktrends/worktrends3_3.html.
24. http://www.catalystwomen.org/press/factsheets/factscote00.html, 1.
25. Another study, based on top-level men and women, cited similar findings. See Tahmincioglu, E. (September 2004). When women rise. *Workforce Management,* 26–32.
26. Washburn, 51–56; Howe; Mui N. (Feb. 4, 2001). Here comes the kids: Gen Y invades the workplace. *New York Times,* sec. 9, p. 1, col. 3.
27. Data Dome, Inc. (2004). WorkForce Trends Newsletter. *WorkForce Trends, 3(2),* http://www.datadome.com/worktrends/workforcetrends3_2.html.
28. Ibid.
29. CIGNA News Releases & Speeches. (March 2, 2004). Benefits of 401(k) plans may be lost on new "millennial" generation; CIGNA survey finds 401(k)s fail to engage America's youngest workers. http://www.prnewswire.com/cgi-bin/micro_stories.pl?ACCT=149478&TICK=CI20&STORY=/www/story/03-02-2004/0002120458&EDATE=Mar+2,+2004. See also CBS news.com, "The Echo Boomers" (Dec. 6, 2004) www.cbsnews.com/stories/2004/10/01/60minutes/ main646890.shtml.
30. The Institute of Management and Administration. (October 2003). Generation Y creates new challenges for A/E firm managers. *Design Firm Management & Administration Report, 3(10),* 4.
31. Weiss, J. (2000). *Organization Behavior & Change,* 2nd ed. South-Western College Publishing, 18–23.
32. Fulmer, W., Casey, A. (1990). Employment at will: Options for managers. *Academy of Management Review, 4,* 102.
33. Flynn, G. (2000). How do you treat the at-will employment relationship? *Workforce, 79,* 178–179.
34. Fulmer and Casey (1990), 102.
35. For a discussion of these issues, see R. Awney. (1920). *The Acquisitive Society.* New York: Harcourt, Brace & World, 53–55; C. Reich. (1964). The new property. *Yale Law Review; 73,* 733; also Supreme Court case *Perry* v. *Sindermann.*
36. Boatright, J. (2000). *Ethics and the Conduct of Business,* 3rd ed. New Jersey: Prentice Hall, 265.
37. Rowan, J. (April 2000). The moral foundation of employee rights. *Journal of Business Ethics, 24,* 355–361.
38. Ibid., 358.
39. Ibid.
40. Jacoby, S. (1995). Social dimensions of global economic integration. In Jacoby, S., ed. *The Workers of Nations: Industrial Relations in a Global Economy.* New York: Oxford University Press, 21–22. Also see Steiner, S., and Steiner, J. (2000). *Business, Government, and Society,* 9th ed. Boston: McGraw–Hill, 618–619.
41. Schmidt, R. J. (March–April 1996). Japanese management, recession style. *Business Horizons, 39(2),* http://www.findarticles.com/p/articles/mi_m1038/is_n2_v39/ai_18124645; Poór, J. (September 1, 2002). HR practices are changing in Central and Eastern Europe. *Mercer Human Resource Consulting,* http://www.mercer.co.uk/summary.jhtml/dynamic/idContent/1067605.
42. Velasquez, M. (1998). *Business Ethics,* 4th ed. Upper Saddle River, NJ: Prentice Hall, 439, 440.
43. Lewis, D. (March 4, 2004). Pay gap shrinks, but women still work for less. *The Boston Globe,* 1.
44. Velasquez, 439, 440.
45. Hackman, R., Oldham, G., Jansen, R., et al. (Summer 1975). A new strategy for job enrichment. *California Management Review, 17,* 56–58.

46. Bjork, L. (March 1975). An experiment in work satisfaction. *Scientific American, 232(3),* 17–23; also, Simmons, J., Mares, W. (1983). *Working Together.* New York: Knopf.
47. Beauchamp, T., Bowie, N. (1988). *Ethical Theory and Business,* 3rd ed. Upper Saddle River: Prentice Hall, 264. Also see chapter 5 in the 6th edition (2001), published by Prentice Hall.
48. DeGeorge, R. (1990). *Business Ethics,* 3rd ed. New York: McMillan; D. Ewing. (1977). *Freedom Inside the Organization: Bringing Civil Liberties to the Workplace.* New York: McGraw-Hill.
49. Beauchamp and Bowie (1988), 260, 261; Beauchamp and Bowie (2001), 369, ch. 6.
50. "Just cause" guideline. *Hawaii State AFL-CIO.* http://www.hawaflcio.org/J-coz. html; Using the seven tests. *United Electrical, Radio and Machine Workers of America.* http://www.ranknfile-ue.org/stwd_jstcause.html.
51. Meyers, D. (1998). Work and self–respect. In Beauchamp and Bowie (1988), 275–279; Beauchamp and Bowie (2001), 256–258.
52. Court of Common Pleas, Mahoning County, Ohio, No. 98CV1937, 2000; Anderson, T. (May 2001). Elsewhere in the courts . . . *Security Management, 45,* 105.
53. Werhane, P. (1985). *Persons, rights and corporations.* Upper Saddle River: Prentice Hall, 118.
54. Des Jardins, J., McCall, J. (1990). A defense of employee rights. *Journal of Business Ethics, 4,* 367–376.
55. Ibid.
56. Zall, M. (May/June 2001). Employee privacy. *Journal of Property Management, 66,* 16–18.
57. Post, J., Lawrence, A., Weber, J. (1999). *Business and Society,* 9th ed. Boston: McGraw-Hill, 378.
58. Dalton, D., Metzger, M. (Feb. 1993). Integrity testing for personnel selection: An unsparing perspective. *Journal of Business Ethics, 12(2),* 147–156.
59. Carroll, A. (1993). *Business and Society: Ethics and Stakeholder Management,* 3rd ed. Cincinnati: South-Western, 371, 372.
60. Samuels, P. (May 12, 1996). Who's reading your e-mail? Maybe the boss. *New York Times,* 11; also Guernsey, L. (December 16, 1999). On the job, the boss can watch your every online move, and you have a few defenses. *New York Times,* G1, 3.
61. For a list of specific rights, guidelines, and Web sites regarding telephone, computer, and (e)mail monitoring, see: Privacy Rights Clearinghouse. Employee mentoring: Is there privacy in the workplace? http://www.privacyrights.org/fs/fs7-work.htm.
62. Forster, J. (December 21, 2004). Instant messaging causes a problem for companies. *The Standard-Times,* L2, http://www.southcoasttoday.com/daily/12-04/12-21-04/102ca270.htm.
63. Martin, J. (March 1999). Internet policy: Employee rights and wrongs. *Human Resources Focus, 76,* 13.
64. Ibid.
65. Zall, 18.
66. Minarcek, A. (June 29, 2004). Taboo on office romance fading. *Cox News Service,* http://www.azcentral.com/ent/dating/articles/0629officeromance29.html.
67. Des Jardins and McCall, 204–206.
68. Goldstein, R., Nolan, R. (March/April 1975). Personal privacy versus the corporate computer. *Harvard Business Review, 53(2),* 62–70. In addition to these guidelines, another source that provides drug testing guidelines is M. Bernardo. (1994). Workplace drug testing: An employer's development and implementation guide. Washington, DC: Institute for a Drug-Free Workplace.
69. For an updated list of mandatory guidelines for federal workplace drug testing programs, visit the U.S. Department of Health and Social Services–Division of Workplace Programs Web site at http://workplace.samhsa.gov/fedprograms/MandatoryGuidelines/MG04132004.htm.
70. Timms, E. (June 24, 2001). Bush campaigns to outlaw "genetic discrimination." *Boston Globe,* A5.
71. For an updated discussion on genetic nondiscrimination legislation, visit The American Society of Human Genetics Web site at http://genetics.faseb.org/genetics/ashg/news/018.shtml.
72. Des Jardins and McCall, 213.

73. There are several Web sites to view updated employee, consumer, and employer right-to-know legislation and information across industries and products. These include: http://www.ombwatch.org/info, http://www.healthy-communications.org/rightoknowsidebar.html, and http://enviro.blr.com/topic.cfm/topic/160/state/155.

74. Action on Smoking and Health UK. International developments on smoke-free policies. http://www.ash.org.uk/html/workplace/html/smokefreenews.html.

75. There are several Web sites that update smoking and other workplace facts, legislation, and research. These include: http://www.newstarget.com/002342.html, http://www.news-medical.net/?id=5964, http://www.ash.org.uk/html/press/041025.html, http://www.workplacelaw.net/display.php?resource_id=5113&keywords=, and http://www.ahipubs.com/newsletter/ht/ht11.02.04.html.

76. Eisenberg, M., Ranger-Moore, J., Taylor, K., Hall, R., et al. (Feb. 2001). Workplace tobacco policy: Progress on a winding road. *Journal of Community Health, 26,* 1, 23.

77. Karr, A., Guthfield, R. (January 16, 1992). OSHA inches toward limiting smoking. *Wall Street Journal,* B1.

78. DeGeorge, 322–324.

79. Velasquez, M. G. (1988). *Business Ethics: Concepts and Cases,* 2nd ed. Upper Saddle River: Prentice Hall, 388; also see the 4th edition (1998), 463–467.

80. Carroll, 371, 372.

81. U.S. Department of Labor–Office of the Assistant Secretary for Policy. Employment Law Guide–Plant closings and mass layoffs. http://www.dol.gov/asp/programs/guide/layoffs.htm.

82. Fletcher, M. (May 21, 2001). Employee leave and law. *Business Insurance, 35,* 3.

83. Ibid.

84. Online federal and state legislative updates of the FMLA can be found on the following Web sites: http://www.ellnfonet.com/fedarticles/10/5, http://www.dol.gov/esa/programs/whd/state/fmla, and http://www.ppspublishers.com/articles/gl/FMLAeligibility.htm.

85. Kanowitz, L. (1969). *Women and the Law.* Albuquerque, NM: University of New Mexico Press, 36; also quoted in Velasquez (1988), 324; and Velasquez (1998), 387–392.

86. Fehrenbacher, D. (1978). *The Dred Scott Case.* New York: Oxford University Press.

87. Velasquez (1998), 375.

88. Lewis, D. (November 26, 2000). Revisiting equal pay. *Boston Globe,* G2.

89. Des Jardins and McCall, 377–382.

90. Feagin, J., Feagin, C. (1986). *Discrimination American Style,* 2nd ed. Malabar, FL: Robert Krieger, 23–33; Velasquez (1998), 391.

91. J. Krasner. (May 20, 2001). Hitting the glass ceiling. *Boston Globe,* G1.

92. Polek, F. J. (May 21, 2002). Keeping step with the USA Patriot Act. *Sheppard, Mullin, Richter & Hamilton LLP,* http://www.smrh.com/publications/pubview.cfm?pubID=176.

93. Ibid.

94. Noah, T., Karr, A. (November 4, 1991). What new civil rights law will mean: Charges of sex, disability bias will multiply. *Wall Street Journal,* 31.

95. U.S. Equal Opportunity Commission. Title VII of the Civil Rights Act of 1964. Charges: FY 1992–FY 2000, at http://www.eeoc.gov/stats/vii.html.

96. Excerpts from: Supreme Court opinions on limits of Disabilities Act. (Feb. 22, 2001). *New York Times,* A20.

97. Discrimination interviewer questions sometimes illegal. (May 20, 2001). *Boston Globe,* p. H2.

98. Lewis, G2.

99. DeGeorge, 322–324.

100. Ibid.

101. Updates on affirmative action, EEO, and discrimination legislation can be found at http://www.dol.gov/dol/topic/hiring/affirmativeact.htm.

102. *Bakke* v. *Regents of the University of California.*

103. Mollins, C. (July 17, 1995). Shaky freedoms: The U.S. supreme court challenges liberalism. *McLean's,* 22; and Gwynne, S. (April 1, 1996). Undoing diversity: A bombshell court ruling curtails affirmative action, *Time, 147,* 54.

104. Wilgoren, J. (March 28, 2001). U.S. court bars race as factor in school entry. *New York Times,* http://www.nytimes.com/2001/03/28/national/28MICH.html.

105. Steiner and Steiner, 656.

106. Kjos, L. (December 16, 2004). Analysis: Affirmative action stirs debate. *The Washington Times,* http://www.washtimes.com/upi-breaking/20041216-023249-7254r.htm.

107. Strom, S. (October 20, 1991). Harassment rules often not posted. *New York Times,* 1, 22.

108. Finkelstein, K. (May 25, 2001). TWA to pay $2.6 million to settle harassment suit. *New York Times,* B6.

109. Machlowitz, M., Machlowitz, D. (September 25, 1986). Hug by the boss could lead to a slap from the judge. *Wall Street Journal,* 20; Wermiel, S., Trost, C. (June 20, 1986). Justices say hostile job environment due to sex harassment violates rights. *Wall Street Journal,* 2.

110. Hayes, A. (October 11, 1991). How the courts define harassment. *Wall Street Journal,* B1; Lublin, J. (October 11, 1991). Companies try a variety of approaches to halt sexual harassment on the job. *Wall Street Journal,* B1.

111. Mastalli, G. (1991). Appendix: The legal context. In Matthews, J., Goodpaster, K., Nash, L., eds. *Policies and Reasons: A Casebook in Business Ethics,* 2nd ed. New York: McGraw–Hill, 157, 158.

112. Long, S., Leonard, C. (October 1999). The changing face of sexual harassment, *Human Resources Focus,* S1–S3.

113. Ibid.

114. Ibid.

115. http://www.blr.com is an excellent source of training for human resources employees and employers. This section is also based on the work by Long and Leonard.

116. Foreman, J., Lehman, B. (October 21, 1991). What to do if you think you may be guilty of sex harassment. *Boston Globe.*

117. Johannes, L., Lublin, S. (May 9, 1996). Sexual-harassment cases trip up foreign companies. *Wall Street Journal,* B4.

118. Maatman, G., Jr. (July 2000). A global view of sexual harassment. *HR Magazine, 45,* 158.

119. Steeley, B. (September 2000). Evaluating your client as a possible qui tam relator. *The Practical Litigator, 11(5),* 15.

120. Hoffman, H., Moore, J. (1990). Whistle blowing: Its moral justification. In James, G. *Business Ethics: Readings and Cases in Corporate Morality,* 2nd ed., 332. New York: McGraw-Hill.

121. Ibid., 333.

122. The Brown & Williamson papers can be found at http://www.library.ucsf.edu/tobacco.

123. Sass, R. (2001). The killing of Karen Silkwood: The story behind the Kerr–McGee plutonium case. *Winter Relations Industrielles, 56,* 222.

124. *Haley v. Retsinas,* 1998 U.S. App. LEXIS 4654 (8th Cir. Ct., March 16, 1998), No. 97–1946; also see http://www.hrlawindex.com/articles/a/w 0525 9.html.

125. DeGeorge, 208–214.

126. Near, J., Miceli, M., Jensen, R. (March 1983). Variables associated with the whistle-blowing process. Working Paper Series 83–111, Ohio State University, College of Administrative Science, Columbus, 5. Cited in Carroll, 354, 355.

127. Carroll, 356.

128. Ewing.

129. See the Brown and Williamson papers.

130. Maatman, 158.

7

Business Ethics, Stakeholder Management, and Multinational Corporations in the Global Environment

We have six billion people on the planet . . . five billion of them in developing countries. The one billion in the developed world has eighty percent of the assets, the five billion have twenty percent. . . . The inequities are considerable and we have 2.8 billion people who are living under two dollars a day, and 1.2 billion under one dollar a day. And we find in fact in so many parts of the world that the equity is in fact diminishing in terms of rich and poor rather than improving.[1]

What do we mean by globalization? Globalization is about an increasingly interconnected and interdependent world; it is about international trade, investment, and finance that have been growing far faster than national incomes.

It is about technologies that have already transformed our abilities to communicate in ways that would have been unimaginable a few years ago. It is about our global environment, communicable diseases, crime, violence, and terrorism. It is about new opportunities for workers in all countries to develop their potential and to support their families through jobs created by greater economic integration.

But it is also about international financial crises, about workers in developed countries who fear losing their jobs to lower-cost countries with limited labor rights. And it is about workers in developing countries who worry about decisions affecting their lives that are made in faraway head offices of international corporations.

> Globalization is about risks as well as about opportunities. We must deal with these risks at the national level by managing adjustment processes and by strengthening social, structural, and financial systems. And at the global level, we must establish a stronger international financial architecture and work to fight deadly diseases, to turn back environmental degradation, and to use communications to give voice to the voiceless.

> We cannot turn back globalization. Our challenge is to make globalization an instrument of opportunity and inclusion—not of fear and insecurity. Globalization must work for all.[2]

There are more challenges ahead, and bigger ones.

> In the next 25 years, world population will go up by 2 billion to a total of 8 billion people, with 98% of that increase in the developing world. The population of Europe will shrink, while that of the United States will go up a little, but largely from migration.

> As we go forward the voices of the poor must be our guide.

> Time is short. We must be the first generation to think both as nationals of our countries and as global citizens in an ever shrinking and more connected planet. Unless we hit hard at poverty, we will not have a stable and peaceful world. Our children will inherit the world we create. The issues are urgent. The future for our children will be shaped by the decisions we make, and the courage and leadership we show today.[3]

7.1 THE CONNECTED GLOBAL ECONOMY AND GLOBALIZATION

The global environment consists of a dynamic set of relationships among financial markets, cultures, political orientations, laws, technologies, government policies, and numerous stakeholder interests. This chapter presents different dimensions of globalization: the driving forces, business opportunities, the "dark side" issues, and debates regarding the positive and destructive ethical effects on consumers and disadvantaged people. Multinational corporations (MNCs) as stakeholders and their host-country relationships are then presented. We conclude by identifying negotiation methods for making ethical decisions taking cross-cultural contexts into consideration.

Globalization and the Forces of Change   Because globalization involves the integration of technology, markets, politics, cultures, labor, production, and commerce, it is both the processes and the results of this integration. The global economy has been estimated at $33 trillion. Although globalization has facilitated economic growth over several decades, this process is also vulnerable to the forces in the environment as discussed in this chapter. The most recent threat to economic stability and growth is global terrorism and the aftermath of continuing national and international security threats and costs. Nevertheless, the technological, cultural, production,

and political factors have to date accelerated global integration. Some of these forces include:

- The end of communism, which has allowed the opening of closed economies. The emergence of China as a global trading partner. The U.S. November 2004 trade deficit was $60.3 billion; the largest share was with China—an imbalance of $16.6 billion.[4]

- Information technologies and the Internet continue to accelerate communication and productivity within and across companies globally. Today it is fairly easy for any company to globalize using the Internet.

- Entrepreneurship and entrepreneurs are more mobile, skilled, intelligent, and thriving worldwide.

- Free trade and trading agreements among nations open borders: Among them are the European Union (EU)—(see Figure 7.1 for a list of these countries); the North American Free Trade Agreement (NAFTA), which encourages large and small businesses to operate in Canada and Mexico; the Association of Southeast Asian Nations (ASEAN), which helps emerging companies to compete with European and U.S. firms; and the World Trade Organization (WTO), which accepted China starting in 2002 and which provides a framework that "creates stability and predictability so that investors can, with more security, plan their activity. . . ."[5] Global trade has tripled over the past 25 years.

- The World Bank and the International Monetary Fund (IMF) offer a conduit for needed capital flows to countries participating in building the global economy.

- As they grow and spread, transnational firms also open new markets and create jobs across the globe. Such transnational giants include General Electric, British Petroleum Amoco, Daimler Chrysler, Shell Oil, Ford, Procter & Gamble, Coca-Cola, and Heinz, to name only a few. An estimated 40,000 to 100,000 multinational companies continue to do business across national boundaries and contribute to the global economy. It is likely these numbers will increase. Where there are new markets, companies will move and be created.

- A shift to service economies and knowledge workers using technologies has also propelled innovation and productivity worldwide.

- "Global terrorism" and counter responses since September 11, 2001 continue to present regions, countries, businesses, groups, and individuals with sizable risks and costs. For example, from an American perspective since the start of the U.S.-led war

FIGURE 7.1   European Union Countries

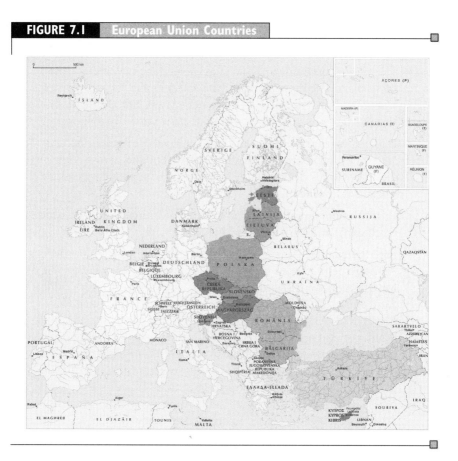

Legend: *Light gray* = **Pre-May 1, 2004 EU Members;** *Dark gray* = **May 1, 2004 Acceding Members;** *Medium gray* = **Post-May 1, 2004 Candidate Countries.**

Source: © European Communities, 1995–2004, http://www.europa.eu.int/abc/maps/index_de.htm.

on Iraq, through March 27, 2005, 1,704 coalition forces have been killed, including 1,528 U.S. military. Before the second election of George W. Bush, the U.S. Congress approved $151.1 billion for Iraq. An additional $60 to $100 billion was expected to be passed after the election.[6] Also, due in part to the Iraq war, a U.S. surplus of $127.4 billion in 2001 has risen to a projected deficit in the 2004 budget year of $477 billion, and is projected at $368 billion,[7] excluding war costs, for fiscal 2005. Add war costs and this figure could climb to almost half a trillion U.S. dollars.

A key ethical question posed by U.S. and coalition responses to post-9/11 and the Iraqi invasion remains: Will the benefits of the secondary goal of creating and spreading democracy in the Middle East exceed the costs incurred? Certainly international business and the commercial aspect of globalization could thrive if this were the case.

7.2 GLOBALIZATION AND BEST BUSINESS PRACTICES

By 2020, the global economy is predicted to grow by 80%.[8] Much of this growth will be driven by corporate activities. Processes of globalization accompanying economic growth present both moral and profitable opportunities for businesses that include and treat stakeholders fairly. The process of what has been termed "smart globalization" involves including local stakeholder interests and resources in international business growth.

"Smart Globalization" Some multinationals have experienced notable failures in their attempts to grow big and fast in developing countries. AT&T did not meet its promise of executing 20 ventures in China. Enron Corporation's $4 billion Indian power plant investment also did not work. General Motors' planned Asia-wide network of auto plants based on its $1.2 billion plant in Shanghai failed. Moreover, "Exxon, Mobil, Cargill, Freeport-McMorRan, and Royal Dutch/Shell became targets of local uprisings over oil, mining, and other projects in Indonesia, India, and Nigeria."[9] A lesson learned: "Being first and biggest in an emerging market isn't always the best way to conquer it. A better tactic is to learn about local cultures—and build a presence carefully." Whirlpool, Citibank, and Kodak have pursued global competitive tactics that set a standard for growing in developing nations: (1) Methodically build a presence from the ground up instead of planning megaprojects, takeovers, and acquisitions. Partner with a savvy local business professional who has a factory and build from his or her strengths. (2) Do extensive homework before starting a business in the developing country by consulting with and learning from local stakeholders: entrepreneurs, bureaucrats, government officials, and grassroots social groups. (3) Forget about targeting the richest 10% of the global population and then marketing to them. There is an international market of 4 billion people who earn less than $1,500 annually. They are the source of future growth, even though few now can afford a personal computer, car, or mortgage. (4) Introduce and help stimulate product use with local populations. Hewlett-Packard offers computer literacy programs from Central Asia to Africa—serving commercial and social need programs simultaneously.

The central premise of "smart globalization" is that globalization can be a double-edged sword.

> The global or globalizing firm has the potential to reap several types of benefits such as the vast potential of a much larger market arena, opportunities to capture scale- and location-based cost efficiencies, and exposure to a multiplicity of new product and process ideas. However, globalization also exposes the firm to numerous strategic and organizational challenges emanating from

a dramatic increase in diversity, complexity, and uncertainty—external as well as internal to the firm. How managers address these challenges determines whether globalization yields competitive advantage or disadvantage and makes the company stronger or weaker. "Smart" globalization is the ability to capture the benefits and minimize the costs and risks.[10]

Several companies are using "smart globalization" practices. Whirlpool works with local distributors in China. The firm's machines have been modified for local tastes, and its basic models now use 70% of the same parts. The company expects that demand abroad will grow 17% to 293 million units through 2009, while flattening in the United States. Citibank in Bangalore, India, works with mid-sized companies to establish retail bank accounts for all their employees—from janitors to top officials—with a $22 deposit. A card is issued for accessing cash, getting loans, and paying bills at local ATMs. In three years, the company has gained 200,000 retail customers, while doubling its base in India to $10 million. Noted strategist C. K. Prahalad notes, "The next round of global expansion is as much about imagination as about resources. Putting a billion dollars down does not involve imagination. With the mistakes of the '90s behind them, the winners will approach the world in a smarter way."[11]

World's Most Admired Companies: Best Practices   The Hay Group annually produces a peer-interviewed and -ranked list of the world's most admired firms for *Fortune* Magazine. Hay Group led this survey in 2004. To understand how and why the most admired companies perform better, the Hay Group sent follow-up questionnaires to senior operating and human resources executives from more than 150 companies worldwide.[12] *Fortune* magazine's list of the 25 "World's Most Admired Companies" for 2004 includes:

1. Wal-Mart Stores (U.S.)
2. General Electric (U.S.)
3. Microsoft (U.S.)
4. Johnson & Johnson (U.S.)
5. Berkshire Hathaway (U.S.)
6. Dell (U.S.)
7. IBM (U.S.)
8. Toyota Motor (Japan)
9. Procter & Gamble (U.S.)
10. FedEx (U.S.)
11. Coca-Cola (U.S.)
12. Citigroup (U.S.)
13. United Parcel Service (U.S.)
14. Pfizer (U.S.)
15. BMW (Germany)
16. Sony (Japan)
17. Intel (U.S.)
18. Walt Disney (U.S.)
19. Nokia (Finland)
20. Home Depot (U.S.)
21. Nestlé (Switzerland)
22. PepsiCo (U.S.)
23. Anheuser-Busch (U.S.)
24. Honda Motor (Japan)
25. Lowe's (U.S.)

Although some of the most admired firms have treated their stake-holders with questionable ethics (e.g., Wal-Mart's alleged unfair dealing with employee benefits and wages), these same firms provide jobs and benefits to local and global economies. Effective business and ethical practices of these companies include the following:

- More than 91% of respondents from the most admired companies reported that their leaders " . . . are honest with each other about the realities of the business, as did 81% of those from the peer group. Both groups also scored high when asked about their leaders' honesty with employees and the willingness of employees to speak candidly with leaders. 'We spend a lot of time communicating with people,' says Smith, the FedEx CEO."[13] It is interesting to note, however, that those surveyed in these companies thought insufficient coaching and feedback were offered to employees.

- Eighty-four percent of the most admired groups reported that their strategy had a clear action plan with clear accountability.[14]

- Eighty-one percent of the most admired firms said that roles and responsibilities at their companies were clear, and 80% reported that their jobs were designed to ensure that no gaps existed in accountability. Fred Smith, chairman and CEO of FedEx stated, "We have a long-term incentive that is tied into our rolling three-year performance. We operate to a very rigorous business-planning process, a formal one that's approved by the board. Each week the strategic management committee measures against last year and against that business plan."[15]

- "Talent management" is viewed as a core accountability for line managers in the most admired companies, not as a human resource responsibility.

Although globalization has provided "triple bottom-line benefits"[16]—i.e., financial, social and environmental results—not all regions and countries have been winners in the globalization process. The countries of the First World—the more advanced industrialized countries—have reaped the major benefits, that is, higher standards of living and increased trade, gross national product (GNP), and gross domestic product (GDP). Singapore, Hong Kong, Taiwan, Korea, India, and several Latin American countries are integrating into the global economy as well. High-level U.S. intelligence analysts forecast that India and China, which together comprise more than a third of the planet's population, will surpass Europe and compete with the U.S. as major global powers by the year 2020.[17] The Second World countries—former communist nations under the previous Soviet Union—continue to struggle out of their planned economies. The poorest Third World countries, which include all of sub-Saharan Africa and much of the

Middle East, South Asia, and Central and South America, continue to struggle with poverty. Criticisms of globalization are discussed in the following section.

7.3 Issues with Globalization: The Dark Side

It is difficult to determine whether the process of globalization is the cause or effect of the forces driving this phenomenon. The process of globalization may be producing "losers" (i.e., countries that cannot share in the wealth- and health-generating processes, activities, and outcomes of globalization because they are either excluded from or ignored with respect to the positive side of globalization—for example, technology development and use, education, and economic development).

Critics generally argue that globalization has caused, or at least enhanced, the following problems: crime and corruption; drug consumption; massive layoffs that occur when companies move to regions that offer cheaper labor; decreases in wages; the erosion of individual nations' sovereignty; and the Westernization (led by Americanization) of culture, standards, and trends in entertainment, fashion, food, technology, movie star role models, ways of living, and values. We will discuss some of these issues related and attributed to globalization.

Crime and Corruption   "In Eastern Europe, traffickers ship girls through the Balkans and into sex slavery. Russians launder money through tiny Pacific islands that have hundreds of banks but scarcely any roads. Colombian drug barons accumulate such vast resources that they can acquire a Soviet submarine to ship cocaine to the United States. . . . [I]t is clear that the globalization of crime is a logical outcome of the fall of Communism. Capitalism and Communism, ideologies that served as intellectual straitjackets for Americans and Soviets, allowed them to feel justified in unsavory proxies to fight their cold war."[18] The Global Trends 2015 Report estimates that corruption costs $500 billion annually, 1% of the global economy. The report also stated that in the illegitimate economy, narcotics trafficking has projected annual revenues of $100 to $300 billion. Auto theft in Europe and the United States is estimated to net $9 billion, and the sex slave business projects $7 billion. Every third cigarette exported is sold on the black market.[19] The Corruption Perception Index—based on the perceptions of ordinary citizens, business leaders, and experts and developed by the nonprofit group Transparency International—shows that the most corrupt countries in 2004 were Turkmenistan, Azerbaijan, Paraguay, Chad, Myanmar, Nigeria, Bangladesh, and Haiti. The United States ranked toward the bottom of the top 20 least corrupt countries, tied with

FIGURE 7.2	The 2004 Corruption Perception Index*

Least Corrupt

Rank	Country	Score
1	Finland	9.7
2	New Zealand	9.6
3	Denmark	9.5
4	Iceland	9.5
5	Singapore	9.3
6	Sweden	9.2
7	Switzerland	9.1
8	Norway	8.9
9	Australia	8.8
10	The Netherlands	8.7
11	United Kingdom	8.6
12	Canada	8.5
13	Austria	8.4
14	Luxembourg	8.4
15	Germany	8.2
16	Hong Kong	8.0
17	Belgium	7.5
18	Ireland	7.5
19	United States	7.5
20	Chile	7.4

Most Corrupt

Rank	Country	Score
1	Bangladesh	1.5
2	Haiti	1.5
3	Nigeria	1.6
4	Chad	1.7
5	Myanmar	1.7
6	Azerbaijan	1.9
7	Paraguay	1.9
8	Angola	2.0
9	Congo, Democratic Republic	2.0
10	Côte d'Ivoire	2.0
11	Georgia	2.0
12	Indonesia	2.0
13	Tajikistan	2.0
14	Turkmenistan	2.0
15	Cameroon	2.1
16	Iraq	2.1
17	Kenya	2.1
18	Pakistan	2.1
19	Sudan	2.2
20	Ukraine	2.2

*The lower the score, the more corrupt.

Source: Transparency International. Transparency International Corruption Perceptions Index 2004, http://www.transparency.org/pressreleases_archive/2004/2004.10.20.cpi.en.html.

Belgium and Ireland. See Figure 7.2 for recent survey results of the global country corruption index. Interesting to note that some of the industrialist leading nations did not rank at the top for non-corrupt activities.

Economic Poverty and Child Slave Labor
"More than 120 million children between 5 and 14 years old work full time. Include children whose work is a secondary activity and the number climbs to 250 million."[20] Child labor exists in both developing and industrialized countries, but mostly in South and Southeast Asia, South America, Africa, and increasingly in Eastern Europe where there is an economic transition from a command economy to a market economy.[21] "Among countries, the big losers are in Africa, south of the Sahara. They are not losing, however, because they are being crushed by globalization. . . . [T]hey are losing because they are being ignored by globalization.

They are not in the *global economy*. No one in the global business community wants anything to do with countries where illiteracy is high, where modern infrastructure (telecommunications, reliable electrical power) does not exist, and where social chaos reigns. Such countries are neither potential markets nor potential production bases."[22] The gap in per capita GDP between the richest and poorest countries in the world is about 140:1. This gap will increase as the shift from industrial- to knowledge-based economies continues to occur. "Any Third World country that wants the benefits of globalization has to get itself organized to acquire those technologies."[23]

Regions of the Ivory Coast of Africa (e.g., Logbogba, Sinfra, Soubre) continue to attract child labor traffickers (those who buy, enslave, and sell children to work on industrial projects and plantations, like cocoa and chocolate production). Annual wages paid for children under the age of 14 are about US $135 to US $165. Poverty is dire in this region. A broad UNICEF estimate is that there are 200,000 children worldwide who are victims of traffickers every year. Ivory Coast law permits children over 14 to work if the work is not dangerous and they have parental consent.[24]

The Third World includes not only all of sub-Saharan Africa, but also most of the Middle East and much of South Asia and Central and South America. "Hunger is common; disease is rampant; infant mortality is high; life expectancy is short."[25] Notable economists from the Group of Eight (leading industrial countries) conclude that solutions to Third World poverty must include ". . . systematic attempts to change incentives at every level in the global system—from the gangsterish Third World governments that exploit their citizens to the international institutions that prop them up through continued lending."[26]

The Global Digital Divide

"The Universal Declaration of Human Rights and Article 19 of the International Covenant on Civil and Political Rights (ICCPR) proclaim the freedom of everyone without discrimination to enjoy access to information. The majority of countries have ratified and accepted the duty to guarantee this freedom by signing the ICCPR.[27] Freedom of expression as a right includes 'freedom to seek, receive, and impart information and ideas of all kinds, regardless of frontiers, either orally, in writing or in print, in the form of art, or through any other media of his choice."[28]

The world continues to have different levels of access to technology. One third of the world's population is disconnected from and has no access to the Internet. This fact continues to broaden the divide between the have's and the have-not's and between the First and Third World countries. Less than 1% of online users live in Africa. Less than

5% of computers are connected to the Internet in developing countries. The developed world has almost 50 phone lines for every 100 people, compared to 1.4 phones per 100 people in low-income countries. Countries excluded from the global economy are those that cannot and do not build access to the Internet. Wireless technologies offer encouraging signs for Third World country access to First World technologies.[29] The EU has committed to concentrate its efforts on formulating information on society policies focusing on EU coordination, Internet governance, and financing.[30] The U.S., technology multinationals, and other regional alliances are also working to fund and supply less-advantaged countries with Internet capabilities.[31]

Critics of globalization, on the other hand, would argue that the technology revolution and the Internet powered by globalization, telecommunications, information, and transportation, integrates the world economy into a networked global village. One consequence is that technological changes increase child pornography as a consumptive practice as well as an industry. Also, new values and ethical standards are influenced and created through cyberspace. "What are the implications for ethics and value systems as a result of the changes and transformations attributed to the technological imperatives initiated by globalization? Has human nature changed as a result of globalization and the technological innovation and market competition? Is there a legitimate basis for a social divide between global regions over ethics and values—or a lack of ethical values?"[32]

Westernization (Americanization) of Cultures

Globalization has brought "Americanization" (some critics say imperialism) to other cultures through fast-food commerce (McDonald's, the *Fast Food Nation* phenomenon discussed in Chapter 4, and Starbucks, for starters). The "McDonaldization of Society"[33] is "the process by which the principles of the fast-food restaurant are coming to dominate more and more sectors of American society as well as the rest of the world."[34] George Ritzer, the author of the book *The McDonaldization of Society*, argues that "McDonaldization affects not only the restaurant business but also education, work, the criminal justice system, health care, travel, leisure, dieting, politics, the family, religion, and virtually every other aspect of society."[35] (Ritzer states toward the end of his book that McDonaldization will someday pass on or "until the nature of society has changed so dramatically that they can no longer adapt to it."[36])

In addition to fast food, the Internet has brought instant exposure to all forms of American culture: entertainment, films, news, music, and art. Values and ways of living underlie these influences and are not always welcome in many countries—France, China, Singapore, and countries in the Middle East to name a few. Serious ethical questions are asked that are related to problems and threats of globalization through Westernization: "Does globalization result in cultural and economic homogenization through a heightened emphasis on consumerism? Do local and global values change as a result of international integration that promotes the conversion of national economies into environmentally and socially harmful export-oriented systems for competition in geographically and culturally transcendent 'world markets'?"[37]

"Affluenza" is a society's "sickness," a "disease" experienced through materialistic overconsumption.[38] Countries like the United States can experience affluenza from so much economic prosperity and access to products and services. Compared to poorer countries, and even some European countries, the U.S. consumption of energy, food, housing space, and other indicators of standard of living is questionable according to critics of globalization. Does the process of "affluenza" through globalization create and change values affecting perceptions and beliefs that everything is for sale?

The World Trade Center attack and the war on Iraq focused on America's image and influence abroad, particularly in the Middle East. Journalists and the media asked, "Who Hates the U.S.? Who Loves It?"[39] One article noted, "Take Iran. In the 1960s the writer Jalal Al-e Ahmad identified what he called a cultural 'illness' that had stricken the country's cities and towns. He coined a new word to describe it: gharbzadegi—'Westsicken-ness,' or 'Westoxication.' He mourned the villager who 'in search of work flees from the village to the town so he can drink Pepsi-Cola and eat a five-rial sandwich and see a Brigitte Bardot film. . . .' Two decades later, the elimination of 'Westoxication' was a central goal of Ayatollah Ruhollah Khomeini. Now Osama bin Laden is accusing Saudi Arabia of becoming Westoxicated by allowing American military forces on its soil."[40] The article continued: "An important feature of this complicated landscape is a broad chasm between the way Americans see themselves and the way they are seen. . . . A good deal of the struggle is over something that has long troubled traditional societies: the invasion of their cultures by powerful outside influences, forces like social mobility and cosmopolitan thinking that can undermine the authority of clans and religious elders, kings and dictators. Americans sometimes call the new influences freedom. Older societies have other names."[41]

Loss of Nation-State Sovereignty

Critics also protest that globalization erodes the ability of governments to protect the interests of their citizens against more powerful multinational corporations. At conflict are the benefits of economic globalization and the laws and institutions within these nations' own boundaries. Part of the debate centers on the argument that market forces are global and must be dealt with by global businesses.

There is also tension over sovereignty between nations and multinationals regarding power and influence. An example was the rejection of the proposed merger between General Electric and Honeywell by the European Commission's antitrust authorities. The merger, it was argued, would have left public interest behind, because these companies bring different legal and regulatory traditions across the Atlantic. Questions raised included: "What right does the European Commission have telling two American companies what they can and cannot do . . . especially when its decision conflicts with the decision reached by the relevant American authority? Sure, [the United States] supports the rule of law, but whose law? Aren't [U.S.] antitrust laws, which reflect our strong market tradition, superior to Europe's, which tend to reflect a strong statist tradition?"[42]

These arguments diminish when evidence is provided that multinationals cannot, and do not claim to protect citizens during wars and regional conflicts; collect taxes; distribute benefits; build roads and infrastructure; care for the environment; or protect the rights of individuals, groups, and the elderly. In fact, governments subsidize and support companies when needed. In the immediate aftermath of the terrorist attack on the World Trade Center, the U.S. airlines suffered sizable financial losses. It is estimated that 2005 losses in the industry will be $3.4 billion, up from $1 billion.[43]

Other industries (e.g., railroad, automobile, agribusiness, aerospace) have also been subsidized by government funds. Still, it is argued that "globalization will continue to chip away at the power of the nation state. As the Europeans know from their experience over the last 50 years, surrendering some degree of national autonomy is a natural and inevitable concomitant of growing economic interdependence."[44] The degree to which nation-states share and/or give up power, influence, and sovereignty to global companies—and the types of power, influence, and sovereignty they do give up or share—is and will be a continuing subject of debate. We continue the discussion of ethical implications of globalization in the next section.

7.4 MULTINATIONAL ENTERPRISES AS STAKEHOLDERS

Multinational enterprises (MNEs) are corporations that "own or control production or service facilities outside the country in which they are based."[45] "In the United States, MNCs [Multinational Corporations] account for more than 60% of the export of goods and 40% of the import of goods. . . . The U.S.-based MNCs employ about 20 million workers in the United States, while U.S. affiliates of foreign companies employ about 5 million workers in the U.S."[46] MNEs also are referred to as global, transnational, and international companies.[47] No distinction is made here among these names. Global enterprises are highly decentralized, operate across a large range of countries, consider no geographic area as a primary base for any particular function, and move to areas to improve competitive advantage.[48]

Companies go global to enhance profit by creating value, building and increasing markets, and reducing costs. Costs are reduced by locating and using raw materials, skilled labor, land, and taxes at lower costs. Value can also be added by joint venturing with other national and regional partners who have market reach, global skills, experience, and resources.

Power of Multinational Enterprises   Although MNEs often reflect and extend their home nation's culture and resources, many are powerful enough to act as independent nations. This section focuses on MNEs as independent, powerful stakeholders, using their power across national boundaries to gain comparative advantages, with or without the support of their home country. Common characteristics MNEs share include: (1) operating a sales organization, manufacturing plant, distribution center, licensed business, or subsidiary in at least two countries; (2) earning an estimated 25 to 45% of revenue from foreign markets; and (3) having common ownership, resources, and global strategies.[49] Because MNEs often span nations, governments, and different types of businesses and markets, their operations are based on a shared network of strategies, information and data, expertise, capital, and resources.[50] MNEs have become the most strategically powerful stakeholders in the race to compete and dominate global industry market shares. "Privately held multinational corporations now represent many of the largest economic entities on Earth, larger than most countries, amounting to about thirteen of the fifty largest economic entities, and about forty-eight of the largest one hundred. Multinational businesses have the ability to avoid or to hamper legal enforcement on certain occasions—by withdrawal or by threatening withdrawal from economically dependent nations."[51] In 1995, almost 70% of world trade was controlled by 500 corporations. One percent of all multinationals own half the total stock of foreign direct investment. About one-third of the $3.3 trillion in goods and services transaction that took place in 1990 occurred with a single firm.[52]

The world's largest companies are shown in Figure 7.3. They include Wal-Mart, British Petroleum (UK), ExxonMobil, Royal Dutch/Shell

FIGURE 7.3	World's Largest Companies		
Search Rank	Revenues Company	Profits ($ Millions)	($ Millions)
1	Wal-Mart Stores	263,009.00	9,054.00
2	BP	232,571.00	10,267.00
3	ExxonMobil	222,883.00	21,510.00
4	Royal Dutch/Shell Group	201,728.00	12,496.00
5	General Motors	195,324.00	3,822.00
6	Ford Motor Company	164,505.00	495
7	DaimlerChrysler	156,602.20	507
8	Toyota Motors	153,111.00	10,288.10
9	General Electric	134,187.00	15,002.00
10	Total (French company)	118,441.40	7,950.60

Source: Fortune.com/Global 500, "World's largest corporations." Also reference Hjelt, P. (July 26, 2004). The Fortune Global 500, *Fortune*, 179.

Group, General Motors, Ford Motor Company, Daimler Chrysler, Toyota, General Electric, and Total. Half of these firms are U.S. based.

The dominant goal of MNEs is, as noted earlier, to make a profit and take comparative advantage of marketing, trade, cost, investment, labor, and other factors. At the same time, MNEs assist local economies in many ways, as will be explained. The ethical questions critics of MNEs have raised are reflected in the following statement by the late Raymond Vernon, noted Harvard professor and international business expert: "Is the multinational enterprise undermining the capacity of nations to work for the welfare of their people? Is the multinational enterprise being used by a dominant power as a means of penetrating and controlling the economies of other countries?"[53] The next subsection addresses these questions in a discussion of the mutual responsibilities and expectations of MNEs and their host countries.

Misuses of MNE Power

Corporations cannot act as if they operate in a social vacuum. Society's values changed after September 11 and in order to maintain legitimacy, organizations were now expected to take into consideration a new social framework where society expected them to go beyond mere financial decisions and do "the right thing". This change is evident from the hundreds of shareholder resolutions, lodged in the last two years, relating to social issues. It is also reflected in the new environment of corporate social responsibility and increased disclosure. September 11 and the endless stream of corporate failures made people question more closely the motives of U.S. corporate management.[54]

Crises since the birth of the multinational corporation after World War II have raised international concern over the ethical conduct of

MNEs in host and other countries. Most recently, the corporate scandals of Enron, WorldCom, and other firms discussed in previous chapters and in the previous excerpt emphasized the legitimacy of global corporation accounting practices (and loopholes) and their stakeholder relationships. And not long ago, the Ford-Bridgestone/Firestone tire crisis was international in nature. These companies were not forthright early on with their consumers about defects known by the companies. Union Carbide's historic chemical spill disaster in Bhopal, India, resulted in thousands of deaths and injuries and alarmed other nations over the questionable safety standards and controls of MNE foreign operations. Nestlé's marketing of its powdered infant milk formula that resulted in the illness and death of a large number of infants in less-developed countries raised questions about the lack of proper product instructions issued to indigent, less-educated consumers. (Nestlé's practice resulted in a boycott of the company from 1976 to 1984.) Also, the presence of MNEs in South Africa raised criticisms over the role of large corporations in actively supporting apartheid or government-supported racism. Because MNEs had to pay taxes to the South African government and because apartheid was a government-supported policy, MNEs—it is argued—supported racism. Several U.S.-based MNEs that operated in South Africa witnessed boycotts and disinvestments by many shareholders. Many MNEs, including IBM and Polaroid, later withdrew. Post-apartheid South Africa has seen the reentry of companies from all countries. Another long-standing moral issue is the practice of MNEs of not paying their fair share of taxes in countries where they do business and in their home countries. Through transfer pricing and other creative accounting techniques, many MNEs have shown paper losses, thereby enabling them to avoid paying any taxes.

As noted earlier, the post-9/11 and post-corporate scandal environment added moral as well as legal pressures on U.S.-based MNEs' tax practices and offshore business movement.

> With September 11 came the clamp down on terrorists and their funding. The likelihood that terrorists would want to move their funds around unnoticed highlighted the importance of countering money laundering. With the focus on finding and confiscating terrorists' funds it was realized that the countries which provided an environment conducive to money laundering were the same countries to which U.S. companies were moving to minimize their taxes. September 11 also brought other issues to the fore. The increased cost of homeland security together with the cost of fighting terrorists outside of the U.S. would mean higher taxes, at the same time that some major U.S. companies were reorganizing themselves so they would pay less tax. September 11 also saw an increase in nationalism and being labeled unpatriotic was not something for U.S. citizens and companies to be proud of. This led to off-shoring being seen as a moral issue.[55]

Critics claim that many multinational corporations are not fulfilling their part of the implicit social contract discussed in Chapters 5 and 6.

Some of these critics include Richard Barnet and John Cavanagh in their book *Global Dreams,* David Korten in *When Corporations Rule the World,* Tom Athanasiou in *Divided Planet: The Ecology of Rich and Poor,* Paul Hawken in *The Ecology of Commerce,* and William Greider in *One World, Ready or Not.*[56] Multinationals' practices subject to criticism include committing corporate crimes, exerting undue political influence and control, determining and controlling plant closings and layoffs, and damaging the physical environment and human health. Evidence regarding these claims showed, for example, that 11% of 1,043 MNEs studied were involved in one or more major crimes over a 10-year period. The crimes included foreign bribery, kickbacks, and improper payments. A small sample of those firms included Enron, WorldCom, Adelphia, American Cyanamid, Anheuser-Busch, Bethlehem Steel, Allied Chemical, Ashland Oil, and Beatrice Foods. Large corporations (along with trial lawyers and labor unions) also have immense influence through political action committees (PACs). The organization Common Cause noted that the majority of soft money contributions to both American parties in 1999 came from corporate business interests. With regard to plant closings and "downsizings," critics are concerned that some MNEs are more concerned with a particular profit margin than with their share of responsibility to community and society. After all, taxpayers support roads and other external conditions that allow corporations to operate in a country. Although corporations are not expected to be a welfare system for employees, critics note that large companies are expected to share in the social consequences of their actions, especially when, for example, plant-closing decisions are made to reap the benefits of cheaper labor in another country. Finally, there is historical evidence that several large corporations have harmed the physical environment and the health of their employees and local communities. Classic crises cases discussed in Chapter 4 regarding asbestos manufacturing, oil spills, chemical plant explosions, toxic dumping, and industrial air pollution demonstrate corporate misuses of the environment in recent history. The external and human costs that communities, governments, the environment, and taxpayers have had to pay for these misuses of power are documented.

In the following sections, two perspectives regarding global corporations' responsibilities—that of the MNE and that of the host country—are discussed.

MNE Perspective   "A rising tide lifts all ships." MNEs enter foreign countries primarily to make profit, but they also create opportunities host countries would not have access to without these companies. Although MNEs benefit from international currency fluctuations, available labor at cheaper costs, tax and trade incentives, and the use of natural resources, and gain access to more foreign markets, these companies benefit their host countries through foreign direct investment and in these ways:

- Hire local labor
- Create new jobs
- Co-venture with local entrepreneurs and companies
- Attract local capital to projects
- Provide for and enhance technology transfer
- Develop particular industry sectors
- Provide business learning and skills
- Increase industrial output and productivity
- Help decrease the country's debt and improve its balance of payments and standard of living

Moreover, MNEs open less-developed countries (LDCs) to international markets, thereby helping the local economy attract greatly desired hard currencies. Also, new technical and managerial skills are brought in, and local workers receive training and knowledge. Job and social-class mobility is provided to inhabitants.[57] Some MNEs also establish schools, colleges, and hospitals in their host countries. For example, although Nike has been criticized for its international child labor practices, it is also true that by contracting with factories abroad, it has helped employ more than half a million workers in 55 countries. Eighty-three percent of Nike's workforce in Indonesia is women who would not otherwise be employed.[58] Another company, Patagonia Inc., gives 1% of its annual sales to environmental groups and gives employees up to two paid months off to work for nonprofit environmental groups. The company also routinely permits independent human rights organizations to audit any of its facilities. The company participates in the Apparel Industry Partnership (AIP) to set standards to expose and monitor inhumane business practices in their industry. Cadbury's is another example of a company that practices high ethical standards abroad. In India, the company hired local workers and instilled new work-related ethical values in its plant.[59]

The MNE must manage overlapping and often conflicting multiple constituencies in its home- and host-country operations. Figure 7.4 illustrates some of the major environments and stakeholder issues the MNE must technically and ethically balance and manage in its foreign location. From the MNE's perspective, managing these stakeholder issues is difficult and challenging, especially as the global economy presents new problems.

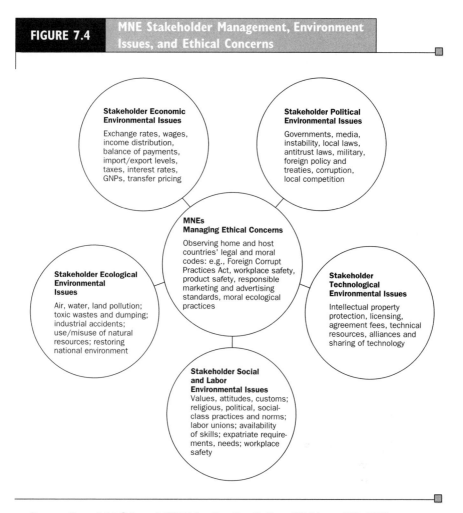

FIGURE 7.4	MNE Stakeholder Management, Environment Issues, and Ethical Concerns

Stakeholder Economic Environmental Issues

Exchange rates, wages, income distribution, balance of payments, import/export levels, taxes, interest rates, GNPs, transfer pricing

Stakeholder Political Environmental Issues

Governments, media, instability, local laws, antitrust laws, military, foreign policy and treaties, corruption, local competition

MNEs Managing Ethical Concerns

Observing home and host countries' legal and moral codes: e.g., Foreign Corrupt Practices Act, workplace safety, product safety, responsible marketing and advertising standards, moral ecological practices

Stakeholder Ecological Environmental Issues

Air, water, land pollution; toxic wastes and dumping; industrial accidents; use/misuse of natural resources; restoring national environment

Stakeholder Technological Environmental Issues

Intellectual property protection, licensing, agreement fees, technical resources, alliances and sharing of technology

Stakeholder Social and Labor Environmental Issues

Values, attitudes, customs; religious, political, social-class practices and norms; labor unions; availability of skills; expatriate requirements, needs; workplace safety

Source: Copyright © Joseph W. Weiss, Bentley College, Waltham, MA, 2005.

MNE executives and other managers also complain of what they consider unethical practices and arbitrary control by host-country governments. For example, local governments can and sometimes do the following:

- Limit repatriation of MNE assets and earnings
- Pressure and require MNEs to buy component parts and other materials from local suppliers
- Require MNEs to use local nationals in upper-level management positions

- Require MNEs to produce and sell selected products in order to enter the country

- Limit imports and pressure exports

- Require a certain amount or percentage of profit to remain in or be invested in the country

Finally, MNEs always face the threat of expropriation or nationalization of their operations by the host government. More recently, MNEs must assume high-stakes risks, liabilities, and responsibilities in the area of safety since September 11, 2001. The airline industry in particular has been hit very hard by this unpredictable crisis. The crisis itself, along with the "fallout" over laxness in safety standards and enforcement, has taken a heavy toll on all U.S. and most international carriers. The price of doing business safely has escalated.

Host-Country Perspective   Six criticisms of the presence and practices of MNEs in host and other foreign locations are discussed here.

1. MNEs can dominate and protect their core technology and research and development, thus keeping the host country a consumer, not a partner or producer. The Brazilian government, for example, has counteracted this by having entry barriers and laws that, since the 1970s, have protected against the complete control of its own electronics industries by foreign manufacturers. It is also argued (or feared) that Japan's MNEs could in the long term dominate certain critical industries (such as the electronics industry and perhaps the automobile industry) in the United States and use American labor more as assemblers than as technology R&D partners.

2. MNEs can destabilize national sovereignty by limiting a country's access to critical capital and resources, thereby creating a host-country dependency on the MNE's governments and politics.

3. MNEs can create a "brain drain" by attracting scientists, expertise, and talent from the host country.

4. MNEs can create an imbalance of capital outflows over inflows. They produce but emphasize exports over imports in the host country, thereby leaving local economies dependent on foreign control.

5. MNEs can disturb local government economic planning and business practices by exerting control over the development

and capitalization of a country's infrastructure. Also, by providing higher wages and better working conditions, MNEs influence and change a country's traditions, values, and customs. "Cultural imperialism" is imported through business practices.

6. MNEs can destroy, pollute, and endanger host-country and LDC environments and the health of local populations. For example, the mining of and dangerous exposure to asbestos continue in some LDCs and in Canada.

Obviously, these criticisms do not apply to all MNEs. These criticisms represent the concerns of host-country and LDC governments that have suffered abuses from multinationals over the decades. Tensions in the relationships between MNEs and host countries and other foreign governments will continue, especially in the least-developed settings. Whenever the stakes for both parties are high, so will be the pressures to negotiate the most profitable and equitable benefits for each stakeholder. Often, it is the less-educated, indigent inhabitants of LDCs who suffer the most from the operations of MNEs.

More global companies are beginning to self-monitor and contribute to host-country education, consumer awareness, and community programs (e.g., Shell has written a primer on human rights with Amnesty International; Hewlett-Packard offers consumer education programs and computer training in host countries).

7.5 MULTINATIONAL ENTERPRISE GUIDELINES FOR MANAGING MORALITY

Guidelines for managing international ethical conduct have received detailed attention and effort over the past four decades in the areas of consumer protection, employment, environmental pollution, human rights, and political conduct.[60] The driving forces behind the development of these published guidelines, or universal rights, include the United Nations, the International Labor Office, the Organization for Economic Cooperation and Development (OECD), the CERES Principles on the Environment, the Conference Board, and the Caux Round Table Principles for Business.

The underlying normative sources of the guidelines that these global organizations developed include beliefs in (1) national sovereignty, (2) social equity, (3) market integrity, and (4) human rights and fundamental freedoms.[61] DeGeorge specifically offers the following guidelines that multinationals can use in dealing with LDCs:

1. Do no intentional harm.

2. Produce more good than harm for the host country.

3. Contribute to the host country's development.

4. Respect the human rights of their employees.

5. Respect the local culture; work with, not against, it.

6. Pay their fair share of taxes.

7. Cooperate with the local government to develop and enforce just background institutions.

8. Majority control of a firm includes the ethical responsibility of attending to the actions and failures of the firm.

9. Multinationals that build hazardous plants are obliged to ensure that the plants are safe and operated safely.

10. Multinationals are responsible for redesigning the transfer of hazardous technologies so that such technologies can be safely administered in host countries.[62]

Other recent developments involving global companies and business ethics include the following: (1) Global companies are developing and using core principles relevant to their business practices; (2) codes of ethics with minimum social responsibility standards (e.g., gender discrimination and environmental responsibility) are being adopted and employees trained on them; and (3) a broad consensus for ethical requirements is being articulated. The Conference Board, a global network of businesses, academic institutions, governments, and nongovernmental organizations (NGOs) in more than 60 countries, is working to define global business practice standards, core principles for doing business across cultures, and the requirements for the support of and cooperation between business and nonbusiness institutions.[63]

Some classic guidelines that continue to influence policies and practices of global companies are presented next. The following MNE guidelines are summarized under the categories of employment practices and policies, consumer protection, environmental protection, political payments and involvement, and basic human rights and fundamental freedoms.[64]

Employment Practices and Policies

- MNEs should not contravene the workforce policies of host nations.

- MNEs should respect the right of employees to join trade unions and to bargain collectively.

- MNEs should develop nondiscriminatory employment policies and promote equal job opportunities.

- MNEs should provide equal pay for equal work.

- MNEs should give advance notice of changes in operations, especially plant closings, and mitigate the adverse effects of these changes.

- MNEs should provide favorable work conditions, limited working hours, holidays with pay, and protection against unemployment.

- MNEs should promote job stability and job security, avoiding arbitrary dismissals and providing severance pay for those unemployed.

- MNEs should respect local host-country job standards and upgrade the local labor force through training.

- MNEs should adopt adequate health and safety standards for employees and grant them the right to know about job-related health hazards.

- MNEs should, minimally, pay basic living wages to employees.

- MNEs' operations should benefit the low-income groups of the host nation.

- MNEs should balance job opportunities, work conditions, job training, and living conditions among migrant workers and host-country nationals.

Consumer Protection

- MNEs should respect host-country laws and policies regarding the protection of consumers.

- MNEs should safeguard the health and safety of consumers by various disclosures, safe packaging, proper labeling, and accurate advertising.

Environmental Protection

- MNEs should respect host-country laws, goals, and priorities concerning protection of the environment.

- MNEs should preserve ecological balance, protect the environment, adopt preventive measures to avoid environmental harm, and rehabilitate environments damaged by operations.

- MNEs should disclose likely environmental harms and minimize the risks of accidents that could cause environmental damage.

- MNEs should promote the development of international environmental standards.

- MNEs should control specific operations that contribute to the pollution of air, water, and soils.

- MNEs should develop and use technology that can monitor, protect, and enhance the environment.

Political Payments and Involvement

- MNEs should not pay bribes or make improper payments to public officials.

- MNEs should avoid improper or illegal involvement or interference in the internal politics of host countries.

Basic Human Rights and Fundamental Freedoms

- MNEs should respect the rights of all persons to life, liberty, security of person, and privacy.

- MNEs should respect the rights of all persons to equal protection of the law, to work, to choice of job, to just and favorable work conditions, and to protection against unemployment and discrimination.

- MNEs should respect each person's freedom of thought, conscience, religion, opinion and expression, communication, peaceful assembly and association, and movement and residence within each state.

- MNEs should promote a standard of living to support the health and well-being of workers and their families.

- MNEs should promote special care and assistance to motherhood and childhood.

Frederick[65] states that these guidelines should be viewed as a "collective phenomenon," because all do not appear in each of the five international pacts they originated from: the 1948 United Nations Universal Declaration of Human Rights, 1975 Helsinki Final Act, 1976 OECD Guidelines for Multinational Enterprises, 1977 International Labor Organization Tripartite Declaration of Principles Concerning Multinational Enterprises and Social Policy, and 1972 United Nations Code of Conduct on Transnational Corporations.

The guidelines serve as broad bases that all international corporations can use to design specific policies and procedures; these corporations can then apply their own policies and procedures to such areas as "[c]hild care, minimum wages, hours of work, employee training and education, adequate housing and health care, pollution control efforts, advertising and marketing activities, severance pay, privacy of employees and consumers, information concerning on-the-job hazards."[66]

7.6 STAKEHOLDER MANAGEMENT: CROSS-CULTURAL ETHICAL DECISION-MAKING AND NEGOTIATION METHODS

"You are a manager of Ben & Jerry's in Russia. One day you discover that the most senior officer of your company's Russian venture has been 'borrowing' equipment from the company and using it in his other business ventures. When you confront him, the Russian partner defends his actions. After all, as a part owner of both companies, isn't he entitled to share in the equipment?"[67] These and so many other international business situations confront managers and professionals with dilemmas and gray areas in their decision making. As one author noted, "Global business ethics has now become the ultimate dilemma for many U.S. businesses."[68]

"Transnationals operate in what may be called the margins of morality because the historical, cultural, and governmental mores of the world's nation-states are not uniform. There is a gray area of ethical judgment where standards of the transnational's home country differ substantially from those of the host country. . . . [T]here is yet no fixed, institutionalized policing agency to regularly constrain morally questionable practices of transnational commerce. Moreover, there is no true global consensus on what is morally questionable."[69] Scholars and business leaders agree that solving ethical dilemmas that involve global, cross-cultural dimensions is not easy. Often there are no "quick fixes." Where other laws, business practices, and local norms conflict, the decision makers must decide, using their own business and value judgments. Ethics codes help, but decision makers must also take local and their own company's interests into consideration. In short, there is no one best method to solve international business ethical dilemmas. From a larger perspective, external human rights and corporate monitoring groups are also needed to inform and advise corporations before dilemmas occur about human rights and methods that can prevent abuses of local workers and private citizens.

External Corporate Monitoring Groups
Corporations and their leaders are ultimately responsible for articulating, modeling, and working with international stakeholders to enforce legal and ethical standards in their firms as they do business around the world. Many do.

However, as noted earlier, gray areas and lack of universal laws and norms leave loopholes that companies and local groups might use as competitive, but harmful, cost-saving advantages (e.g., not providing even "living wages" to the poor women and children they employ, polluting the environment, and using undue political influence to beat out competition). Numerous international groups[70] that work with and monitor MNEs regarding human rights include—but are not limited to—Amnesty International (promotes and advocates human rights), OECD (developed Guidelines for Multinational Enterprises), International Labor Organization (publishes and works in the area of human rights), NGOs (combat corruption, assure adequate labor conditions, and establish standards for economic responsibility), Transparency International (monitors and publishes the international Corruption Perception Index), Apparel Industry Partnership (which develops codes of conduct regarding child labor practices and working conditions related to "sweat shops" and subcontractors), and The Round Table (an executive group formed in Switzerland that published the noted Caux Principles and works with other international business professionals on developing and implementing universal ethics codes). These groups work with, and some are composed of, MNE executives, governments, legislators, local citizenry, and other stakeholders worldwide to inform, monitor, and assist MNEs with ethical global business practices.

> Demands for greater corporate transparency and accountability, as well as anti-corruption measures are fostering significant new accountability, reporting, and transparency initiatives among coalitions of business, labor, human rights, investor, and governmental bodies. . . . A database created by the International Labor Organization and available over the Internet lists nearly 450 Web sites of industry and business associations, corporate, NGO and activist groups, and consulting organizations that have developed and are promulgating a wide range of relevant policy initiatives. These initiatives include a mix of transparency and reporting initiatives, codes of conduct, principles, and fair trade agreements. Responses to these demands are varied. Many companies, particularly those under NGO and social activist pressures to reform labor and human rights abuses in their supply chains, have formulated their own codes of conduct. Notable among these companies are Levi-Strauss, Nike, and Reebok, all significant targets of activism.[71]

In the following section, several guidelines are discussed to complement principles and "quick tests" presented in Chapter 3.

Individual Stakeholder Methods for Ethical Decision Making

> In an international environment, the temptations can be strong, and the laws looser, or less obvious. Pressure from headquarters to make the bottom line can also weigh heavily. "Sometimes people confuse norms with ethics—exploitation of child labour, bribery and kickbacks may be the norm, but that doesn't mean they're right—and that's what companies need to deal with,"

says Joseph Reitz, who is co-director of the International Center for Ethics in Business at the University of Kansas. "There's lots of evidence that companies insisting on doing business in the right way may suffer in the short term, but in the long run they do well."[72] Or do they?

Individual employee and professional stakeholders—when confronted with cross-cultural ethical dilemmas, conflicting norms, and potentially illegal acts in international situations, like the case of Louise in Chapter 3, need guidelines. Professionals and executives preparing to work abroad should ask for country-specific training on regional and local laws, customs, and business practices. These professionals need to know their own firm's acceptable and unacceptable policies and procedures regarding negotiations and business dealings. This section introduces—some—but obviously not all—guidelines—that are a beginning step to becoming aware of the cultural differences and potential ethical consequences from doing business in other regions and countries.

DeGeorge[73] offers the following general tactics that serve as a basic start for preventing, as well as solving, ethical dilemmas internationally:

1. Do not violate the very norms and values that you want to preserve and that you use to evaluate your adversary's actions to be unethical. Seek to pursue with integrity economic survival and self-defense tactics. Winning a tactical battle unethically or illegally is not the goal.

2. Use your moral imagination, because there are no specific rules for responding to an ethical opponent. Stakeholder analysis can help. Explore different options. Use literature, stories, and lives of heroes and saints for creative responses instead of rules.

3. Use restraint and rely on those to whom the use of force is legitimately allocated when your response to immorality involves justifiable force or retaliation. Use minimal force that is justified as the ultimate solution, realizing that force is a reaction to unethical acts and practices.

4. Apply the principle of proportionality when measuring your response to an unethical opponent. The force you use should be commensurate with the offense, the harm suffered, and the good to be gained.

5. Use the technique of *ethical displacement* when responding to unethical forces. This principle consists of searching for clarification and a solution to a dilemma on different, higher levels than the personal (e.g., as discussed in Chapter 1, look at the problems from these levels: international, industry, organizational, structural, and national or legislative policy).

6. Use publicity to respond to an unethical practice, adversary, or system. Corruption, unethical and illegal practices and actions, operates best in the dark. Using publicity judiciously can mobilize pressures against the perpetrators.

7. Work jointly with others to create new social, legal, or popular structures and institutions to respond to immoral opponents.

8. Act with moral courage and from your values, personally and corporately.

9. Be prepared to pay a price, even a high one. Innocent people sometimes must pay costs that others impose on them by their unethical and illegal activities.

10. Use the principle of accountability when responding to an unethical activity. Those who harm others must be held accountable for their acts.

Getting to Yes Solving a moral dilemma in an international context is not easy. Fisher, Patton, and Ury's book *Getting to Yes: Negotiating Agreement Without Giving In* (alluded to earlier in this text) remains a classic primer for negotiating. Their four-step approach includes:

1. Separate the people from the problem.

2. Focus on interests, not on positions.

3. Insist on objective criteria, never yield to pressure.

4. Invent options for mutual gain.

The authors note that it is always necessary to determine your best alternative to a negotiated solution before starting a negotiation.[74]

Building on Fisher, Patton, and Ury's method, Nancy Adler states that formal negotiations, especially in an international or cross-cultural context, proceed through four stages after preparing for a negotiation:

1. Build interpersonal relationships (learning about the people)—separate people from the problem.

2. Exchange task-related information—focus on interests, not positions.

3. Persuade—invent options for mutual gain, instead of relying on preconceived positions, high pressure, or "dirty tricks."

4. Make concessions and agreements—use objective decision criteria.[75]

Understand the Local Culture First   Is local culture important or are people across cultures becoming more alike, especially with globalization and for those working in MNEs? Studies show that although organizations are becoming more alike in their structures and technologies, individuals maintain and even emphasize their cultural behaviors even more. National culture explains more about employees' attitudes and behaviors than does age, gender, role, or race.[76] When communicating and negotiating in different cultural contexts, gaining an understanding of the local culture in preparing for the negotiation is recommended before using any specific negotiation technique. Cultural miscues and disconnects are grounds for creating and exacerbating ethical problems and dilemmas. Consider, then, these cultural differences before problem solving or negotiating with counterparts:

- What are the dominant, underlying values of the culture? (Are groups, families, and collectives and their decisions valued over individuals and individual decisions, or vice versa?)

- How formally or informally are relationships viewed? (Is it necessary to get to know someone before negotiating, or is jumping to the facts first acceptable?)

- How do people understand and value rules versus spontaneity and bending rules? (Do friendships come before rules or are rules seen as unbreakable and applicable to all?)

- How are authority and power viewed? (Is position and status valued more than experience? Is the boss more often seen as being right regardless of "the facts"?)

- Is age respected as indicating wisdom and authority?

- To what extent does the culture avoid or embrace uncertainty and risk? (Are people threatened by ambiguity and therefore avoiding unpredictability?)

Sources that address these and other comparative cultural differences are readily available.[77]

Figure 7.5 illustrates different styles of negotiation among North Americans, Japanese, and Latin Americans, based on cultural values and characteristics. Can you see how ethical problems and dilemmas could arise from communication miscues among professionals from these countries negotiating a complex transaction?

It is also helpful to understand how other cultures perceive, understand, and perhaps even stereotype American cultural characteristics. (Obviously, not everyone from every culture reflects all of his/her national culture's characteristics.) For example, characteristics most

FIGURE 7.5   Cross-Cultural Negotiation Styles

Japanese	North American	Latin American
Emotional sensitivity highly valued	Emotional sensitivity not highly valued	Emotional sensitivity valued
Hide emotions	Deal straightforwardly or impersonally	Emotionally expressive and passionate
Subtle power plays; conciliation	Litigation used more than conciliation	Explicit power plays; use others' weaknesses
Loyal to employer; employer takes care of employees	Little commitment to employer; either side can break lines if necessary	Loyal to employer (who is often family)
Group decision making by consensus	Team provides input to decision maker	Decisions come down from one individual
Face-saving crucial; decisions often made to save someone from embarrassment	Decisions based on cost-benefit analysis; face-saving not generally important	Face-saving crucial in decision making to preserve honor and dignity
Decision makers openly influenced by special interests	Decision makers influenced by special interests, but often not considered ethical	Inclusion of special interests of decision maker expected and condoned
Not argumentative; quiet when right	Argumentative, but impersonal, when right or wrong	Argumentative and passionate when right or wrong
Written statements must be accurate and valid	Give great importance to documentation as evidential proof	Impatient with documentation, seen as an obstacle to understanding general principles
Step-by-step approach to decision making	Methodically organized decision making	Impulsive, spontaneous decision making
Good of group is the ultimate aim	Profit motive or individual benefit is ultimate aim	What is good for group is good for the individual
Cultivate a good emotional climate for decision making; gel to know decision makers	Decision making impersonal; personal involvements seen as conflict of interest and avoided	Good personal relationships necessary for good decision making

Source: From *International Dimensions of Organizational Behavior,* 4th edition, by Adler. © 2002. Reprinted with permission of South-Western, a division of Thomson Learning: www.thomsonrights.com. Fax 800-730-2215.

commonly associated with Americans from the different nationals reveal interesting patterns (e.g., although Americans were largely seen as industrious, inventive, intelligent, decisive, and friendly by an interview sample of French, Japanese, Western Germans, British, Brazilians, and Mexicans, Americans were also seen as nationalistic, rude, and self-indulgent by Japanese; sophisticated by western Germans; nationalistic by Brazilians; and greedy by Mexicans).[78] Becoming self-aware of one's cultural characteristics (attitudes, values, behaviors, and other's perceptions of us) is an important step toward business transactions in order to prevent and negotiate ethical dilemmas.

Four Typical Styles of International Ethical Decision Making

At a more macro level, George Enderle[79] identified four distinctive international ethical decision-making styles that companies often use when making decisions abroad: (1) *Foreign Country style*: a company applies the values and norms of its local host—"When in Rome, do as the Romans do"; (2) *Empire style*: a company applies its own domestic values and rules; this can be an imperialistic practice; (3) *Innerconnection style*: a company applies shared norms with other companies and groups; national identities and interests are transcended and blurred, as when states make commercial decisions and rely on NAFTA or the EU members to offer agreed-on processes and solutions; and (4) *Global style*: a company abstracts all local and regional differences and norms, coming up with a more cosmopolitan set of standards and solutions for its actions in the host country.

The Foreign Country and Empire styles have obvious drawbacks in reaching ethical decisions. The Foreign Country style may result in gross injustices and inequities that are inherent in the norms adopted. Some local country norms and business practices, for example, do not prohibit child labor. The second style is a form of imperialism that disregards local norms and practices. The Global style, seemingly the "right answer," also presents problems. This style imposes its own interpretation of a "global morality and truth" on a host culture and norms. The Global style can also suffer from shortcomings shared by the Foreign Country and Empire styles. The Interconnection style "acknowledges both universal moral limits and the ability of communities to set moral standards of their own. It balances better than the other types a need to retain local identity with the acknowledgment of values that transcend individual communities. The drawbacks of this style are practical rather than moral." Companies and individual employees usually do not have quick or direct access to a commonly shared local, national, and international source to advise on a particular issue. Of the four styles, the Interconnection style appears to be less arbitrary and absolutist.[80] Another option is creative ethical navigation (which Donaldson and Dunfee term "integrative social contract theory" or ICST). This is not really a "style" of decision making; rather, it is the process of a decision maker navigating among "hypernorms," company interests, and local norms, as explained in the following section.

Hypernorms, Local Norms, and Creative Ethical Navigation

It would be helpful to have a set of norms that everyone agreed on. *Hypernorms* represent such an ideal. "Hypernorms are principles so fundamental that, by definition, they serve to evaluate lower-order norms, reaching to the root of what is ethical for humanity. They represent norms by which all others are to be judged."[81] Hypernorms relate to universal rights: for example, the right not to be enslaved, the right to have physical security, the right not to be tortured, and the right not to be discriminated against.[82] However, the problem even with hypernorms is that when "rights," local traditions, country economic systems, or business practices conflict, decisions have to be made; in such cases, it is necessary for a manager or professional to use his or her hypernorms as a starting principle, but then to be creative in considering the local context and competing norms. Reaching a win–win situation without violating anyone's norms is an ideal goal. An example of such a troublesome gray area, along with a suitable solution, is offered by Donaldson and Dunfee:

> Consider another situation confronted by Levi-Strauss, this time involving hypernorms connected with child labor. The company discovered in the early 1990s that two of its suppliers in Bangladesh were employing children under the age of fourteen—a practice that violated the company's principles but was tolerated in Bangladesh. Forcing the suppliers to fire the children would not have insured that the children received an education, and it would have caused serious hardship for the families depending on the children's wages. In a creative arrangement, the suppliers agreed to pay the children's regular wages while they attended school and to offer each child a job at age fifteen. Levi-Strauss, in turn, agreed to pay the children's tuition and provide books and uniforms. This approach allowed Levi-Strauss to uphold its principles and provide long-term benefits to the host country.[83]

Figure 7.6 illustrates Donaldson and Dunfee's "Global Values Map," which portrays the zones groups may consider to creatively navigate among and reach agreement on competing norms and business practices.[84] At the center of the figure are "hypernorms," which are basic values acceptable to all cultures and organizations. The next concentric circle represents "consistent norms," which are culture-specific values but still consistent with both hypernorms and other legitimate norms. Ethical codes of companies, such as Johnson & Johnson's Credo, are examples of consistent norms. Moving away from the center of the circle to the outer circle, one encounters inconsistent norms, which may conflict with hypernorms and/or local business practices. Outside the concentric circle are illegitimate norms—values or practices that transgress hypernorms (e.g., exposing workers to asbestos or other carcinogens). In the "moral free space," a company can creatively explore unique solutions that satisfy all parties.

FIGURE 7.6 Global Values Map

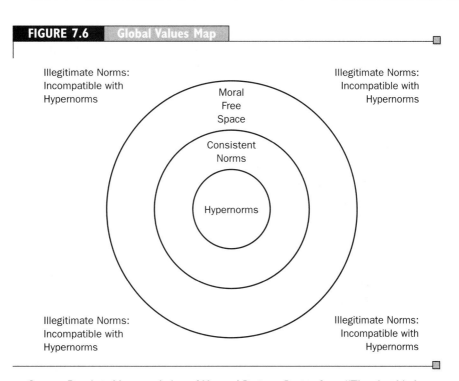

Illegitimate Norms: Incompatible with Hypernorms

Illegitimate Norms: Incompatible with Hypernorms

Moral Free Space

Consistent Norms

Hypernorms

Illegitimate Norms: Incompatible with Hypernorms

Illegitimate Norms: Incompatible with Hypernorms

The previous example of Levi-Strauss illustrates a process using Figure 7.6. Levi-Strauss had to decide among a "hypernorm" (child labor is wrong), its own company norms ("consistent norms"—children cannot be hired or used by company suppliers), and Bangladesh suppliers' child labor practices ("illegitimate norms") to reach an agreement that would benefit the children and their families. Levi-Strauss entered the "moral free space" and worked out what seems to have been a "win–win" situation for all parties involved—and an arrangement that brought no harm to any party.

Finding such creative solutions to international moral dilemmas involves balancing and combining business pressures, legal enforcement, and political will. A company attempting to make tough decisions with local groups could also seek to do so with the cooperation of other companies, local government officials, or even an external human rights group as the Interconnectedness style of decision making would suggest. The ultimate decision may very well entail *no compromise* after reflecting on the situation, the hypernorm, and a company norm. Still, the methods discussed here can enable a decision maker—individual or global or company team—to look for options without getting trapped into blind absolutes, amoral gray zones, or relativism. Entering "moral free space" requires flexibility and negotiating. The embedded process in Figure 7.6 also enables a company or individual decision maker to use the principles and quick tests discussed in Chapter 3.

SUMMARY

The global environment consists of a dynamic set of relationships among companies, financial markets, cultures, political ideologies, government policies, laws, technologies, and numerous stakeholders.

There are estimates of between 40,000 to 100,000 multinational companies doing business across national boundaries and contributing to the global economy. It is likely these numbers will increase. Where there are new markets, companies will be created and go.

Globalization is the integration of technology, markets, politics, cultures, labor, production, and commerce. Globalization is both the process and the result of this integration. The global economy is estimated at $33 trillion. As the complexity and volatility of the global environment increases, the probability of ethical dilemmas and conflicts is also enhanced. The 9/11 attacks and the U.S.-led international "War on Terrorism" exemplifies the economic, legal, moral, and social pressures businesses face as a result of these events. Several industries continue to struggle for survival and profitability.

Forces that have accelerated globalization include the end of communism and the opening of closed economies; information technologies and the Internet, which accelerate communication and productivity within and across companies globally; entrepreneurship and entrepreneurs who are more mobile, skilled, intelligent, and thriving worldwide; free trade and trading agreements among nations; the flow of money through the World Bank and the International Monetary Fund (IMF), which offers a conduit to bring needed capital to countries participating in building the global economy; the growth and the spread of transnational firms, which open new markets and create local employment; a shift to service economies and educate workers using technologies, which has also propelled innovation and productivity worldwide. Given the attacks on September 11, 2001, and the threat of other organized attacks on individual, country, and corporate interests in all countries, a question asked is: Will globalization and accelerated business integration across national borders be slowed or rejuvenated through new and changing business, governmental, and entrepreneurial alliances?

Major corporations play significant economic and ethical roles in helping rejuvenate the global and local economies. "Smart globalization" strategies and processes are used by several companies and include the following: (1) methodically building a presence from the ground up instead of planning takeovers and acquisitions; (2) doing extensive homework before starting a business in a developing country by consulting with and learning from local stakeholders; (3) forgetting about targeting the richest 10% of the global population and marketing to the 4 billion people internationally who earn less than $1,500 annually and are the source of future growth; and (4) introducing and helping to stimulate product use with local populations.

The "dark side of globalization" includes such issues as corporate crime and corruption, child slave labor, Westernization (Americanization) of values, the global digital divide, and loss of nation-state sovereignty. Also, critics argue that the "McDonaldization of Society" delivers cultural values as well fast food. This is a debatable issue and is discussed in the chapter.

The power of MNEs or global companies lies in their size, economic prowess, and ability to locate and operate across national borders. MNEs offer benefits to their host countries by employing local populations, investing capital, co-venturing with local entrepreneurs and companies, providing enhanced technology, developing particular industry sectors, providing business learning and skills, and increasing industrial output and productivity.

MNEs also abuse their power by committing corporate crimes, exerting undue political influence and control, determining and controlling plant closings and layoffs, and damaging the physical environment and human health. Guidelines drawn from more than four decades of international agreements and charters were summarized to illustrate a consensus of host-country rights that have been used to help MNEs to design equity into their policies and procedures.

Finally, principles from *Getting to Yes: Negotiating Agreement Without Giving In* were extended to include understanding cross-cultural characteristics of decision makers to prevent ethical dilemmas and negotiate complex business transactions. A creative model was summarized enabling companies to reach agreements among conflicting hypernorms (universal rights), consistent norms (company ethics and values codes), and illegitimate norms. Being able to balance local cultural norms, a company's norms, and competing business practices involves creative and responsible navigation and decision-making skills based on personal, professional, company, and universal values.

QUESTIONS

1. Briefly characterize the emerging competitive global business environment and identify some of the forces that define it. What is different about the global environment today than before September 11, 2001?

2. What is "globalization?" What are some of the forces driving this process?

3. Does globalization result in cultural and economic homogenization (alikeness) through a heightened emphasis on consumerism, or is this an exaggeration? Explain and defend your position.

4. Do local and global values change as a result of international integration? Why or why not? If so, in what ways? Offer a few examples.

5. Do you believe that globalization "promotes the conversion of national economies into environmentally and socially harmful export-oriented systems for business competition" that is not in the best interests of consumers? Why or why not? Defend your position.

6. Select two global companies mentioned in this chapter and locate their corporate Web sites. Find their codes of conduct or ethics statements. Download these and evaluate whether or not they serve any practical purposes or help meet the companies' social responsibility goals and why.

7. Explain what the "dark side of globalization" means. Offer some examples. Offer an additional issue that could be considered a dark side of globalization. After doing so, offer a realistic solution that could either eliminate, change, or transform the dark side of your issue.

8. Explain the differences in perception and experience with regard to moral issues for (a) a host country viewing an MNE and (b) an MNE viewing a host country. Which perspective are you more inclined to support or sympathize with? Why?

9. In a paragraph or list, describe dominant cultural characteristics of yourself as could be seen from another country or regional perspective. Include some of your core values. Then proceed to the next question.

10. Using your description from question 9, what difficulties or misunderstanding based only on your answer would you predict that you might encounter when negotiating an ethical dilemma with someone who had opposite cultural characteristics? Explain.

11. Find an example from the media, cinema, or someone's experiences of an international dilemma a person or company has had in a host country, and apply the process of the "Global Values Map." Evaluate how well you believe the process could have worked in the example you found.

EXERCISES

1. Argue and defend your positions on the following statements:

   (a) A "global set of ethics" is impossible. Each culture and region of the world should have its own ethics as well as values and cultural differences.

   (b) To succeed, globalization must involve justice and fairness practices from First World countries toward Third World nations and peoples.

   (c) Although it is preferable that transnational and multinational companies act ethically, it is really not practical in every region of the world, including the U.S.

   (d) MNEs cannot financially afford to follow the guidelines in Section 7.5; it would be too costly for them.

   (e) When two MNEs are both right on a controversial issue—for example, violation of patent or intellectual property rights—ethics should be avoided, and other, more concrete issues should be used to resolve the dispute.

   (f) Without transnational companies and MNEs doing business in poorer countries, peoples of those countries who are striving to survive would suffer even more.

2. Offer an example of and explain why one of your own values or an ethical standard you deeply believe in and follow might conflict with a different cultural or regional ethic in, for example, China, Russia, the Middle East, or the U.S. (if you are from a different culture). How flexible would you be, or not be, in negotiating one of your core beliefs in another culture? What would be your constraints to be flexible and change your value-based position? Explain.

3. Evaluate and argue different sides of this statement: "McDonaldization is not a 'bad' thing. Everyone has a choice of what and how much to buy and consume. People are lucky to have a low cost food option as McDonald's."

Ethical Dilemma   Jane's New Assignment

You (Jane) are a 29-year-old single woman who has an MBA and has been working in your current marketing position for a year. Your firm has recently opened a new pilot branch in Moscow. The CEO of your company believes there are real growth opportunities for your firm's products in that region and also wants visibility there. The company has decided to launch a small office there for visibility as well as to introduce the product. You are one of the most outgoing and talented marketing professionals in your firm. It is believed that you'll make a positive impression and represent the company well. There is a small community of American business professionals there who will assist you.

Country values there are very different from what you are accustomed to. You overhear a discussion between two of your male colleagues who were recently in that country completing arrangements for the office. One says, "Jane's going to have some interesting challenges with the men she has to do business with. . . . It's like the Wild West." The other answered, "Yeah, she's got some real surprises coming." Your research suggests that country laws and norms on issues you take for granted (like women's rights and sexual harassment) are not well defined.

You have a conflict over wanting to advance with your company but not wanting to take this assignment. You are aware that the CEO has his mind set. In fact, you've already had a discussion expressing your concerns and fears. He brushed your issues aside when he told you earlier, "Jane, try it. You need the international exposure and experience." The second time you approached him with your concerns, he blurted out, "Look, Jane. I understand your concerns, but this is important to me and our company. There are some people there who can help you. I know it's going to be a challenge. But after a couple of years, you'll thank me." You still don't feel right.

Questions

1. What do you do, and why?
2. If you do decide to go, what specific preparations should you make?
3. If you decide not to go, draft out the dialogue you would have with your CEO.

Ethical Dilemma **Who's Training Whom?**

You are attending a sexual harassment training seminar for local managers in your company's branch office in a Middle Eastern, predominately Muslim country. You were flown over with the trainers to observe their techniques and become familiar with the training materials because you, as a new human resource staff member, would be expected to give this course. The course has been a success for managers in the United States. The same materials have been perfected and are being used in the United States. The instructors call on local Muslim managers (men and women) to role play and openly share stories about sexual harassment that involved them or that they had heard about. Near the end of the half-day session, several of the host country employees uncharacteristically walk out. The trainers are dazed and become upset.

QUESTIONS

1. What do you think went wrong?

2. What would you do in this case if you were one of the trainers?

3. Read the epilogue following, then return and answer this question: "Assume the trainers have been briefed on the research you just read. Who should do what, if anything, with the Muslim managers after this cultural mishap? Why?"

EPILOGUE

"In 1993, a large U.S. computer-products company insisted on using exactly the same sexual harassment exercises and lessons with Muslim managers halfway around the globe that they used with American employees in California. It did so in the name of 'ethical consistency.' The result was ludicrous. The managers were baffled by the instructors' presentation, and the instructors were oblivious of the intricate connections between Muslim religion and sexual manners.

"The U.S. trainers needed to know that Muslim ethics are especially strict about male/female social interaction. By explaining sexual harassment in the same way to Muslims as to Westerners, the trainers offended the Muslim managers. To the Muslim managers, their remarks seemed odd and disrespectful. In turn, the underlying ethical message about avoiding coercion and sexual discrimination was lost. Clearly sexual discrimination does occur in Muslim countries. But helping to eliminate it there means respecting—and understanding Muslim differences."

Source: Donaldson, T., Dunfee, T. (Summer 1999). When ethics travel: The promise and peril of global business ethics. *California Management Review.* 41(4), 60.

CASE 21

OLYMPIC ATHLETE DRUG TESTING: CREATING AN ANTI-DOPING CULTURE AND FAIR COMPETITION

The Doping Edge　The Olympic Games have been a showcase for athletes' achievements since their inception in ancient Greece. Countries send their strongest and best competitors to the Olympics, hoping they will bring home prestige, global recognition, and sponsorships. Pressure for athletes to do whatever it takes to win is part of the contest.

The strength and power of an athlete's mind and body are the keys to winning. When an athlete reaches the point where willpower and mental strength are no longer enough to push the body to its limit, chemical enhancements or doping can provide a desired boost. Taking a drug in order to enhance one's performance—or doping—pushes an athlete's body beyond normal activity and poses the risk of serious harm. Doping also gives athletes an unfair advantage over other athletes who play without the aid of performance-enhancing drugs.

Gaining an Athletic Edge: A Historical Perspective

Since the origin of the Olympics, athletes have pushed themselves to the limit in order to achieve greatness. Competitors in the sacred games of Athens died of injuries sustained while trying to win. Other forms of competition, such as the jousts of medieval England, also resulted in the death or injury of an opponent for the chance at glory. As time progressed, the brutality of sports lessened, but the need to go to extremes to win has remained. In modern times, sports medicine does its best to prevent and heal injuries so players can continue. It also creates chemical enhancements that are used by some athletes to improve their performance.

Pinpointing when drug or substance abuse became a part of training to compete in events such as the Olympics is a difficult endeavor. The ancient games of Greece ran from around 900 BC through 393 AD. Competitors may have taken herbs and juices during these games as a form of performance enhancement. Revivals of the games started in 1852 in Britain with the Much Wenlock Games and in 1859 with the Pan-Hellenic Games in Greece. Various types of amphetamines already existed by this time, and it may be assumed that due to lax regulations, use of them was prevalent.

The birth of the "modern" Olympic Games came under the guidance of Baron Pierre de Coubertin. He wanted to bring the ancient games of Greece back in order to strengthen sports worldwide and to "assure their independence and durability and, moreover, to allow them better to fulfill an educational role which was their duty in the modern world." He helped establish the International Olympic Committee (IOC) in 1894, and the first Olympic Games began in 1896. The IOC, formed as an independent international group, governs the modern Olympic Games and defines and enforces the general policies of the Olympics. The first Committee had 15 members chosen for their knowledge of sports and their positions in their representative countries. Today, the IOC is composed of members representing over 80 countries world-wide. The IOC is still an independent group, and its various committees administer all policies and enforcement.

Surprisingly, the IOC did not begin to test athletes for use of per-formance enhancing drugs until 1967, even though proof exists that athletes used them before this time. For instance, beginning in 1956, the Soviets provided steroids to all their Olympic athletes. Many drugs and chemicals—such as strychnine, caffeine, cocaine, and alcohol—were used to improve performance and lessen pain. In the 1960 Olympics, 29-year-old Knut Jensen, a cyclist from Denmark, became the first Olympian to die during the Olympics due to drug use, after taking a mixed dose of amphetamines and nicotinyl tartrate. In 1961, the IOC established the Medical Commission. During the 1964 Olympics, cyclists were tested for stimulants, but they were the only group of athletes examined.

When 29-year-old amphetamine user Thomas Simpson died while ascending a mountain as part of the 1967 Tour de France, the IOC finally recognized the seriousness of drug enhancements, and that doping was having a negative impact on fair play. With an estimated 25% of athletes worldwide abusing some sort of chemical enhance-ment in 1967, the Medical Commission of the IOC was reconstructed and began testing all athletes competing at the Olympics, beginning with the 1968 Olympic Winter Games in Grenoble and Summer Olympic Games in Mexico City. The early tests were only for amphet-amines—stimulants that allowed users to push their bodies beyond the point when a non-user would be exhausted. Another type of chemical enhancement—hormonal supplements such as anabolic steroids—became widely used during the 1960s. However, anabolic steroids were not banned until 1975, and the first testing for them occurred at the 1976 Montreal Olympics when eight athletes were disqualified for using them.

Anabolic steroids are testosterone-based chemicals that increase muscle and bone growth; promote muscle mass, strength and stamina; and allow athletes to recover rapidly from strenuous exercise. Athletes can use them during training to help bulk up and to work more intensely. The problem with testing for them during the Olympics is that their use is undetectable unless the athlete uses them while at the

Olympics. Athletes who trained with anabolic steroids will test negative as long as use is terminated a sufficient length of time before the Olympics begin.

In 1986, the IOC added blood doping to its list of banned procedures and enhancement methods. Blood doping—a procedure that removes and then replaces blood prior to competing so that more hemoglobin would form—was introduced to athletes during the 1970s as a way of adding oxygen to the blood before competition. Drugs that increased hemoglobin such as erythropoietin (EPO) were banned as well, beginning in 1990.

Since the Medical Commission's inception, it has followed its own Anti-Doping Code. The Medical Commission developed a list of substances that were not allowed and completed testing for them. Banned substances and methods included amphetamines, steroids, some nutritional supplements, blood doping, and EPO. The list grew as drugs were developed, used, and detected. The code also established rules for testing and sanctions. Testing required a blood sample and urine sample, which could be done before or after competition. For any action to take place against an athlete, he or she had to test positive for a banned substance. The IOC could prevent athletes with positive drug test results from competing as well as strip them of their victories and records.

Realizing that their efforts had not been sufficient, the IOC began to take alternative steps. On November 10, 1999, through an initiative led by the IOC, the World Anti-Doping Agency was formed with the mission to establish a uniform policy against drug use in sports and to get all sports federations to adhere to it. As stated on its Web site: "The World Anti-Doping Agency (WADA) seeks to foster a doping-free culture in sport. It combines the resources of sport and government to enhance, supplement, and coordinate existing efforts to educate athletes about the harms of doping, reinforce the ideal of fair play and sanction those who cheat themselves and their sport."

As a result of the IOC's drug testing at the 2000 Sydney Olympic Games, nine athletes were disqualified during their competitions, seven were disqualified before competing, and 40 athletes were not even allowed to go to Sydney for failing drug tests in their own countries. The more than 50 disqualifications in these Olympics encouraged the IOC that they were heading in the right direction by expanding drug-testing efforts.

In 2002, the IOC invited WADA to the Winter Olympic Games in Salt Lake City. The Agency observed how the IOC carried out and controlled all of its anti-doping activities. The IOC and WADA worked together to develop a program that would permit the testing of athletes outside of pre-competition immediately before the Olympics begin.

The IOC and WADA also developed an Anti-Doping Code based on the original anti-doping code of the IOC and Medical Commission. Beginning with the 2004 Olympic Games in Athens and all those to follow, the IOC will follow the Anti-Doping Code of WADA. In 2004, WADA had testing agreements with 26 Summer Olympics, all 7 Winter Olympics International Sports Federations, the International Paralympic Committee that represents 13 sports, and 6 other recognized federations. WADA believes that all sports federations will implement the Anti-Doping Code before the 2006 Winter Olympic Games in Torino.

For the Olympics in Athens, the IOC authorized WADA to carry out all the testing on athletes. Athletes could be tested at any time or place without warning—while competing in Greece, before entering the country, at venues outside of Greece and the Olympics, and after the final competition. Testing at the 2004 Athens Olympics resulted in 24 drug violators being caught during the actual competition—a record for the Summer Olympics. Charles Yesalsis, a Penn State University professor of health policies predicts that "the worst abuses of drugs in sports are yet to come at the 2008 Summer Olympics in Beijing" with so-called designer drugs.

WADA's Anti-Doping Code and Ways to Get Around It

The Anti-Doping Code of WADA presents a stronger stand against doping than any previous code. The IOC revised its older code to resemble WADA's rules. The Medical Commission is still responsible for implementing the code. Under the code, athletes are held responsible for any substance that enters their body. Not knowing, not having intent, or being negligent are not acceptable excuses for testing positive for a banned substance. If an athlete refuses a test, does not make his or her schedule and whereabouts available to the IOC, or fails to show up for a test, he/she is in violation of the Anti-Doping Code. The athlete cannot have a banned substance in his or her possession either, regardless of whether it was used.

All of these provisions are similar to the IOC's original code, except Article 3 of the Code, "Proof of Doping." Under the previous IOC code, athletes who tested negative for a performance-enhancing drug were allowed to compete and keep whatever they won. If athletes tested positive, they could not compete or forfeited their victories. Athletes had to be proven guilty by test results. Article 3 of the WADA Anti-Doping Code states that, "The standard of proof shall be whether the IOC has established an anti-doping rule violation to the comfortable satisfaction of the hearing body." By allowing a less stringent standard—that of "comfortable satisfaction"—proof beyond a reasonable doubt by a positive test for doping is not required for the IOC to take action against an athlete. This opens up the possibility of banning or sanctioning an athlete on the basis of a paper trail linking him or her to illegal drugs—perhaps through a trainer. A trail of documents, such as e-mails, calendars, and drug schedules can all be used against an athlete to comfortably satisfy a board examining the evidence and determining an athlete's fate.

In the United States, for example, several cases occurred where athletes tested negative, but other evidence suggested possible drug use. Marion Jones, Tim Montgomery, and Kelli White were investigated by the United States Anti-Doping Agency (USADA) for using the previously undetectable steroid tetrahydrogestrinone (THG), allegedly distributed by the Bay Area Laboratory Co-Operative (BALCO). For instance, in March 2003, Kelli White, a sprinter, "asked BALCO founder Victor Conte for a full-scale drug program," including THG. She subsequently accepted a two-year ban from the sport because she knew the USADA had paper evidence linking her to doping.

THG "was undetectable until track coach Trevor Graham submitted a syringe of it to American drug-testing authorities." Gary Wadler, a researcher and member of WADA, says, "Without the syringe, we wouldn't have known about THG. It would have never been found out had somebody not delivered the product." Wadler adds, "The fact that it happened with one [synthetic steroid that was previously undetectable] indicates to me there are others. Whether it's one, 10, or 20, no one knows."

On the horizon is athletic performance enhancement through gene therapy. Consider the work of Johns Hopkins University molecular biologist, Se-Jin Lee. Lee has achieved promising results after investing nearly a decade of time researching "how to manipulate a gene in a way that would increase muscle growth, in hopes of helping those suffering from degenerative diseases such as muscular dystrophy, cancer, and AIDS." Lee points out that he has received inquiries regarding the possible application of his work in sports. This raises the possibility of yet another avenue by which athletes can make the playing field uneven.

Reactions of Interested Parties   The aim of WADA and the IOC is to promote drug free sports and create a level field for competition. Anything that meaningfully contributes to realizing these objectives would seem to be warmly embraced by all interested parties. But is it? Citing weightlifting and track as examples, David Wallechinsky, author of *The Complete Book of the Summer Olympics*, observes that "the sports that have caught and cracked down on their drug cheats have not prospered from showing integrity." The image of the nation is reflected in the behavior of its athletes. An implication or proof of doping for any athlete can reflect negatively on that country and its other competing athletes. With the lax standard of "comfortable satisfaction," athletes are more likely to be found guilty of doping—perhaps wrongfully so—and to lose competition and endorsement opportunities. Likewise, athletic trainers who may be connected to a drug company or drug therapy but have never implemented it as part of Olympian training, may face losses similar to those of the athletes.

Spectators of the Olympics Games and other sporting events go to see something spectacular accomplished. The use of performance-enhancing drugs by an athlete who wins or does well in a sport may or may not have a drastic impact on their followers. Fans may not care as much about who uses performance-enhancing drugs as long as there is a good game or race. Do fans want to watch an exciting competition or one that is played fairly? If fair means no doping, perhaps most fans would accept that. However, if a fan favorite is involved in a doping scandal, will there be negative effects? Will the fans lose faith in the athlete, the sport, or in the system that has caused the athlete to be accused of doping?

Questions for Discussion

1. What are the ethical issues associated with the use of performance-enhancing drugs?

2. Why would an athlete want to use performance-enhancing drugs when he/she knows the risks involved? Would you use performance-enhancing drugs to improve your competitive chances? Why or why not?

3. Under IOC and WADA rules, athletes can be tested for banned substances at any time or place without warning. What purpose does this serve for the Olympic movement and for competitive sports in general? Is it fair to athletes? Why or why not?

4. What do you think the future holds with regard to efforts to subvert the intent of the IOC and WADA anti-doping policies and procedures?

Sources

This case was developed from material contained in the following sources:

About WADA: WADA fact sheets. *World Anti-Doping Agency*, http://www. wada-ama.org/en/dynamic.ch2?pageCategory_id=17, accessed February 13, 2005.

Associated Press. (August 29, 2004). Doping cases at the Athens Games. *Boston.com*, http://www.boston.com/sports/other_sports/olympics/articles/2004/08/29/doping_cases_at_the_athens_games/, accessed February 13, 2005.

Brennan, C. (June 10, 2004). Anti-Doping Agency taking right steps. *USA Today*, http://www.keepmedia.com/pubs/USATODAY/2004/06/10/485109, accessed March 25, 2005.

Guttmann, A. (1988). *A Whole New Ball Game: An Interpretation of American Sports*, Chapel Hill: The University of North Carolina Press.

Horovitz, B. (2001). Drug scandal shines spotlight on image. In L.M. Messina (ed.), *Sports in America*, New York: H.W. Wilson Company, 181–184.

International Olympic Committee. (July 30, 2004). IOC anti-doping rules applicable as per today. *Olympic Movement: IOC Medical Commission*, http://www.olympic.org, accessed August 2, 2004.

International Olympic Committee. (April 6, 2004). *The International Olympic Committee Anti-Doping Rules Applicable to the Games of the XXVII Olympiad in Athens 2004.*

Nuwer, H. (1994) *Sports Scandals*, New York: Franklin Watts.

Robbins, L. and Longman, J. (June 15, 2004). Lower standard of proof angers athletes and lawyers. *New York Times*, 153(52881), D2.

Searle, C. and Vaile, B. (1996). *The IOC Official Olympic Companion 1996*, London: Brasey's Sports.

Ungerleider, S. and Wadler, G.I. (June 20, 2004). A new world order in elite sports. *New York Times*, http://www.shorel.com/nytimesopedjune2004.pdf, accessed March 25, 2005.

Weir, T. (December 8, 2004). Drug-free sports: Do the fans care? *USA Today*, http://www.usatoday.com/sports/2004-12-07-drug-free-sports_x.htm, accessed February 13, 2005.

CASE 22

SWEATSHOPS: JUST A PROBLEM IN DEVELOPING NATIONS?

Sweatshops: An Assault on Human Dignity—Somewhere in the World

Working conditions in sweatshops "are undeniably poor and human rights violations are rampant. Workers suffer from dangerous equipment, and safety procedures are few or nonexistent. Hours are long and the workweek is a full six or seven days. But agitating for better conditions results in termination of employment. Thus, given no leverage for negotiations and few economic alternatives, workers are forced to accept the sweatshop lifestyle or suffer even more abject poverty."

Although sweatshops are found in numerous industries, ranging from toy manufacturing to television and telephone parts manufacturing to food processing, they have become most notoriously famous within the footwear and apparel (or garment) industries. In these two industries, easy portability of work and technology from one region to another, or one country to another, has facilitated the ongoing presence of and reliance on sweatshop factories. For instance, from a historical perspective, apparel manufacturing has been a very mobile industry, migrating from Britain to New England in the United States, to the southeastern United States, and to Mexico and Asia, "with makers in a constant search for less-expensive workers, often called 'the race to the bottom.'"

In this "race to the bottom," clothing wholesalers and retailers have developed a manufacturing supply chain of a large number of contractors and an even larger number of subcontractors, all with the aim of securing the absolutely lowest cost possible. Each move on the "race to the bottom" has been more fleeting than the preceding one, but that may now be changing with the increasing economic presence of China in the global marketplace. China's population of 1.3 billion people, coupled with its system of internal work visas, ensures a supply of low-wage workers for years to come. Thus, for the foreseeable future these advantages will give China the lead in the "race to the bottom."

In the late 1990s the media often portrayed sweatshops as the omnipresent "seamier side" of developing countries' economies. Some of the most infamous sweatshops were in Honduras, Indonesia, Thailand, and Vietnam. The sweatshops in these developing countries were characterized as being set up to exploit the poor for the benefit of the rich—somewhat like a reversed modern-day Robin Hood, who robs the poor to give to the rich. One media account illustrates this quite well: "One has only to visit the wretched colonias growing up around spotless maquiladora factories in Mexico or see the young women locked into lethal Bangladeshi sweatshops for 80 hours per week to see how the system is rigged to prevent shared benefits."

Although sweatshops have undeniably been a part of the economies of many developing nations, are those the only locations where sweatshops flourish? Do sweatshops exist in countries with developed economies and among leading, industrialized nations of the world?

Sweatshops in Developing Nations   Transnational corporations (TNCs) often source their products from factories in developing nations where there is forced labor—debt bondage and prison labor—and the blacklisting, firing, beating, torture, and killing of unionists. Other common characteristics of the sweatshops patronized by TNCs include discrimination against women; physical, psychological, and sexual abuse of workers; exposure to unhealthy and dangerous work; and forced and excessive overtime. "The worst problem for most workers is that their wages don't meet basic needs. In China, Vietnam, Indonesia, and other countries, base wages range from 20 to 30 cents an hour." The economic needs of many workers in the developing world are so desperate that they cannot refuse work, no matter how dangerous or unsafe. "Forty percent of the world's population, almost 3 billion people, live on less than $2 a day, with 1.3 billion living on less than $1 a day."

Workers in factories in the developing world "are often subjected to uncontrolled chemical exposures, high noise and temperature levels, unguarded machinery and other safety hazards, as well as ergonomic hazards from long hours of intensive manual assembly tasks. Worker training on the nature of these hazardous exposures and how they can be reduced or eliminated is virtually unknown."

There are seemingly endless instances of sweatshops in the developing world. "In Thailand, workers producing children's clothing for Nike, Levi Strauss, and Adidas recently reported having to work up to 110 hours per week. Managers made them swallow amphetamines ('speed') so they could work up to 48 hours straight before collapsing." In another instance, "a manufacturer of McDonald's 'Happy Meals' toys was charged with employing 13 year olds, working them 16 hours a day for three dollars." Moreover, there are reports of sweatshops where workers were injected with contraceptive drugs, and pregnant workers were pressured by their employers to have abortions.

Tennessee-based VF Solutions, an apparel manufacturer, was in line to receive a $100 million contract to produce firefighter uniforms for the New York Fire Department. VF Solutions subcontracts work to Latin American sweatshops, according to Charles Kernaghan, president of the National Labor Committee. Kernaghan, who exposed the use of child labor in the production of Kathie Lee Gifford's clothing line, asserts that he found Latin American sweatshops where workers were taunted by screams to work faster and the drinking water was tainted with human feces.

All of these sweatshop examples reflect deplorable conditions and direct assaults upon human dignity and human rights. An excruciatingly painful toll is exacted from the workers at the lowest rungs of the "economic food chain" for the exorbitant benefit of others higher up and at the top of the "economic food chain."

Do these deplorable conditions and assaults upon human dignity and human rights exist only in developing nations that are struggling to advance economically, or are they "alive and well" in more economically advanced nations?

The Chinese Connection China, poised to become a superpower in the global economy, has fueled its economic engine, at least in part, by using sweatshops to fulfill contracts for many companies that have outsourced the production of their goods. For example, Gap, Inc. reports that its problems with contract manufacturers occur most frequently in China. In 2003, 73 of 241 Chinese plants were evaluated by Gap as "needing improvement" or "requiring immediate attention" with respect to sweatshop conditions.

A good deal of China's increasing strength as an economic powerhouse can be attributed to its extremely large, low-wage labor force. As the world's most populous country, with 1.3 billion people, China has a seemingly inexhaustible supply of workers. However, much of China's population lives in impoverished conditions. "In 2000, about 47% of China's population had incomes of about $3 or less a day, estimates the World Bank."

In China's footwear industry, for example, workers average 11 hours per day, often with no days off, and a staggering amount of wages are owed but not paid to migrant workers. Chinese migrant workers submit to degrading work conditions at miserly pay because it is usually a step up the economic ladder.

The nature of China's sweatshops is perhaps best illustrated with the case of a Northern Ireland apparel firm that subcontracted the production of British army uniforms to a Chinese manufacturer. Cooneen Watts and Stone, an apparel manufacturer located in County Fermanagh, Northern Ireland, received a £50 million, five-year contract to produce combat uniforms for the British military. Cooneen Watts and Stone subcontracted the work to a Chinese manufacturer described by one social analyst in the following less-than-flattering terms: "The crumbling concrete buildings of People's Liberation Army Factory Number 3533 look more like a gulag than the base of an international business. The migrant workers, dressed in drab dark blue uniforms, shuffle around the remote mountainside complex under the glare of security guards, who ensure that strict production quotas are met. There is no air conditioning in the factory . . . the women endure temperatures higher than 40°C in summer. Junior workers are paid a mere £32.50 a month, senior workers get £39, and clerical staff earn up to £50. But they must pay to sleep in dormitories and for their simple rice meals."

Given that China, an emerging economic superpower, is not immune from sweatshops, what about the advanced, industrialized world?

Sweatshops in Developed Nations   Peter Laarman, an observer of global economic conditions, takes an interesting perspective on the linkages among outsourcing, technology, and the existence of sweatshops. Laarman argues that technological changes have made nearly every job vulnerable to outsourcing. He reasons further that "[i]f workers in Bangalore use the same or better technology as U.S. workers but receive one-tenth the pay, jobs will flow back to the U.S. only when labor costs here decline to the same level." Laarman's observation suggests that sweatshops in developed nations might be an inevitable evolutionary consequence of technological advances in a globalized economy.

Developed nations need not await the natural evolutionary consequences of globalization to embrace sweatshops. Sweatshops in developed nations are already here! Indeed, sweatshops never left the scene. Reflecting on the declining strength of unions in the late twentieth century, one social commentator points out that "without unionization and state guaranteed workers rights, the sweatshop has reigned as a dominant figure on the American landscape," especially in the apparel (or garment) industry. Another analyst who described New York City's garment industry, noted "[l]ike sweatshops of long ago, safety and health violations, along with the use of child labor and coercive methods, have remained hallmarks of the modern-day sweatshop." Little has changed other than who is exploited. "Although the ethnic groups have changed over time, much has not: the long hours of toil, the abysmally low wages, the health hazards, the withholding of pay, and the intense vulnerability of immigrant workers."

U.S. Locations   Recruiters of Eastern European illegal immigrants promise good jobs in the U.S. "only to deliver them into the hands of subcontractors, who allegedly violate overtime and Social Security and worker's compensation laws." In Los Angeles, an estimated "120,000 workers toil in thousands of tiny factories that routinely violate federal minimum wage, health, and safety laws." Workers at Liberty Apparel, located in New York City's Chinatown, "say they sewed for 14 or 15 hours a day and were never paid for much of their work." In addition, they only had 10-minute lunch breaks, poor ventilation, and no air conditioning. The workers also assert that Liberty "is hiding behind the subcontracting system to circumvent state and federal laws governing wages and working conditions."

Consider a September 2004 report prepared by the University of California at Berkeley's Human Rights Center and Washington, D.C.-based Free the Slaves. According to this report, at any given time in the United States "[a]t least 10,000 laborers from more than 38 countries are forced to work for little or no pay and in miserable conditions in sweatshops and restaurants, on farms, or as domestic help and prostitutes." An estimated 14,500 to 17,500 people were trafficked into the U.S. in 2003 to work in these types of jobs. "Most cases are in populous states like California, Florida, New York, and Texas which have large immigrant communities. Traffickers target poorly regulated industries which rely on cheap labor and use fraud, coercion, and violence to maintain control over workers." China, Mexico, and Vietnam were major sources of illegal immigrants for the traffickers. In one case, a Mexican woman was lured to the United States with promises of a job and free room and board. Instead, she ended up working in a Los Angeles sweatshop. "[S]he was forced to work 17-hour days making silk party dresses and was given one daily meal of rice and beans, She was paid about $100 a week and was forced to pay off a 'debt' of $2,550 to the trafficker," who also regularly beat her.

Canada In Toronto, Canada, approximately 8,000 immigrant women, mostly from Asia, sew garments in their homes for subcontractors that supply clothing wholesalers and retailers. "The women are paid by the number of garments they produce: about $3 for a shirt, between $4 and $5 for a dress. They provide their own sewing machines and pay for the electricity to run them." The average hourly earnings for these women is $7, which is 15 cents below the minimum legislated by the Ontario Employment Standards Act. "These home workers get no benefits or paid vacations. If they start to produce at a higher speed, the subcontractor cuts the price paid for each unit." Thousands of additional immigrant workers are struggling under similar conditions in Winnipeg, Vancouver, and Montreal. "This employment system is illegal, but the women are almost powerless to do anything about it. Most speak little English or French and know nothing of the laws that might protect them. They are isolated from one another so [they] cannot organize. And, most are desperate for the little money they earn."

Combating Sweatshop Conditions   Given that sweatshop conditions exist around the world, what can be done to counter these assaults upon human dignity and human rights that affect the most vulnerable people in the "economic food chain"?

In the United States, student-led anti-sweatshop demonstrations and protests have pressured some 200 colleges and universities into adopting "no-sweat" purchasing policies—especially for clothing emblazoned with the schools' logos. Ten universities in Canada also have "no-sweat" buying policies, as do several U.S. and Canadian cities. The Worker Rights Consortium (WRC) campaigns against sweatshops and helps to police factory compliance with "no-sweat" codes of business conduct. The WRC "does complaint-based and spot monitoring of plants that supply goods to its over-100 member universities."

In March 2004 the Play Fair at the Olympics Campaign was launched by a coalition of social activists and an international confederation of trade unions. The coalition called on the International Olympic Committee "to ensure that products displaying its five-ring logo are made by companies that observe 'fair labor standards.'" The coalition targeted second-tier brands such as Asics, Mizuno, Puma, and Umbro because Adidas, Nike, and Reebok had already been "named and shamed" in the anti-sweatshop campaigns of the late 1990s.

In 2003 the Fair Labor Association (FLA), whose members include companies such as Adidas-Salomon, Eddie Bauer Inc., Levi Strauss & Company, Liz Claiborne Inc., Nike Inc., the Phillips-Van House Corporation, and Reebok International Ltd., as well as about 175 colleges and universities, began publicizing audits of factories regarding possible sweatshop conditions, including labor and human rights violations. These publicized audits put "pressure on Wal-Mart, Disney, Gap, and every other company that does labor monitoring, to release their audits, too."

In May 2004 Gap Inc. issued its first social responsibility report in which it acknowledged that "many of the overseas workers making the retailer's clothes are mistreated and [the company] vowed to improve shoddy factory conditions by cracking down on unrepentant manufacturers." Gap uncovered "thousands of violations at 3,009 factories scattered across roughly 50 countries," including unacceptably low pay, psychological coercion and/or verbal abuse, lack of compliance with local laws, workweeks in excess of 60 hours, poor ventilation, and machinery lacking operational safety devices. Gap CEO Paul Presser says, "[w]e feel strongly that commerce and social responsibility don't have to be at odds." Gap insists that its contract manufacturers address all violations, including substandard pay, when problems are discovered. Business relationships are terminated with those contract manufacturers that repeatedly fail to comply. In 2003 Gap severed relationships with 136 factories, including 84 in China and Southeast Asia.

SweatX, an anti-sweatshop clothing brand established by Ben Cohen, co-founder of Ben & Jerry's ice cream, hired experienced, motivated garment workers to work in a new plant, paid them a living wage with full health benefits, got them involved with UNITE (the garment workers' union), and educated them in the virtues of cooperative ownership. Although the venture failed in May 2004 after 25 months of operation because of "pretty serious mismanagement," Cohen and his advisers believe that much was learned that would enable another start-up business of a similar nature to be successful.

These are some of the more notable efforts that have been undertaken to combat sweatshop conditions around the world. They have met with varying degrees of success. Ultimately, true success only will be found in putting the brakes on the "race to the bottom," and in establishing an acceptable minimum level of conditions and compensation for workers on the lowest rungs of the "economic food chain"— acceptable minimums that will ensure them a living wage, protect their rights, and respect their dignity as human beings.

Questions for Discussion

1. Why are sweatshops so common in the developing world?

2. Looking to the future, how are sweatshops likely to influence China's emerging role in the world economy?

3. Why do sweatshops exist in advanced, industrialized nations?

4. Are all retail operations in developing countries "sweatshops"? Obtain an example of a company in a developing country that subcontracts or directly runs a legitimate manufacturing facility using low-cost labor but pays living wages in that country.

5. What is a reasonable objective (or set of objectives) for addressing sweatshop conditions throughout the world? Explain your answer.

6. What do you think is the most viable approach for effecting meaningful change in sweatshop conditions throughout the world? Explain your answer.

Sources

This case was developed from material contained in the following sources:

Appelbaum, R., and Dreier, P. (July 19, 3004) SweatX closes up shop. *Nation*, *279(3)*, 6–7.

Berstein, A. (June 23, 2003) Sweatshops: Finally, airing the dirty linen. *Business Week*, 100–101.

Borden, T.G (Spring 2005) A book review of *Sweatshop USA: The American Sweatshop in Historical and Global Perspective*. *Working USA: The Journal of Labor and Society, 8(3)*, 374–375.

Brown, G. (April 2004) Vulnerable workers in the global economy. *Occupational Hazards, 66(4)*, 29–30.

Frager, R.A. (October 2004) A book review of *Sweatshop USA: The American Sweatshop in Historical and Global Perspective*. *American Historical Review*, 1207–1208.

Guynn, J. (September 24, 2004) University of California report details sordid trafficking in workers. *Contra Costa Times*, accessed from Newspaper Source database at http://search.epnet.com/login.asdirect=true&db=nfh&an=2W60277746413 on March 7, 2005.

Jobs from hell. (October 2004) *Canada & the World Backgrounder*, accessed from MasterFILE Premier database at http://search.epnet.com/login.aspx?direct=true&db=f5h&an=15087204 on March 7, 2005.

June, A.W. (July 4, 2003) In its first major report, anti-sweatshop group cites violations. *Chronicle of Higher Education*, *49(43)*, A23.

Laarman, P. (November 16, 2004) Ethics of outsourcing. *Christian Century*, *121(23)*, 50.

Liedtke, M. (May 13, 2004) Gap acknowledge labor violations. *The Washington Post*, accessed from Newspaper Source database at http://search.epnet.com/login.aspx?direct=true&db=nfh&an=WPT189069689704 on March 7, 2005.

Malone, S. (February 8, 2005) Tempest in a t-shirt: Book offers new look at globalization. *WWD: Women's Wear Daily*, *189(28)*, 15.

No sweat. (August 21, 2004) *Economist*, *372(8389)*, 51.

Parry, S. (November 21, 2004) Exposed: Appalling Chinese sweatshops where 800 women are paid as little as £1 a day to churn out substandard uniforms for the British army. *Mail on Sunday*, 36.

Port, B., Lombardi, F. (September 5, 2003) New York Fire Department may buy from uniform firm accused of using sweatshops. *New York Daily News*, accessed from Newspaper Source database at http://search.epnet.com/login.aspx?direct=true&db=nfh&an=2W63326889762 on March 7, 2005.

Rodriguez, J. (November 7, 3003) Always low wages: Exploitation of illegal immigrants is everywhere.

San Jose Mercury News, accessed from Newspaper Source database at http://search.epnet.com/login.aspx?direct=true&db=nfh&an=2W702028737087 on March 7, 2005.

Samuelson, R.J. (April 5, 2004) China, trade and progress. *Newsweek*, *143(14)*, 47.

Sun, L.H. (September 23, 2004) U.S. has 10,000 forced laborers, researchers say. *The Washington Post*, accessed from Newspaper Source database at http://search.epnet.com/login.aspx?direct=true&db=nfh&an=WPT229997474104 on March 7, 2005.

Weber, L. (July 9, 2004) Factory workers urge boycott of New York City clothing maker. *Newsday*, accessed from Newspaper Source database at http://search.epnet.com/login.aspx?direct=true&db=nfh&an=2W63807397023 on March 7, 2005.

Wells, D. (September/October 2003) Global sweatshops & ethical buying codes. *Canadian Dimension*, *37(5)*, 9–22.

Wells, J. (May 22, 2004) Social responsibility report looks good on Gap. *Toronto Star*, accessed from Newspaper Source database at http://search.epnet.com on March 7, 2005.

Yesilevsky, A. (May/June 2004) The case against sweatshops, *Humanist*, *64(3)*, 20–22.

Notes

1. Wolfensohn, J. D. (February 16, 2004). Financing the Monterrey Consensus—Remarks at the conference: Making globalization work for all. *The World Bank Group,* http://web.worldbank.org/WBSITE/EXTERNAL/NEWS/0,,contentMDK:20169719~menuPK:34472~pagePK:34370~piPK:34424~theSitePK:4607,00.html.
2. Wolfensohn, J. D. (April 2, 2001). The challenges of globalization: The role of the World Bank. *The World Bank Group,* http://web.worldbank.org/WBSITE/EXTERNAL/NEWS/0,,contentMDK:20025027~menuPK:34474~pagePK:34370~piPK:34424~theSitePK:4607,00.html.
3. Ibid.
4. Crutsinger, M. (January 12, 2005). U.S. trade deficit soars to all-time high. *The Washington Post,* http://www.washingtonpost.com/wp-dyn/articles/A4687-2005Jan12.html.
5. Koppel, N. (September 15, 2001). China in accord on entry to WTO. *Boston Globe,* C1.
6. Bennis, P. and the IPS Iraq Task Force. (September 30, 2004). A failed "transition": The mounting costs of the Iraq War. *Institute for Policy Studies,* http://www.ips-dc.org/Iraq/failedtransition/A_Failed_Transistion-webver.pdf.
7. Campbell, I. (March 12, 2004). The costs of terrorism. *SpaceDaily,* http://www.spacedaily.com/news/terrorwar-04f.html. Also, see "Fazio Says U.S. Deficit Pledge Is Crucial for Dollar," Bloomberg.com, February 19, 2005, www.bloomberg.com/apps/news?pid=10000085&sid=aa2oWzadD1jw&refer=europe.
8. Bender, B. (January 14, 2005). Study sees rivals to US power. *The Boston Globe,* A9, http://www.boston.com/news/world/asia/articles/2005/01/14/study_sees_rivals_to_us_power/.
9. Engardio, P., with Kripalani, M., Webb, A. (August 17, 2001). Smart globalization. *Business Week,* 32. Quotes in this section are taken from this article.
10. Gupta, A. K., Westney, D. E. (2003). *Smart Globalization: Designing Global Strategies, Creating Global Networks.* San Francisco: Jossey-Bass. http://www.wiley.com/WileyCDA/WileyTitle/productCd-0787965324.html.
11. Engardio, 32.
12. Hjelt, P. (March 8, 2004). 2004 global most admired companies. *Fortune, 149(5),* 38–58.
13. Ibid.
14. Ibid.
15. Ibid.
16. Elkington, J. (1998). *Cannibals with Forks: The Triple Bottom Line of 21st Century Business—Conscientious Commerce.* Gabriola Island, British Columbia: New Society Publishers; see also www.sustainability.com/philosophy/triple-bottom/tbl-intro.asp.
17. Bender, A9.
18. Smale, A. (August 16, 2001). The dark side of the global economy. *New York Times,* 3.
19. Ibid.
20. Child Labor 101. *International Labor Organization,* http://www.us.ilo.org/teachin/ilou/ilou101.cfm.
21. Ibid.
22. Thurow, L. (August 7, 2001). Third World must help itself. *Boston Globe,* F4.
23. Ibid.
24. Onishi, N. (July 29, 2001). The bondage of poverty that produces chocolate. *New York Times,* 1.
25. Warsh, D. (July 29, 2001). The next 50 years. *Boston Globe,* E2.
26. Ibid.
27. Article 19 states: (1) Everyone shall have the right to hold opinions without interference. (2) Everyone shall have the right to freedom of expression; this right shall include freedom to seek, receive, and impart information and ideas of all kinds, regardless of frontiers, either orally, in writing or in print, in the form of art, or through any other media of his choice. (3) The exercise of the rights provided for in paragraph 2 of this article carries with it special duties and responsibilities. It may therefore be subject to certain restrictions, but these shall only be such as are provided by law and are necessary: (a) for respect of the rights or reputation of others; (b) for the protection of national security or of public order *(ordre public),* or of public health, or morals.

28. Peacock, A. (2004). The Digital Divide and Human Rights–What the EU should do at the World Summit on Information Society, 2005. *The Open Society Institute's EU Monitoring and Advocacy Program,* http://www.eumap.org/journal/features/2004/infohr1/infohr/peacock.

29. Shadid, A. (January 24, 2001). Third World nations threatened as digital divide grows, report says. *Boston Globe,* D2.

30. Peacock.

31. For more information on Information Society, the Digital Divide, and Information Communications Technologies, visit the following Websites: http://www.globalcitiesdialogue.org, http://carbon.cudenver.edu/~mryder/itc_data/dig_div.html, and http:/www.internetworldstats.com/links10.htm.

32. Imamkhodjaeva, O. Globalization modules: Globalization and ethics: Prospects for a democratic world order. *Rochester Institute of Technology,* http://www.rit.edu/~global/glob-oidin-ethics.html.

33. Ritzer, G. (2004). *The McDonaldization of Society,* 4th ed. Thousand Oaks, CA: Pine Forge Press.

34. Ibid, 1.

35. Ibid, 2.

36. Ibid, 212.

37. Imamkhodjaeva.

38. Post, Lawrence, Weber, 485.

39. Sciolino, D. (September 23, 2001). Who hates the U.S.? Who loves it? *New York Times,* 4–1.

40. Ibid.

41. Ibid.

42. Tyson, L. (July 14, 2001). The new laws of nations. *New York Times,* A15.

43. DiCarlo, L. (January 24, 2005), Airline losses may triple past estimates, Forbes.com, www.forbes.com/services/2005/01/24/cx_ld_0124airlines.html.

44. Tyson, A15.

45. United Nations. (1973). *Multinational Corporations in World Development,* 23.

46. Weidenbaum, M. (May 2004). Outsourcing is a good thing—mostly, *USA Today,* www.findarticles.com/p/articles/mi_m1272/is_2708_132/ai_n6019795.

47. Czinkota, M., Ronkainen, I. (1989). *International Business,* 338. Chicago: Dryden.

48. Weidenbaum, 203.

49. Sturdivant, F., Vernon-Wortzel, H. (1990). *Business and Society: A Managerial Approach,* 189–190. Homewood, IL: Irwin.

50. Vernon, R., Wells, L., Jr. (1986). *Manager in the International Economy,* 5th ed., 2. Englewood Cliffs, NJ: Prentice Hall.

51. Palmer, E. (June 2001). Multinational corporations and the social contract. *Journal of Business Ethics, 31(3),* 245.

52. Mayer, D. (Winter 2001). Community, business ethics, and global capitalism. *American Business Law Journal, 38(2),* 215–260.

53. Vernon, R. (1971). *Sovereignty at Bay.* New York: Basic Books.

54. Johnson, J., Holub, M. (October 2003). Questioning organizational legitimacy: The case of US expatriates. *Journal of Business Ethics, 47(3),* 209.

55. Ibid.

56. Meyer, 215–260. Citations for the following section are also taken from Meyer.

57. Czinkota and Ronkainen, 346–347.

58. Akst, D. (March 4, 2001). Nike in Indonesia, through a different lens. *New York Times,* 3.

59. Beyer, J. (September 1999). Ethics and cultures in international business. *Journal of Management Inquiry, 8(3),* 287–297.

60. This section is based on Frederick, W. (1991). The moral authority of transnational corporate codes. *Journal of Business Ethics, 10,* 165–177.

61. Ibid., 168–169.

62. DeGeorge, R. Ethics in personal business—a contradiction in terms? *Business Credit, 102(8),* 45–46.

63. Berenbeim, R. (October 2000). Globalization drives ethics. *New Zealand Management, 47(9),* 26–29.

64. Frederick, 166–167.

65. Ibid., 167.

66. Ibid.
67. Puffere, S., McCarthy, D. J. (Winter 1995). Finding the common ground in Russian and American business ethics. *California Management Review, 37(2),* 20–46; Donaldson, T., Dunfee, T. (Summer 1999). When ethics travel: The promise and peril of global business ethics. *California Management Review, 41(4),* 45.
68. Davis, M. (January/February 1999). Global standards, local problems. *Journal of Business Ethics, 20(1),* 38.
69. Maynard, M. (March 2001). Policing transnational commerce: Global awareness in the margins of morality. *Journal of Business Ethics, 30,* 17, 27.
70. Cattaui, M. (Summer 2000). Responsible business conduct in a global economy. *OECD Observer, Issue 221/222,* 18–20; Berenbeim, R. (September 1, 1999). The divergence of a global economy: One company, one market, one code, one world. *Vital Speeches of the Day, 65(22),* 696–698; Morrison, A. (May 2001). Integrity and global leadership. *Journal of Business Ethics, 31(31),* 65–76; Palmer, E. (June 2001). Multinational corporations and the social contract. *Journal of Business Ethics, 31(3),* 245–258.
71. Waddock, S. (April 2004). Creating corporate accountability: Foundational principles to make corporate citizenship real. *Journal of Business Ethics, 50(4),* 313.
72. Integrity, on a global scale. (February 10, 2003). *The Economist,* http://www. economist.com/globalExecutive/Education/displayStory.cfm?story_id=1562708.
73. DeGeorge, R. (1993). *Competing with Integrity,* 114–121. New York: Oxford University Press.
74. Fisher, R., Patton, B. M., Ury, W. L. (1992). *Getting to Yes: Negotiating Agreement Without Going In,* 2nd ed. Boston, MA: Houghton-Mifflin.
75. Adler, N. J. (2001). *International Dimensions of Organizational Behavior,* 4th ed. Cincinnati, OH: South-Western/Thomson Learning.
76. Lubatkin, M., Calori, R., Very, P., Veiga, J. (1998). Managing mergers across borders: A two-nation exploration of a nationally bound administrative heritage. *Organization Science, 9(6),* 670–684; Laurent, A. (1983). The cultural diversity of Western conceptions of management. *International Studies of Management and Organization, 13(1–2),* 75–96.
77. See Hofstede, G. (Summer 1980). Motivation, leadership, and organization: Do American theories apply abroad? in *Organizational Dynamics* and *Cultures and Organizations: Software of the Mind: Intercultural Cooperation and Its Importance for Survival.* (1991). London: McGraw-Hill; Hampden-Turner, C., Trompenaars, F. (1997). *Riding the Waves of Culture: Understanding Diversity in Global Business,* 2nd ed. New York: McGraw Hill; Hall, E. T. (1976). *Beyond Culture.* Garden City, NY: Anchor Press; Adler, N. J. (2001). *International Dimensions of Organizational Behavior,* 4th ed. Cincinnati, OH: South-Western/Thomson Learning.
78. Adler, J. (July 11, 1983). What the world thinks of America, *Newsweek,* 44–86.
79. Referenced in Donaldson, T. and Dunfee, T. op. cit., 48.
80. Ibid.
81. Ibid., 63.
82. Donaldson, T. (1989). The *Ethics of International Business,* ch. 5. New York: Oxford University Press.
83. Donaldson and Dunfee, 62.
84. Ibid.

Index

Page numbers followed by *f* denote figures.